PENGUIN BOOKS

EUROPEANS

Jane Kramer has been a writer for *The New Yorker* since 1964. She is the author of *Off Washington Square*, *Allen Ginsberg in America*, *Honor to the Bride*, *The Last Cowboy*, and *Unsettling Europe*. In 1981, she won the American Book Award for nonfiction. She is married to the anthropologist Vincent Crapanzano, and they have a daughter, Aleksandra. She lives with her family in Paris and New York.

EUROPEANS

JANE KRAMER

PENGUIN BOOKS

PENGUIN BOOKS
Published by the Penguin Group
Viking Penguin, a division of Penguin Books USA Inc.,
375 Hudson Street, New York, New York 10014, U.S.A.
Penguin Books Ltd, 27 Wrights Lane,
London W8 5TZ, England
Penguin Books Australia Ltd, Ringwood,
Victoria, Australia
Penguin Books Canada Ltd, 2801 John Street,
Markham, Ontario, Canada L3R 1B4
Penguin Books (N.Z.) Ltd, 182–190 Wairau Road,
Auckland 10, New Zealand

Penguin Books Ltd, Registered Offices:
Harmondsworth, Middlesex, England

First published in the United States of America by
Farrar, Straus & Giroux, Inc. 1988
Published in Penguin Books 1990

3 5 7 9 10 8 6 4 2

All of the selections in this book
originally appeared, some in slightly different
form, in *The New Yorker*.

LIBRARY OF CONGRESS CATALOGING IN PUBLICATION DATA
Kramer, Jane.
Europeans/Jane Kramer.
p. cm.
Reprint. Originally published: New York: Farrar, Straus & Giroux,
c1988.
ISBN 0 14 01.2808 5
1. Europe. 2. Europe—Biography. I. Title.
[D842.K7 1990]
920.04—dc20   89–23208

Printed in the United States of America
Designed by Cynthia Krupat

For the staff of The New Yorker, *and for all the other people, in Europe and America, who have helped me, advised me, indulged me, and, in many ways and over many years, contributed to this book*

Contents

Foreword

With Paris as her base, Jane Kramer has taken all Europe as her province. Between 1978 and 1988, under the modest heading "Letter from Europe," she wrote a series of masterly reports for *The New Yorker* from France, Germany, England, Austria, Italy, Switzerland, Portugal, Greece, and Hungary. More than thirty of those reports are now assembled in this book. Her method was odd. Instead of approaching the various countries head-on or with any view to dealing with them comprehensively, she approached them obliquely and idiosyncratically, choosing subjects—stories, people, situations—for no reason other than some profound personal interest. The paradoxical result is that the many parts fall into place to form a coherent whole: a portrait of Europe at this particular moment in history. She is undaunted by complexity, and appears to delight in making the complex understandable. Many of the Europeans she writes about are heroic, and some are less than that: Pierre Mendès France, on the one hand, and Klaus Barbie, on the other; French Resistance members and German terrorists. She composes a memorable picture of her Portuguese concierge, Mme Gonçalves, by closely following the woman's transient thoughts and feelings and reactions to large events over a period of years. She explores the labyrinthine scandal involving the French bank known as Paribas, and the equally labyrinthine banking problems of the Vatican. She tells the story of the struggle that the citizens of the West German town of Schlitz engaged in to keep the U.S. Army from storing nuclear missiles in a nearby mountain, thus making the town itself a nuclear target. She adroitly makes her way through the intricacies of a vast financial swindle devised by a Milanese psychoanalyst named Armando Verdiglione and carried out under the impressive auspices of his own Foundation of International Culture. Another story, replete with all the contradictions and ambiguities of French politics, is about how Jean-Marie Le Pen and his Front National (with the slogan "France for the French") moved into the political life of the small city of Dreux in 1983 and, by exploiting the resentment its French citizens felt toward the thousands of foreign workers living there—Algerians, Moroccans, Tunisians, Turks, and others—managed to get rid of the progressive, severe, incongruous Socialist mayor, Françoise Gaspard, and replace her with a conservative local banker with whom they had formed an alliance. She is also drawn to eccentrics: the little-known French "novelist of complaint" Emmanuel Bove, who was admired by Rilke and Beckett; the "not quite French banking intellectual" Pierre Moussa; the peaceable revolutionary Otelo Nuno Romano Saraiva de Carvalho. She lights up two musical bypaths: the story of Luis Mariano, a Basque tenor who was a matinee idol earlier in this century and who was adored by Anna Silva, a Théâtre du Châtelet wardrobe seamstress who worked on "the lace and the braid and the gold and silver piping on Luis Mariano's fabulous costumes"; and the story of Frankie Ntoh Song, the leader of a popular Paris rock-music group from the Cameroon called Ghetto Blaster. She provides a penetrating study of the Kurt Waldheim case. One chapter is titled "Being German." And indeed she writes brilliantly and convincingly about what it is to be German and what it is, too, to be Swiss or French or English or Austrian. Her sense of national character is as dependable as her sense of individual character. She knows Europe, and Europeans.

Jane Kramer is sensitive to political nuance, alert to social change. She is fond of details, but every detail counts, so she is never trivial. If there is humor or irony anywhere to be found in a given set of circumstances, she will find it. At the center of her writing style is wit, and at the center of the wit are a powerful intelligence and an elegance of diction. A number of her epigrammatic statements come to mind. She writes, "The Germans loved Adenauer. He turned their evasions into something positive, and persuaded them, with his stern calm, that rituals of guilt and expiation could be undermining and indulgent." Again on Germany: "It is as if the wall had given Berliners the kind of freedom prisoners and kindergarten children have—had made them, by definition, not responsible. They are bound not so much by a common cause as by the shared pleasure of unaccountability." Referring to Paris, she writes, "It is hard to imagine another city whose intellectuals could be promoted like rock stars or reigning quarterbacks—inspiring the most avid, fan-club sort of curiosity, cultivating groupies, posing for *Paris Match* with sultry, heavy-lidded looks and shirts unbuttoned to the waist." Again on France: "Frenchmen from Diderot and the Encyclopédistes to Fernand Braudel and the Archivistes have considered themselves, by birthright, the arbiters and cataloguers of Western civilization—its official overseers, so to speak— but this does not mean that Frenchmen, either by tradition or by temperament, have ever had any real enthusiasm for the facts about civilization, neutral and unadorned." About England she writes, "The 'right' people here have always thrived on the cachet of poverty, the way they have thrived on being dotty or barmy or whatever other word they choose for symptoms that are usually called crazy in the less fortunate. They have had the confidence of class to see them through their aberrations and their overdrafts." And: "There is something touching about Margaret Thatcher and her enthusiasms. She seems to believe in Milton Friedman the way an English schoolgirl believes in Hobbits." About Switzerland she writes, "It is the responsibility of the Swiss to prosper. They take it on faith that the survival of any goodness in the world depends on the survival of the Swiss franc." And: "What the Swiss offer, beyond the obvious pleasures of their country and the services of their banks and tax havens, is a kind of theater of rectitude." I am tempted to quote more, but I will leave further discoveries to the reader.

Ostensibly, Jane Kramer is a journalist; she writes factual reports on timely matters. Again and again, however, she crosses over into the literary realm; the timely becomes timeless, and her work can be read with rapt interest years after it was written. Reading Jane Kramer, from the beginning, has been an adventure for me: the new, enthralling stories; the unfamiliar people who emerge as vivid presences; the fresh insights; the sudden vistas; and always, always the beauty and clarity of her prose.

William Shawn

SEVEN
EUROPEANS

JOSÉPHINE GUEZOU

My friend Joséphine Guezou cannot forgive the Germans. Joséphine is a Breton villager of sixty-four, with a sick husband and a dipsy uncle around the house, five children, eleven grandchildren, and (at the moment) forty-one rabbits to worry about, and normally she does not have time for old antagonisms. I spent a few weeks in her village this summer —it is a gray stone village on a little estuary of the English Channel —and I know that one reason I felt at home there was that Joséphine worried about me, too. She looks after her villagers the way Mme Gonçalves, my concierge, looks after our Paris street, except that Mme Gonçalves is a professional and tends to regard local life as a challenge in housekeeping, whereas Joséphine is an amateur, a natural backwater busybody, who makes herself useful because she can't resist her neighbors' domesticity. Joséphine makes the rounds of the village and the nearby farms in a bright-blue Deux Chevaux, pinning up messages. She lets the vet know that one of the cows is sick at Crec'h Le Coz. She puts the artichoke farmer on the road to the market town in touch with the mason who wants to borrow the farmer's truck to haul some firewood to his grandfather's cottage. She writes on the back of used brown wrapping paper, which she gets from her cousin at the *quincaillerie*, starting small and shaping her letters carefully but always letting loose at the end with an enormous and enthusiastic JOSÉPHINE. There is satisfaction in that signature. It graces barn doors and village mailboxes like a royal seal, conferring a kind of confidence in the day's arrangements. Joséphine began writing messages for the village in 1942, when she was a ruddy young woman of twenty-four and her husband —the husband who is sick now, with a bad heart and failing eyesight

—was underground with the Resistance, coming out in the dark to blow up German trucks or set flares for the Free French soldiers who would parachute into the artichoke farmer's fields at night, carrying cyanide pills and radio batteries and instructions straight from Charles de Gaulle, across the Channel. Joséphine offered herself to the Resistance with a stubborn and good-natured curiosity, just as she offers herself to the village now. She bought a grammar book and practiced writing. Soon no one in the commune moved against the Germans unless his orders were signed with her enormous JOSÉPHINE. The mayor and the policeman and the butcher who spied for them were bewildered, but they never stopped to consider why Joséphine—she had a bicycle then—was always pedalling across the countryside at odd hours. They knew that Joséphine was incorrigibly useful, that she liked bursting into other people's houses. They knew that anyway she had to deliver the oysters she dredged at low tide to trade for eggs and bread for her little boys. Certainly they never imagined that Joséphine was JOSÉPHINE. The Germans had a meeting, and brought in experts to break the JOSÉPHINE code, but the only code in Joséphine's messages was the fact that they were all written with her little boys' red crayon, and by the time the Germans thought to search for a red crayon Joséphine had given it to the goat and the goat had eaten it.

Joséphine still writes her messages in red. (She has switched from crayons to red felt-tip pens, which she buys at a stall in town at the Friday market.) And she is still writing about Germans, though most of the Germans who concern her now were not alive forty years ago, and Joséphine—out of politeness, she says—has learned to spell "*Guten Morgen,*" "*Guten Abend,*" and "*Auf wiedersehen.*" They are couples, mainly, and sometimes families. They come in the summer in groups of six and eight, and even ten, and they rent the new white cement house that Joséphine has built for her only daughter, Marianne, with the savings of a lifetime, and that Marianne and her husband are slowly furnishing with food processors and fitted sheets and electric lettuce dryers for their old age and their dying. Joséphine has always known where *she* was going to die. She wanted her daughter to have that same important information, in order to give her life its proper quality and her work its proper conclusion in her own village, her own *pays,* among her own people, and so Joséphine built the house. She sometimes says that the reason her interest in the sea stops at the oyster beds she dredged in wartime is that the treacherous North Breton currents kill so many of her neighbors before their time and rob them of the death they planned. In Joséphine's day, people left the sea and farmed if they had the good luck to get hold of some land of their own. They had to plant their cabbage and their artichokes in sandy coastal soil and graze their milk cows in fogs so thick that the only way to gather them in, most winter days, was by sniffing, but they could still get by if they worked hard. Now there is not much profit in farming the little peasant freeholds along the estuary. The oldest of Joséphine's four sons gave up his few acres and joined a merchant fleet, and comes home to his family only four or five times a year. Her second son is a kind of sea sweeper, working a rig that skims the oil slick from the Channel waters. Her last two sons are fishermen. But Marianne married a village boy to Joséphine's liking, and the two of them moved to Rennes and went right to work in a cheese factory—and Joséphine knows that one day they are coming home to their own house, with its clumps of pink and blue hortensia by the front wall, because Joséphine has thought to provide her daughter with the dowry of a peaceful dotage. While they are in Rennes—making money, raising children, *Gastarbeiter* in their own province—Joséphine pays their mortgage with the rent she collects from Germans on holiday.

Joséphine is not in business, like the old cartwright across the road, who moved his family into a shack and put their fine stone house on the market as a summer cottage. She watched the cartwright's boy grow up and go off to the big *lycée* in town and then to the university in Rennes, and, of course, she voted for him when he ran for town councillor, even though he lived far away in Limoges by then and showed up in the village only to campaign. She assumed that the councillor was coming home eventually. He had worked so hard to buy back the family house, she says, and his curly-headed Paris wife had even sent out Christmas pictures of all the neighbors standing in front of the saplings he planted in the back yard. That was ten years ago. Nine years ago, the councillor started renting his house to Parisians and bought himself a little villa in the South of France. Joséphine says that the house has lost its heart with its family—by which she means that it is getting sad and shabby, that the saplings are storm-bent and stunted, that the dish towels are frayed and losing their loops because no one is around on winter nights to mend them, that the upstairs bed is broken and resting on a log and the stuffing is falling out of the couch near the fireplace and the kitchen curtains are torn, and that there is no more wood in the woodpile. *Voilà*, Joséphine always says when she points it out to her Germans, there is a house without a family. It is part of Joséphine's little ritual of welcome. She greets the Germans at the village bar-and-grocery store, and then she asks them home for pound

cake and a glass of wine, pointing out the councillor's house on the way.
The councillor's house makes a proper contrast to her daughter's house,
which has a neat mowed lawn and rows of dahlias and zinnias and
pansies that confront the street like an audience. She likes to make the
Germans smell her daughter's sheets, fresh from the clothesline, and
feel the thick quilted pads on every bed and count the plates in the
lacquered armoire in the dining room and try the cupboard underneath
the kitchen sink in order to admire the new aluminum garbage pail
from a Prisunic in Rennes, which pops open automatically whenever
the cupboard door opens. She says, carefully, *"Tochterhaus,"* so they
will understand. She wants them to know that this is a house for
coming home to. She hopes they will not break the glasses and burn
the enamel pots, the way the Germans who came for the last two weeks
of July in 1979 did, or adopt a tomcat that sprays all over the sitting-
room upholstery, like the Germans that August.

Joséphine is still a little afraid of Germans, so she tries never to talk
about the war or the German soldiers who moved into the village in
'44, after the Allies landed, and ground out their cigarettes on the pine
floors and used for firewood whatever furniture they didn't need. Now
that she has built her daughter a house, Joséphine tends to think of those
soldiers as demented vacationers—as tourists run amok in other people's lives and houses. It gives a kind of home truth to her war memories
and, in a way, explains her experience. Early this spring, she confessed
to the rental agent in town that she was sometimes uneasy having
Germans in her daughter's house. The agent, a pretty young woman
with a sideline in Common Market contraband involving the smuggling of local smoked salmon across the Channel to be sold as discount
Scotch salmon, offered to find Joséphine British tenants—respectable
salmon dealers from London—but Joséphine thought it over and said
no, she would make do with the Germans she had. July's Germans
came and went, and then August's Germans arrived—three hearty
couples from Dortmund, who drove into the village with windsurfing
boards strapped to the roofs of their little Audis and immediately put
on rubber wet-suits and disappeared over the rocks in the direction of
the Channel. Joséphine liked them. She looked after them as if they
were outsize children. She gave them leeks from her kitchen garden and
told them stories and left them notes whenever she felt a storm blowing
up, so they would not drown in their toy sailboats or leave her daughter's best towels on the clothesline. Then, one night, the Germans had
a party. They drank a lot and decided to race their Audis around
Joséphine's daughter's garden. They rutted the lawn and flattened the

dahlias. Cleaning up, they broke the aluminum garbage pail, and left it swinging from the cupboard door like a hanged partisan. The next morning, Joséphine drove to town and bought a red crayon. She left her message on the mailbox for everyone to see: *"Attention, Allemands! La maison de ma fille n'est pas un bordel. Mon pays n'est pas un bordel. Vous n'êtes pas gentils. C'est moi qui vous le dit.* JOSÉPHINE."

August 1982

FERNANDE PELLETIER

The trip south from Paris to the Pelletier farm takes just a few hours now that a little Air Limousin De Havilland Twin Otter meets the Paris plane at Limoges. From Limoges, you can fly to the town of Brive-la-Gaillarde in ten or eleven minutes, and after that it is an easy, pretty drive down the Vézère River into the Périgord, past the village I will call Sainte-Lucie and the hamlet of Sainte-Lucie-le-Pont and, finally, up the steep dirt road that ends at the Pelletiers' Périgord farmhouse. Fernande Pelletier talks sometimes about "flying to Paris for the day," and then she howls with laughter until the dogs come running in to investigate and Fernande herself has to sit down with a glass of water, to recover. The idea of flying to Paris for the day is Mme Pelletier's idea of something so preposterous, so improbable, that laughing about it is a way of laughing at life, or at herself, if she is disappointed or confused or is feeling helpless because someone in the Common Market has traded, say, a butter-and-milk quota for a beet-sugar quota and the world has intruded again on the hundred acres of France that her family has farmed for centuries. Before the Common Market, there used to be only what she regarded as natural intrusions on the Pelletier farm—wars or plagues or phylloxera.

Fernande Pelletier was in Paris for a day in 1964. She and her husband, Georges, drove here with their son, who was four and slow in talking and had an appointment with a famous Paris doctor. They left the farm at three in the morning, arrived at noon, found the hospital, saw the famous doctor (who said that he didn't know why the boy was slow), and headed home without another stop. It was not that Paris intimidated the Pelletiers or put them off. The Pelletiers had a book of photographs of Paris. They knew Paris from their book and from the evening news and from the pictures in *Le Pèlerin*, the Catholic weekly that Fernande's mother gets in the mail on Fridays. It was simply that they never thought to stay in Paris and look around—just as they never think to look around Brive, say, or Périgueux after a weekly market or around Sainte-Lucie after a sheep sale. The Paris of doctors' appointments and all the other business of daily life is not the Paris that Fernande Pelletier means when she talks about "flying to Paris for the day."

Seven years ago, I met an old sherry vintner in Jerez who talked about flying to New York for the day. It amused him to imagine getting on a Concorde in the morning, enjoying a glass of his best sherry at the Knickerbocker Club, and heading home in time for a good night's sleep in the carved-oak bed where his father and grandfather and great-grandfather had slept before him. He must have been about ninety then, because he described skating on the Neckar with his friend Alfonso XIII when they were both at boarding school in Heidelberg at the turn of the century. He remembered the long fall trips from Jerez to Heidelberg. He went in his father's coach, north through most of Europe, and while he couldn't say—not at the age of ninety—exactly how many weeks he was in the coach each fall, he did not find anything odd about the trips he made and the time they took. He liked the time of travelling. He found it consistent (his word) with the occasion.

It may be that only the middle class is really comfortable about starting a day at home and, with not much more than a case of jet lag to show for it, ending up on another continent in a couple of hours. There are still people in Europe who are profoundly *located*, and they are mainly peasants like Fernande Pelletier and old aristocrats like the vintner in Jerez. Their little jokes about flying to Paris for the day or taking the Concorde to New York for a glass of sherry at the Knickerbocker Club are really the same story—a way of reminding themselves that the world beyond their land and their attachments may control their fortunes but that it has nothing at all to do with who they are or with the rhythm and etiquette of an appropriate life.

The first time I visited the Pelletiers, I took the train. Fernande was curious about the trip, because she had taken a long train trip herself in the summer of 1955, when she and Georges got married and went to the Pyrenees for a week and stopped in Lourdes for the blessing of the Virgin. Fernande never took another holiday. She thinks that there is one allotted holiday in a peasant's life, and that is a honeymoon spent in pursuit of blessings. Sometimes she can hear a train passing above

Sainte-Lucie-le-Pont in the morning, but she rarely sees it now that she has sold the sheep that used to graze in pastures with a view of the railroad tracks. In the old days, she would take her sheep and her dogs and a copy of the racing news out to one of those far pastures of the farm, and she would watch for the train and think about her weekly bet and about her honeymoon and the *pension* at Lourdes where she discovered how disappointing love was compared with Mass in the grotto or the sight of a ton of corn filling the family's orange metal crib after a good harvest. The farm was still her father's then. His name was Olivier Tricart, and he was a blunt, intelligent man (*"C'est quelqu'un,"* people who knew him always said), a man of dignity and authority, and a proud farmer. *"Nous, les paysans,"* he would begin when the other Sainte-Lucie farmers came to him for advice. Today in Sainte-Lucie, the farmers call themselves *cultivateurs* and refer to their farms not as farms but as *exploitations agricoles,* and it is mainly the young farmers —who go off to agricultural school in places like Périgueux, or even Limoges, and meet boys and girls from the city and talk about coming home as "returning to the land"—who use the word "peasant." They say *"nous, les paysans"* the way Parisians on my street say *"nous, les intellectuels."* There are two or three young farmers starting out now in Sainte-Lucie-le-Pont. They come to consult Fernande, just as their fathers used to consult M. Tricart, and when they talk excitedly about "ecology" and "natural farming" it amuses Fernande, because she knows they are really talking about the kind of farming everybody has to do these days to stay alive. She worries about her son, Maurice, who is twenty-five now and has so little of the excitement, the sense of starting an adventure, that those other young farmers have. She thinks that the life of a farmer starting out should be full of feeling and excitement, because it has to supply the memories to sustain him later on.

Fernande likes to remember the day that she and Georges took over the farm from her father. It was the fall of 1972, and M. Tricart had decided to celebrate his seventy-fifth birthday by retiring. Not that he was stopping work—he was stopping to enjoy a long last word against the government. At his birthday dinner, he signed over his entire property to Fernande—it cost him a gift tax of about three thousand francs, or, at the time, about six hundred dollars—and announced that he had saved the Pelletiers the price of at least twenty acres in inheritance taxes. Fernande concluded that she had twenty acres coming to her. She took out a loan at the Crédit Agricole in Sainte-Lucie and bought the land at a good price from her neighbor and admirer Pierre Lagorce, an old farmer who had had his eye on Fernande since she was a rosy girl with a flock of sheep and he was an ardent husband with a complaining wife. It happened that Fernande had something of her father's authority. She tried it out on Georges, who was a sweet-tempered, diffident sort of person, much happier when he was out somewhere on his tractor than when he was in the barnyard giving orders to someone else. She paid the bills, ordered the feed and the fertilizer, kept the books, bid on the sheep they bought at auction, and bargained with the three hard men from the farmers' union who ran the marketing cooperative. People with business on the farm would pay their respects to Georges, off by himself in a tobacco shed or a cornfield, and then they would head for the farmhouse and M. Tricart and his daughter. Fernande was nearly forty-two when she took over the farm. She was getting stout, but her cheeks were still rosy and her hair was as red and curly as it was when Lagorce first saw her, sitting on a rock with her dogs at her feet and her sheep all around her, studying the weekly racing form. She won nine thousand francs in the pari-mutuels that year, and bought a Deux Chevaux with some of the money. She drives it today; it is a kind of talisman. When she puts on her old duffel coat and a pair of mud boots and gets behind the wheel of that Deux Chevaux and goes bumping up the road with her bottle-red hair poking out of a plaid kerchief, she looks the way she must have looked the year she got her farm, and her horse came in, and she had a shy husband for nighttimes and a lusty old lover for the afternoons.

There is something young about Fernande at fifty-four, an awkward optimism that makes her touching. This year, she is feeding ducks for foie gras. Last year, it was geese as well. The year before, she had 120 veal calves in one barn, and was feeding them corn from her own hand. She is raising tobacco, too—not just the dark tobacco her father planted years ago on three acres up the hill from the farmhouse, where the soil is particularly fine, but light tobacco, which is not a Common Market surplus crop and brings a high price at auction. She is thinking about pressing oil from any walnuts which she doesn't sell. She used to make sunflower oil, but, with the price she gets now, it is not worth her time to go on with it, and, besides, she wants to see what walnut oil will bring if she puts it in little tin jars marked *"Fabrication Artisanale"* and sells it to a co-op for fancy-food stores. She is also thinking of saving walnut *brou*—the dark, fibrous casing around walnut shells that stains farmers' hands brown at harvest time—and selling it in Belgium, where it is bottled as "winter tanning lotion" and put on the cosmetic counters of expensive department stores. There are three acres of walnut trees on the farm, and it is getting hard for Fernande to compete with California walnuts, which come from huge farms and are artificially dried in only forty-eight hours; her walnuts are better, but she dries them naturally, and that takes three straight weeks of decent weather.

Still, the price of walnuts does not upset Fernande the way the price of lamb does. She has always thought of herself as a sheep farmer, despite her three acres of tobacco and her three acres of walnuts, not to mention her twenty-four acres of corn, her twelve acres of wheat, her twelve acres of barley, her sunflowers, her kitchen garden, her fruit trees, her six cows, her two pigs, her geese and chickens and the eighteen hundred ducks that pass through her barns each year to help keep France in foie gras and pâté. She is not a woman who regrets, she likes to say, but in spite of herself she regrets that there are no more sheep grazing out by the Vézère, and no lambs suckling in the pasture behind the barn. She gave up sheep in 1983. By then, she had 360 ewes and their lambs, and she was using a couple of prefab hangars to feed another fifteen hundred baby lambs, to be sold as Roquefort spring lamb when they got to eighty-five or ninety pounds. That spring, her ewes suddenly started dropping, and after the blood tests were in an inspector from town confirmed what Fernande herself suspected, once she was seeing two or three aborted lambs every time she left the house —and that was brucellosis. There was no insurance—Fernande was saving money in 1983—and no way for her to claim damages from the man who had sold the infected sheep to her. In the end, she got 225 francs from the state for every ewe she slaughtered—it was called a *prime d'abattage*—and 300 francs for each of the few that were still healthy and could be sold. It was not much money. No one wanted her lambs after that, and for a while, she says, she was close to ruin. She blamed herself. She blamed stray sheep crossing the Pyrenees from Spain and breeder sheep imported from Australia, because sheep that were not French were, to her mind, diseased to begin with and survived only to spread their diseases around. She blamed the Communists, because people said that rich Communist farmers here were buying weak, sickly sheep from Eastern Europe in order to give their friends a chance to earn some hard currency. By now, she doesn't blame the brucellosis. She says that brucellosis was merely the *coup de grâce* to her career as a sheep farmer, since there was no way to make a living from sheep anyway once the English had started selling their Common-wealth lamb in France at a lower price than she or most other small French farmers could afford to ask. It does not console her that there was also no way for a small English farmer to match the low price of all the good French fruit at an English supermarket.

Fernande Pelletier keeps going, and keeps her farm going, and in her way—with or without her sheep—is prosperous. The neighbors say she has a *"grosse exploitation."* To them, she is a rich woman. She has that "extreme love of the soil" which Tocqueville wrote about— that "illuminating attachment" of a French peasant to his land which is probably the most profound attachment of the civilization. When a farmer like Fernande—when anybody French—talks about France, that person is talking literally, talking about soil and trees and vines. The idea of La France, which is held so fervently here and mocked so insistently abroad, is drawn from that experience of the countryside. Strangers are astonished at this. They decide that the French are primitive under their immense sophistication, but what they describe as primitive to their friends at home is really an identification of soul and place of great ethnographic purity. Every Frenchman has his *pays,* his corner of the provinces, his ancestral soil, even if that soil belongs to somebody else by now or is confined to the flowerpots of a family farmhouse that has been restored by bickering cousins for country Christmases and August holidays. Fernande would not know what to make of the abandoned countryside in southern Italy or Spain or Portugal. The idea of a French family abandoning its corner of France is as strange, as unnatural, to her as the idea of a ewe abandoning her lamb or a mother her child. She considers the land of France a trust and the peasants who tend it the custodians of that trust.

In a way, they are. It has been three hundred years since the nobility began to leave the countryside, keeping their châteaus for hunts and holidays, and gradually selling off their fields to pay the potlatch cost of court life in Paris and Versailles. By the Revolution, most of the local *châtelains* in France were people who could not afford to move to town, and half the farmland was peasant freeholds. The family across the valley from the Pelletiers can trace their births and their bans and their funerals in village records back to 1300. Their farm was surveyed in the 1700s and the deed to it entered at the *mairie* seven generations ago. Georges Pelletier's family goes back that far in *its* village, over on the south side of the Vézère. And Pierre Lagorce, who spent seventeen days in school in 1920 and only learned to sign his name in 1969, when he took out a loan for his daughter's dowry, was once the owner of 150 acres and a dilapidated château with twenty-five rooms. His daughter did well with her dowry. She married a plumber and lives in a house in town and, according to Fernande, puts on terrible airs and pretends that the family was a noble family once —the de la Gorce family, she says—and suffered some mysterious calamity. The truth is that M. Lagorce bought his château a few days after the war, and the only family that suffered a calamity was the one that sold it to him for a few hundred dollars. Lagorce talks a lot about working, but he is at his best at the Pelletiers' kitchen table with a glass of wine in his hand and a discourse to deliver. Working itself never agreed with him. He was not happy as a *châtelain*. He lived in an old farmhouse on his land, out of sight of the château and the walls that needed pointing and the roof that needed tiling. He let the trees and the fields go. Eventually, he sold the place to a young vicomte from Paris who was a passionate farmer, and he went to work for the vicomte as part of the bargain—an arrangement that consisted of Lagorce "supervising" and the young vicomte and his vicomtesse getting up with the sun to build walls and dig up rocks and plant flowers while their supervisor slept.

Fernande's family worked for the château once. It was before the Revolution, and the Tricart family was what the French call *en métayage*, which means that they were sharecroppers, turning over half their harvest to the château according to the terms of yearly contracts that they could never extend and never anticipate. After the Revolution, they began to rent the land they farmed. They were *fermiers* then —tenant farmers, with a proper lease in the *notaire*'s safe, and the knowledge that they would never have to ruin another Christmas wondering whether their *châtelain* was going to throw them out on December 31. They started to buy their land, acre by acre, the year Fernande got married. Her father wanted the land for her. He wanted to settle it on her, the way he would have settled a chest of sheets and tablecloths on an ordinary daughter. That land has been the romance of her life —not the affable husband who runs errands for her on his tractor, or the garrulous old lover who has overstayed his welcome by a quarter of a century, or the son who, at twenty-five, is often as slow as he was at four, when his mother took him to the Paris doctor and asked if he was going to talk.

Fernande and Georges had an understanding. They never talked about it, but it was agreed that when they married Georges would turn over whatever land he inherited to his brothers and sisters, so that Fernande and her land could stay together. Or, rather, it was accepted that Fernande's attachment was stronger. Certainly she would never have sold her farm, the way Lagorce sold his to the vicomte. As it is, she is reluctant even to share it with Maurice—or with her daughter, Mercedes, who is married and lives in Tulle and has a family of her own. Other farmers in Sainte-Lucie-le-Pont are overjoyed if their sons stay home, the way Maurice did. They do everything to please them. They are paterfamilias at the table, but on the farm they cede their authority. Lately, in Sainte-Lucie, they are signing contracts with their sons so that father and son become a kind of family cooperative —a GAEC, or *groupement agricole d'exploitation en commun*—and are partners, dividing the family's property and its profits along with the work there is to do. Fernande does not approve of this sort of arrangement. Perhaps she does not trust anybody else to love the farm as she does. Or perhaps she does not expect the farm to outlast her optimism for it, now that the Pelletiers have had to give up their sheep for ducks and some of their dark tobacco for light tobacco and their sunflower oil for walnut oil, and the man at the Crédit Agricole in Sainte-Lucie —he was sent to the village after losing a couple of million francs through bad loans in one of the big-city branches—says to concentrate on crops that haven't made the EEC agenda, and the man down the street at the state agricultural office says no, it is more important to concentrate on the quality of the crops they already have, and their deputy says that small farmers are the future of the Common Market, and their mayor tells them that farms like theirs will be obsolete by the end of the century.

Twenty-five years ago, there were two and a half million farmers in France. De Gaulle was President. He was provincial and puritanical and profoundly Catholic. He had, Fernande says, "farmers' values," and he believed that those values were France's power. He held them insistently, while the rest of Europe was abandoning the countryside for the city, the farm for the factory, the reality of property for the illusions of paper capital; and because of this France entered the Common Market shrewdly, at great agricultural advantage, "sacrificing" the industrial advantages to Germany. The Minister of Agriculture then was Edgard Pisani, and most people who know anything about French farming consider Pisani the best Agriculture Minister the country ever had. In his way, he was a visionary. His particular vision was the ideal French farm—an *exploitation familiale* that could be farmed to its potential by the members of one family working together and that could support that family completely. He talked about *la tâche primordiale* —the primordial task of farming—and at the same time about an entirely new relation between the French farmer and his land, and between the collectivity of French farmers and what he called "the space of the nation." Pisani's rhetoric was thick, but, simply put, what he wanted was to see each ideal French farm join with the other ideal French farms in its neighborhood, creating chains of cooperatives and collectives, and linking the farmland of France by region and husbandry and local culture. He resigned from the government in 1968, and broke with de Gaulle in 1969 and joined the Socialists, but by the time he did, French family agriculture had been eased into the century and spared the kind of brutal modernization that was turning farmers in most of Europe into a disaffected proletariat. Oddly, the prototype for Pisani's ideal French farm was the ideal English farm—eighty or a hundred acres of intensively cultivated land, which compensated for its small (by England's colonial standards) size through the extravagant attention of its farmers. French farmers had a fine tradition of *main-d'œuvre* themselves, and Pisani's genius was to encourage it in ways that never undermined the technology that was really changing their lives. The fact that they could think of France as a breadbasket, and not a container truck or a carton for square tomatoes, was a measure of the extent to which de Gaulle and his minister had reassured them that the France they knew, the old France—*la France profonde*—was the real source of their prosperity, and that the changes that frightened them were changes only on the surface of their lives.

When France made its arrangements with the Common Market, in 1962, the country was as close to being self-sufficient in food as any place in Europe except, maybe, Sweden, which was not a member. French farmers were in the business of feeding France, the way they had always been. They were not really in the business of exporting food, and certainly none of them dreamed that in twenty-three years there would be a million tons of surplus butter sitting in Common Market freezers and another million tons of powdered milk in Common Market silos. They thought of "export" in terms of the Brie and the Roquefort and the château wines and the first-press olive oils they sold to fancy stores in London and New York. Most of the grains and the milk and butter they produced—the survival foods—stayed in France. What the French call *concurrence*—the dropping or balancing of trade and tariff barriers to create a competitive common market, in which, say, a French string bean could cost in Hamburg what it cost in Paris —began in 1962, when they sold cereal grains in Germany for what would have been the market price at home. In 1968, French milk became Community milk. Meat was put *en concurrence* during the sixties and seventies (although the *concurrence* was adjusted according to what sort of meat it was), and was followed, in the last few years, by wine and fruit (with more complicated adjustments and readjustments). For a while, French farmers were thriving. They were expanding their farms and in some cases doubling their crops—and they were making money doing it, because everyone else in Europe was buying. They were joining storage collectives and marketing cooperatives, and —the Pelletiers do this—were getting together with other farmers to invest in expensive harvesters and corn chutes and tractors that they could never have bought alone.

People like the Pelletiers discovered credit in the early days of the Common Market. Maître Prot, the *notaire* in Sainte-Lucie, says that most of the local farmers had never used a check before 1962. They kept a big wallet full of franc notes, and when they went out they attached it, for safety, to a chain on their vest, and did their business and paid their bills that way. But once the Crédit Agricole opened a branch in Sainte-Lucie they joined and started writing checks, and then they started borrowing money to pay for what they bought with those checks. Fernande herself had a checking account and two loans paid up before she had electricity on the farm, or even running water. She may have decided that borrowing money was less shameful, in the end, than no lights and no toilet and a yard that looked like the *basse cour* of a set for some medieval movie. By the time she went to the bank for money for Pierre Lagorce's twenty acres, the Crédit Agricole had six hundred clients in Sainte-Lucie, and those clients were also buying new land and, with it, new machines, and they were farming efficiently enough to let a few of their children leave home—the way Fernande let Mercedes leave for Tulle and marry an arms-factory worker. All told, since 1960 a million French peasants have left the land they farmed or their parents farmed. (During those twenty-five years, the agricultural yield in France has nearly doubled.) One reason they left was that they had somewhere to go. There was a labor shortage here in the 1960s and 1970s. Factories were recruiting—first the million new French workers and then a few million immigrant workers—because back on the farm the workers' parents were buying machines and wiring the house and starting to buy the gadgets these factories produced. The honeymoon between agriculture and industry—with farmers making more money with less manpower and using it to buy the sorts of things they had never thought about until their children moved to towns like Tulle and Lille and Clermont-Ferrand and started making them —was a little like France's honeymoon with Germany when France was the only breadbasket in the EEC and Germany was the machine shop. In twenty years, both honeymoons were over. The idea of "Europe" had been moving only as long as no one suffered from it, or thought he suffered. "Europe" itself ended up in the kind of family fight where everyone divides the pots and pans and the flatware and tries never to meet again except at funerals.

The fact is that people like the Pelletiers think of themselves as French farmers, not European farmers. When English lamb (which often means New Zealand or Australian lamb) or Italian wine arrives in Sainte-Lucie selling for less money than the Pelletiers' lamb or their neighbors' wine, they say that France is threatened, not that "Europe" is served. The agreements that have been signed in Brussels since 1962 by politicians determined to promote the interests of France, say, or Germany or England while defending the rhetoric of "Europe" have got so complicated by now, so elaborate, that it is much easier to add to them than to explain them, let alone make them work. Every formula for fair subsidies or quotas seems to create a new set of inequities to replace the ones it was supposed to remove (one Community bureaucrat called the EEC Gödel's proof), and every national gesture seems to offend "Europe" as much as Europe's gestures offend its members. Of course, the commitment to a European community grew out of the Second World War—out of a common experience of demented nationalism and the impulse, after that experience, to soften borders and create connections. People in Europe knew that any real economic recovery would have to be shared. Jean Monnet could speak convincingly of "European unity," because they never expected to be undone by nationalism again, especially the fairly respectable kind of nationalism that seems to be the common experience now. The charter of the EEC is clear—any European state that meets Community criteria involving democratic elections, civil and economic freedom, and human rights is eligible for membership—and so is the assumption of the men who signed it that belonging to "Europe" is the best way to keep on meeting those criteria. When Greece gets rid of its colonels, or when the Generalissimo dies in Spain, the EEC is under a kind of contractual obligation to let that country in. The country applies, and its application is welcomed with a lot of speeches and a lot of tight smiles —and then the members get together and argue for years about how to protect themselves against their would-be partner. Everybody knows vaguely that the EEC is a good thing. Presumably, Spain and Portugal, which are trying to join now, know, too. But it is hard for people in the Community to explain exactly why it is such a good thing when they spend so much of their time trying to get around it.

The arrangements and rearrangements and exceptions and exemptions and subsidies that have made lamb chops coming from England a better buy in Sainte-Lucie than Fernande Pelletier's lamb chops are coded and stored in the Common Market computer, and perhaps a few people in Brussels understand them. They are beyond Fernande. She has asked about them in Sainte-Lucie. She asked the manager at the Crédit Agricole; he is a little odd, because of his disgrace, and he looked cross and peered at Fernande in case she was a spy from the *caisse* in Paris posing as Mme Pelletier and trying to catch him out in another bad loan, and finally he said, "Madame, it is illusory to expect that international agriculture is going to adapt itself to your small enterprise." He told her to accept the fact that, with a hilly piece of property like hers, and only a couple of acres of really "serious" soil, she would never be able to compete with an English sheep farmer, let alone with any of the thousands of big one-crop farms in France. He said he had seventy-four sorts of loans, with seventy-four different sets of terms, at his disposal, and that he was certain they could find a nice one— although he did acknowledge that the rules about lending money were a little stricter under Mitterrand than they had been under Giscard, who rarely paid attention. Polyculture was the answer, he said. This year, people at his branch of the bank were thinking in terms of three specialties per farm: one vegetable crop, one pasture animal, and one *exploitation hors sol*—which literally means "off the ground," and which in Fernande's case means plants or animals that do not use land, like hydroponic tomatoes or veal fattened in a feed pen. The manager told Fernande to "spread her risk" (*"Diversifiez vos investissements, Madame"*) and accept the realities of the market, and choose crops that the Pelletier family could raise on a hundred acres but that a robot on a thousand acres could not.

Fernande thought about what the bank manager had said. That night, she talked it over with Georges and with Pierre Lagorce, who had started eating at the Pelletiers' when his wife died and now that he was "retired" was around all day, offering advice (which was often good advice) and keeping Fernande company, so that Georges could disappear on his tractor and do the farming. Lagorce had been gossiping about some new neighbors in Sainte-Lucie-le-Pont—two Dutch couples who shared a house and, apparently, their affections. It was a scandal of great interest to Lagorce and to the Pelletiers, who believed that rich city people usually bought country houses in order to be depraved in private. Fernande does not talk about her own household arrangements, although she certainly considers it much more respectable to be eating with Georges *and* Pierre Lagorce than it would be to be eating with Lagorce alone. In a way, the Pelletiers have come to regard Lagorce as if he were an old relative with nowhere else to go —an embarrassment, maybe, but, in the end, their charge. Lagorce regards himself as indispensable. When Fernande complained that they were already as "polycultural" as they could get, considering that they had grown or raised or fed just about every plant or animal the area could support, Lagorce said that polyculture was not their problem anyway—their problem was that they were not *hors sol*. And then Maurice spoke up, and said that *he* had heard about *hors sol* at some point during his year as an apprentice on a "scientific farm." Usually, nobody pays much attention to Maurice except his wife, Clémentine, and *she* always tries to pay attention—if they are at supper, say, or in bed, and she isn't busy doing anything important. Clémentine is the daughter of dirt farmers from the next village, and (it is acknowledged) she is not a beauty. She never expected to find a husband, let alone a husband who was tall and handsome in a blank, cheerful sort of way, and the heir to a hundred acres. Three years ago, she married Maurice in the church in Sainte-Lucie-le-Pont where Fernande had married Georges in 1955, and like Fernande, she spent a brief honeymoon at Lourdes—after which she was put to work on the farm, feeding the ducks in the barn and washing up after meals and doing the laundry and keeping the family accounts in Fernande's big green ledger, and doing all the other things that are expected of a daughter-in-law without a dowry. She was paying attention when Maurice said that, to his mind, force-feeding eighteen hundred ducks for foie gras in a small barn was farming *hors sol*. She even blushed, because the word "mind" sounded so intelligent. But Pierre Lagorce disagreed. He said that feeding ducks in a barn was not, in itself, *hors sol*, and the next afternoon he called everybody into the barn to demonstrate what a real *"exploitation hors sol"* was. He fastened one of the duck coops to a rope. Then he threw the rope over a rafter. And while everybody watched and Clémentine made careful notes in the ledger, he hoisted the coop a few feet off the ground—*"Voilà, hors sol,"* he said—and left it there and tipped his blue beret and waited for congratulations.

Once or twice a year, Fernande invites her neighbors Odette and Paul Martignac to a big Sunday lunch. The Martignacs are what people in Paris would call *petits hobereaux*—little provincial nobles. They live in a château down by the Vézère, and possess a title on Odette's side and a Gaullist officer on Paul's, and are a couple with *"un peu de race,"* as Fernande puts it. They always drive to the farm in a 1967 Peugeot, but they like to look as if they had been out hunting and had just dismounted—in hacking jackets and jeans and leather riding boots. The Pelletiers, for their part, dress for the occasion. Georges puts on his Sunday suit, and Fernande puts on the outfit she copied from a picture in *Le Pèlerin* six years ago—a yellow-and-green plaid kilt and a dark-green blouse to go with it. As soon as she says hello, she covers her outfit up with her old nylon housecoat and starts stirring and beating and basting in the kitchen, and never thinks to remove the housecoat until the Martignacs are gone.

The Martignacs are important farmers for Sainte-Lucie-le-Pont. They have corn and wheat, and thirty acres just in walnut trees —that means a harvest of thirty tons a year to dispose of—and Paul Martignac has even been to California to look at some of the astonishing walnut farms where the trees are tended by machines and the nuts are dried in forty-eight hours. The nuts taste terrible, he says, but by now they sell as well as the Martignacs' nuts, because nobody else seems to care about the difference. Someone in California told Martignac about the Diamond Nut Company, which produces eighty thousand more tons of walnuts in a year than all the farms in France put together, and he has been depressed about this ever since he came home to Sainte-Lucie-le-Pont. He worries about his farm, and about the family furniture and the family portraits on his walls. There are robbers around Sainte-Lucie—*brocanteurs* who arrive at night in trucks and make off with your antiques to sell at flea markets to important Paris dealers —but Martignac says that, given the nut competition from California, he will never be able to afford alarms for his château and will have to depend on his aging cocker spaniel, Irène, to defend his treasures. Thinking about his pictures and his Louis XV candlesticks and his set of twenty-four dining-room chairs that may or may not have put in time at Fontainebleau makes him nervous when he is out at the Pelletiers', say, having Sunday lunch, but he always accepts their invitation and is always easy with them and talks a lot and exchanges local gossip and enjoys Fernande's cooking. He and Odette, who is a handsome woman with long black hair in a bun and her mother's emeralds pinned to her hacking jacket, do not acknowledge Pierre Lagorce at the Pelletiers' table. Martignac consults with Georges about the weather and the crops and the criminals in Mitterrand's government, and Odette Martignac talks to Fernande about food, and the women exchange recipes, and then everybody compares the Martignacs' strawberry wine with the Pelletiers' walnut wine and gets a little drunk and barely notices that Pierre Lagorce has started talking, too. Sunday lunch at the Pelletiers' runs from noon till three or four in the afternoon when there is company. It begins with fresh foie gras and Fernande's foie-gras pâté, and then, if it is the mushroom season, there is a gratin of *cèpes* and maybe a mushroom tart, too, and afterward one of Fernande's fat ducks or a corn-fed chicken from the yard, and cheese, of course, and the glazed apple turnover from her grandmother's recipe book (which is often charred now that Fernande is teaching Clémentine to make it) and an ice-cream bombe with two flavors in the middle. There is wine from the *cave*, and, after dessert, cognac and Armagnac and coffee and, always, a plate of ordinary chocolates that Fernande drives all the way to Brive to buy at the confectioner's, and, being the only part of the meal she pays for, are what she assumes has made it special.

Fernande likes having company. Eight years ago, she added a big new room to the farmhouse to be her company room, and fixed it up until, to her mind, it was just like the living room the young vicomtesse from Paris had put together when she bought Lagorce's château. Fernande had helped the vicomtesse with that room—she had unpacked the plates and the pictures and the walnut side tables and had fitted together the stone fireplace that the vicomtesse had found, in pieces, at a convent auction—and once they had got the room in order and Fernande was used to everything in it being so old she decided to admire the room as much as she admired the vicomtesse. Actually, Fernande would have preferred a modern room for herself, something easy to wipe down, but not long afterward—it was a year when her sheep were selling well—she asked Georges and Pierre Lagorce to strip the beams and the tiles from two old barns on the farm, and went out looking for a stone fireplace of her own and a brass chandelier for the ceiling. Her room looked a little bare, though, so she improved on the vicomtesse's salon. She bought smoked glass for the windows, so that everything outside was blurry and romantic, and you couldn't see the old machines and the tractor in the barnyard. She ordered fringed lampshades from a farm-wife catalogue, and velvet armchairs the color of tarragon mustard, and a couple of brand-new "Oriental" rugs that were much more cheerful than the vicomtesse's faded carpets, and after

Maurice got married she added seven rubber plants that George's sister
had sent as a wedding present, tied with pink-and-white taffeta bows
and trailing ribbons on the floor.

Fernande thinks the room is perfect now, but she never uses it if
the family is alone. When the telephone in the room rings, she stands
to answer it and talk; she is not really comfortable in her velvet chairs
—the way she would not be comfortable in one of the twenty-four
chairs in the Martignacs' dining room. Odette Martignac has never
invited the Pelletiers for a Sunday lunch at her house, and if she did
Fernande would feel awkward and embarrassed and would never invite
the Martignacs to the farm again. The rules in Sainte-Lucie-le-Pont are
severe, though probably less so to the people who follow them than to
the people who try to write them down, and according to those rules
a *châtelain*— Fernande considers the Martignacs *châtelains*— can visit a
peasant in the peasant's house and sit comfortably at his table but the
peasant can never sit down at the *châtelain*'s table without doing a
curious kind of damage to their relations. There is a common culture
in France, and Fernande can open a family album begun in 1847 and
read her great-grandmother's notes for scalloping a sheet or making a
chestnut mousse or the fine menu for her mother's confirmation, in 1913,
but what is shared is not class but appreciation. Appreciation and
discretion and delicacy and assurance. Fernande's mother has a great
deal of delicacy. She is eighty years old, and beautiful, and her face,
framed by the black scarf and the collar of the long black cardigan she
put on when M. Tricart died, is delicate, and so are the flutter of her
hands and her laugh, like a chirp, whenever something funny or outra-
geous is happening in the house—whenever, say, Pierre Lagorce starts
talking. Sometimes she says she wishes she had "gone" with M. Tricart,
but there is nothing morbid about her. She feels not so much out of
place as out of her proper time in the house she used to manage. When
she is thinking about M. Tricart, she will disappear into the *cave* and
dust the dining-room furniture that was part of her dowry—and that
Fernande uses now for storing preserves and drying apples. There is
a table of blackened oak, and there are two massive sideboards with little
doors and balconies and pillars all over them which Mme Tricart calls
her Henri II sideboards, because that was how the man in the furniture
store described them in 1926, when she and *her* mother went shopping
for something that nobody in Sainte-Lucie-le-Pont was apt to have. She
has never understood why Odette Martignac looked so disappointed
after she climbed down into the *cave* to see the sideboards for herself.
Mme Tricart comes from Limoges and is the only one in the family

who has ever—if the word applies—travelled. Once a year, when she was a bride, she used to leave Sainte-Lucie-le-Pont for Limoges to see her father, who was a carter and carried barrels of wine from the great Bordeaux châteaus to the Limoges merchants. Now she never travels. She rarely goes out of the house at all. She stays in the kitchen, cooking or knitting or looking at the pictures in *Le Pèlerin* or daydreaming. When there is company, and the Pelletiers are eating in their big new room, she will join them as long as she can sit at the place nearest the kitchen door, and the only thing she insists on anymore is that the television set stay in the kitchen, so she can watch *Dallas* and *Dynasty* from her old chair at the foot of the kitchen table. Her only excursions now are her annual visits to the *notaire*, Maître Prot, who is nearly eighty, too. She admires Maître Prot for his clarity. She still talks about the day her husband bought his first tractor and Maître Prot came out to the farm himself and explained so beautifully what "depreciating one's tractor" meant: he told Olivier Tricart to think of the tractor as if it were the oxen that used to pull his plow and lived for twenty years and lost a little of their value every year as they got older.

Last fall, Maître Prot sat behind his big Empire desk in Sainte-Lucie and received Fernande and her mother and talked with tears in his eyes about "*vous braves paysans.*" Maître Prot was born in Sainte-Lucie, and he could see what happened to his old friends when an agricultural adviser arrived from Toulouse or Limoges or one of the other big towns and told them to raise beef, and, on his next visit, to forget beef and grow tobacco, and then, when tobacco prices fell, to switch to grazing sheep—that is, until cheap lamb started coming in from England, and he had to come back and explain that there had been a *petite erreur,* and that he should have said walnuts or snails or foie gras. Maître Prot was the mayor of Sainte-Lucie-le-Pont for a long time. It was during his last year at the *mairie* that the local chapter of the big farmers' union, the Fédération Nationale des Syndicats d'Exploitants Agricoles, joined a roadblock against trucks carrying foreign meat through the Périgord. That was also the year some Sainte-Lucie farmers tried to do what the farmers down in Cahors had done to protest against the foreign meat—drive their sheep to the prefecture and open the door and let the animals in. Maître Prot did not know what to advise Fernande then, and he did not know what to advise her in December, when she and her mother came for their yearly visit and Fernande announced, suddenly, how much she missed her sheep and said she was unhappy in a barn feeding ducks, even with a daughter-in-law to do it for her. He told Fernande that she could buy new sheep and feed them well and still lose so much money because of the *concurrence* that she would have to sell them—and then discover in a year or two that French lamb was in demand again. Right now, the government was paying farmers about fifteen hundred francs for every milk cow they slaughtered, and Maître Prot wondered what was going to happen when people needed milk again and raising cows was profitable and those farmers who had worried about a surplus in 1984 had slaughtered all the cows they had.

There is no doubt that Fernande and the other farmers in Sainte-Lucie-le-Pont could plan better and work better and get the kind of quality in their meat and produce which may be their one hope against the dizzying competition from abroad. Fernande knows this, but she also knows that life was much simpler for a farmer when Maître Prot and her father were young men. The smart young farmers today are trained to plan better and work better, and even so—unless their farms are enormous—they eventually have to forget about raising cows or sheep or planting their own wheat, and turn their barns into feed hotels for strangers' animals on their way from their mothers' milk to the slaughterhouse. That kind of work is shaming to a real farmer, and in the end it is not much more secure than keeping a pasture full of Charolais cows and a bull in the barn and raising their own calves. They borrow to begin with. They buy too much feed or too many machines or take on too many animals. Like their parents, they end up fattening veal or lambs on ninety-day contracts or stuffing ducks or geese with corn for foie gras or incubating snails, and then discovering that it is the wrong market for veal or baby lambs or ducks or snails. They are left with rusty machines and three loan payments a year to make to the Crédit Agricole so that no one will come to claim those machines or the cars and television sets and electric stoves that were bought so proudly on expectations of a good life.

This year, Fernande is paying the interest on two bank loans. She is paying what amounts to seven hundred dollars in taxes to Sainte-Lucie-le-Pont and a land tax of four hundred dollars to the village of Sainte-Lucie, which is a cantonal seat with eight incorporated hamlets like Sainte-Lucie-le-Pont, and a population of twelve hundred, and she is paying a house tax and a tax to a town forty miles away to which Sainte-Lucie is attached for obscure bureaucratic purposes, and another two thousand dollars for social security and health insurance. She could pay less if she itemized her taxes. Clémentine—who is happiest when she can sit on one of the velvet chairs in the company room with Fernande's ledger in her lap, adding and subtracting and in general

savoring the numbers that belong to Maurice's family—wants to prepare a proper tax form for her mother-in-law, with columns and calculations, but Fernande wants to sign the simplest standard form the state
provides and have done with it. She is like her father in this; she wants
the last word when she is doing business with the government. She
knows that someone in Paris is bound to check her taxes if Clémentine
complicates them—and deprive her of the great pleasure of cheating on
her declaration.

Lately, Fernande has been thinking a lot about the way she ended
up at home on her father's farm—by now a kind of father to the family,
too. She loves the highland of the Périgord, with its dips and its rises
and the patches of landscape that catch her storybook memories and
make her wait for the knights of some imaginary gentle time to pitch
their pointed tents and start their games while their ladies wave pretty
scarves and sigh. She loves the riverbanks and the old steel bridge in
Sainte-Lucie-le-Pont, and even the weather that is always turning.
Sometimes she feels the appropriateness of her life on the land, and then
when she talks about it she is blunt and eloquent and sentimental
—and I think of Millet, who painted peasants like her and talked about
how planting wheat and sowing potatoes was noble. There are other
times when Fernande shrugs and says that there was nothing for her
to do but farm. She was a schoolgirl during the war, and was sent off
with the other village girls to a convent in the hills while their mothers
stayed home with the animals and their fathers either were taken prisoner of war or were put to work in factories or disappeared into the
Resistance. There were nights when she heard German soldiers on the
road and German guns in the distance, and once she and her friends
at the convent saw a group of farmers run out of the woods and
dynamite a bridge along the Germans' route. She remembers the nuns'
telling them that Germans had stopped at Oradour-sur-Glane, up in the
Haute-Vienne, and shut the women and children in a church and killed
them all, and how after that, whenever there were steps on the road at
night, they hid in the cold *caves* of the convent, too terrified of the rats
to cry. She was fifteen when she came home to Sainte-Lucie-le-Pont,
and, she likes to say, she was *"très, très collet monté"*—very straitlaced
and prudish. For a while, the only times she saw her neighbors were
Sunday mornings, when the family walked the three miles down from
the farm to the village church. Then her grandmother died, and she was
in mourning for a year, and then her grandfather died, and she was in
mourning for another year, and finally another grandfather died, and

one of her uncles, too—which meant that Fernande Tricart wore black and stayed at home until she was nearly twenty-five and met Georges Pelletier at a neighbor's wedding. He was the first young man in the house since the family had put away its mourning bands, and Fernande wondered when there would be another—and told her father to settle the marriage contract. She wanted to have a wedding with bridesmaids and a trainbearer and a hundred farmers dancing, like the one the neighbor had. When the wedding was over, and she had been to Lourdes and collected her blessing, she settled down to her old duties on the farm and took her orders from her father until he died and she started giving the orders herself. It may be that she has kept her hair red all these years—even though the sun on the dye turns it orange and gives it strange metallic splotches—in order to keep her future open. When this year's Agriculture Ministry adviser came to the farm and told her that the Israelis were now exporting foie gras to France —cheap foie gras, which could ruin the market for Fernande's foie gras —Fernande just smiled at him and offered him a glass of her walnut wine and said that she was not going to be discouraged or confused, the way she was sometimes when she turned on the evening news and heard about its costing France more money to give away food surpluses to people starving in Ethiopia than to let the surpluses rot at home. She told him she knew all about how French farmers should cut their harvests and reduce their costs. She had read (she thinks it was in *La France Agricole*) that less than 15 percent of the farmers in France study anything at all, let alone farming, after high school, but she did not know why studying was so important when the ducks that Pierre Lagorce had lifted *hors sol* were doing just as well as the ducks that Maurice, with his year on a scientific farm, was raising on the barn floor.

France right now accounts for about a third of Europe's food, and in Fernande's part of France wealth *is* food, not killing your cows or cutting back your harvest. Fernande believes that she is rich when her granaries are full and her animals are having babies. Her sense of who she is is something she can measure directly against the corn in her cribs and the dry tobacco plants hanging in her sheds. She would never vote for a Socialist, but the fact is that the only Agriculture Minister she has approved of since Edgard Pisani was Mitterrand's first Minister of Agriculture, Édith Cresson, because Mme Cresson stood up to the union that was protecting the interests of the big farmers, and spoke for the farmers like Fernande, and for *their* land and the dignity of *their* commitment. Édith Cresson was not a realist. The average French farm is about sixty acres; by the end of the century, it will be ninety or a hundred, and, as the people at the Ministry here in Paris say, "the farm pyramid will turn over"—by which they mean that there will be bigger farms and fewer farmers, and that those farmers will be specializing in the kinds of experiments they learned about in agricultural schools. They will know how to produce a pig like the pigs in China, which have five more piglets in a litter than French pigs do, or hybrid corn like the corn in America. There will be discipline in French farming then. Competition will be harsh, and a farm will survive on its cost-plus figures, not on the courage of its farmers.

January 1985

EMMANUEL BOVE

It is about a half-hour walk from my street to the cemetery in Montparnasse, and it is a walk that people in the neighborhood make often, because so many interesting characters are buried there. Abbé Grégoire, the radical priest of the Revolution, is in the cemetery, along with his old adversary Claude François Chauveau-Lagarde, the lawyer who defended Marie Antoinette and Charlotte Corday. The painters Gérard and Girodet are there, and the historian Augustin Thierry, the explorer Jules Dumont d'Urville, and the astonishing doctor Matthieu Orfila, whose essays on the properties of arsenic inspired a generation of poisoners. Like Père-Lachaise and the cemetery in Montmartre, the cemetery in Montparnasse is a kind of tombstone history of the last hundred and fifty years of the capital. Jean-Paul Sartre's ashes were buried there in 1980. Thousands of students marched in his funeral cortège through Montparnasse, and got to know the place, and a lot of them come back now to visit. They come when the weather is good, to read and walk around with a *pain au chocolat* and enter into a kind of custodial communion with their hero. There is always a flower on Sartre's grave; Simone de Beauvoir left a rose on the day of the funeral, and afterward the students took over.

My neighbor Véronique Lavali, who rents a *chambre de bonne* on the sixth floor and is getting her doctorate in Japanese, had an odd experience at Sartre's grave. One day, she stopped by with a potted geranium, and was just walking off to the Métro when an old man in overalls tapped her on the shoulder. His manners were correct, Véronique says. He asked if she would mind stepping behind one of the big mausoleums across the road and taking off her stockings. He needed her stockings, he said, but he would give her a nice new pair in exchange. Véronique says that she looked down at the stockings she had on, which were snagged from boots and had a run starting, and —being a warmhearted Niçoise anyway, and not prudish, like the Parisians in her class—she obliged him. The old man put her stockings in his pocket, presented Véronique with a little shopping bag from the Prisunic, and hurried off down a path between a row of tombs. A few days later, Véronique was back in the cemetery studying and the same old man appeared; she took off her stockings again and got another new pair. After that, their meetings were, as Véronique puts it, "established." The old man was solicitous. He would ask occasionally if the stockings fit, and once he wanted to know if she preferred a change of shade. Véronique says that she used to imagine him alone with her stockings—alone in a shabby room, somewhere on the edge of Montparnasse, with Véronique Lavali's big, round Niçoise legs on his mind and her stockings for company and stimulation. The thought pleased her, in a way. It made her feel sophisticated and tolerant, and I think she has never really forgiven the old man for telling her, at last, that what he used those stockings of hers for was cleaning tombstones. Cleaning tombstones was his job. People hired him to keep their crypts and their mausoleums polished, because according to cemetery rules a family that neglects its graves for more than five years is presumed dead, as it were, and its "concession"—its space in the ground— is sold. He uses lime to do it. As he said to Véronique, everyone in the cemetery business knows that nylon stockings are the best lime filters you can find. He buys a batch of stockings every couple of months, and adds the price to his bills, and, inasmuch as for *his* purpose old stockings do just as well as new ones, he has taken to trading. He may have decided that exchanging stockings with pretty young students who come to the cemetery to lay flowers on the graves of geniuses was a way of contributing to the culture. Véronique admits that it is a gallant gesture, though a strange one, maybe a little inappropriate, a little blunt in its innocence. She calls it *"un geste Emmanuel Bove."*

Emmanuel Bove was a French novelist who died in 1945, when he was forty-seven years old and had written twenty-eight books about the sort of *paumé* characters who usually end up in potter's fields. He himself, however, is buried in the cemetery in Montparnasse, over in what is called "the Jewish Section," in the family vault of Louise Ottensooser Bove, his second wife. The vault is one of those proper French mausoleums with a grillwork door, a stained-glass window, and a kind of altar for flowerpots and watering cans, but there are never any flowers. It has a desultory look to it, a look of being without a family. Last fall's leaves are scattered over the stone floor, and there are cobwebs in the corners—not much to suggest that an important French literary personage is buried there. Some of the people who admire Bove —people who began to read him in the seventies, when he was "discovered" and republished and written about in *Libération* and *Le Monde* under headlines like HAVE *YOU* READ EMMANUEL BOVE?—have made pilgrimages to the cemetery. They stop at the grave-registry building near the main gate, wait while a couple of clerks leaf through old ledgers and yellowed dossiers, and eventually make their way to the mausoleum, but apparently they find the gloom and the cobwebs and the leaves rather *Bovien,* and hesitate to interfere.

Bove wrote his first novel, *Mes Amis,* at twenty-four and introduced the French to what could be called the genre of impoverished solitude. *Mes Amis* was about being lonely with no moral or emotional resources, about encounters that failed because the people who wanted them had no capacity for honor or clarity or compassion. It was a ruthless, almost a clinical, description of failure, and it was startling in a country where being lonely was ordinarily either an occasion for phenomenological discourse or a highly stylized practice—being lonely in a café, say, or being lonely with a flower in the cemetery in Montparnasse. There was not much of a tradition for incapacity in French literature. The Russians could turn their failed encounters into rueful, humorous, illuminating stories, and the Germans understood those encounters as harsh paradigms of modern man, but there was nothing illuminating or paradigmatic about *Mes Amis*— and this is why the book was a sensation. Bove was mildly famous for a while. He won the Prix Figuière, and some of the best publishers in the country—Emile-Paul, Fayard, Calmann-Lévy, Gallimard—began to court him. He kept on writing, and publishing, for the rest of his life. When he died, he was forgotten. Yves Rivière, who publishes art books here and who inaugurated the "discovery" of Emmanuel Bove eleven years ago with an edition of three Bove stories illustrated by Jean Messagier, Bram van Velde, and Roland Topor, says that he simply died at the wrong time —that in 1945, with all the other French writers looking to their reputations after years of war, Bove's reputation was "unattended." Bove's old friend the writer Emmanuel Roblès says that Bove suffered "a betrayal of destiny." Philippe Soupault, the Dadaist, who knew Bove, too, says that he was "too discreet to be remembered."

The people who did remember Bove in those days, after the war, made a kind of group. They liked the mystery of the man. The fact that most of them knew nothing about him was part of his attraction. Bove was said to have been shy and silent and reclusive—Soupault says "too discreet," but other people say "pathologically discreet"—and his admirers saw him as the original novelist-cum-antihero. For them, he was as *Bovien* as the condition of his tomb is now. They liked to think of him among the drifters and hangers-on and hustlers in the old novels of his they passed around, and they considered him father to writers like Samuel Beckett (who is only eight years younger) and Jean Genet. Beckett in fact read Bove and liked what he read enough to praise it, but they were not friends. Bove's friends were not at all *Bovien*. They were lively and engaged: Roblès, Soupault, Jean Cassou, who wrote about art and ran the Paris Museum of Modern Art for a time and was a Resistance hero, the writer Marcel Aymé. Aymé died in 1967, but the others are still around. Some are very old, and, being old *and* distinguished, they expect the visits they get to be a kind of homage. They do not much want to spend them reminiscing about anybody but themselves.

Soupault is eighty-seven. He lives in an old-age home out near the Porte d'Auteuil, and shares his room with an enormous tinfoil ball, which he started putting together years ago from cigarette-package liners and pieces of aluminum foil and got attached to, and sometimes, talking about his friend, he shakes his head and says that Emmanuel Bove was not the only one who was forgotten. Cassou is eighty-eight. He lives with his books and his paintings in the big old flat near the Sorbonne where he raised his family, and always wears the black-and-green silk bar—black for mourning, green for hope—of the Compagnons de la Libération. Being a Compagnon carries great honor. It was de Gaulle's personal decoration, and it means that the General himself commended you for loyalty to France and great bravery against the Germans. There were only a thousand Compagnons. Cassou talks about how, even now, meeting on the street or at a café, they will greet each other with a *"Bonjour, Compagnon."* He would really rather talk about things like that than about Emmanuel Bove, but he wrote a fine preface to *Mes Amis* when Flammarion republished the book eight years ago, and in that he talks about the incredible "naïveté" of the unhappiness in a Bove novel and about Bove's own taste for "modest despair." There is a snapshot of Rilke, taken in the garden at Valmont just before he died, framed and hung on Cassou's living-room wall, and Cassou says it did not surprise him at all that his friend Rilke admired *Mes Amis*. It may be that the desultory appreciations of Paris in the book reminded Rilke of Malte Laurids Brigge's Paris, or even of his own.

This is the way *Mes Amis* begins: "When I wake up, my mouth is open. My teeth are greasy; it would be better if I brushed them at night, but I never have the courage for it." Victor Bâton, *mutilé de guerre,* is getting up. He starts the day with meticulous anomie. He is cold and rheumy. His eyelids are stuck. His nose is running. The ceiling of his attic room is leaking on his beard. Victor likes to scrutinize himself. His "friends" are really a catalogue—or a litany—of his misencounters, and Victor records them the way he records waking up, with an almost lewd self-absorption. But the idea of having a friend pleases him. He says he is looking for one. He sleeps with Lucie, who runs a bar on the rue de Seine. He hopes that afterward she will make him a cup of coffee in her bar, and feels sorry for himself when she does not. He meets a rich man, who offers him a job. He starts bothering the man's daughter on her way home from school, and when the man gets mad and fires him he wonders again why people always hurt his feelings. He tries out three or four other "friends" before the neighbors start to complain about him and the landlady gives him notice and the book ends, with Victor climbing back into his damp bed in the attic, complaining. He says that he does not see how he will ever find the friends he wants. By then, it is hard not to agree with him.

Mes Amis is considered Bove's best novel. There is a cautious formality, an etiquette, to Victor Bâton's misencounters which makes them (Samuel Beckett's word) "touching." It is easy to see why Rilke liked the book. The sensibility is more German than French or —Bove's father was Russian—Russian. Peter Handke, the Austrian writer, and Wim Wenders, the German filmmaker, talk about Bove now with the same sense of familiarity Rilke felt, talking to Cassou, sixty years ago. In France, it is more often the artists like Topor and Messagier who feel this familiarity reading Bove. For them, the very concrete and very precise language in a story by Emmanuel Bove is a language that addresses the eye, a language that the eye can read as images. Topor started to read Bove because a writer he knew— a writer with a "taste for agony," Topor says—described him as "a master of morose images," and Topor, who is an acknowledged master of morose images himself, was curious. He bought his first Bove in 1963 for a few francs, and his second for not much more. A first-edition Bove —if you can find one—costs six or seven hundred francs nowadays, and there are standing orders with every *bouquiniste* in town.

At about the same time that Topor was illustrating one Bove and
Handke (who got *his* first Bove from his French translator, Georges-
Arthur Goldschmidt) was turning another into German, a writer from
Brittany by the name of Raymond Cousse took up the cause of Emmanuel Bove. Raymond Cousse is an insistent, ebullient character, and he
is known here for his causes. One of them is critics. (A couple of years
ago, he published a book of his letters to all the critics in France he did
not admire.) Another is the comic monologues he likes to write. (Every
few years, he shepherds a one-man play called *Stratégie pour Deux
Jambons* around the world, performing it himself.) When Cousse discovered that he and Emmanuel Bove shared a birthday—it is April 20
—he became a passionate and protective advocate. He started tracking
down the Bove family. He put together a bibliography and then a
working chronology of Bove's life. He talked the people at Flammarion, his publisher, into putting out a Bove book every year or two,
with himself as editor of the series. He said that when he started
working on his bibliography not even the Bibliothèque Nationale had
all the Bove novels. He told them that Emmanuel Bove was a missing
piece of the patrimony, and that it was their duty to retrieve it. People
in Paris were asking "Who is Emmanuel Bove?" but the fact is that no
one really knew until this inquisitive and exhausting Breton told them.
It turned out that Bove was indeed discreet. He worried all the time
about money, and in general felt sorry for himself. He had no particular
politics and no particular enthusiasms, like Catholicism or Marx. He
was not part of *le discours.* He was, as Topor likes to say, *un caractère
pâle.*

Bove was born in 1898 on the Boulevard de Port-Royal. His real
name was Bobovnikoff, and his father, Emmanuel, was a Jewish émigré
from Kiev who, family wisdom had it, was an important nihilist in
exile. His mother was the chambermaid who cleaned his father's hotel
room. She was a hefty girl from Luxembourg, and Bobovnikoff must
have been fond of her, because she produced a second son, Léon, in
1902, four years before her lover settled down with a young English-
woman named Emily Overweg and had a son by *her.* Emily had money
—her father was the British consul in Shanghai, and she herself was a
painter—and she also had charm and a lot of tolerance. Her son, Victor,
still lives in Paris. He is a courtly lawyer of seventy-eight who rides,
mornings, in the Bois de Boulogne, and goes on *randonnées* in Switzerland. A couple of years ago, when he was riding in the Valais, he
galloped onto the road, wearing his Croix de Guerre, and saved a girl

whose horse had run away with her. Victor prefers the classics to
Emmanuel Bove. "Perhaps I attach more importance to grammar, to
fluidity of style, than Emmanuel did," he says. "Emmanuel was fond
of the imperfect subjunctive. But the imperfect subjunctive three times
in one sentence—*c'est l'horreur.*"

Emmanuel Bobovnikoff presented himself in Paris as a literary
man. His documents said "without profession," but he did in fact write
one book. It was a tourist dictionary for rich Russians coming to Paris
for the World's Fair of 1900, and while it was not exactly a piece of
nihilist literature, it did well, being full of useful phrases, on the order
of "I would like to reserve a table at Maxim's" and "Do you have a suite
facing the Parc Monceau?" and "Take me to the House of Callot."
Bobovnikoff was not much interested in his son Léon. Léon was a little
simple—someone Bove might have invented later on. (Léon is eighty-
three now and lives alone in a cottage in Versailles, where he keeps a
record of his life, filling one small school notebook every week with
what he considers the important information—what time he goes to
bed, how many trips he makes to the market, the price of the tomatoes
he buys there, the phone calls he makes, the busy signals, the answers,
and the disappointments.) Emmanuel did much better than Léon with
the Bobovnikoffs. His father liked him, and Emily Overweg seems to
have adored him. She put him into the École Alsacienne, which is the
finest private school in Paris. When the family moved on to Geneva,
she took him along, and when the First World War began she sent him
off to boarding school in England. He was in England when his father
died, of tuberculosis, and he did not get back to Paris until the year he
was eighteen. Cousse has made a list of some of the odd jobs Bove had
in Paris that year—tram conductor, taxi driver, dishwasher, unskilled
worker at Renault. Bove was poor again (wartime devaluations had
nearly ruined the Overwegs), and for a while he was under suspicion,
because of what was referred to then as a *patronyme douteux.* The Paris
police arrested him in the end. He spent a month in prison, and got out
only because he had been drafted. Raymond Cousse thinks that his
exhausting commutes between wealth and poverty are what made him
so nervous later on.

Bove had two writing lives, a little like his two childhood lives.
One was the life he spent working on what became the twenty-eight
Emmanuel Bove books. The other (it was a short life) he spent working
under a pseudonym on cheap fiction that he could turn out fast; he
would put his watch on the table and pace himself at a hundred lines

an hour, eight hundred lines a day, one book every week and a half. He was married by the time he started writing. His first wife was a schoolteacher named Suzanne Vallois—he borrowed the "Vallois" for his pseudonym—and they had a short, terrible marriage and two children, who rarely saw their father once the marriage was over.

Bove published his first short story in 1923. Colette read it and asked him for a novel for the collection she was editing then at Ferenczi. Bove showed up with the manuscript of *Mes Amis.* It was Colette who established Bove in Paris. He took to sitting around at the Flore and got to know Charles Henri Ford and André Breton and all the Surrealists and Dadaists, but he was obviously not the sort of cheerful bohemian one likes to imagine in Paris in the 1920s, having a good time. Colette did not really know what to make of Bove ("Your friend Bove," she told Soupault once. "Take him away; he's much too quiet for me"), but she liked his books, and the way he wrote them amused her. He would choose a title. Then he would write his name under the title. If the arrangement pleased him, he would move it down to the middle of the page. The next morning, he would start to think about a story that matched. He read a lot in those days. He kept a diary. He liked silk shirts, which he would buy by the half dozen when he was flush and try to sell to his friends when he ran out of cash. He moved a lot. He either borrowed houses or apartments or lived in hotels. Except for the shirts, he rarely spent his money. He never invited anybody home. The men didn't mind. They put it down to poverty or timidity, or even "spirituality." Jean Cassou says that life on the Left Bank then went café, *tabac,* gallery, bistro, bed, and that with a life like that it was hard to get mad at anyone. Everybody was cultivating eccentricity, and being droll and secretive and a little cheap was what made Bove a *personnage.*

Marie-Antoinette Aymé, Marcel Aymé's widow, says that if no one was ever invited to the Boves' for dinner it was because the house was dirty. Emmanuel, as she calls him, was so neurasthenic that even the sound of a vacuum cleaner distressed him, and consequently vacuum cleaners were forbidden. She says that what men like her husband called Emmanuel's sensitivity was really Emmanuel's black thoughts, and black thoughts do not go well with the pastel silk and Empire clocks with which Mme Aymé—who was such an exemplary *femme d'intérieur* that her husband really never had to leave the house for his inspiration—likes to decorate her life. She got to know Bove in 1936, when he rented a place in Cap Ferret, south of Bordeaux, near the Aymés' summer house. He used to walk the beach with Marcel Aymé

in the afternoons, and Mme Aymé suspects that her husband helped
him with the rent, or that a relative of one of the Rothschilds in the
neighborhood helped him. The Bove she liked was Louise Bove, his
second wife. Louise was a sculptress. She was not a particularly good
sculptress, but she was lively and worldly—Bove had met her at the
Dôme, in 1928—and as a young woman she was beautiful. Victor
Bobovnikoff says she called *le tout Paris* by its first name, so that he
never really knew whom she was talking about when she told her
stories. She knew the art world the way Emmanuel Bove knew the
literary cafés. She went to the Beaux-Arts with Betty Parsons. She
lunched with Louise Leiris. She drank with Picasso. Her family was a
rich banking family from Alsace, and she had "brought Bove money,"
as Cassou puts it, but she was fashionably, passionately Communist all
her life. She kept a picture of Stalin in the house, and planned vacations
by the sea for workers' orphans, and Sundays in Paris she went from
door to door selling *L'Humanité*, the Party paper—though, according
to Victor, never without her gold bracelets and her fur coat. In Cap
Ferret, she shocked the fisherwomen by smoking and wearing bloomers. She kept a cigarette lighter tucked into a leg of the bloomers, and
she would reach up and pull it out and start to smoke while she was
waiting in line at the village *laiterie* with the porcelain chamber pot she
used as a milk pail. She called her husband Bobby—"*à l'anglaise,*" she
said. Bove wrote her letters and, when he was not being irritable, signed
them with his new name, and Louise saved them in an old suitcase. The
suitcase was under her bed when she died, in Paris, in 1977, and the
letters were still in it, along with sixteen pages from Bove's diary and
twenty unpublished fragments and proofs and manuscripts. They are
the Bove archives, so to speak. The rest of Bove's papers were left in
a house in Cap Ferret, and the house was either sacked or burned
—no one is really sure—by local Fascists when the war started.

Cousse has included the diary and four of the thirty-one letters
in a little pamphlet that was published along with last year's Bove, a
collection of stories called *Un Soir Chez Blutel*. The diaries are "literary." They are all about sensibility and about what Bove read and
what he thought about what he read. Bove has a lot to say about
chagrin, and he complains about the trouble he has creating characters with a sense of humor. ("I have a tendency to melancholy, I have
to watch it.") He admires *Robinson Crusoe*. He wants his heroes to be
like Robinson, fighting to survive, fighting to be esteemed and honored, so that their past vanishes. The letters are love letters, a little
stiff, a little whiny, not very inspired. But the letters that Cousse left

out of his pamphlet, the irritable letters, are interesting. Bove was used to women looking after him. It was Louise who wrote to his first wife when he wanted to see his children—and who got the refusals and the complaints and the demands for money that ended, "Your husband, Madame, has responsibilities"—and it was Emily Overweg, his stepmother, who usually saw the children for him. Emily liked the girl, Nora, but she reported to Bove that the boy, Michel, was grouchy. Nora married a journalist and went to work at the University of Paris. She is retired now, and lives in the country. Michel was a mason. He married a pious Catholic who did not approve of the other Boves at all, and they live near Toulouse. If you call to ask about Emmanuel, they talk about depravity.

In July of 1940, Bove moved Louise, who was already in danger as a Communist and a Jew, out of Occupied France and to a *centre de clandestinité* in Lyons. In 1942, when the South was occupied, he moved her again, to Algiers. Emmanuel Roblès, who met Bove for the first time in Algiers, says that he never talked about why he had come but that everyone knew it was for Louise. There were a lot of French writers in Algeria by 1942. Bove's old friend Soupault was there, and, among the others he knew, André Gide, Marcel Sauvage, Henri Jeanson, and Antoine de Saint-Exupéry. They used to meet at Edmond Charlot's bookstore. Charlot was only twenty-seven at the time, but he had credentials. He had been arrested and interrogated by the Vichy police, and had spent two years in a camp, and the little storefront where he printed and sold his friends' books became a kind of clubhouse for the intellectuals who were in Algeria then, cut off from the Free French and waiting for a chance to fight. They called themselves the National Committee of Writers, and when Bove arrived they made him a member.

Roblès thinks that Bove was already dying in Algiers. He was always a little hunched over, with his hands behind his back, and he talked softly, as if he were trying to save his strength and his voice —a strange figure, Roblès says, for a Mediterranean city where most people shouted and gesticulated and waved their arms around. Roblès lived in a suburb called Bouzaréa. It was in the hills, about six miles from town, and Bove had rented a room there as a place to write. Roblès would see him on the bus sometimes, or in the baker's, buying a baguette, and one day he asked Bove what he did up in Bouzaréa all day, and Bove replied that he was writing a novel. That was the most they ever talked about Bove's writing except for one day when Roblès

wanted to know if the novel was coming along, and Bove said *"Oui."*
Roblès worried about Bove, because he was getting paler all the time,
and coughing. Bove's friends at Charlot's bookstore thought he might
have cancer, but he probably had tuberculosis, like his father. (In the
end, his death certificate said "cardiac arrest following attacks of malaria.") Louise brought him back to Paris in 1944, two months after the
Liberation. They had nowhere to go, so she took a cab to Victor
Bobovnikoff's empty apartment on the Avenue des Ternes and asked
the concierge for the key. When Victor arrived in June of 1945
—after five years as a prisoner of war in Germany—the concierge
stopped him at the door to say that his brother was inside, dying. Victor
took a room in a hotel, and stayed there until Louise called him with
the news that Bove was dead.

Louise Bove was fanatic on the subject of her husband. She wanted
to see Bove properly honored—his genius acknowledged and his memory restored. Occasionally, people would come to the apartment on the
Place des États-Unis that she shared, as a widow, with her sister Colette,
and they would ask about making a movie from one of the novels or
about reprinting a story, but Louise always named a price "worthy of
Emmanuel," and that was more than anyone would pay. In the end,
the only money she earned from her husband's writing was the four
thousand francs that Yves Rivière says he spent for the three stories he
bought in 1972. The only "biography" was an eighty-page master's
thesis written by a Belgian Jesuit at the University of Louvain.

The Ottensooser sisters' apartment was an old *Seizième* apartment,
big and kind of dark, and the two women gradually filled it up with
what Rivière, who went there to ask for the stories, calls "many dead
things." Mary Blume, the American journalist, used to visit sometimes,
figuring that the old women were lonely, and Topor used to visit, too.
The sisters made an odd, complementary couple. Louise got fatter and
fatter over the years (at the end, she had a pacemaker and could hardly
walk), and Colette got thinner and thinner—pickled, Topor says. They
were always arguing, because Louise was such an ardent Communist
and her sister was an ardent Gaullist who had spent the war in London
decoding messages for the General. Louise drank wine; Colette, who
was an Anglophile, drank tea and sherry. Louise Leiris remembers
Louise Bove—she calls her *"la petite grosse"*—during those last years.
She would turn up at an opening at Louise Leiris's gallery on the rue
Monceau and buttonhole the guests and tell them all about her husband.
The year she died was the year Flammarion published *Mes Amis*.

Reputation is a cruel French specialty. The French may never stop reading Proust or Stendhal or Flaubert, but it is unlikely that people who could take up Marx, Freud, and Saint Augustine in the course of a few years and, in succession, drop them are going to stay passionate about Emmanuel Bove. The great pleasure of Bove for most of them was in the discovery.

His novels tend to blur, at least in memory, and perhaps the Bove enthusiasts of today are more interested in the man than in the books anyway, because Bove's affection for his curious genre is really the most exceptional thing about them. Once, when Bove was having trouble starting a novel, the publisher Jean Fayard dropped by and said to concentrate on finding a terrific subject, the way the Russian novelists used to do, and Bove replied that, to his mind, it was tone, not subject, that had made their books so good—that in the end there was not much difference between a plot of Dostoevsky's and the story line of a French comic strip. His problem was not so much that tone obsessed him; it was the particular tone he chose. His books are elegant reproductions, but what they reproduce is the same state of stunted perception. His people are innocent in the way that cows are innocent. They have no "character." They mean no harm, but they are petty and attached to misery as if attachment were a form of combat. Their eccentricities turn out to be peculiarities, their kindnesses turn out to be solicitations. They are full of grievances, like Emmanuel Bove.

In 1926, Bove lived for a while in a bleak little Paris suburb called Bécon-les-Bruyères, between Courbevoie and Asnières, and when he left he wrote a story about it. He said that in Bécon-les-Bruyères it was hard to imagine a woman sleeping in her lover's arms, or a stamp collector counting stamps, or a housewife dusting for a party, a young girl dressing up, a poor man opening his mail to discover he has made a fortune. In Bécon-les-Bruyères, "the happy moments of life are absent," and maybe, one day, the place will disappear and no one will remember it: "The town I leave today is as fragile as a human being. Maybe it will die in a few months, on a day when I have missed the newspaper. No one will tell me. And, thinking about all the people I have known there, I will believe that it still exists. I will believe that for a long time—until one day I learn, suddenly, that it has been gone for years."

May 1985

FRANKIE NTOH SONG

Frankie Ntoh Song made his first guitar out of some twigs and rope he found in the bush outside Douala, and strung it with rusty wires stripped from the brakes of an old bicycle at the repair shop down the road from the mission school of the Cathédrale Pierre et Paul. Frankie's father was the handyman at the mission. The family lived in a little house on the mission grounds—ten workers for the price of one, Frankie says now. His mother sold *beignets* to the priests and nuns and the Dominican friars, and sometimes to the elegant Jesuits at the mission *collège,* where the sons of the important Bassa village chiefs went for a Catholic education. His sister helped with the *beignets.* He and his six brothers swept the classrooms at the mission grammar school, and once a week, when everyone at school got a malaria pill (and had to take it right there, with the teacher watching), he was sent to the pump in town for "swallowing water" and carried it back in a heavy calabash on his head. He served at Mass, and since he was good at climbing trees, he also picked the missionaries' mangoes from the trees in the cathedral garden. He was not allowed to take mangoes for himself—not even the ones that fell to the ground and splattered when he was up on a branch and lost his footing. There was always a priest attached to Frankie when he did his chores—a priest whose job seemed mainly to consist of keeping Frankie honest. There was a "marketing priest" and a "cathedral-business priest" and, if the missionaries wanted mangoes, a "mango priest," who gave Frankie one mango at the end of the day and sent him home with it to his mother. It was as if the great civilizing mission of the Church of Rome in Africa were concentrated on the small person of Frankie Ntoh Song. Frankie's people—they were a riverain Bassa people from southwestern Cameroon—measured their land and their rights to the land by river boundaries. As they understood it, the mango trees of Douala belonged to everybody born there, but the Church said no, the trees belonged to the Bishop of the Cathédrale Pierre et Paul, and really to the Pope and to the Church in Rome. The Church taught Frankie sin and property. He stole mangoes, and whenever he did he had the sense of having stolen something. "I don't know why, but the thing that stays in my head—the thing that's always in my head—is the mango trees," he says. Sooner or later, whenever Frankie talks, he comes back to the mango trees. The mango trees were there, and the priests certainly hadn't planted them, and Frankie says that it makes no sense that he was not permitted to take mangoes for himself. It makes no sense that when he did take one he felt so terrible.

Frankie is a musician now. He is thirty-two and lives in Paris and plays the keyboards in a group called Ghetto Blaster, which is one of the best new African groups around. He wears an Afro and a pencil mustache, and he owns a pair of soft black leather trousers, soft pointed leather boots, and a golden identification bracelet with links the size of mango pits. He talks with ease about the influence of James Brown and Otis Redding, about the "funky-jazzy" sound of the Temptations and the Commodores and all the other Motown groups he admires, and about the new, "Afro-urban" sound that Ghetto Blaster is trying to articulate. The sound is affecting. "You hear African music, you have to dance, man" is Frankie's explanation for it. It is not a question of whether you want to dance. It has nothing to do with whether you *can* dance. Dancing is something that happens to you when you hear the rhythms of West Africa. Your feet move the way your leg moves when the doctor taps it with a hammer. One of the things that Frankie wants to do while he is here in Europe is go to Rome and make the Pope dance. He has already been to Rome twice, for concerts. He was there at Eastertime this year, and he can imagine Ghetto Blaster in St. Peter's Square, playing their song "Preacher Man" while the Pope dances. As Frankie describes it, the music will enter John Paul II. It will possess him like an irresistible ancestral spirit. He will start to dance, and he will keep on dancing to the Ghetto Blaster beat until Frankie and his friends release him. It is Frankie's moment of power, his great moment of reconciliation and revenge. "Let me tell you, we play, he dances—*pourquoi pas?*" Frankie says.

Lately, the word around Les Halles and Beaubourg and the Place de la Bastille and the other places where Paris kids gather is that if you want to be *branché*—plugged in—you have to be *branché Africain*. You have to have *le black feeling,* or pretend to have *le black feeling.* You have to hang out in the African-music section at FNAC and discuss the latest tapes by Ray Lema and Youssou N'Dour, and have gone to demonstrations for Fela Anikulapo Kuti, a Nigerian saxophonist with twenty-seven wives and a revolutionary palaver who has just spent two years in jail for the illegal possession of sixteen hundred British pounds. A couple of years ago, no one in Paris had *le black feeling* except, understandably, the blacks who live here. Paris is black the way Los Angeles is Chicano. For every African legally in Paris—the official figure for the city and its suburbs is under a hundred thousand adults with *cartes de séjour*—there are five or six Africans who have entered illegally or managed to come as "tourists," and have simply disappeared into the city and its squats and its black suburbs. There are more Malians in the workers' suburb of Montreuil than in any place in Mali except Bamako, the capital. There are more Senegalese in the back streets of Montmartre and Belleville and Ménilmontant than in most Senegalese towns. People figure that if you include the Antillais, who have French passports and can come and go as they want to, there are at least a million and more likely a million and a half blacks living in the Île-de-France.

The Africans came here as factory workers and as students and because Paris was the place that young Africans longed to go. They were isolated and alienated and not much loved by Frenchmen. They were hired off the books, and usually they lived in sixth-floor *chambres de bonne* or in abandoned ateliers converted by enterprising French landlords into what were delicately called *foyers immigrés.* There were Senegalese *foyers* near the Gare de Lyon (and there are still huge *foyers* between Nation and the Porte de Montreuil) where entire villages were transplanted. Eventually, these *foyers* were "sold," and the immigrants ended up with African landlords who were just as enterprising as the French, and just as ruthless. The immigrants paid for protection, and then for mediums and sorcerers to protect them against their protectors. "Resolve your problems," the black classifieds in Paris said. "Enemy(ies). Money. Work. Fidelity. Customers. Complexes. Affection. Disenchantment. Exorcism. Chance. Success. Drivers' Licenses. Cards. Exams. Sentimental Complications." Friday night in Montreuil or on the Boulevard Barbès was not much different from Friday night in Douala. The men with jobs got paid and bought a bottle and went dancing. The women with jobs got paid and did the marketing and fed the children, and then they went dancing, too. It was a way to commemorate the end of a week of exhausting work or exhausting evasions of work, and it was just as much of a ritual for Africans here as sitting under a tree and sharing a calabash of palm wine on Friday night was a ritual for the old men in Frankie's father's village, twenty-five miles by canoe from the Douala missionaries. The music that Africans played in their *foyers* was not always "African." It was often a mixture of their own local drum rhythms and the harmonies of foreign groups that they had heard on the radio back home. If they came from Zaire, or from countries that used to belong to France, like Senegal or Mali or the Ivory Coast, the chances are there was a lot of Antilles zouk in their music, and traces of the cheap pop melodies that French singers like Serge Gainsbourg and Johnny Halliday recorded. If they came from Nigeria or Cameroon, they knew Jamaican reggae and English rock, and even some American jazz. They played bongos and tam-tams and koras and box guitars, and dreamed of amplifiers. They kept their radios on loud, day and night, and liked nearly everything they heard. They liked the way James Brown sang, because James Brown had what in Paris argot is called *les tripes*—big gut feelings. They liked the way Jamaicans rapped about revolution, and they liked the way Herbie Hancock played his keyboard synthesizer against complicated rhythmic patterns that were pure Africa—"techno-roots," they called it. They liked the scratchy .45s the Bembeya Jazz National band mixed in Guinea with a single microphone, and they liked the smooth "soul makossa" sounds that came from Manu Dibango's saxophone in a twenty-four-track Paris studio. Manu Dibango moved here from Cameroon in 1949, and stayed. In a way, he is the grandfather of *le black feeling*. Africans say that he carried the sound of Africa to Paris in his saxophone case. They hang his picture—Manu in his tweed cap and his expensive shades—in makeshift nightclubs in the Cameroon bush (nightclubs with names like Soul Jungle), and in workers' squats in Paris where Senegalese and Guinean *griots* play on ancient instruments that have been handed down, like sacred objects, over generations.

Frankie remembers the day he first heard Manu Dibango on his father's radio. He was fourteen and had quit school and was selling *beignets* for his mother at a stand near the Jesuits' *collège*, but he knew a little about keyboards from having watched the organist at Pierre et Paul whenever he served at Sunday Mass, and he was getting lessons of sorts from a neighbor who owned a box guitar and a "pianica" that worked something like a mouth organ—you had to blow through a tube and play your chords at the same time. The chords that Frankie learned were do, fa, and sol—C major, F major, and G major. He practiced them at home on a keyboard that one of his brothers drew for him on a piece of paper, with the chords marked and the fingering pencilled in. He never did learn to read music. It is understood among Frankie and his friends that if you are black reading music ruins your creativity, and, besides, Frankie is a cynic where most music audiences are concerned. "If you play good, they clap, and if you play bad they clap," he likes to say. This was true when he was fifteen and gave his first concert—he was a reluctant guest soloist with the Jesuits' school orchestra—and it was just as true when Ghetto Blaster played for a thousand Trotskyite students last Saturday night at the Palais de la Mutualité.

Frankie's first job playing was in a little nightclub in Douala. He used his neighbor's box guitar and sang what the owner wanted —which turned out to be James Brown's "Papa's Got a Brand-New Bag" and a Johnny Halliday version of Otis Redding's record "Knock on Wood," with "Aussi Dur Que le Bois" for a title. It was clear to Frankie that he needed improving. He went back to his neighbor. ("I went to my big brother," he says, because it is Frankie's policy to insist that all Africans are his brothers and his sisters, and it takes a while to figure out whether he is talking about the neighbors or the Dominicans or his own family.) He asked his neighbor how to change chords. "Make a major chord," his neighbor said. "Now take the finger in the middle, move it back a bit, just a bit, and that's a minor chord. Now take the *first* finger, move it back a bit, just a bit, and that's a flat chord. Now take the same finger, move it not back but up a bit, just a bit, and that's a sharp chord." It was Frankie's last music lesson. He went home and practiced. He used his ear. If he thought "minor" but didn't sound minor, he would take his middle finger and move it back a bit, and it must have worked, he says, because whenever he played people started dancing. Soon is was not his chords that bothered him anymore, it was the fact that his shoes had holes in the front and his shirts were hand-me-downs from his older brothers. He says that appearing in public like that, in such terrible clothes, was much worse than having a repertoire of only three chords, with variations. He was so ashamed of his clothes that one day he broke down and took some money from his mother's pocketbook and bought a suit for himself. His mother was furious. Like most African mothers, she didn't really believe in music. She thought of music—not the music you heard in church or at the *griot*'s house but the kind of music Frankie played—as something that gangsters and layabouts did to amuse themselves. Music like that was not something a responsible young man, with obligations to his family, thought seriously of taking up. Frankie's mother did not believe that people like

King Sunny Adé, in Nigeria, or Youssou N'Dour, in Senegal, would get rich from music. She did not believe that one day they were going to be big men at home. It may be that her hard African life had cheated her of *le black feeling*. She did not really understand why Frankie —she called him Bernardin, which was his Christian name, after St. Bernard—wanted to dress up when he went to the club to play, or why he talked about having a feeling that was special, a feeling that seemed to contradict the poverty around him. There is a song going around Paris now—an Ivoirien who goes by the name Cophie wrote it—about a man with a new universe in his head, a universe where there is no drought or famine or despair, no war or animosity, only brothers and sisters with plenty to eat, and rain for bathing. The man with a new universe in his head makes an appointment to see the important men who are in the business of building new universes, but he knows that he must not arrive at his meeting on foot, looking like a poor African. He has to arrive in a long Rolls-Royce, looking like the sort of man who can make a new universe pay. He has to inspire confidence, and there is no way he can inspire confidence. He cannot afford a long Rolls-Royce—not even for the afternoon. He has to walk to his meeting, and the important businessmen laugh when they see him, and say "Who is this poor African who wants us to build a new universe?" and they send him away. One of the Ghetto Blasters says that Frankie, talking in his soft, insistent voice about mango priests and old shoes and dancing Popes and brothers and sisters, is really looking for a new universe. "Let me tell you," Frankie says, "I needed shoes."

Frankie left Cameroon on September 21, 1975. He is often vague on dates, but September 21 is one date he remembers. That morning, Frankie crossed the border into Nigeria in the company of three other musicians and a Nigerian "manager," who had invited them to play in his fine new club in a city called Aba. That afternoon, Frankie discovered that the fine new club was a pile of sticks and cinder blocks waiting for him and his friends to put it up. He had what amounted to four dollars in his pocket. It got him to Onitsha, the market town of the old Biafran state and the headquarters of the Fifth Brigade of the Nigerian Army, and that night in Onitsha he met a bass guitarist from Cameroon named Willy N'For, who played in the brigade band—it was called The Pentagon—and whom Frankie knew at once for a true brother. Willy came from a mission, too—only his missionaries were evangelicals from New Jersey. They ran a school called the World-Wide Missions School, in Muyuka, and they were not notably disposed toward any music except hymns. The car at the World-Wide Missions School

was used for collecting Willy and his friends when they sneaked away
at night and booked themselves into the local clubs as a teenage rock
group called the Gentles. Willy knew how to play the box guitar and
the trumpet—his father was a policeman and a fine trumpet player,
Willy says—but once when the Gentles decided to give a real concert
he rented a six-string acoustic guitar and started improvising bass
chords, and after that he figured he had found his instrument. He had
time to reflect, because the principal of the World-Wide Missions
School suspended him for his playing and put him to work clearing
bush for a garden. He spent two weeks in the bush and thought about
music. "I thought about Fela and Manu, about the African musicians
I was hearing," he told Frankie. "I thought, Wow, so Africans can play
like that! I never knew how rich African music was—how jazzy, how
African. I thought, I'd better do music."

There was a party that night at Willy's. It began at ten and went
on until morning, and by the time Frankie recovered, his new brother
had persuaded the lieutenant who ran The Pentagon that what the band
needed was a keyboard man with three chords and a repertoire of
American funk and the lyrics of the Temptations in his head. There
were not many civilians in The Pentagon. For a while, all that Frankie
and Willy had to do was sleep all day and celebrate all night and
occasionally join the band for a concert in the officers' mess, but
Frankie and Willy played so well together that the lieutenant decided
there was money in The Pentagon for him. It does not seem to have
occurred to the lieutenant that six years after a civil war in which at
least a million Biafrans died people in Onitsha would be disinclined to
make merry to the music of the Nigerian Army. He started booking
The Pentagon into Onitsha nightclubs, where they played either to
empty rooms or to murderous audiences. It was not a good feeling,
Frankie says. He and Willy and their civilian friends had to "resign"
from the band by flashlight at four one morning while the lieutenant
was distracted. (The lieutenant was distracted because his commander
had just been taken away and shot as a conspirator in an attempted coup
d'état.) They made it to the town of Port Harcourt. There were six of
them—enough for a group—and so they introduced themselves around
as the Mighty Flames and went looking for a manager to buy them
instruments.

When Frankie came to Paris as a Ghetto Blaster, the first thing he
wanted to know was who would own the instruments he was going to
play. It was the first thing Willy wanted to know when he joined

Ghetto Blaster, and the first thing P. P. P. Kiala Nzavotunga, the lead guitarist, wanted to know, too. There are eight musicians in Ghetto Blaster, and half of them—all but the two saxophonists, the drummer, and the percussionist—depend on complicated electronic equipment that costs a fortune. The percussionist, Udoh Essiet, plays with a pair of short wooden sticks and two simple congas that were made for him in Nigeria, and, according to Willy, who has a gift for description, he is "the pure real shock of Africa" at the heart of Ghetto Blaster's jazzy, eclectic sound, the way the saxophonists are "the color that arranges it." Willy himself plays a Yamaha BB800 bass guitar and a Lag Black Bass hooked up to a Peavey Combo amplifier, and Frankie uses a big Roland JX-8P synthesizer and a DX7 Yamaha synthesizer, and sometimes, in concert, he adds a Korg Remote keyboard for wandering around the stage and dancing. If you asked either of them the main difference between playing with a group in Paris and playing with a group in Nigeria, he would probably say that a musician in Paris can leave with his instruments any time he decides to go—and no one will throw him in jail for stealing. In Africa, playing with a group is a kind of indenture. Whoever owns the equipment owns the men who use it.

The manager of the Mighty Flames was an Ibo whom everybody called Right Time. Right Time had been an important man in Biafra. He could still name his terms, and the terms he made with Frankie and Willy and the rest of the Mighty Flames were room, board, and instruments in exchange for service. He had them sign a contract. The contract said that they were buying their instruments, month by month, with their salaries, but it didn't say what those salaries were or what the instruments cost or how long it would take to own them. None of the Mighty Flames had a copy of the contract anyway. It disappeared into Right Time's safe, along with whatever passports or papers they had, and for the next four years they played in Right Time's nightclub, made his records, and slept on amplifier cartons in his storeroom, which was a hanger with a leaky mud roof, no toilet, and water only once a week, on Saturdays. Right Time showed them his big house, but he never invited them in for a meal and some conversation. He never listened to them "with a good heart," Willy says. He liked them to play cheap Ghanaian high life instead of their own meandering music. And he liked having them where he could keep an eye on them. When they finally did leave, late in 1980—they drove to Lagos with the instruments to give a concert and decided to stay—he had them arrested. Frankie and Willy went to jail in chains.

There were millions of people in Lagos then. Frankie says that you

WHT16-47193

EUROPEANS

34FG4H0010EX

Location   Totes   Tote 2461 Item 0
Description   This item is in good condition. All pages and covers are
readable. There are no stains or tears. Dust jacket is
present if applicable. May contain small amounts of
writing and/or highlighting. Spine and cover may show
signs of wear. May not contain supplementary items
such as CD's or DVD's. We ship within 1 business day.
Big Hearted Books shares its profits with schools,
churches and non-profit groups throughout New
England. Thank you for your support!

ASIN   0140128085
Employee   eliana

If anything is incorrect, please contact us immediately at
customerservice@bigheartedbooks.com and we will
make it right. Thank you again for your purchase and
please leave feedback online!

could "see the money flowing"—which in a way was true, since the big
British and American oil companies were bringing in wells right off the
coastline. Nigerians were making fortunes as contractors or consultants
or "facilitators," or simply as 10 percent guides to the appropriate open
hand, and as soon as Frankie and Willy got out of jail and free of Right
Time Frankie looked around and said to Willy, "Oh boy, may we go"
—which was pidgin for "Let's go where the action is" and in practical
terms meant "The action is here." It was fashionable in Lagos at the
time to own a group. All the important musicians owned groups
—big-band groups with singers and dancers and pretty girls to look at
and plenty of brass to make things loud—and all the important businessmen wanted to own them. Most of the groups played in a quarter
called Yaba, near the port, which was Lagos's downtown. King Sunny
Adé had a club there, and so did Fela Anikulapo Kuti. (Fela's club was
called the Shrine, and Fela supposedly kept his musicians faithful the
way Right Time did—by locking up their passports.) It is easy to
recognize the music that came through Lagos on its way to Europe. It
is like the town. It has a hard edge, and there is something close to jazz
in it, and something like blues. It is weak on melody, but its rhythms
are so persistent and complex, and "turn" so fast, as musicians say, that
it is hard to tell when a phrase begins or when it ends. Willy likes to
say that Lagos music "drops"—that it hits the ground and picks you
up instead of floating around in the air alone, like a lot of the music that
came to Paris straight from Zaire or Cameroon without a Lagos stop.
A lot of that music is soggy and banal—what the French call variety
music. It was, as Frankie says, a matter of transportation.

Martin Meppiel and his brother Stéphane were divers on an oil rig
off the Nigerian coast when they started going to the Lagos clubs and
getting to know the music. They were young, and they were seeing
the world, and the world they especially wanted to see was the Third
World. The brothers came from an old French Communist family.
Their father had quit the Party in 1968, but their mother was still a
member. She was a film editor and had been to Cuba, and she gave the
brothers what in Africa were considered excellent Third World credentials. Martin was addicted to Africa. He says that whenever he
wasn't in Africa he was somewhere trying to get to Africa. He would
work in France, say, driving for a rock group, and as soon as he got
paid he would buy a car—preferably a Peugeot, because West Africans
like Peugeots—and then he would take the car to Africa and cross the
desert and sell it in Niger or Nigeria or Benin for enough money to

stay a couple of months and pay his plane fare home. Eventually, he started diving, because diving from a platform in the middle of the Gulf of Guinea was not something many people wanted to do, and so it paid handsomely. There was a colony of young French leftists in Lagos in the early 1980s. They were there for the adventure and the music, and because Lagos was a freewheeling and anarchic town that suited their mood and their style and their politics. Martin Meissonnier, who wrote about African music for *Libération* and is now a producer for Ray Lema and a lot of the other important African musicians, was working as Fela Kuti's manager. Katrin Lesevre, Martin Meppiel's wife, was one of Fela's sound engineers. Pascal Imbert, who works for the record company Celluloid now, was helping to organize Fela's tours. They were all fascinated by Fela Anikulapo Kuti. He was their E.T., Martin Meissonnier says. Fela was often half naked when he played. He wore necklaces made of iron rings. He waved his saxophone like a rifle and sang about the great African revolution while his wives crawled around on their knees, like handmaidens, carrying his equipment.

In 1981, Stéphane Meppiel and his mother made a short movie set to a Fela song called "Authority Stealing," and a year later Stéphane made a longer movie, *Music Is the Weapon*, which was about Fela himself. In the course of making those movies, Stéphane got to know Kiala Nzavotunga, who was working as Fela's lead guitarist. They began to talk about what would happen if the Meppiels took a couple of French musicians they knew—musicians with Paris and New York experience—and put them together with Kiala and some of his friends and told everyone to play. The more they talked, the more appealing the idea sounded. It took a while to organize, but one morning early in the spring of 1983 a caravan of old Peugeots arrived at the Nigerian border carrying the Meppiel brothers, a movie production crew, the French musicians (one of them, Stefan Mikhaël Blaëss, plays guitar with Ghetto Blaster now), and so much sound equipment that it took Martin Meppiel two days to persuade the customs officer to let the caravan in. The group put itself together in a Lagos nightclub called the Black Pussycat. Kiala brought his friends, and his friends brought *their* friends, and after they had all been improvising for a couple of weeks they painted the name "Ghetto Blaster" on the wall behind the bandstand. They had their first concert, at the Black Pussycat, that May. By June, Martin and Stéphane had sold their cars and used the money to fly six of the Ghetto Blasters to Paris—where they settled down in a houseboat on the Seine that belonged to the brothers and their father. By December, Ghetto Blaster was playing at Phil'One, a

club in a shopping center at La Défense which was considered particularly *branché* at the moment. Two months later, they recorded
"Preacher Man" for Island Records.

Ghetto Blaster was polyglot. Four of the group were from Cameroon—Frankie, Willy, a drummer named Nicolas Avom, who answers
to Ringo, and an alto saxophonist named Félix Priso, who answers to
Féfé. The tenor sax, Steve Potts, was an American black. Udoh was an
Obon from Nigeria. Stefan Blaëss was French, but his mother came
from Casablanca, and Kiala was Angolan by origin, but *his* mother had
raised him in Zaire, because of the Portuguese at home. There was a
woman from Benin, too—a singer called Betty, who was with Kiala for
a while and with Stefan for a while, and had a belting voice and
apparently a belting character. She drank, and exasperated everyone
who knew her. She died suddenly last year, when she tripped on the
houseboat ladder, hit her head, and drowned.

At first, Martin Meppiel left the group alone on the houseboat. He
went on tour to America with Sunny Adé, and by all accounts Ghetto
Blaster had a party that lasted the three months that he was gone. They
fought and fired each other and then made up and hired each other
back, and once they took on a fast-talking Ghanaian who wanted to
turn them into a high-life backup band. When Martin came home, they
had a discussion *à la Yoruba*, which means a discussion that gets loud
very fast. It was the first of many discussions. For one thing, the
Africans in Ghetto Blaster had trouble rehearsing. The kind of rehearsals they liked were the rehearsals where you brought your beer and
your joints and your women and your records and had a party, and
then, when everybody was laughing and dancing and high and ap-
preciating you—then you rehearsed. They had their "Africa" in
Udoh's drums. ("Udoh was their security, their metronome," Martin
says.) They had their "Afro beat" from Kiala and Ringo, who had
played for Fela, their rock from Stefan, their makossa from Féfé, their
jazz from Steve, and their funk from Frankie and Willy—and no leader
to tell them what to do. There were times when Willy wanted to lead
the group and times when Kiala wanted to lead it, and the only way
they knew to settle the argument was to announce that Ghetto Blaster
was a new sort of African group, a democratic group, and everyone in
it was equal. The one thing they did agree on then was that a big
houseboat on the Seine, where friends could crash and there were
always guitars and amplifiers lying around, was Africa without any of
Africa's hassles. Willy says now that the hardest thing for most of them
was getting used to French recording studios—to the empty rooms, the

glass booths, and the serious engineers who sat alone at their control panels and did the difficult mixing of traditional and electronic sounds. But Willy knew that unless they got used to it they would end up with terrible records, and no work except an hour of playback once or twice a month at some embarrassing *"soirée Africaine"* at Le Palace or L'Observatoire. "It was a big problem, because being alone in a studio feels too cold for an African," Willy says. "There is not enough to blow his mind in a studio. He has to learn to blow his own mind. That's what he has to learn in Paris."

There is a publisher here named Jean-François Bizot who likes to say that the first step any African takes in Paris involves a hustle. Bizot owns the magazine *Actuel* and a big piece of a radio station called Radio Nova, both of which promote black music and black chic and *le black feeling*, and though he himself is white and French, as well as being an heir to the Rhône-Poulenc chemical fortune, he is considered a master hustler of the black-feeling scene. Bizot is what is called a *soixante-huitard.* He "made his 1968," as the French say. The *Actuel* he started then went on to die with its causes, and once the glamour was gone from being a Maoist or a Tantrist or a pacifist or a psychedelic or simply stoned, Bizot's readers were at a loss. *Le black feeling* arrived in Paris just as Bizot was looking around for something new to engage them, and in 1979 he started again, with a magazine that was slick and shrewd —a little sensational, a little satirical, a little political, a little porno- graphic—and took black feeling out of the *foyers immigrés* and put it into a sunny office down the street from the Bastille, with a staff of beautiful black girls for class. It is unlikely that many of the African factory workers in Montreuil buy *Actuel.* Musicians buy it, and rich students from Zaire and the Ivory Coast buy it, and so do Parisians who want to know where *le black feeling* is happening and how to get there and what to wear when they go. When a movie about black feeling called *Black Mic-Mac* opened last month, Bizot put out a guide to *"l'ambiance Afro-Antillaise à Paris,"* and 150,000 people asked for copies.

It may be that if you are black and in Paris it is hard to make your feeling pay without a Frenchman behind you. There are record compa- nies here with names like Safari Ambiance, and clubs with names like Black and White and La Plantation. There are promoters like Serge Kruger, who plays black music on a station called Radio Tchatch and at a disco called Le Tango, and who presents a "black evening" every Tuesday at Le Palace—distinguished mainly by the fact that four black girls dance on platforms and a couple of rented tigers are occasionally paraded around the dance floor. There are designers called Laurence Olivier and Wilfried and Ambrozzio for the men from Zaire and the Congo who get dressed up on Saturday nights and have "elegance contests." (The men call themselves Sapeurs, after *saper,* the old Paris slang for dressing up, and they form a make-believe brotherhood called the Société des Ambianceurs et des Personnes Élégantes. Their ideal is a "Sape" who flashes labels from Dior and Versace and Montana and wears crocodile shoes so valuable that he has to keep them at the bank in a safe-deposit box.) There are fifteen-year-old entrepreneurs who, for seventy francs an hour, will teach an anxious classmate how to distinguish a makossa beat (Cameroon) from a juju beat (Nigeria) or a mandingo beat (Mali). By now, it is expected that any African musician who wants a reputation outside Africa will get on a plane to Paris, play the clubs here, give a concert, and cut a record (or at least get himself a contract to cut a record) before he considers going home. "Making the international circuit" is what Parisians call it.

There are English and American music critics who say that the African groups that Parisians like so much are really ordinary rock groups—guitar, bass guitar, keyboard, and drums—with the native instruments thrown in like spice, for flavor. Certainly there is not much harmonic complexity in most of the African music you are likely to hear on Radio Nova or find on cassettes at FNAC. (The exception is Ray Lema, who was trained in classical piano and composition and is in the process of writing an African symphony.) The international circuit that Parisians talk about can take the rhythmic—really the polyrhythmic—complexity that African music does have and reduce it to French pop standards, to a kind of rock monotone. Unless a group is tough and confident, like Ghetto Blaster, it can make that music as banal as elevator songs.

Right now, Frankie and Willy live in a suburb called Bondy, about ten miles out of Paris. They have an apartment on the ninth floor of a big housing project filled with immigrants, and they share it with two African "sisters," who complain about the noise they make when they practice. Frankie and Willy miss the houseboat. They have not been able to live there since February of 1985, when Martin Meppiel called another one of his discussions *à la Yoruba* and in the course of it announced that he wanted his boat back, that he was beginning to have nightmares about Ghetto Blaster, that he needed a break from Ghetto Blaster for a while. The break lasted a year. Martin and Katrin had a baby, and the three of them went to Cuba, where Martin got interested in a Cuban group, Los Van Van, that had started out as a kind of backup band for Castro's sugarcane-cutting marathons. Ghetto Blaster drifted for a while. They went on tour. They went on television. They rented time at a sound studio on the rue de Bagnolet, toward Ménilmontant, and started rehearsing. They were working there on their first LP when Betty died. They went from the funeral to the studio and decided the time had come to discipline themselves and their disparate sounds into something particular. They gave their old songs—songs with names like "New Generation" and "Life Is Just a Party"—a nerve and energy to take the place of hers. When the record was ready, they called it *People.* Early this spring, Martin started managing the group again.

Frankie and Willy like to talk about the old days on the houseboat —the days when Kiala was writing "Life Is Just a Party," and Ghetto Blaster was truly *branché,* having plugged the boat into a streetlamp on the quai in order to get electricity free. They miss having a place of their own to practice even more than having a place of their own to live —though it is hard enough for any African to find a flat in Paris, and if he does find one he usually has to send a Frenchman to rent it, because white Parisians do not extend *le black feeling* to the subject of real estate. Most of the Ghetto Blasters have girlfriends here. Féfé lives with a woman from Cameroon, and they have three small children. Udoh lives with an American blues pianist, and Kiala is getting married to a girl from New Jersey with an art-history degree, and has started practicing Tibetan Buddhism. Willy sees a Swedish saxophonist in Mory Kante's backup band. Frankie's girlfriend is a dancer from Cameroon who goes by the name Chantal. Frankie says that at first most of the women the Ghetto Blasters met in Paris would say to them, right away, "We are not like *your* women. We don't walk on our knees for a man, like Fela's wives." And the Ghetto Blasters would have to explain that African women *like* to serve, that African women have plenty of power —and wait to see if anyone believed them. As far as Frankie and Willy are concerned, the women in Paris—even the African women— are puzzling. The "sisters" in Bondy are puzzling, and the neighbors in Bondy are even more puzzling. Frankie and Willy cannot get over the fact that they live in a building with hundreds of neighbors who never talk to them, not even in the elevator. When Willy thinks about the loneliness here, he puts his hands to his face and hides. He wants to cry, and doesn't want anyone to see him crying, and when that happens Frankie stiffens and takes Willy's sadness and turns it into something instructive and a little hard—something like a judgment. "They want us to be getting together, black and white," Frankie will say. "But we're suffering, and they're not suffering, so how can we be getting together? Let's wait until we're *all* not suffering. Then maybe we can see about this getting together." And Willy will sigh, and say, "Oh, man, they want to discover us. They want to know, Who is this African?" He will feel better, talking. He has an idea—a "spiritual" idea. He wants to find "a voice to come out with," a voice in music, that will let everybody know who this African is.

Willy is small—loose, boyish, and appealing—and he has a shy charm. He wears jeans and a fisherman's gray sweater and a green beret to rehearsals. When he plays his bass guitar, he closes his eyes and croons and moves around, listening to himself, as if the pleasure that music gives him were something precious and surprising. Frankie never shuts his eyes when he is at his keyboard. He sits up straight, with his legs extended in his soft black leather pants, and his ankles crossed and his feet still. He is in charge of himself. He watches everyone. Martin has said that Willy is the "soul" of Ghetto Blaster—that it only became a group with Willy there—and some of Martin's friends say no, Kiala is the soul of Ghetto Blaster, and others say that the soul is Udoh. But when Ghetto Blaster rehearses, the power is Frankie's. He sets up his gear in the middle of the rehearsal room, between Udoh and the saxophones, climbs onto a stool, and in a way takes over. There is a kind of controlling tension in Frankie. It has nothing to do with what he says or does, or how he plays. It has to do with his posture and his regard, with something cold in his look that can demolish the group, and with something in his quick, wide smile that can unite it. The group plays better when Frankie laughs. He laughs suddenly, as if some secret of his, some intuition, had delighted him. The laughter warms the studio, and when it stops the musicians are anxious—everyone, that is, but Willy, dancing around with his eyes closed, listening to himself.

Willy and Frankie are inseparable. They are inseparable the way the sweetness and the anger in Africa are inseparable. When people ask Willy about Africa, he says, "Man, you got to meet Frankie," and when people ask Frankie about Africa he says, "Man, you got to meet Willy." Willy trusts everyone, and Frankie is wary—and trust and distrust are really the Afro beats of Ghetto Blaster music. When the two of them were in jail in Nigeria, the older prisoners put them through an initiation. They were told to walk on their knees, like Fela's wives, and Willy has never forgotten the fact that he walked on his knees and Frankie refused—and no one touched him. He is solicitous of Frankie, and he listens when Frankie talks. Frankie's edgy pieties about Africa give Willy a kind of definition and comfort, the way Willy's intelligent good nature gives Frankie some of the balance and resilience he needs. Frankie came late to Ghetto Blaster. He had trouble with his papers, and Martin had to fly to Lagos to get him, and so he arrived on the houseboat months after the others came. Willy was used to the Paris cold by then, but Frankie suffered. There were nights when it was so cold on the boat that Frankie would be stretched out stiff, under blankets, and the group would think that maybe he had died, and Udoh would have to go up and shake him and say, "Hey, Frankie, you alive?" Frankie's African name Song means "the moon when it is full." Willy's African name Manga was the name of a great chief—Rudolph Douala Manga Bell—who fought to save his people's land from the German Kaiser. Their mothers never used those names; they called them Bernardin and William, and now Frankie and Willy wonder why, because there is power in their African names, and both of them feel that power. When people here talk about the reputation Nigerians have for being corrupt, or Zairians for being evasive, or Senegalese for being tough in business, Frankie shrugs his shoulders and says, "Everyone in Africa finds his way out of the bullshit in different ways," and then he invokes that part of them all which is "Africa" and is immensely calm— he calls it "polite"—in its power.

The French are not calm. Willy remembers walking into the Black Pussycat in Lagos the day he met the Meppiels, and finding all those Frenchmen, with their sound equipment and their expensive cameras, running around and smoking cigarettes and looking so strange and worried—looking "not free." He had never seen such nervous people, he says—not even the week he went to New York with Sonny Okosun's band and stayed at the Empire Hotel on Broadway, and rode in long, long cars with bars and television sets in them, and ate in a restaurant in Brooklyn that had bodyguards standing around outside with guns, frightening everyone. Frankie and Willy have decided that the French know nothing about real power. Ringo and Kiala wear dreadlocks, but Frankie says there are people in Africa *born* with dreadlocks, people with the power of prophecy. They are so powerful, Frankie says, that they have to have a big ceremony, with sacrifices, any time they want to cut their hair—and that is nothing compared with the power the people in Willy's village have, which is the power of sending thunder. Frenchmen are always asking Frankie and Willy to *explain* that kind of power, but Frankie says that he cannot explain African power to a Frenchman any more than the bishop in Douala could explain to him why Jesus was able to walk on water. He is suspicious of people who have been so keenly interested in Africa and in what they could take from Africa that now they even want to take the secret of African spirit and call it *le black feeling*. Willy tells him that they will always be strangers here. He may be making the problem worse, as Frankie says, by letting the French get to him, but even Frankie tends to agree with Willy that it may be time soon for Ghetto Blaster to be moving on, maybe to New York. Willy has told him that in New York everybody is the same, everybody is *American*—that in New York there are no strangers.

When the Pope dances, Frankie will be ready to go.

May 1986

DR. VERDIGLIONE

The Milanese have a reputation for sophistication, but they like to think of themselves as plain, provincial people, at the mercy of fast-talking southerners like Armando Verdiglione. Verdiglione is a Calabrese. He came to Milan, checked out the *Weltanschauung,* and made his pitch with the right amount of hard sell and obfuscation. By thirty, he had set himself up as a fashionable psychoanalyst. By forty, he had convinced so many Milanese that health and happiness—he called it "your personal intellectual itinerary"—were something you bought, like growth stocks, by investing in him, that he owned a chunk of the city which included a choice corner (the one with the view) of the Piazza del Duomo and extended out into the suburbs to Senago and the summer palace of the seventeenth-century cardinal Federico Borromeo. Last year, when the police arrested him for fraud, extortion, and assault, he was a local personage in the manner of Giorgio Armani and Fiorucci—or maybe Michele Sindona. He had a wardrobe of violently striped suits and three-toned patent-leather shoes, and he kept a fat, ten-inch cigar stuck in the middle of a face that was as soft and bland and petulant as a teenage guru's. It was hard to miss Armando Verdiglione if you were young and trying to be trendy and hung out on the via Montenapoleone, looking at clothes and drinking espresso at the Caffè Cova. Armando Verdiglione was an impresario of his own celebrity. He lived on that opulent street of shops, in an outsize panelled flat done up with the edgy dignity of people the old Milan rich refer to as *emergenti*—a couple of boardroom tables, a couch assaulted by zigzags of printed flame stitch, and a library filled with the books of psychoanalytic "theory" he wrote so fast, and so unintelligibly, that it

looked as if Armando Verdiglione's real inspiration had been an active
Ouija board, not Freud, and certainly not "Dante, Ariosto, Peano,
Vico, and Pirandello," which was the list he gave when he was trying
to persuade people that psychoanalysis was not therapy but "culture,"
and that consequently his patients were not really patients at all when
they bought him palaces but simply paying cultural conversationalists.

Armando Verdiglione used to lead a busy Montenapoleone life.
He took his coffee and brioche at the Cova at nine-thirty every morning, and after that he had a lot of people to see. He had to see his
entourage of "Verdiglionian psychoanalysts," and his friends from the
banks and the advertising agencies and insurance companies and fashion houses, who were the city's other *emergenti*, and who seemed to
believe, like his patients, that an investment in Verdiglione was going
to save them from a conspiracy between the Communists and the
Catholics to deprive them of their money, on the one hand, and their
fragile status, on the other. He had to see his friends from the Socialist
Party, who were looking for something cultural to attach to, and, in a
city soaked with politics, had offered him a political umbrella on the
assumption that "something cultural" was Armando Verdiglione. He
had to see the editors at Spirali (Spirals), his publishing house, who put
out a monthly magazine devoted in large part to the thought and
triumphs of Armando Verdiglione, and a collection of books that included Armando Verdiglione's complete works as well as the high
points of his "international cultural congresses." He had to lunch at
Savini with the pretty young women who put their money in Spirali,
and in the holding companies and limited partnerships he had put
together in the interests of a big personal itinerary for everyone, and
who in return had "graduated" from his instruction and were now
psicanaliste themselves, with patients of their own in various stages of
distress and solvency. Some of those patients—there were four or five
hundred small stockholders in the companies of the Armando Verdiglione Foundation of International Culture—had raised two and a half
million dollars to buy Verdiglione his view of the Duomo's lacy façade.
The Piazza del Duomo was the headquarters of the Armando Verdiglione Foundation of International Culture. The handouts called it "a
place and a time to discuss the cultural issues which in Europe since
1978 have marked the turning point from disciplinary, ideological and
sometimes patriotic as well as provincial universalism to industrial,
namely artistic and cultural, internationalism, with the specificity of
scientific discourse that internationalism implies."

The Piazza del Duomo was where everyone started out on his

personal itinerary—where the pretty young women had consulting
offices and gave courses called "Reading Verdiglione," and where Verdiglione himself held forth, Monday nights, at a weekly "psychoanalysis seminar," sitting behind microphones on a podium that resembled
a state monument from 1935 and talking about things like "the maternal
phantasm" and "the language of the structure of the symptom." But
eventually that itinerary would lead to the Villa Borromeo, which
Verdiglione had bought with another four million dollars' worth of his
admirers' investments and promissory notes made over to a holding
company he modestly called Kolonos, after Sophocles' birthplace and
Oedipus' last refuge. Verdiglione claimed that the Villa Borromeo was
the world's first "true psychoanalysis clinic." He thought the dimensions of the place were appropriate—the marble fountains and the birch
parks and the stately, pilastered façade, the ochre cornices, the twenty-
one drawing rooms that he could name Sala New York, Sala Tokyo,
Sala Jerusalem, and Sala Paris, after the cities of his most important
congresses. There was plenty of space for cultural conversation at the
Villa Borromeo. Patients could rent a bedroom, and analysts an office,
and sometimes they all got to mingle with French media *philosophes* like
Bernard-Henri Lévy and Philippe Sollers, who showed up at what
Verdiglione called his "manifestations of the Second Renaissance,"
either for the trip or for the publicity or perhaps in the suspicion
(intellectuals in France are given to this sort of insecurity) that they
might be missing something chic or *sérieux* if they stayed at home.
Occasionally, the patients at the villa were joined by real celebrities.
Elderly literati like Jorge Luis Borges and Eugène Ionesco would arrive
in Senago for a couple of weeks' vacation and discover themselves at
a conference called something like "Finance and Science," expected to
talk for an hour every afternoon to an audience of Verdiglionian analysts, Milanese analysands, and bewildered businessmen who had paid
a lot of money to hear them. Giorgio Bocca, the *Repubblica* columnist,
says that the single most interesting fact to emerge from the Verdiglione affair was that for seven days, a nice room, and all expenses paid
you could get any Nobel laureate in the world onto an airplane.

Whatever Armando Verdiglione was selling varied with the times
and the market and the fickle enthusiasms of the Milanese, who were
his real clientele. The Milanese say in their defense that they have
always had trouble distinguishing between gurus and charlatans. They
go on television panels and write letters to the editor complaining that
all the institutions of Italian life, from the family to the Church to the
Mafia, have primed them to meekly turn over their money and their

faith to people they have terrible trouble understanding. They like to point out that thousands of Italians are *arancioni*—"orange people" —and wear saffron robes and worship a disreputable Indian known as Bhagwan Shree Rajneesh. One of the orange people sits on the secretariat of the Italian Radical Party—the Radicali. He has told the other orange people to join the Radicali and get their guru elected something important, like Prime Minister, and the Milanese say that when you compare the Second Renaissance with an operation like that it is hard to accuse Verdiglione of anything. But Verdiglione was special. He was not selling God or karma or phony stocks or Florida swamps or any of the charlatan's classic offerings. He was a Cagliostro, selling a new kind of protection. Sometimes he called it "psychoanalysis" and sometimes "culture" and sometimes "the word," and after he was arrested and decided that the state had coopted the word—"the demonization of the word," he said—he called it "the cipher." What made him special was that nobody, not the analysts and their patients or the prosecutors and the judges or the French *philosophes* who wrote letters defending him to the Italian President and sponsored an appeal on his behalf to the European Court of Human Rights—nobody, possibly not even Armando Verdiglione, could say for sure what he was talking about.

Armando Verdiglione was born toward the end of the Second World War in a village called Caulonia. His father was a blacksmith, and his most illustrious relative was an older brother named Guido, who in 1945 put together his own army, took over the village, and proclaimed the Red Republic of Caulonia. Armando does not go back to Calabria much anymore. Perhaps it was not his preferred personal itinerary to be the baby brother of a revolutionary, because, as a boy, he wrote gloomy poems and had spiritual crises and went on a pilgrimage to the Madonna di Serra San Bruno, and even talked about becoming a missionary someplace far away, like Japan. His mother sent him to the Jesuits in Sicily for proper spiritual instruction, but, according to a reporter who went to Palermo and tracked down Verdiglione's spiritual adviser, the Jesuits considered him "too Catholic to be a believer and too much of a Jesuit to become one." He arrived in Milan in 1964, with a letter from his bishop, and apparently let it be understood that he was from a "princely family." Four years later, he had a degree in modern literature from the Catholic University here. He was bright and wrote easily even then. He lived in a Church dormitory called the Augustinianum, and people who knew him say he paid his way by writing theses to order for his classmates and by selling lecture notes. Last summer, when he was in jail and was going on about the history of persecuted genius (Socrates, Cicero, Galileo, Verdiglione), he began writing tracts in which he talked about racism and about how people in Milan despised southerners like him. (The first tract was *The Word on Trial*, and then came *What Am I Accused Of?* and *The Misadventures of a Psychoanalyst.*) He could name everyone who had ever called him swarthy or smarmy, or even dark, or had joked about an *oscura* mind in a *scuro* body, or referred to the round lapels on his striped suits as "designer Calabrese," but the fact was that Verdiglione had cultivated his southern style, with what might have been irony or contempt for convention, or even cultural commentary, but in all likelihood was innocent preference. His classmates in Palermo had called him Pomatina, because of the way he slicked his hair, and his classmates in Milan thought that the cigars he smoked were "pestilential." He was not much liked at college. He did not "make his 1968," as the Europeans say, by striking and demonstrating and occupying buildings and otherwise preparing for the revolution, but he seems to have learned something from the people who did, because the congresses—he liked to call his meetings "congresses"—that he orchestrated later on resembled nothing so much as 1960s sit-ins. You could walk into a Verdiglione congress and—no matter what the posters said about its being a meeting on semiotics or psychoanalysis or insurance—sing a song or make a speech or show home movies of your sex life or announce the arrival of UFOs or start shouting about oppression. The difference was that the students of 1968 called it participatory democracy, while Verdiglione charged for the experience and called it the Second Renaissance.

In 1968, Verdiglione got a job teaching Italian literature in a local high school. He told his class about structuralism and linguistics and a lot of other glamorous French things the class had never heard of (one of his old students says that in those days Verdiglione was altogether *dans l'air du temps parisien*), and started introducing himself around Milan as a linguistics scholar. Most people believed him. Franco Fornari, who was president of the Freudian institute here, invited him to give a series of lectures on "psychoanalysis and linguistics" to his training analysts, and after that Verdiglione also started introducing himself as a psychoanalyst, and sometimes even as a training analyst. (Legally, there is nothing to prevent anybody in Italy from calling himself a psychoanalyst.) The Milan psychoanalysts—orthodox Freudians, and not an expansive group to begin with—were furious. Apparently, Dr. Fornari ordered Verdiglione to stop using the institute's name to solicit patients, and when Verdiglione ignored him

Fornari called Verdiglione a *magliaro*, which is one way of saying a Calabrian hustler, and appealed to an older analyst named Cesare Musatti, who was the paterfamilias of the Milan Freudians (Musatti is ninety now and still consulting), to do something. Dr. Musatti summoned Verdiglione to talk about honor. Not much later, Verdiglione left for Paris.

It is hard to discover what, exactly, Verdiglione did in Paris or how long he was really there. Sometimes he says he was on a grant to study semiotics at the École des Hautes Études en Sciences Sociales. Sometimes he says he was studying with Maurice Merleau-Ponty (who had died in 1961), or with Georges Bataille (who had died in 1962), or with Claude Lévi-Strauss or Jacques Derrida. Of course, in Paris "studying with" can mean anything from writing your thesis under someone's direction to sitting in on his lectures with five hundred curious Parisians to simply reading his books. Lévi-Strauss taught until he was seventy-four and thinks that a hundred thousand people must have sat in on his lectures at one time or another. Verdiglione registered as a doctoral candidate at the Hautes Études every year from 1970 to 1976, and listed the semiologist Julien Greimas as his "director of studies," but Greimas says that Verdiglione was only around for two of those years, and that he never submitted a thesis or got a doctorate. No one at the Hautes Études today remembers him. The people who do remember Verdiglione in Paris met him in 1972, in Jacques Lacan's famous waiting rooms on the rue de Lille, when he was commuting from Milan for monthly sessions of Lacanian analysis.

Jacques Lacan was the "linguists' psychoanalyst." He changed the way the French read Freud—most people would say he introduced the French to Freud, because the French Freudians were a tiny group, and no one else in the country knew anything about Freud, or wanted to, until Lacan started writing and teaching and practicing. He was much closer to the structuralists and semiologists of postwar France than to any of his own colleagues. It was his theory—expounded over thousands of pages of "Séminaires" and "Écrits"—that words themselves were the real subject of a Freudian analysis. He believed that language camouflaged the desires it had already subverted, and the dramas and traumas of what he called "the Freudian tale," and he talked and wrote an involuted, mystifying, and sometimes illuminating prose that —he seemed to be saying—was language calling language into question. He was a conjurer, and he was always performing. He liked to be driven to his seminars at the Hôpital Sainte-Anne in a Porsche and hide in a café until everyone was fidgety and getting nervous—

and then he would rush in, out of breath, and talk about something like the sunrise in Baltimore or the columns of the Pantheon. He produced in people a kind of semantic vertigo, but they must have liked it, because half of Paris started turning up at those seminars, and they had to be moved to a big auditorium at the École Normale Supérieure, and then to the Faculté de Droit, and even then—it was after Brigitte Bardot became a regular—you had to be in line by seven in the morning to get a seat.

Lacan's patients, who followed him around dutifully, concluded that *le style Lacanien*, like *le discours Lacanien*, was a way of shocking them out of their expectations and assumptions. (Orthodox Freudians who knew Lacan pointed out that he was a cranky and impatient man and may have preferred his patients shocked speechless to sitting in his office talking at length and boring him.) Some Lacanian analyses went on long distance, like Verdiglione's. The Lacanian hour lasted anywhere from a couple of hours to a couple of minutes, for therapeutic reasons only the doctor could anticipate, but his patients considered themselves so well served by this ephemeral contact that after Lacan died, in 1981, a group of rival analysts talked about putting a notice in *Libération* to the effect that Dr. Lacan was continuing his practice —only from farther away. There were days when Lacan would simply sit at the desk in his consulting room, reading the newspaper or fixing his bow tie or pouring tea from a Wedgwood teapot—and occasionally stare out the door at some invisible "other" (he called the unconscious "the discourse of the other") behind the people who had collected in his waiting rooms as the day went on. In the end, those patients got to know each other at least as well as they knew their doctor. Jacques-Alain Miller, who married Lacan's daughter and now presides over the École de la Cause Freudienne—a revived version of Lacan's psychoanalytic society, the École Freudienne—remembers Verdiglione from his waiting-room days. He says that there were maybe ten people commuting from Italy to the rue de Lille to be analyzed or supervised or simply "received," and that none of them got along with Verdiglione, even though he was "not so obnoxious" in Paris as in Milan. Lacan saw Verdiglione for about two years. According to Miller, he was trying to "discipline" Verdiglione—presumably through the connection to himself and to a "Lacanian network." According to Cesare Musatti, Lacan was "smart but a little crazy. He took students very nonchalantly. He didn't care if after two months you said, 'I am a Lacanian analyst now.' "

Cesare Musatti has a theory about Verdiglione. He says it is very easy to imitate "dissidence" in psychoanalytic circles, and this means that the language of psychoanalysis—and especially arcane "dissident" language, like Lacan's—is open to all sorts of manipulations and deceptions, including self-deception. Verdiglione claims now that he never was a Lacanian. "I have passed Freud, and I have passed Lacan," he likes to say. But he believed, if not in Lacan, then in his own ability to pull off a "Lacan" in Italy, and Dr. Musatti thinks this gave him a certain power as a healer. Verdiglione made people feel better— at least for a while—because that was what he told them he was doing. He had a "Lacanian" practice here before his own sessions with Lacan had even started, and his patients then—back when business was small and he was still calling them patients—thought he was a fine clinician. (On the other hand, fifteen years ago in Milan not that many people knew what a clinician was, or even what psychoanalysis was, besides being something you lay down for and paid for by the hour.) They had very little choice anyway. If you lived in Milan in the early seventies and wanted the cachet of a Lacanian analysis, either you went to Armando Verdiglione or you went to Lacan's Italian translator, Giacomo Contri, who was indisputably astute but was involved in the politics of a very conservative Catholic group called Communion and Liberation—and that connection made a lot of analysands nervous. It was clear in Paris which Italian Lacanians were in favor, because in Paris Lacan had admitted Contri and Muriel Drazien, an American woman with a Rome practice, to his École Freudienne, and he had refused to admit Verdiglione, no matter how often Verdiglione asked. It was not so clear in Milan. Lacan wanted to have an institute in Milan and establish *his* Freud in Italy. He was a conceited man, and, whatever he thought of Verdiglione, he knew that Verdiglione had a following of "Lacanians" here—maybe the biggest following of Lacanians. When the time came to put together that Italian institute, he informed Contri and Drazien that Verdiglione would be joining them as a director.

Contri says now that he has made an *autocritica*. He has decided that Verdiglione's real problem was not crime but rejection, that Verdiglione was always getting rejected, and that rejection exalted him and, like a psychotic or a junkie, he needed bigger and bigger rejections —getting arrested and going to jail in handcuffs—to satisfy him. At the time, however, all that Contri knew was that he wanted to reject Armando Verdiglione. Muriel Drazien, who was a serious young woman from New York, didn't think much of Verdiglione *or* Contri. She says the three of them were like the states of Italy before the Risorgimento—ambitious, different, divided. They met a few times and eventually signed some papers for a school to be called La Cosa Freudiana. They did manage to hold one meeting, with thirty people, and then they argued publicly and La Cosa Freudiana dissolved. Around that time, Verdiglione held the first of his congresses, "Psychoanalysis and Politics."

Armando Verdiglione is not a charismatic man or an attractive man or a man of any noticeable charm. It is hard to imagine him in the sunshine. He is short and sallow, and until he went to jail he was always plump—not fat or stocky but plump and smooth, like a flashy little Buddha carved in wood. He has a look that you sometimes see in hospitals—a look psychiatrists associate with lack of affect. It is a look of intense and aggressive disregard. In Verdiglione, it passed for confidence at first, and then for success, because nothing embarrassed Verdiglione and no one intimidated him. He founded something called the Freudian Collective for Semiotics and Psychoanalysis. He gave seminars with an entrance fee of five or ten dollars. He saw to it that his patients brought their friends, and his old *liceo* students brought their friends, and that they all sat still while *il professore* said whatever came into his head and called it "discourse."

People who heard Verdiglione talk say that his words were like potshots—sometimes they hit reality and sometimes not—but everyone figured he was saying something brilliant, because he always spoke in the company of intellectuals whose names they knew and who seemed to be listening. Verdiglione had discovered early on that intellectuals like to get invited places, that they like to see their names on posters, like politicians or rock stars. He collected names in those days, names like Socrates and St. Catherine and Gödel and Semiramis to drop in his lectures, in between the references to "signs" and "signifiers" and "the transfinite"—and also fashionable Paris names like Gilles Deleuze and Octave Mannoni and Marcelin Pleynet to come to Milan and hear those lectures. He acquired lists of smart people the way a catalogue company acquires lists of customers, or a candidate acquires lists of voters. He seemed to know that only a few of the smart people would bother to complain, and even fewer would think to call their lawyers, if they saw their names appropriated as Verdiglione "authors" or "sponsors" or (his favorite) "collaborators." He knew, in fact, that most of them would go along for the sake of being cited in such good company.

Verdiglione's collection was at its most beguiling in the early eighties, when he was using a system of mailings and promotion based on the simple premise that anyone who didn't actually reply to his invitations saying no could be said to have accepted. There were four hundred names on the International Board of Collaborators he published at the front of his magazine, *Spirali* (before the phone interviews and conference transcripts and unpaid reprints and the articles about Verdiglione and even the articles by Verdiglione). They ran a gamut from wrong people (Bob Guccione) to dissident people (Vladimir Bukovsky) to important Third World people (Léopold Senghor), and the one thing most of those people had in common was that they had never heard of Armando Verdiglione. By then, the posters for Verdiglione's congresses—like the congress called "Sex and Language," at the Plaza, in New York in 1981—listed under "participants" everybody who had been invited, and under "invited" (presumably) everybody who had refused. But by then it was obvious that a lot of people would cheerfully give a ten-minute talk on "The Indissoluble" or "The Syntax of Enjoyment" or "Pen, Pencil, and Penis" or "Pornography and Cinema of the Semblance" in return for a week at the Plaza at the expense of banks and businesses, and even governments, that were convinced Armando Verdiglione was Italy's answer to Masterpiece Theatre. Some of those people would even pay to see their name on a speakers' program with names like Michelangelo Antonioni, Luciano Berio, Milan Kundera, and William Burroughs (whether or not they came) and get to make a speech in simultaneous translation.

Piero Bassetti, who runs the Milan Chamber of Commerce, says that Verdiglione's genius was to "finger the *emergenti* whose real financial activity was spending." Verdiglione made these people feel like intellectuals, and even like aristocrats, by selling them a world that was so arcane, so "Lacanian," that nobody else could understand what they were saying. Italians have a great respect for obscurity, for long and difficult words and the *dottori* who use them, and Verdiglione talking "Lacan"—talking about "the submission to the guarantee of the ineffable" or "the ear as metaphor for the representation of 'the listen' "—was not so different in the end from the judges and doctors who used to talk in Latin so that people would find them priestly and intimidating. In Italy, a man who sounds obscure can pass for a cultivated man, and the more obscure he sounds the more cultivated he seems. This may be why the Milanese took up Armando Verdiglione as if he were a Fendi fur or a pink plastic lamp from Ettore Sottsass's Memphis studios. By 1976, Verdiglione was established here. He was Dr. Verdiglione or Professor Verdiglione or anything else he chose to call himself. He had renamed his "collective" the Italian Psychoanalysis Association. He had Feltrinelli publishing his conferences. He was starting to

meet the lawyers and accountants who later on would turn his real
estate into a foundation. He was training a group of avid, if often
unstable, young patients as psychoanalysts. Those patients were beginning to see patients of their own, and were putting their money and
their patients' money into the association. Armando Verdiglione was
getting so well known in Milan that when he announced his first
International Psychoanalytic Congress two thousand Milanese paid for
tickets to hear him talk about madness.

A psychoanalyst here named Elvio Fachinelli says that the trouble
with Verdiglione's own personal itinerary was that it really was an
itinerary. Verdiglione took his show out of Italy for the first time in
1977, and after a few years there was nowhere left for him to go. He
was compulsively extravagant. (His admirers said "baroque" and "the-
atrical" and "in the tradition of the Counter-Reformation.") The first
time he came to New York, he got out one of his American lists and
invited everybody on it for champagne and lobster at the Waldorf. A
few months later, he was back with sixty French and Italian reporters,
and then he brought in his team of "international intellectuals" and
booked them into the Plaza. The bill at the Plaza was a quarter of a
million dollars, and no one ever found out who paid it—though Alitalia
admitted having helped out with the Italian airfares, and Air France
with the French airfares, and it turned out that the Banco di Roma and
what Verdiglione calls "industry" had contributed to a big party at the
Metropolitan Museum. (Not to be outdone, the French Foreign Minister told his cultural attaché in New York to throw a bigger, better
party, and Verdiglione arrived with three or four hundred guests.)

Verdiglione does not like answering questions about money.
When people ask about the women who are said to support him
—his first "fiancée" was a disciple named Giovanna Sancristoforo, and
now his fiancée is a textile heiress named Cristina Frua De Angeli, who
says that coming, as she does, from an industrial family, her own
personal itinerary would naturally combine "psychoanalysis and business"—he either changes the subject or talks about Freud and Marie
Bonaparte and how everybody in Vienna was jealous. He is said to have
paid bills in New York with Banco di Roma sacks filled with dollars,
but the only sack he chooses to discuss is something that has to do with
comparing the unconscious to a contraceptive. Sometimes he says that
talking about money is a way of avoiding talking about "sex" or "the
voice" or "parricide," or whatever word he happens to be promoting.

Other times he says that money has been the big taboo in "European discourse," and that he has broken it.

A couple of years ago, a story went around Milan to the effect that Verdiglione's bank sacks were sacks of money that he was laundering for the Mafia. People believed this until someone pointed out that the Mafia had more efficient ways of laundering money than Armando Verdiglione. As it happens, the only Mafia that Verdiglione tapped was the one Italians call "the Socialist Mafia," which is run mainly from Milan by a group of Milanese *emergenti*—most notably, the old Prime Minister, Bettino Craxi; the mayor of Milan, Paolo Pillitteri, who is Craxi's brother-in-law; and the young Socialist Party vice-secretary, Claudio Martelli, who is Craxi's protégé. The Italian Socialist Party has very little to do with European socialism, or even with old Italian socialism. It was slow to revive once the war was over, and by the time it did revive it was to all intents and purposes a new party—with the same sort of clientele Verdiglione was courting. It is considered an aggressively corrupt party, even by Italian standards, because the Socialists bought into the political spoils system so much later than the two big parties—the Christian Democrats and the Communists— that most of Italy was given away by the time they arrived. The Socialists went into *la cultura* and *lo sport* and *la moda* as if they were dairy monopolies or state electric companies, and they peddled influence for people like Verdiglione, whom the old politicos had never even considered. It is unlikely that many of them read the "dialogues" in which Verdiglione discussed Adam and Eve, William of Malmesbury, Sylvester II, Albertus Magnus, Thomas Aquinas, Alexander Pope, Abraham ibn Ezra, Giordano Bruno, Lord Byron, Kant, Leibniz, Paracelsus, Jacques Offenbach, and the Goddess of Dawn with somebody called the Coder and somebody else called Encoding. But they saw to it that the bankers they knew gave Verdiglione credit, and that their friends at the Ferrovie and the insurance companies contributed to the Freudian cause, and that advertising agencies the party used put ads in *Spirali* and helped out with expensive congresses like "Sex and Language" and the Tokyo congress called "Sexuality: Where Does the East Come From, Where Is the West Going?"

Piero Forno is a forty-year-old public prosecutor with more experience interrogating terrorists than interrogating psychoanalysts, and neither the time nor the money nor the requisite chic to receive a celebrity's invitation to the Second Renaissance. In fact, Piero Forno had never heard of Armando Verdiglione until the spring of 1985, when he was told to investigate some charges involving a training analyst from Verdiglione's group and a patient of the analyst's who had signed over $170,000 worth of bank loans, promissory notes, and IOUs in exchange for shares in three of Verdiglione's real-estate companies. The analyst was a doctor from Padua named Fabrizio Scarso, who had moved to Milan to practice after a couple of years on Verdiglione's couch. The patient was a dentist from Puglia named Michele Calderoni, who had moved to Milan to study and—whether or not he was sick to begin with—had ended up in a schizophrenic ward after a couple of years on Scarso's couch. When policemen raided the Villa Borromeo, looking for Scarso, they found torn-up checks in Verdiglione's wastepaper basket—and Verdiglione himself hiding behind a chair in a room with the lights turned off.

Forno spent about a year on the case. He interviewed dozens of patients ("the victims"), and in the end he arrested Verdiglione, along with Scarso and four other analysts in Verdiglione's entourage. The charges he brought against them ranged from extortion and fraud to *circonvenzione di incapace, abbandono di incapace,* and *violenza privata.* When the case was tried, he recommended that the court consider a second trial, because he also wanted to charge twenty-six associates of the Armando Verdiglione Foundation of International Culture with criminal conspiracy.

The case of Michele Calderoni was a model of what one reporter called "the Verdiglione method." The first year of the dentist's analysis was apparently uneventful, although his lawyer has said that Calderoni was having trouble because of the "pressures of dental school." (Verdiglione, who can get carried away into lucidity when he talks about the case, says that Calderoni was having "woman trouble.") When Calderoni had been in analysis for about a year, Scarso talked to him about the possibility of his becoming an analyst himself. Scarso sent him to see Verdiglione, and that, according to the prosecution, was when Verdiglione asked for money. At the time, Calderoni had six thousand dollars in the bank. Verdiglione took it. A few weeks later, he arranged for the dentist to raise forty thousand dollars in loans from six banks —loans that were guaranteed by Scarso and some of the other foundation analysts. Eventually, Calderoni turned over $125,000 more. He borrowed some of it, at 20 percent interest, using his dental practice as collateral, and the rest was in IOUs made out to the holding companies Kolonos and Spirali and to another company, called Klinein (from the Greek "to bend"), which Verdiglione had set up to rent space and sell "services" (like catering and translating and linens) to businesses that wanted to use his headquarters for meetings of their own. Calderoni signed so many IOUs—Italians call them *cambiali,* and buy them, notarized, in tobacco shops—that his bill at the local tobacconist's was nearly seventeen hundred dollars. His lawyer claims that trying to meet those IOUs was what was driving Calderoni crazy. He says that when Calderoni complained, Scarso threatened to stop analyzing him if he stopped "investing." Scarso denies this, but the fact is that by the beginning of 1985 Calderoni was in terrible shape, and no one was looking after him properly. He was having hallucinations, and he would sit alone in his room laughing to himself.

Calderoni's sister, who was the original plaintiff, says that one day that winter a van arrived at his apartment, driven by a foundation factotum by the name of Mario Latino. Latino seems to have been a combination driver, electrician, analyst, and escort (he was once charged with raping a patient, and acquitted) at the Villa Borromeo. He took the dentist, his clothes, his books, and his furniture to Senago —apparently so Calderoni could pursue his personal itinerary in a more congenial cultural environment—but Calderoni lasted only a month there. His family thinks that the people at the villa got frightened, seeing how sick he was, and let him go. The day he came home, he was so disoriented that his sister called a doctor, and the doctor persuaded him to check into the hospital. A day later, the bankers started calling her.

What bothered the investigators and prosecutors most about the case was that neither Scarso nor Verdiglione—who was supposedly supervising Scarso—had consulted another doctor about Calderoni or let his family know how sick he was. It looked as if they had something to hide, something more important to them than a dentist with a woman problem. The more the prosecutors thought about the case —and about Verdiglione and his analysts and his Foundation of International Culture and his holding companies with Greek names and "shares" that apparently could be neither sold nor reclaimed—the more familiar it seemed. It reminded them of the case of the philosophy professor Toni Negri, who was arrested in 1979 and charged with "masterminding" terrorist plots at the University of Padua. Negri had demanded to be tried as an "ideological prisoner" instead of a criminal conspirator, and now here was Verdiglione demanding to be tried as "a prisoner of the word." The prosecutors thought they had another conspiracy on their hands, no matter how much Verdiglione complained that it was psychoanalysis on trial, or culture, or transference

(Giovanni Caizzi, the chief prosecutor, kept interrupting testimony to talk about "bad transference"), or how often he told reporters that psychoanalysts had been better off in Stalin's Russia and Hitler's Germany than they were in democratic Italy, where there were "thought police" everywhere.

In a way, Verdiglione was right when he said that psychoanalysis was on trial. It was clear that the *magistratura*—Forno and a colleague named Francesca Manca, who had done the investigating; Caizzi, who had taken over in court as prosecuting attorney; and the three judges, who found Verdiglione guilty last July—considered psychoanalysis a slippery, if not a sinister, business. It was as if there was something unhealthy about a world where people revealed the most intimate details of their lives to someone just because he called himself an analyst —someone who then proceeded to discuss those intimate details with *his* analyst or, even worse, with a whole group of analysts claiming to be making up a "theory of the clinic." Some of them thought it was bad enough that Italians still felt compelled to kneel in dark booths talking to priests about whether they masturbated or fornicated, or whether they respected their mothers. In Italy, the *magistratura* is a public profession: being a prosecutor or a *giudice istruttore* or a judge of the tribunal means that you are a civil servant. The Italian courts are arbitrary, sometimes corrupt, and almost always political, with the Communists and the Catholics demanding their share of the jobs and their share of decisions, but in cities like Milan there is a generation of young prosecutors and judges who have done as much as anyone in the country to help stop terrorism, and they are admired by a lot of Italians for their determination and courage. They are not worldly people. They tend to see decadence where other people see Marx or the Mafia, and they believe they can clean up Italian life as if it were a kitchen floor —with scouring and a lot of pressure. They would probably look at psychoanalysis as a conspiracy whether it was Verdiglione or Freud on the witness stand.

The state had one idea, which was brought home when two of Verdiglione's analysts "repented" in jail (in Catholic Italy, people who turn state's evidence are called *pentiti*) and dictated some forty pages of accusations against him. The idea was that Verdiglione had "used" Freud—that he had used the confidentiality of the couch and the conventions of training analysis—for criminal purposes. You chose an analyst, the argument went. Maybe it was an analyst you knew from one of Verdiglione's congresses, someone who had sat on a stage right next to Borges or Elie Wiesel—someone not too bright, and even a little dissociated, who had been transformed by proximity into someone brilliant. Your analyst was soothing and, you assumed, correct, until one day he said to you, "Giovanni"—or Giovanna—"you will never resolve your problems lying on this couch. You have to integrate your analysis into a cultural activity, something that will give meaning and direction to your life. You have to enter the Armando Verdiglione Foundation of International Culture." Now (the argument went on), suppose you asked your analyst what your "cultural activity" could possibly be, seeing that 90 percent of all the activity at the foundation seemed to belong to Verdiglione, and anything left over was reserved for the celebrities who took their vacations at the Villa Borromeo. Your analyst was ready. He "knew" your secrets. He would say to you, "Giovanni, you dream of painting. You think you are a podiatrist" —or an accountant or a kindergarten teacher—"but your true self is an artist, and it so happens that Armando Verdiglione is looking for an artist to paint pictures of the Second Renaissance. That is your *spazio*, your true cultural activity." Well, by then you were delighted. Armando Verdiglione was the answer to your problems. He was going to transform you from a podiatrist into a painter, and all you had to do was join this foundation of his, which had psychoanalysis for an ideology (or, if you preferred, a theology). Then and there, you fell in love with your analyst. It was the beginning of what Caizzi liked to call your "bad transference." You were in love with the foundation and with psychoanalysis and with Armando Verdiglione and with yourself. You gave up podiatry to paint the Second Renaissance. You understood from Verdiglione's speeches that "culture" was everything. Culture was art, theater, factories, insurance companies—though arguably not podiatry—and it cost a lot of money to organize.

The time had come to start paying, because Verdiglione had projects that were also your projects, from the point of view of your new itinerary. He had a dozen holding companies, a Chinese box of companies—one company founded to buy shares in another company founded to buy shares in a third company founded to buy shares in a company that owned an expensive piece of real estate. The companies sounded good, because they were not called Senago Real Estate or Duomo Properties. They were called Delfi and Kolonos and Freud and Pirandello. They sounded like the sort of companies you would expect to visit on your itinerary. Say you had five thousand dollars. Your analyst would tell you that five thousand dollars was not much money, but he would take it anyway, and after a few days he would ask you again—and you would find five thousand dollars more.

Finally, when there was nothing left, he sent you to Armando Verdiglione. He sent you to the glamorous flat on the via Montenapole-one, the flat you had read about in *Oggi* and *Panorama*, the flat where Lina Wertmüller dropped in of an afternoon and the Prime Minister's relatives—if not the Prime Minister himself—were said to have discreet Sunday-afternoon analyses. You arrived, nervous and excited. To your astonishment, Armando Verdiglione knew as much about you as your analyst did. He was a little cross with you, in fact. He had thought you understood that a proper investment in the Second Renaissance was not five thousand dollars but, say, fifty thousand dollars. He said to you, "Giovanni, what is a mere fifty thousand dollars when it's your life as a painter we're talking about?" He told you about his new "department of art" at the Piazza del Duomo, which was going to make your reputa-tion, and about how you would be speaking soon at his international congresses and having lunch with famous international intellectuals and seeing your paintings reproduced in magazines in Tokyo and New York. And when you thought about this you saw his point exactly. You said, "*Professore,* you are right. What's fifty thousand dollars when I'll be rich and famous soon?" And then you and Verdiglione made plans. You talked about getting loans, because Verdiglione knew bankers through his important political friends, not to mention through his congresses on "banks, art, and culture" and his talks on "banking and the unconscious." In the end, you went to those bankers, and you got your loans—never one big loan from one bank but a lot of small loans from a lot of banks. It was your analyst who guaranteed those loans. He knew the bankers, too, because he was in debt to them himself. He had invested two hundred or even three hundred thousand dollars in the Second Renaissance. In fact—from the state's point of view —the only difference between you and your analyst was that your analyst fell for the scam first.

The scam, of course, was a reconstruction—something plotted out like a game of Clue on the third floor of the Milan courthouse. The real patients had stories that were much more sordid. One woman said that after she refused to ask an uncle of hers for money Verdiglione humil-iated her at one of his "psychoanalysis seminars," announcing to every-body there that she and her uncle had committed incest. She claimed that Verdiglione had threatened her mother, too, saying that her mother would never see her again if she didn't pay. Another woman claimed that Verdiglione had beat her. Some patients said he threatened them with going mad. There used to be a crime in Italy called *plagio* — plagiarism. It meant literally borrowing someone else's will "to reduce him to a state of total subjection," and it was used (liberal Italians would say misused) to describe a kind of psychological extortion or incitement. *Plagio* was taken out of the criminal code in 1981, but it looked like what the prosecution had in mind last year when Verdiglione and his analysts went on trial. The prosecution knew that the patients Forno had interviewed—including five whom he persuaded to press charges along with Calderoni—might be less credible as witnesses than their analysts, and even less credible than Armando Verdiglione. The one thing in their favor was the possibility that psychoanalysis had made them that way.

Verdiglione did a lot of writing about his trial. There were his three tracts, and then there was a series of special issues of *Spirali* — it is now *Spirali del Secondo Rinascimento*. Those issues were bordered in gray, like mourning testimonials, and they included one issue Verdiglione called "Musatti and the Monster of Florence," which was an attack on the old analyst who had dressed him down for fraud twenty years ago. Sometimes it seemed as if Verdiglione blamed Musatti for the trial. Sometimes he blamed "Milanese corporatism" (because people in Milan didn't understand that private capital was responsible for all the great Italian adventures, from Christopher Columbus's voyages to his own) and sometimes "Milanese Calvinism" (because people in Milan were "critics of the probable"). Mostly, though, he blamed Milanese Communism—which was odd, considering that Milan has been a Socialist town for eighteen years. He said that the real power here was Communist. He said that Piero Forno was a Communist, and that the judges were Communists, and that Giorgio Bocca and all the other columnists and reporters covering his trial were Communists, and that the expert witnesses in the trial—two psychiatrists and an anthropologist—were Communists. (Elie Wiesel told Verdiglione that it was an "honor" to be attacked by the Communist Party.) Finally, even one of his own lawyers was exasperated. The lawyer says now that one of the three experts *is* a Communist, but then so is one of every three Italians.

Verdiglione got four and a half years. He was in jail in San Vittore until the end of July, and then confined to his apartment, and he took it as "a symbol of the sickness of the civilization" when Giovanni Pescarzoli, who was the presiding judge at his trial, refused to let him telephone Ionesco to discuss proofs. (The judge said that calling up Ionesco would undermine "the reeducative function" of the sentence.) In February, the Court of Appeals basically confirmed that sentence, and then, in a gesture that only the Milanese seemed to understand, expanded Verdiglione's house arrest to include the whole country —which amounted to provisional liberty. It may be that by February the Milanese were finally finished with Armando Verdiglione. Nobody here cared where he went or whom he called, and soon the only place besides *Spirali* where you could read about the Verdiglione affair was in the French papers. Some of the French writers he used to publish bought a page in *Le Monde* to tell the President of Italy that they were *"Pour Armando Verdiglione."* (Bernard-Henri Lévy, who had called the "persecution" of Armando Verdiglione a battle in the war between the "cosmopolitans" and the "totalitarians," thought up the appeal.) They pointed out that anyone smart enough to have published *them* was clearly a lover of freedom and an editor of great talent, not to mention a contributor to *"la qualité du dialogue Franco-Italien."* They talked about "moral lynching," and how Verdiglione's only crime was his independence from "the machines that control and share the politico-ideological life of Italy." Six weeks after the appeal ran, Verdiglione was in Rome at a Radical Party convention. He had decided to join the Radicali, like Toni Negri, who had discovered the party after four years in jail on "pretrial detention." Negri was elected to Montecitorio as a Radical deputy and freed with parliamentary immunity—and got on a plane for Paris. Verdiglione did not mention Negri. He talked about his friend Enzo Tortora, a television talk-show host who had also been "persecuted" by the courts—for drug and arms dealing for the Mafia. Tortora had got ten years to Verdiglione's four and a half, but he was out in less than a year, and by then he had also discovered the Radicali, who put him on their secretariat, with (among others) the orange person and a terrorist *pentito*. The Radicali got Tortora elected to the European Parliament, and *he* has diplomatic immunity—which may be what Verdiglione hopes to have before the court hands down an indictment for criminal conspiracy, or the bailiffs arrive.

Verdiglione owes a fortune. He has sold his apartment. His Social-ist friends have disappeared, and so have his banker friends and his insurance friends and his industrialist friends, and not many famous people have been dropping by lately to reassure him. He has got thin. No one sees him at Savini anymore, or at fashionable parties. Cristina Frua De Angeli looks after him at home. She has taken over his confer-ences and his correspondence and his self-promotion, and she instructs a clutch of handmaidens whose personal itinerary seems to be waiting for Armando Verdiglione to revive. For a while, he shared the offices on the Piazza del Duomo with a public-relations firm, and once a singles' club called the Together Club took over the Villa Borromeo for a "disco ball," but now both properties have been seized by the court, and sooner or later he will have to sell them. He went into debt last summer to settle three-quarters of a million dollars on "victims" who would otherwise have sued him; officially, he was buying back their shares in Delfi and Kolonos, or in the little investment funds called Freud, Galileo, Pirandello, and Vico. The analysts who were arrested want to get paid, too, and their shares add up to more than a million and a half dollars. All of them are out of jail now, and all of them need the money—and if they are indicted in a criminal-conspiracy trial they could also sue Verdiglione for damages. Even Verdiglione wants to sue someone. He is thinking of the producers of a television show called *Drive In*—which is a kind of Italian *Saturday Night Live.* The hit of *Drive In* these days is a psychoanalyst who wears terrible loud suits and smokes cigars and slicks his hair and steals his patients' watches as soon as they lie down and close their eyes. He is always trying to sell them property. The sign on his door says "psicanaLEASING," and his name is Dr. Vermilione.

June 1987

ANNA SILVA

My neighbor Anna Silva has not lost Portuguese so much as she has learned, in over twenty years in Paris, to feel in French. She may talk Portuguese to the other concierges on the block, and write letters to her son, Raul, in Portuguese, but her exclamations are the exclamations of a native. When Anna is startled or excited, she says *"Dis, donc?"* When she is sad, she shakes her head and says *"Ah, Seigneur!"* When she counts the small blessings of her hard and unaccountably tragic life, she says that at least she has had *"du pain, du vin, et du Boursin,"* instead of saying whatever people say in the mountains near Bragança, where Anna (I have changed her name) was born. She sits with her sewing, in the concierge's lodge of an old apartment building around the corner, trying to comprehend that life, which has left her alone and lonely and far from home, and the trying confuses her. It makes her dreamy and distracted. Sometimes she turns on the television set and stares patiently at the screen, as if she were waiting for François Mitterrand or Jacques Chirac or the Antenne 2 weather girl to advise her. Sometimes she picks up the phone to call Raul, in Cleveland—that is, until she remembers how much a call to Cleveland costs, or that mothers in Cleveland are cheerful, independent people who exercise and play cards and never disturb their children with the burdens of grief and age. Sometimes she simply clears a space on the narrow bed that doubles as her couch and sewing table, and opens a round red biscuit tin in which she keeps the pictures and papers and correspondence of a lifetime. She rummages in the tin until she comes to a tinted postcard of a handsome man—middle-aged and a little thick at the waist, but handsome —dressed up in the golden doublet and tail-tipped ermine cape of some imaginary, composite court and century. The man is wearing a bright, black, wavy hairpiece. His face is framed by a petal ruff, which hides the beginnings of a double chin. His eyes are clear, though. His eyebrows arch. His smile is extravagant. He has a set of perfectly capped and whitened teeth. The man's name is Luis Mariano, and Anna says that in his day he was the toast of Paris. He starred in eighteen movies and recorded more than five hundred songs, but what he did best —what made him the toast of Paris—was sing in musicals at the Théâtre du Châtelet. Mariano made the kind of musicals the French call *opérettes à grand spectacle*—lavish, fantastical period musicals with simple songs, complicated plots, a production number for every change of scenery, and exotic names like *Le Prince de Madrid* and *Le Secret de Marco Polo* and *La Caravelle d'Or*. He was a matinee idol for twenty-five years. It is said that when he toured the provinces theater managers had to put up signs backstage saying DÉFENSE AUX FIGURANTES DE TOUCHER M. MARIANO, and that even in sophisticated Paris thousands of women got together every week to listen to their Luis Mariano records and exchange their Luis Mariano gossip and compare their Luis Mariano scrapbooks. Anna never had a scrapbook, but she has kept her postcard of Mariano for eighteen years. There is a message just for her on the postcard. It is scribbled across the doublet—thus avoiding the white ruff and the whiter smile—and it has the tenor's famous signature, with an *L* that loops around and trails like a ribbon, underlining everything. The message says: *To Anna, for remembrance.*

Anna is vague about most things that affect her, but she has never forgotten the day she got her postcard. It was December 19, 1969, and *La Caravelle d'Or* was opening at the Théâtre du Châtelet. Anna watched from the wings that night. She watched while an ailing fifty-five-year-old Luis Mariano turned himself into a dashing young Don Pedro of Bragança and wooed a beautiful French princess and went to war against his wicked brother and ("to general rejoicing," the program says) was crowned King of Portugal. He was crowned in his doublet, his ermine cape, and a pair of green satin pantaloons trimmed with fat emeralds and gold braid. Anna was especially proud, she says, "because there was gold all over Luis Mariano" and, in a manner of speaking, she had put it there. In those days—those *golden* days, she likes to say, by way of a small joke—Anna was the seamstress in charge of "sewing-machine decorations" at the Théâtre du Châtelet, and most of the lace and the braid and the gold and silver piping on Luis Mariano's fabulous costumes was attached at Anna's big Singer in the Châtelet costume room. "Personally attached," Anna says now.

Anna was married for thirty-four years and lost her husband in an accident. She bore two children and lost one. She worked for twenty years to build a house, and after it was finished vandals broke in to steal the television, and set the house on fire. But when she talks about loss, when she tries to explain what grief is, she always comes back to the fact that Luis Mariano got sick and had to leave *La Caravelle d'Or* and, a few months later, died—the word in the costume room was that he died from a Rumanian youth cure—and took the "sunshine" in her life with him. By now, Luis Mariano is as vivid in Anna's memory as the husband who carved tombstones for a living and loved flowering trees, or the child who died, or the new villa north of Lisbon, tiled and shining, before the vandals came. She feels a connection to Mariano that, in her mind, sets her apart from his more or less official mourners —from the thirty-three thousand women in Luis Mariano fan clubs, who call themselves Marianistes and make pilgrimages to his tomb, in the village of Arcangues, and show his movies at weekend "homages to Mariano" at the Lille fairgrounds. Anna married Lourenço Silva in the chapel at the Monastery of Jerônimos in Lisbon—just where Luis Mariano hid his beautiful princess in *La Caravelle d'Or*. She and Lourenço lived for nineteen years in a little house near the monastery, and when they moved to France, to earn the money for their villa, she carried a letter of introduction from one of the Jerônimos Fathers. For Anna, there is something mystical—something whose meaning just eludes her—in the fact that the last time Luis Mariano sang at Châtelet he was Don Pedro of Bragança, center stage in a papier-mâché-and-plywood monastery, wearing satin pantaloons and a golden doublet that Anna Silva had embroidered.

Anna is sixty-seven years old, and since Lourenço died she has dressed in mourning, like the women of Bragança, in a plain black dress and black stockings. She wears two rings—a thin gold wedding band and a thicker silver-anniversary band—and a silver medallion, blessed by John Paul II, that one of our neighbors gave her after a Rome vacation. Sometimes she wears a watch—but only when she decides to wear her glasses, too. Anna cannot read very well without glasses, and she certainly cannot read the faded gold numerals on a lady's 1947 wristwatch. She seems to prefer not reading to the thought of herself with a pair of eyeglasses on her nose. She will go to the fruit-and-vegetable stand on our corner with a long marketing list that she has written out in the privacy of her lodge, and hand the list to the Portuguese boy who always waits on her, and always cheats her, asking him, *s'il vous plaît*, to read it for her, saying, in her timid, stubborn way, that she has left her glasses at home. I do not know whether this is vanity, or whether it has to do with Anna's reluctance to see a harsh world any more clearly than she has to. Anna is a modest woman. She is so discreet, in her black dresses and her two plain rings, that in a neighborhood like ours, with its Left Bank mixture of migrant workers, local shopkeepers, and old Paris money, her discretion could pass for the understatement of a woman the French would call "a woman of a certain age." But I know that she is vain about some things. She is vain about her hair, which used to be brown but is blond now, and sometimes—if I have been in New York and managed to stop at the hairdressers' supply house near my office—a color that Anna refers to as "American blond." Anna dyed her hair for the first time in 1967, when Luis Mariano was singing Goya in *Le Prince de Madrid,* and a pretty soprano—she was an understudy to the Duchess of Alba—would pay Anna to come in early and color her hair with a paintbrush and a bottle of something blond from America. One day, the soprano invited Anna to try the color on herself. Anna has kept the brush she used. She is still using it. It was one of the paintbrushes in Goya's secret studio in the Chapel of San Bernardino—the studio in which he painted the naked Maja five nights and two matinees a week for eighteen months while singing a duet and preparing for a bullfight and worrying about the Inquisition.

Luis Mariano—his real name was Mariano-Eusebio González y García—was born in the Basque city of Irún, in northern Spain, in the summer of 1914, just after the war broke out in Europe. His father was a Spanish mechanic who lived in Bordeaux but had headed home that summer to avoid fighting—and who seems to have spent the next twenty years shuttling the family back and forth across the border, unable to decide which country was safer. No one knows how "Basque" Luis Mariano was—there are no typically Basque names in the family—but he made his reputation as a Basque, and to his fans he was pure Basque, by which they meant that he was ardent, impetuous, honorable, pious, brave, romantic, noble, and a dozen other operetta qualities. The Basque country of their imagination had no borders. It produced no rain and no violence—no separatists or terrorists or secret revolutionary armies with unpronounceable names. It was a sunny and entirely bucolic place where high-spirited young tenors like Luis Mariano were always dancing in their village squares or bursting into song in their sweethearts' gardens or making ardent vows to the Virgin. Certainly no one who could sing got old in the Basque country. Mariano was six when Anna was born, but he dropped those six years in 1936 to avoid the draft—the family was back in Bordeaux in 1936—and once he became the toast of Paris and a famous stage lover he dropped as many more years as his roles demanded and his paunch allowed. The result was that he inspired in women like Anna a kind of modest, comfortable, maternal passion. There are women who began to love Luis Mariano when they were little girls, and kept on loving him while they aged and he got younger, and now those women are like the mothers of some handsome and heroic soldier who died (faithful to them) before his time. According to my friend Jeanine Parzy—Mlle Parzy works in a bank in Lille, and she is president of all the Marianistes in the Pas de Calais and Belgium—there are always fifty or sixty women in Arcangues on a summer day, taking advantage of their *congés payés* to make a pilgrimage to the famous tomb and "discover Mariano, before our eyes, in the sun and the flowers and the beautiful Basque colors." Mariano owned a farm in Arcangues—a "Basque" farm, with a swimming pool and a chapel and a hundred acres. He left it to his chauffeur—the chauffeur's name was François Lacan, but Mariano called him Patchi—and the chauffeur's son Marianino, whom Mariano had adopted. Nothing has changed there since he died, Mlle Parzy says, except the milk cows, which used to be named for Mariano's leading ladies.

Luis Mariano had a nice clear tenor voice with no particular character. His contemporary Marcel Merkes, who is sixty-seven and still singing on the provincial circuit, had a much more interesting voice than Mariano. And it was Georges Guétary (Guétary was Gene Kelly's rival in the movie *An American in Paris*), not Mariano, who had the important reputation abroad and got to sing on Broadway. Mariano couldn't act and he couldn't dance, but there was something about him that none of the competition seemed to have. *"Il portait le soleil,"* Anna says when she tries to describe him, and that is what Mlle Parzy says, too, and just about everyone else I know who saw him. They say that the sun was in him. It was in his terrible toothy smile and in the way he sang his songs (many of them were written by a French dentist named Francis Lopez, who provided a Basque history of his own for the purposes of their collaboration), and it literally warmed an audience. People who loved Luis Mariano would save for a year to come to Paris when he was performing. They would sit in the big theater on the Place du Châtelet, with its crystal chandeliers and its "royal" boxes and its three thousand plush seats, and have the romance of their otherwise cautious and correct lives.

There are intellectuals who maintain that Mariano was not truly *populaire*—the way Edith Piaf, say, was *populaire*—but the fact is that their concierges and their butchers and their postmen and the plumbers on their block either went to Châtelet or wanted to go to Châtelet when Luis Mariano sang, and it would be difficult to prove that those people are any less *le peuple français* than the street waifs and four-in-the-morning truckers whom Paris intellectuals romanticize. Besides, it is hard to find a Paris intellectual who never went to Châtelet, as a boy, with his grandmother, or who never broke a date because of a Mariano movie on television, or who never knew *La Belle de Cadix* by heart or which words rhymed with "Mexico" in the famous finale of *Le Chanteur de Mexico* (*torero, nouveau, tropicaux, bateau, crescendo, bolero, galop*). People here have been going to *opérettes* since Jacques Offenbach moved into a wooden shed across the street from the Paris World's Fair of 1855 and invited the tourists to Les Bouffes-Parisiens for an evening—*"une soirée légère et plutôt gaie"*—where everybody sang and danced and said malicious, delicious, witty things to everybody else. (Offenbach and his librettists, Henri Meilhac and Ludovic Halévy, are said—by the French—to have been the Rodgers and Hart of the Second Empire.) Offenbach's musical theater was his antidote to the pompous offerings at the Opéra Comique. He established a genre. The *opérettes* that Parisians liked best were written by people nobody remembers, and had names like *La Mascotte* and *Les Mousquetaires au Couvent* and *Mam'zelle Nitouche*. Some of them were dreadful, and none of them was very good, or very demanding, but they suited the times. The new rich of the Second Empire had money to spend and not much culture, and they wanted to be worldly. Mainly, they wanted to forget that their parents had lived it up at country cattle fairs and had gaped at the jugglers and tumblers on the Pont Neuf when they came to town. Their insecurities survived the Empire. When Franz Lehár brought his *Merry Widow* to Paris, it had the longest run of any production in the city's history.

Mariano came to Paris—it was Occupied Paris—in 1942. He had studied for a year at the conservatory in Bordeaux, and had already sung with a Basque choir in a movie called *Ramuntcho* and made two records with the chorus of a Spanish tango orchestra, but Marianistes consider that his proper début was Christmas Eve, 1943, when he sang Ernesto in a special performance of Donizetti's *Don Pasquale* at the Palais de Chaillot. They are not troubled by the idea of Luis Mariano carrying the sun to an audience of opera-loving German officers —and neither, apparently, was Mariano. He saw to his career in Occupied Paris, and then he fled to Les Landes during the bombings and celebrated the Liberation by singing the "Marseillaise." On Christmas Eve, 1945, he made his "second début." He opened—in a little theater on the rue de la Gaîté called the Casino Montparnasse—in Francis Lopez's operetta *La Belle de Cadix.* By all accounts, it was not an *opérette à grand spectacle.* It was written fast, to fill a hole in the theater's season, and it was put on with a four-man orchestra and eleven singers wearing homemade costumes that Mariano had designed. Lopez, who is seventy-one now and lives in an orange penthouse on the Boulevard Haussmann, with palm trees and pelicans painted all over the front hall, and sheets of plastic on the furniture, says that *La Belle de Cadix* made them "top number one" in Paris. (He usually adds that he was already top number one, owing to a song called "Allons, Petits Soldats de France," which he had dashed off for a troop show in 1939, when he was a young dentist in the French Army.) They were booked for six weeks, but by the time they closed there were 800,000 Marianistes in France, and Luis Mariano was shopping for his first Cadillac and Francis Lopez had stopped pulling teeth. People were walking around Paris singing the song about the beauty from Cadix. They were dancing to it in basement clubs and at Saturday-night street balls, and listening to it on the butcher's radio while they stood in line with their ration books waiting to buy their weekly meat allowance.

Anna was born in Trás-os-Montes in 1920—the year that Luis Mariano chose for his birthday. Her father was a peasant. He owned eight acres of stony mountain land an hour's walk from the nearest village and about fifty miles from the city of Bragança; an ancient farmhouse with mud floors and animal stalls under the kitchen; a vegetable garden; and an assortment of sheep, cows, goats, and pigs. He had a wife and thirteen children. Nine of those children survived. Anna, who was the seventh, says that they ate "everything the earth gave us," even the maize they were supposed to save for pig fodder. Each September, at the village fair, they sold some calves and lambs for a winter's supply of grain and staples and, if there was anything left, woollen cloth for making winter clothes. Each January, they slaughtered four pigs to be smoked and cured. Anna had two jobs—getting up at four in the morning to milk the cows and make fresh cheese, so that the family could have a bowl of cheese with their bread at breakfast, and passing the rosary for mealtime prayers. She went to school in the village for a few years, but the walk was long—especially the walk home, up the mountain—and there was already too much work for her at home. She stopped—all the girls in the family stopped school—as soon as she could read and write and knew addition and subtraction and her multiplication tables. Her mother ran the farm, because even then there were not many men in the north of Portugal who could afford to stay at home. Men married and fathered their children, one a year, and then they left, looking for work, looking for better land, looking for anything to ease the poverty of their lives in that stony and remote corner of Europe, where—the saying went—nothing had changed in a thousand years except the priests and the policemen. Peasants in Trás-os-Montes slept in the stalls with their animals, for warmth, and were often dead of work and disease at an age when the Lisbon rich were just settling down and getting married.

It was such a humiliating life, at least for Anna's father, that while he was still at home he hired a feeble village boy as a goatherd rather than herd the goats himself or have his sons herd them. Anna was six when he went away. He sold a field and went to Brazil with one of his brothers, and the children climbed to the top of the mountain carrying stones and built a shrine to protect him. He stayed in Brazil six years, working as a waiter in Rio, and when he came home, not much richer for his troubles, he sold another field and left for Brazil again, and died there. Anna's brothers left, too, as soon as they could pass for men. Her three oldest brothers went to the iron mines north of Lisbon, and two of them died there, in a cave-in. Vasco, who came next and was her favorite brother, ran away and joined the Navy. (Anna says it was the year that Luis Mariano began to practice his famous *écriture d'artiste*, with its long *L* and its letters slanting backward, signifying a pleasing combination of modesty and ambition.) Vasco got so seasick on his first cruise out that he ended up in a Lisbon hospital. He was discharged by an admiral whose brother, a professor of jurisprudence, needed a maid for his family. The admiral asked Vasco if he had any sisters at home in Trás-os-Montes to take the job.

Anna moved to Lisbon after the harvest that year. She was fourteen. She sewed dresses for the professor's wife and knit pink sweaters for the professor's two daughters, and she showed such an aptitude for the work, such stubborn patience with a needle, that the professor paid for her to spend a couple of weeks with a neighbor's maid, learning piping and tucking and embroidery, and mastering the many uses of a foot-pedal sewing machine. Anna loved the professor's family. His daughters behaved. His wife wore perfume, and silk underwear, and took a bath with bubbles every afternoon, after her siesta. The professor himself spoke softly. Like Luis Mariano, he was respectful and commanding at the same time. He had a bottle of wine at lunch and a glass of port after supper, but he never drank himself into a rage, like the men at home, and smashed his glass and hit the women in his family. He was the first gentleman in Anna's life, and his wife, she says, was the first real *senhora*. His wife had long black hair—Anna would comb it back for her and roll it into a chignon—and a clear, high forehead, and she was beautiful. There is a picture of her in Anna's biscuit tin. It was taken in Spain, on a holiday, and in it she is all dressed up in Moorish clothes for an "Alhambra portrait." Anna thinks that the shadow on her cheeks makes her look like Carmen Sevilla, who was Mariano's leading lady in the movies of *La Belle de Cadix, Andalousie,* and *Violettes Impériales,* and, according to the press agents and managers who were entrusted with Mariano's manly image, the great and unrequited love of Luis Mariano's life.

It is Anna's "disposition," she says, to look after people. She is uneasy on her own, but she tends the periphery of other lives with grace and even authority, which may be why she was so content as a maid in Lisbon. The repression in Fascist Portugal seems to have passed in Anna's mind for a kind of civic discretion, because she keeps a postcard of Oliveira Salazar's simple stucco house in her biscuit tin and likes to say that while she does not know anything about politics she knows that Dr. Salazar was a pious man and made "Christian laws." (The last time Anna went back to Lisbon, she was shocked to discover young women swimming topless just across the highway from the presidential palace, and the law she has in mind is one requiring women at the beach to wear modest, one-piece, skirted bathing suits.) Anna's only real sadness in Lisbon, she says, was the sadness of seeing her brother Vasco leave for Brazil. She was twenty when he emigrated, and he was going to send for her as soon as he had the money, but it was two years before he even wrote, and then there was no ticket for Anna with his letter. There was a snapshot of him, in a striped suit and white shoes, with a bride on his arm—a Brazilian bride, dressed in a smart, short dress with a peplum and padded shoulders and smoking a cigarette through an ivory holder. Anna says now that she never intended to move to Brazil. She will talk at length about Luis Mariano wooing Carmen Sevilla on a warm Andalusian night or sambaing through the gardens of Acapulco singing "Chica-chica-aie-aie-aie" (it was, so to speak, his vocal signature), but she has no appetite for real adventure. She preferred her life in Dr. Salazar's Lisbon, where the official love songs were laments called *fados* and anyone sambaing through town singing "Chica-chica-aie-aie-aie" would have been arrested as a Communist.

. . .

Anna met Lourenço Silva in 1942. She looked out of her window
in the professor's house and saw a young man carting a slab of striped
black marble down the road, and a minute later the young man was at
the back door, cap in hand, asking directions to the parish cemetery.
Lourenço carved beautiful tombstones, Anna says. He had an eye for
color—it showed in the way he planned a garden, and in the way he
would design a grave with, say, a white marble Lamb of God and a pink
marble Holy Spirit and a couple of green marble twining vines. He was
barely nineteen, and skinny, with a widow's peak and a pointed nose
and a long, pointed chin that gave his face an odd sort of downward
direction. But to Anna there was something romantic about him. He
was limp, like the sailors in American movies. He never stood up
straight. He slumped into some imaginary wind and flung his arm
across anything that was close enough to support him—a friend, a
tombstone, the back of a chair—and at the same time he kept two
cigarettes burning. In his wedding photograph there is one cigarette
hanging from his lower lip and another cigarette between his fingers,
and he is leaning on Anna—who is squat and solid in a shirtwaist gown,
a white mantilla, and a crown of wilting orange blossoms and silver
leaves. Anna was twenty-six when she married. She was happy to have
a husband. She held Lourenço up and stared into the professor's camera
with the beginning of that stubborn, almost defiant timidity which is
so exaggerated in her now.

The professor paid for the wedding. He found the Silvas a little
house near his own house, on the sea road out to the Monastery of
Jerônimos, so that Anna could get to work in time to brew his breakfast
coffee and stay late whenever his wife had a party. Anna rarely saw her
own family anymore. I imagine that her mother had wanted her to
marry someone from the Trás-os-Montes—someone with fields of his
own and a job waiting in Brazil—instead of a rubbery Lisbon boy who
was still apprenticed at a tombstone factory. But it may be, because
Anna was plain and had never been courted until she met Lourenço,
that her mother had started to think of her as the spinster daughter who
would come home and take over in her mother's old age. Anna never
talks about her mother. When she talks about the wedding, she talks
about how beautiful the professor's wife looked, in her fur cape and her
high-heeled, open-toed lizard-skin platform shoes. Or she talks about
how beautiful the chapel at Jerônimos looked, lit by candles. Luis
Mariano had just closed at the Casino Montparnasse, and it is reasonable
to suppose that by March 12, 1946, when Anna and Lourenço celebrated

their wedding, with salt cod and dancing at a restaurant by the sea in Cascais, even the bands in Dr. Salazar's dour Portugal had *La Belle de Cadix* in their repertoire.

Lourenço was young, but he dreamed of being retired. He wanted to leave Portugal. He wanted to get a job in a rich country, carving expensive tombstones for rich people, and make enough money to forget about tombstones and go home and build a villa and plant an orchard of flowering trees. He wanted to smoke his cigarettes in tranquillity while Anna cooked his *bacalhau* and sewed his clothes. Once, when he was sixteen, he and two friends had stowed away on a freighter bound for America, but they were discovered six days into the crossing, and never even got off the boat. Then—it was the year he met Anna—he tried to emigrate to Portuguese Africa. He applied for Angola—there were recruitment posters for "Angolanos" all over the Lisbon tramway—and then for Mozambique and then for Guinea-Bissau, but for some reason he never got permission to go. Finally, he wrote to Anna's brother in Brazil. Vasco had bought himself a ranch in the province of Goiás, and he was making money. He had already sent Brazilian working papers to three of his brothers. Anna was sure that he would send them to Anna, too. He promised to send them. Every year, he wrote a letter promising, and every year Anna wrote a letter asking again. Anna had a boy, who died in his crib, and then she had Raul, who was born in 1950—the year Luis Mariano was voted one of the twelve most important men of the half century; the year he made his first movie with the beautiful Carmen Sevilla; the year he had his appendix out and someone stole it from the operating room and sold it on the Marianiste black market for the price of a Picasso, and Mariano's mother moved into the hospital with his Teddy bears and his stuffed Babars to see that the rest of Luis Mariano was safe. Lourenço went on writing his letters and carving his tombstones, and dreaming of an orchard full of flowering trees.

One day—it was 1965, and Raul was fifteen and just starting high school—Lourenço got a letter from an old friend who worked in Paris. His friend wondered if he knew that Paris was full of cemeteries. What was even more interesting, Parisians were always ordering new tombstones for their cemeteries, because the city dug up every grave that was left untended for over five years and auctioned off the plot, and this was extremely good for the tombstone business. Lourenço left that week for Paris. He was smuggled across the Portuguese border into Spain, and then across the Spanish Pyrenees into France, by a professional, who charged two thousand dollars for his services and split his profits with

a Spanish border guard. Lourenço had to cross the Pyrenees on foot
—right through Luis Mariano's wonderful Basque countryside, Anna
says now—with eight or nine other immigrants. It was early October,
and the weather was still good, but as soon as they got to France they
were left alone in the mountains with no food and no water, and one
of them died. Anna says that Lourenço nearly died himself. He
weighed a hundred pounds by the time he found a town with a train
station. His first real food in a week was a ham sandwich he bought on
the train to Paris, and his first bed was a hammock in an abandoned
warehouse, near a rail siding east of the city, where a group of French
patrons hid their illegal workers from the immigration police. Lourenço
"volunteered" as a carver for six months before his new *patron* gave
him a work contract, and once he had the contract he had to go back
to Portugal with it and apply for a French visa for himself and a
residence permit for Anna and Raul.

   They lived at first in a sixth-floor *chambre de bonne* near the Place
Pigalle and then in an immigrants' hotel. Anna was unhappy. She
missed the professor and the professor's wife and daughters and the
professor's house, and she missed her own house. She took her letter
from the Jerônimos padre to a priest at one of the Pigalle churches, and
the priest read the letter—it said that Anna was a "militant parishioner"
—and agreed with Anna that the Place Pigalle, with its whores and its
nightclubs, was not the proper Christian climate in which to raise a
teenage boy. He sent Anna across Paris to another priest—a priest at
Saint François Xavier des Missions Étrangères—who sent her to a
gérant in the parish, and the *gérant* looked around the neighborhood
and finally settled the Silva family into the little courtyard lodge where
Anna lives now. Anna was what the French call a demi-concierge. She
sorted the mail twice a day, and kept the courtyard and the three entries
off the courtyard washed and swept and the brass on the bannisters
polished, and in return she got the use of the lodge, a small salary, and
the understanding that she would really be working somewhere else.

   Anna did not know French yet, but one of her new neighbors was
a Portuguese maid who cleaned dressing rooms at the Théâtre du
Châtelet and talked all the time about Luis Mariano. Anna heard about
how kind and glamorous Luis Mariano was. She heard about how sad
everyone at the theater was that things had not worked out between
Luis and the beautiful Carmen Sevilla, and about the vow Mariano had
made—the vow never to love anyone again except his mother, his sister,
the Virgin, his chauffeur, and the little boy called Marianino, who was
like his own child. She heard about Mariano's three Cadillacs and two

Jeeps and his Rolls-Royce, and about his Basque farm and his country houses and his three Paris studios and the enormous building he owned in downtown Madrid. She heard about the famous smile that *portait le soleil* and the famous voice that *portait le soleil*, too. And one day —when the courtyard was cleaned and the mail sorted—she took the Métro to the Place du Châtelet and met her friend and saw Luis Mariano herself. It turned out to be a day when two of the Châtelet cleaning women had a terrible argument. They rolled around on the floor, kicking and scratching and punching each other, while Anna and her friend shook their heads and talked about how irritable French-women were. The women screeched *"Putain!"* and wailed so loudly that the rehearsal—it was a rehearsal of *Le Prince de Madrid*—stopped. Not even Luis Mariano, with his biggest smile, could calm them. By the end of the afternoon, Anna had a job cleaning the theater.

Anna learned French at Châtelet. She had a gift for it. Her French was better than Raul's, even though Raul was at a French school and speaking French for seven or eight hours every day. And it was much better than Lourenço's, because the only French that Lourenço both-ered to learn was the words that had to do with marble and cemeteries. Anna's phrasing was precise, and even subtle, and her voice was deli-cate and clear, with hardly any accent. Luis Mariano, who had a thick Spanish accent, was surprised to learn that she was Portuguese. Once, when she was straightening his dressing room, Mariano asked her to sew a button on his blazer (she remembers the blazer, because it had the crest of his farm, in Arcangues, on the pocket), and she told him about herself, about her sewing machine in Lisbon and the clothes she had made—the embroidery and the tucking and the fine stitching —for the professor's wife. The next day, Mariano took her to the costume room. There were a dozen seamstresses working in the Châte-let costume room, but none of them had Anna's patience for fine, close work, and none of them was Portuguese. Most of them were French, and belonged to parties and unions and workers' committees, and they were always demanding their overtime and their Catholic holidays and their Communist holidays. They were never as obliging as Anna, who had an immigrant's terror of being turned away and sent home, and spoiling her family's chances for a better life.

Anna and Lourenço began to save for their villa in 1967, the year *Le Prince de Madrid* opened and Anna—she likes to say it this way —was "discovered." They bought five acres of land, not far from the sea, about forty miles north of Lisbon, and the next summer Lourenço went home and cleared the land, and the summer after that he started planting. He planted vines and built an arbor. He planted an apple orchard and then a pear orchard. A few years later—on a rise that he and Anna had chosen as the site for their villa—he planted a small grove of lemon and orange trees. Then he thought about a flower garden. He seems to have had an almost English sense of gardening. At any rate, he did not much like the gardens he had seen in France—the rows of marigolds and the sculptured hedges and the carefully clipped trees. He scattered seeds and waited for surprises. He planted for spill and charm.

At first, Lourenço rented a room for himself in the nearest town and walked out to his trees and flowers every morning, with his tools and fertilizers in a wheelbarrow. There was a farm about half a mile from his land, and he stopped there in the evening and got to know the family who owned it. Eventually, he started staying with them. He was an important person in his new neighborhood—the *marbrier* who lived in Paris, and had a boy spending the summer with the family of a Lisbon professor, and a wife sewing for Luis Mariano. Anna says that, even there, everybody knew about Luis Mariano. They knew about his cows named Carmen and Annie and Martine and Ludmila, and about his two million records, and about the concerts he gave in cities like Mexico City and Montevideo, where 150,000 people would fill a soccer stadium to hear him sing. They knew that every day he received a bunch of violets from a lady who had seen his movie *Violettes Impériales* forty-seven times and had taken the same seat at Châtelet—front row orchestra, fifteen seats to the left of the center aisle—for every Sunday matinee of every Mariano performance. They knew that he never sang on Good Friday, and that he always carried a statue of the Black Virgin of Castile on his trips. They knew that he opened his concerts with a song dedicated to his mother—"Maman, Tu Es la Plus Belle du Monde"—and that once a year he spent a whole day praying at his father's tomb.

In Lourenço's professional opinion, it was not much of a tomb. Judging from the pictures, Lourenço was sure that a Spaniard had carved it. He had a plan—he told it to Anna—to make a perfect tomb and sell it to Luis Mariano. He was certain that a man with two million records to his credit, a man who was said to be the *fils naturel* of the Spanish King Alfonso XIII, would have a lot of money to spend on his tombstone, and Lourenço Silva would be a lot closer to retiring from the tombstone business and coming home for good. He wanted Anna to tell her friend Luis Mariano about his tombstones, and about how all the truly prudent people in Paris were ordering their tombstones early, before the supply of good marble—the tender pinks and the brilliant greens—was gone. Anna listened to Lourenço, in her maddening, meek way, and ignored him. She wanted him to have his villa and his flowering trees and the gentle life they had worked so hard for, but she did not want to leave the Théâtre du Châtelet—not yet, not while Luis Mariano was singing. And she certainly did not want to think of Luis Mariano dying, even if dying involved a beautiful tombstone that was really a little marble theater, with a curtain and an orchestra of angels and an altar, like a stage, covered with Lourenço's sculptured flowers. Anna preferred to think about the gold flowers she had stitched up and down the arms of Mariano's green satin jacket when *Le Prince de Madrid* went on tour, and about the gold tassels on his red cape, and the gold ruffles and ribbons she produced a few years later for *La Caravelle d'Or.* Besides, as Mariano got younger (or Anna got older) it was hard for her to think of him as an ordinary, mortal man. The first time she saw him looking frail, she says, was the day he came to the theater after his Rumanian youth cure, and everyone started talking about the injections he had had in Rumania—*accélérateurs cardiaques,* the seamstresses called them—and about a mysterious woman doctor known as Doctoresse Aslan, who had invented those injections so that rich and celebrated people like Mariano could live forever.

Mariano had gotten thin in Rumania. He had never been thin before. In fact, he was always working out and getting massaged and going on diets. He had been dieting ever since a critic for *Je Suis Partout* —a collaborator who had to flee to Argentina during the Liberation —saw him in *Don Pasquale* in 1943 and wrote that the young tenor Luis Mariano was built like a boxer, short and squat and chesty like so many of the *"étrangers bien nourris chez nous."* And he had trouble dieting. Whenever he came home from a concert tour or a vacation, he would be ten or fifteen pounds heavier than when he left, and would have to start dieting again. This time was different, Anna says. The costumes she decorated for him in September of 1969—when he posed for his *Caravelle d'Or* postcard—were loose by October and much too loose by December, when the operetta opened. Mariano stayed with *La Caravelle d'Or* for two months. After that, he was so sick that he stayed in bed all week and performed only on weekends, to keep the production going. In May, he stopped performing at all. The critics complained that Luis Mariano was getting old, and he answered them, sadly, "But I have always tried to be young in spirit. In the end, isn't that what counts in a business like mine?"

Mariano died on Bastille Day, in the Hôpital Salpêtrière. His doctors conferred, and agreed on a diagnosis of "generalized hepatitis, aggravated by cerebral hemorrhaging," and then he was flown to Arcangues and buried by his parish priest, next to his parents' graves and under what Lourenço ruefully observed to be another very ordinary tombstone. His friends had wanted to bury him in his coronation costume from *La Caravelle d'Or*—the finest costume Anna ever worked on—but the manager at Châtelet refused to give up any costume, or even sell one, and Mariano was buried in a plain black suit, the kind of suit old Basques bought for their weddings and wore to their funerals. Anna knew then that the "golden" days at Châtelet were over. Even the obituaries said so—and she read them all. The obituary in *Le Monde* talked about the old, strict laws of operetta, according to which Luis Mariano had led his audiences into a land where shepherds as happy as princes got to marry princesses as pretty and sweet as shepherdesses, and "sadness turned to gladness in the time it took to sing a graceful song." The one in *France-Soir* talked about the famous smile, so full of *gentillesse* and simplicity, that no one would see again, and the famous voice, with its "mysterious power to move an audience to bravos and tears." The obituary Anna liked best was the *Paris-Match* obituary. It said that there had been two Parises since the war—the Left Bank, avant-garde Paris, where people listened to jazz and danced the Twist and sat in cafés talking politics, and the Paris "on the other side of the river," which belonged to Luis Mariano.

Raul Silva got married after Mariano died. He married an American girl he had met at a café near the Institut Catholique, where he was taking French classes, and they moved to Cleveland, to her parents' house, as soon as Raul got his visa. The girl's name was Florence. She was a crisp, nervous person, without much patience, but she was a good Catholic, ready to spend her honeymoon on a pilgrimage to the Trás-os-Montes, and Anna could see that she was practical when she suggested using some of the Châtelet flowers to decorate the church for her wedding. She and Raul borrowed a truck from the tombstone factory and drove to the theater, and they left with enough lilies for the church *and* the wedding lunch. Anna was comforted, she says, to know that it was Châtelet flowers at the altar of Saint Francois Xavier des Missions Étrangères for Raul Silva's wedding. She still has one of the flowers; she keeps it in an envelope with the wedding snapshots and a picture of Florence at a church in Bragança, worshipping the Virgin and wearing an ermine cape (a little like the cape Mariano wore when he was Don Pedro of Bragança) that the church provided for the occasion. She has the menu from the lunch, too. It was held in a private room at a pretty restaurant near the theater, where tourists often ate after a Luis Mariano performance. Anna had never been to the restaurant, but she walked right in the day Raul announced that he was getting married. She asked for the manager. She said that she was a *couturière* at Châtelet, the *couturière* who put the gold on Luis Mariano's costumes, and the manager gave her a special price on a wedding banquet for sixteen. It came with champagne, three red wines, and eight courses, beginning with *foie gras en brioche* and ending with a tiered white wedding cake with a spun-sugar bride and groom.

The restaurant is still the same, but the old Théâtre du Châtelet —the theater of *opérettes à grand spectacle*—went bankrupt sixteen months after Mariano died, and the lease changed hands, and the seamstresses were let go. By now—two leases later—the city has taken back the building, and turned the theater over to the mayor's *conseiller culturel*, whose seasons run from imported modern-dance companies to French amateur nights. Anna never goes there anymore, unless she is on her way to Printemps during a January sale and stops at the Place du Châtelet for a cup of tea when she is changing trains. No one at the theater remembers her, and she says that not many people there even remember Luis Mariano. Every year on July 14, she lights a candle for Mariano in the chapel at Saint Francois Xavier des Missions Étrangères, and three months later she lights a candle for Lourenço, who died in Lisbon the year after he had finished building their villa and had finally retired to smoke cigarettes and look after his flowering trees.

Anna was back in Paris when Lourenço died. It was October of 1980, and she was nearly sixty—the age at which she could start collecting her concierge's pension and her social security from the French government. She was working full time as a concierge then—working so hard and saving so conscientiously that it made no sense to lose that social security for the sake of a few extra months at home. Sometimes she says that if she had been in Portugal, cooking for Lourenço and doing the marketing, maybe Lourenço would be alive. He was always helpless in the house without her. He never shopped ahead, and he couldn't cook or clean, so while he was waiting for Anna to retire he stayed with his friends from the farm, and only lived in the villa in August, when Anna was there. He was driving to town with the farmer to pick up cigarettes and a bottle of milk when a car, speeding around a curve, hit them. The farmer was barely hurt (he broke an ankle), but Lourenço was unconscious by the time the ambulance came. And what Anna wanted to know when she had the news—the question she kept asking—was whether Lourenço had gone out late at night mainly for the cigarettes and only incidentally for the milk, or mainly for the milk and only incidentally for the cigarettes, because cigarettes were his own affair, his own bad habit, whereas milk was something that would have been taken care of if Anna had been home. There would have been fresh milk in a pretty blue pitcher in the German refrigerator in the shining tile kitchen in their new villa—and Lourenço would not have crashed. The question haunted Anna on the long train ride home to Portugal. It was the first thing she asked Lourenço when she managed to find him in the hospital, but Lourenço, lying on a hospital cot with tubes all over him, couldn't remember anymore.

Lourenço spent a bad month in the hospital. It was a poor, over-crowded Lisbon hospital, nothing like the Hôpital Salpêtrière, where dozens of important specialists had fretted and conferred over Luis Mariano, ordering tests and making diagnoses. Lourenço kept telling Anna that he was fine. He would wake up suddenly and ask for ciga-rettes, or for a piece of Gruyère—he was partial to Gruyère—or he would tell Anna to get the car fixed or water the flowers or remember to prune the trees. And then he would groan with pain and fall asleep again. Anna gave up, finally, on the hospital. She called the town firemen to take Lourenço to his villa to die. He lived at home for an hour. The firemen propped him up in a chair on the balcony, overlook-ing his lemon trees, and the priest arrived to give extreme unction, and then he died, Anna says, with a cigarette in his mouth and another cigarette between his fingers.

There are days lately when Anna cannot remember very clearly. She can talk about the pilgrimages she made as a little girl, or the day she carried a rock up the mountain to build a shrine to protect her father in Brazil. But she cannot talk about Lourenço Silva's funeral, or about the lawyer who took her savings to settle the problem of insurance after the people in the car that hit Lourenço produced a "witness" to say that the accident had been Lourenço Silva's fault. She never saw the lawyer again, or the money, or, for that matter, Lourenço's car, and whenever I ask her why she gets vague and shakes her head and says "*Ah, Seigneur!*"—life in Portugal is like that. She does not know why her life "disappeared" so quickly and so completely. But she knows that after all those years in Paris she had "lost the habit of Portugal." She had forgotten that lawyers in Portugal will take your money and then stop answering your phone calls; or that witnesses will appear two weeks after an accident and no one at the police station will think to ask them why, if they were there, they hadn't rushed to a telephone to report that someone was lying, dead or dying, in the middle of a country road; or that important specialists will not show up at the hospital for tombstone cutters, even tombstone cutters who have been to Paris and built a villa on five acres of flowering trees. She had lost, if not the language, then the appropriate measure of Portuguese cynicism. "*C'est une autre mentalité,*" she tells me whenever she comes back from an August at home.

She goes, though, because she is proud and does not want to stay alone in her lodge in August, with none of her tenants around and all the other concierges in the neighborhood off visiting their children. Raul goes camping with his children in August, or rents a cabin on a lake. He wants his children to have proper American vacations, not the kind of vacations the children of immigrants have, looking after grandmothers who arrive in plain black dresses and black stockings, smelling of French courtyard disinfectant. Anna has been to Cleveland twice in seventeen years. Once, when Lourenço was alive, they went for Christmas. They drove in the snow through pretty suburbs where every window was lit with strings of Christmas lights, and every yard had a Christmas tree and a sleigh and reindeer. Anna says that she felt at home in Cleveland at Christmas. She says that the only difference between a Portuguese Christmas in Cleveland and a Portuguese Christmas in Paris is that in Paris you eat *bacalhau* on Christmas Eve and in Cleveland you eat pork roast. She would like to have gone again, but the next year Raul and Florence went skiing at Christmas, and the year after that they took a charter to the Virgin Islands. In the end, Anna did not go back to Cleveland until after Lourenço died, and then it was in August, and she was alone in the house all day, because Raul and Florence had decided to work that August and had taken their vacation in July, and her grandchildren were at camp.

Anna had always thought that the family would be together in Portugal in August. She had fixed up a bedroom in the villa for Raul and Florence—a white room with voile curtains at the window and a white crocheted bedspread—and a big pink room for the two girls and a blue room for their brother. But Raul was not interested in Portugal anymore. He and Florence and the children came to see the villa one summer—it was the summer Lourenço retired—and he drove around the neighborhood, and the only people he saw were old couples, like his parents, working on their houses before they had to go back to jobs in Paris or Lille or Clermont-Ferrand. He must have been bored, Anna says, because he never came again. Anna waited for him the summer his father died, and she waited for him last summer, after the robbery and the fire.

She expected him then because there was work to do—the vandals had slashed the furniture and ripped up all the clothes in the closets, looking for money—and it was much more than she could manage alone. She did not mind losing a television set, she says. What hurt her was that everything she loved was ruined—burned or shattered or torn apart—from the little flannel-covered bed warmers in her grandchildren's beds to her framed wedding portrait to the best sewing machine she ever had. She was alone when the insurance agents drove out from Lisbon to inspect the damage. She had no receipts to show them, and before she knew what was happening she had signed a paper agreeing to a settlement of a thousand dollars for her ravaged house. When she called Raul, in Cleveland, he said that the Portuguese mentality was *merde*. It was another mentality. And there was nothing Anna could say to that, because it was just what she always said herself.

On the way back to Paris, Anna made a pilgrimage to Arcangues. It was closer to Biarritz than to the Basque country. Anna bought roses from a Biarritz florist who specialized in flowers for Luis Mariano's tomb, and then she took a bus that stopped near the Arcangues cemetery, in a special lot for the pilgrims, and checked into a pilgrims' hotel. The next day, she joined a group of Marianistes from Belgium for a walk to the famous farm. She saw two "Luis Mariano look-alikes" at the farm, and after dinner that night she saw Mariano himself, in his Châtelet costumes, in a picture book the Belgians passed around for signatures, and heard a tape called *Mes Premières Opérettes*, which included his love song about the nightingale—the *rossignol de mes amours*. Before the Belgians left, they told Anna that 1989 had been set aside as Luis Mariano Year. There was going to be a big homage to Mariano in Lille that winter, and a summer of celebration in Arcangues. Anna was embarrassed, she says, because she had thought that 1989 was only the year of the French Bicentennial.

There is a picture I like of Anna and Lourenço on their balcony in Portugal. Raul took it when he flew over with his family to see the villa eight years ago. The color has faded, as it sometimes does with old Polaroids, but you can still make out the fresh pale green in the faïence tiles that Anna chose for the front of the house, and the pink and white blossoms on the fruit trees, and Anna's American-blond hair. Lourenço is standing almost exactly the way he stood for his wedding portrait. He is loose-limbed and smoking two cigarettes—and he is leaning on

Anna. But the change in Lourenço, at fifty-six, is remarkable. There is an easy confidence about him now. He looks quite good in his khaki slacks and his open-necked sports shirt, and it is hard to see in him the skinny apprentice of twenty-three in a shiny wedding suit, or the immigrant worker posing with a couple of other immigrants outside a Paris tombstone factory. There is a difference in Anna, too. She is almost fifty-nine years old, and she is getting stout, but, standing on her balcony, in a long print skirt and a soft shirt and the string of pearls that Lourenço bought at the Bon Marché for their thirtieth anniversary, Anna is beautiful. There is a look about her that I have never seen in Paris. It is a look of being finally in her own house, the mistress of her own life—in a country where a real sun shines and real flowers scent the air, and the sound of the nightingales singing is broken by the hum of a brand-new electric sewing machine, with attachments. Anna keeps the picture in her biscuit tin, but she never takes it out, the way she takes out Luis Mariano's postcard. She does not know why, but it is easier to look at Luis Mariano when she is feeling lonely in her Paris lodge than to look at a picture of Anna and Lourenço Silva on the balcony of the villa that Anna was going to call the Golden Caravel.

August 1987

OTELO

Everyone in Portugal calls him Otelo—everyone except the military-prison guards who bring him cigarettes and coffee and call him Sir or Major and surreptitiously salute him. His name is Otelo Nuno Romano Saraiva de Carvalho. He was one of the three young officers who led the peaceable Portuguese revolution that began in the morning on April 25, 1974, to the sound of a folk song on the radio and the sight of 210,000 soldiers putting red carnations in the barrels of their rifles, and ended that afternoon with the overthrow of the oldest, longest Fascist regime in Europe. Today, he is fifty-one and a prisoner in an Army fort at Caxias, just outside Lisbon, serving fifteen years for what (at least in the law of those few Western countries that haven't jettisoned the concept) amounts to the "moral authorship" of a terrorist gang. Otelo has an attachment to Caxias, almost an affection for it, because he was the officer who liberated the prison in 1974. It was a political prison then, fitted out with torture chambers and "coffin cells" carved into the thick stone walls and underground tunnels, linked to a system of electric pumps, where prisoners lived for months in water —first to the knees, then to the waist, the chest, the chin—until they broke and signed confessions for the policemen who patrolled in rowboats, with the pens and paper in their pockets. Otelo always calls those policemen "the terrorists." Often, when he is sitting by the window of the visitors' room on the third floor of Caxias, smoking a cigarette and looking down through yellow bars into the prison courtyard and reminiscing with a friend about the revolution, he will shrug and say, "Remember how full of joy I was to liberate this fort from the terrorists."

Otelo is not a sophisticated man. He does not understand why those terrorists are free and he is not. He and his Army friends had managed to put together a secret revolutionary movement, with a cell in every unit at home and in the colonies, and then to calibrate their revolution so precisely that three-quarters of the Portuguese military moved at the same moment—it was twelve-twenty in the morning —and the rest surrendered without a shot fired. People who are skeptical about Otelo—people who do not believe that Otelo was an innocent bystander to the bank robberies and the killings that began here seven years ago in the name of April 25—point out that the real Portuguese revolution was not the work of an innocent or stupid or entirely trusting man. But the fact remains that only six people died in the revolution, and one of them died by accident and the other five were killed by Fascist secret police. Otelo and his friends (they called themselves the Armed Forces Movement, and everybody else called them "the captains of April 25," although they were actually captains, majors, and a few colonels) did not kill anybody. In Africa, they put down their guns and ended thirteen years of colonial war, which is what most of them had joined the revolution to do. At home, they bought carnations. There were no witch-hunts. Most of the old Fascists went into comfortable exile for a couple of years and then came home to collect their pensions. The torturers changed jobs. Some of the political police became night watchmen, and a few did well as private detectives, because there were a lot of women in Portugal who wanted to know where the revolutionaries went when they were supposed to be at meetings discussing Mao, or organizing people's factories, or practicing direct democracy on occupied farms.

Otelo wanted everyone to love the revolution. He was headstrong, and he probably talked too much about "people's power" and becoming "the Castro of Portugal" and about collecting reactionaries and throwing them into the Lisbon bullring, but he had an extraordinarily gallant and benign notion of what a revolution should be. Once, he was visiting Mozambique—he grew up in Mozambique—and got a call from a woman he had known since grade school. The woman was not a friend. She disapproved of Otelo's freewheeling, left-wing, populist politics, and she certainly didn't want to give Mozambique back to the Africans, the way Otelo did, but her husband was brutal and drank, and he had beaten her, and she swallowed her pride and her politics and called Otelo for protection. Otelo sent three large commandos to discuss the situation with the husband. The commandos lifted him up and dropped him on the floor a couple of times, and then they put him in a jeep and drove him to the Lourenço Marques jail, where he spent the next six months. Otelo was the Revolutionary Commander of Lisbon then. As such, he deployed the Portuguese armed forces, and personally commanded five thousand marines, paratroopers, and commandos in the country's only fully operational unit, which was called COPCON. He believed in a free Africa and in *o povo,* the poor people of Portugal —and in what he still calls "the military virtues" of honor, loyalty, and physical and moral courage. He believed in protecting women from drunken husbands.

I should say right now that I am a friend of Otelo's. I met him during the revolution and inspected the tunnels of Caxias with his permission, and was rescued by some of his COPCON soldiers —they used to patrol Portugal in black berets and yellow bandannas and snappy camouflage clothes—one night when ten hypnotized crocodiles in the ring of a provincial circus woke up and made for the audience. I have followed his career through an abandoned coup of "workers, soldiers, and sailors" in November of 1975—a sort of revolution within the revolution, because to Otelo's mind *o povo* had not been getting enough of a direct experience of their own power—and through three arrests, two presidential campaigns (he got 17 percent of the vote the first time and less than three when he ran again), and a pursuit of "popular democracy" that left him in a small, gray Lisbon office, with three plastic carnations on his desk, a fantasy "Global Project" for protecting Portugal from Fascists, and a motley party of his own, which was infiltrated by informers and terrorists. He has eaten at my house and argued about politics with my husband and talked to my daughter about where the best beaches in Mozambique are. I have always liked him. Everybody likes him. Mário Soares, who was Prime Minister when Otelo was arrested and is the President of Portugal now, claims to have voted for him in the 1976 presidential elections. The judge who investigated his case voted for him, too. The prosecutor, who made her name with his trial, called him a "sweet man," and the "repenters"—the *arrependidos*—who turned state's evidence against him, called him naïve and tenderhearted. His friends from the Army said "Poor Otelo," and shook their heads, and did nothing. *O povo* said "Poor Otelo," and did nothing. The president of the Lisbon bar complained about the terms of his indictment and the conditions of his detention, and then did nothing. Otelo was arrested in 1984, and for three years what people mostly did for Otelo was gather at the Caxias gates on April 25, at precisely twelve-twenty in the morning, and light candles and sing the beautiful song called "Grândola," which had signalled the start of the Portuguese revolution.

I think that Otelo is a fool of revolution, the way people in Mother Russia were fools of God. He never got over the fact that the revolution stopped, and that when it did stop *o povo* were not much richer or happier or more in control of their lives than they were before. Most Portuguese agree with him that they never "finished" the revolution —at least, according to the never-never rhetoric of April 25, which had to do with perfect justice and perfect harmony and perfect democracy and perfect socialism. They do not like thinking about that twenty-four-hour utopia, and Otelo, in his way, was the last man to remind them. He was the last captain of April 25, acting out the country's confusion and exposing the painful choices that the revolution had put to everyone. He made the Portuguese uncomfortable, talking on into the 1980s about common power instead of the Common Market. They were not unhappy to see him go to jail—the only victim of the Portuguese revolution, someone called him—and to be able to say "Poor Otelo" and talk about how they had voted for him eleven years ago.

The summer before the revolution, Otelo bought the first home he ever owned. It was a small apartment in a project in Oeiras, a new town not far from Caxias, and it was built by an English developer while Otelo and most of his neighbors were still away in Africa, fighting. The Englishman figured that a lot of young officers in Mozambique and Guinea and Angola would want a Lisbon base, someplace safe for their families, because once the fighting reached the colonial cities there were not many wives like Otelo's wife, Dina, who were willing to stay in Africa with their husbands. The apartments he built were cheap, with low mortgages and easy terms, and the officers could afford them. The days when officers their age had money of their own were gone. They no longer came to the Army with latifundia and old Lisbon palaces, like dowries. They were the sons of clerks—like Otelo, whose father worked for the Lourenço Marques post office. Or they were the sons of workers, who wanted to get ahead in the world and thought the Army was the best way. Otelo calls this "the proletarization of the Army," and says it meant the end of the regime. He says that once the wars began in Africa the "gilded misery" of a Portuguese officer's life was of no interest to the sons of the upper classes, that it belonged to a place like Oeiras, with its projects spread over a couple of miles of dry scrub flats, and looking more like public housing than a proper suburb—or the headquarters of an Armed Forces Movement.

Otelo moved to Oeiras after a tour of duty in what is now Guinea-Bissau. He had lost a daughter in Guinea. She was seven years old, and she died from a malarial brain fever, and Otelo's hair turned gray overnight. It was his third tour in Africa, and he says he was a "totally different man" from the man who had first gone out in 1961, when the fighting started. He believed, in those days, that Portugal had a mission in Africa. He says that all the soldiers believed it—that even after a couple of years of terrible bush fighting they believed that they were heroes, defending Portugal in Africa. His first "revolutionary action" was to refuse to order his platoon to shoot Africans who jeered at them on the road, cut off the Africans' heads, and impale them on spikes, as a "lesson." His first "revolutionary consciousness" was the horror he felt when practically the whole platoon volunteered to do it anyway. He has an orderly mind—an officer's-logbook mind—and he lists what could be called the stations of his enlightenment by time and place and outcome, as if they were military engagements. The incident of the impaled heads was "Angola, June, 1961, four months after the fighting started." Then came "first contact with intellectuals"—with young *milicianos* who had been pulled out of universities at home and sent to Africa as conscript officers, and who hated the war, and the regime, and began talking politics to officers their own age, like Otelo. It was something they never would have done at home. Otelo began to read in Africa. He read the counter-insurgency texts that were supposed to teach the Portuguese troops what the enemy thought, and then he read the enemy—African revolutionaries like Amílcar Cabral, in Guinea —and then the historians who wrote about the enemy. He read a translation of Basil Davidson's *Liberation of Guiné*, and was so taken with the book that he stole it from the command post for his library. He understood then that the terrible attrition in Africa—he says there were seven thousand Portuguese dead, thirty thousand Portuguese disabled, and a hundred thousand deserters who had literally disappeared—would only stop when the Army stopped taking orders. By the time he settled down in Oeiras, he was busy recruiting for the revolution. By the revolution, he was going to transform Portugal.

Otelo thought that his revolution would be all things to all people —freedom for the Africans, land for the peasants, wealth for the workers. His Portugal was a loaves-and-fishes world where the people ruled under the benign patronage of an Army that rejected power but kept the powerful at bay with its infectious, intimidating satisfaction. For a while, he was the closest thing to a popular hero that Portugal produced. It was known that his soldiers travelled with pads of blank arrest warrants in their pockets, that they threw businessmen in jail, that they assisted a little too enthusiastically when *o povo* were occupying farms in the Alentejo, or Lisbon factories. Once, when they wanted a newspaper, they tried an occupation themselves. (They had taste; it was *Expresso,* the best paper in the country.) But they were gentlemen compared to the soldiers in divisions the Communists controlled. The Communists came out of fifty years of clandestinity as if Fascist Portugal had been a time capsule. They were rigid and covert. They believed in the authority of the Party and the memory of Stalin—and they considered Otelo an affront to both. They feared Otelo as a rival and despised him as an *esquerdista*—a leftist—and for being open and irrepressible and anarchic, and everything else a Communist is not. It gave him great cachet among the bourgeoisie. For a while, everybody courted Otelo. (He was chic, the German papers said.) *Milicianos* home from the war courted him. Intellectuals home from exile courted him. Revolution watchers and revolution groupies courted him. At one time, he was advised by a counterculture filmmaker from California, a rich Brazilian Marxist married to a French countess, and a *chercheur* from the École des Hautes Études, in Paris, who specialized in something called "the sociology of defense." If he was impressionable, so were his advisers. They talked to Otelo about a new Army in which the soldiers would elect their generals, an Army that would be "the people at arms," but it was old-fashioned military glamour that impressed them. They liked running around Portugal with Otelo. They liked the uniforms and the salutes and the cheers and the reflected glory. It was a chance to practice machismo in a noble cause.

Otelo is a handsome man. He is short and thickly built, but he has the force of short, solid Latin men—the kind that Picasso and Casals had, and that always seems to remind people of a bullet or a bull. It was said in those days that Otelo moved around Lisbon like a bullet. There was a tremendous energy in him. He loved drama, and he had an actor's presence—he took over a room or a street or a stadium just by being there. He liked telling people that he had always wanted to be an actor. His grandfather was passionate about theater. He cut a ridiculous figure, Otelo says, because he was fat and ugly, with tiny arms. But he gave up his job to study acting at a conservatory in Mora, in the Alentejo, and then he went on tour in Africa, and died there at forty-four, playing Shakespeare in the Angola bush. He left the family penniless. Otelo's father had to emigrate at seventeen to find a job—which may be why, when Otelo was seventeen and announced that *he* was going to New York to enroll in a famous school called the Actors Studio, his father replied that there was no prestige and no money in an actor's life, and refused to lend him the fare. Otelo went to Lisbon, and military school, instead. He still talks about the play he did at military school. It was called *O Acto e o Destino*. It was written by a Fascist, but it was the first, and probably the last, production in the history of the Portuguese Army, and Otelo had the leading role. His big scene was a long barroom monologue about the heroism of Portuguese foot soldiers in Mozambique, and I have heard him describe it with more vanity than I have ever heard him talk about anything, including the revolution.

The next time Otelo got to perform was in 1981. He had been stripped of his command, and he was brooding about his Global Project, and a friend named Alberto Seixas Santos (who is now the head of films for Portuguese television) decided it was time to make a movie about "Otelo's revolution," the revolution that ended on November 26, 1975, when Otelo dropped out and saved the country from civil war, and the people at arms surrendered to a general named António dos Santos Ramalho Eanes—and what Otelo calls "bourgeois democracy" was finally established in Portugal. Otelo, playing himself, stole the movie. He was eloquent and funny, and so persuasive that no one who saw it seems to have thought very much about the astonishing things Otelo said. The movie, which was called *Gestos e Fragmentos*, went to the Venice Film Festival, and Otelo's friends say they wish it had been a better movie—up to the standards of Otelo's performance—because then maybe it would have played New York and someone from the Actors Studio might have seen it and called Otelo and started him off on a new career. Otelo had nothing to do in Portugal but mourn his revolution. "I wanted to declare the socialist nature of the revolution, and all that Portugal declared were bourgeois elections," he used to say. He missed his Army "at the vanguard of the proletariat"—the Army that went straight from a war in Africa to a war against misery and injustice, the Army that "put the law in a drawer and speeded up the solution to the people's problems." He was always getting into trouble. He behaved as if it were 1974, and Portugal was waiting for freedom —and whatever he did would be judged gratefully by history. He had no one really to advise him. Most of his old advisers had left him when he lost his power. They were not around to pick up the pieces of a "people's coup," or to explain to Otelo why a military vanguard polic-

ing a free civilian state is a contradiction in terms. They were back in
countries where people are not arrested for "moral authorship" or
"ideological influence" and where *o povo* are the maid and the gardener.

Ten years ago, Otelo started writing down his Global Project.
Portugal was still suffering in 1977. The revolution was over, but fifty
years of incalculably backward Fascist rule had left the country bankrupt. No one was investing in Portugal. There were no more jobs.
Workers and their families were starving in the big cities, and a Fascist
militia was training just across the border, in western Spain. It seemed
then that everyone in Portugal who was not actually a Fascist was
worrying about Fascists' taking over, the way they had taken over in
1926, ending the only democracy that Portugal ever had. Mário Soares,
the Prime Minister, spoke in the parliament about the danger of a
Fascist coup. General Eanes, who had been elected President the year
before, talked about it in the Council of the Revolution, where all the
important captains of April 25 but Otelo sat watching over Portuguese
democracy. Otelo himself sat in his flat in Oeiras and thought about
what *o povo* could do if the Fascists came. His Global Project reads like
an elaborate boys' game—a revolutionaries' Dungeons and Dragons
—but it must have sounded reasonable, and even ordinary, to someone
like Otelo, who had put together a real revolution. Otelo drew up plans
for four organizations—four "autonomous structures," he called them
—to stay on alert for a Fascist coup. Two were armed, secret structures
—one in the factories, and one in the barracks, to seize weapons and
keep troops sympathetic to the Fascists from moving out to fight. The
third was an "open structure"—a United Organization of Workers
—to enlist the parties of the left in "the political mobilization of the
masses." And the fourth was a structure that Otelo called Oscar, and
should have called Otelo, because it had to do with the installation of
a revolutionary *chef d'état-major*. According to Otelo's plans, these
autonomous structures were going to keep in touch through a kind of
people's coordinating committee, the Political-Military Directorate.
They would get their money from an import-export company selling
Portuguese shoes and Portuguese cheeses in the Third World, and
from friendly countries making contributions to a bank account in
Switzerland.

Nothing about the Global Project stayed very secret. Otelo talked
about it to a lot of his friends, and he registered his import-export
company and had checks printed. People from his "armed civilian

structure" took over the workers' commissions in their factories, and apparently some men and women went to Algeria for training, but Otelo claims that none of them was ever armed, and that his "armed military structure" was never even organized—which may be a way of saying that no one wanted to join. The United Organization of Workers *was* organized. Half a dozen little left-wing parties—each with its own politics and its own agenda—came together and fought and split and came together again for what one of my Lisbon friends calls "a bad theological discussion between politically marginal people with nothing to do but argue about the sex of angels." They argued so much that the United Organization of Workers had to keep a hundred people on its central committee, and those people ran from worker priests to militants who wanted to start another revolution. They would never have lasted as a group, and anyway, in the end Otelo wanted to have his own party. Otelo's party was the Forças da Unidade Popular, and it was called FUP. Hundreds of people joined. Many of them knew Otelo from 1975, when they were in a group called the Partido Revolucionário do Proletariado and volunteered for the "revolutionary brigades" that tried to turn Portugal into a popular democracy governed by revolutionary councils of workers, soldiers, and sailors. They said they had given up "the armed struggle" for what on the far left is generally called "the struggle for the institutions" (meaning getting jobs and getting elected), but they still had friends from the brigades who wanted to continue the revolution as they saw it.

On May 1, 1980, a gang calling itself the Forças Populares de 25 Abril announced its arrival on the scene with a crazed manifesto about repression in Portugal and hundreds of small, "symbolic" explosions all over the country. A few days later, they proceeded to a bank robbery, and eventually to a murder. It was the first of many robberies and many murders, and no one who knew Otelo well—no one who had seen him fight in Africa, or worked with him in the revolution—believed then that he had anything to do with them. FP 25 had arms caches and bunkers stocked according to terrorist handbooks. They got money from Qaddafi, and had dealings with Basque terrorists and Baader-Meinhof and the Irish Republican Army. They shot at the wrong people and panicked in a confrontation and kept getting themselves arrested and made up rules for themselves that said you could rob a bank on your own initiative but you had to ask your "district director" if you wanted, say, to shoot someone in the feet, and your "national director" if you wanted to kidnap someone or kill him.

Otelo denounced the violence. He issued a statement saying that the Forças de Unidade Popular had nothing to do with FP 25 or with any of its crimes, and after that, he says, there was chaos in the party. Half the people in FUP were furious. They told Otelo that whatever they—or he—thought of terrorists, these terrorists were brothers in the revolutionary cause. They called Otelo's statement "an insult to the true fighters of the revolutionary left." They threatened to leave the party if he issued another. Otelo says they put it this way: "The brothers in FP 25 have their ways, and we have our ways, and it is not our role to denounce them." That was the argument, and Otelo calls it "the voice of the majority." He says that he had no option but to keep quiet.

It may have been Otelo's first real experience with popular democracy. He was like the head of his ideal, imaginary Army—he was the general chosen by his troops, and he had no authority left to lead. All of the other captains of the revolution had come to terms with what they called "the realities of life after April 25." They made their arrangements with the people in power, and went about their work and were passed over for promotion in favor of more amenable, more dependably conservative officers—and some retired, but none was surprised when the Council of the Revolution was disbanded and no one thought to thank the captains for giving Portugal back to the politicians, not even the politicians, who had nothing to lose. Otelo reminded them of their humiliation. He talked about his little party as if it were another Armed Forces Movement. He seemed to believe that the spacey, angry people who wandered in and out of his office held the same values that had briefly bound the captains of April 25. He believed that they were honorable and loyal and would never betray a comrade. It was not his nature to betray them. He must have known that some of them were involved with the terrorists from FP 25. His old friends warned him. Friends of Otelo's say that as early as 1982 they could name the people in FUP who knew all about the FP 25 holdups, and that they told Otelo to get out fast. They say he "accommodated" those holdups, or, at least, ignored them—that at first he trusted the people around him, and in the end he had no power to stop them. Otelo admits that FP 25 was trying to recruit people in his party (the prosecution claimed that five or six FP 25 "operationals" actually joined), and that some of those people were attracted to violence. He kept them around, he says, to try to convince them that violence was wrong.

The police came to Otelo's apartment at six in the morning on June 19, 1984. Otelo opened the door in his bathrobe and let them in,

and the family watched while the policemen—there were three of them
—searched the apartment. It is not a big apartment, but it is full of
pictures and books, and there are a lot of carvings that Otelo and Dina
collected during their three African tours, and I think it must have
surprised the policemen—that vivid, intelligent clutter in a drab apartment block in the middle of Oeiras. The police were very correct, Otelo
says. They did not touch Dina's framed Turner prints, or her Picasso
lithograph, or the pale abstract oil with a broken *V*, for the broken
victory of the revolution, or even the big red painting Otelo had got
as a gift from the Mozambican artist Malangatana—which is a painting
about Mozambique under Portuguese rule, and is crowded with lurid,
embryonic figures spying on each other. They did not rip up the
African hangings or open the smooth hardwood African boxes or
unglue the snapshots in the family album. They missed the interesting
things, like the pictures of Otelo on a trip to the front in northern
Guinea. That was when he first met Vasco Lourenço—the second
captain of the revolution—and both of them had their pictures taken
by a *Stern* photographer named Gerd Heidemann, who got famous
later on for peddling a set of forged "Hitler diaries." Otelo always liked
to show those pictures to company.

The policemen were interested in anything that might connect
Otelo's Global Project to the terrorism in Portugal, and specifically in
anything that connected Otelo or his party or his project to the gang
called FP 25. They took Otelo's "diary." It was two spiral pads, the kind
stenographers use, but Otelo had indulged his old logbook habit of
writing everything down, and the pad contained a list of all the appointments he made and all the meetings he went to between January of 1982
and June of 1984, including some twenty meetings with people from
the Political-Military Directorate of the Global Project. They also took
what the prosecution referred to at Otelo's trial as "arms"—a subma-
chine gun that Fidel Castro had given him the year *Time* put Otelo on
the cover. They took checks and papers printed with the name of his
import-export company, which supposedly had business in Libya, Algeria, Liberia, Iraq, Angola, Mozambique, Togo, and Cameroon. They
took a how-to book about the construction and provisioning of Basque
"people's prisons." The next day, they took Otelo. They had not found
anything to prove that Otelo was a terrorist, or had committed terrorist
crimes, or approved of terrorism, or was even a "moral author" of
terrorism, but they booked him on suspicion of being "the founder and
political leader of a terrorist association," and brought him to Caxias,
and held him for twenty days in solitary confinement. His lawyer saw

him once—for half an hour, with an agent of the Portuguese security police listening—but nobody else got to see him until the president of the Lisbon bar protested. Otelo stayed in detention, awaiting sentence, for the next three years.

There were anywhere from fifty to a hundred people in FP 25, and by the time Otelo was arrested they had committed, or claimed to have committed, or were suspected of having committed—or someone claiming to be them had committed—dozens of crimes of the sort that terrorists call "actions," including as many as twelve killings, twenty bombings, and eleven armed robberies. Their "signature" was a star with a fist and a rifle inside it, and their manifesto ended with the words "Against the violence of the bourgeoisie . . . the violence of the workers! The fight continues!" In fact, very few of them were workers. Most of them were criminals or addicts or dropouts or police informers, and a few, apparently, were ex-commandos who had once served under Otelo in COPCON and were unable or unwilling to adjust to ordinary civilian life after their heady year and a half as heroes. They had no politics of their own, let alone the politics of a fighting proletariat. They were willing to mouth whatever politics their leaders invented for them, but they made no gestures. They never occupied a supermarket and distributed the food to poor people, the way revolutionaries in South America did, or gave away any of the money they stole. They were simply, thoroughly, contemptible, and in fact no one on the far left outside of FUP tried to justify them. Somebody called them "a Portuguese joke on terrorism," and eventually there *were* jokes about them—jokes that began with, say, "What's the difference between an action by Baader-Meinhof and an action by FP 25?" and ended as gruesome commentaries on the inadequacy of the Portuguese. The police knew who they were and where to find them. The day before Otelo was arrested, there was an FP 25 roundup, and the police locked up about thirty terrorists—adding, for good measure, most of the people on FUP's "political council," one nun, and a priest from a Catholic farming cooperative whose crime was having once sat on the crowded central committee of Otelo's United Organization of Workers. Policemen searched their houses and their offices and ended up with hundreds of what they entered in evidence as "terrorist documents." At FUP, they found twenty-eight documents with Otelo's writing all over them. They were old documents that described the Global Project, but Otelo had taken them out and marked them up for a secret meeting that was held a couple of weeks before the roundup. It was the first real "plenary session" of his Political-Military Directorate, and it took place in a safe house in the mountains near Porto, and everybody came in a mask with eyeholes and was identified by a number. Otelo's number was 7. He noted it in his diary, just as he noted the date—June 4, 1984 —and he wore his mask, though it is hard to believe that anyone in Portugal over the age of ten would not have recognized the voice of Otelo Saraiva de Carvalho, even in a safe house in the mountains, far from home. Otelo's story is that he went to the meeting to explain to his Directorate that the Fascist alert was over—that it was clear the Fascists were never coming back, and there was no more need for any "armed structures," and the Global Project would have to be revised or abandoned. He made his margin notes and his revisions and what he calls his "new analyses," and copies were distributed, and at the meeting, after a lot of arguing, twenty-eight of those corrected copies were approved. Otelo says that the arguing was mainly over his idea of dropping "armed structures" from the Global Project. He told the court that as soon as it started he suspected, for the first time, that the project was infiltrated by terrorists from FP 25. The prosecution said that FP 25 *was* the Global Project—that when FP 25 robbed a bank or stole guns from an Army depot or shot a businessman Otelo Saraiva de Carvalho was in charge.

In a way, Otelo's trial was Portugal's *compromesso storico*. For the first time since the revolution, the Portuguese Communists and the old Portuguese right got together and agreed on something, which was that with Otelo in prison the lingering romance of April 25 would be over —out of sight and mind. In Portugal, the Communists and the reactionaries have this in common: they are *ancien régime* creatures. They prefer maneuvering in the creaky, tractable institutions inherited from fifty years of corporatism to competing in the political marketplace of a free country. It is hard to see how Otelo or his party, or even his dotty Global Project, was threatening to the Communists. They had their vote—it is 11 or 12 percent, and rarely changes—and they controlled their trade unions and, through them, a million obedient Portuguese workers. They were well placed in the bureaucracy—in the courts and even in the judiciary police. But they wanted to be the only left in Portugal when deals were made and power was negotiated. They may not have plotted against Otelo to begin with, but it was in their interests to see Otelo ruined. It was especially in their interests if, while disposing of Otelo, they could take some credit for saving Portugal from terrorists.

The Communists got involved in the police investigation of FP 25 after some guns were seized that linked the gang to a faction of the PRP and its "revolutionary brigades"—and thus, indirectly, to Otelo. A special unit of the police infiltrated the gang, and through it, as one Lisbon reporter said, they "infiltrated the infiltrators" of the Global Project. Eventually, they infiltrated FUP, and started building their case against Otelo. Two of the *arrependidos* who testified at the trial were police informers, a third informer was shot and killed, and a fourth—he testified that Otelo and François Mitterrand were plotting to overthrow Sésé Séko Mobutu and take over Zaire—said *he* was informing because Otelo had betrayed the revolution by rejecting the armed struggle. There was never conclusive evidence against Otelo. The testimony of any "repenter" is suspect, and the presence in FUP of five or six terrorists who knew the Global Project, or were inspired by it, or were even connected to its "armed civilian structure," is, legally speaking, circumstantial—just as Otelo's presence at meetings to which terrorists came is circumstantial. It is obviously a crime to raise an "armed civilian structure," which is simply another way of saying an illegal army. But Otelo was not arrested for raising an army. He was not arrested for any specific "actions." No one accused him of violence, or of ordering violence. Even the judgment against him noted his belief that the only justification for violence in Portugal would be "an unconstitutional attack against the state by the far right." He was arrested —on the evidence of those two *arrependidos* and of a drug addict under indictment—for being the "political leader" of a terrorist gang that was represented in the membership of his party, and as the author of that gang's vicious ideology.

Many people here believe that, in the end, Otelo was arrested because the Prime Minister was out of town. Mário Soares is a shrewd politician. He was not a very successful Prime Minister, although he tried three times, but he was successful at his own power and his own image, and it is not in his image to be the man who put away the hero of the Portuguese revolution. He would never admit to being conned by his own government in the Otelo affair, but it is likely that he *was* conned. The day Otelo was arrested, Soares was on a plane to Tokyo. The last thing he had managed to do in Lisbon before he left was to convene a "crisis cabinet" and go over a long list of suspected terrorists. The Justice Minister wanted them arrested, and so did the Interior Minister, the Attorney General, and the heads of the judiciary police and the Republican Guard. Mário Soares, in particular, wanted them arrested. Soares was convinced that Communists were behind FP 25. As a Socialist, he hated the Communists as much as the Communists hated

Otelo, and he was certain that they were using terrorists and terrorism to undermine the government—especially because the government was his.

The story in Lisbon is that Soares approved the list as soon as he saw the name Dias Lourenço. He took it to refer to António Dias Lourenço, the editor of the Communists' newspaper, *Avante*, and apparently no one at the cabinet meeting enlightened him—although the name on the list in fact belonged to an FUP militant called Joacquim. In any event, Soares approved. He got on his plane, and the security police started arresting—and *then*, the story goes, Otelo's name was added to the list, along with the names of three other FUP leaders and an engineer at a fish factory, who was discreetly released a couple of months later. People who were with Soares in Japan say that the first he heard about Otelo's being arrested was when someone telexed the news to the Portuguese Embassy. They say he got mad for a while, and then, characteristically, turned his attention to himself and decided that it was not the moment for magnanimous gestures. Now that he is President, and by way of being an elder statesman, he prefers to talk about "healing Portugal" and about "the two Otelos"—"Otelo the symbol of the revolution" and "Otelo the terrorist." When people write to Soares—important Socialists and foreign jurists and professors —asking him to intervene for Otelo, he sends them a form letter printed in several languages for the occasion. It begins with a word of praise for the first Otelo, and ends by saying that they would surely agree that political power has no place in the judiciary of a free country, and that "it is thus for the courts to decide whether Mr. Saraiva de Carvalho is guilty or not, and I hope that justice will be done."

The prosecutor assigned to Otelo's case was a young woman named Candida Almeida, who is attached to the Attorney General's staff and is supposedly close to the Communist Party through her contacts on the board of the magistrates' union, which the Communists control. Candida Almeida says that Otelo's name was always on that mysterious list—that the reason he wasn't arrested right away was to give her a chance to listen to wiretaps she made when news of the other arrests went around, and to read the documents the police had seized. Then, she says, she gave the order to arrest him, too. There was also the problem of finding the right judge to sign the warrant and charge Otelo. (In Portugal, the examining judge is called a "judge of instruction," because he directs the "instruction," or investigation, in a criminal case, and decides which charges apply and whether to recommend the case for trial.) There are ten examining judges in the Lisbon courts, but the one Candida Almeida wanted for Otelo was a man named Martinho Almeida Cruz—a man with what the Portuguese usually describe in French as a *louche* reputation. Almeida Cruz made the Lisbon scene. Candida Almeida spent all night trying to find him. Otelo says she found him at four in the morning in a Lisbon bar.

The "instruction" lasted seven months. It covered seventy-six indictments and filled twenty-five thousand pages, and when it was over Candida Almeida submitted her official accusation to the court. She was an exotic presence, at least in the dour precincts of the Lisbon *magistratura*. She got to be known, like Otelo, by her first name. Everybody talked about Candida's wild black hair and her bright-blue eyelids and her red toenails, and the day I met her at the courthouse she had on a low-cut hot-pink T-shirt, a pink scarf, fringed with beads, around her hips, and a pair of baggy black harem pants, a little like outsize diapers. But there was nothing exotic about her performance. She was single-minded, and excited by the attention. One of the defense lawyers, João Araujo, said that, whatever the real politics of the trial were, it was the little personal ambitions like Candida's that finally counted most. He said that none of the lawyers—himself included —wanted to miss the notoriety. He called Almeida Cruz a *palhaço* —a clown—who mainly wanted to get a job abroad. He said that Candida wanted attention, that her boss wanted to stay on the good side of a magistrates' union run by Communists, that the presiding judge, whose name was Adelino Salvado, wanted one "success" in his other-wise mediocre dossier, so he could get promoted, and that the auxiliary judges wanted to clear their names. There are usually three judges in a criminal trial here—the presiding judge, and two auxiliary judges who are supposed to be picked by lot. But the fact is that both auxiliary judges in Otelo's trial were under investigation themselves by a special "high council" of the *magistratura*. One of the investigations was dropped when Otelo was convicted, but everybody in Lisbon knew about the other. The judge in *that* investigation had supposedly got drunk in a nightclub in Santarém and literally gambled away his shirt. He "borrowed" a gun, ran shirtless into the street, and robbed the first bus that came along. He returned to the nightclub so pleased to have some money that he kissed the drummer. The drummer pressed charges against the judge for spreading germs.

There was probably no way Otelo could have won. The trial was staged against him. It wore him down and wore everybody else out, including the Portuguese press and the few people who had originally tried to help him. It began on October 7, 1985, nearly sixteen months after his arrest, having been postponed half a dozen times—in part because of prosecution strategy and the complications of pursuing a "collective crime," and in part because of a series of prison breaks, new arrests, and new murders, including the murder of a witness. It ended twenty months later, on May 20, 1987, and during those twenty months the director of prisons was shot and killed by terrorists, and Almeida Cruz was sent away to a safe job in Brussels with the Portuguese delegation to the Common Market—which may have been the understanding to begin with. Most lawyers had assumed that the charges against Otelo would be dropped during the instruction, on technicalities: Otelo's twenty days of solitary confinement; his lack of access to counsel; Almeida Cruz's persistent release of "evidence" when the instruction was still sub judice. But after a while people got bored and they began to forget about Otelo, and then Otelo made one of his extravagant "captain of the revolution" gestures that reminded too many Portuguese of the time he had talked about throwing reactionaries into the Lisbon bullring. On the first anniversary of his arrest, he wrote to the other prisoners—they were in a state prison, where conditions were terrible—calling them *companheiros* and giving them advice on raising money and hiring lawyers, and then telling them to take heart and celebrate the anniversary with him. When one of those prisoners escaped, he left the letter in his cell. The police found it, and eventually *Expresso* got hold of a copy and published it—and after that a lot of Otelo's friends gave up on him. They said there was nothing anyone could do for Otelo anymore—not when he persisted in that kind of stupid, stubborn, suicidal solidarity. They said that Otelo was pure, the only one of the captains who was really pure, but that maybe in the end purity was not a very politically useful virtue.

António Barreto, a sociologist I know who taught in Switzerland until the revolution and came home as Minister of Agriculture in the first Socialist government, says that maybe Otelo's tragedy was that he existed for Portugal only as a revolutionary leader—and to be that revolutionary leader he had to believe in revolutionary solidarity whether there was a revolution or not. He had to worry about his "troops," because worrying is what leaders do. He refused to denounce the terrorists on trial with him, even when they were "repenting" and making deals and testifying against him—and getting their own sentences suspended. He refused to stand alone. He could have come to court in his uniform, with all his medals and decorations on, and announced that as a father and guarantor of Portuguese democracy he did not recognize the court's right to judge him politically—that in fact, given the disregard for his civil rights during the instruction, he did not recognize its right to judge him at all. Manuel de Magalhães e Silva, the lawyer who represented the farming priest (and got the charges against him dropped after the priest had spent two years in exceptionally punishing detention), thinks that Otelo might have got somewhere that way. But Otelo never made what lawyers call a political defense. He never explained why he wrote a Global Project, or why he covered for the people he knew, the way the captains had covered for each other in the months before April 25, 1974. He never distinguished his battle plans from the ones the *arrependidos* claimed to have taken from him. The terrorists were killers, but they were amateur killers, gratuitous and wanton. They had none of Otelo's military virtues—or, indeed, his military discipline. And, despite the verdict, no one was able to prove that they were Otelo's people. The closest anyone came was when Martinho Almeida Cruz flew to Switzerland to examine a Global Project bank account. He was expecting to find eight hundred thousand dollars that the terrorists had robbed from a Brink's truck. He found a hundred dollars.

Major Vítor Alves was the third captain of April 25. He was the strategist and in many ways the brains of the revolution, and he lived down the street from Otelo in Oeiras—which gave the revolution a kind of family headquarters. He figures that, politically, Otelo would consider him "the other side." He had nothing to do with the "people's coup," and he never thought much of "direct democracy" or the idea of a country run by revolutionary councils of soldiers, sailors, and workers. But he is working to help Otelo now. He says that maybe this is another military virtue: "We have a special friendship. It doesn't prevent us from arresting each other, but we are still friends." Alves retired at forty-seven, when the Council of the Revolution was abolished, and then went briefly, and disastrously, into politics for a party that Eanes founded. He retired, he says, because he could accept Portugal's forgetting its captains but he could not accept Portugal's humiliating its captains. He saw—"in the extraordinary contempt of the law *for* the law" during Otelo's trial—a sign of contempt for them all.

A lot of Portuguese are troubled, like Vítor Alves, by what seems to be an almost conscious policy to destroy the symbols of April 25. Vasco Lourenço was "disciplined" last April 25 because he gave a speech saying that the Army would defend Portugal again if democracy was threatened; he spent the next five days in jail. Eanes, in his way, was disciplined, too. Once the civilians took over, Eanes sat in the President's palace in Belém and was asked out mainly to cut ribbons and review schoolchildren—and no one even told him about Otelo's being arrested until the afternoon after it happened. Some people blame the right wing of the military for trying to marginalize the men who gave democracy back to Portugal. Some people blame the political right, and talk about right-wing bombings after the revolution which have never been prosecuted, and about a "double standard" for Portuguese justice. Some people blame the Communists. Some blame the Americans—because America tends to pressure its allies into "cleaning" their armies of what it considers leftist officers. And some blame history. "It was naïve, perhaps, to think we could have gone a long way together," Vítor Alves says when he talks about the revolution. "We were so different. We were caught by the left, the right, the Socialists, the Communists. We were a bottle of champagne badly opened, but we are not murderers."

António Eanes is a Catholic, and he calls Otelo "a sin in the collective conscience." He says that he regrets never giving Otelo something useful to do, never finding a proper job for the headstrong soldier who had failed as a revolutionary because he wanted a revolution that would cause no suffering to anyone. Otelo would have made a fine diplomat. He was close to Samora Machel in Mozambique, and to a lot of other important Africans. He went to Africa nearly every year (that is, every year he wasn't under house arrest of one sort or another). He and his wife and children had their vacations on Machel's beautiful white-sand beaches, and while they were there Otelo always did something wonderful. He arranged loans. He persuaded Portuguese engineers to come to Mozambique and teach and build. He invited Mozambican students to the universities in Lisbon and Coimbra. He cemented friendships. There must have been a way for Portugal to use him well, to give him a little status and a little glory—to concede the glamour that had attracted the revolution watchers and the revolution groupies.

There was nothing glorious about Otelo's trial. The presiding judge was a conservative man, not very independent and under a lot of pressure from the prosecution. He was quite reasonably scared of the terrorists to begin with, and people say that Candida Almeida convinced him that the only way to avoid reprisals was to make sure everyone on trial was put away for a long time. He copied her two-hundred-page accusation nearly word for word in his own *despacho de pronúncia*. He presided over a "high-security courthouse"—it was built for the trial in a Lisbon suburb called Monsanto—and after the first day he saw to it that the prisoners were separated by nets from the bench and the public, and even their own lawyers. There was never much of a public anyway, given that the trial lasted nearly two years and there was nowhere to park a car and the only bus in Monsanto was diverted a quarter of a mile away. Anyone who wanted to follow Otelo's trial had to walk, and even then there were only thirty or forty places, way in the back of a long, narrow room. Dina Carvalho never went to the trial. She is a physiotherapist at a Lisbon hospital, and she had no time off—and now she says she wouldn't have gone anyway. It was too painful. Occasionally, the children went—Paola, who is twenty-six and getting a doctorate in sociology, and Sergio, who is twenty-two and studying engineering. They are nice children, and they make a nice family—cheerful and brave and loving. They have what Otelo would call the military virtues, but I would call them family virtues. The family has held together through war and displacement and revolution and now disgrace, and they are proud of each other and anguished for each other, and they want Otelo home from what Dina, lately, calls "this impossible, inglorious fight."

Portugal is becoming radical in ways that Otelo never imagined. The people running the country now are young economists who love "the market" and talk as if the real revolution was Portugal's discovery of a truly pitiless capitalism. There is an odd euphoria here. António Barreto says that the people fighting for "the market" are really fighting *against* some mythical welfare state that Portugal never was. They are saying the state cannot provide for everybody, when the state never had a chance to provide for anyone. Portugal is still a terribly poor country. There is no real equality. The "five families" of the old oligarchy are back in force—and style—but 20 percent of the people are still illiterate, and the government, going through rites of privatization, is offering up the public sector to a country that still depends for its income on the remittances of a million and a half migrant workers. It may be that the Portuguese are dazzled by the "prosperity" of their first years in the Common Market—the years of credit and subsidy before some other country applies and the bills come due.

For better or worse, Portugal belongs to its civilians now, and this has given back to the captains of April 25 a little of their old solidarity. Five years ago, Vasco Lourenço was not speaking to Otelo. He kept Otelo from joining the other captains of April 25 for their annual parade, and Otelo cried, and they stopped speaking. But Lourenço testified for Otelo at his trial, and so did Eanes—although it was Eanes himself who had arrested Otelo after the "people's coup" in 1975 and, during the ten years that he was President, had done as much as anyone in Portugal to keep Otelo out of the way and out of any power. Just before the instruction ended, Almeida Cruz went to one of Eanes's friends, a Major Sousa e Castro, and offered to drop the charges against Otelo if Otelo could be persuaded to admit his guilt and leave Portugal. Eanes refused to see him. Then Almeida Cruz went to Caxias and asked Otelo, and Otelo said no. Otelo tells me that he was counting on "justice" to exonerate him. He was going to "defend the prestige of the democratic institutions." It is not in his character to go quietly into exile for the sake of what other people would call his freedom. He could be pardoned by the President, except that first he would have to serve out half his sentence—and anyway there is no indication that Mário Soares thinks Otelo is innocent. He could be amnestied by the parliament. His sentence is severe, given the fact that one of the auxiliary judges—it was the nightclub judge—wanted to acquit him. (When he heard the sentence, the judge cried, "I have been betrayed.") It seems especially severe when you consider that two FP 25 terrorists who were convicted for actually committing crimes got only seventeen years to Otelo's fifteen, and the *arrependidos* got off entirely. Otelo says he would accept an amnesty (he would have no choice, actually) even if it made the state look magnanimous, which is precisely what the state would want. His case is on appeal now. If he loses, he will be automatically discharged from the Army and moved from Caxias to a state prison, where there are no soldiers around to call him Sir and buy his cigarettes and salute him. Candida Almeida has 140 more terrorism cases pending—cases that have to do with specific crimes, in specific places—and there are warrants out for Otelo as the "moral author" in forty of those cases, which means that even if he wins his appeal he could be arrested again the minute he leaves the courtroom.

Moral authorship is an ambiguous notion, and it can open the law to all sorts of manipulation and political and public pressure. It has to do with guilt by influence and guilt by association. Most jurists with any sense prefer to keep that kind of guilt "moral" and leave it out of their courtrooms and penal codes. Germany went through its arguments about "moral authorship" during the worst of the Baader-Meinhof years, when there were hot lines for anonymous informers and people who knew people who knew terrorists were being hauled out of bed in the middle of the night and thrown in jail. Italy had *its* arguments during the Brigata Rossa years, when a philosophy professor at the University of Padua named Toni Negri was arrested as a "terrorist mastermind." Moral authorship can be a convenience—a way for states to "solve" terrorism by locking up the people whose ideas alarm them along with the people who put those ideas, or say they do, into practice. Portugal calls them the "politicals" and the "operationals," and charges them with a kind of collective crime, and sends them to prison together.

Otelo does not mind prison, he says, but he is determined to be free. He wants to win a "public victory," and an amnesty may be his only chance unless a parliamentary commission clears him or the Attorney General drops the other charges against him—or his appeal is still pending on January 22 next year. The law in Portugal says that a case has to be decided within three years of the *despacho de pronúncia* or the prisoner goes free, and January 22, 1985, was the day Judge Adelino Salvado formally pronounced the accusations against Otelo. A group of European jurists was just in Portugal trying to arrive at some strategy to help him. People from the European Committee for the Defense of Refugees and Immigrants, who know Otelo's work in Africa, are trying to help him, too. They sent a professor from the law faculty at Oldenburg to observe his trial, and they are sponsoring an appeal to the Court for Human Rights in Strasbourg—but mainly what they try to do is organize Otelo's friends abroad into some sort of coherent international defense for him, and every few weeks, from their Basel office, they mail "Otelo reports" around the world. They were shocked at first by the apathy in Portugal. They were shocked that even Otelo seemed to accept it.

Otelo says sometimes that he doesn't believe in the revolution anymore. He wants to know if *o povo* anywhere have managed to keep a vision of a better life for very long. He is not worn out, he says, but he is troubled by "the futility." He thinks about "the dignity of the masses" and about how to maintain that dignity, and wonders if his heroes, like Che Guevara, are still in the hearts and minds of the poor people they died for. He was so proud of his own people—of the peasants in the Alentejo and the workers in Lisbon and Setúbal and all the soldiers and sailors home from Africa. None of them has written to him, or sent a telegram, or made a phone call, since he went to prison. None of *o povo* has demonstrated or gone on strike. It is the "bourgeois intellectuals" who stand at the gates of Caxias with their candles, singing revolutionary songs. I always laugh when Otelo talks about bourgeois intellectuals. "You bourgeois intellectuals," he will say. "You are the only ones who fight. You are the only ones who care about fair trials and due process." When I tell him that that's what bourgeois intellectuals do—worry about things like due process—he says that if there is ever a *real* democracy in Portugal no one will be allowed to say a word against bourgeois intellectuals. This is something he guarantees.

November 1987

FIVE CITIES

HAMBURG:
TERRORISM IN
GERMANY

Ulrike Meinhof was a journalist when she left Hamburg ten years ago. She was already a celebrity then—a reigning radical among the reporters here—and she was much courted by the worldly *Bürger* of the city, who were entertained, and maybe a little chastened, by her furious polemics against their values. Even now, a lot of them claim Ulrike Meinhof as their own, the way they might claim Helmut Schmidt, the West German Chancellor, who got his start in Hamburg, too. They make elaborate distinctions between the "purity" of Ulrike Meinhof's political passion and the mindless passion of the various gangs that have terrorized the country in her name.

Hamburg is an arrogant, anglophilic city. For centuries its merchant ships have sailed the sixty-eight miles down the Elbe to the North Sea and on to England, and it is not really surprising—considering the euphemistic genius of a people who can call their atomic-waste depots "disposal parks"—that there are Hamburgers around now who refer to the Second World War as an "unfortunate interruption" in an old relationship. People here like to compare their city to an English city —to Bath or, better still, Kensington. They ignore the fact that the English themselves tend to think of Hamburg, with its notorious Reeperbahn, as one of the sin cities of the Western world. Hamburgers strolling at dusk along the promenade at Övelgönne can look across the Elbe at the surreal silhouette of one of the biggest industrial complexes in Western Europe, but there is still a party at the university most years on Queen Victoria's birthday, and the town fathers pursue a turn-of-the-century English style that, for all their good intentions, is entirely German in its earnestness. The guest who does not bring flowers to his hostess is not apt to get invited back in Hamburg. The stranger who does not think to put on black tie for dinner at the Hotel Vier Jahreszeiten ruins everybody else's party. This is a city of manners and title and a great deal of *"Herr Professor Doktor"* and *"gnädige Frau,"* and yet the people here refer to the Jeanne d'Arc of German terrorism as Ulrike.

Ulrike was different, they say. Ulrike was an intellectual, and impressionable, like all intellectuals. Poor Ulrike would still be entertaining Hamburg with her magazine columns and her angry charm if she had not fallen into bad company—the company, that is, of Andreas Baader, Gudrun Ensslin, Jan-Carl Raspe, and the eight or nine others in the first group that called itself the Red Army Faction and that everyone else called the Baader-Meinhof gang. Baader, by all accounts, started out in terrorism as a restless child of the *Kleinbürgerstand,* with a gift for manipulating the various social guilts of his more delicately bred conspirators. It was apparently his only gift. For a while, he had got by on a kind of petulant macho—one of the countless hangers-on in the Berlin student scene of the 1960s—but when he discovered that the radical life had its rewards in girls and glamour he began to preach a politics of praxis, having little to offer in the way of thought. No one could have expected Germany's armchair left to see itself in the swaggering persona of Andreas Baader—or, for that matter, in Gudrun Ensslin, the girl who taught Baader the rhetoric of their particular revolution. Ensslin was a pastor's daughter with an odd, fanatical imagination, and she evidently thought of their little band as "chosen" to exorcise the country's capitalist devil. As for the next group of "Baader-Meinhof" terrorists to appear—the "second-generation" terrorists, Germans call them—most of them came out of a patients' collective at Heidelberg University's Psychiatric-Neurological Clinic. *They* followed a psychiatrist guru by the name of Wolfgang Huber—a kind of Leninist R. D. Laing, who convinced the people in his charge that the society was their real disease, and apparently inspired a lot of them to try to cure it. And as for the "third-generation" terrorists—the ones who in six months last year killed Germany's Chief Federal Prosecutor, the chairman of its second-biggest bank, and the head of its association of industrialists—they are a self-appointed hit squad for a revolution none of them has yet been able to articulate. Whatever the jargon of their ransom notes, they are as much a punk phenomenon as a political one, and they horrify most older people on the left here, who blame them, reasonably, for the backlash the entire left endures after each gloating act of third-generation violence.

It is only ten years since Andreas Baader, Gudrun Ensslin, and a couple of their friends hid fire bombs—set to explode after closing time —in two department stores in downtown Frankfurt, to protest what they called *Konsumterror:* the terrorism of things, the brutality of a society that seemed to value the objects in its shops more than the lives of children in Vietnam. But the reason people keep talking about terrorist generations is that there is no way, really, for any liberal and compassionate German to associate the burning of an empty store with, say, the ritual murder of a kidnapped businessman. People here have made a memory cult of Ulrike—she hanged herself in prison nearly two years ago—because Ulrike was the first, and last, of the terrorists who could have been any one of them. She represents for them a kind of grim but oddly logical correlative to the bad conscience that they claim to share. She was the journalist who bolted, the only one, in a city of journalists—*Die Zeit* is published here, and so are *Der Spiegel* and *Stern,* along with three of the notorious dailies of the Springer Press— and she left her friends and her colleagues feeling guilty and relieved and a little dull. Some of them had just helped make Willy Brandt the new West German Chancellor. They were busy proselytizing for an *Ostpolitik* that would finally open the borders of the two Germanys to a little tolerance. Radical chic—or *Schickeria,* as the Germans call it —was the proper chic among Ulrike Meinhof's old Hamburg friends when she took the rhetoric of their columns and their parties and put it into practice. Her new friends came from the world of realpolitik, and in May of 1970 she joined them to "liberate" Andreas Baader from the inconvenience of a prison term—leaving for good an unfaithful husband, an extravagant household, and a Marxist journal called *Konkret,* which had been getting money from the East Germans before Ulrike's husband decided he could do better by spiking its politics with photographs of naked girls. After that, she seemed to embrace her alienation. She went off with Baader and Ensslin to the Middle East to train with Palestinian guerrillas. She tried to send her two small daughters to a camp in Jordan where the Popular Front for the Liberation of Palestine was raising children for the revolution to come. In two years as a fugitive, she learned to shoot, bomb, forge, and steal with considerable facility. In three years as a prisoner awaiting trial, she went through hunger strikes and forced feedings and long, deranging bouts of solitary confinement.

By the time she died, in the spring of 1976, half the students in the country had a poster of Ulrike Meinhof hanging in their rooms —Ulrike backed against the brick wall of a prison courtyard, dressed in a worn regulation shift, her hair clipped short, her hands gripped above her head, and her dark eyes narrowed into a stare so haunted and accusing that it is hard not to turn away. That image seems to be the one hold that any of today's terrorists have on the country's conscience. Ulrike is a kind of common denominator—without her a vicious underground would lose whatever revolutionary mystique it still can claim, but then without her a lot of Germans might not be asking themselves why the new, democratic Germany of the "economic miracle" turned into such a sterile and alienating place.

There is no way for Germans to avoid talking anymore. After thirty years of nearly phobic silence among people frantically rebuilding a society and at the same time unable or unwilling to examine what they were rebuilding or even how they were going about it, the fact of terrorism on German soil has given Germans the beginnings of a vocabulary for talking about themselves. They are genuinely frightened by the violence in the middle of their economic miracle— their *Wirtschaftswunder*. A Hamburg businessman with a meeting in Frankfurt will still travel all night by train or car to avoid being blown up in an airplane—though it is five months now since Baader, Ensslin, and Jan-Carl Raspe died, evidently by suicide, in Stammheim Prison, and the Red Army Faction threatened to avenge them by blowing up one Lufthansa plane in flight for each dead terrorist. Some companies grounded their executives when word went around that the terrorists actually had a tidy stockpile of Russian SAM-7 missiles—forty-pound, shoulder-held missiles—to do the job. The government, on the other hand, encouraged *its* people to fly, as a show of confidence in its ability to stop the terrorists from blowing up anything. And the end of it all, so the story goes here, is that now when a bureaucrat and a businessman have a meeting the bureaucrat falls asleep from tranquillizers while the businessman falls asleep from exhaustion. In Bonn, there are as many soldiers wandering through the Bundestag as there are deputies, and the Chancellery is floodlit and patrolled as if it were Lon Nol's palace and the Khmer Rouge were at the gates. In Cologne, which has turned into a kind of headquarter town for German industrialists—the Federation of German Industries meets in Cologne, and Hanns-Martin Schleyer, who was the head of the Federation when terrorists kidnapped him and slit his throat last fall, lived there—every important businessman has at least one bodyguard. (Otto Count Lambsdorff, the Economics Minister, always comes to Cologne with four bodyguards.) In Frankfurt, which is the country's banking center, bankers have started varying their routes to the office in the morning, and even the head of the bank that belongs to the sixteen trade unions of the Deutsche Gewerkschaftsbund is supposed to be on a terrorist hit list. It is hard for any German to be confident about his credentials these days —when he reads that a man like the Marxist philosopher Jürgen Habermas, whose institute is just outside Munich, has been vilified for speaking out against the violence.

A few deranged children of the New Germany have actually succeeded in terrorizing the country, and, inasmuch as they bomb and kill and kidnap with impunity, they have forced the lid on a Pandora's box of social problems—not the least of those problems being the lingering fondness of a lot of Germans for peremptory solutions to all the others. There has not been a week in the past five years without some incident involving terrorists or terrorism—from car thefts and raids on passport offices and Army depots to bank robberies and shootouts. But then there has hardly been a week in all those years when some aspect of the country's young democracy has not been called in question as inadequate to the emergency. Whatever the lessons of Nazism, a high regard for the rights of citizens in times of social stress is evidently not among them. Many Germans still think of civil rights and civil order as conflicting concepts, and when the two do seem to conflict—as they well might in a country with perhaps a hundred terrorists operating underground and getting help from about a thousand active sympathizers—there is no doubt that the priority is order. *"Hier herrscht Ordnung"*— "Here reigns order"—is a kind of national homily in Germany. It is the way a proud hausfrau talks about her parlor or a father admonishes a child who has left his skateboard in the driveway, and it is still the way most Germans would like to talk about their country. The first Baader-Meinhof group called itself Communist. Now, as often as not, the terrorists describe themselves as anarchists —though Bakunin himself would have trouble recognizing them and would probably assume that other Germans saw them as a threatening but basically aberrant phenomenon. But since Hitler, Germans have had an understandable problem in distinguishing what is aberrant from what is symptomatic, and they are having that problem now as they try to come to terms with terrorism and their own responses to it. The fact that anybody in Germany is willing to take the civil liberties that were so meticulously framed in the West German constitution and place them at the discretion of the state is certainly symptomatic of something unmended in German attitudes about power—at least it is for those Germans who are getting alarmed by what they read and hear.

The real argument in Germany cuts through class and politics, and is less about "left" and "right" than it is about authoritarian and libertarian strains in the society. Helmut Schmidt, of course, is a Social Democrat, but his prestige, even in his own party, does not come from any confrontation with the Christian Democratic opposition over witch-hunts in the universities and the press for the spiritual "mothers and fathers" of terrorism, or with the police over the tremendous license policemen have been taking lately in their pursuit of terrorist sympathizers. That prestige comes from his image as a tough, law-and-order Chancellor—the Chancellor who sent German commandos to Mogadishu, Somalia, last fall to storm a hijacked German jet and free German hostages. Social Democrats like Schmidt, with an instinct for the real priorities of the country's voters, are trying to court the backlash away from the Christian Democrats, though Schmidt's government, which is a coalition of Social Democrats and Liberals, seems practically benign in any comparison with the so-called Christian parties.

Franz Josef Strauss, the strongman of the Christian Social Union, still gets to run Bavaria in return for leaving the conservative field to Christian Democrats in the other *Länder,* and Strauss and his people have practiced a kind of Tyrolian McCarthyism for as long as most young Germans can remember. Augusto Pinochet, the Chilean dictator, gave Strauss an honorary doctorate of laws this winter. Strauss was probably the only politician of any importance in Europe who would have taken it, and he was certainly the only one who would have come home, as he did, calling today's Chile "a form of freedom." But, for all his red-nosed, lederhosen bluster—Idi Alpine is what the left calls him —Strauss is not the caricature he seems. There is an audience for his kind of paranoia; it is the same audience that applauds the vicious, cheap-shot patriotism in Axel Springer's newspapers. Last year, Christian Democrats took over Frankfurt, which had been a preserve of the Social Democrats since the war, by persuading enough voters that the old government, having been corrupt and fairly ruinous to the city, had thereby undermined the sort of God-and-family values that produce obedient (non-terrorist) children and compliant citizens; and now Alfred Dregger, the Christian Democrats' own *Sturm und Drang* man and their party boss in Hesse, is trying to take over the *Land* with the same slogans. Germans say that "another Schleyer" could put the Christian Democrats in power in Hesse and Lower Saxony this year, and if it did, the Bundesrat—which is the upper house of the West German parliament and is filled by the governors of the various *Länder* and their appointees—would have enough conservative, Catholic votes to veto any progressive legislation in the Bundestag.

Schmidt obviously knows this. He is a thoroughly pragmatic politician—the kind of man Germans call a *Macher*, the kind of man who, in a crisis of confidence like the one in Bonn this winter, over spies in the Defense Ministry, could rebuild a cabinet in twenty-four hours, without wasting a moment in self-recrimination or despair. Schmidt has none of Willy Brandt's old illusions about the moral force of the liberal intelligentsia in the Social Democratic Party, or even of the party's own socialist wing. He was raised in Hamburg. He worked his way up through the party here and in Bonn, and ended up as the Finance Minister in the Brandt government, and he is not likely to forget that the millions of German workers who vote Social Democrat —whatever claims those workers may make to participation in the boardrooms of German industry—are creatures of a prosperous welfare-state capitalism and a hysterical mass press, and as conservative in their values as any of their American counterparts. Terrorism is what alarms them. They do not worry very much if a law gets changed in the name of fighting terrorism, or if the state takes uncommon license with the law it has.

Last fall, after the Schleyer kidnapping, German policemen raided thousands of apartments—as often as not on the ground of "present danger," which meant without search warrants. And they might have raided more if the big new American computer that the Federal Criminal Police had just installed in its Wiesbaden headquarters had not had a lot of trouble communicating with the Siemens computers in the local precincts. The police claimed that they were entirely within the law in those house raids, and cited in their defense Article 34 of the German penal code—which is a kind of extenuating-circumstances law involving crimes against the person committed under threat of danger to "life, health, or freedom." The law had been written into the code in 1968 to protect people acting in self-defense from persecution by the state, but now the state was claiming that in *its* present danger Article 34 was an enabling law that applied to itself. The state had already cited the article in defense of wiretaps and the monitoring of conversations between terrorist prisoners and their lawyers. After the kidnapping this fall, it was even cited to justify what Germans called the *Kontaktsperre* —a new Bundestag decree by which the state could deny prisoners the right to see their lawyers for as long as fourteen days without a court review of the ban, and longer if the court approved it. Germans have always tended to reify the state, but, for a lot of people here, the logic involved in the state's claiming for itself the rights of a citizen was as grotesque as it was alarming. The house raids became a cause célèbre after policemen with machine guns searched the studio of a young painter who turned out to be Heinrich Böll's son—he had evidently let some friends spend the night at his studio once or twice, and when those friends turned up later on someone's list of terrorist sympathizers, young Böll became a suspect, too. It was only one incident in a nasty game of accusation and denunciation which had been going on since the police set up terrorist-information hot lines for people who preferred to do their accusing anonymously. ("To the denunciators of apartment Liebigstrasse 75!" a classified ad in the *Giessener Allgemeine* this winter began. "We are, according to the police, no terrorists. Denounce all you like.") But Heinrich Böll amounts to a national treasure, something on the order of the Alte Pinakothek, and after the raid Helmut Schmidt felt called on to invite Böll to the Chancellery —along with the writers Günter Grass, Max Frisch, and Siegfried Lenz —to try to calm him down.

Still, some very decent people here admit to being in a kind of double bind when it comes to civil rights and the abuses of those rights. They say it is hard to feel particularly concerned about the sanctity of anyone's apartment when they board a plane wondering if they are going to survive takeoff, or open the morning paper to read about the Karlsruhe police dismantling a terrorist missile that was within minutes of being launched. (The missile in Karlsruhe was aimed at the office of Germany's new Chief Federal Prosecutor; terrorists had shot and killed the old prosecutor five months earlier.) They also say that it is getting hard to read righteous lectures in *Le Monde* every other day about "Fascism" in German law and German prisons, knowing as they do that French prisons are not noticeably pleasant, and that the French penal code does not trouble itself much with the civil rights of the accused. Or to welcome a Bertrand Russell tribunal with much humility when no Eastern European country would even let the Russell people cross its borders.

The problem for Germans old enough to have any memory of the war is that the Nazi past loads the present with implications, and confuses it, leaving them without much confidence in their responses now. They seem to have as much of a Weimar complex as a complex about Hitler. When the Bundestag, say, agrees to change the law in ways that give the state discretionary power over basic civil rights, they are apt to think first of the chaos of Weimar—having been taught at school that that chaos "produced" Hitler—rather than the cowardice of Weimar, and end up grateful that their new government, being well intentioned, is not asking for more power than it is. Only four of the 224 Social Democrats in the Bundestag voted against the *Kontaktsperre* last fall, and they were taken to task for breaking the party's parliamentary discipline—something that had rarely happened here since a group of socialists voted against extending war credits to Kaiser Wilhelm. There were no dissenting votes two years ago when the Bundestag amended the penal code to make propaganda for violent acts against the state as punishable as the acts themselves, even though freedom of speech seemed to be the issue then—and what, exactly, constituted propaganda varied, and still varies, considerably from *Land* to *Land*. This winter, a *Gastarbeiter* in a town near Hagen got three months in jail for calling Schleyer, who was already dead, a name that did not sit well in Rhine-Westphalia. Last summer, a student at Göttingen took the nom de plume of Mescalero and published a piece about his "furtive joy" at the news that Siegfried Buback, the Chief Federal Prosecutor, had been murdered; twenty-one professors around the country who reprinted Mescalero's article in a broadsheet—making no comment of their own but adding, rather stupidly, Rosa Luxemburg's famous description of *her* joy over the assassination of a czarist general—and distributed it were told to sign public apologies or lose their jobs and, in some *Länder*, face criminal charges.

Actually, the police had been seizing books and papers and arresting the people connected with them long before the propaganda law. A radical publisher in West Berlin by the name of Klaus Wagenbach —he was once Ulrike Meinhof's publisher—saw three of his house's books confiscated over the past few years, and had to go to court to clear himself. One of those books was written under the pseudonym of the Red Army Faction "collective" by a lawyer named Horst Mahler, who started out with the Baader-Meinhof group and now, in prison, has been born again as what seems to be a kind of Maoist pacifist. The second was a famous "apprentices' calendar," which, with its down-home recipes for factory sabotage, got the sort of attention among fashionable radicals here that *The New York Review of Books* got when *it* published a blueprint for making Molotov cocktails. And the third book—no one has ever managed to figure out exactly why it was banned—was about the Haymarket Riot of 1886.

A lot of the new laws have to do with the rights of lawyers who defend terrorists or people accused of some association with terrorists. Group defense in terrorist trials—which was a terrorist invention to

begin with—has been stopped. And now no one charged with a terrorist crime can have more than three lawyers representing him. Klaus
Croissant, the Baader-Meinhof lawyer who was charged with conspiracy, fled to France last summer, and was extradited in November,
apparently had fifteen or twenty lawyers working with him before the
law was changed. Cases like Croissant's get a good deal of publicity
among liberals abroad, but German liberals tend to be skeptical about
a man who once had eight of the sixteen terrorists on Germany's
most-wanted list working in his office—including Susanne Albrecht,
the girl who brought a bouquet of roses to her godfather, the chairman
of the Dresdner Bank, and then, evidently, shot him. Their real worry
involves the kind of new law that foreigners rarely read about in the
newspaper. Lawyers are now forbidden to take on more than one client
in any terrorist case, and one lawyer was actually excluded from a
recent trial because he had filled in for a day for a colleague with a cold.
The state is also claiming the right to exclude defense lawyers from
terrorist cases on the ground of *suspicion* of conspiracy with their
clients—something it was already able to accomplish simply by pressing charges, without the necessary evidence.

    As early as 1972, a lawyer named Otto Schily, who is probably the
most distinguished civil-rights lawyer in West Germany, was excluded
from the Baader-Meinhof trial on unsubstantiated charges of having
carried a letter from Gudrun Ensslin to Ulrike Meinhof when Ensslin
was in prison and Meinhof on the outside. There was no law on the
books then which covered the grounds of his exclusion, and Schily was
eventually reinstated as defense counsel, but six years later the state
shows no signs of formally dropping its investigation. Another civil-
rights lawyer, Hans-Heinz Heldmann, is going to stand trial soon on
charges that involve "defaming the state." And the trial of Kurt
Groenewold, a radical lawyer here in Hamburg, has already started.
Groenewold was one of the original lawyers hired to defend the
Baader-Meinhof group. He had been Ulrike Meinhof's divorce lawyer,
and her friend, and now he is charged with having run an "information
network" for his clients, but he was actually disbarred by his Hamburg
colleagues some three weeks after his exclusion from the Baader-Meinhof defense, in 1975—and that was a full year before he was charged
with anything. Groenewold says that some sixty German defense lawyers are now under indictment for crimes like "disrespect for the court"
and "slander against the state." When those lawyers do stand trial, they
will have to contend with harried and often frightened judges who have
spent the last several years listening to their political patrons carry on

about a legal conspiracy to sabotage the state in its pursuit of terrorists. None of this, of course, is going to encourage other lawyers—lawyers who want to stay in practice, anyway—to take on cases that involve terrorists or, more important, people accused of helping terrorists or even one another. And probably none of this is going to discourage terrorists, either, since people who shoot strangers and plot to blow up airplanes are unlikely to be thinking rationally about getting caught, let alone about finding the perfect lawyer if they are.

Lawyers here complain that criminal cases of any sort are hard to argue. They say that a feeling for due process is underdeveloped in German law, that justice in Germany, as it is in fact in most of Europe, is dominated by the courts, responsible to some ideal of Truth—*Wahrheit*—but not to any reasonable criteria for fair trial. They say that the stuff of German Romanticism is the first principle of West Germany's penal code. These things concern them much more than the satisfaction of a few terrorists. No one here was immune to the horror of Mogadishu or the Schleyer kidnapping; Germans literally do not see how a country like Italy survived last year with two thousand terrorist crimes. But German trial lawyers say they have a special problem —the problem being that too many people here expect their laws to clean up terrorism for them, as if terrorism were a little dirt on the floor or a bad smell. Germans believe in the efficiency of their institutions, and even now they have a hard time associating Hitler and a lost war with the fact that so many of those institutions failed. A uniform or a title or any other emblem of official authority still carries a kind of infallibility in Germany. People are frankly startled when foreigners, say, question the suicides at Stammheim Prison last October. Foreigners, at least at first, tend to assume that Baader, Ensslin, and Raspe were murdered by prison guards or policemen, or forced to kill themselves. Another Stammheim terrorist, named Irmgard Moeller, survived *her* "suicide" and now claims to have been drugged and stabbed, and there are all sorts of rumors going around about the three who died. The most elaborate rumor has Andreas Baader being flown to Mogadishu with orders to persuade the hijackers that Bonn was ready to release thirteen terrorists for the lives of the Lufthansa hostages. When Baader failed, the story goes, the police flew him back to prison and killed him and his two friends to keep them quiet—and the proof of it all seems to be that Baader was wearing sand-caked street shoes instead of his usual sneakers when his body was discovered. There are obviously people here who believe this sort of story. A lot of students do, and so do people from the small, radical-Communist parties that Germans call "K groups" to distinguish them from the official West German Communist Party—a dreary, orthodox cousin to the East German Party which was set up in 1968 when Bonn was trying to smooth the way to relations with Eastern Europe. The rest of the German left tends to agree with everybody else that the three terrorists killed themselves. Sometimes the explanation is that committing suicide was "in character" for the terrorists; usually, though, it is that no German prison guard or policeman with a mind to murder four terrorists would ever bungle the job so thoroughly that one survived.

The problem for foreigners in Germany is that so much of the propaganda they read and hear turns out to be true. The claim that a lot of second-generation terrorists were clinically schizophrenic or that the third-generation terrorists are rich kids with no real ideology but violence may sound like right-wing fantasy, but it is mainly accurate. So are the claims that those terrorists are part of an international network that runs from the Popular Front for the Liberation of Palestine to the Japanese Red Army and the Italian Red Brigades and the Irish Provos; that they train in guerrilla camps in the Middle East, get money from fanatics like Libya's Colonel Muammar Qaddafi, and buy missiles on the Swiss black market; and that they are on easy terms with an underground of "specialists" in Western Europe who can forge their passports and their papers, change the motor numbers on their cars, and make whatever weapons they have trouble buying. It is true, too, that after their trial the Baader-Meinhof gang did not suffer much in prison. Andreas Baader had a few hundred books in his cell, along with a typewriter, a radio, and a stereo, and he even shared a bed occasionally with Gudrun Ensslin—at least, according to the guards who discovered them one night and beat up Baader. Nor were the prisoners, by then, particularly out of touch with their admirers; records show that from the middle of 1976 to the middle of 1977 eighteen Baader-Meinhof prisoners had twelve thousand visits and phoned or wrote to the outside some sixty-five thousand times.

But then the stories that the left tells about prison conditions *before* the Baader-Meinhof trial are true, too. There is no limit on detention in Germany, and no plea bargaining. A prisoner has to wait to stand trial for as long as it takes the prosecution and his own lawyers to prepare briefs on every charge against him, not merely on the first charge or the most serious. Baader and Meinhof and their friends were in prison for three years before *their* trial started. And until legal and public protests stopped it they were kept in a kind of isolation— empty, white, soundproofed cells with the lights on day and night

—that some psychiatrists called torture. The judges chosen for that famous trial were making their careers on it. The presiding judge was biased and prosecutory and frankly indulged the prosecution and the police, who were said to have withheld evidence and known to have monitored the conversations between the Stammheim prisoners and their lawyers. The left is accurate, too, in claiming that the agreement everybody calls *Berufsverbot*—it dates from 1972 and establishes common criteria, for the federal government and the various *Länder*, for keeping radicals out of civil-service jobs—is still in effect in most of Germany, despite the fact that the Social Democrats, at least, have officially disavowed it. In some conservative *Länder* these days, anyone whose politics offends the local bosses is a radical, and a threat, whether he wants a job as a bus driver or a university professor, and anyone who is a radical is by definition a *Sympathisant* of terrorists—and this means that in a country where 13 percent of the jobs are civil-service jobs of one sort or another a jealous colleague or a neighbor with a grudge or simply an ambitious politician has tremendous power over other people's lives. The director of the municipal theater in Stuttgart almost lost his job last year because a few people saw him donate a hundred marks to a fund for fixing Gudrun Ensslin's teeth. The mayor of Stuttgart saved him, but then the mayor happens to be General Rommel's son and a popular, liberal Christian Democrat, and even he was putting his career on the line by speaking out for a little compassion and common sense.

In Bonn, the idiom of recrimination affects everything the government does. The country's family law still needs revising. Women were given equal familial rights years ago, in the late fifties, but the legislation of children's rights was put off once the terrorists appeared and so many people started railing against "permissiveness." The Bundestag was finally going to vote on new laws for children last year—in part because the incidence of child abuse has been uncommonly high in Germany, and children's advocates have been fighting to extend the jurisdiction of the state over the children of violent or neglectful parents. But then the government dropped its bill—which was a good, comprehensive bill—after the spring elections. Schmidt wanted to dampen any opposition arguments about Social Democrats' destroying the sacred institution of the German parent, and the new, coalition bill before the Bundestag now is timid by comparison. Not that parents themselves are so well protected by the law when in one *Land* schoolchildren have had to answer questionnaires about their parents' relationship and their parents' politics. Three years ago, parliament approved the appointment of a federal Ombudsman for Privacy, and a brilliant young law professor from Frankfurt named Spiros Simitis, who was already the Privacy Commissioner in Hesse, agreed to take the job. Simitis asked for a staff of twenty, and announced that the main responsibility of his new commission, as he saw it, was protecting citizens against illegal invasions of privacy by the state, and especially by the police and the secret services. The cabinet, meanwhile, limited his staff to eight people, including two secretaries and a chauffeur. Simitis resigned in protest before he even took office.

Old friends in Hamburg like to say that there was something consummately German about Ulrike Meinhof, preaching community against society, soul against civilizaton, the absolute good against the merely ethical. They say that the mystique she made of a kind of clarifying violence was right in the tradition of the great German Romantics—from her liberation of Andreas Baader to her prison suicide. More likely, that mystique had to do with the very specific evasions of postwar German society and the conviction among all young radicals of her generation that the country's Nazi past had never really been repudiated. They had watched East Germany coopt the rhetoric of anti-Fascism at a time when their own parents still talked about the generals who plotted the bunker coup against Hitler in July of 1944 as if they were the flower of the underground. The fact that Communist power in East Germany played to a great extent on war guilt—played on a repudiation so intense and unremitting that it could become a kind of substitute for the revolution the country never had—did not matter very much to those young West Germans. Party cynicism in the German Democratic Republic seemed a little beside the point to students who were discovering that some of the men in charge of the successful new advertising agencies in Frankfurt had got their training in Goebbels's Propaganda Ministry, or that the head of one of West Germany's big synthetic-rubber companies, a man much decorated by the government, had been accused of committing atrocities on foreign workers in the war, or that Adenauer's State Secretary in the Chancellery was one of Hitler's official commentators on the Nuremberg Laws and the person who introduced the letter "J," for Jew, into German passports. Schleyer himself had been an officer of the S.S. in Czechoslovakia—but this was something that young Germans learned only last fall, after Schleyer was kidnapped, and by then Schmidt's "crisis staff" had made the decision that saving Schleyer was not its priority. The chances are that their parents didn't know who Schleyer was, either.

Their parents belonged to a generation that had learned at school that Hitler did not start persecuting German Jews until the war turned, at the end of 1943.

Actually, West Germany never had much chance to confront its conscience. The Cold War followed so fast on the war Germany had fought that within a year or so of the surrender it was more rewarding to hate Communism than to hate Fascism. The Eastern front had by then become a field of honor, the place where Hitler's war turned into the defense of Germany—the place where patriotism and anti-Communism could be profitably confused. America, funding the reconstruction, had made a decision early on that it was safer to bet on Germans who, if not actually ardent Nazis, had never been demonstrably anti-Nazi than on anyone associated with the German left. The left—or what remained of it—had been the greater part of the resistance, and expected to be honored. Now, suddenly, the left in many of its traditional shapes and sizes fell under the cloud of Communism—when in fact it was hard in those first postwar years to find many Communists at all in the new Federal Republic. Most German Communists who survived the war had made their way to East Germany. The big migration in the late forties and the fifties involved the eleven million *Volksdeutsche* and East Germans who fled to the Western sectors for asylum, and those refugees, like most of the people in West Germany already, were the same men and women who had tolerated, if not supported, the Third Reich. Hitler's majority in 1936 was still the majority in 1946. There were simply not enough other Germans around in 1946 to take over from them, and this meant that there was no way, short of a revolution, to really change the management of the country. It also meant that the project of "cleansing Germany's soul," which people like Ulrike Meinhof took up so much later, was in fact a fantasy of foreigners. Willy Brandt, who took office in 1969, was the first West German Chancellor who could actually claim to have fought the Nazis. Brandt spent the war in the Norwegian Army, and though he did not bear arms, there are still people here who agree with Franz Josef Strauss that Brandt was somehow treacherous to have put on an "alien uniform" while the rest of his generation suffered at home for twelve years defending the fatherland from Communists. After the war, they clearly preferred the healing, paternal hand of a Konrad Adenauer—someone who could protect the country from its history. Adenauer convinced the Germans that the energy of their anti-Communism was itself proof of a new democracy at home. It was easy enough for him to do, inasmuch as most West Germans were never more than a few hours from the reality of the German Democratic Republic—Hamburg is only half an hour's drive from East Germany—and West Berliners had daily confirmation of their worst fears about the people's paradise on the other side.

The Germans loved Adenauer. He turned their evasions into something positive, and persuaded them, with his stern calm, that rituals of guilt and expiation could be undermining and indulgent. He was seventy-three years old when he became the first Chancellor of the Federal Republic, and he had all the privileges of the patriarch. His people built their "temporary" capital at Bonn because he had a house there and liked the town and, after all, knew what was best for the country—which was a solid, Christian Democratic setting for its new government. They took for common cause his rhetoric of reunification, though reunification was something the Cold War absolutely contradicted. Adenauer himself knew that Russia would never tolerate a neutral and united Germany, and he had good reason to believe that the Germans, after their insane war and humiliating defeat, lacked the proper democratic instinct and even the stability to run one. Germany had hardly been a nation to begin with. Bismarck invented it in 1871, taking a grab bag of kingdoms and duchies and principalities and free city-states—twenty-five of them in all—that had never really got along and putting them together as the home base of a new empire. For seventy-four years, "Germany" was a marriage of convenience, a partnership for power. And now, with the only capital that Germany ever had cut off and occupied, with families forced from their homes into a kind of ideological geography and West Germany itself a Cold War corridor, defended like some Gaza Strip of Western Europe, the idea of one Germany had more to do with a lost future than a real past.

The historian Karl-Dietrich Bracher, who teaches at the University of Bonn, says that in the end the only identity left for West Germans was economic. He says they fled into economics, really, making economic consensus the basis of a new democracy that had no other rationale—neither the social revolution of the left's dreams nor the united Germany of the nationalists'. Certainly today the Bundesbank is as much a symbol of the West German nation as the parliament in Bonn, and the remarkable Deutsche mark the nearest thing the Germans have to a Marianne or an Uncle Sam. They have made a kind of ideology of their economic miracle, because what the *Wirtschaftswunder* did was define the boundaries of the state for people who at the time were not even sure if a German passport meant citizenship in the new Federal Republic or the old Weimar Republic—people whose splendid capital city had been reduced to a function of the balance of East-West power and whose land was at the service of vast Occupation armies. Even now, there are more than 200,000 American NATO troops in Germany. Their presence, over the years, may have humiliated a lot of Germans, but it did remind those Germans about the pleasures of power that did not depend on a myth of the pure *Volk*, or even on a Bismarckian chauvinism. The Germans took on the values of the Occupation and eventually took them over, until the country began to look like their own remorseless version of the United States. Hamburg is deceptive, with its industry safe and sculptural across the Elbe. For all the building and rebuilding that went on here in the fifties and sixties, the elegant old plan of the center city has mainly been preserved. The real New Germany is the Germany of the infamous Autobahn, of speeding trucks, and of factories that have pushed their way into the bombed-out hearts of towns like Düsseldorf and Cologne —it is the Germany of the modern megalopolis, driven by the aesthetic of its own sprawl. Its triumph is a city like Frankfurt, which was gutted by the war, then half rebuilt in the architectural potlatch of the giant banks and businesses of the *Wirtschaftswunder*, and finally finished off in the name of progress by a succession of greedy local governments. The shell of Frankfurt's glorious opera house, lit at night like the set for a *son et lumière* about destruction, makes its own sad comment on the graceless towers that surround it now. Even the crime in Frankfurt is the new crime of German reconstruction—Frankfurt's underworld belongs to a mafia of enterprising Turks and Yugoslavs who came in the wave of two and a half million foreign workers and found Germany too profitable to think of going home.

By now, Germany has the strongest economy in the world, and the strongest currency. The Deutsche mark that the dollar made controls the dollar these days on the world market. And America depends on Germany to protect that sinking dollar with its own policies. Saudi Arabia and Kuwait and the oil sheikdoms depend to a great extent on German trade to channel their petro-dollars into Western Europe. The Common Market depends on Germany to finance its projects. (Germany agreed from the start to meet some 28 percent of the Common Market budget, which is almost entirely an agricultural budget, and by now the cost of guaranteeing its neighbors' produce and its neighbors' prices is enormous. Last year, Germans watched the Common Market unload their butter surplus, at a fraction of its free-market value, in the Soviet Union—which quickly made a big profit selling that butter to Italians.) Italy itself floats, from crisis to crisis, on German credit. And yet the mark keeps going up—in terms of purchasing power, wages in Germany are the highest in the world—and it goes up so consistently that while the rest of Europe struggles to pay oil bills that are five times what they were a few years ago the Germans can pay for their energy completely with what they sell to the oil-producing countries. No one here can say precisely why the *Wirtschaftswunder* continues. There are a million people out of work—some 4 percent of the working population—though economists tend to halve that figure in their projections, saying that a few hundred thousand of those people are unemployable and should be registered on the welfare rolls, and that probably a few hundred thousand more are making the most of a year on unemployment compensation, which amounts to around three-quarters of a worker's last net income, tax free. Then, too, the wage increases that German workers demand, and get, in their yearly negotiation ritual with the German Employers' Association have squeezed profits —and this does not do much to encourage investment in German industry, despite the fact that there is no capital-gains tax on investments held for more than six months. Germany, by rights, should be suffering some by now. The high price of the mark should be making German products too expensive to compete abroad, and yet they do compete—in part because of their quality but mostly because the oil countries that buy so much from Germany these days can afford to pay anything at all for what they want. Actually, Germany's new markets are expanding. As long as they do expand—which means as long as the world's new rich would rather spend eighty thousand of their petro-dollars for a Mercedes than twenty thousand for a Cadillac—Germans are not going to have to worry very much about the killing price of their own currency.

Hamburgers sometimes credit the British with the *Wirtschafts-wunder,* inasmuch as it was the British who made off with whatever old machinery they could salvage from the ruins of German industry in 1945, leaving Germany with no choice but to replace everything, and America anxious to see that it was done fast. Germany had nothing left *except* its industrial potential. There are virtually no resources in the country—coal and a little iron and not much else. German agriculture had been undermined by the mobilization and then by the war, and after the surrender in 1945 less than 15 percent of the population was living from the land. By the fifties, in fact, when the European Economic Community wrote its charter, Germany was more than willing to subsidize someone else's farms in return for the kind of arrangements that supported the scope and priorities of that industrial potential. The

French myth of a breadbasket economy was a little bucolic for modern German tastes anyway. What Germany wanted then, and got, was a clear field to develop the most sophisticated industrial plant in the Western world; its goal for the end of the recovery was to be able to export a quarter of its gross national product in the form of German factory goods and, in crises like the oil crisis ten years later, to be able to underwrite its new expenses by exporting more.

When Germany met that goal—and American industry, with its vast, traditionally captive domestic market, looked on, complacent —the government pronounced the country officially "recovered." The trouble was that a new generation of students, and a lot of young men and women just out of university, were not at all convinced that Germany had recovered any of its human values in the process of recovering its solvency. Many of them had joined the Social Democratic Party —or, as students, the Socialist German Students Union, which was supported by the Social Democrats until it broke away because of a fight over representation at party congresses—hoping to find a platform for their own ideas. What they found instead was that the old German party of the Socialist International had little to do with the left they had imagined in their students' clubs and classrooms. They found that little by little the Social Democratic Party had changed its mind about the issues that involved them—NATO, rearmament, atomic bombs on German soil. They found, in fact, that the Social Democrats were beginning to believe in the values of the recovery, that whatever socialism their party had in mind stopped at West Germany's borders —that the party could fight for its workers, and get them boardroom clout and remarkable state services, and still share the conservatives' appetite for the new economic empire that had replaced the older, failed forms of German conquest. The Social Democrats had always rejected the notion of a popular front of socialists and Communists, and, for that matter, the notion of an international class struggle; now the Deutsche Gewerkschaftsbund had dropped its rhetoric about a workers' movement, in Germany or anywhere, and started demanding a big piece of the *Wirtschaftswunder* for itself. Most self-respecting German workers, anyway, thought of "the proletariat" as something subversive that the Russians were exporting. In 1968, a housepainter in West Berlin shot and nearly killed a young pacifist named Rudi Dutschke—a refugee from East Germany who was leading student protests against the Vietnam War—and gave as his only reason the fact that he could not stand anything that "Communists" like Dutschke stood for.

There is no way to compare the young German left of the 1960s to the New Left in America during those years, though Germans do it all the time. The causes were the same—the bomb and then the war in Vietnam—and a lot of the protest style around the Free University in West Berlin was lifted from American colleges. Germany had its Yippies in the form of a group called Subversive Action, which was much given to pudding bombs and costumes; its counter-conventions in the form of an Extra-Parliamentary Opposition on the campuses; and, of course, its communes. But the movement that called itself the New Left was really more of a response to issues than a left, and it dissolved with its causes, leaving a handful of Weathermen and one small Symbionese Liberation Army, whereas the young left in Germany represented something—a tradition, a population, an ideology —and to exclude it, as the Social Democrats seemed to do, amounted to a kind of social amputation.

Obviously, the Social Democrats wanted to win elections. By 1966, they had enough votes so that the Christian Democrats, having fought with the Liberals, needed them to form a government, and by 1969 they were ready to form a government themselves. Willy Brandt was their candidate for Chancellor—as mayor and champion of beleaguered West Berlin, as old friend to the martyred American President, Brandt had an image and a reputation abroad that none of the other Social Democrats could touch. Everyone in Western Europe and the United States knew his name and could recite his virtues. He was their "good German," and, in fact, he was an admirable German, a man of great sympathy and conscience. By being familiar, he reassured the Americans, who were still terrified of "socialists" in any part of Western Europe and consequently preferred to think of the urbane, exuberant Herr Brandt as a kind of German Kennedy. The irony of his popularity abroad was not lost on the powers of the Social Democratic Party, who were beginning to believe that Brandt was one of the few real socialists among them. But for the young, his candidacy was a vindication —a chance that maybe, after all, their protests had been heard. They counted on Brandt to restore the conscience of a country whose first postwar loan had been a hundred-million-Deutsche-mark credit to the South Africans—to open West Germany to a more humane future. The fact that their own parents went cheerfully along, making money, never really sharing their outrage about Vietnam, never risking anything in protest, seemed to explain a lot to those young Germans about the dinner-table evasions of their growing up and the excised pages of their grade-school history books. It was hard for them now to believe that the same parents who refused to stand up and say "This is bad"

or "That's wrong" in the free Germany of the 1960s had had the
courage to protest at all in the Germany of Storm Troopers and concentration camps. But they could believe in Willy Brandt. Brandt was
the father who had joined the war against Hitler, the father who would
later fall to his knees and weep in the Warsaw ghetto, the father who
seemed to be saying that the country's moral problem was not just
reconciliation with the West but reconciliation with the peoples Germany had murdered.

Those students were willing to trust Brandt with their future.
They were moving out of the classroom and into the world at the same
time that Brandt left West Berlin for the Bonn Chancellery, and they
made a public decision to take a chance on a new Germany and a new
Social Democratic Party—to abandon their opposition, and make what
they called "the long march through the institutions." They applied for
jobs in the civil service, joined the staffs of Bonn ministers and local
mayors, became the teachers and bureaucrats in a thousand little towns.
Those young Germans were euphoric after Brandt's election. Their
country was prosperous, their government stable, their constitution
exemplary—and their expectations enormous. It is hard to exaggerate
their disillusion after a few years of marching through West Germany's
institutions and finding that very little of the tone and quality of German life had changed. What they found at the end of their long march,
in fact, was not a place for their politics but a *Berufsverbot* that Brandt
himself had signed, under pressure from the right *and* some of his own
Social Democrats. They found that the *Ostpolitik* was not just a question of the young refugee in Munich getting to see his mother back in
Dresden but a question of the West German government getting to
ratify postwar settlements without having to sign a peace treaty that
acknowledged the division of the country, and of German industry,
with all the Western clients it was likely to have for a while, getting
to ensure its new markets in the East. The *Ostpolitik* was Willy
Brandt's great vision, but it happened in large part because German
business let it happen. In the end, the young Germans who loved
Brandt found that his power was more symbolic than practical, not
because Brandt was weak, necessarily, but because the values of the
recovery were so much stronger. Brandt turned out to be a dreamer,
not a *Macher*. He had staked his political life—and spent his energies
—on opening West Germany to the East, and in the process he neglected West Germany and its own problems. He was wonderful on the
rostrum of the United Nations or on a peace mission, but he was no
match for the seasoned compromisers in the back rooms at Social

Democratic headquarters. He could never have hoped to meet the expectations he inspired, or even deliver what he promised—or, more likely, what young German socialists and liberals thought he promised —because the new consensus was based not on shared values but on shared economic interests, and Brandt had neither the aptitude nor the sympathy nor the time for the complexities and compromises of modern monetary politics. He could have survived whatever romantic scandal reporters here claim was used by the party to force his resignation in 1974. He might even have survived the "official" scandal—that scandal being that Günter Guillaume, his friend and aide in the Chancellery, was in fact a captain in the East German Secret Service. Brandt had given the Social Democrats their biggest vote in party history when he won the 1972 elections, but now the party wanted to get down to the business of running Germany for the next fifty years or so and was demanding a tough manager as Chancellor—and Brandt was tired, and in the end turned out to be the champion of all causes but his own.

It is not really surprising that terrorists surfaced during Brandt's Chancellery. People in Hamburg who are in their thirties now often say that if there had been anything resembling a European left in Germany—a real Socialist Party or a receptive Social Democratic Party or even a strong socialist wing within that party which was ready to stand for something and vote for it instead of backing out of its confrontations with the opposition—people like Ulrike Meinhof might have been absorbed into some sort of useful political life. They remember that Meinhof's first arrest had to do with the Vietnam War protest —she had marched with Rudi Dutschke in West Berlin and, when Dutschke was shot, joined the people who attacked the Springer Presse Haus there, claiming that Springer papers like *Bild*, with their hysterical appeals to the patriotism of working-class Germans, were the real assassins. They remember, too, that Gudrun Ensslin started out in West Germany's Ban the Bomb movement, and even put in time as a volunteer in Willy Brandt's campaign headquarters; that Jan-Carl Raspe once lived peaceably in a commune and wrote quite a good sociology thesis about the problems of working-class children.

In a way, people here are right to say that the first Baader-Meinhof group was making a kind of desperate and belated resistance to the German past, but the terrorism in Germany now is much too complicated in its causes, and much too gruesome in its consequences, for anyone's easy explanations to hold. Certainly it makes very little sense to blame the Social Democrats for disappointing the German left when to everybody else here the Social Democrats *are* the German left.

Even now, not enough people who consider themselves on the left are willing to admit that West Germany, by anybody's standards, is a free country—and was a very free country ten years ago when Brandt was running for the Chancellery and Baader was getting to know Ensslin and Raspe and Horst Mahler in Berlin. They tend to forget that if Germany were as reactionary as they claim, a Strauss or a Dregger, not a Helmut Schmidt, would be their new Chancellor. There are a million university students in the country, and a lot of them are as alienated by their fantasies of German life as by the reality around them, and too often they indulge in a wild theoretical projection of past horrors onto any discussion of civil liberties now. Terrorism in Germany today plays into the hands of Fascists, and nothing else. The problem for everybody else is less terrorism than the lack of a kind of broad social confidence—confidence to call Andreas Baader, say, a criminal and at the same time confidence to preserve freedoms under threat, confidence to accept dissent as something absolutely ordinary in a democracy. Charles de Gaulle could say of Jean-Paul Sartre, "He, too, is France." When that sort of thing happens here, Germany will be much closer to recovery.

March 1978

PARIS:
LE DISCOURS

Parisians read the paper the way an old Baptist goes to church—
for the terror and solace and satisfactions of the instruction. It seems
to be in their character. Parisians think of themselves as heirs to a
history of great events rather than of small and sometimes even ignoble
incidents, and so they tend to translate the details of their national life
into important pedagogic matériel, having to do with civilization and
its future. One of the first duties of the French press, in fact, is to
distract them from a fatal suspicion that France and civilization may not
be entirely synonymous as concepts. Jean Daniel, who runs the weekly
Le Nouvel Observateur, will talk about, say, unemployment in America
or England as "unemployment," but unemployment in France
becomes "a question of civilization." For André Fontaine, the editorial
writer at *Le Monde*, French influence in the oil sheikdoms is a question
of civilization, too—but so, for that matter, is the success of the annual
picnic for *Le Monde*'s typographers.

It is expected of people like Daniel and Fontaine to make this sort
of pious, hyperbolic statement. Frenchmen from Diderot and the Encyclopédistes to Fernand Braudel and the Archivistes have considered
themselves, by birthright, the arbiters and cataloguers of Western civilization—its official overseers, so to speak—but this does not mean that
Frenchmen, either by tradition or by temperament, have ever had any
real enthusiasm for the facts about civilization, neutral and unadorned.
It is the *imaginaire*, and the imaginative act of evaluating and describing, that excites them. They are romantics, under cover of their own
belief in themselves as rationalists. The confusion in their lives has

nothing to do with the left and the right, as they would have it. It has to do with Voltaire and Rousseau—and it has been going on for centuries, because the French, finally, are an anarchic people, given to excess, who live in great, bourgeois dread of their excesses. They may drive too fast and eat too much, but their most earnest efforts, from French grammar to the French state, have to do with controlling themselves, containing themselves, calming themselves with elaborate ideologies and systems. They believe in their systems, and to keep believing they will deny that anything in the world exists unless they have had something definite to say about it, somewhere to place it in the categories of their thought, some way to decide its value to themselves. To the French, literature means precisely those titles that Gallimard prints across the delicate, gold-line spines of the Éditions les Pléiades. Philosophy is the collective taste of the Academy. Music is mainly the taste of Pierre Boulez, who came home from New York three years ago to a job that translates loosely as President of French Music. And news, to be serious, must by some miracle of subject or timing accommodate what people here call *le discours*—by which they mean that persistent discussion about reality which keeps a professional Parisian intelligentsia entertained and earning money while "reality" goes on, for good or ill, right or wrong, regardless of the talk.

All this makes a big business of opinion. Paris, with a quarter the population of New York City, still has eight major newspapers (even though most of those papers lose money), four national news weeklies, and hundreds of journals and reviews of varying inscrutability, intention, and mischief—from Philippe Sollers's *Tel Quel* to *La Vie Catholique*. Twenty-seven thousand books are published here every year. Three state television networks—TF1, Antenne 2, and France 3—devote over a third of their programming to news and documentaries and are planning more. And Parisians themselves always seem to be reading something, watching something, hurrying through traffic with rolls of magazines and papers tucked up under their arms—the way sentiment and the movies usually have them carrying loaves of bread. *Le discours* is the city's software. The trendy thought has replaced the mantelpiece Sèvres as status symbol for a whole new bourgeoisie that has moved "up" to Paris from the country over the past ten or twenty years, trading its roots in the dying popular culture of the provinces for a popularized official culture, an intellectual *bon goût*—decreed, like the right clothes or the right stereo, by a local cottage industry that packages the life of the mind to sell.

It is hard to imagine another city whose intellectuals could be promoted like rock stars or reigning quarterbacks—inspiring the most avid, fan-club sort of curiosity, cultivating groupies, posing for *Paris Match* with sultry, heavy-lidded looks and shirts unbuttoned to the waist. The French have always adored intelligence. They take the act of thinking to be something swashbuckling and erotic. They warm to a fancy thought as if it were d'Artagnan swinging from Cardinal Richelieu's chandelier. Their children learn in grammar school that it was France's philosophers, and not France's rabble, who fought and won the Revolution. *La vie littéraire,* which was lived so scandalously well by Gustave Flaubert and Charles Baudelaire and Victor Hugo, is a social form for scholars, too, here. Henri Bergson was considered "literary," and so were Maurice Merleau-Ponty and Roland Barthes, and so, now, are Michel Foucault, with his elegant shaved skull, and Jacques Lacan, with his cranky shamanism. It is not surprising, then, that a silly pop philosopher like Bernard-Henri Lévy should turn up on T-shirts and posters or that an aging *enfant terrible* like André Glucksmann rushes around looking, at forty-two, like a Berkeley senior who has slept in his jeans and neglected to wash and wants everyone to know that he has been much too busy rescuing boat people or smuggling dissidents' memoirs to bother. They are both products of a long tradition of bourgeois *philosophes* who can consider themselves public figures because their judgments are taken as a kind of verbal realpolitik by everybody else. They mirror, in a way, the dilemma of a middle class that is now the majority in this country but that still feels blocked in its priorities by the very concrete power of the state, on one side, and of labor—for all practical purposes, the French Communist Party —on the other. The *philosophes* represent a third force, real or imagined, for that middle class. They articulate for it those few simple and disturbing facts of French life that were most ignored during the past twenty years of ideological obsession but were probably the source of more middle-class anxiety than any fine points of ideology—one simple and disturbing fact being that in France, almost by definition, institutions like the state and the Party will always prefer injustice to disorder. Their forum is *le discours,* rather than the parliament or the Party congress, but they enjoy an authenticity as leaders because *le discours* is an article of faith in Paris life, and supports its practitioners the way the Church supports its clergy—through the faith and contributions of the public.

Last year, a journalist at *Le Matin* named Jean Bothorel wrote a book, *La République Mondaine,* to say that the country was playing worldly word games with itself. Then Régis Debray wrote *his* book, *Le Pouvoir Intellectuel en France,* saying yes, that intellectuals in France fed on the establishment they pretended to scrutinize, trading critical distance from the institutions of the society for their own notoriety in that society as "philosophers." But people here read their books mainly as entertainments. They were a couple of writers exercising an old, honored literary license to *épater le bourgeois,* and all they accomplished was that, for a while, *le discours* became its own new subject. Actually, Debray was in Nicaragua at the time, a celebrity camp follower of the Sandinistas—some of whom undoubtedly had grown up on stories of Debray's days in the Bolivian hills with Che Guevara and then in prison. Debray's friend Pierre Goldman—an outlaw anarchist in the tradition of Jean Genet who had spent six and a half years in prison himself, on murder charges, and, in the course of being convicted and then acquitted, had written a famous prison memoir called *Souvenirs Obscurs d'un Juif Polonais Né en France,* and become a literary cause célèbre, too—was the one person in Paris to point out that only a *grand bourgeois* like Debray could have afforded the money and the time to visit somebody else's revolution. Goldman was shot last fall by right-wing assassins—one of the groups taking "credit" calls itself Honneur de la Police—and died on the street outside his flat. As for Debray, he posed for snapshots dressed up as a guerrilla, in fatigues and cartridge belt, and the snapshots were duly published, and at the same time he made a great point of refusing to go on television to discuss his book. It was his gesture, he said, against *médiologie*—a word he likes to use to describe the corrupting power of the media in intellectual life. He did not want anyone to miss that gesture, or ignore it. Accordingly, he wrote articles with titles like *"Lettre du Corrumpu au Corrupteur"* and gave interviews to the Paris papers repeating that he could still be counted on to refuse to publicize himself.

Actually, French television turns over "intellectuals" as if they were Charlie's Angels, fresh and different every season. Three million people stay home on Friday night for *Apostrophes,* the literary round table that Régis Debray boycotted, and publishers here claim that a few minutes on *Apostrophes* will sell an extra twenty thousand copies of any book—no matter how dreary the book *or* the discussion. *Apostrophes* is a kind of national occasion. There is a whole new generation in France whose mental life follows the seasonal schedulings of Bernard Pivot, the host of *Apostrophes* and a literary impresario of long standing who started out in culture, as it were, as a gossip columnist for *Le Figaro Littéraire*. It is not just media celebrities like the "new philosophers" —the *nouveaux philosophes*— who teach by television, causing so many French adolescents to assume that the death of Karl Marx was something that happened when Pivot did a show with Glucksmann. Politicians find this sort of easy intellectual glamour useful, too. Valéry Giscard d'Estaing may be too busy with affairs of state to say, for example, whether or not he took a quarter of a million dollars' worth of diamonds from Jean-Bédel Bokassa back when Bokassa was still the Emperor Jones of Bangui and Giscard the Finance Minister for Georges Pompidou—or whether his old Interior Minister, Michel Poniatowski, suppressed evidence of a plot against the life of a well-born, well-connected swindler named Prince Jean de Broglie, who was then murdered, or why his Labor Minister, Robert Boulin, drowned himself in a pond at Rambouillet over a minor real-estate scandal. But the President was able to spare enough time last summer to give himself a crash course in Guy de Maupassant so that he could acquit himself as a man of letters on *Apostrophes*. Certainly the literati here were more amused than impressed by the spectacle of Giscard d'Estaing chatting on television with a couple of de Maupassant scholars sufficiently distinguished for the presidential company, though not, of course, so distinguished as to detract from the presidential preeminence. The fact remains that within a few days the Pléiades edition of de Maupassant was sold out all over France, and by the end of a week it was even hard to find a Livre de Poche of any of his work in the bookstores.

The people who bought the books—voters whom Giscard has to woo and who now associate their President with every French schoolboy's favorite writer—are precisely those new teachers and managers and technocrats whose political interests lie not with the production systems of the working class or the administrative systems of the traditional *grande bourgeoisie* but with what can probably be called the country's systems of eloquence. A few years ago, they identified with the rhetoric of the left. Marx was their lingua franca, their security in an intimidating capital. Now they have discovered the Gulag. They talk about human rights as if the liberty of individuals were a new idea that someone had last year after the Socialists and the Communists argued. Now they would rather see the President of France receive American hostages' wives in a Louis XVI drawing room at the Élysée than Fidel Castro, in his khakis, make a long speech about revolution in the Havana soccer stadium. They are sick, and suspicious, of their old political vocabulary. They have discarded the left like the rich-peasant look that it was for most of them, and are prepared to be mollified by someone who will occasionally talk to them about whether it was more agreeable to have been born Maupassant or Flaubert.

This is the sort of talk that reassures the French lately. It is easy, clubby, not too complicated. It has the sort of bogus intimacy about it that inspires confidence. And it distracts people from the fact that their parliament has been in one budget deadlock after another for the past three years; that their President, making his energy arrangements day by day, has had to bluff a presence in the Middle East; that, for that matter, France itself will probably sell its soul along with its guns for oil before the year is out. People here are going through the xenophobia of hard times, dragging a stubborn French anti-Semitism out of the closet, acknowledging the incantatory mumbo-jumbo of a *nouvelle droite* philosophy that mixes some feudal economics with a sociobiological mystique about the Aryan gene pool. They are turning away from the millions of migrant workers from Southern Europe and North Africa whom France has almost wantonly imported, and they are turning away from the hundreds of thousands of refugees from their old colonies in Southeast Asia whom France, just as wantonly, refuses to admit in anything more than token numbers.

France has only state television. TF1 is the "popular" channel, with a dose of official culture once a week on *Au Théâtre Ce Soir*. Antenne 2 is the "serious" channel, with programs like *Apostrophes* and *Les Dossiers de l'Écran*. And France 3 is the "experimental" channel, with local news and culture—the one to watch for a poetry reading in Oc or an inspirational debate on freedom for Brittany. What the people who run these networks have in common is a conviction that they provide the only "objective" source of information in a country where the nearest thing to a journal of record is *Le Monde* and the rest of the press is openly a tribune for the prejudices of its various editors and owners. Television people here boast a lot about being "condemned to objectivity"—if by nothing else than by the diversity of the public they have to please. They like to talk about the native wisdom of "the people," about French television's function as a kind of *maison de rendezvous*, introducing opinions to their proper clientele but forcing no one into bed. In fact, French television seems to have found its own safe level somewhere between Italy's state television system, in which the left and the right divide up all the jobs, from network director to studio grip, and no one without a party card would think of applying, and the British system, which current media mythology holds to be a paradigm of truly independent public television, despite the fact that its independence has been dampened some by Margaret Thatcher's 300-million-dollar budget cut and her firing of the five BBC symphony orchestras. Television here *is* independent, insofar as its administrators have a common interest in preserving their right to run it and will fight for that monopoly. Most of them have been trained to privilege at one of the *grandes écoles* that still separate the few thousand children who will run France from the million *universitaires* who will serve it, and privilege here has priority over any politics—over left and right, over socialism and Giscardism and Gaullism, over whatever rhetorical chapel people claim.

The political pressures on French television executives have less to do with jobs and budgets lately than with personalities and questions of exposure. François Mitterrand, the Socialist Party Secretary, pirated a radio frequency last year because the networks had refused him air time for a speech, and he was indicted for it. On the other hand, when a group of *nouveaux philosophes* wanted to have their say about the bankruptcy of socialism, three years ago, word apparently went around the networks to let them have it. Everyone watched television that year —what with legislative elections coming up—and this was fine for the television producers, and fine for the government, which kept its majority in the Assembly, and fine for the *nouveaux philosophes*, who were philosophers mainly in that they got away with describing themselves that way. This kind of collusion—the state's exploiting intellectuals while intellectuals exploit the institutions of the state—is what Debray tried to examine in *Le Pouvoir Intellectuel en France*. There was something terribly smug about the début of the *nouveaux philosophes*. It stirred the old national myths about intellectual influence in public life, but the currency of the exchange was not influence at all but celebrity and profit.

The state is the employer of first and last resort here, and there are actually very few Paris intellectuals who do not work, directly or indirectly, for the government. It is a matter not just of state radio and television but also of the *lycées* and colleges and universities where they have always taught, the ministries and bureaus where they are *conseillers d'état*. Since Napoleon, the ruling class of France has given its sons to the state the way Italians give sons to the Church, and, inasmuch as the French still practice a kind of Napoleonic state capitalism, that "state" means banking and business and industry as much as government. Very little important business is conducted here in which the state does not figure as an investor, an underwriter, a banker, or a partner —including the business of information. But there probably could never be a *Berufsverbot* in France, the way there is in parts of Germany —an arrangement that gives government the right to fire anyone whose thinking the people in power at the time consider subversive. The French are fierce about their right to ideology, and their fierceness translates into a social contract, because very few Frenchmen, in the end, will risk that right just for the privilege of censoring a neighbor. It is not really in the interest of the state, anyway, to fuss much about the ideological enthusiasms of its employees. The business of the French state is to preserve and perpetuate its own autonomy—which includes seeing that its investments flourish. It cannot afford to sacrifice its talent (or its profits) because of family squabbles that will end, sooner or later, by themselves. The state here is a little like property in a Jane Austen novel: it is meant to survive generations of its custodians and their various attitudes.

André Malraux once said that in France ideas were guests— *hôtes de passage,* little celebrities invited in for a while but rarely allowed to overstay their welcome. There are not really many ideas here for which people will risk their own security—besides, perhaps, the "idea" of the state and the rather Jacobin "idea" of the Communist Party. Despite the whoops and the feathers, there were no deaths here in May of 1968. The famous *événements* were a kind of happening. They had the energy of a passion play but not a passion. They were, rather, a poignant moment in France's history—which may be why they are so affectionately remembered now. May 1968 did not produce a revolution; it released a generation of *fils à papa* with the confidence, the contacts, and the money to make their reputations as revolutionaries before the public's interest was exhausted. Jean-Édern Hallier, one of the most agitated of the 1968 *gauchistes,* married an heiress and could therefore finance his own newspaper, which he called *La Cause du Peuple.* From Mao, Hallier was converted to Ecology, and from Ecology to Independence for Brittany. Just now he is a Pagan, and celebrates his Celtic past with expensive campaigns for the European Parliament and occasionally writes for right-wing journals. Of course, not everyone can keep up like that. Lévy, even with a family fortune in African wood to maintain him, had to give up *his* newspaper, *Imprévu,* after about three days and an enormous bill from Drouant, which had evidently served Lévy and his staff as a kind of corner cafeteria, sending up champagne and fancy finger sandwiches. As for the others, Daniel

Cohn-Bendit spent the last few years working in a Frankfurt bookstore, and some of *his* old friends say they are going to start a "post-Marxist" journal, once they have raised the money. Some have dropped out and are farming in the Var, making cheese in communes on choice Vaucluse property, preaching Nature now instead of Revolution.

The rhetoric is anxious here, and French is a language that encourages this sort of anxiety, this sense of vast hermeneutical space, like an apartment house or a garage, always waiting to be filled, always changing tenants. Paul Valéry once said, *"Il n'y a pas une parole qu'on puisse comprendre, si l'on va au fond."* And probably no one but a Frenchman, talking to other Frenchmen, could have said that and been understood. French makes its points by tone, by pause, by phrasing and syntactical play. William Carlos Williams's instruction to American poets— "No ideas but in things"—would sound here like someone imposing debating rules in a *grand salon.* People in Paris use language to mystify and shine, like a bright balloon, performing best at its least substantial. And this is just as true when they are discussing factory conditions and the lumpenproletariat as when they are writing poetry. In fact, in Paris it is often considered a mark of intellect to be *illisible.* Philippe Sollers's *Tel Quel*—which is subsidized by Éditions du Seuil, sells about six thousand copies, and has taken up Marx, Mao, structuralism, psycholinguistics, Freud, St. Augustine, Solzhenitsyn, and the Free World, roughly in that order, over the past ten years—is considered the last word in the Paris *discours,* the Yves Saint Laurent of thought, and not really because of the brilliant piece it will sometimes run but because so few people can understand a word in the magazine. *Tel Quel* sets a standard in obscurity. Occasionally, someone of the stature of Foucault will get away with clarity—with the kind of prose that suggests a clear head and a disciplined intelligence. But prose like that rarely does very well as mythology for the masses, and so it has few political uses. The cult of the *illisible* has made a market not in philosophers but in *nouveaux philosophes* and other facile literary performers with a talent for translating the current conflicts of the intelligentsia into catchy rhetoric that anyone can use. The "new" egalitarianism against the "new" Fascism. Monotheism against paganism. Judeo-Christian civilization against *Übermensch* culture. Humanism against genetics. Marx against magic. Montaigne against Marx. And those *hommes moyens sensuels* of the discourse are there to explain it all on television, in cashmere turtlenecks and designer jeans, and in "philosophy" books that make the best-seller list in *Paris Match.*

Books are fetishes in France. Jacques Monod's *Le Hazard et la*

Nécessité sold a quarter of a million copies. Bernard-Henri Lévy's *Le Testament de Dieu* sold more than two hundred thousand. And people whose reading rarely runs deeper than that will still buy Claude Lévi-Strauss and Roland Barthes and Jacques Lacan for their coffee tables —precut emblems of belonging. French publishing, consequently, is an odd business. Editors here may do the work of getting books to the printer, but the glamour attached to "serious" publishing belongs to resident intellectuals under contract to direct collections, and they are often writers themselves—like Lévy, who publishes books of *nouvelle philosophie*, including his own, for Grasset. The idea, presumably, is that the books a particular house intellectual likes are going to share something—a perspective, an aesthetic—and that each imprint will define a movement or a school. What actually happens is that most collections make a celebrity of their intellectual and all the other writers are identified through him. Their books become *his* books, little spin-offs of a master thought, a master category—though as often as not he is window dressing for his publisher, a name to impress the public while the company makes its real money somewhere else. Seuil publishes Barthes and Lacan, and Sollers himself directs a collection there, but Seuil counts just as much on a long list of books about music and musicians, which the French, surprisingly, buy by the hundreds of thousands. And Plon makes *its* real money not from the conservative historians on its list but from a cheap series of sex-and-spy novels by a man named Gérard de Villiers, all of them featuring a hero of remark-able erotic accomplishments known as Son Altesse Serenissime, and a cover photograph of an undressed girl caressing a pistol or a rifle. By now, de Villiers sells at least seven million books a year. M. de Villiers has made so much money for Plon that he was able to buy a major block of stock in the publishing house a few years back and see to his own political and literary tastes—which will probably be known one day as *macho droite* and discussed in learned journals.

Finally, *le discours* perpetuates itself in the Paris press—the news-papers and the magazines where the vedettes of the apocalypse write their essays and their columns while staff reporters grumble and occa-sionally try to hold on to their news space by adding *"écrivain-philo-sophe"* to their bylines. Reporters here have discovered that the self-scrutiny of the born-again bourgeois who used to scorn them sells at least as well as news. Their papers traffic in "thought" now, as much as in information, and even the best reporters occasionally give in to a temptation to stay in print by making a media bohemia out of life in the back rooms at Socialist Party headquarters, or on the editorial board at Seuil or Gallimard or Grasset, or in the stacks of the Bibliothèque Nationale. There is a kind of Jamesian quality to Paris life lately, with the women—like Ariane Mnouchkine, the director, and Anne Bragance, the novelist—tending the gentle realm of art while their men buy and sell ideas as if ideas were negotiable securities on the Paris Bourse. In a sense, they are negotiable. *Le Matin*—the paper that Claude Perdriel, who publishes *Le Nouvel Observateur,* started three years ago—increased its newsstand sales by nearly a third during the five days of a series about the *nouvelle droite* and its theoreticians. *Le Monde,* which turned its second page into a section called "Idées" after Jean Bothorel began a "Commentaires" page at *Le Matin,* ran so many elaborate exegeses of the *nouvelle droite* that it eventually had to print a bibliography so that people could keep them straight.

The spectacular début of this latest right wing in France is worth considering, because even now that it is over no one knows to what extent it was a media event, a stopgap in a flagging discourse, and to what extent it reflected a real shift in the ideological status quo, one that the reigning pundits had simply neglected to notice earlier. The word "new," this time around, seemed mainly to distinguish the current crop of ideologues—their "pure" European ideal is a sort of cross between Parsifal and Arthur Jensen, with impure leanings toward Yukio Mishima in his loincloth, about to disembowel himself—from a traditional Catholic bourgeoisie that considers itself the proper right in France and, in the end, holds most of the same prejudices. The new *nouvelle droite* had actually been around for years. Its quarterly review, *Nouvelle École*—which involves misreadings in ethology, mythology, and Kultur, and lists as its advisory board a few responsible academics and a virtual *Who's Who* of Europe's Fascist intelligentsia—first went to press in March of 1968, two months before the *événements.* Its "study club," GRECE (which stands for Groupement de Recherches et d'Études pour la Civilisation Européenne), has been holding big yearly colloquiums at the Palais des Congrès and by now has four or five thousand members.

It stands to reason that only forty years after Vichy there would be some nostalgia, somewhere in France, for its old simplicities. But the *nouvelle droite* apparently took Paris by surprise, and people here tend to date it from around 1978, which is when Alain de Benoist, the editor of *Nouvelle École,* won the essay prize of the Académie Française for his "theoretical journalism" in a book called *Vu de Droite,* and when de Benoist's friend Louis Pauwels, planning a new weekly magazine for *Le Figaro,* made de Benoist his first columnist. Pauwels was a packager himself, an entrepreneur of slick, pseudoscientific mysticism. He was responsible for a book called *Le Matin des Magiciens* and had already produced a glossy magazine for the moneyed occult crowd. "California French" is the way somebody described Pauwels at the time. *Le Figaro*, peddling its new magazine with the Sunday paper, gave him a captive audience of some five hundred thousand Frenchmen on whom to test the strength of an old observation of Georges Pompidou's that there was quite a career to be made by some enterprising fellow as a right-wing journalist.

Le Figaro had been Paris's "other" paper since the war, the serious conservative reply to *Le Monde*'s rigorous, radical propriety. The money behind it was old money from the North of France, and the people connected with it were respectable and occasionally remarkable men and women. Raymond Aron wrote a column in *Le Figaro*. Claude Mauriac was a mainstay of *Le Figaro Littéraire*. The changes at *Le Figaro* really began five years ago—long before anyone there had heard much of Pauwels or de Benoist—when a publisher named Robert Hersant from a little town near Nantes bought the paper. Hersant had been a collaborator, and was officially censured. But he had made some money during the war, and eventually he used it to begin to build a publishing empire for himself. He started out with papers in the provinces and then moved on to Paris. By the time he bought *Le Figaro*, he already owned the Paris dailies *France Soir* and *L'Aurore* and eleven big provincial papers, and, all told, controlled some 20 percent of the newspapers in France. Still, he had seemed willing to leave *Le Figaro* pretty much alone until he started talking to Pauwels about a magazine. Raymond Aron quit around that time, with a moving public protest. He was the only important writer who did, though, despite the fact that some of *Le Figaro*'s best journalists were Jewish and that the new magazine quickly took up an argument—in the interest of what is euphemistically referred to here as "national reconciliation"—against airing the American mini-series *Holocaust* on French television. People like Aron were probably right in saying that the most alarming "new" thing about the *nouvelle droite* was its access to a major newspaper. Certainly this is the first time since the war that any extreme-right group has had the cover and prestige and audience of a powerful Paris paper at its disposal.

Aron, who is seventy-six, writes a weekly column for *L'Express* now. But *L'Express* itself has changed a lot since Jean-Jacques Servan-Schreiber edited the magazine. Servan-Schreiber decided to go into politics ten years ago—he ran three times for the National Assembly and lasted twelve days as Minister of Reform in Jacques Chirac's cabinet—and in 1977 he finally sold *L'Express* to the conservative English businessman and publisher Sir James Goldsmith. Most journalists are prepared to move around these days. Marcel Julien, who was director of Antenne 2, has gone to work for Hersant as his "chief of culture." Olivier Todd, who spent years at the socialist *Nouvel Observateur*, is at *L'Express* now, with Jean-François Revel for an editor and a group of colleagues devoted to exposing a Soviet conspiracy to rule the world. The weekly *Le Point*, for its part, was started by writers who left *L'Express* after Servan-Schreiber—practically a radical in his day —sold it, and yet *Le Point* is the most traditional of the French weeklies and is considered by now the reliable voice of the country's Catholic, business bourgeoisie. As things turned out, one of *Le Point*'s founders and its literary editor, François Nourissier, eventually left the Catholics there for the Druids over at *Le Figaro Magazine*. But the circle of exchange was really closed when André Fontaine invited Alain de Benoist to state the case for the *nouvelle droite* on the "Idées" page of *Le Monde*.

Everybody wants to state his case in *Le Monde*. *Le Monde* arbitrates *le discours*. There is no paper like it in France, because no other French paper is quite so purposeful. No other French paper is so frankly pedagogic. The people who write for *Le Monde* may have changed jobs and politics a dozen times getting there, but once they arrive they tend to become solemn and steadfast and a little supercilious—to take their vows as professor-priests to the country, guiding the French in the proper evaluation of their history. Jacques Thibau, who wrote a long book about the paper, says that *Le Monde* is the moral equilibrium of the bourgeoisie, and that is precisely what the people at *Le Monde* think, too. The one reporter to demur publicly is a man named Michel Legris, who spent sixteen years on the paper before starting on a scurrilous but often accurate account of life at *Le Monde* and of some of its meaner office politics. He was turned down by every publisher in town until, so rumor has it, Gérard de Villiers persuaded the board at Plon to take the book, which was published in 1976 and called '*Le Monde*' *Tel Qu'il Est*. Legris has been out of a job since then.

Le Monde is, in fact, a kind of public trust. No one "owns" *Le Monde*, or has ever owned it. The homely brick building in the cul-de-sac at 5 rue des Italiens was built by the owners of an earlier newspaper, called *Le Temps*, which turned Pétainist in the Second World War and was dissolved by Charles de Gaulle at the Liberation of Paris. *Le Monde* began on the day de Gaulle handed the plant and

the presses over to his old friend Hubert Beuve-Méry—a Resistance
journalist of great intellect and courage and an ardent Catholic in the
tradition of France's Catholic progressives—with a mandate to start a
new paper for a new, free country. There were nine "founders" of *Le
Monde,* and together they worked out an odd but durable cooperative
charter. First, they allocated 40 percent of the company stock, which
is voting stock and has no negotiable value, to an ongoing founders'
advisory board—but with the stipulation that businessmen and politicians be permanently excluded. (The board has fifteen members now,
and is supposed to represent some sort of national collective wisdom
for the paper.) Another 40 percent of the stock is divided, by rank and
seniority, among the editors and writers—the *rédaction*—of the paper.
Nine percent goes to the administrative officers and their staffs. And,
finally, 7 percent goes to the editor in chief—the *directeur*—and four
percent to the man who looks after the paper's finances. Beuve-Méry
retired in 1969, leaving Jacques Fauvet as his successor, but there was
no apparent successor to Fauvet on the paper, and Fauvet, who is
sixty-seven now and was supposed to retire at sixty-five, asked to stay
until the end of 1982—by which time, he assumed, his staff would have
to agree on someone. They finally did agree this month, on their
seventh ballot since February. The third director of *Le Monde* will be
Claude Julien, a Catholic radical of fifty-five who used to be the paper's
foreign editor and now runs its monthly supplement, *Le Monde Di-
plomatique.*

The succession at *Le Monde* was never a simple problem of conflicting politics—though this is the way the rest of the press described
it, talking about the left versus the moderates on the staff, the anti-
Americans versus the pro-Americans. The politics of most people with
any power at *Le Monde* have long since taken on the paper's missionary
character. Those politics are pastoral, paternalistic. They have to do
with a kind of Christian populism—like Beuve-Méry's in the fifties and
sixties, like Claude Julien's now. They translate easily as "socialism
with soul," which is how they are described most often here, but they
are certainly as strongly influenced by de Gaulle and Beuve-Méry as
by any socialist doctrine. *Le Monde* writers can practice the most terrorizing cant: Fontaine is "for" the Sermon on the Mount, as he informed
Benoist. Jean Genet, on special assignment in Stuttgart, was for the
liberation of West Germany by Andreas Baader and Gudrun Ensslin.
Various bureau chiefs, in their time, have been for the liberation of
Cambodia by the Khmer Rouge, for the liberation of the Lisbon newspaper *Republica* by its typographers' union, for the liberation of Que-

bec Province by terrorist *citoyens*. This is not innocence or malice but a kind of blind Christian pride. *Le Monde*, like the remarkable fathers of France's far-flung missions, has staked out a Third World for itself to save and sponsor—its white man's burden, its Calvary, the proper field for its protective cover and its forgiveness and, of course, its influence. People on *Le Monde* tend to react to abuses of power in that world with the enlightened tolerance of a wellborn curé among the savages in a Graham Greene novel, and this is why the paper often sounds so sanctimonious, so snobbish. *Le Monde* practices a kind of international double standard—rigorously *gauchiste* abroad, more cautious in the rest of Europe, and increasingly conservative the closer a story gets to French soil and French pocketbooks. There was a time when *Le Monde* protocol was to avoid calling anyone a dictator who was not "established"—which meant, it turned out, established by the Americans. This was naturally agreeable to other dictators, like Muammar Qaddafi, whose oil France wanted, and it was really not much different from Giscard's dropping in on the oil sheikdoms, celebrating with the PLO, announcing a new French authority in Middle Eastern politics. The paper and the President are both in the business of salvaging old illusions. And so, even in opposition, *Le Monde* remains something of an official newspaper, looking after the rhetorical glory of the nation, regardless of governments that come and go.

For two years, people at *Le Monde* were caught up in the drama of the succession. Candidates announced themselves, campaigned for a while, and exhausted their prominence. Foreign correspondents came in from the cold with gratuitous punctuality to look them over and make their own deals for the future. The first straw votes of the *rédaction* ended in a draw, and even now, the only thing certain about Julien's tenure is that he is going to have tremendous influence on *le discours*, on the national preoccupations, on what France's sense of itself over the next ten or twenty years is going to be.

Le Monde confers a kind of honorary degree—even on its targets. It accredits them, the way it accredited a *nouvelle droite*, with its space and outrage. It gives them their moment in *le discours*. Attention is what the French value most, and this, as Gregory Bateson said to his daughter in one of the zany and instructive conversations he called "Metalogues," is why Frenchmen wave their arms about when they talk —so that no one will get frightened and run away before they finish talking.

June 1980

ZURICH:
ZWINGLI'S GOLD

Zurichers know that history begins with the consciousness of property. They want to believe in the history they learn in school—which has to do with a nation nobly born one summer morning seven hundred years ago when three grave elders from the clans of Uri, Schwyz, and Unterwalden came down out of the mountains to pledge themselves to federation and freedom from the invading armies of the House of Hapsburg. But the history in which they feel at home invokes a Switzerland more in the style and spirit of its astonishing citizen-priests, like Ulrich Zwingli, who on another morning, in 1525, officiated at the Reformation of Zurich by dumping all the statues at the Grossmünster into the river Limmat—the saving grace, so to speak, about Zwingli being that he had already stripped those wicked Catholic objects of their gold and silver and their precious stones, turned the treasure over to the Zurich Town Council, and in the process started what has come to be called, reverently, Swiss banking. The conversion of art to property, of sacred to profane wealth, that accompanied the conversion of Zurich's Catholics to Protestantism does not seem to have distressed the people here. Gold, to a proper citizen of Zurich, is going to have the same special quality whether it is cast as a Virgin's crown or melted down into a tidy bar to fit a sixteenth-century exchequer's coffer.

Ulrich Zwingli understood his Zurichers in ways that Calvin —who was, after all, a foreigner from Picardy, preaching his brimstone sermons with the license of an imported *signoria*— never managed with his Genevese. Calvinism travelled better, in the end, but it was Zwingli who domesticated the Reformation, who fit it to the once and future native character in a memorable disputation with a colony of Anabaptists who wanted to settle here. Zwingli argued that the Anabaptists, fervently sharing their wealth and their wives in the name of Christian innocence, were in fact heretics and communists, and he proved it to the satisfaction of his town councillors with a long testimony about the commandment "Thou shalt not steal"—which, he claimed, was really God's eccentric way of saying that private property was sacred.

The Swiss, Protestant or Catholic, German-speaking or French-speaking or Italian-speaking, are all in a way children of the Zurich Reformation, because, whatever their fiercely held differences, they have all learned from Zwingli that they are worthy, and that their worthiness is somehow attached to the proper material context— that the good is like a tender Alpine violet and will only flower in a rich, nurtured, and protected soil. It is the responsibility of the Swiss to prosper. They take it on faith that the survival of any goodness in the world depends on the survival of the Swiss franc, and Zurich is still the city most particularly devoted to that end. Zwingli's Grossmünster, in the old town, looks down on cobbled medieval streets and out over the Limmat and the flags of the guildhalls on its quais to a gilded mile of the Bahnhofstrasse, where one in every seven buildings is a bank and the most extravagant distractions from the business of money are the *truffes du jour* at Sprüngli's. The first of the Bernese Alps rise in the southwest with a kind of picture-postcard authority—just close enough to reassure the people here of their protection. Even the Zurich See, with its sailboats and paddle steamers and shivering summer bathers, does double duty as a watery halfway house for the sealed storage tanks of food and fuel and medicines that the Swiss believe are going to see them through everybody else's nuclear apocalypse.

Zurich is a beautiful city, a congenial and in its way a welcoming city. It is not hard to imagine James Joyce at his table at the Café Kronenhalle or Lenin padding through the stacks of the Municipal Library. Goethe liked to write in Zurich. So did Schlegel and Rilke, Alexandre Dumas and Victor Hugo and Mme de Staël and even, sometimes, Casanova. Revolutions in art and politics have been plotted in the *Konditorei* of Zurich's comforting neutrality. The cavernous "socialist cafeteria" on the Werdplatz still serves Steak Café de Paris and fried potatoes to the hundreds of workers and students and visiting intellectuals who sit at its long wooden tables every night trying to appear conspiratorial. Theodor Pinkus's ancient cooperative bookstore on the Froschaugasse literally sags under the weight of all the tracts that generations of Marxists and Trotskyites and anarchists have left there, hoping to inspire a revolution somewhere else. Zurich has always offered up the calm climate of its neutrality to foreign activists and artists as a kind of service, the way its banks offer up the calm climate of numbered accounts and secret currency transfers to Arab sheiks and American mafiosi now. All Zurich asks is that whatever seditious or delicious thoughts are nurtured in the fugitive peace of the city be taken away quietly, exported like tourist clocks or chocolates, so that in the end the twenty thousand brooms of the municipality will have nothing more disreputable to dispose of than the few, last pencilled traces of a polemic or an erotic poem.

With its charm and its probity, its banks and its bookstores, Zurich is the bridal bed in a marriage of convenience between a mountain people with a shrewd instinct for folklore morality and a greedy *Ausland* that has found the folklore attractive for its purposes. A dozen other small countries, from Lebanon to Costa Rica, have tried over the years to set themselves up as bankers to the world, with all the assurances of discreet and oligarchic democracy, but the fact is that only the Swiss have been able to satisfy their clients with the right mix of steel and guilelessness. What the Swiss offer, beyond the obvious pleasures of their country and the services of their banks and tax havens, is a kind of theater of rectitude. They have chosen to believe that their neutrality is unselfish; that their Army and their Alps, and not the conveniences of an open Switzerland, are what protect them. They believe that it is their own industriousness and their own prudence that support the Swiss franc and create that standard of stability against which every other hard currency is measured. They are a conscientiously decent people, but they are no less cynical than, say, the Costa Ricans. It is rather that they are so completely, so almost theologically convinced of the depravity of others that the perception itself amounts to a kind of proof of immunity. Their politics at home, their cool simultaneous practice of the social contract and the secret banking code have to do with a national double standard which holds that the Swiss be rigorous and fair in their domestic life but at the same time free, if not committed, to exploit the greed of foreigners, who are, almost by definition, a species doomed to foolishness. The Swiss are a little like those Indian tribes that keep the word "people" or "human" exclusively for themselves. It is the duty of every Swiss citizen to survive the mess the world continues to make of itself, and so if he happens to help finance that mess in order to finance his own survival—that is of no particular consequence to anyone. The Swiss are quite willing to take their service charge and their interest on foreign scams. What they consider a real breach of national propriety is to organize scams of their own. People were genuinely humiliated here last year when bankers from the Schweizerische Kreditanstalt, or Crédit Suisse, confessed to having swindled depositors out of some $840 million, and were quick to point out that the Crédit Suisse affair had originated at the bank's Chiasso branch—which is to say practically in Italy. They said that a complicated swindle like Chiasso's, involving bogus investment funds and holding companies in Liechtenstein and forged stocks and guarantees and documents, had a kind of baroque Italian style to it, that Italy, after all, was only two streets south of Crédit Suisse's Chiasso office. Four of the five embezzlers were, in fact, from Italian Switzerland, and feelings here about Italian Switzerland are such that when a mother warns her daughter about the dangers of a mixed marriage she is not talking about the new African exchange student at the University of Zurich but about some young seducer from Lugano. Zurichers tend to avoid the fact that the mastermind of the Chiasso affair was a good German Swiss named Ernst Kuhrmeier and that the money lost was mainly the sort of flight money—imported illegally across the Italian border—that is the stuff of respectable Swiss banking and Swiss investment capital and has helped make Switzerland, with six million people and with water as its most important resource, the fifth-richest country in the world.

Zurichers are right in saying that a scandal like Chiasso's is not their style at all. Zurich is what purists most often have in mind when they talk about the quintessential "Swiss" city. Geneva has lost too much of its distinction to an occupying army of tax exiles and international *fonctionnaires*—eleven thousand *fonctionnaires* in all—and their families to be considered particularly "Swiss" anymore. Besides, Geneva is in the Suisse Romande, dipping into France, and the Genevese themselves are an edgy, independent élite who have always kept to their own culture. Bern, for its part, longs for culture. People from Bern will talk about the twenty theater companies in town before they think to mention the parliament or the Federal Council, but Bern is still, hopelessly, a government city, given over to the ministries and archives of the Federation and to a commuter population of politicians and lobbyists who put up in bleak, overpriced hotels and run for the train as soon as parliament adjourns. Basel, at the Rhenish hinge of Switzerland, Germany, and France, is a port and border town in a landlocked, mountain-blocked country. Its wealth is old shipping wealth, and there is a kind of exuberant provincialism about Baselers that lends itself to Fastnacht carnivals and flea markets and students sunning themselves on the steps of the city's marvellous museum. The exuberance of Basel is something very different from the calm enthusiasms of Zurich. Zu-

rich is securely Swiss in its values. It does not attract rich Arabs, the
way Geneva does, or retired American Army colonels, like Lugano.
Movie stars and millionaire pop novelists are not apt to take up tax-
dodge residence in villas by the Zurich See when all their friends are
building chalets with private discothèques in Vevey and Gstaad. Zurich
is a city of discreet, domestic virtues. A city where the man who
directed the Swiss National Bank through the dollar float and the first
winter of the oil crisis takes in his neighbors' cats while they are on
vacation. A city where the mayor goes on television to complain that
too much "bad news" is making people gloomy, and wants to know
why the local press cannot be more considerate. A city where the
citizens were shocked when their children began rioting last summer,
mainly because, as they explain it, no one had found anything to riot
about in Zurich since a general strike in 1918. A city where the women
have had the vote for only eleven years and still consider themselves
fortunate because they were two years ahead of so much of the country.
Actually, Zurich has sent a woman, a Social Democrat, to parliament,
but the truth is that most Zurichers would rather see a woman in Bern
making laws than a woman at home signing checks of her own or
—until a few years ago—getting a passport without her husband's
permission. Women who want to control their money have to draw up
special marriage contracts with their husbands. Those contracts are
very much the custom here, because even now a woman in Zurich does
not open a bank account without her husband's signature or keep the
interest on her capital if her husband wants it or even order a checkbook
unless her banker decides that she is not the sort of woman who will
use it foolishly. Extravagance, like war, is for foreigners. The Swiss will
profit by it, but they will not indulge in it themselves.

The Swiss invented neutrality, and they did it mainly to keep their
young men home, herding cows and making Emmentaler and cultivating the republican virtues. For centuries, Switzerland's peasants, recruited in the flush of what was considered a superior Alpine hardiness,
had been the best mercenaries in Europe, exceedingly adept at making
war and taking plunder. One of the great strengths of the Reformation
in Switzerland, in fact, was its appeal to poor cantons that were getting
poorer because all the young men who might have spent their energies
at home had been recruited and sold by local aristocrats or priests to
live and die in the camps of foreign armies. It is difficult now to think
of Switzerland as a poor country, but the Swiss remember a thousand
years of poverty, and this may be why they tend to associate their

prosperity with the fact that they stopped fighting. In 1815, the Congress of Vienna established and guaranteed "everlasting neutrality" for Switzerland. The Swiss had lost their state treasury to the French Revolution, and then thousands of their soldiers to Napoleon's Russian winter. By 1815, Switzerland had nothing left to sell but its services—a new way to save itself by serving others.

The Swiss Constitution forbids citizens to fight anywhere, in any war, even as volunteers. A Swiss contingent of the International Brigade was raised in clandestinity during the Spanish Civil War— it was part of the Thälmann Brigade—and Bern, to this day, refuses to lift its official condemnation of the Swiss who fought in Spain, even of the 146 among them who died fighting. Well into the 1940s, Swiss doctors who wanted to set up field surgeries for partisans in Yugoslavia, say, or Maquisards in France had to get themselves out of Switzerland like contraband war matériel. Switzerland made it safely through the Second World War with its railroads running and its bank vaults and hotels open, but that safety in the middle of a brutally warring Continent was a Swiss prerogative, jealously guarded. Switzerland had room for everyone's money and almost no one's immigrants. It was a Swiss —the head of police administration in the Ministry of Justice—who concluded that a "J," for "*Juden,*" on German-Jewish passports would help Hitler to control the flight of Jews from Germany. Ten years later, with the war over, there were only twenty-nine thousand Jews in Switzerland; thousands more had reached the border, to be turned away.

People in Zurich do not talk about the ethics of their neutrality in the Second World War. The subject is a kind of national taboo. It raises questions that the Swiss do not permit themselves to ask now because they did not ask those questions forty years ago. When war broke out in Europe, most Swiss had already decided that self-sacrifice, even to a just cause, was impractical and even inappropriate—something Switzerland could not afford. It was not that the Swiss were pacifists. People here have always admired military power, and for a while they especially admired German military power. When Kaiser Wilhelm II rode through Zurich in 1912 in his high boots and imperial helmet and all his bars and stars and Iron Crosses, people gave him one of the biggest rallies in the city's history. But in 1940, when France fell to Germany and Switzerland discovered itself surrounded, the first radio message of the Foreign Minister to the Swiss people was a famous "invitation to silence." It is fashionable here now to regard the war-not-fought as a kind of redeeming national experience, the first real experience as a nation for people whose own passports describe them as citizens of their father's native village and only incidentally as citizens of Switzerland. The Swiss were obviously drawn close during those years in their distaste for the war and for Hitler and in their determination to survive both. The government did take in some refugees—mainly the sort of people who could be counted on to leave once the war was over —and treated them with the glacial courtesy of a *grand hôtelier* forced by circumstance to run a hostel. In 1946, Switzerland sent out accurately detailed bills for room and board, fully expecting to be reimbursed by the Dutch countesses and Danish diplomats it had accommodated. The Swiss thus turned neutrality into a kind of hospitality. They ran the best cloak-and-dagger spas and at the same time indulged in stern and often satisfying displays of principle that threatened no one who had any real power to retaliate.

A few years back, a local writer named Nicolas Meienberg and some friends made a movie about a dim provincial soldier from Saint Gallen, *Ernst S.*, who had sold the Germans some commonplace Swiss Army artillery shells for four hundred francs and was executed as a traitor—an example to his countrymen—at the same moment that a group of Switzerland's most important bankers and industrialists were drafting letters to the Federal Council demanding a more accommodating official attitude toward the Third Reich. *Ernst S.* was a quiet, shocking movie. Some people said that it should not be shown, that it was unpatriotic—the film critic for the *Neue Zürcher Zeitung,* for one, opposed Meienberg's application for the kind of government grant that goes almost automatically to filmmakers here—and the reason they gave for their disapproval was that it was more important to remember that a traitor to Switzerland had been properly shot in 1942 than that some of their neighbors in 1942 were making money on German trade. Switzerland, surrounded, sold its wheat for German coal. Swiss railroads carried corn from Rotterdam to the German front in Italy. The Swiss merchant fleet covered the North Sea and the Atlantic, carrying German cargo. A family here by the name of Bührle, which owns companies like Bally now, made part of its fortune selling arms to the Nazis and used it afterward to soothe the city with a beautiful new Kunsthaus. Three of the richest families in the country made *their* fortunes speculating in corn and grain for the German Army.

The Swiss say that they could not very well have refused to do business with the Germans, that the German war plan was to take Switzerland anyway—from the east, after conquering Russia—and that by selling to them they were really buying time. Germany needed

Switzerland's railroads to supply the *linea gotica*. The Swiss were going to destroy their railroad tracks and tunnels if Germany invaded, and the Germans knew it, but, even then, the war folklore had Switzerland's Army and not its railroad tracks or, for that matter, its docility keeping the Reich at bay. The Army is at the heart of what writers like Meienberg call the "Federation folklore"—the folklore that creates a nation for people whose circles of identity weaken considerably the farther away they get from the solid core of their communities.

The Army here is a militia, a citizens' force convoked in 1817 and then, in 1848, written into the first Swiss Constitution. By now it has sixteen hundred career officers and takes up nearly 9 percent of the federal budget, but it is still, most importantly, a symbol of the Swiss citizen at arms, defending his family and his home. It is as much a part of the national zeitgeist as snowcapped mountains or brass cowbells or the soft rush of a brook through the Jura woods. Every able-bodied man in Switzerland is on active duty in the Army until at least the age of fifty. People with special skills or medical deferments can sometimes join the civil defense instead, but conscientious objectors go to jail. They are considered dangerously antisocial—and not simply by the Army. The Swiss took up the question of conscientious objectors three years ago in a national referendum and voted, by a 62 percent majority, against any easing of the punishment. It is only foreigners who confuse Switzerland's neutrality with pacifism. Switzerland, at any given time, can call up a reserve of 640,000 soldiers, and those soldiers will be ready for action, having put in four months of basic training and, depending on age and rank, one to three weeks of training most years after that. The Swiss are proud to be soldiers. They live with their rifles propped against the wall and their uniforms, cleaned and pressed, waiting in the bedroom closet, hearty players in the harmless drama of a great deterrent force in a country no one wants to attack, a country that has long since seen to its indispensability. War games are played with the high seriousness of amateur sports. They go on by the Zurich See and in the mountains of the Engadine and the quaint villages of the Bernese Oberland, where the grass is thick and soft and the good food gratifying after a day's maneuvers. They are a chance to get together for the militia captains and colonels and brigadier generals who otherwise sit in parliament and on the boards of banks and of international conglomerates with headquarters in tiny "tax cantons" like Zug and Glarus and Graubünden. There is no conflict of interest for people in the Swiss Army because nearly every soldier is, technically, just a private citizen in the reserve. Gustav Däniker, who ran a big advertising and public-relations firm and had the Army for a client—along with a lot of other clients with Army contracts—is now a major general, training officers. He likes neutrality. He says that being Swiss is "like being on a bus without paying," and most people here would agree with Däniker that Switzerland has got the best of its bargain with a bad world.

While bigger countries plan for the eventuality of their wars, Switzerland plans for the eventuality of its survival. Civil defense amounts to an obsession here. People are passionate about their bomb shelters and about the barracks and storerooms and hospitals they build deep under the ground of their big cities or hollow out of their mountains. It is as if the discipline and sobriety and common sense that characterize respectable Swiss citizens from Heidi's grandfather to the clerks and accountants in Robert Walser's short stories had finally fulfilled themselves in the heady vision of a holocaust that the Swiss sit out, underground, administering intravenous glucose to each other, sharing Red Cross bandages and brandy, apportioning the food and the water and the comic books, and shooting anyone who comes pounding on their thick steel doors. It does not occur to many of the Swiss that a world which blows itself up might be a failed experiment, cosmically speaking—a world not worth surviving. The Swiss do not like to consider the possibility that the future belongs to the kinder folk of some as yet undiscovered *Star Wars* planet. For the past fourteen years, it has been illegal to build a house or office or hotel here—or any building where people live or work or come together—without either putting in a private shelter or paying the city to provide one. There are shelters now for more than 95 percent of the people in Zurich. The biggest shelter in town is a parking garage called the Urania, which can house ten thousand people in an emergency and includes among its many attractions a morgue and a police station complete with cells. Most people prefer their own shelters. Zurichers use them as laundry rooms or wine cellars, but they keep them stocked according to the 320-page civil-defense manual that every household in Switzerland must own and that is itself one of the Federation's most engaging exercises in rhetoric, with a chapter headed "We Will Not Be Caught Napping" and lists of all the important "temptations" against constant vigilance—pacifist monks, for example, or citizens' initiatives to cut the military budget, or a Swiss version of the Mothers' Strike for Peace. There is even a demonstration shelter here, with heavy equipment on display and an "infirmary" full of wounded dummies, all of them painted bloody or black and blue, like Sicilian street-procession sculpture, and a permanent exhibit of drawings by Zurich's schoolchildren.

Drawings of happy families playing cards together in their shelters while enemy planes drop hydrogen bombs on their houses. Drawings of mushroom clouds exploding in some lurid scribbled distance while Zurich sleeps, peaceful and secure and underground.

The Swiss have never been very interested in one another's culture. Zurichers learn French in school and people in Geneva learn German, and then they diligently refuse to speak the language they have learned. It is not so strange to hear a couple of businessmen or students carry on for an hour in English because neither one wants to give in and accommodate the other. People in one part of Switzerland rarely read the books or magazines or papers of another region, or consult its scholarship, though intellectuals from the Suisse Romande have at least been trying to encourage some exchange. Writers here in Zurich never talk about an audience in Lausanne, say, or Fribourg. The recognition a Zurich writer wants is not from the Genevese who can read his German, or put it into French, but from the critics in Munich and Hamburg and Frankfurt. He would gladly give up half of Switzerland for a place in the catalogue at Surkamp, the Frankfurt publishing house, which happens to be owned by a family of Swiss merchant traders and consequently supports a lot of German-Swiss writers.

Some of the most interesting artists in the country now are filmmakers—people like Alain Tanner and Yves Yersin in Geneva and Rolf Lyssy and Thomas Koerfer in Zurich. In a way, the filmmakers have been forced together, forced to be "Swiss," and not simply because of the high cost of making movies but because the images they explore are bound to be images that all Swiss recognize. Koerfer, who is one of the youngest of the new filmmakers, calls them "images of citizenship" —images of landscape, say, like the Alps, which have been associated for so long with the country's most traditional values that they are narrow, partisan, nearly political images by now and need to be rediscovered to be seen freely.

Some of those images, like the values they announce, are close to caricature. Youngsters here were not as silly and rhetorical as they first seemed when they talked about "liberating the images of Zurich" and then took off their clothes to streak, naked, past the opulent shops of the Limmatquai—which is what a lot of them did last summer. What turned into a kind of teenage guerrilla war, with the riots here this fall, began really as guerrilla theater: a couple of hundred kids "occupied" the steps of the Zurich Opera House and made a nuisance of themselves and a mess of everybody else by pelting the city's best-dressed opera lovers with eggs and tomatoes. Zurich was about to vote a special grant of sixty million francs to restore the opera, and these *Schlüsselkinder,* as the Swiss sometimes call them—most of them already offered up to the tedium of trade schools and apprenticeships that are still the tradition in a country where less than 7 percent of the population goes to a university—wanted a grant of their own for what they could only describe as an "autonomous youth center." The fact is that Zurich, with just three-quarters of a million people—half that in the township proper —and an annual culture budget larger than New York City's, had never really bothered about enlightening or even entertaining its youngsters. Money to turn an old, red brick ITT factory, across the lake, into a kind of open community center had been channelled and rechannelled, when it arrived at all, and by this year most of the "Red Factory" was in use as ateliers and workshops for "established" artists and directors, and as commercial craft studios. The one big room that the local young-sters wanted for their rock concerts had been turned over to the Zurich Opera as a set storeroom. What they got, instead, after their summer protests was a few months' lease on a condemned warehouse in one of the seediest neighborhoods in town.

The youngsters who have done most of the rioting here are not very articulate as to what exactly they do want from an "autonomous" center. Some want their own studio and theater space. Some want the rock concerts they were promised. Some want a safe house for selling dope. Some simply want to get away from their parents, because apart-ments are so scarce and so expensive in Zurich lately that most young people have to live at home until they marry and have children of their own. They are not really a group at all, and it seems to be against their principles to choose leaders to negotiate for them, but the city fathers could easily have calmed them down with a little understanding and appreciation of the rankling boredom of their lives as baby Swiss citi-zens. Instead, the generation that had sat out the Second World War quite literally rose to this one. People saw the glass of broken windows on the Bahnhofstrasse and talked, darkly, about a new Kristallnacht. They treated their children like the vanguard of a foreign army. For a while, they even managed to embarrass the police, who tried to ignore the worst of their orders and actually talked their way out of one showdown in the middle of the bridge from Bellevueplatz to Bürkli-platz which would have ended up with everybody in the river. But the mayor and his council saw to it that the police met the next demonstra-tions with armored personnel carriers and rubber bullets and blasts of tear gas that hung in the humid summer air and provided tourists with the amazing sight of Zurich's bourgeoisie weeping copiously into its *Geschnetzeltes mit Rösti* at the city's best restaurants. Zurich is still in a state of shock. Not fear but shock. The police have settled into what hundreds of the Zurichers who have been injured or arrested this fall say is a stubborn and routine brutality, patrolling the city in their battle gear, scaring passersby, chasing anybody in a funny sweatshirt or a pair of old bluejeans off the streets. The biggest department store on the Bahnhofstrasse has started an advertising boycott, cutting its ads in newspapers like the *Tages Anzeiger* that do not take up the call for *Ruhe und Ordnung* as enthusiastically as the merchants think they might be doing. Good citizens now talk about censoring the press. They find it reasonable that the editor of the *Thurgauer Zeitung* should lose his job for refusing to fire four controversial writers. They are not overly concerned that the local Minister of Education should try to seize a videotape of the Opera House demonstration which a group of anthropology students from the university made for their "community media project," or that the district attorney may have shot the earlobe off a demonstrator who "provoked" him, or that the police chief in Lausanne, say, or the manager of a dress shop here in Zurich should lose *his* job for protesting the harshness of the official response to a couple of hundred angry and confused youngsters. People in Switzerland identify profoundly with their conventions. Social distress is unimaginable to them, and so they call it criminal.

It is not surprising that Zurich supports five important psychoanalytical institutes and many of their graduating psychoanalysts. People here save their eccentricities for the couch. Unhappiness shames them. They have based too many of their institutions—from the Swiss family to Swiss democracy—on a conviction that those institutions will reflect not the compromises of individuals living together but a kind of sublime accord. They tend to believe in "the people against the person," as one of the local psychoanalysts put it—in a collective will as solid as any of their mountains or their shelters.

Democracy in Switzerland does not really involve the concept of an opposition. The half-dozen major parties vary so much from town to town, from canton to canton, that they stand mainly for a lot of inherited local networks under common names. Officially, the Social Democrats in Switzerland have a popular majority and the conservative parties—from the Freisinnige Party of the old business establishment to the various Christian *Volksparteien*—have a majority coalition in parliament, but none of this makes much difference in the end because the parties have long since agreed to agree on nearly everything. They run Switzerland together. The conservative coalition in Bern does not "hold" power against a Social Democratic opposition. Its leadership is not, technically, in office. There is no Prime Minister, and the Swiss Presidency is mainly ceremonial, a way of getting someone to sign letters and to meet other peoples' Presidents on their state visits and give dinner parties for delegations from the Chinese writers' union. The job passes, yearly, from minister to minister on the Federal Council —a kind of permanent "emergency government" which, by parliamentary formula, always includes two Social Democrats, two Freisinnige conservatives, two Christian Democrats, and one farmer from the Swiss People's Party. It is a formula that gives Switzerland, in effect, a collective Presidency. The Swiss, in Rousseau's phrase, are a "passionately reasonable" people. They prefer to wait out the working life of a fool or a martinet on the Federal Council than to encourage trouble at the heart of the benign and oligarchic family that is their government. They have not even bothered to provide themselves with procedures for bringing down a government they disapprove of—no parliamentary no-confidence votes, no national referenda on the subject. Having settled once on a fairly acceptable balance of power and interest, they are unlikely to change their voting habits any faster than they changed the time on the famous cathedral clock in Basel, which, according to Boswell, ran an hour ahead of the rest of Switzerland for centuries while the town councillors debated the pros and cons, the risks and satisfactions and consequences, of resetting it.

Most of Switzerland works like that—"making haste slowly," as they say here. There are still two cantons where only the men vote, and in five of the country cantons the citizens still gather in a ring, a *Landsgemeinde*, once a year to make laws and elect their leaders by a show of hands. Hundreds of towns and villages are run by meetings, too, including 138 of the 171 little *Gemeinden* in the canton of Zurich. Zurich's own mayor, Sigmund (or "Sigi") Widmer, is a history teacher from the Landesring, the party of the Swiss consumer movement, who governs the banking capital of the world as if it were a fairly successful cottage industry with a union problem.

The politics in Switzerland are homely and lively and collusive. People forfeit opposition policies because they know, in the end, that their security and their wealth depend on the confidence they inspire elsewhere. They are the happy family in a world of divorces. They do not expect their parliaments or councils to argue out their differences for the public record any more than they expect their wives to contradict them at a dinner party. The political fights are fought, and the consensus hammered out, by "pre-parliamentary commissions" of lobbyists from the five economic-interest groups—farmers, employers, the banking and industrial elite, the Schweizerischer Gewerkschaftsbund, and the federation of small businesses and trades—that are called "peak associations" here. And inasmuch as those lobbyists are often deputies or senators, too, the arrangement tends to give a few hundred people most of the political and economic power in the country. The Swiss normally do not talk about this much. Jean Ziegler, a sociologist and armchair radical and, officially, Social Democratic deputy from a town in the Suisse Romande, wrote a book about Swiss multinational involvement in the Third World—*Une Suisse au-dessus de Tout Soupçon* —and upset everybody so much that even the secret policemen tailing him around Bern will occasionally break into his conversations to scold him. It is not so much Ziegler's hyperbole or even his arrogance that seems to distress the Swiss. It is his indiscretion. He is one of the few politicians on the Swiss left to actually behave like a member of an opposition, and so no one in any party trusts him to keep the family closets closed. His colleagues say that he was hustling Switzerland's secrets for his own celebrity when he wrote his book. They are not talking about Nestlé's 800-million-franc-a-year profit or about the balance sheets of a few Swiss holding companies. The secret is that people in Africa or South America might be suffering some to keep those balance sheets healthy.

There is a public-relations man in Zurich named Ernst Cincera who circulates a blacklist telling his clients who the latest leftists are, what journalists are subversive, whom to boycott, whom to fire. Cincera and his staff provide a kind of unofficial espionage service on behalf of the people Americans used to call a silent majority and the Swiss call a preventive minority. These are the people who can be counted on to vote no on a referendum to liberalize family law, say, or strengthen the Constitution—the people who keep the country from progressive excesses and who therefore want to have on hand the name of the cartoonist whose drawing of William Tell betrayed a suspicious disrespect for the national hero. They have to look hard to find much real subversion here. Youth riots like Zurich's have little to do with the sort of healthy, subversive spirit that creates an avant-garde of its own in art or politics. The claustrophobia of the young is real, but it is not the mountains or the foehn that shuts them in—it is a kind of suffocating contentment around them. They long for friction. Life is good here in such obvious ways that they seem a little crazy, even to themselves, when they complain about it. They cannot point to anything specific, like poverty or oppression, to corroborate their unease. They can only sense that the complacent, collusive citizenship all around them is unnatural to their young age, that a social contract so coolly and successfully elaborated as Switzerland's can be the triumph of their society and still leave other kinds of liberty unexplored.

Certainly no one else seems to complain here. Most of the 500,000 workers in the country's labor unions keep to a no-strike policy the unions made in 1937, and it is usually metalworkers from the Suisse Romande, with old anarcho-syndicalist roots, who try to strike now and then, if only to keep the tradition going. Collective bargaining here was once described by Beat Kappeler, the young Economic Secretary of the Gewerkschaftsbund, as a yearly ritual in which "no one adventures and no one loses." The unions settle for modest raises—about 2 percent a year lately—and reasonable cost-of-living guarantees, and sometimes seem to be more alarmed than industry about the way the appreciation of the franc cuts into industry profits. Workers voted recently against a shorter workday for themselves—"in the best interests of the economy," they told the newspapers—and supported a referendum to increase the price of bread. It is impossible to imagine this sort of forbearance in Britain, say, or Italy, but Swiss workers get a lot for it. They get practically guaranteed employment. (The unemployment rate in Switzerland is 0.2 percent.) They get an economy that can still absorb the shock of having its currency almost triple in price since 1973—after forty years of a fixed exchange rate of 4.30 francs to the dollar. They get an inflation rate that rarely goes past 2 or 3 percent and a per-capita income of $15,455.

Of course, Swiss workers are highly skilled workers. There is no real underclass, no Swiss lumpenproletariat besides the few thousand rural women who still work for sweatshop wages in the country's textile mills. The Swiss import their underclass. Base labor is Spanish, Portuguese, Italian, Yugoslav, and now Turkish. Some of it is even French. One in every six people in Switzerland is a foreigner. Some 300,000 of the foreigners are agency bureaucrats and businessmen and tax exiles, but 700,000 are workers, and they are subject to one of the harshest immigration policies in Europe.

Six years ago, there were nearly a million *Gastarbeiter* here. The Swiss have sent about 300,000 of them home since the oil crisis—which amounts to 12 percent of the labor force—because, like most of industrial Europe, the Swiss discovered that they could buy their oil with the money they saved firing foreigners. The day workers and the workers who cross the border from France or Italy or West Germany on nine-month visas, without their families, had no claims on the state at all. The contract workers, or *Jahresaufenthalter*, were simply let go when their contracts expired, or, at best, kept on just short of the ten-year stay that would have given them the right to residency permits and eventually—if they could pay for it—citizenship. The Swiss have already had three national referenda on proposals to expel foreigners. They voted on the first one in 1970, long before Switzerland had to worry about its oil or about exports no one could afford because a pricey franc was making everything Swiss so expensive. The referendum then was the brainchild of a small right-wing party called National Action, which was fairly insignificant in itself but evidently tapped a xenophobic strain in the Swiss, because 46 percent of them voted in favor of throwing out foreign workers. It is a mark of either progress or prosperity that at the last of these referenda, in 1977, only a third of the people who voted said yes.

The Swiss are always voting. They are so worn down by their direct democracy—with its citizens' initiatives and its referenda —that a lot of people who have had to put in their first few Sundays as grownups at the polls, trying to make sense of a bewildering variety of local and cantonal and federal proposals, have simply stopped voting on anything but their own particular enthusiasms. The canton of Schaffhausen now makes its pin money fining citizens who do *not* vote —a kind of reverse poll tax or, more accurately, a luxury tax on staying home. Men who campaigned bitterly against letting women vote will say that they were protecting the gentle sex from the terrible burdens and responsibilities of citizenship, but it is possible that they were just making sure of a woman in the house to cook the Sunday dinner. Only 41 percent of the voters showed up for a referendum on taking three northern districts from the canton of Bern and creating a new canton, called Jura, for the 67,000 French-speaking Catholic peasants and watchmakers who lived there, but the Swiss considered that a good turnout—reflecting the fact that the creation of a canton was a serious and highly emotional business, involving self-determination and religious liberty and the tremendous job of dismantling and redesigning the dome of the Bundeshaus rotunda, with its stained-glass cantonal crests, to include the new crest of Jura.

There is no Supreme Court, in the sense of a constitutional court, in Switzerland. The Federal Court sitting in Lausanne can comment on the constitutionality of laws, but it cannot rule on them, and so the constitution itself has become a kind of working brief, always redescribing and redefining its authority. By now, it is a bulging document. Legislators often carry it around in a scrapbook, with paste-ups of the ninety amendments that have passed the majority of Swiss people and Swiss cantons since the last constitutional revision, in 1874. The rule of thumb—in a system where any piece of legislation is put to a popular vote if its opponents can collect fifty thousand signatures—is that the government is going to be more liberal than parliament, and parliament is going to be more liberal than the people. "Preventive minority" is delicate, as descriptions go, since most Swiss consider it a duty to vote down anything that comes from Bern. They reject some 60 percent of the laws put to them, and still more constitutional amendments, because constitutional amendments mainly broaden the jurisdiction of the federal government and the cantons get to vote them down even if the country as a whole likes them. It took fifteen years for Switzerland to pass a federal civil code. The federal penal code took twenty-four years. Work on a new constitution began in 1965 and is unlikely to satisfy everybody in Switzerland till sometime into the next century. Actually, the Swiss reject their own proposals even more often than the government's. They have not said yes to a citizens' initiative—which is a way of changing the constitution through a referendum organized by a grass-roots group, like the ecologists, or by a political party—in thirty years.

There is undeniably something moving about the ruddy elders of Appenzell or the velvet-vested cowherds of the Oberland or even the portly burghers of Zurich walking out on a Sunday after church to make a solemn choice about the cost of bread or the right of the federal government to cut a hiking path through their canton or the wisdom of establishing a federal riot police or of abortions on demand or nuclear power plants or a ban on cars the second Sunday of every month. This exhausting exercise in citizenship takes place in the more folkloric reaches of Swiss democracy. It sets a kind of moral landscape for Switzerland's real business—a Reformation landscape, out of Max Weber, for a country that sells its nuclear technology to places like Pakistan and Argentina and wants to export its own spent fuel before any radioactivity can leak into the fresh Swiss air, a country that pays its deputies only twenty or thirty thousand francs a year in the knowledge that most of them will make up for it in one of the Swiss-registered banks or companies which, by *code d'obligation*, have to have a "51 percent resident" board of directors.

· · ·

There are 474 banks registered in Switzerland—96 of them foreign banks—with 4,896 branch offices among them. About eighty thousand people work in those banks. Their total assets come to 440 billion francs, which is more than twice Switzerland's gross national product, and half of that money is in the accounts of foreigners—a house of bank cards built on what the Swiss call "the principle of confidentiality" and "the freedom of currency exchange," or laundering and hiding money. Lately, there has been pressure on the banks from American tax collectors chasing mafiosi, but it is still up to the tax collectors to prove a degree of criminal intent if they want figures, and even then the most they can get from the banks is figures, not cash. Flight capital, in any event, will arrive, by routes that make it possible for an honest Swiss banker to avoid knowing who the worst of his clients are.

Honest Swiss bankers are really office managers at heart—bureaucratic and fussy. They prefer to think of the banking apparatus here as a kind of social service, not as a marketplace for felons and fiddlers and tax fugitives and money hawkers. The gnomes of Zurich, left to their own common sense, would never have dropped the gold standard seven years ago. Edwin Stopper, who was head of the Swiss National Bank at the time, was evidently shocked into a heart attack by the dollar float, and soon retired to the relative calm of the Bank Leu, which is merely the sixth- or seventh-biggest bank in the country. Stopper complained then that the Swiss franc was going to replace gold as a standard and that this would put a burden on the franc—which is in short supply in the best of circumstances—inflating its value to satisfy a market of speculators and leaving the domestic economy in a "disagreeable and even irritating" position. This, of course, is what happened. Swiss businessmen had to risk their reserves to meet costs and stay at all competitive on the world market, and since then Swiss bankers have had to orchestrate their policies like conductors—playing on themes and restraints and resolutions to keep the franc steady and at the same time keep the foreign capital in Switzerland fluid. Last year, with too much foreign money on their hands, they put a 100,000-franc limit on foreign accounts. The law of the moment read that foreign depositors had forty-eight hours in which to invest "productively" any capital over that 100,000—which meant in gold or in Swiss bonds or shares in Swiss companies or Swiss-registered companies—or pay a 40-percent interest charge to keep their capital in francs. This year, with the franc falling slightly, the bankers abolished the law, saying that the "informal arrangements" they had made with national banks in other countries

—arrangements about buying money and covering transactions in important trade currencies—were more agreeable, friendlier finally, than formal rules and regulations about liquidity.

There is probably no country in the world that can afford to do without Switzerland. The Swiss National Bank, at the top of the Bahnhofstrasse, is often mistaken for the national crafts center, down the street, where tourists go for wooden cows and aprons with mountains or fondue recipes printed on them, but there is no mistaking the feeling about midtown Zurich, near the Bank. It is a feeling that somewhere close, just around a corner, the ex-President of a small banana republic is entering a bank with the state treasury in his pocket. Or perhaps a commissar with a cardboard suitcase full of foreign-exchange currency from the Moscow black market. A drug-and-numbers racketeer who wants to clean the money his daughter will need at Princeton for the spring semester. A cabinet minister from Pretoria converting his profits on the Zurich gold exchange to a stash against a black future. Or, of course, the perfectly respectable factotum of any one of a thousand foreign businesses and corporations and holding companies here. There are five hundred American companies alone with offices in Zurich. Companies registered here not only can buy and sell and change and hide their money but can negotiate their own low Swiss taxes and enjoy the convenience of the best university hospital in Europe and a fine airport for trips from Paris or São Paulo or New York or wherever their impresarios live. Those impresarios like to come to Zwingli's Zurich. They feel rigorous and wholesome here. They take their children to the old guilds' festival of Sechseläuten and wait, shivering, in a field by the lake while important Zurichers in medieval costumes light bonfires under a big cotton snowman of Uncle Winter with his corncob pipe and a wicker basket for a cap. They buy their children goose-down comforters and chocolate truffles just across the street from the banks where they buy their gold.

December 1980

LONDON:
A SENSE OF LOSS

There is a sense of loss here. It has come over the city as a kind of quickening sadness, like one of those early spring evenings that suddenly light the blackened stones of Parliament and the Embankment with streaks of gold. Everybody has an explanation for it. People talk about "the decline"—which is the fashionable London phrase lately —as if the country's distress were a moment in some historical aesthetic, something to survive and savor. Or they talk plainly about the price of groceries and children's coats, and in the end sound just as evasive and rhetorical, because there is much more to this distress than high prices in a ravaged and ravaging economy. It is as if Londoners were grieving for themselves, for the decency they have always held, as an article of faith, to be a particularly *English* quality, for the civility, the fairness of mind and spirit, that they believe is finally what sets them apart from millions of smarmy and disreputable Europeans waiting just across the Channel to corrupt them. They seem to be suffering from a loss of faith in the British character. They have counted on character, the way a conquistador might have counted on God, to see them through their wars and their empires and their homelier domestic crises, and many of them assumed that Great Britain's latest crisis—2.5 million unemployed, race riots in Brixton, Ulster close to civil war, Labour turned viciously against itself, a Prime Minister devoted to what is probably best described as up-against-the-wall economics—was going to be another one of those tonic afflictions that used to marshal the reserves of British character to come to the rescue when the common good was on the line. They talked about the unemployment queues and the ten thousand bankruptcies and the burdens of an inflated currency as something "good for you," like cold showers at boarding school or a just war, or even Charles de Gaulle. They seemed to welcome some of that bracing austerity in their lives, and they set themselves little mortifications of the flesh and spirit to make them feel at one, in sacrifice, with the potash miners near Whitby and the steelworkers in Consett who had lost their jobs. I know a cheerful, rather plummy historian in Kensington who stopped drinking for a couple of weeks and was much discussed by friends as an object lesson in self-discipline and making do and the resilience of the upper classes under pressure. I know a tender and eccentric Dorsetshire lady, a writer of one-act plays about cats and the dark side of table manners, who decided that her life of classically genteel poverty was inappropriate to the spirit of the "new" hard times, and who wanted to share the rigors of those times by doing something more unpleasant than playwriting—she took a job in town answering the telephone for a young man engaged in peddling pornographic cassettes to South Americans. I know people in London who are turning vegetarian, people who are closing down their weekend cottages, people who have started to take in boarders while their children are away at school. But theirs are helpless, delicate gestures—Chekhovian gestures choreographed at the country house of British character —and have no correlatives in the Council flats and the New Towns that are English life for so many English men and women. Oxbridge England has always played at hard times. The "right" people here have always thrived on the cachet of poverty, the way they have thrived on being dotty or barmy or whatever other word they choose for symptoms that are usually called crazy in the less fortunate. They have had the confidence of class to see them through their aberrations and their overdrafts. And so they were able to persuade themselves that pulling through was a kind of national sport, that in the end the energy of the working class, like their own energy, would always spend itself in patriotic rituals. They have lost this innocence now—about the country, about each other—without ever really having understood how much of it was arrogant and willful. It was an innocence that took need for graciousness, envy for enthusiasm, serving for service. And it was of much use to them in the brutal exercises of an expanding empire, securing for England, more than for any other colonial power, that sentimental psychic space between ruler and ruled, owner and worker, in which the social contract could invent its necessary euphemisms. The English produced the most class-ridden society in Europe, and in some ways the most aggressively self-deluded—and for centuries managed to hold it together by pretending that responsible social cooperation was a natural expression of Englishness, rather than the protective accommodation of citizens to one another in a free country. Now that psychic space is gone.

Americans look to England as a model. They study the first two years of Margaret Thatcher for some clue to the next four years of Ronald Reagan. They see a mirror of Chrysler's troubles, say, in British Leyland, which could not be coaxed to solvency by a few pat changes in the economic rhetoric, or even by a year or two on the public dole. Americans share with the English that conscientious befuddlement, that sanguine, profitable naïveté, which has let the English make wars and build empires and plot whole continents like kitchen gardens —all the while ignoring the cost in human terms because they knew that the *fellahin* and the *dukawallahs,* and even the homegrown workers and soldiers of their adventure, had sacrificed themselves proudly in a common cause, and not out of poverty or desperation or surrender. England is America's lesson in an imperial liberalism worn like horse blinkers against the disconcerting truth of why people work and suffer. England's image of service has been as potent a resource as the coal in Wales or the oil off the coast of Scotland, but it was good only for the life of the ruling class that carved it into the value system of the country. As long as the people who ran Great Britain—left or right, Labour or Conservative—were the rosy amateurs of an Oxbridge *Weltanschauung,* unworldliness was the hallmark of the country's institutions and the snobbery of its official attitudes, and "playing the game" was its most appropriate cliché. British rule has always been self-referential. To boys who had learned their own game as bowlers and batsmen at Eton or Winchester, the game in Yorkshire's quarries or Manchester's slums was just a rougher version of it—with stress and sweat appropriate to the station of the players.

Life in the mines or the smelters as a variation on the theme of sportsmanship—that was the assumption of a ruling class that ruled as avocation and asked only that its subjects pretend to serve in the same spirit. It was an assumption that made rebellion unseemly and social disgust ungenerous. It laid the ground rules of a civil service and a Foreign Office that would "launder" class, so that unfortunate but promising children from state schools and undistinguished families would have a back desk or a properly remote country where they could overcome their roots and their envy and their worst vowels and whatever unruly instincts might tempt them to compete or supplant or overthrow. It meant that chippy young men sent off to some dreadful outpost of empire came home a few years later with their sense of themselves and their identity tied firmly to a conviction that the world was a *tableau vivant* to please the tastes and standards of the aristocrats who ran the Foreign Office.

The difference in England now has less to do with the loss of power abroad than with the fact that a whole new class of men and women has started demanding to run the country at home. There have been changes in the leadership of both big political parties, and for the first time these changes involve class as much as policy. The terrible split in Labour after a conference in Wembley last January was not a simple matter of left wings and right wings and union wings of the party. The trade unions stifle the economy here. In the past, they have usually settled for that kind of negative power, leaving the Parliamentary Party—that is, Labour's Members of Parliament as a group —to be the statesmen and to live stylishly in London. But after Wembley it was clear that a lot of tough old trade-union bosses had been making new arrangements with a party left, in and out of Parliament, that offered them the promise of a nationalized Great Britain, controlled in its production by the Trades Union Congress and choreographed in its policies by the grass-roots constituencies of the country —the so-called Constituency Party. The arrangements made at Wembley gave the unions 40 percent of the votes in Labour's electoral college and left the Parliamentary Party and the Constituency Party to divide up the rest. Those arrangements were bound to change. The Labour Members of Parliament, meeting on their own, voted two to one against them. They said that Labour could not afford defectors —certainly not among its sitting Members—and most of them were convinced that people would in fact leave the party in protest. Thirteen Members, of course, did leave it for a new Social Democratic Party, among them David Owen and William Rodgers, who joined Roy Jenkins and Shirley Williams to complete the Gang of Four, which is what everybody calls the new Social Democratic leadership. These are liberal, educated, worldly politicians, and, taken as a "gang," they tend to prove the point that, left and right wings notwithstanding, a lot of the trouble in Labour has had to do with class—with young Fabians who head down from Oxford directly to the House of Commons and with aging armchair socialists who have rich wives and pretty Ladbroke Grove houses. Tony Benn may be the strategist of Labour's new "egalitarian" platform, but he would have been Viscount Stansgate if he had not renounced the title in 1963. Benn is part of a generation that grew up in the *noblesse oblige* days of the British left. Those days ended when the war did, and since then grass-roots power in the Labour constituencies has gradually been appropriated by a left different from the one Tony Benn grew up in—a left that will never see the inside of White's or tread a grouse moor, a left full of sulky ideologues with equivocal accents and polytechnic diplomas and just enough in the bank to pay the rent on a bed-sitter. The lumpenpolytechnic, people call them. Or the polytechnocrats. They are, at any rate, a world of bitterness away from the elegant young men who used to offer themselves up to working-class constituencies on the ground that they would make a better impression in Parliament than the locals. The polytechnocrats may have more in common, in the end, with the Tory proles—the cheeky back-benchers who put a Grantham grocer's daughter named Maggie Thatcher into No. 10 Downing Street when the gentlemen who used to settle the Tory leadership among themselves, and from their own kind, could not come up with a candidate anyone else was likely to vote for. Mrs. Thatcher had to do her time in the Tory constituencies, earning party power. She herself does not have much to say to Old Guard Tories like the diplomat at Whitehall who wanted what he called "the Rhodesia thing" settled, because it was "such a cloud over the Office."

There is vast closet wealth in England. A few dukes here and there may take in paying guests and turn their gardens into "safari clubs," and Piccadilly traffic may be snarled by Volvos now instead of by Rolls-Royces, but enough of England's rich have had the wit and the accountants to survive the punishing taxes of the last Labour years —taxes that got as high as 98 percent on unearned income—without ever having to sacrifice their faith that their own good times were good for everyone. Those benign patriarchs of the Conservative Party made their peace with the century by spending everyone's money but their own on the common good. They were sentimental about money the way Tories have always been sentimental about money, but Mrs. Thatcher has never been noticeably sentimental about anything, and neither have the sort of people who voted her into office—who include, in fact, some three million of the twelve million workers in the trade unions that originally founded the Labour Party and still pay 80 percent of Labour's bills.

Every week for almost a year, the *Sunday Times* has published a body count of the past week's employment casualties called "Jobless Britain." There have been weeks when ten or twelve thousand workers were laid off, weeks when just one bankrupt factory or closed dockyard cost five thousand jobs, weeks when no worker, anywhere in Britain, could say for sure that he was safe. Six hundred and fifty of the fifteen hundred Whitby potash miners lost their jobs in one week. Five hundred of the two thousand workers at the Glasgow plant of Collins, the publishing company, went in another. Even Rupert Murdoch, pouring three countries' worth of cheap-tabloid profits into the *Times* and its supplements, has had to start laying off typographers to keep the papers from another year of thirty-million-dollar losses. There is no logical reason for England to be going broke. Its North Sea rigs pull up a hundred million tons of oil a year—which means that for accounting purposes England is self-sufficient in oil and one of the few countries in the West with no balance-of-trade debts to the OPEC states. The Minimum Lending Rate—which is equivalent to our discount rate and is the gauge that economists use here—is no higher than France's, say, and for the moment a point lower than America's. Clearly, there is more to the bankruptcies and layoffs and shutdowns than the high cost of money. Half the population pays relatively low rent to live in Council housing, and in theory everyone has access to the free hospitals and doctors of the National Health Service, to free schools, to a hundred other perks and social services. And yet the country seems as fragile as a tea rose in the shadow of a Birmingham factory. The bankruptcy rate is close to what it was during the worst years of the Depression. More people are out of work than at any time since 1933, and mainly they come from the same kinds of jobs in the same places—the mines and shipyards and heavy-machinery plants of the North Country and of Wales and Scotland. They come from factories where conditions have not changed much since the Industrial Revolution—or, if they are lucky, since the more inventive days of the Great Depression. It is as if the English themselves, in a kind of misguided native pride, conspired to keep their industry out-of-date. After the war, they seem to have decided that they had nothing to learn, or even borrow, from the technology of neighbors like the French, who had capitulated, or like the Swedes, who had bought their peace as dropouts, or certainly like the Germans, who had lost.

When Mrs. Thatcher took over the government two years ago, with a program for what Labour called "dismantling the public sector" —the industries that the state owns or subsidizes or in one way or another guarantees—people talked about the end of socialism in Britain as if this were something that had actually been accomplished, neatly, at the polls. Mrs. Thatcher had persuaded them that she could put Britain, share by share, on the market, but she had no understanding with, or even authority over, the trade unions, and therefore no assurances to offer buyers. The result, of course, was that no one bid. Now she is in the predicament of having to underwrite a padded bureaucracy and a huge public sector, of which she disapproves, while presiding over the worst period that private industry, which she likes, has ever seen. The most interesting thing about Mrs. Thatcher's plans is probably that anyone believed in them—believed that a complicated state economy like Britain's, which by now is part of a fabric of attitudes and expectations, could be transformed at will into its opposite. It is obviously easier to nationalize than to denationalize. Marshal Tito managed denationalization, to some extent, with his famous Economic Reform of 1965, which converted Yugoslavia's state farms and factories into free-market workers' cooperatives, but even then the cost in human terms—one in every five Yugoslav workers out of a job—was enormous. Tito probably would have lost his own job in a country like Britain, where the state depends, in the end, on the voters' appetite for compliance. Democracy does not make for the easy "dismantling" of economic structures.

There is something touching about Margaret Thatcher and her enthusiasms. She seems to believe in Milton Friedman the way an English schoolgirl believes in Hobbits. She planned a triumphant offering of British Airways stock on the open market. She wanted to auction off the monopoly on delivering mail. At one point, she even would have sold an entire Nottinghamshire village, which had been left to the government as a historic trust—taking, as it were, the long view of her prerogatives as Great Britain's elected landlady. The village happened to be distinguished for a rare system of medieval strip-farming, and consequently there was a good deal of *Sturm und Drang* among the country's medieval historians—a group not normally given to wild public protest—before Mrs. Thatcher was persuaded to withdraw it from her portfolio of "negotiable properties." That portfolio still includes not only British Airways but also, among other things, British Rail, British Steel, the telephone company, and the mail service. Mrs. Thatcher is determined. After two years of disappointment, she still thrills to the logic of profit. She talks like a Jay Gould or a Cornelius Vanderbilt, but so far all that she has been able to sell is a few bus companies and resort hotels that British Rail owned and operated. British Airways, which was the plum in her portfolio, lost close to two billion pounds this past fiscal year. British Steel is so beleaguered that Mrs. Thatcher cannot even give away the steelworks at places like Consett—which, in fact, she tried to do. The Consett plant itself closed in September—one of the latest in a series of steel-industry shutdowns that have put ninety-six thousand men and women out of work.

In Britain, the public sector produces more than one-third of the national income, and Mrs. Thatcher, who believes in tight money, has already had to borrow what amounts to nine billion dollars over her industry budget to keep open what factories she can. The government under Mrs. Thatcher has ended up as its own best client, and the money supply that she was going to squeeze—squeezing with it the inflationary sponge of costs and waste and salaries—is actually going up by 22 percent a year.

Mrs. Thatcher has managed to get by until now because she taps a very real fear of organized labor among the country's petite bourgeoisie. She shares that fear herself. Her attitude does not make for a very useful or discreet politics, but it underlines the fact that a lace-curtain and Prince-Charles-and-Lady-Di-plate population still aches for gentility and thus subscribes to a politics of dissociation from the working class. England has never had a real social revolution. Cromwell's republic came (and went) too soon in Britain's economic history to transform the country's class—which is to say its management—structure. The great commune of 1871 was in Paris, not London. The country that had served Karl Marx as the model for the classic industrial state of *Das Kapital* survived its own Industrial Revolution and its Great Depression, its two world wars and the rise and fall of its world empire, with its old ruling class intact, with the ambitions of its bourgeoisie cleaned up like mob money in a Bahamian trust, and with very little room, real or psychological, for the sort of relentlessly philistine energies on which the rest of postwar Europe recovered. Great Britain has lived for a hundred years off the proprietary rhetoric of the Industrial Revolution, but the fact is that a hundred years ago European engineers were already writing that Britain's industrial plant, its new North Country technology, was neither as innovative nor as efficient as the new technologies in France and Germany, and were predicting that industry here would suffer from the contempt in which educated Englishmen held it, from the hothouse gamesmanship of England's managers. The reality is not so different. Business is still despised in England. People from the right schools and the right families do not usually run factories or manage corporations. There is still more cachet attached to a hairdresser or a punk designer than to a Jay Gatsby of British finance. And this is a fundamental fact of class that has nothing to do with politics. The left and the right have both suffered from a *défaillance*—from a gap between the almost literary class postures of their parliamentary leaders and the hardscrabble task-at-hand realities of power and solvency. In fact, there has been a tolerance, and even an enthusiasm, among Tories for the nationalizations that began in 1946 with Clement Attlee's Labour government, and one good reason is that a job with a state company like British Leyland or British Airways translates easily into service to Queen and country, and so is rather like a job in a ministry or at the Foreign Office, carrying no common associations of new money or of greed or aggressiveness—of being "keen," as the English say. The proper way to be in business in England is *noblesse oblige;* to be in business any other way is still one of those social burdens that used to complicate the prospects of some otherwise worthy daughter in a Jane Austen novel. There is, on the other hand, a distinction, even a pride, in maladaptation. Denis Thatcher, the Prime Minister's husband, was director of a subsidiary of Burmah Oil during the years that the company was going broke buying supertankers, and people talk about this now as if the connection were somehow appropriate to his present status. "We're just not good at growth here," they will say, and cheerfully concede that whatever choice they make will be the wrong one, because "we have no instinct for that sort of thing."

Still, when traditional Tories talk about disasters in state industries they tend to forget that they were often the people who ran those industries and ran them into the ground. They forget that it was a Tory Prime Minister, Harold Macmillan, who chose to celebrate the fragile prosperity of the late fifties with what, for Britain, was an orgy of public spending—that it was Macmillan, as much as Attlee or Harold Wilson, who endorsed the high expectations of the British welfare state. They blame the trade unions, because the unions—with their paralyzing strikes, their bloc votes for sale at Labour Party congresses, and their exploitations of the whole costly apparatus of the welfare state—are such logical targets for any public bitterness. Or some of them blame the Common Market; they used to blame it for freezing out British products and now, as members since 1973, they blame it for agricultural arrangements that hurt British fishermen and sheep farmers and for "harmonization" codes regulating parts and weights and packaging which make British machinery obsolete. They still blame the war, because the war forced the rest of Europe's industries to modernize, so to speak, by destroying them. And they blame their own new "radical right wing"—by which they mean Mrs. Thatcher and her friends—because they themselves have been accomplices in the Labour experiment, enjoying the ease and the guarantees, if not always the responsibilities, of public management. The state as an employer has spared them the disgrace of the marketplace, and so they do not like Mrs. Thatcher, who was evidently supposed to throw out the bath-water but leave them with the free run of the nursery.

Margaret Thatcher is a politician of high and alarming principles. At fifty-five, she is just young enough to qualify as a postwar Tory. She came of age politically in the 1940s—which means that she had no adult experience of the Depression, of the poverty and the anguish it in-volved. To older people in the party, she seems to lack that decent measure of social guilt which makes them vote for free school lunches and baby bonuses and big printings at the Bank of England to raise salaries when a strike spreads. She seems to accuse them of dealing in expectations and illusions as cavalierly as the trade unions do. She has few heroes among them. *Her* hero is the wartime Winston Churchill. Talking about Churchill's defeat at the polls in 1945, Mrs. Thatcher is as close to bathos as she ever gets. She is determined to fight her own war against Britain's eclipse, and so she has no time for the sort of Tory paternalism that treats Britain as its own last colony. To Mrs. Thatcher, the Harold Macmillans of her party are a little like sultans who order pretty pink walls put up and flowering trees planted along the roads of their kingdoms so that they never have to notice the slums and the suffering of their subjects.

Britain has been buying time with old symbols of abundance —which is why politicians like Mrs. Thatcher attach so much impor-tance to exploiting new ones. The image of a British oil rig standing alone in a treacherous and stormy sea is one of those new symbols —perhaps the only one Britain has—and they use it whenever they talk about the future. In fact, Britain has about ten to twenty years' supply of oil in the North Sea. The job of bringing it up is risky—people die every year on the rigs—and expensive. The government has had to pay its way by setting high tariffs and barrel-landing taxes. Only 11 percent of the available drilling sites have been licensed, and some local econo-mists say that over the long term Britain would be better off developing the sophisticated industries for which it has the skills—computer soft-ware or biomedical technology or microchips. (Microchips have taken on such a mystique here that people talk about starting a "microchip economy," as if England were a little one-crop country that had simply got its seeds mixed up.) They say that Britain, with the right planning, could buy any oil it needed from the Arabs and still come out ahead. The real value of oil wealth is political. The thought of an oil rig in

Britain's own North Sea waters is one of the few things that can be counted on to distract the British from the fact that old neighbors down the street in, say, Keighley are now bitterly at odds because one of them will have to be laid off to save the other's job. The most that can be said for Mrs. Thatcher in places like Keighley is that she makes no excuses to those neighbors. There is too much of the self-made—"I did it, you do it"—woman in her for her feelings about unemployment in Keighley to be anything but political in the strictest sense. She operates out of a kind of pure and unpatronizing insensitivity, and she has no social philosophy, no humanitarian confusions, to blunt her argument. Christopher Hitchens, of the *New Statesman*, tells a story that has Maggie Thatcher touring the schools in a run-down North London borough and trying to explain oxidation to the boys in a chemistry class (her own degree, from Oxford, is in chemistry) by asking them to consider what happens when they eat an egg with a sterling-silver spoon. Callousness like this is genuine. Workers who voted Tory may rail against Mrs. Thatcher now, but they are not distressed by her contempt for poverty; they are distressed because they expected her to cure them of poverty at the expense of other workers, and she failed. More than half the workers in the Trades Union Congress belong to white-collar unions or to the public-service syndicates known here as "dirty-white-collar" unions. They are the sort of people who (when they are not out on strike themselves) tend to be especially resentful of strikes that affect them—strikes like the long coal miners' strike in 1974 that brought down Edward Heath's government. They do not aspire to solidarity with an industrial proletariat. They have no longings for the "white heat" of technology, as Harold Wilson put it. They do not much care that Lancashire's woollen mills are closing at the rate of three a week, but they care a lot that Mrs. Thatcher gave way to the mineworkers' union this winter and kept open twenty-three of the country's oldest and least productive coal mines because she was unwilling to risk the sort of confrontation that finished Heath. They are people who voted Labour in the past and felt betrayed by politicians like Wilson and James Callaghan, whose rhetoric made them confuse public spending with public improvement, distribution with ownership, a few years' prosperity with social revolution. It is not hard to imagine the appeal of a Maggie Thatcher, arguing incentive and preaching a miraculous new doctrine called monetarism, which was going to revive British industry and British glory and reverse the incredible rate at which Europe had cut into domestic markets, flooding England with European goods and buying, they were told, so little in return.

The British are not the investors that Americans are. They do not gamble on the stock market or deal in risk capital. When they have money to invest, they invest it in property. They read Keynes, but they tend to take their economics from the Galsworthy novels that they loved at school, and with Mrs. Thatcher's abolition of foreign-exchange controls two years ago a lot of them hustled their money out of the country and into Krugerrands or Canadian real estate or American factories and banks and ranches. This was not what Mrs. Thatcher expected. Nor did she expect that a lot of Arab oilmen and Iranians in exile, moving their capital into England, would spend so much of it on Britishness instead of on Britain—on buying big Georgian houses off Grosvenor Square and expensive stud farms in the country. What she did expect from her exchange reforms and her capital-gains reforms and her corporate-tax reforms was active capital investment in British industry, but, as it happened, no one invested—not even the industrialists. British industrialists were simply not prepared to spend money on anything as risky as their own businesses or the government's businesses. And the petro-millionaires from Saudi Arabia and the sheikdoms, by shrewdness and temperament, knew better than to spend *their* money in the City when they could buy London itself, or at least make better interest on that money as short-term financiers. Mrs. Thatcher ended up presiding over a recession. She kept saying that unemployment was going to "discipline" inflation, but by early this year it was clear that one of the few things unemployment had disciplined was production. Too much sterling was in real estate or overseas or simply in the bank. The pound was "too expensive to spend," investors said, and "too expensive to borrow." Small, private companies, however energetic and resourceful, could not pay more and more each month for materials and oil just to have the satisfaction of funding up to 50-percent pay raises for a disabled public sector and at the same time underwriting the welfare costs of an 86-percent rise in unemployment. The companies that survived at all were not making any profit. They were caught in a vicious circle of paying a little less in taxes and a lot more for everything else, including the loans that might have seen them through. Compromises like Mrs. Thatcher's compromise with the coal miners rankle these small companies. They know by now that the compromises the state makes are inevitably compromises with the state's own employees (schoolteachers actually got about 8 percent more money than they were meant to, because a comparability board that was supposed to adjust state salaries to the level of salaries in the private sector made a mistake in its calculations), while the best that *they* can do to keep from going under is to fire a few more people and cut back on another set of orders. To them, Thatcher economics must begin to sound like Santayana's definition of fanaticism: "redoubling your efforts when you have forgotten your aim."

There is no shortage of money here. There is a shortage of desire. People are reluctant to put much faith in the idea of a new industrial capacity for the country when the old capacities have been ignored or unexplored or—as in the case of Britain's aircraft industry under Callaghan's government—absorbed by the state for its own access to industry's profits. Partly, it is lack of imagination that keeps so many people who think of themselves as capitalists terrified of capitalism. (W. H. Auden, who spent five years as a schoolmaster to some of the children of England's old money, liked to describe them as the real cream—"rich and thick.") Partly, it is the fact that England's new-money people—people in sales and advertising and in boom industries like construction and electronics—have been schooled in egalitarianism but not in any egalitarian public philosophy. New money has produced a bourgeoisie that never rose against an *ancien régime,* and the sons and daughters of that bourgeoisie now see themselves enlisted as middlemen, if not mercenaries, in a class war they want no part of. They read about Lord Vestey and the various Vestey sons and cousins—the richest family in the realm, polo-playing friends to the Consort—manipulating their way through Bermuda companies and Uruguayan trusts in order to live for sixty years without the bother of paying normal income taxes, cleared of trouble with Inland Revenue by the House of Lords. And mainly what those second-generation bourgeois learn from the story is to put their own money in Bermuda, too. They see labor as being so volatile that one small wildcat strike that began at a mine in Wales this winter could spread across the country and into Scotland and within a few hours involve more than fifty thousand mineworkers. They are used to this by now. The strikes that finished Callaghan, two winters back—"the winter of discontent," Londoners call it—spread even faster. The Prime Minister left for Guadeloupe after Christmas, fairly confident of his government, and came home to find the entire country on general strike and London itself with no garbage collectors or hospital workers or bus drivers, or even gravediggers. Londoners these days are not apt to turn on the telly for many more speeches about restraint and cooperation as being "natural" expressions of the social contract between the state and its workers.

This means, of course, that a lot of Englishmen will not—and often cannot—borrow money to put into their own companies. A government that sets commercial interest rates intentionally high does not give people much incentive to risk the money they do borrow on improving a business that could go under any day. And consequently the percentage of gross profits that companies reinvest in their physical plant, as opposed to, say, wages or advertising or dividends, is about the lowest in Europe. Monetarists like Mrs. Thatcher's Industry Minister, Sir Keith Joseph—"the mad mullah of money," reporters call him —say that in the end high-cost capital will reward efficient reinvestment by forcing business to be a lot more careful with the loans it takes and the capital it has. But in a way the "natural" price of a loan is only a function of the person who wants it. Its value reflects the kind of equation he makes between money and wealth. Americans, having neither a mystique of property nor a long tradition of bowing before the value of property, adjust to high interest rates when they have to. They tend to think of property mainly as something that translates into dollars. They borrow cash—some of them were borrowing at a prime rate of nearly 22 percent a few months ago—and they buy on margin, and when they have the money they want, native ethic compels them to spend it on making more. The psychology of money in America is a kind of salary psychology, an income psychology. America's plastic banking, the stupefying debt supported by a house of credit cards, rests on an assumption that everybody will be making more money in the future, and it has nothing to do with the credit system in England, with its courtesies and its overdrafts, which rests on class consciousness and commitments, and often on the assumption of property behind a loan.

The English clearly consider Americans frivolous in these matters. No one who has ever set foot in the Victoria and Albert Museum or watched the guests at a London dinner party check the heft of the silver —or, for that matter, spent time in an old British colony with people who have lost their imperial mission but not their houseful of sustaining imperial purchases—doubts that British materialism is a sacred institution, like the Church of England and the monarchy, and can make the acquisitive inclinations of others seem slapdash by comparison. Materialism here is just that—attachment to the material world. And the English think of money mainly as something that translates into a piece of that world—into property. They let their bills run at the tailor or the poulterer not because they are larcenous but because they really do not regard the cash they owe with the seriousness that they regard the suit or the chicken or, it goes without saying, the property on which their credit has been established. This is not merely something the rich do—turning their evasions into an aesthetic and their bank statements into a kind of financial *Yellow Book*. It amounts to a national attitude that affects lives and occasionally destroys them—an attitude that right now the government can exploit by withdrawing a worker's supplementary benefits if the worker has managed to acquire enough "property." Officially, anyone who has worked for more than two years and is laid off under the redundancy laws—"redundant" being a legal euphemism here for "fired"—can collect a lump-sum compensation payment amounting to at least two weeks' salary for every year, up to twenty years, of work. In practice, if he wants to collect certain other benefits he must prove "poverty" to the satisfaction of the state. This means that owning liquid assets worth more than a thousand pounds can disqualify him.

The wealth, especially in London, is in houses. A row house in Camden Town, bought by a worker for the equivalent of ten or fifteen thousand dollars in the sixties, now goes for as much as two or three hundred thousand. That kind of property represents enormous wealth to the worker, but it is probably all he has or will ever have. And there is no practical reason for him to sell it: another house in the neighborhood would cost him just as much. Right now, he has to pay heating bills on his house which are six times higher than they were before the oil crisis, and real-estate taxes that probably reflect the fact that his trendy new neighbors, who just paid $300,000 for houses on either side of his, have "upgraded" the neighborhood. He cannot afford to be an amateur about money, like those new neighbors. He can moonlight. He can cheat on his taxes. And if he works for the state, as one in four British workers does, he can "fiddle."

If perks are job benefits, fiddles are benefits to which one helps oneself, and helping oneself has become a national habit, an addiction, and has produced a kind of fiddle junkie, greedy and glassy and demoralized. Constantine Cavafy supposedly once said to E. M. Forster, "You English must never lose your money—otherwise you'll become dirty thieves like us." It is an anecdote that the British have been quoting, in a rueful way, lately. They want to be good sports, but they are rueful because they truly believed that corruption was something that began with the wogs at Calais—a specialty of those tin-pot Catholic countries that England used to defeat in wars. "What's the fiddle? What can I take home? And what time can I knock off?" These are the first three questions a British worker asks about a new job—or, rather, the first three questions he used to ask, back when there were new jobs to be had. Fiddling shows up as a kind of letting go of social affect. The sort

of people who shop on Mount Street and take their tea at the Con-
naught complain about it as a certain lack of civility. The people who
do their shopping on Oxford Street during lunch hour talk about the
pushing and kicking that go on at bus stops and wonder why no one
queues anymore—queuing being the local symbol of cosmic harmony,
like the end of Prospero's tempest or a stage sunrise after the last battle
in *Macbeth*. It is a common assumption here that nationalized industry
is a fiddle—that the rolls are padded, the hours forged, and the work
ignored. So is the civil service, at its more ordinary levels. The mechanic at Victoria Station who leaves at one in the afternoon to moonlight as a plumber has to have a friend to sign him out properly, and
he owes that friend something. The repairman at the Electricity Board
who takes a few days off each month will have his arrangement with
the assignment clerk who obligingly fills out his schedule with a list of
fictitious customers. The telephone man who installs new phones on
the quiet and at half the official price needs a mate at the company
warehouse to slip him those phones when he needs them.

    None of this is much different from petty corruption anywhere,
in any city, but in London it means that something "not done" is being
done. It is part of the decline that people talk about. (The Irish in
Camden Town like to say that England has saved them from God but
the fiddle has sent them to the Devil.) At any rate, it is impossible to
calculate the cost of this corruption, which is not so much corruption
on a grand scale as a series of little daily dishonesties, none of them
amounting to much alone. What *is* possible to calculate is the extent
to which a union pads its shop quotas or the way a city department
adjusts its staff recommendations to the fact that its budget, and often
its supervisor's salary, is going to depend directly on the number of
people carried on the books. One reason that three million workers and
at least as many shopkeepers and small businessmen and local entrepreneurs, from cabbies to blacksmiths, voted Tory at the last election
was that the fiddle had begun to affect them, and they were encouraged
by Mrs. Thatcher to blame Labour for the habit. Mrs. Thatcher promised them alternatives to the fiddle. She promised tax breaks, and as
soon as she won she reduced income taxes in the lowest tax bracket
from 33 to 30 percent. In the end, though, she took much more than she
gave. She paid for that 3 percent tax break by nearly doubling the Value
Added Tax—which is the British sales tax—to 15 percent, and also by
forcing up mortgages to 15 percent, so that families saving three pounds
a week in income tax often ended up spending ten pounds more on
mortgage interest. Just this March, in the third budget of her adminis-

tration, she raised the excise tax on liquor, gas, and cigarettes by more than 10 percent, and then she effectively raised income taxes, too, by overriding an old law that had allowed families to adjust their deductions to the inflation rate. She has cut important social services—school subsidies and health care and libraries and public housing—by cancelling two billion dollars' worth of new projects and by leaving old ones with their old budgets, which in purchasing terms means as much as 20 percent poorer every year. She has forced people to be willing to work for less money by letting them price themselves out of the jobs they had, but in the process she has endorsed an economy where there are no more jobs for them at any salary. She has realized the worst clichés about a divided Britain, with its poor industrial North and its bucolic South. Unemployment in the North is up to 16 percent of the labor force by now—20 percent in some towns—while in the South it is only 7 percent, and the most serious complaint in some southern villages is about high French tariffs on the local lamb chops.

There is one thing that everybody who grew up in the Labour Party agrees on, from the moderates who left it to start the Social Democratic Party to the old-time syndicalists who still rule the enormous fiefdoms of the Trades Union Congress, and this is that the class war in Britain has been at the heart of the country's troubles. It is this conviction, finally, that separates Labour people, and even ex-Labour people, from the Tories—the conviction that class, in its peculiar British exaggerations, is a force for social evil which cannot be simply acknowledged politically, as the Tories believe, or corrected politically, as the Liberals do, but must be purged from public consciousness before England is a healthy place to live. The class war has ruined relations in British industry—to the extent that there were any relations to begin with. Industry is unproductive here because the British worker has so little stake in the social whole. His stake is private, grudging. His leverage is the strike, the demonstration, the shutdown—not the contribution he makes. His resentment (like Maggie Thatcher's) has a long tradition. He is alienated not only from a job but from a whole network of appreciation and affect. He is "labor"—just that. He may be British to the core, but there is a pub-pride bluster to his Britishness that is likely to set his children street-fighting against the newest black and Asian immigrants.

People here look at industry in Sweden or in Germany or in France and puzzle over the high production quotas—the work energy, as it were—in those countries, forgetting that there is more to work energy than sleek new plants or a Weberian ethic, or even the Jacobin gaze of a French Communist foreman on his closed shop. There is a kind of equality of attitude. The Swedish worker, like the German worker and the French worker, is *somebody*— to himself, to his culture. He has a place and a stake in his country's future, and his children have at least the illusion of an open future of their own. He believes that he belongs to what is often described—awkwardly—as the new European meritocracy. His status may be as much a function of public hypocrisy as of public philosophy, but there is still a vigorous measure of self-esteem in him.

A lot can be said, and has been said, against the British trade-union movement. Peter Jenkins, of the *Guardian*, calls it a friend who has been on the booze too long—there is nothing you can do for it, no way to help it, and so you give up on it to save yourself. British unions are xenophobic, and they exploit resentment. They are often run by people who (the saying goes here) couldn't open a whelk shop in Brighton. They are less involved in brotherhood these days than in a scramble for pieces of a pie that can no longer feed them all. And by now they have started to fight among themselves for the pie. "The war of all against all," someone put it when the railroad unions started trying to do each other in because each wanted the labor monopoly at British Rail.

Eighty years ago, unions here invented the British Labour Party as their political arm. Eventually, they promised the party to enforce a kind of self-denying ordinance against strikes and social agitation if Labour governments delivered the goods to them—but they have contrived to strike and agitate during every Labour government in the party's postwar history. They control the party this way and, of course, by means of the thirty million pounds that the unions contribute yearly to the Labour Party's coffers. Every one of the twelve million workers in the Trades Union Congress owes his union a political levy along with his dues. He can take the time and trouble to "contract out" of his levy if he wants to—evidently, three million members did last year —but the union can pay the levy for him and in this way add his clout to its vote at party conferences and caucuses. The unions have appropriated so much power, in fact, that no Labour Party leader since Hugh Gaitskell had challenged their authority and won until the Gang of Four managed a kind of Pyrrhic victory by walking out on them. And yet there is still a strong conviction among liberal people here that the trade-union movement, for all its faults and tyrannies and corruption, may be the only hope for a decent deal for the majority. It is a conviction that the unions, at their worst, are still the British workers' best protection, because no one else is going to look after the boy in the coal mines or the grandmother in the textile mills—certainly not Labour's Oxbridge intellectuals sitting in Parliament and talking about their mission to lead the masses to a better world.

Part of the nostalgia that people feel, now that the Labour Party has so furiously divided, has to do with this old belief in a trade-union movement that would liberate a working class and, in so doing, liberate a nation from its stale equations of class and expectation. Nostalgia was not enough, though, to hold the party or the movement together. The politicians who walked out of the Labour Party made a point of complaining about "social Fascism" in the party's new policies and about unfortunate totalitarian impulses in some of its new spokesmen. They said that there was no room for discussion, let alone dissent, in the new Labour hierarchy. They said, for example, that social ownership of industry was not necessarily state ownership but, rather—and possibly more to the point—an equitable distribution of industry's benefits and resources; the party's latest platform, on the other hand, is all about nationalizing two hundred of the country's biggest private companies. Then, too, the Social Democrats did not give much priority to unilateral disarmament, nor do they consider NATO an especially compromising alliance, the way Tony Benn does and the new party leader, Michael Foot, seems to. And, despite the fact that Common Market arrangements ignore most of Britain's claims and exploit its weaknesses, they accepted the fact that 40 percent of Britain's trade is now with "official" Europe, that Germany has replaced America as Britain's biggest customer, and that to quit the Market at this point would probably be to hand England back to its old playschool industrialists and its most crippling chauvinists. The new Labour establishment, for its part, seems more distressed by the fact that Roy Jenkins got a virtually tax-free salary of sixty thousand pounds when he was running the Common Market, and Tony Benn—warming to his role as a kind of Savile Row Robin Hood of the Labour left—seems to think that if Britain abolished the Honours List and the House of Lords, the country would quickly take its place among the "other" Third World socialist republics and find in their trade networks a substitute for the Common Market. But even the most bitter defectors from the party —people call them "the peelers," to distinguish them from "the stickers," who dissent but stay—talk sadly about "the end of Labour as we knew it." They may see nothing but opportunism in the marriage of convenience made at Wembley between the old union bosses and the young clubhouse Marxists from the Labour hustings, but a lot of them left Wembley weeping all the same.

The anguish in the Labour Party is real. Members in Commons are torn, because they have always had the power to choose their own leader, who becomes the party leader and potentially the Prime Minister, and the new party rules take that power from them. They were free to choose the candidates, too, whenever a constituency opened up or a by-election was called, and the party, traditionally, approved their choices. They have always given themselves a kind of tenure, making a good, safe Labour seat a lifetime job, and they were rarely subject to constituency review, short of having a sex scandal or a bank heist in the family, and almost never subject to challenge from their own parliamentary colleagues. Like deputies or congressmen anywhere, they formed a clique, and over the years that clique has come to be a university, and even an Oxbridge, club. By the 1970s, nearly 70 percent of all the Labour Members in Commons were university graduates—in all of Great Britain in the 1970s, only 7 percent of the population went to university—and more than half of them came from Oxford or Cambridge, which accept students on the basis of a special examination that is not apt to be stressed in the curricula of comprehensive high schools in working-class neighborhoods of Scotland, say, or Wales, where Labour always gets its best majorities.

Education, in fact, is a real issue behind the rhetoric of the party split—this despite the fact that it was Shirley Williams who, as Harold Wilson's Minister of Education, fought for the new comprehensive-school system that is causing so much of the Labour bourgeoisie to bolt the party with her now. England has been unique in postwar Europe for the inequities of its school system. Other Europeans seem to take some pride in the fact of institutions where *tous se rencontrent*, as the French say—institutions where the children of a country come together and where performance, at least for the moment, stands some chance against origin and wealth. Those institutions are usually the schools and the Army. England has had no draft since 1960, and as for the schools here, children from good families have gone to public schools and a handful of exceptional grammar schools for so many generations that they speak what amounts to a different language from the working-class children they will eventually confront as employers or, in the case of Labour, represent in Parliament. They have an education in "England" but virtually no education in the real country they have been promised to rule. They buy their place in the queue, as the saying goes, with high tuitions at schools that get to maintain charity tax status while organizations like Amnesty International pay taxes, because they are considered political by the Charity Commissioners. The rest of the country's children used to run a gauntlet called "streaming," which meant that children in state schools were tested at the age of eleven and their futures decided then and there by the local school boards. If they did well on those tests, and were nice children, they might go on to grammar schools and prepare for university or for the good polytechnics in cities like London and Manchester. The rest of them—that is, three-quarters of the eleven-year-old children in the country—were streamed into demonstrably inferior local schools and never got another chance.

There was no doubt about the need for a change in British education when Shirley Williams, following Anthony Crosland's lead, absorbed the grammar schools into a system of local comprehensive schools, but often all that their change managed to accomplish was to deprive those working-class neighborhoods with grammar schools of the only institutions they were proud of, and a lot of bright working-class children of the one opportunity they had for the education they deserved. It made those children a litmus generation in cities where the people most capable of and articulate about standing up to a mediocre school board were now sending their own children off to private schools and boarding schools as young as possible to avoid "sacrificing" them to other people's Labour principles. Some teachers say that the comprehensives isolated working-class children more, if anything, than they had been isolated in the old system. Others—Molly Hattersley, for one, who runs a big London comprehensive and is head of the country's comprehensive-school principals' association—say that comprehensives were the only way to assure those children of any academic attention at all. There are parents, though, who mainly blame the teachers, not the system, saying that too many British teachers, out of normal schools and second-rate polytechnics and practicing a kind of punishing self-made socialism, resent the ten or twenty middle-class children in a class of one or two hundred, begrudge them the time and the encouragement it would take to prepare them for university examinations, and in general act out a kind of class rage, refusing to educate a new elite, as they see it, and making a dubious equation between classroom democracy and education at the lowest common denominator.

In a way, the children of wellborn Labour Party liberals became a kind of metaphor for their parents' complaints about the party. When the parents said that England's new comprehensive schools were no more "educational" than those expensive public schools where the girls got chilblains and the boys got flogged and everyone developed character—that the point of the comprehensives was not academics but social integration—they were also saying that they did not want to stay in a Labour Party that would soon be run by people who were integrated and ignorant and therefore susceptible to easy sloganism, people desperate to belong and untrained to think for themselves. They were right about slogans. Labour's split in March was accompanied by a lot of catchy rhetoric about a workers' state, but in most ways the crisis in the party was England's old crisis over class and power.

There is obviously no fair way to elect a leader in a parliamentary system. People vote directly for their leaders only in presidential states like France, and those states, in the main, are fairer only in that they situate inequity somewhere else in the political process. Every so often, there is talk here about changing to a system of proportional representation, the feeling being that this might break the stalemate pattern of British politics and encourage new kinds of coalition, giving smaller parties—like the Social Democrats or the Liberals or, for that matter, the Communists and the Trotskyites—a share of parliamentary power proportionate to their share of the national vote taken as a whole. Proportional systems make complicated politics, though, in any country. They do not have much of a track record for stability, and they seem to release amazing possibilities for collusion and corruption. The system that exists in Britain is open less to corruption than to interpretation. Roy Jenkins and Shirley Williams and their friends say that Labour in Parliament represents a much larger public than the Labour Party itself—for the simple reason that millions of people with no official connection with the party voted Labour in parliamentary elections—and that consequently the Labour Members' choice of a leader and potential Prime Minister most accurately reflects that public's interest and preferences. Labour in the constituencies, on the other hand, claims that its public is in fact often unrepresented in Parliament —especially in districts where the Labour vote was heavy and the Tories won by only narrow margins—and so party workers now want *their* say in choosing Labour candidates and leaders. As for the trade unions, *they* take it on faith that Labour belongs, as it were, to labor. They tend to look at the Labour Party as a sort of closed shop that produces politics. They pay their money to put their own men into party power—though rarely their women, Britain's trade unions being about as feminist as Margaret Thatcher, who managed to appoint two women to a government of fifty-five state secretaries, ministers, and lawyers—and so they are not overly concerned with questions of, say, "democratic consultation" when a union secretary is about to cast a bloc vote at a party congress in the name of a quarter of a million members. Then, too, there is still that Labour idea of the London Conference of 1918—the idea of a great national political party of social-ist consensus. That idea is resonant enough today to have landed a model Oxbridge radical in the party leadership. Michael Foot, who has had the job since October, is a Methodist preacher's son. He is a man of weakness and charm and a fuzzy, fiery pacifism that seems to do better for itself in antinuclear parades than in antinuclear negotiations. A worrier. A waffler. A romantic of sixty-seven who represents the earnest and gently hypocritical myth of an England that is fading. Tony Benn is a Labour pro more in the psychological genre of a Margaret Thatcher. They are the natural antagonists. They stand for punishing times, bad sportsmanship, and a brutal politics. They know the power of a union bloc or a party constituency to mobilize people as weapons, and they do not waste too much time on democratic niceties. They have neither the time nor the patience for the fretful confusions of an older England, grieving for itself.

May 1981

WEST BERLIN: THE WALL

KEEP SMILING!
NEW YORK HASN'T GOT A WALL!

Someone sprayed this on the Berlin Wall last month, not far from the no-man's-land of barricades and tank traps and police dogs on the other side, which was once the Potsdamer Platz, the center of the city —Times Square, people used to call it back in the days when both squares were doing better than they are now. The graffito was in English, so it could have been the handiwork of an American— a soldier, say, or a tourist. Tourists come to Berlin just to see the wall. They expect their money's worth of spray-paint sentiment, and they are apt to supply it themselves if they are disappointed. Berliners tend to avoid the wall, or at least to ignore it. They have lived with the wall since the morning—twenty years ago last August 13—when thousands of East German soldiers and factory workers appeared suddenly on the streets of the city and sealed off the Western Sectors. The wall is a fact of Berlin life by now, grotesquely normal, cutting Berlin in half, like a jagged line drawn by a demented giant. A generation of Berliners has been born to the sight and sensitivities of a divided city. They accept the fact that their world is an enormous cell—185 square miles, bounded by 100 miles of barbed wire and white concrete. They live an island life, and if a friend or a parent gets depressed or wakes with nightmares or goes crazy they are likely to call his symptoms *Mauerkrankheit*, or wall illness. They rarely join the tourists who climb the wooden steps to the rickety little platform near the Potsdamer Platz to look down into the eastern half of the city. Berliners avoid the wall precisely because it *is* a fact of life. What is intolerable to them now is not the wall itself but the fact that the wall has lost its drama. In a way, they are proud that strangers find the wall alarming. They have a kind of nostalgia for the invigorating fear that *they* felt back in the days of the Berlin blockade, when planes were landing every two minutes, carrying not just food and fuel but a measure of self-esteem to a city that a lot of Germans had rather hoped would disappear under Russian bulldozers, taking the past with it, as it were—taking with it twelve unspeakable years of German history. Berlin in 1948 was no longer the doomed capital of two lost wars but the capital of a new war, a cold war. The blockade had suddenly made Berliners heroes. It had turned the blitzed capital of Hitler's Reich into a freedom fortress in the malignant East of Soviet power. It lent the rhetoric of the frontier to the experience of an otherwise meaninglessly divided city, and the Berlin Wall completed that rhetoric. The wall gave people here a sense of mission. It made a virtue of their ambiguous citizenship. It was a hundred-mile concrete correlative of the complications and the valor of being a West Berliner —guarded by an occupying army, attached for all practical purposes to a country that could then be reached only by sealed railway car or by air shuttle, out of touch with, and even out of sight of, a million of one's closest neighbors. *"Ich bin ein Berliner,"* John F. Kennedy said after the wall went up. Berliners repeated it in the first flush of a seductive new identity, leaving unresolved the identity of friends, and even family, across the wall, who had no choice now in the matter of who *they* were. There were sixteen million Germans left in the German Democratic Republic on that August 13, and the wall was really intended for them —to keep them home. More than three million people had fled East Germany by 1961—some eighteen hundred a day during that final summer. I know two brothers, men in their fifties, whom the war and then the wall separated. "So I am on the wrong side again," the brother in East Berlin wrote in a letter after the wall went up. Ten years passed before the brothers saw each other again, and by then each was a good party man in his own Berlin, with a job in government. Besides, by then an agreement had been negotiated between the four occupying powers —Britain, France, the United States, and the Soviet Union—and while it mainly concerned Allied access rights and transit traffic, it did pro- duce a kind of local détente. The Quadripartite Agreement, as it was called, went into effect in June of 1972, and after that West Berliners with the time and the checkpoint patience and the hard currency could cross over into East Berlin to see friends and family, and even do some business, and East Berliners who had retired could move west and let

West Germany pay their pensions. It meant, too, that the brothers I know could send presents to their nieces and nephews, and even get together for Christmas dinners and for family funerals—though always in East Berlin, since East Berliners without official or "approved" business in the West rarely get to cross over into West Berlin, and most of them have given up applying to their government for permission. But 1961 was the last time that either of the brothers mentioned "sides" or talked politics. There is nothing now to talk *about*, the brother in West Berlin says; he seems to miss the tension of the Berlin blockade and the old border crises—the tension of those terrible, heroic, *political* moments, which the Agreement reduced to the status of little disturbances in daily life. A lot of West Berliners miss the tension. They sense that there is a kind of monstrous irrelevance to West Berlin today, that the subsidized and spacy energy of their city is in fact the energy of an imploding claustrophobia. They sometimes say that from the point of view of morale they were better off before the Agreement—that it was the Agreement and, with it, Willy Brandt's *Ostpolitik*, the policy of reconciliation with East Europe, that first suggested to the West that life in walled Berlin was "normal."

There is nothing normal about Berlin. Its *raison d'être* is emergency—emergency is mainly what has made the queer arrangements of life in West Berlin tolerable—and without it the city seems to suffer from a kind of civic emptiness. In a way, the idea of a "normal" Berlin has been more undermining than liberating. It is an idea that suits West Germans better than West Berliners, because Berlin is West Germany's hair shirt, a permanent object lesson in the consequences of the country's past savagery, and West Germans prefer their object lessons calm and at a safe remove, providing sentiment, and even shame, but not the discomforts of enacted penitence. They are willing to pay for that preference. In fact, they paid nearly ten billion Deutsche marks last year—about 55 percent of West Berlin's budget—in direct subsidy to the city, and billions more in indirect subsidies like tax breaks and bonuses and special business credits, which the government here prefers to call "promotions." Intellectuals in West Berlin say that these subsidies are a form of blood money, that maintaining Berlin has been the most dramatic, if not always the most convenient, way for West Germany to clear its conscience—a way of buying out of the slow, dispiriting business of moral recovery and historical reflection, so that West Germans can get on with the more pressing business of their celebrated economic miracle. They grumble about the cost, especially now that inflation in the Federal Republic is higher and the mark is falling, but most of them know that ten or eleven billion marks a year is not such a heavy price to pay for purity. It is the Allies, after all, who have to maintain a Berlin garrison of twelve thousand soldiers—more than half of them American—and keep the runways clean at Tempelhof Airport.

The Occupation of Berlin began with the conquest of the Reich, and for America it was even then more symbolic than strategic. Eric Warburg, the head of the Hamburg merchant-banking dynasty, who had spent the war attached to the intelligence branch of the United States Army, and was concerned with the disposition of Western power, was one of the people who urged the Allies to trade their presence in Berlin, if necessary, for the obvious—and not only to a merchant banker—advantages of a West German Elbe and, with it, control of shipping on Central Europe's most important waterway. The argument for occupying Berlin had to do with a kind of moral strategy—with *la grande revanche* of Charles de Gaulle and the Free French, who had had their own capital humiliated under Nazi Occupation, and with some sort of tangible, final victory for an exhausted Britain, and especially for London, after years of German blitz. That argument was much more powerful. The Russians took Berlin, and then the rest of the Allies arrived to share it, eventually pulling back to the present borders.

Today, West Berlin is for all military purposes indefensible, but in spite of that, 1,900,000 people—half of them postwar settlers—have been encouraged to stay here and plan their future here, and they understandably demand to be defended somehow. They are terrifically indulged. West Germany tends Berlin like the hothouse flower it is —always out of season, under a bell jar of soft jobs and subsidies. Berliners are cynical. They have come to enjoy the fuss, and West Germans, for their part, have come to resent *them* and the financial burden they represent—not to mention the guilt—though most of their outbursts against Berlin and Berliners are followed by effusive and even teary protestations of affection, as if the subject of Berlin were automatically an exercise in self-censorship. Straining toward respectability, West Germans do not know what to make of this city which reacts so splendidly to trying times but takes up "normalcy" with a kind of kinky torpor that mocks their earnestness.

Berlin's history as the capital of a united Germany was, like that of united Germany, a seventy-five-year disaster. Berlin was nearly synonymous with war—or, rather, with interludes of peace so brief, so fragile, that people today unconsciously extend them, taking, say, Wei-

mar Berlin well into the 1930s, forgetting that the Berlin of Wystan
Auden and Christopher Isherwood was already Hitler's Berlin, too.
Certainly Berlin never mellowed as a city or a culture. It was always
provisional, and it is still provisional—which may be why people who
live here prefer its unsettled, edgy tone to the aggressive propriety of
other German cities. Berlin at its best was a vulgar town, lively and
tough and popular. It thrived on new money and on new blood
—qualities that Germans today can speak of with chilling sentimental-
ity, as if Berlin had always cherished the Jews and the Slavs who gave
the city so much of its wit and temper.

The *Gastarbeiter* in Berlin today—230,000 foreign workers and
their families—are in a long tradition of immigration to Berlin. The
Turks who were recruited after the wall went up to fill the jobs that
had belonged to East German workers have a lot in common with the
Poles who started coming here a hundred years ago to take the jobs that
no one else wanted. Berliners complained then about the Poles, who
they said were lazy and backward, and they complain now about the
Turks—120,000 Turkish peasants from Anatolia—because cities like
Frankfurt and Hamburg and Düsseldorf, recruiting earlier, got all the
Italians and Yugoslavs and Greeks.

Still, Berliners make do. It is one of the things about them that
alarm the bourgeoisie in West Germany, which has the space to keep
its own *Gastarbeiter* relatively out of the way, in workers' suburbs and
factory stalags. West Germans suspect Berlin of arty, foreign, and
erotic tendencies—of having a bad influence on children and the national rectitude. With its foreigners and its students and a couple of
hundred thousand free spirits of one sort or another who, when
pressed, will frankly describe themselves as "freaks," Berlin is like a free
port of the mind, a trip in every sense. It is as if the wall had given
Berliners the kind of freedom that prisoners and kindergarten children
have—had made them, by definition, not responsible. They are bound
not so much by a common cause as by the shared pleasure of unaccountability. They improvise their reality. They assume that their city
is a European New York. They talk about island nerves, and about the
special humor of the born survivor. They talk about walled-in West
Berlin as if it were Manhattan in a blizzard or a blackout or during a
garbage collectors' strike. They say that a sense of what-are-we-doing-
in-this-crazy-place inspires the same sort of gruff and democratic col-
legiality they associate with New York from American magazines and
movies. They talk about the anarchic intelligence of the place. They
make Berlin wisecracks and Berlin jokes. (East Berliner goes to a de-

partment store and asks for scissors. Salesman says, "No scissors are on the third floor. On this floor we have no shoes and no stockings.") They refer to the West German bourgeoisie as if it were a breed peculiar to the Federal Republic. They say that the boring people—the serious people who want to make serious careers and raise serious German children—move quickly to the West but that everything interesting that happens in and for Germany happens here. They say that they have a hot, subversive culture—a counterculture—and they try to ignore the fact that about a third of the population of West Berlin is old-age pensioners and bureaucrats. They brag, but then they have few options besides bravura. They often refer to themselves as *freischwebende Intellektuelle*—free-floating intellectuals. They miss an acknowledged kinship with their counterparts in East Berlin, but a lot of them still associate a sense of *Volk* and common culture with Nazism and its perversions of identity. Artists and intellectuals who leave East Germany—they are about the only people besides pensioners who *can* leave, the feeling in the German Democratic Republic being that good minds and independent imaginations constitute a public nuisance —often prefer to stop and settle in West Berlin, "in the shadow of the wall," as they sometimes put it. A lot of them are reluctant to leave a city of so many contradictions and ambiguities and fertile tensions for the pervasive *Bürgermentalität* of the Federal Republic. "I think Berlin is the world," the young writer Thomas Brasch said after he had moved from East to West Berlin at the suggestion of his Minister of Culture, who gave him two days to stop publishing or start packing. "I try not to be *more* than what I write. I want to write deep, not wide. And here, where I live, I find the world. Fascism and Communism. East and West. Jews and Christians."

West Berlin literally rose from its rubble. Modest estimates in 1945 put the destruction of prewar industrial Berlin at between 75 and 80 percent—some of it bombed away by the Americans and the British and the rest stripped by the Russians, who were under orders to send home anything useful or inventive that was left. The new Berlin was built on politics, and on American money. The Kurfürstendamm, running like a village high street from the ruins of the Kaiser Wilhelm Memorial Church to the ponds and meadows of the Grunewald, replaced the Friedrichstrasse, in the Russian Sector, as the place to shop and eat and stroll. People who before the war had watched the world go by from smart cafés at the corner of Friedrichstrasse and Unter den Linden took up their tables at Savignyplatz instead. The restoration of

East Berlin was a subdued affair; its new public buildings had the sort of severe banality that Communist governments tend to associate with proletarian authenticity, and in some ways the most interesting change in the city in thirty years was the recent restoration of Frederick the Great and his horse to their pedestal on Unter den Linden. (The East German government has now officially recognized the existence of Frederick, in keeping with a new policy of what it calls "developed socialism.") East Berlin today is shoddy and dull, but then West Berlin is shoddy and garish. West Berlin is as provisional, in a way, as it seems to feel. There is an almost colonial look to a lot of the buildings off the Kurfürstendamm, as if they had been built for settlers with somewhere else to go in the end and would need only a little bougainvillea in front to fit nicely in Rabat or Tunis. As for the new "public" Berlin, the enormous exposition hall that opened in 1979 to lure trade shows and conventions to the city turned out to look like an aluminum lunchbox. The Berlin Philharmonic, designed by an architect from the port city of Bremen, looks like a beached boat. There are parts of Dahlem given over to Army barracks and bungalows, split-levels and supermarkets, which could be any base anywhere in America. In Dahlem, it is hard to imagine that neighborhoods like Kreuzberg and Schöneberg and Wedding—old neighborhoods, near the wall—are still so derelict. *Gastarbeiter* live there, and so do squatters, just minutes away from the lovely parks and woodlands (a third of West Berlin is still kept clear by zoning laws) intended to disabuse Berliners of their longing for old, forbidden countrysides beyond the wall. There is a famous strip joint in a porno district of Berlin which caters mainly to soldiers and foreign workers and to Third World diplomats, who have special checkpoint privileges and can easily cross over from the East at night for some Western vice. In it, every customer sits alone in a little room and peers through a keyhole at the same girl taking off her clothes. Berlin, in a way, is like that girl shivering in the center of a circle of keyholes: it belongs to no one and to everyone. Its geography, its old place in the Prussian landscape, has been replaced by a kind of psychic space. It is as maddeningly open-ended as a night prowl begun at a keyhole by a lonely diplomatic clerk from Bulgaria or Angola.

West Berlin is, to begin with, a legal fiction, constantly under negotiation and revision by Occupation officials and Bonn ministers and local politicians. It runs itself, in a way, according to the needs and conveniences of the moment. Thirty-six years after the war, Occupation law is still officially the law of West Berlin, and judicial rhetoric has to do with sectors, not borders. But the West Germans claim Berlin as a *Land*, or German state, under their constitution, and add, by way of a footnote, that federal jurisdiction has been "temporarily suspended" by the Allies, thus keeping their claim active. In the same way, they keep their claim to a united Germany active, too. Officially, Bonn is still their "provisional" capital. Officially, East Germany does not exist for them as a foreign state; they call their embassy in East Berlin a *ständige Vertretung* (a permanent mission) and their ambassador a *Missionschef*. It has been the common assumption that no compassionate community of Germans can exist as long as there are two Germanys, and so it is still heretical to suggest that the real German recovery can occur only when it is openly accepted that there are now two German states, and that in all likelihood there will continue to be two German states in our lifetime. Günter Gaus, who opened the first West German mission in East Berlin in 1974 and stayed for nearly seven years, suggested as much in an interview in *Die Zeit*, but Gaus, of course, was Willy Brandt's man in East Berlin and shared Brandt's passionate concern for a humane policy toward East Germany. Helmut Schmidt replaced Gaus late last year with his own man, Klaus Bölling, and Bölling is a loyal party man, unlikely ever to embarrass his Chancellor in one of the country's most important newspapers.

East Berlin, for its part, considers itself the capital of the German Democratic Republic, and *its* particular fiction is that someday, somehow, all of Berlin will fall under its jurisdiction. The Occupation powers, in turn, are careful to preserve *their* Berlin fiction, which holds that East Berlin is still the Russian Sector of an unresolved war zone, and not anybody's capital. America, for instance, still calls its embassy in East Berlin an embassy *to*, not *in*, the German Democratic Republic. And in the end what all the euphemisms and odd prepositions add up to is a convenient cover for a lot of human anguish and a diplomatic conundrum.

The Occupation armies, small as they are, keep very much in evidence in West Berlin. The British wax their cars, and the French dress up in their fanciest uniforms whenever they have messages to deliver or calls to pay. The Russians, on the other hand—in keeping with their contention that East Berlin is no longer under Occupation authority but belongs entirely to the G.D.R.—have long since pulled back most of their troops to the edge of town, where they tend to get lost in the Prussian forests. The soldiers one sees in East Berlin patrolling the wall are German soldiers. Karlshorst, in East Berlin, is still the site of the major Soviet command headquarters in East Germany, but most of the 400,000 Russian soldiers in the G.D.R. are off in the countryside. The Russians, in a sense, have made the wall their proxy in Berlin. Only 170,000 East Germans have managed to escape since 1961, and they have made their way to the West mainly through other Eastern European countries. Not many people are willing to attempt the wall itself anymore—there are twelve thousand East German soldiers on patrol, and six hundred East German attack dogs. Seventy-two people have died trying over the past twenty years, and the price of success these days runs to roughly twenty thousand dollars for "arrangements." Germans on both sides of the wall call this lucrative trade in lives "the refugee business"; in fact, it is many businesses, the biggest of them run by a Berlin entrepreneur who has long since taken himself, and his bank account, to Switzerland.

West Berlin has thus settled into a state of permanent instability. The Allied military keeps its old extraordinary privileges. Questions of military housing and services and education still fall under Occupation law. The Berlin Document Center, which contains the Nazi archives, is still in Dahlem, run by the American mission. Mainly, though, the military leaves West Berlin to its own problems. Berlin has a parliamentary system of government, complicated by the fact that in an emergency Bonn can intervene—as it did last January, when the Social Democratic mayor lost a vote of confidence in the city's parliament and had to resign: Helmut Schmidt stepped in with a new mayor to run the city until new elections could be held. The city follows West Germany's constitution and the Federal Republic's legal code— the difference here being that laws passed by the Bundestag in Bonn are also put to the West Berlin parliament and to the Allies, who have a formal veto power. Negotiations of authority that do go on usually involve the courts and questions of judicial jurisdiction. Two years ago, for example, a woman who lived in a nicely wooded suburb in the American Sector petitioned a visiting judge from New Jersey— a Federal District Court judge named Herbert Stern, who had just convened the United States Court for Berlin, for the first time in its history, to hear a hijacking case—to enjoin the United States Army from completing a new housing project in her suburb. The case Judge Stern was hearing involved an East German who had stolen a Polish plane and flown it to Tempelhof, the airfield in the American Sector of Berlin, which is, by Occupation law, under American administration. No one knew for sure whose case it was or whether extradition was in order. (One of the problems was that West Germany had nowhere, legally, to send the hijacker, since it does not recognize East

Germany; besides, its constitution forbids the extradition of any German national to a "foreign" country.) Several federal judges from
America had already begged out of going to Berlin before Judge Stern
was drafted, and Stern, to the distress of his drafters, turned out to be
rather strenuously radical as a jurist. He convened a jury of Berliners
and at the same time guaranteed the hijacker due process under American law—and then the Americans put him on a plane and flew him
home before he could get to any more cases, including the case of the
woman defending her suburban woods. The woman, on the other
hand, warmed to this new idea of due process for Berliners under the
laws of the United States. Her lawyer—a young partner of Otto Schily,
who had guided the defense during the first of the Baader-Meinhof
trials and is considered Germany's preeminent civil-rights lawyer
—took the case of the housing project through the American District
Court system, right up to the Court of Appeals in Washington, where
the woman finally lost.

It is obvious that the West Berlin government was well out of a
case involving hijacking and extradition claims and hostages—what
with 320 West Germans in East German prisons and the East Germans
already furious because West Germany had refused to extradite a girl
from the G.D.R. charged with killing her father. It is obvious, too, that
people here are going to want some say about any exploitation of the
city's "wilderness," especially since it is the only wilderness they are
ever likely to have. And it is obvious that most people will adapt
eventually to confusions of authority—will come to accept the political
uses of confusion and, when they can, make good use of it themselves.
(When Stefan Aust, a young news producer at North German Television, was refused access to information about the shooting of a suspected terrorist in West Berlin in the late sixties, he called an American
lawyer, who demanded the records he wanted under the American
Freedom of Information Act.) The trouble is that a lot of Berliners have
adapted too well. They have been spared the inconvenience of discipline in their lives and of competence in their jobs, and by now no one
seems to expect these things of them. About a quarter of all the salaries
in West Berlin are paid directly by the government, and a lot more are
either subsidized by the government or are guaranteed by the government. West Berlin sends deputies to Bonn, and those deputies keep
busy behind the scenes in party politics—being ineligible, under Occupation law, to vote on any of the legislation put to the Bundestag
—but mainly Berlin is a kind of farm team for West German politics.
People are sent to Berlin to try out, as it were, for the Federal Republic,

and if they acquit themselves well here—which is not so har
with a little work, in a city that is practically bonded against inadequacy
—and show their loyalty to the party that sent them by not complaining, they are awarded with a ticket home and power somewhere else.

The trip through any of the Berlin checkpoints can take a few
minutes or an afternoon, depending on what the guards at the eastern
end of the checkpoint had for lunch or on the situation in Poland, but
either way it is a psychologically wearing trip. Millions of people from
the West—West Berlin *and* West Germany—have crossed into the
G.D.R. over the past ten years. The traffic was running at about seven
million crossings a year until October 1980, when the East Germans,
worried by social revolution in Poland and wanting to discourage visits
from the West—and the news and talk that usually come with them
—doubled (and, in the case of West Berliners, tripled) their currency-
exchange fee. Then the number of visits started falling. Usually, West
Germans get into East Berlin with much less fuss than West Berliners
—who, oddly, have an easier time than other Germans getting into the
rest of the G.D.R. West Berliners complain about checkpoint frisks and
long delays, but what they complain about most is the strain of maintaining ties in East Berlin, knowing that they will be the ones to do the
crossing—that the burden of friendship rests with them—since it is
almost impossible for an East Berliner to cross over on a visit. East
Berlin has its elite, and obviously that elite has its privileges. The
Berliner Ensemble wants to play New York and will probably get there
with no more trouble than it has getting to Budapest or Prague. But
it is not likely to play West Berlin. Writers like Wolfgang Kohlhaase
and Christa Wolf are more likely to turn up in residence at the University of Iowa or apartment-sitting on Central Park West than at the Café
Paris, off the Kurfürstendamm, where a lot of West Berlin's writers
come to drink and talk. Actually, it is easier, and takes less time, for an
intellectual in East Berlin to fly to London than to get permission to
see his friends twenty minutes away in Charlottenburg. The problem
for an East Berlin intellectual is that his government suspects that, like
most other East Berliners, he is going to measure success not by the
standards of colleagues in Prague or Moscow but by the standards of
colleagues across the wall in chic neighborhoods like Charlottenburg.
His government, in fact, would rather that he leave for good than
import the kind of longing that is bound to show in his work and color
his influence.

Thomas Brasch says that if people in East Berlin began to talk about the wall, the government would have to tear it down—which is another way of saying that the problem of longing is simple: longing spreads. Still, it has been twenty years since East Germany bothered to jam the radio and television transmissions from West Berlin. The lure of the West—its fine freedoms and its shallow luxuries—is part of the daily life of every East Berliner with a radio or a television set. East Berliners keep a sort of body count of friends and neighbors who have been arrested trying to flee to the West and sent to prison. And yet at night they sit down to West German television news and programs and commercials. The State Opera buys fabric for its costumes at the Ka De We—the Kaufhaus des Westens, West Berlin's best department store—and the people who go to the opera follow the sales and the styles at the Ka De We and are up on the night life along the Kurfürstendamm. Nights in East Berlin are quiet. The streets are dimly, economically lit. There is a soft, almost nineteenth-century glow to the suburbs, as if some painter a hundred years ago had caught the city in a haze of gaslight and fog. Visitors find this "old" Berlin quaint and calming. They ask their friends to show them "Brecht's Berlin" —the proletarian Berlin. They look for the ancient quarter where the city's workers once lived—dense, squalid, full of a life that in the visitors' minds is always set to Kurt Weill music. But that Berlin is gone, bombed in the war. No worker in East Berlin today thinks of himself as a prole anyway. He likes the Western euphemism—*Arbeitnehmer,* or "work-taker"—which makes of work a kind of gracious, voluntary gesture. He saves his money for a big veneered wall unit that will look like the wall units that appear to him in such a dazzling variety of shapes and sizes on West Berlin television. His children arrive at the theater or the museum on their school trips dressed to the last child in imported bluejeans. Those children face a planned and packaged future —East Germany, like Russia, wants to choose careers for its children, educate them accordingly, and then send them off to wherever the state needs them—but some of them escape by forming rock bands. A lot of them, in fact: East Germany today is said to have more rock musicians under the age of twenty-five than it has young Communists.

Intellectuals here say that despite the harshness of official East Berlin—the "Communism with a Prussian face" of Western cartoonists —there is often a more humane quality to daily life across the wall, a respect for common people and common pleasures: the intimacy and the feeling of solidarity that men and women who live under oppressive or illegitimate regimes sometimes seem to have. It is a feeling that defecting East Berlin intellectuals miss. Whatever they despise in the official East German state, they know that the material passion of West Germany has pushed back a necessary consciousness of the Nazi past. They know that a generation of West Germans has drugged itself with prosperity, and that—however cynically, however politically—East Germany remembers the war, and sees to it that its children know that Erich Honecker, the East German Communist Party Secretary, was a resistance hero who suffered ten years in Nazi prisons while Helmut Schmidt was growing up in the Hitler Youth and then in the Wehrmacht. Some of the older men and women in the Party in East Berlin are Jewish. Their ties to the Party and its orthodoxies have to do with the 1930s and with an anti-Nazi movement that found a home and a *raison d'être* in the Communist underground. They do not know what to make of youngsters like Thomas Brasch, who broke publicly with his Communist father and landed in jail for his part in East Berlin's version of the 1968 *événements*, or like Wolf Biermann, the poet and folksinger whose concerts on the Alexanderplatz were East Berlin's version of Bob Dylan's Berkeley concerts during the Vietnam War —or, for that matter, like anyone who says that there must be alternatives in life to fighting devotedly for the Communist state and fighting devotedly against it.

Wolf Biermann lives in Hamburg now, singing sad songs and writing sad poems about the corruptions of exile. Here in West Berlin, people rarely talk about corruption. They talk about *Filz*. Whenever something shady or merely stupid happens here, people shake their heads: "*Der Filz.*" Nothing gets done properly in West Berlin because of *Filz*. The more something costs, Berliners say, the less adequate it is bound to be—and this is because of *Filz*, too. *Filz* means "felt," the cloth, but in Germany the word is mainly used to describe a social fabric in which the threads of authority and personality and profit have been pressed together so tightly that they are now inseparable. *Filz* is not exactly corruption. *Filz* is a kind of greedy and ingenuous collusion among people whose ideas about conflict of interest are structurally undeveloped.. Hamburg, for example, has a little over a hundred thousand bureaucrats on the public payroll; West Berlin, not much larger, has nearly twice as many, and these bureaucrats have settled in for life, primarily to make jobs for one another outside the bureaucracy. After a while, no one can fire them from the government. It is their reward for staying here, not for service—a way of making sure that they have no reason to go back to West Germany, where most of them came from. Bonn pays them an extra 8 percent on their salaries as a kind of hardship allowance (actually, everybody in West Berlin gets this allowance), and if the bureaucrats court the right people and get to be ministers in the government—and if they last as ministers for a while —they can draw a lifetime ministerial pension and never really have to work again. Then, too, as ministers and deputy ministers and commissioners they sit on the boards of utility companies and banks and construction firms that the city either owns outright, like the Berliner Bank, or controls, like the electric company. It is considered reasonable here for an undersecretary in the Ministry of Housing and Construction, say, to sit on the board of a construction firm in which the city has an interest and to send that firm Ministry jobs and contracts. *Filz* is everywhere in West Berlin, binding the city like a social contract. There is theoretically room here for four million people. In actuality, only two million live here. Some eight hundred buildings—nearly all of them belonging to the government—are boarded up and unoccupied, yet the construction business in West Berlin is the liveliest business in town, being more conducive to *Filz* than any other. Not so long ago, one of the construction companies here was given a city contract to develop some choice land on a little Berlin lake and sell it, in plots, to people whom the government was trying to woo away from the Federal Republic. To nobody's surprise, it was soon discovered that a government undersecretary from the Housing Ministry had picked up a plot for himself at 130 marks a square meter, which was about thirty marks a square meter below the market price. What did surprise Berliners was the fact that the undersecretary made the becoming and unique gesture of asking to be demoted. They assumed that the land must have been worth more to him, in the end, than the remaining possibilities of his position. Like the undersecretary, everybody in West Berlin seems to have made some sort of provision for himself. The unions have made their arrangements with the government and its banks to keep their membership inflated far beyond the needs of the city. The intelligentsia keeps *its* membership inflated, too—the State Theater alone has four hundred "civil servants" on its payroll. And it is hard to find a politician in Berlin who does not collect something in cash or status or influence. Peter Lorenz, who was chairman of the Christian Democratic Union in West Berlin in the seventies (he was kidnapped in 1975 and held for six days against the release of some jailed terrorists), is considered a prototype of the Berlin politician. He was paid an honorarium as the local party chairman, and a salary as a deputy in Berlin's parliament, and at the same time he was retained as a lawyer by one of West Berlin's two state radio stations. But *Filz* creates the sort of network that easily crosses party lines, and when the local coalition of Social Democrats and Free Democrats fell apart last January it turned out that Lorenz was also making money as a lawyer for Dietrich Garski, the Free Democratic architect and real-estate developer whose wheeling and dealing had caused the trouble. Garski had borrowed 115 million marks from the city of West Berlin. He said that he was going to finance the construction of a couple of military academies for the Saudi Arabians—some of whom took ten million of those marks in commissions for the "contract" that Garski had to produce at home. Nobody seems to have asked Garski (who has disappeared in the meantime) what he was doing in the Arabian-military-academy business, or why, or how he planned to pay back the 115 million marks. The mayor of Berlin, Dietrich Stobbe—who had taken over in 1977 after *his* predecessor resigned because of a construction scandal—had approved the loan. The deputy mayor had also approved it, and so had the Finance Minister for West Berlin, who is now making 170,000 marks a year as director of one of the city's banks. Stobbe fired his Finance Minister once the scandal broke—and immediately moved to make him leader of the Social Democratic faction of the city parliament. (It was a job that lasted about a week and ended when the government ended.) Stobbe himself resigned and was put away into a safe party job. And Hans-Jochen Vogel, the federal Justice Minister in Bonn, was ordered to Berlin by Helmut Schmidt to save the city for the Social Democrats.

Willy Brandt, of course, was the great mayor of West Berlin. People still associate Brandt with the heroism of the city under siege, and there is not much heroism left here to associate with anyone anymore—only what Berliners call border politics. No ambitious politician these days *chooses* Berlin, but no ambitious politician can refuse to go there. Helmut Schmidt's new party secretary, Peter Glotz, put in his time in West Berlin as a Science and Research Minister while he was making his way to Bonn and federal politics. Schmidt used him again here during the Garski scandal as a combination trouble-shooter and informer; it was evidently Glotz who decided that, whatever Vogel might think of the idea, no one but Vogel would do to replace Stobbe as mayor and redeem the Social Democrats in West Berlin. (This is a piece of party gossip that Berliners learned when someone with access to the spy equipment the Allies use for listening in on East Berliners bugged a telephone conversation between the Chancellor and Glotz and sold a transcript of it to a local tabloid, owned at the time by a

Persian rug dealer.) Vogel had a reputation for honesty and for an almost excessive diligence. He was not exactly radiant as a personality, but he had done so well as a Social Democratic mayor of conservative Munich in the early sixties (Brandt once called him the last Prussian from Bavaria) that he got almost 80 percent of the vote when he ran for a second term. Glotz apparently persuaded Schmidt that Vogel could keep Berlin in the party, and this was especially important to Schmidt, because Berlin has always been a fairly reliable gauge of the strengths and weaknesses and flexibility of the coalition of Free Democrats and Social Democrats that now lets Schmidt run the country. That coalition, which had looked so good after the federal elections late last year, was already in trouble by January of this year, when the West Berlin government collapsed. Schmidt was losing favor. He was paying the price of old successes he could never match. He had seen Germany through the worst years of the oil crisis. He had covered each increase in the cost of fuel with an increase in industrial production that fairly accurately matched the expanding appetite of the OPEC states for German goods. By 1978, West Germany was the only country in Western Europe with no debt to those states—in fact, with a surplus of eighteen billion marks. Germans had come to believe that this sort of accommodation to the cost of fuel could go on forever—which meant that they blamed the government when OPEC increases of the past few years finally left Germany with a corresponding deficit. Today, that deficit—thirty billion marks—is close to the highest in Western Europe, but even so it is less than the increase in the country's oil bill, and this means that Schmidt has managed rather well. There was certainly no way he could meet the expectations of his welfare state *and* pay for his oil *and* please both the Free Democrats in his coalition, who were arguing for industrial incentives during inflationary hard times, and a growing left wing in his own Social Democratic Party, which did not approve of the sophisticated strategies of those Free Democratic welfare-state capitalists and wanted a "socialist" solution having vaguely to do with disarmament and neutrality and various ecological enthusiasms. Schmidt had not really been well for a year when he was operated on in October and got a pacemaker. There was the old problem with his heart muscles, and after the federal elections his doctor had ordered him off cigarettes, which made him grumpy, and he had gained weight, which made him grumpier, and then he had lost some twenty pounds by dieting, which, according to his friends, made him impossible. Schmidt is part of a generation of Germans whose rejection of the past involves a kind of passionate pragmatism, a contempt for ideology of any sort. He is comfortable with business-men and bankers from Cologne and Düsseldorf who have a cost-plus definition of human progress and no illusions about the social contract. He is comfortable with union bosses at the Gewerkschaftsbund in Frankfurt who trade political compliance for the protection of cost-of-living guarantees and health benefits. But he has no patience for the heady, romantic strain of the German left that for him evokes the old Berlin of Marxist intellectuals like Walter Benjamin and, years later, the Berlin of Willy Brandt. Brandt's own failings—his penchant for lost causes and his fuzzy judgment, and his difficulty, sometimes, in distin-guishing between friends and courtiers—have been taken up as virtues by a lot of people in the Social Democratic Party, and not only its young radicals and its old Marxists. There is a liberal and gently urbane bourgeoisie among the Social Democrats that grew up with Brandt and made its money with Schmidt. It is middle-aged now, and is used to that money. The people in it feel particularly deprived by the inflation at home and by the fluctuations of the mark as it affects their standing at the beach in Quogue or in the art galleries of Tokyo, but as Willy Brandt's children they tend to associate their malaise not so much with oil economics as with a kind of moral retribution for Helmut Schmidt's impatient character. The more things cost, the more they blame Schmidt's pragmatism, his bad temper, his fondness over the years for martinets like Valéry Giscard d'Estaing and Cold War conservatives like Ronald Reagan. And Brandt, at sixty-seven—with his radical girl-friend and his new Third World economics and his peace missions to Moscow and his equivocation about NATO armaments in Germany—has suddenly come in from the cold of political eclipse as his party's conscience.

Schmidt, for all his hard-edge and hard-line politics, has had trou-ble keeping the party together in a lot of cities. Just this spring, the young Social Democratic mayor of Hamburg—Hamburg is Schmidt's home town and political base—quit his job because of pressure from Schmidt's people in Bonn to approve the construction of a nuclear power plant at Brokdorf, in nearby Schleswig-Holstein. And in Berlin thousands of Social Democrats dropped out of the last election alto-gether ("producing politics by saying we do not want to join," as someone put it) or joined the Alternativler—an odd lot of anarchists and Marxists and Spontis (for "spontaneous"), not to mention ecolo-gists, feminists, gay activists, and, mainly, well-bred liberals fed up with parties and politicians—which collected ninety thousand signatures, entered the elections as a kind of anti-party, and, in the end, won over

7 percent of the vote and nine seats in the local parliament. The Berlin Social Democrats did not like Vogel much. They knew that he wanted to be Chancellor one day. They knew that he had no desire to leave the safety of his ministry in Bonn for a suicide mission into West Berlin politics. And they knew that, as a loyal party man, he had no choice except to take his orders and go—which was just the sort of thing they had come to resent about the Social Democrats under Schmidt. Vogel spent his four months at the Rathaus under the testy scrutiny of several hundred Berlin bureaucrats who had never before had to account for themselves and were worried that they might have to begin now. He looked uncomfortable, and he talked uncomfortably about his mission in Berlin—about the two million brave Berliners who were not going to be abandoned by their government. In fact, he tried to help. He ordered a temporary truce with the squatters, who had already occupied 160 empty houses in Kreuzberg, Schöneberg, and Wedding as what they called *Instandbesetzer*—"house restorers." (At the time, most of the policemen sent to evict them refused to go anyway.) He saved rent control—Berlin is the last big German city with effective rent control, and there is still a shortage of cheap housing here, despite, or possibly because of, the eight hundred empty buildings and the "new towns" like Märkisches Viertel, near the wall, which have got so expensive that few working-class families can afford them. He cancelled plans for a peripheric highway just inside the wall, which would have had no exits and nowhere to go but back into the city.

All told, Vogel was caretaker mayor for four months of earnest hatchet work. He ditched half his coalition's candidates for reelection and fired all but three of the ministers in the cabinet he had inherited from Stobbe, but in the end—with the son of the chief of police squatting in Kreuzberg and Willy Brandt's son Peter writing the foreign-policy platform for the Alternativler—it was clear that, after thirty-five years of almost constant power, the Social Democrats had lost all their authority. Now there is a new, Christian Democratic mayor named Richard von Weizsäcker. He took over in June, a month after the Christian Democrats won the election—or, more accurately, after they won more seats in the parliament than the coalition of Free Democrats and Social Democrats—and finally managed to put together a minority government. People like von Weizsäcker, even though he comes from Baden-Württemberg, and not Berlin. He is pleasant and correct. A "civilized centrist," someone in the opposition called him—although admittedly that was before von Weizsäcker decided to evict eight squatter households this fall and a teenage boy was crushed to death by a bus in the course of street fighting between the squatters and a contingent of two thousand riot policemen. Berliners in his own predominantly Catholic party like von Weizsäcker because he is a churchgoing Lutheran—a past president of the West German Evangelischer Kirchentag —and Berlin, unlike the rest of West Germany, which is half Catholic, is a Lutheran town. But mainly they seem to like him because he is already much more of a "Berliner" than Vogel, having been sent here before, in 1979, to run for mayor, and having lost.

On paper, Berlin is the first industrial city in Germany—which means only that more Berliners work in factories than people in other towns do, and that more of the income here comes from that work. Actually, Hamburg, with its oil refineries, has a bigger industrial turnover than Berlin, and the small cities of the Ruhr form an almost unbroken industrial chain that is much larger than West Berlin's 120,000 acres. Berlin industry is a statistic, affected by the depression in the city's other sectors and by the fact that everything within the wall is "West Berlin," whereas the industrial complex in a city like Hamburg takes in areas that have become townships of their own. Eighty percent of West Berlin's "exports" go directly to the Federal Republic, but they make up only about 3 percent of the national product. Some 100,000 of the 300,000 West German workers who came here after the wall was built have gone home. And the kind of industry those skilled workers served has been leaving, too, at a pace that quickened after 1972, when Berlin was "normalized"—no longer on West Germany's conscience, and not really important anymore for its public relations. Before the Quadripartite Agreement, smart businessmen wanted their headquarters in Berlin. Berlin was the symbol of free enterprise surviving in the middle of Communist Europe, and was as valuable an association for a West German company as a television association with Shakespeare's plays or with Pavarotti's tenor voice is for IBM or Exxon. In a way, détente made West Berlin an unnecessary overhead for German businessmen. With their best workers streaming back to the Federal Republic and being replaced by *Gastarbeiter* out of peasant villages in Anatolia, they started to phase out precision industry here, leaving the city and the *Gastarbeiter* to the mass production of cheap machinery and to the sort of piecework that would multiply the cycling of goods and equipment through Berlin in order to take advantage of the city's special tax allowances and subsidies. When a shirt made in West Germany is shipped to Berlin, as some shirts are, for its buttons to be sewn on, people here can be fairly sure that the government has made the trip worthwhile for the shirtmaker—and that the shirtmaker has long since moved his parent plant to the comfort and convenience and security of the Federal Republic. There is no business elite in West Berlin; there are only middle managers. The elite here is intellectual, and while it makes for an interesting scene at Kempinski's Grill Room or Fofi's Estiatorio, it has nothing to do with the limousine-and-body-guard society of Düsseldorf and Cologne, or with the splash of nou-veau-riche Munich, or with the chilly hierarchies of merchant-banking Hamburg. The people with power in Berlin are a political middle class —pompous and mediocre. This accounts in part for a kind of local "freak chic," which holds that it's gauche to feel important. The ideal Berlin freak is a new-wave and leather-jeans drifter with a high I.Q. and an anarchic disposition, who changes places from one week to the next with the bartender who waits on him or with the cabbie he hails, stoned, at three in the morning. Half the businessmen in Berlin could trade jobs with that cabbie, too, and no one would know the difference—except, maybe, the pedestrians. The entrepreneurs of the "new" Berlin are gone—the men who were speculating on its future as the West's most active trade link with Eastern Europe. Less than 2 percent of the city's products go to East Germany now. The merchant houses that were going to manage volume trade between the two Germanys and the two Europes manage, in fact, only about 20 percent of German trade with the East, despite the temptations for East Bloc businessmen to come here: closeness to home; permission to exchange their soft currency for marks or dollars; permission to stay in the West—with its porno movies and nude bars and weirder varieties of prostitution than a Bulgarian commissar is likely to have even heard of—without a visa for thirty-one days; the simple pleasure of roaming around a big, brassy town with no curfew and no closing hours. The trouble is that most Eastern businessmen seem to find West Berlin as beside the point as their Western counterparts do.

Still, Bonn keeps the incentives for investment high, and picks up new incentives when investment falls off. By now, investing in indus-try here is a little like investing in industry in Puerto Rico or Northern Ireland or the Mezzogiorno—more profitable than productive. A com-pany setting up a branch in West Berlin gets about twenty thousand marks outright from the government for every hundred thousand it invests. There is accelerated depreciation. Credit is easy and cheap, a lot of it still tied to postwar recovery programs like the Marshall Plan. Industry here can usually expect to make back its investment after three or four years. There are businesses that set up complicated and expensive plants in West Berlin, take their credits and tax breaks and subsidies, and then literally dismantle the plants and ship them in pieces to new headquarters in Darmstadt or Munich—and end up spending half of what it would have cost them to build in Darmstadt or Munich to begin with. Then, there are the businesses that come to Berlin, establish the cheapest operation possible, and use their profits to finance expansion at a classy parent company in the south. Berliners talk about one company that is known around the world for the precision drills and bores it manufactures at its headquarters near Stuttgart; in Berlin, the same company mass-produces crude tools in ten-thousand-piece lots for quick profit in the Third World, and this is especially galling to people here, because Berlin used to be the German city famous for precision machines and tools. Foreign companies like IBM have subsidiaries that make typewriters, say, in Berlin, but they make their computers somewhere else. The big companies keep pulling their headquarters out. There are no research-and-development centers here anymore, no marketing departments. The Schering pharmaceutical firm is the only important company with headquarters in Berlin. And of all the companies with plants here, only Daimler-Benz makes any of its key components in West Berlin—and Daimler-Benz has a rather eerie nostalgia for the city's *Hauptstadt* days, as is clear to anyone who sees the giant Mercedes star revolving over Berlin on its tower, like an electric harbinger of the Second Coming.

Economists here make this equation: no headquarters equals no top personnel equals no real energy or imagination equals no "rationalization" of industry in the interests of a competitive, self-sustaining society. The workers who argue about cooperatives and co-determination and risk are in places like Darmstadt and the Ruhr; Berlin workers want security. They do not much care about things like inventiveness or expansion. They are not overly distressed when a company suddenly moves out, bag and baggage, leaving an empty factory as the only proof that it was ever there at all. The trains to Berlin are full of *Gastarbeiter* each September, and thousands of sealed trucks carrying West Berlin products still make their sedate run through the G.D.R., but nothing alters the fact that there were 280,000 industrial workers in West Berlin in 1974 and today there are 180,000. Workers in West Berlin right now make cigarettes—something the Anatolian Turks can do with simple machines and no secret circuits or components—and they process packaged food and manufacture low-quality electronic gadgets. The real business of West Berlin (the only growth industry) seems to be in brains—the business of education and culture and, of course, counter-

culture. There are local economists who maintain that the way for the
city to revive—to break the vicious and debilitating circle that runs
from subsidy to *Filz* to failure to more subsidy—is with its one proved
and successful product: its scholars and scientists and artists. They want
the city to specialize in the manufacture, so to speak, of highly sophisticated mental labor for the West German market—and to divert the
vast amounts of money spent on industrial promotion to giving Berliners a better life. There are already two enormous universities in Berlin
—the Free University and the Technical University, which includes a
teachers' training college and an art institute—with seventy-five thousand students between them, and staffs of nearly thirty thousand. There
are 185 research institutes of one sort or another, like the Max Planck
and the Wissenschaftszentrum, with nearly five thousand full-time fel-
lows. And there is what Berliners call "official culture"—a 315-million-
marks-a-year culture budget that seems to cover everything going on
in town, from the Deutsche Oper to the rock concerts to the tents for
the latest "alternative" circus to a mysterious happening called Festival
of Fools.

Obviously, conventional industry has nowhere to expand here.
The wall stops it. Even as it is, people complain about industrial pollu-
tion. They suffer from an endemic claustrophobia that leaves them
terribly concerned about the little space, the little air they have. Bonn
has tried to relieve some of this claustrophobia over the years with
subsidized plane fares—220 marks ($98) round trip to Hannover, 350 to
Frankfurt—and with delicately negotiated access highways across East
Germany to the Federal Republic. (West Berliners hate the car trip.
They claim that the G.D.R.'s hundred-kilometer-an-hour speed limit
—a little over sixty miles an hour—is much too slow to drive and makes
them nervous.) But it is clear by now that even the workers no longer
believe in the myth of Berlin as a great industrial city. Only now is an
Autobahn to Hamburg—the shipping center for West Germany and
presumably vital to its factory cities—being constructed. When Günter
Gaus negotiated the right to construct the Autobahn a couple of years
ago, every politician in town complained that he should have been
negotiating for a road straight to the countryside around Dannenberg,
where a lot of Berliners have their weekend houses.

Right now, nothing else about Berlin is quite as real as the wall.
Not the economy. Not the politics. Not the American Army and its
bungalow suburbs, where teenage wives from the Ozarks live out their
tour of duty on a diet of alcohol and doughnuts—and, it is said, some-

times do go crazy looking at the wall and beat their babies. It is not just
the drugs or the famous "scene," or even the draft exemption enjoyed
by every resident of the city, that draws so many young West Germans
to Berlin—it is this unreality, this sense of psychic as well as physical
distance from the real German world, where a crude prosperity seems
to count for so much more than reflection and balance. A lot of these
young Berliners sound completely vacant when they talk about themselves or about what they want here, but then they lack a kind of
citizenship—they lack that sense of nationality that has not simply,
aggressively ignored the past but has confronted and come through it.
Berlin, in a way, corroborates their confusion. Behind its wall, it is the
freest city in the world. For the young, life here is a life lived against
official culture and official politics—a way of leaving home and still
collecting one's allowance. They sense, accurately, that everyone here
is in his own way just as cynical, just as subversive as they are—
the tenured bureaucrat, the coddled German worker, the farmed-out
corporate manager, the dissident intellectual. West Berlin's protest-by-
instinct population supports a daily underground newspaper—*Tages-
zeitung,* which everyone calls *Taz*—along with two thousand "alternative" businesses, including taxi cooperatives and punk bars and
macrobiotic grocery stores and even laundries. It supports the sort of
people who moved into an abandoned movie studio a few years back
and became an "arts collective"—and were so successful that now the
Social Democrats keep trying to subsidize them. It raised a million and
a half marks for dissidents in El Salvador last year, and it contributes
regularly and heavily to something called Netzwerk, a kind of counterculture slush fund for alternative-scene people who need money
—teachers, say, who lose their jobs because of politics, or ecologists who
want backing to manufacture windmills. Netzwerk operates like a
combination insurance company and investment bank—an idea, most
Germans would admit, that could have come only from Berlin, the way
the idea of squatters spread to West Germany from Berlin, and the idea
of centers for battered wives, and, for that matter, most of the radical
ideas in West Germany's cautious and conservative culture. For West
Germans, in fact, May of 1968 came from the Free University of Berlin
—which is the ultimate Berlin phenomenon, since it owes its existence
to the formal division of the city in 1948 and to a mass exodus of students
and professors from Humboldt University, in the Russian sector. It was
General Lucius Clay who installed some desks and blackboards in an
Army administration building in Dahlem, and gave the new Free University the official protection of the American Berlin Brigade—a piece

of history that would undoubtedly stun most students at the Free University now. Clay had expected, at the most, fifteen thousand students. Today, there are forty-five thousand, and there are so many professors that it will take another ten years for any tenure lines to open. Still, things have been quieter at the university lately. People like Otto Schily, concerned about civil rights in West Germany, worry that students here are *abgestumpft*—dulled, indifferent, most of their old ardor gone. Günter Gaus, who took the job of Minister of Science and Research here for a few months before the election and is now advising the Social Democrats on international affairs, says that the "alternative" enthusiasms of students now are remarkable for being so *un*political —that they reflect the disappointment of a generation that gave up its revolution to make what it called "the long march through the institutions" and got, according to today's students, so little for it. Gaus himself worries about a kind of cult of irrationalism among students now. They remind him of young Germans at the beginning of the century, who were idealistic and peaceful and loved nature and, on principle, despised technology—and were so intensely, arrogantly unpolitical that it took only thirty years to turn their Wandervögel into the Hitler Youth. The young in other German cities are still "recoverable," as the politicians say, for party politics. They are the anti-nuke people and the anti-NATOs and the pacifist left of the Social Democratic Party and the young parents protesting the expansion of the Frankfurt airport. But in Berlin that group went over to West Germany when Willy Brandt did. The young in Berlin today look at the politicians who run the country, and conclude that the line between pragmatism and opportunism has long ago been crossed. They drop out. They squat. They pass the hat for Solidarity when they are demonstrating against American cruise missiles or Alexander Haig. They confuse their causes. Students here used to spend forty or fifty hours a week sitting on committees they invented in the name of popular democracy. Now, according to one of the teachers at the Free University, they are very sensitive, they can't bear tension, they sulk like children when anything is demanded of them.

Students come to Berlin—more than half the students at the Free University are from West Germany—looking for a scene, because West Germany is in many ways a country without a scene. They find that Berlin is a scene without a country. The best of West Berlin is a transplant, brought over with the subsidies and the tax breaks and the sealed trucks full of Common Market pears and oranges to complete the illusion of a rich and normal life. Many of the good artists and writers and musicians here are paid to be here. They are imported—and with imagination—but apart from Peter Stein's Schaubühne, which is one of the great theater companies of Europe, and the monument of Herbert von Karajan's Berlin Philharmonic, the city buys much more "Berlin culture" than it produces. It may be, as people who leave Berlin for Hamburg or Munich claim, that culture in Berlin is as stale as the government—that Berlin has to import its artists and performers the way the political parties have to import their politicians. Or it may be that by now the city has a chronic case of *Mauerkrankheit*, which leaves it nervous and insecure and in need of large doses of entertainment as well as attention from the outside.

Berliners are neurotic, guilty people—like New Yorkers. It is one of the things that a busy West Germany cannot forgive them for. In West Germany this fall, people were talking about Schmidt's new budget, with its twenty-billion-mark cuts in social services and pensions and corporate credits, and complaining about the ten billion marks that will still be going to support Berlin, where the tax on salaries is 30 percent less than the tax *they* pay, and the tax on corporate profits almost 25 percent less, and where one con man can not only bring down the government but disappear with money that West Germany probably supplied. But in West Berlin this fall people were talking about the implications of an exhibition here concerned with Prussian history and culture, and about whether an art gallery on Meinekestrasse was right or wrong in mounting a retrospective of Arno Breker, who flourished under Adolf Hitler. A few hundred of them bought space in the local papers and signed a protest against the gallery, and then the gallery tried to sue for libel, claiming that the words "Nazi exhibit" in the protest damaged its reputation, not to mention its honor, and then the West German Sculptors' Association got involved. In some ways, this is still the capital.

December 1981

MME GONÇALVES

MME GONÇALVES

My concierge is Portuguese. She comes from Trás-os-Montes, the northeasternmost province of her country—a region of stony, arid land and peasant freeholds and such poverty that half the population has had to emigrate in the past twenty or thirty years. Mme Gonçalves (I will call her) went to Angola with her husband. They bought some cows and kept a little dairy farm outside Luanda, and, being simple, faithful people whose politics echoed their parish priest and their own wary isolation, they did not think much about whether they were wicked *gros colons*, oppressing Africans, until the revolution started in Angola and their two young sons had to leave the farm to fight. The Gonçalves sons are in Brazil now, working in factories. Mme Gonçalves put them on a freighter out of Cabinda in 1973, when the fighting was terrible, and then she and her husband fled. They went to Zaire, which had been advertising itself in the Luanda papers as a "land of promise," and then they went home to Portugal, where there was no work and no housing —and not much of a welcome, either—for the *retornados* of Europe's last great African empire. They ended up in France, along with a million other Portuguese, looking for jobs.

Mme Gonçalves is a tiny, tidy woman—correct and delicate. Strangers on the block often take her for a Frenchwoman. She knows that Parisians always prefer a woman to a man as their concierge —that they think of a good woman, vigilant behind the curtains of a little lodge on the *rez-de-chaussée*, as somehow setting the proper tone for a courtyard. And so she is formally the concierge here—guardian of the mail, gatekeeper to everybody's company. Actually, like most of the Portuguese concierges on the block, she has turned the building over to her husband. M. Gonçalves strolls his courtyard as if it were the *praça* of some little private village of his own. He is so familiar to the neighbors now—with his long, woebegone Trás-os-Montes face and his big ears and his sudden wide, wide smile—that most of them have stopped complaining about the courtyard door's being always open, so that he can tip his cap and say *"Bom dia"* whenever anybody passes. Mme Gonçalves herself works as a maid, days, for a diplomat around the corner, making better money. Nights and weekends, she takes in sewing. She does not really believe that she has found a home here. She thinks that some calamity—a war, perhaps, or the kind of poverty she knew as a girl in Trás-os-Montes—will uproot her, that she will have to pack everything and move again. But the truth is that after eight years here she is practically Parisian. Like the Parisians on the block, she talks about immigration as something that has to do with foreign workers on yearly contracts with the big factories outside Paris and Lyons and Clermont-Ferrand, or with Indochinese refugees, or with the West Africans and North Africans who arrive in the *métropole* looking, perhaps, for old colonial attachments as well as jobs. She has never considered our street in the middle of Paris—or the people on it—as being in any way connected with the violent new demography she sometimes hears about on the TF 1 nightly news. Our street is respectable. It is a busy street, busy with shops and stalls and local commerce, and ending in a market. Jacques Hillairet (a ninety-five-year-old Army colonel who, at fifty, decided to spend his retirement documenting the history of every house on every street in Paris) describes it in his *Dictionnaire Historique des Rues de Paris,* noting one by one the carved wooden double doors that open onto deep and surprisingly eccentric eighteenth-century courtyards. Most of these famous doors are thick with paint now, and most of the old houses, by the looks of them, had a couple of extra stories added to them during the Second Republic—"1848 public housing," Edgar de Bresson, the filmmaker, who lives in the quarter, calls it. That extra height gives the houses (which, after all, were once important, even stately houses) a kind of gawky charm—like French boys grown too tall for the good gray trousers they have to wear to school. It saves the street from seriousness, makes it gay and rather lovable. At any rate, it is the sort of street that Parisians love—part *quartier populaire* and part *quartier bourgeois,* which means that the restaurants are good, and, usually, the plumbers. Everybody knows everybody else, everybody gossips. Mme Gonçalves admits that there have been changes here during her eight years. Some-times she mentions approvingly that "important people"—rich people

—have been moving in. Or she worries about the children on their way to school who have to pass the new bookstore down the block toward Raspail, where two middle-aged women of obvious refinement sit behind a long glass table, presiding over a connoisseur's display of illustrated first editions of sadomasochistic literature. She speaks of changes, but she does not find anything unusual in the fact that a fifty-four-year-old peasant from Trás-os-Montes and Angola can be seen on the street most evenings after the eight o'clock news walking to fittings with an old broom on which the skirt and culotte lengths appropriate to this year's fashion have been marked off in bright-red ink. It would surprise her to learn just how much the life of the building and the block *has* changed in eight years. Late in the afternoon, as soon as she gets home from the diplomat's house, she and her husband make their own *passeio*. The first butcher they pass comes from Paris, and then there is the butcher from Auvergne, and then the butcher from Dahomey. The grocers on the street are Arab, Berber, and Italian. The two plumbers are Italian, too, and the man who works at the corner hardware store and lives across the street is Portuguese. The waitress at the café next door comes from Sri Lanka, the family serving *entrecôte aux clous de girofle* at the restaurant a little farther on is Tunisian, and the boys carrying late deliveries from the drugstore and the local wine *négociant* are Vietnamese boatpeople. The neighbors whom the Gonçalveses consider exotic are mainly the Parisians, who have always been here: the fussy spinster, say, who manages the laundry *à poids*—twelve francs a kilo of wash, or nine francs if you are willing to collect it wet—and the old couple at the *poissonnerie*, who still get up at four every morning to choose their fish at the wholesale market in Rungis.

October 1981

Mme Gonçalves wants to boycott the gas company. She has been stopping everyone in the courtyard to say that, as a decent Catholic woman, a mother of sons, our own diligent custodian, she cannot in conscience cooperate with a government that plans to buy its gas from the Russians—by which she means that we should not expect her to deliver our bills from Gaz de France, or the little reminders that follow them, or even the last warnings that come a week before the company turns the gas off. Mme Gonçalves wants to send them back with the postman, marked "Address Unknown" or "Please Return" or "Dead," or whatever happens to sound right in the French-Portuguese patois she started improvising for herself—a kind of private lingua franca —the day that she and M. Gonçalves arrived in Paris. Mme Gonçalves is a friendly woman, but she hates Russians. She associates Russians with the fiends and demons who are so busy torturing sinners in the lower left-hand corner of the Last Judgment calendar she always receives at Christmas from her sister in Trás-os-Montes.

Back home in that remote and fairly medieval corner of Portugal, Mme Gonçalves learned about Russians even before she learned about Protestants. The first Protestants she actually saw were a family of Baptist missionaries—and that was in Angola. She was invited to the mission once, on a Sunday, and was astonished to discover that a family pretending to Christianity should sit down to Sunday dinner with a dour prayer and no wine on the table and a meal that smelled, she says, like the municipal swimming pool. When she learned that the missionaries had "purified" the salad and the vegetables in chlorinated water, she concluded that Protestants were peculiar people, and possibly retarded, but of no real consequence.

Communists, on the other hand, were of considerable consequence. When Mme Gonçalves was a girl, her parish priest saw two Communists at the jail in Bragança, where he was administering last rites to an old peasant who had been caught poaching so often that, at the age of seventy-five, he had decided to move to jail permanently and spare himself the inconvenience of being arrested again and beaten and put on trial. The priest told the parish children stories about red devils who came at night and kidnapped naughty boys and girls from their beds and ate them up at a long banquet table in a pagan fortress called the Kremlin. Years later, on her dairy farm near Luanda, Mme Gonçalves repeated those stories about Communist bogeymen to her own boys when she tucked them in at night, and they shivered in their beds, terrified and delighted, and asked for more. Everybody in Angola said that it was the Communists in Russia, sending Agostinho Neto their guns and their money, and the Communists in Cuba, sending him their best soldiers, who finally stole beautiful, bountiful Angola from the Portuguese. Mme Gonçalves herself blames the Communists for the fact that she had to abandon her dairy farm; for the fact that there were no jobs in the new, free Portugal when she came home to Trás-os-Montes after the revolution; for the fact that Portuguese soldiers put red carnations in their rifles and never stopped the strikes and the shortages and the mysterious fires that ruined the harvests that year in provinces where peasants still kept tinted photographs of António Salazar on the kitchen wall; for the fact that the province was disrupted by groups of rich young students driving up from Lisbon in their sports cars and demanding that families that had been feuding comfortably for centuries organize into cooperatives and share their land and tractors, and even the little money they had.

When the Gonçalveses finally took up residence in the concierge's lodge that runs the length of our cobblestone courtyard—starting with the outdoor taps, where servants washed the dishes and the sheets a hundred years ago, and ending at the row of privies, where tenants now store everything from firewood to inflatable motorboats—she consoled herself with the thought that here, at last, was a respite from the problem of Communists. True, there were strikes in France, just like the strikes at home, and people here also tended to blame the Communists, but the strikes here never really interfered with the life of our quarter, with its busy shops and markets, or with Mme Gonçalves's own new sideline—taking up the neighborhood's hems and letting down its hems, tightening its trousers and loosening its trousers, padding its shoulders and narrowing its shoulders, according to the season's fashion. Mme Gonçalves has doubled her spending money since Christmas shortening bluejeans for the teenage girls on the block, not one of whom will leave her house this winter without a pair of little red pumps and jeans shortened to display the appropriate amount of Argyle socks—synthetic Argyle socks that the Americans have been producing for the French market in combinations of pinks and purples and turquoise blues which would certainly alarm any Scot who saw them.

Mme Gonçalves is careful to leave a big hem in the jeans she shortens. She is a mother herself, and sympathizes with the mothers here and their expenses. Besides, she considers the French a people of helpless frivolity. She fusses over her tenants, and over the diplomat around the corner whose house she cleans, and the neighbors anguishing about their hems and their heels, and spending more money on their lunches than on their churches. She thinks of them as children themselves—children who could not get by without her common sense and her indulgent services. She is a woman of such extravagant experience—a Portuguese peasant who lived for twenty years like a châtelaine, with a cook and a maid and a gardener and a houseboy of her own, and then ended up as maid, concierge, and seamstress to a lively old Left Bank neighborhood just as it was being taken up by moneyed intellectuals looking for "authenticity"—that she takes a long view of their circumstances and her own. It has saved her from bitterness. It has turned humiliation into a kind of maternal exercise, though it did not stop her from losing everybody's telephone bills after President François Mitterrand had four Communist ministers named to the cabinet. The telephones in the building went dead, mysteriously, one by one last fall. And one by one the tenants talked politics and telephones with Mme Gonçalves: the Niçoise student from a converted sixth-floor *chambre de bonne* who sells vegetables at the street market to pay her way through a doctorate in Japanese; the Italian plumber from the third floor; the retired general from the wing across the courtyard; the young man on four who recently turned his apartment into a combination ashram and crash pad for local Krishna worshippers and needed a working phone to keep in touch with his guru, in Key West.

This time, they are talking in advance, hoping to intercept next month's mailings from Gaz de France in a way that will not compromise Mme Gonçalves's principles. In fact, most of them agree with her that it was somehow shameful for France to sign a trade agreement with the Soviet Union only a month after the military coup in Poland —especially an agreement that runs well into the next century, committing France to buy from the Russians as much as a third of all the gas it is going to use for twenty-five years. And Mme Gonçalves, holding forth at her doorstep, nods and reminisces with them about how well the building behaved at Christmastime, when nearly all the tenants put candles in their windows for Catholic Poland and attended demonstrations and made sure that none of their children scribbled on the poster that went up across the street—a weeping face turned sidewise to become a map of Poland. Last week, someone pasted a notice over that poster—a big *affiche* purportedly coming from Gaz de France and urging everyone to phone in the make and model number of his gas stove and heating system, because the gas company was about to start adjusting or replacing them, free of charge, to receive the "new" gas from Russia. Evidently, not very many people stopped to consider why gas piped in from Siberia would require a different kind of stove from, say, gas piped in from Algeria or the North Sea or any of the other French sources. They simply started calling, and the number they called turned out to be the Russian Embassy, which did not find the joke as amusing as the people who thought it up did. The Russians disconnected their phone.

France already buys some 15 percent of its natural gas from the Russians. Nearly every country in Western Europe buys gas from Russia. Germany and Italy had already signed their contracts for Siberian gas when the military took over Poland, on December 13 (and everybody said then that business was business, and congratulated the Germans, especially, on a good bargain). France's own contract grew out of ten years of energy anxiety—and partly out of common sense, partly out of an eager naïveté among businessmen who wanted their fuel guaranteed and politicians who wanted the credit for providing it. Mainly, though, it had to do with the fact that Russia needed to sell a lot of gas to finance (with French loans for French equipment) a three-thousand-mile pipeline from Siberia and was willing to sell it fairly cheap—at a price that gave France leverage with other big suppliers, like Algeria, which had to lower its own prices in the end.

People here know this. They have stopped speculating about the economics of the agreement. They speculate instead on what kind of effect it may have on French policy. They wonder how Mitterrand would respond now to an Afghanistan or a Poland. They want to know just what—in a country as concerned as Mitterrand's France is with its civilizing mission and its historical integrity—the practical morality should be. Not Mme Gonçalves. She *knows*. She is the Solzhenitsyn of the block. She will not listen to the commentators on the TF 1 nightly news who try to persuade her that France will end up controlling Russia with its hard, Western currency. She is convinced that Leonid Brezhnev is going to turn the gas off the first time Mitterrand dares to cross him. She imagines Brezhnev sitting in the snow in Urengoy with his hand on an enormous faucet.

February 1982

Mme Gonçalves followed the war in the Falkland Islands. English house guests at the diplomat's around the corner turned on a big shortwave radio every hour and listened to news of the war on the BBC, drinking Vittel water instead of the white Burgundy they always used to drink when they came to Paris, as if to mark the sober tone of the occasion with an appropriate beverage. Everyone sat down to lunch with the radio going (on the dining-room sideboard, next to the Haviland bowl with a rim of blue-and-gold peacocks and a mended crack that Mme Gonçalves keeps discreetly turned to the wall). And whenever the radio was on Mme Gonçalves was not supposed to use the vacuum cleaner or the washing machine, which sends great spurts of noise through the diplomat's apartment and announces each change of cycle with a kind of gear grinding (something like a car jammed into reverse) that always makes his Briard, Loulou, and his Cavalier King Charles Spaniel, Ivy, howl.

Actually, Mme Gonçalves first learned about the war in the Falklands when the diplomat's wife told her to start picking up *Libération* along with the other morning papers and the warm brioches and the fresh milk from the *crémerie* she always takes with her breakfast coffee, because *Libé,* she had heard, was reporting "the war" in some detail. Mme Gonçalves knew from the Cambodian tax inspector who runs the corner newsstand that *Libé* is a radical sort of paper, disrespectful of authority, given to comic strips of naked politicians cavorting with statues, and apt to put a picture of J. R. Ewing on the cover right next to a picture of the President of the Republic—not at all the sort of paper for an elderly Parisian diplomat and his delicate wife. She concluded that something very special must be happening in the world for people like that to start reading *Libé.* She herself started to read through *Libé* on the way to work, although it is still hard for her to read in French, as indeed it is hard for her to understand anyone in Paris who does not happen to have been born and raised, as she was, on a farm in Portugal. She also insisted that M. Gonçalves do something about collecting their television set from the repair shop in Montparnasse where she had sent it in March for a new picture tube. M. Gonçalves does not have much energy for errands. He is *fatigado,* Mme Gonçalves will say, shaking her head, when she hurries home from work at the end of the afternoon, ready for a *passeio* up and down the block, and finds her husband just as she left him in the morning, slowly strolling the cobblestone courtyard of our building, supervising the comings and goings in his mild, distracted way, nodding to neighbors who pass the open courtyard door. He has been *fatigado* since the fighting turned savage in Angola. It is her way of saying that loss has rattled her husband and made him as vague and cheerful as a backward child. This psychic weariness of his—this Trás-os-Montes *Weltschmerz*—is one of the reasons Mme Gonçalves is interested in wars like the Falkland war, which have to do with settlers and farms and cattle. The conversations she heard these past two months at the diplomat's—conversations about battleships and fighter planes and the relative atrocities of napalm bombs versus splinter bombs—seemed to her beside the point. To Mme Gonçalves, the point was whether the Falkland shepherds would be killed or would have to start wandering until they found their way to a concierge's quarters in some Paris neighborhood or, as her sons did, to a Brazilian factory.

Mme Gonçalves is interested in colonial claims and attachments and betrayals. She observes the world as if it were one of the *feuilletons* that run for weeks on television and end, suddenly, not in treaties but in small, corrupting family tragedies. And it was instructive to her that so many of her French neighbors on the block—not the diplomats or the rich intellectuals who prefer fixing up its funny old apartments to finding proper bourgeois housing on, say, the Avenue Georges Mandel, but the shopkeepers and the artisans who have their caning shops and upholstery ateliers in courtyards just like ours—were quite oblivious of the fact that a war was going on.

Not even Mme Gonçalves's friend Mme Lenoir seemed to notice the war in the Falkland Islands. Mme Lenoir is the local nurse. She gives shots and cough medicine and rheumatism massages to the neighborhood and keeps everybody up to date on the state of the little chalet in the Haute-Savoie that she has been preparing, over thirty or forty years, for her retirement in 1986, two days after Pentecost. Once a month, Mme Gonçalves gets a shot from Mme Lenoir for stomachache. She and the nurse have come to know each other fairly well in the course of those monthly shots—two women far from home and getting on, but each in her own way indispensable to a lively street on the Left Bank of Paris. Usually, they talk about the medicine they knew as farm children—garlic around your neck, a cross on your door against the evil eye, a village priest with the right exorcistic enthusiasm, poultices of mud and herbs which would surely have done as well, applied to Mme Gonçalves's sore stomach, as any injection in her arm. But this month Mme Gonçalves wanted to discuss the Falkland Islands. She asked Mme Lenoir her opinion on the latest news, and Mme Lenoir said that to her mind France should never have lost to Wales in last week's soccer match.

Walking home after her shot, Mme Gonçalves met Mme Caillot, from the hardware store, and asked the same question, and had to listen while Mme Caillot, who has no wealth to speak of but considerable respect for the concept, complained about wealth taxes under the socialists. And as for Véronique Lavali—the student who rents the *chambre de bonne* on the sixth floor—she had missed the news of the war entirely, and, in fact, had spent the evening at a play about two antiwar Air Force pilots. It was a hot evening, and Véronique, being a blooming and exuberant Niçoise girl, had stopped in the courtyard, tucked up her skirt, and taken off her stockings, and was wiggling her toes under the cool water from one of the outdoor taps where servants used to wash the building linens (and where Mme Gonçalves still washes out her sheets and towels). Véronique wanted to talk about the play. She told Mme Gonçalves about a scene she liked: the superpowers were carving up the world, country by country, on a big war map, and they went at it until only the Falkland Islands were left. She said that the audience had found the scene *très pertinent*, but when she started to describe the map the Falkland Islands turned out to be Iceland.

Mme Gonçalves knows that a lot of people here consider the Falklands almost French, because the first Falkland colonists were French whalers who sailed from Saint-Malo with a charter from Louis XV that guaranteed their rights to the islands and to the waters around them. The old general from the wing across the courtyard told Mme Gonçalves that just the other day someone had actually claimed Les Malouines (as they are called here) for France in a letter to *Le Monde.* Mme Gonçalves finds it odd that French students, educated boys and girls who go to antiwar plays and should know their geography —especially geography that once, at least, was French geography —could turn the world upside down and put Les Malouines in the North Atlantic. Mme Gonçalves was a married woman in Angola before she could read or write. She started out with her own boys, using the textbooks they brought home from school, and she is still attentive to books, to newspapers and magazines, to almost everything printed. She reads not so much for information or amusement as for security, for something to relieve her of her own unsettling experiences. There is no telephone in the concierge's lodge, and Mme Gonçalves does not intend to pay to install one, but she collects phone books. When she shops at a new store or meets a new neighbor on the street or serves a new guest at one of the diplomat's lunches, she always looks up the name in one of her phone books, and is always reassured when she finds it—printed, permanent, buffered by a million other names and addresses against anonymity and uncertainty. For Mme Gonçalves, pages are more reliable than reality. Angola is still the same orange as Portugal in the atlas that the Gonçalves got as a bonus when they joined a Christmas savings club in Luanda. Zaire is still green for Belgium, a European color, but when the family fled Angola and stopped in Zaire, there was nothing Belgian at all about it, and then Mme Gonçalves knew for sure that they would be leaving Africa. Brazil is orange, too, like Portugal, but Mme Gonçalves has two Brazilian daughters-in-law she has never seen—Bahia girls, used to big-city privacies—and, unlike good Portuguese daughters-in-law, they may not want the Gonçalveses when the Gonçalveses have finally saved enough money to emigrate and grow old quietly near their grandchildren. She suspects that now the Falklands will change their color, too. She is drawn to the process. It is a fascination she shares with some of the other foreigners on the block—the butcher from Dahomey, the Berber greengrocer, the two boys from Vietnam who deliver for the wine store with trim little pushcarts that look like skateboards with handles. In Paris, the differences between colonizer and colonized mean less than this binding colonial fascination. The war in the Falklands was in its way a laboratory for their own history, just as it was a laboratory for the remarkable new weapons that seemed to excite the diplomat and his house guests. It clarified a whole catalogue of friends and enemies and antagonisms. Mme Gonçalves, for instance, hates the Spanish—the Portuguese have hated the Spanish since Spain ruled Portugal in the seventeenth century—and she thinks of Spain mainly as a long road to cover quickly on her way to Trás-os-Montes every August. Insofar as Argentina is a Spanish country, she cannot see any merit in its claims or its adventures. She was distressed to hear from the Italian plumber on the third floor that he had cousins in Buenos Aires who were Argentine and wanted to own the Falklands (though none of them would think of visiting the islands as long as there were calm seas and palmy beaches in Uruguay), because the idea of Spanish-speaking Italian South Americans complicated her prejudices. So did the idea of Catholic Argentina, since she believes that any claim that Catholics make against Protestants—even a Spanish claim—is surely in the Church's interests. On the other hand, she knew that the Pope went to England and said Mass with Protestants. She saw the newsreels that day and concluded that in some way he had raised their claim to the Falklands to a kind of Catholic legitimacy. Then, too, the Falkland shepherds and their children—she saw them in *Libé* every day, piling sandbags, helping the British dig their trenches—moved her. She knew from her own experience that they were happier at home, on their wet and windy islands, herding sheep for a trading company that probably underpaid them, than they would ever have been in England, looking for jobs, looking for the sort of welcome she looked for in Portugal and never found.

A friend who was born in Argentina and has lived in England and France says that to her mind the real difference between French colonialism and English colonialism is that Frenchmen believe in a kind of immortal nationality, called The French, whereas Englishmen believe in an immortal nation, called Great Britain. Certainly the French colonized in the conviction that being French was the highest human good. They preached a kind of sublime identification to their colonials.

Thirty years ago in Algeria and Mali and New Caledonia, local children were sitting at French desks in little French schools, following the same French schedule as any child in Paris or Lyons, memorizing the course of French rivers and the milk production of French cows, making lists of French kings and calling all this their history. Being French was a quality, an achievement, an exercise in style and desire, like French Catholicism or French socialism. It was a quality that travelled like the white Burgundy in the diplomat's cellar, doing fine as long as it was never shaken and never traumatized, and, in fact, it proved to be a fairly durable quality. It inspired resistance and revolution, but in the end it left most revolutionaries resolutely Francophile. Being English, on the other hand, had to do with a place and with a language used to describe that place. Colonials were never educated to *be* English. To be English, they had to sail to England and breathe the air and read the history on English benches and in English libraries. In their own countries, they were not Englishmen but wogs who spoke English. The Englishmen who *were* sent out, like the Falkland kelpers, clearly could not carry an immortal nation with them. They could only carry a marvellous language to evoke it. Even today, the fact of battleships and ocean liners sailing to islands so remote that the journey alone took nearly two weeks has prompted fewer questions about English ships in far-off seas than quotations about those ships and those seas. The quotations were accurate as to courage and decency on what was, after all, the right side of the war, but they had nothing to do with the realities of a trading-company lobbying in Westminster and a small colony of shepherds, seven thousand miles from any recourse, who were mainly ignored before the Argentine invasion and were subject to elaborate restrictions on their rights as British citizens. England went to war for reasons that in the public mind had less to do with Margaret Thatcher or Francis Pym than with Shakespeare and Donne and Byron. The rest of northern Europe, one suspects, went to war vicariously, because the Falkland Islands provided Europeans with a rare occasion to be openly absolute about their values and even about their virtues. It was not, as one of the diplomat's English house guests put it, a moment for "blood in the teacup." Voltaire was much quoted here during those weeks. After the British started using Hamlet to explain themselves, the French started using Voltaire to explain Hamlet: ". . . *Une pièce grossière et barbare, qui ne serait pas supportée par la plus vile populace de la France et de l'Italie.*" But the best and possibly the last word on the mad-dogs-and-Englishmen syndrome came from a historical memoir by a fifteenth-century diplomat. Mme Gonçalves found it in *Libé*: "*Naturellement, les Angloys qui ne sont jamais partyz d'Angleterre sont fort collericques.*"

June 1982

Mme Gonçalves had an economic crisis last month. Until then, she had never thought of needing money as having an economic crisis. She thought that there were rich people in the world, like the French who are her neighbors now, and poor people, like the Portuguese peasants who were once her neighbors in Trás-os-Montes, and travellers of fortune, so to speak, between wealth and poverty. Mme Gonçalves always thought of herself as one of those travellers. She had a personal economics, if the word applies. She believed that the circumstances of prosperity were given, like geography. In a way, she believed that people like herself merely occupied prosperity—*hôtes de passage*, the French would call them—until stronger or smarter people came along and took it over. Talking about Angola, she would always describe a kind of occupation—a squatters' holiday in a sunny and abundant country where cows that would have wasted on the rocky soil of northern Portugal got fat and creamy on rich savanna grass. She said that the war she fled finally, leaving everything behind, happened because the prosperity called Angola was in dispute, like a legacy of a choice pasture or a high-walled *potager*. She believed in wars in Angola and poverty in Portugal, but she did not believe in French economic crises, although she heard about them every night on the news and read about them—*la crise économique!*—every morning in the headlines at the corner kiosk.

When Mme Gonçalves came to Paris, her French was mainly a collection of little rituals of accommodation. She took the measure of the Frenchman (the butcher, say, or a tenant on our courtyard) and improvised according to her own appraisal and the Frenchman's tolerance. Now that she is fifty-six and a grandmother, she feels entitled to some discomfort in others. There is a kind of negative fluency to Mme Gonçalves's French lately. She sweeps through any conversation she does not want to have at an inspired level of incomprehensibility and leaves the clerks at the post office and the meter readers from the gas company stuttering helplessly. Her French has nothing at all to do with the French in which economic crises are invoked and grave statements issued from the Élysée.

Mme Gonçalves always thought of that sort of French as background, a little like the drone of fado on Portuguese radio. It went with the heavy silver forks and platters and the dusty bottles of white Burgundy at her diplomat's lunches. It was decorative and dispensable, like the camel's-hair overcoat and the deep-red cashmere scarf that François Mitterrand likes to wear when he has his picture taken on a lonely road in the provinces and talks to reporters about "the patrimony." When it came to proper French, Mme Gonçalves might have been described as a disciple of the Swiss linguist Ferdinand de Saussure. De Saussure was the founder of modern linguistics. He took a formal, systemic approach to language, and he was not much interested in the word as it relates to its object out there in an empirical world. Neither was Mme Gonçalves. For Mme Gonçalves, proper French was a kind of pure and timeless commentary, following its own logic, untroubled and undisciplined by reality. It could be as satisfying as a costume *feuilleton*, as cathartic as a Trás-os-Montes funeral, but it had no power over Mme Gonçalves—it had nothing to do with polishing the diplomat's silver after lunch and tying it up in plastic bags, or sweeping the courtyard every day, or comparing the prices of vegetables at the Tuesday open market on Boulevard Raspail. It was at the market, on the Tuesday before Christmas, that Mme Gonçalves discovered she was having an economic crisis. The salt cod she needed for Christmas Eve (the Portuguese always have a Christmas Eve *bacalhao*) was up to fifty-three francs a kilo, and the turkey she needed for Christmas Day was nearly as expensive, and Mme Gonçalves was short of cash anyway, because not many of the women on our block—women whose clothes she usually hems and tucks—had bought new dresses for the holidays. Mme Gonçalves took the cod but not the turkey. That night, she announced to all the neighbors she saw that she was having an economic crisis. She described it as something on the order of an act of God or a guerrilla raid in Angola. She did not know what an economic crisis was doing, suddenly, in the life of a respectable concierge with business on the side and five weeks' paid vacation every summer and two grown sons, working hard in Bahia, who had actually flown to Europe in June on a World Cup charter, as if crossing the Atlantic Ocean for soccer games were an old Gonçalves-family practice.

Mme Gonçalves does not know Pierre Bourdieu. She sometimes passes his office, at the Maison des Sciences de L'Homme, on her way to the Raspail market, and it is likely that over the years she has passed Professor Bourdieu himself, having a sandwich at the café across the street, or even doing some shopping of his own along the Boulevard, but she has no idea that having an economic crisis changed her, as it were, from a Saussurian to a Bourdieuian. Pierre Bourdieu has the chair in sociology at the Collège de France. He is the most eminent sociologist in the country. He is concerned with symbolic power. Three years ago, he wrote a remarkable book called *La Distinction*, which was really an explication of France's own "culture" of class and status and its symbolic uses, and just this winter he published a collection of essays on a theory of language—*Ce Que Parler Veut Dire*—that in many ways is a reader's guide to Mme Gonçalves's rhetorical distress. Bourdieu talks about an "economics of linguistic exchange"—a kind of spontaneous science having to do with the relation between what linguists call our grammar and the marketplace, as it were, for that grammar. He says that the language we use represents a kind of capital (something like a Raspail greengrocer's stock or the gold under a rich peasant's mattress) and depends for its authority and its value on a market and on a masterly anticipation of that market. It depends, in other words, on whether anyone is buying what we have to say and the way we say it. Bourdieu would say that people like Mme Gonçalves, being broke lately, have had to buy the sort of fancy and intimidating economic crisis that once merely entertained them on television.

Charles de Gaulle, of course, was the great speculator in the rhetoric of a modern France. Bourdieu says that de Gaulle had the right capital. He was military and high-minded and affectingly lugubrious. He could overawe. His *espace*, as the French say, was appropriate to his discourse. It was the space of righteous triumph, of a war against evil fought and won. Bourdieu says that de Gaulle could talk about raising the price of artichokes and make it sound like a proud sacrifice for God and country. He could make his realpolitik sound like grand symbolic gestures, whereas François Mitterrand, who admires de Gaulle and tries hard for Gaullist style, makes grand symbolic gestures and ends up sounding as if he were making crude and cynical politics. Bourdieu likes to compare de Gaulle and Mitterrand. So do many of the people on my block. Mitterrand's rhetoric has worn them out and made them nervous. They think that rhetoric should soothe reality, not describe it. They miss the kind of economic crisis that de Gaulle used to supply twenty years ago—one that made everybody feel patriotic, and encouraged the French in the uppity xenophobia of wallflowers at a superpowers ball. Mitterrand, sitting at the General's desk and affecting the same gravity, reminds them mostly of unemployment or inflation or the price of cod. There is no market in France for gravity that does not satisfy. Montesquieu called gravity *"le bouclier des sots"*—the shield of fools. Sacha Guitry, paraphrasing Montesquieu, called it "the happiness of imbeciles." The fact is that in France successful seriousness demands practitioners who contradict themselves by a kind of infectious confidence in the terrible things they have to say. De Gaulle believed that the world would end with him—and France—sitting out the apocalypse. He was a con man on a grand scale, which was why real democrats, like Pierre Mendès France, could never stand him. Mitterrand seems too uneasy at the game to see it through. His nerves betray him. His careful gestures—the fine Cifonelli suits, the essays of Montaigne that he keeps open on his lap on the presidential plane, so that Carlos Fuentes and Gabriel García Márquez and the other writers he likes to take along on trips will know him for an intellectual—betray him, too. When he goes to Burundi or Rwanda and makes a speech about France and Africa and great common cause, the people who run Burundi or Rwanda start fidgeting. They wonder what the French President is up to, what he is apt to take away in trade tomorrow. When he talks about great common cause at home, people conclude that things are much worse than they suspected. Even a Portuguese grandmother from Trás-os-Montes who thinks that Socialists are really Communists with baptism certificates knows that socialism is not supposed to mean sacrifice and hardship. Mme Gonçalves has finally bought her economic crisis on the linguistic exchange, and is just beginning to recover.

January 1983

Mme Gonçalves is busy following the Bulgarian connection. She believes that the Bulgarians hired Mehmet Ali Agca to shoot the Pope on May 13, 1981. The idea of the Bulgarians is soothing to Mme Gonçalves. She says that if Bulgarians were responsible for the attack in St. Peter's Square, then perhaps Bulgarians were also responsible for the attack in Portugal a year later, when a crazy priest came at the Holy Father with a bayonet. That attack especially distressed Mme Gonçalves. The fact that the crazy priest was not Portuguese but Spanish—and therefore, to Mme Gonçalves's mind, the sort of person one would expect to go mad and turn murderous over a point of *intégriste* doctrine, like the restoration of the Latin Mass—did not really justify what she considered a serious lapse in Portuguese hospitality. She was ashamed that anyone would feel free to kill a Pope in her own country. She did not see how a people who managed to have a revolution nine years ago without firing a shot could lose their reputation now unless important foreign conspirators were involved.

Mme Gonçalves takes a proprietary interest in John Paul II. She wants the neighbors to know that when the Pope came to Portugal he made the same pilgrimage to Our Lady of Fátima that she had made, as a bride, just before she left her family and her friends in Trás-os-Montes to start her new, married life in Angola. She tells them that when the Pope came to Paris he hurried through Mass at Notre-Dame so that he could pray right here in the neighborhood, at the Chapel of Our Lady of the Miraculous Medal, where a young Sister of Charity called Catherine Labouré saw the Virgin in 1830, and where Mme Gonçalves often prays to the Virgin to cure her stomachaches. Mme Gonçalves has been told by the nun who once sold her a piece of Catherine's skin that in his student days in Paris the Pope made many pilgrimages to the glass sarcophagus where Catherine—St. Catherine now—is on display. She herself discovered Catherine one day when she was out shopping for a jar of plums-in-Armagnac (it was for a dinner party at the diplomat's) and ended up at Dupeyron, on the rue du Bac, down the street from the chapel. By now, praying for her stomach on the rue du Bac is a sort of spiritual supplement to the monthly shots she gets from Mme Lenoir. Like the Pope, Mme Gonçalves believes in a proper mixture of pilgrimage and medicine for long life and in a strong resolve against Communism. She has followed John Paul II on television in the course of the seventeen foreign pilgrimages he has undertaken in the four and a half years of his papacy. She was listening to the news last November when he called himself a "pilgrim messenger who wants to travel the world to fulfill the mandate Christ gave to the Apostles when he sent them to evangelize all men and all nations." She says that that was when she knew for sure that John Paul II preferred the shrines and saints and sweetness of his pilgrimages to any stone-cathedral piety—that stone cathedrals were just official detours on his true path to the worship of the Virgin. Watching him again this month, in El Salvador, she remarked to Véronique Lavali, who often drops in on Mme Gonçalves for the eight o'clock news, that the Pope always seems rosier and happier in "Catholic" countries than he does at home in the Vatican. She said that he had not looked like himself "at home" since last Good Friday, when he celebrated the Stations of the Cross in the Colosseum.

March 1983

Mme Gonçalves was tear-gassed and lost her broom on May 24, during a student demonstration on the Esplanade des Invalides. She was crossing the esplanade at the rue Saint Dominique, on her way to pin up hems for a neighbor of ours who had moved in March, and she was carrying the broom she always uses for her measuring stick. Mme Gonçalves has a real measuring stick in a trunk at her sister's house in Portugal. She is a practical and thrifty woman, who would never think of spending money for another just because she happens to be living in Paris now, and she would have expected any French policeman to understand this—to understand exactly why a middle-aged Portuguese concierge was crossing the Esplanade des Invalides during a demonstration with an old broom on which the skirt lengths appropriate to the season's fashions had been marked off in bright-red ink. Besides, three weeks ago Mme Gonçalves did not take French student demonstrations very seriously. She had no empathy with the students who were demonstrating here all spring, marching through town in their American jeans and bandannas chanting *"Trop de concours, pas de temps pour l'amour"* and stopping occasionally to set fire to a car, as if they were stopping to eat a hot dog or a cinnamon crêpe.

Nine years ago, when the Gonçalveses moved to Paris, people still talked about a "Revolution of 1968." Mme Gonçalves was terrified. She had just fled one revolution, in Angola, and she had dropped in on another revolution, in Portugal, where there was no work for old colonials like the Gonçalveses and not much of a welcome, either. In fact, Mme Gonçalves remembered May of 1968 as the month the fighting got terrible near her farm, and the Gonçalveses lost two cows to the guerrillas and had to camp for a week with the Protestant missionaries, who took the bottles of *vinho verde* that M. Gonçalves had brought along with the bedding and threw them into the bush and then told the Gonçalves boys to pray hard, because Christian martyrdom was at hand. When she got to Paris, she asked the tenants in our building about *their* May 1968. She wanted to know if any of their friends had been hurt, and if there had been looting on the block, and she was startled to hear them get nostalgic and talk about what a wonderful time 1968 had been, and about which of the children on the block had helped occupy the Sorbonne and which women had formed a committee to take them sandwiches.

There was only one protest last month that interested Mme Gonçalves, and that involved the *petits patrons*—the small shopkeepers—who shut down on the afternoon of May 5 to protest the socialist government's tax and credit policies and price controls, which they claim are ruining them. Two shops on our street are already bankrupt. My friend Albert, who sells fluffy retro clothes to the girls in the neighborhood, has pasted a *bail à céder* sign over the poster of Jean Harlow in his window and is waiting to sell his lease and move to Guadeloupe and open a piano bar. Albert went on strike that afternoon. So did Ferdinand, the butcher, who came to Paris from Auvergne five years ago and took over the *boucherie* just up the block from our building and moved his family into the two-room flat behind the refrigerator closet. Ferdinand is an ardent follower of Jacques Chirac, the mayor of Paris, whom he associates with a life free from Socialists, Communists, taxes, and pornography. It was Ferdinand who went from shop to shop, organizing the other merchants on the block, and who held forth, lunchtimes, across the street at the Bar des Sports, passing out strike bulletins from his union, the Syndicat National de la Petite et Moyenne Industrie. Ferdinand is a terrible butcher. He hacks at his meat as if it were destined for the stockpot on his grandmother's wood stove, and Mme Gonçalves says that once she saw him sell some scraps he was saving for a neighbor's dog to a stranger who stopped in asking for boeuf bourguignon. But he works hard, and so does his plump, blond wife, who sits all day on a stool behind the counter and keeps the books and minds the cash drawer and covers for him with the customers whenever he slips out to the Bar des Sports for a glass of wine. In their stubborn, country way, they will not accept the fact that life in Paris, which seemed so agreeable once, so full of prospects, has come to be as punishing as their life at home. Mme Gonçalves says they were the first people on the block to close on the afternoon of May 5. By one o'clock, all the *petits patrons* were closed except the Berber grocer, who is saving for a house in Tafraout, and who said later that he was not going to lose an afternoon just to please a butcher who bought his vegetables from an Italian. That night, two "strike coordinators" paid the Berber grocer a visit, overturned his fruit stand, stomped on his tomatoes and his oranges, and poured his olive oil all over the floor.

Mme Gonçalves knew that there would be students demonstrating on the twenty-fourth. Véronique Lavali was going to demonstrate, despite the fact that the demonstrations were against a new education law—a law introducing qualifying exams and curriculum quotas for second-year university students—that did not in any way affect Véronique, five years into her doctorate. Véronique considers herself a Trotskyite—not a Party Trotskyite, like the angry-looking characters who peered at her through locked gates and around corners on her visit to the headquarters of the Parti Communiste Internationaliste, over on the rue du Faubourg-Saint-Denis, but more of an Early Trotskyite, like the ones in Alain Resnais's movie about Stavisky, which she has seen four times at the Cinémathèque. She says that the Trotskyites here are *"pas du tout gai,"* but she decided to march with them anyway on May 24, because she could not, in conscience, join the bourgeois students who were convening on the esplanade, and who she knew had been organized by right-wing politicians counting on the fact that none of them knew enough about politics to notice.

Mme Gonçalves had thought of avoiding the esplanade—of walking up to the Avenue de Tourville and around the Église du Dôme, where she and M. Gonçalves once saw Napoleon's sarcophagus —but she changed her mind when she saw that the esplanade was quiet. There were policemen everywhere. Some of them were lined up, like a barricade, at the corner where the rue Saint-Dominique opens onto the esplanade, but they stepped aside politely and let Mme Gonçalves through. The problem was that policemen were also lined up across the rue Saint-Dominique on the other side of the esplanade, and those policemen would not let Mme Gonçalves out again. She tried to ask the policemen why they had let her into the demonstration if they were not going to let her leave. She told them that it was ridiculous for the police to let people onto a big open space like the Esplanade des Invalides if the police were so worried about having them there that they all wore helmets and carried shields and tear-gas cannisters. She was still talking when fighting started on the Pont Alexandre III. People were throwing stones and sticks, and Mme Gonçalves heard a kind of popping sound, and then another popping sound—it was tear-gas cannisters going off —and then hundreds of students started running up the esplanade, coughing and crying and covering their faces with scarves and handkerchiefs. Mme Gonçalves nearly fell in the rush of people. She wanted to run, too, but the students were going fast, in their tennis shoes and jeans, and they kept bumping into her. The tear gas caught her in the eyes and burned her throat, and she had to use her broom as a kind of blind man's stick to find her way back to the sidewalk. She says now that she never meant to shake her broom at the policemen who were blocking the rue Saint-Dominique. All she wanted was to go home before the shooting started. She could not imagine that the afternoon would end without shooting, any more than she could imagine that it had begun because a few students didn't want to take a test. But her throat kept burning and she had no kerchief for protection. She started to push through the police line. Two policemen raised their shields to stop her. And Mme Gonçalves shook her broom at them, scolding, the way she always shakes it at the old drunk who wanders into our courtyard late at night and sings. One of the policemen grabbed the broom and stared through his riot visor at the strange red markings. Then Mme Gonçalves ran. She was back in the courtyard, splashing cold tap water on her eyes, when Véronique came home, dispirited. The student demonstrations were over. It was getting on toward exam time, and there were not likely to be more until fall.

June 1983

EIGHT STORIES

THE PLACE DAUPHINE

The Place Dauphine is a secret garden, a little wedge of sandy park and chestnut trees near the tip of the Île de la Cité, just below the Palais de Justice. Children who live on the Place sometimes play on the steps of the Palais, getting in the way of the lawyers and judges and important police commissioners who stop to talk there, but their parents usually have no interest in the Palais—unless, of course, they are judges or lawyers or important police commissioners themselves. When the Palais de Justice was restored, in 1840, the Place Dauphine was a livelier neighborhood than it is now. It was smelly and dense and full of village activity, with the workers and craftsmen and peddlers of the neighborhood living alongside a few bourgeois families who had always considered themselves more interesting, being Place people, than their decorous friends over in the Sixteenth or the Seventh Arrondissement. Gradually, though, the bourgeois families took over. The houses that enclosed the Place were restored to some of their old Henri Quatre detail, and the rents were raised, and now the neighborhood is fashionable and expensive, and most of the workers and craftsmen have had to leave. It is still a neighborhood of great charm, and of special privacy, with its quirky rooftop views of the Seine, and its chestnut trees, and a kind of misty gray light that mellows late on fall afternoons and makes the ground glow. The people who live on the Place today, and on the two quais—the Quai des Orfèvres and the Quai de l'Horloge—that are, in a way, its sidewalks, are for the most part discreet people, bound by real estate and breeding, and even those who might be meddlesome or indiscreet outside the Place tend to dissolve into propriety when they come home. *"On s'entend bien ici,"* people on the Place like to say. They still think of themselves as villagers—as villagers who talk things over, solve their own problems, and have no need of the attention of the outside world, by which they mean the rest of Paris, separated by the Seine from their own few acres of the First Arrondissement. In fact, they rarely interfere even with one another. They look across the Place at each other's doors and into each other's windows. They note the comings and goings, the deliveries and the dinner parties. They literally cross paths whenever they cross the Place, and so they depend on a strict etiquette of cordiality, knowing that there is no space in their neighborhood for unpleasantness.

People on the Place Dauphine say now that this discretion of theirs, this instinct not to interfere, is the reason they paid so little attention to the two reports they found in their mailboxes late last spring under the letterhead of the Comité de Sauvegarde de la Place Dauphine—reports that talked about "hordes of Yugoslav pickpockets" on the Pont-Neuf, "undesirables" who preyed on passersby and had to be "eliminated" from the neighborhood. Most people never even got to the Yugoslavs in the first report. They read that Mme de Roux (at 21 Place Dauphine) was worried about pigeons dirtying Place Dauphine windowsills and eating flowers on Place Dauphine chestnut trees, and then they tossed the report away, thinking vaguely that it must have been at least five or six years since they had got one like it.

The Comité de Sauvegarde de la Place Dauphine began like any of a dozen other local groups here. Some neighbors remember getting together in 1968 because the city planned to build a new subterranean parking lot directly under the Place—and that would have meant cutting down the famous chestnut trees. For a while, they kept on meeting to settle the other problems of the Place, such as how to ensure a proper restoration of Place façades, and, eventually, what the proper hour was for Place restaurants to be putting out their trash cans and their sacks of garbage. One big argument they had was about dogs. Some of the people liked dogs and owned dogs, and even walked their dogs among the chestnut trees, and some of them disliked dogs, and thought of dogs the way they thought of pigeons—as a species that had evolved specifically to offend a few hundred fastidious Parisians who lived on a little common on the Île de la Cité. Life on the Place was fairly calm through the seventies. Housefronts were classified by the Beaux-Arts, and thus protected. The old Place restaurateurs and antique dealers remained, but no one could open a new boutique and make a fortune selling musk candles and home-glazed pottery to tourists. There was some crime on the Place. A couple of young Germans showed up on the Quai de l'Horloge every summer with *their* dogs in tow, and they frightened people walking along the quai and, when they could, robbed them. Occasionally, French boys, working the quais from the crowded safety of the Pont-Neuf, would rob someone, too. Simone Danloux, who runs a bookstore on the Place du Pont-Neuf, was robbed a few times —but never, she says, by "hordes of Yugoslavs." It was the Yugoslavs who caused the trouble on the Place Dauphine. That is, it was the offspring of a couple of Yugoslav gypsy clans that seem to have settled down in their caravans on the outskirts of Paris. They send their children into town mornings—to the Pont-Neuf, say, or the big Métro stations—to pick pockets and steal handbags instead of sending them to school, where the profits are smaller. Gypsies tend to know the law that concerns them, and the law in this case is that no one under the age of thirteen can be detained in France. Not many of the Pont-Neuf Yugoslavs are over ten or, at the most, twelve years old. They work in groups, these gypsy children. They spot some obviously foreign woman sightseeing on the bridge and they gather around her, chattering, begging, tugging at her skirt while one of them grabs her bag, slips it under a newspaper, and disappears into the crowd. By now, the local policemen know them well. They chase them and scold them and get a handbag or two back when they can, and the little gypsy girls giggle and shriek and announce to everybody watching that the policemen are trying to get them into bed. The children think of stealing as a kind of *métier,* the police say, and they like to show off. French television has filmed them working the Métro. *Le Figaro* has published pictures of them snatching bags, and there have been articles about them in *Le Monde* and *Le Nouvel Observateur.* The Comité de Sauvegarde de la Place Dauphine says that Edith Cresson, the Minister of Agriculture, even got up in the Assembly one day to talk about "the Yugoslav problem"—though no one on the committee can swear to the fact that Mme Cresson was talking about ten-year-old gypsy pickpockets, and not just unemployed Yugoslav farmers. The fact is that there are sixty-eight thousand Yugoslavs in France. There are migrant workers from all over Yugoslavia. There are Serbs and Croats and Macedonians and Slovenes, and at the most only a few thousand of those Yugoslavs are gypsies—gypsies who entered France without passports, driving their caravans (the French call them mobile shantytowns) across the mountains from Italy, and showing up at the nearest *gendarmerie* to register as stateless persons and qualify for residence under the country's generous and, at the moment, controversial interpretation of the Geneva-convention rules on refugee status.

Most Yugoslavs in France are here to work in factories and save money and eventually go home and build themselves new houses in their native villages and never work again. Some of them are in Paris doing piecework for clothing designers around the rue du Faubourg Poissonnière, and, by chance, one designer who owns an atelier on the Faubourg Poissonnière and uses a lot of Yugoslavs is a woman from the Place Dauphine. Her name was Aline Hercberg when she moved to the Place, seven years ago. Now her name is Aline Hercberg-Sullivan, because she married an Irishman named Garratt Sullivan, and the two of them exchanged names along with wedding rings. Mme Hercberg-Sullivan has been a refugee of sorts herself; she spent the war, hidden and disguised as a "French" child, in the Pyrenees, far from home. Her parents come from Poland. "Polish Jewish Bolsheviks" is how she likes to describe them. They moved to France some sixty years ago and became furriers in Paris and, in a way, joined the Parisian Jewish bourgeoisie. But they kept their sympathies for poor people and oppressed people and people like Jews and gypsies, who were so often outcasts and exiles. Aline Hercberg-Sullivan grew up in Paris and inherited those sympathies. She went to Israel and spent three years studying Hebrew and working on a kibbutz, and finally she came home and began designing dresses and then producing the dresses she designed, and she did so well that she was able to buy herself a charming triplex on the Place Dauphine which, according to Place gossip, had once briefly belonged to Yves Saint Laurent. She is still what the French would call *une femme très sensible.* She has a horror of prejudice. She likes the Yugoslavs and the Turks who work for her. She does not blame those Yugoslavs for the sleight of hand of a couple of dozen delinquents on the Pont-Neuf, any more than she blames those Turks for murders committed here in the name of Allah by a handful of Middle Eastern terrorists.

Aline and Garratt Hercberg-Sullivan do not belong to the Comité de Sauvegarde de la Place Dauphine, but Aline does contribute to an organization called MRAP—Mouvement Contre le Racisme et pour l'Amitié Entre les Peuples. MRAP grew out of an underground group that was concerned with saving Jewish children during the Second World War, and gradually became a group against racism of any sort, and over the years Aline has advertised her dresses in MRAP's magazine, *Différences,* because she liked the work MRAP was doing and wanted to support it. Albert Lévy, the man who runs MRAP now, is a militant of the French Communist Party, and so are some of the people on his staff. His board—which is an honorary, not an advisory, board—is pointedly not Communist. The board of MRAP is chic. For artists and intellectuals, it has people like Jean Lacouture and Edmonde Charles-Roux and Alain Resnais and Iannis Xenakis and Maurice Béjart. For Socialists, it has Gisèle Halimi and Pierre Joxe, who is head of the Socialist delegation at the National Assembly and who lives off the Place Dauphine himself, on the Quai de l'Horloge. It even has a former Gaullist deputy named Alain Terrenoire and an academician who was so eager for the credential that when his predecessor at the Académie Française died he wrote to Lévy and asked to replace the man on the MRAP board, too. It is assumed that MRAP is going to be more agreeable about fighting racism in a moneyed neighborhood like the Place Dauphine than in a workers' town, where the Communist Party could be embarrassed by a lawsuit. The Party is notoriously xenophobic at its grass roots, and MRAP did not file charges in either of two landmark cases of the past few years where Communists were involved—one having to do with a mayor from the *banlieue rouge* outside Paris who led his colleagues and constituents to sack a dormitory where some Mali immigrants were camping, and the other having to do with Communists who publicly accused a Moroccan family that had been living peacefully in their town for five years of peddling drugs to local youngsters. Lately, MRAP has taken up the Palestinian cause. A number of Jews in the movement are disturbed by this. Some quit two years ago, after terrorists bombed a synagogue on rue Copernic and killed four people, and MRAP released a statement that seemed to them to blame the conservatives, who were still in power in France that fall, more than it blamed the terrorists. The ones who stayed did blame the government for ignoring what they called "the rise of racism and Fascism." They told friends who had left MRAP to consider the implications of remarks like the one their Prime Minister, Raymond Barre, made after the bombing. Barre denounced the "odious crime that was aimed at Jews going to synagogue and made victims of innocent Frenchmen walking along rue Copernic."

Aline Hercberg-Sullivan thought of MRAP when she got her second report from the Comité de Sauvegarde de la Place Dauphine in the mailbox, and so she phoned its offices, on the Rue Oberkampf. On August 13, a lawyer from MRAP's judicial commission formally charged the Comité de Sauvegarde de la Place Dauphine with incitement to racial hatred and discrimination.

There is no doubt that when the Comité de Sauvegarde de la Place Dauphine started meeting again last spring there were problems to solve. There was, of course, the problem of the pigeons that distressed Mme de Roux. There was the problem of the annual Pont-Neuf street fair, which always spilled over onto the Place, and which the committee wanted to replace with "more cultural activities." But mainly there was the problem of security, which became the problem of the "hordes of Yugoslav pickpockets." One woman on the Place says that last spring she was counting fourteen or fifteen robberies a day from her back window, which overlooks the bridge. Another woman says that she was counting ten, anyway. Yet no one actually seems to have seen any Yugoslavs (or people they considered Yugoslavs) on the Place Dauphine itself—and the Place is so well studied by its inhabitants that they know which strangers from the Sixth, just across the bridge, show up for a few minutes in the evening to walk their dogs.

Twenty-two people came to the first spring meeting of the Comité de Sauvegarde de la Place Dauphine. Six people formally excused themselves, including Louis Joxe, the minister who negotiated Algerian independence for Charles de Gaulle and who is Pierre Joxe's father. The people who came elected Louis Joxe their *président d'honneur*. They elected themselves officers. Their new working president was a businessman named Jean-Claude Le Sant, with a real-estate-management company on the Place, a construction company in the suburbs, and an active interest in Jacques Chirac's neo-Gaullist party, Rassemblement pour la République. Le Sant has a vision of the Place Dauphine that seemed to please the people on the committee. He talks with feeling about little stones poured in concrete over the dirt and the grass in some agreeable, easy-to-clean pattern; maybe a flower garden with a fence around it; no dogs; no cars; no old men from the Samaritaine, across the bridge, playing *boules* at lunchtime. But Le Sant is a busy man, admittedly impatient with details. When Françoise Ballé, the new secretary of the committee, walked over to his office, at 14 Place Dauphine, with the minutes of that first meeting, Le Sant glanced at them and then signed them with her and ordered a few hundred copies run off on his office copier, and soon everybody on the Place had a copy.

There are people on the Place who say that Françoise Ballé could be a Yugoslav herself—a kind of laundered and respectable gypsy —with her bright black hair pulled back and the silky red dress she sometimes wears and the flush of agitation on her dark cheeks. They know, of course, that Françoise Ballé is French. Her father had a little bait-and-tackle shop on the Quai de l'Horloge. (Some of the Place people who are annoyed at Françoise Ballé now for her exuberance

about the Yugoslavs have taken to calling it "a little worm shop.") Boys
and girls who grew up on the quai twenty or thirty years ago still
remember going off to the bridge at dawn with a can of M. Ballé's
special worms and with M. Ballé's special tackle, but after M. Ballé died
his wife and daughter became converts, as it were, from worms to tea,
and now the name of the shop is Thés d'Arcy. The Ballé women seem
to associate tea with propriety. Some of their neighbors say that they
control the Place with tea. Everybody buys tea from the Ballés, as if by
way of precautionary expiation for some unknown offense that they are
likely to commit one day. If they happen to dislike tea (a lot of the
French do), there is always Ballé jam, at twelve francs a jar, and an
assortment of fancy spices that come in test tubes, corked on top, and
consequently require the purchase of a shelf to keep them right side up.
As secretary of the Comité de Sauvegarde de la Place Dauphine, Françoise Ballé made a natural vigilante, and her minutes of the first meeting
—it was on May 25—were a catalogue of small social observations.
There was the reference to concierges who broke the garbage code.
There was the reference to Vincenzo Marsiglia—he owns a local restaurant called Il Delfino—as Vincenzo du Delfino. There was the association of Mme de Roux, one of the aristocrats, so to speak, of the Place
Dauphine, with the pigeon problem, as if Mme de Roux's particular
distaste for pigeon droppings added tone and weight and solemnity to
the argument against them. But, for hyperbole, nothing matched Françoise Ballé's passages about Yugoslav pickpockets and about the committee's determination that the prefecture send policemen to patrol the
Place and "ramasser ces indésirables et les diriger où il se doit." She must
have been pleased with her minutes, because a few weeks later she
wrote another report to the neighborhood, this one about the meeting
she and Jean-Claude Le Sant had just had with the police commissioner
and about the commissioner's thoughtfully setting up "an important
operation" to clear the neighborhood.

There is no doubt about the xenophobia in France today. Crime
is rising, and the fact of a couple of million immigrant workers in the
country means that the French are thinking less about the problems
immigrants have in being poor and foreign and far from home and
often unwelcome than about the probability of immigrants' being
criminals. Besides, unemployment is rising, too—because of economic
hard times and two devaluations of the franc, and also because a craven
economic policy on Giscard's part has been followed by a stubborn
policy on Mitterrand's. People in France—as in Germany, as in En-

gland—forget easily that the foreigners came in to do the jobs they themselves despised doing. Now they conclude that the foreigners stole those jobs from them. They conclude that the foreigners are terrorists, because so many terrorists are foreigners—and because France has in fact suffered eighteen terrorist murders in the past seven months. They look at what is really an enlightened policy of political asylum and blame it for the deaths at Jo Goldenberg's restaurant this summer. Eventually, they begin to turn the word "refugee" into something suspect and the words "political refugee" into a kind of synonym for "killer." Simone Signoret, coming home to her apartment on the Place Dauphine from a trip to Poland, read the committee's reports and said that what distressed her most was a reference to the gypsy children on the Pont-Neuf as "children of political refugees."

Georges Kiejman, a lawyer who has tried some of the country's most important political-rights cases, talks about a *banalization du mal* in France today. He says that the further the country gets from the really expressive examples of racism in its recent history—war in Algeria and Nazi genocide—the more racism here turns into the kind of ordinary, daily, even unconscious prejudices that do not scare other people very much but can make libertarians like himself uneasy. Certainly France needed the law against racism which it finally got ten years ago. The last French law to deal specifically with what kind of newspaper one could publish and what kind of open letter one could leave in a neighbor's mailbox had been written in 1881, and over the years even that law was applied with less and less diligence. By the late thirties, papers like Robert Brasillach's *Je Suis Partout* were publishing special issues on Jews in France (*"Les Juifs sont des étrangers"*) which involved the most vicious and grotesque caricatures. People like Simone Signoret—who grew up here in the thirties and who has been involved for years in civil-rights causes—are going to be sensitive to notes about "undesirables" on their doorsteps. But a lot of people do not see anything really terrible about calling thieves undesirables or people from Yugoslavia Yugoslavs, whether or not they come in hordes, and whether or not, being gypsies, they call themselves Yugoslavs to begin with.

On December 9, the case of the Place Dauphine and the Yugoslavs will come to trial in a court at the Palais de Justice. Jean-Claude Le Sant, who, as president of the Comité de Sauvegarde de la Place Dauphine, is responsible for its actions under French law, is being sued for twenty-four thousand francs and the committee itself for another twenty-four thousand, and MRAP is asking—it always does in such cases—that Le

Sant pay for the publication of any judgment against him in four newspapers and magazines of MRAP's choosing. Meanwhile, the committee is collecting witnesses. There is talk of a witness who was robbed in his wheelchair by Yugoslavs, talk of a witness robbed in his moving car. One of the two women who sit at their windows on the quai counting pickpockets is going to testify. The other woman refuses. She says that she does not want to get involved. Some of her friends on the Place Dauphine feel that way, too. They will buy their tea and jam from the Ballés, but they refuse to look silly publicly in front of liberal friends. Most Place people simply regret that the old neighborhood courtesies broke down when it came to the Yugoslavs. They are people like the waitress at Chez Paul who said the other night, *"Le tribunal? Je n'aime pas ces choses sophistiquées."*

Garratt Hercberg-Sullivan is going to testify for MRAP. No one on the Place has volunteered to testify with him, and he doubts if anyone will, inasmuch as since August no one on the Place has even talked to him about it. No one has said "You're right" or "I admire you" or "I don't admire you." No one has offered any encouragement or understanding (or even criticism) of the gesture he and Aline made. One woman on the Place did talk briefly last month about walking over and "having a chat with that nice Hercberg girl, letting her know how we do things on the Place Dauphine," but in the end she decided against it.

Aline Hercberg-Sullivan was busy anyway last month with the Paris *prêt-à-porter,* spending her time with friends and customers from overseas. She says that she never actually asked MRAP to bring the committee before the tribunal; she just looked at those first reports, she says, and got mad and picked up the phone on impulse, and she does not regret it at all. She and her husband have heard their neighbors on the sidewalk outside their living room, and heard them stop and whisper, and knew that they were pointing out the "denouncers' " apartment. People have been stopping like that since word went around the Place that the "denouncers" were the foreigners—less a reference to Hercberg, as it happens, than to Sullivan—at No. 21, the arty foreigners with the salmon-pink shutters. Garratt Hercberg-Sullivan says that he and Aline don't know many of their neighbors anyway, not having a dog to walk or children to call in from the Palais's steps at dinnertime. They know the people at Chez Paul, where they often eat after a long day's work. Now Garratt Hercberg-Sullivan also knows Robert Cointepas, the proprietor of a local wine-and-sandwich bar called the Taverne Henri Quatre, having stopped in for a drink a few days after

MRAP filed charges, and having been asked by Cointepas, "Is your name Sullivan?" When Garratt Hercberg-Sullivan nodded, Robert Cointepas called his wife and said, "It's him, all right. I win the bet."

Garratt Hercberg-Sullivan himself was robbed last year on the Place Dauphine—or, rather, his truck was robbed. Garratt has a business importing Irish salmon and Irish oysters, which he delivers to restaurants in a new insulated truck that he sometimes leaves outside his apartment at night so he can get an early start the next morning. There were thousands of francs in salmon and oysters in the truck when he went to sleep the night of the robbery. In the morning, he was seven thousand francs poorer, and even his delivery trolley was gone. He has no idea who robbed him, but he assumes that if it had been a horde of Yugoslavs he would have heard something.

November 1982

THE IRON MOUNTAIN

One day last spring, after the snows had melted and the streams of Oberhessen were flooding some of their winter swell, Willi Schäfer drove three miles from the town of Schlitz to a wood at the southeast foot of a little mountain called the Eisenberg—the iron mountain —to check the condition of the paths. Willi Schäfer comes from Schlitz and works at the town hall as a "minister of tourists," thinking up pleasant things—things like walks over the Eisenberg—for people in Schlitz to do. Every spring, three thousand of those people take Willi's big annual walk, and a few days before the walk Willi covers the mountain himself, putting up arrows and marking out an itinerary. He was just turning into the wood that day when he came on three or four American Army officers standing around a camp table in a clearing, looking at what seemed to be maps of the mountain, and about fifty American soldiers pacing trails and scrutinizing soil and measuring the terrain with odd-looking instruments on tripods. Willi counted four jeeps, two cars, an Army bus, and a helicopter in the clearing before the officers stopped him, telling him in perfect German that they were on a "secret action" and must be left alone. Willi came home with the news that the American Army was buying Schlitz's mountain.

There had been rumors about the Eisenberg for months—rumors that ten thousand American troops were moving from a base at Baumholder, in the Rhineland, to the Eisenberg. There were rumors about a "master restationing plan" that would shift the concentration of U.S. Forces in West Germany from "safe" bases in the south and the west to bases in towns like Schlitz, near the East German border. There were rumors about a new NATO "war plan" involving the deployment of

108 Pershing II missiles and 96 cruise missiles in West Germany. There were even rumors that some of those missiles were coming to the Eisenberg, though the fact is that the deployment, which began this month, was always intended for Baden-Württemberg and Rhineland-Palatinate.

Back in February, the nature club—the Schlitz League for the Environment and the Protection of Nature—had a meeting at the community center to talk about the rumors. Six hundred people showed up, and every one of them seemed to have already heard a story about Americans on the Eisenberg. They had heard that the Eisenberg trails were blocked. They had heard about barbed-wire fences and bivouac tents and Special Forces patrolling the mountain with bayonets and machine guns. Some Green Party organizers from Fulda—the Greens in Germany are often given to hyperbole—told them about "Nazis stalking the woods with killer dogs." Those Schlitzers were fearful and distressed, and their distress was unusual for a town as used to the American Army as Schlitz was. Every year, thirty or forty war games come through Schlitz and the sixteen villages of the township of Schlitzerland. Schlitz children grow up counting the fighter planes that swoop down over their *Marktplatz* and chasing convoys through the stone streets of the old walled town. American tanks silt up the Schlitz River in the spring. American helicopters leak kerosene. American armored cars crack Schlitz's curbs and cornerstones. And there are days when military code transmissions jam the radio stations in Oberhessen and thousands of American soldiers line up at the Schlitz community center to use the showers.

About 250,000 American soldiers are in Germany right now. Seventy-five thousand of those soldiers are in Hessen. Most are at bases in south Hessen near Frankfurt, where the V Corps of the U.S. Army Europe and Seventh Army has its headquarters, but thousands are at bases in Oberhessen—some people call it north Hessen or east Hessen —in the foothills and valleys of a range of mountains that is cut by the Fulda River to form a long, low corridor from Thuringia, in East Germany, into Western Europe. Army strategists call this corridor the Fulda Gap. They think of it as a kind of natural war zone. Napoleon used it for his retreat from Russia. Patton used it to push back the Wehrmacht in the spring of 1945. Today, NATO uses it for bases and for tactical-nuclear-weapons depots—soldiers call them atomic-artillery depots—and for war games and maneuvers that follow the Gap right up to the East German border. Schlitz is in the middle of the Fulda Gap, some twenty miles from the border and halfway between a squadron of the 11th Armored Cavalry Regiment, which is usually called the Black Horse Regiment, in Bad Hersfeld and the regiment's headquarters in the city of Fulda, where the S.S. once had its officers' training school. Not many of the maneuvers in the Fulda Gap miss Schlitz and its sixteen villages. There are red-and-white coded military signs on country roads all over Schlitzerland. There are mysterious manhole covers—set in groups of three, sealed into the road—at important turnings, like the turning from Schlitz to the bridge to Fulda, which Schlitzers say are atomic demolition mines. No one knows if they really are mines and, if they are, whether there are warheads in the mines and what keeps them from exploding or what keeps people from coming by at night and digging them up and, say, selling them to the Libyans. No one knows what would trigger these mines in the course of a battle or in the course of avoiding a battle. Atomic demolition mines are obsolete by NATO standards, but NATO keeps them in West Germany, and people in Schlitz find this odd. They find it odd that there is a crossing of six-lane superhighways in a landscape whose major traffic problem is the five o'clock rush of milk cows coming in from pasture. The government says these superhighways were built to accommodate millions of foreign workers driving home to Turkey or Yugoslavia in the summer, but people in Schlitz say that they were built for troop convoys. This year, the government is starting to lay tracks for a 170-mile railroad—from Hannover to Würzburg—that will run through countryside like Schlitzerland, where few people ever travel, and will be six tracks wide in places into the bargain. People in Schlitz assume that this is simply the government's way of clearing land for the atomic tanks and mobile missile launchers of some neighborhood "theater nuclear war" that is going to destroy them all.

Most people in Schlitz have lived with armies for as long as they can remember. They were born into the Wehrmacht and they grew up with the Occupation. They welcomed Hitler, and they welcomed the armies that liberated them from Hitler. These Oberhessen peasants spent eight hundred years as vassals of a family of counts who claimed to be protecting them from enemies, so they tended to believe in enemies, and to welcome people who talked to them about enemies. Siegfried Klee, the mayor of Schlitz—a Social Democrat who comes from Wiesbaden and studied at the University of Bonn—says that even now his biggest problem with Schlitzers is the predisposition they have to obey anyone who gives them an order, whether it is a count or an American captain on maneuvers or the mayor himself, so long as the order involves an enemy. Having an enemy has always been their way of describing a world they did not know and had no power to control, and hearing about that enemy from someone with power—even from someone with terror at his disposal—seems to give them a kind of dim, complicitous security.

The farmers and brewers and linen weavers of Oberhessen are not much known for independence or ingenuity. They explain to strangers that they are like the weavers in Gerhart Hauptmann's play *The Weavers*. Not many of them have read the play, or know anything at all about the Silesian weavers' revolt in 1844 that inspired it, but they do know that Gerhart Hauptmann was a famous writer who told about punishing lives and poverty that might have been their own. They talk about the play cheerfully, as if they had inherited from Hauptmann's weavers a kind of celebrity as sufferers.

Willi Schäfer was thirteen when he left school and started weaving. He worked a twelve-hour day in a local linen factory, and in 1958, after eleven years of working, he led the weavers of Schlitzerland in their first strike since the war. It lasted more than three months, shut down three local factories, and got Willi fired. He says now that getting fired was his great chance and his education, because he had to leave Schlitz to find a job, and he ended up in Frankfurt, working on a construction gang, building skyscrapers for the economic miracle that Germans call their *Wirtschaftswunder*, getting involved in the sixties peace movement, walking in Easter marches and wondering what people in Schlitz would say if they could see Willi Schäfer parading up and down in front of the *Bahnhof* with hippies and feminists and professors chanting "Make love, not war." A few years in Frankfurt turned Willi into something of a foreigner—which may be why he was so active in the group that got together to save the Eisenberg from the American Army. Most people in the group—they called it the Eisenberg Action Community—were foreigners by village standards, foreigners and intellectuals. Jörg Brehm and Meertinus Meijering were scientists who had come to Schlitz—Brehm from Lower Saxony and Meijering from Holland—to work at a Max Planck Institute limnological station, and use the Eisenberg's brooks and springs and swamps for their research on running-water systems. Heiner Müller was a dentist who had come to Schlitz from Frankfurt because he dreamed of taking over a quiet country practice and raising his family in the countryside. Gudrun Pausewang Wilcke was a writer who had spent twelve years in South America before she came to Schlitz to settle down and write a famous book about the town and its "last children" after a nuclear war. Bürgermeister Klee had come to Schlitzerland for the Social Democrats, the way any good politician might be sent out to the hustings for his party—because he had sophistication and skill the locals lacked. Children growing up in Schlitz have to leave for their last two years of *Gymnasium*. They go to Fulda, twelve miles away, or Lauterbach, nine miles away, and if they are able to go to a university it usually means that Schlitz has lost them for good. The "intellectuals" who have been coming to Schlitz lately come for the things those students flee— for the isolation, the calm, the tidy charm of a red-roofed medieval village with a sweep of green and golden mountain behind it, for the brooks and the beech, the black woodpeckers and the owls, and the sight, on December mornings, of wild and rutted trails across a meadow, left by boars that dug for roots by moonlight and disappeared into the forest at dawn.

Schlitz sits in the middle of the Germany that Bismarck put together for his Prussian Kaiser. It is halfway between Munich, in the south, and Hamburg, in the north, and Dresden, in the east, and Aachen, in the west—an accident of geography that made Schlitz a marketplace, a kind of European caravansary, and gave it a prominence that lasted until Yalta. The division of Germany in 1945 turned Schlitz from a crossroads town that did its business with Thuringia, and even Leipzig, into a border town. The roads to Schlitz stopped suddenly at the edge of Schlitzerland. Its trade in the East was cut, literally, by barbed wire and attack-dog runs and sentry towers—by stretches of diamond fencing designed to contract on touch and slice your hand off. That fencing was invented by Germans in the West and, in the spirit of *Ostpolitik*, sold to the East German government.

Schlitz is a pretty town, with old half-timbered houses and a church that was consecrated in 812, during the reign of Charlemagne. It has a *Zwiebelturm* like a bright-blue onion, and four castles, and a brewery that has been printing *Schlitz* on its bottles since the sixteenth century. Once, the brewery and the four castles belonged to the counts of Schlitz. So did a big still that produced alcohol of such astonishing kick that it made money for the counts for four or five centuries. So, in fact, did the fifty-five square miles of farmland and woodland and villages called Schlitzerland. In one way or another, everybody in Schlitzerland worked for the counts except some free farmers and the linen weavers, and the linen weavers were usually women whose husbands farmed for the counts or brewed for the counts or worked in the counts' castles. Now there are four private linen factories on the edge of town, and three hundred Schlitzers work in them, weaving dish

towels and sheets for hospitals in West Berlin and little linen doilies that
are supposed to keep hair spray and makeup off the backs of the seats
in Lufthansa planes. The Schlitz family has been around since the
twelfth century at least—church records talk about a Herr de Slitese
getting married in 1116—and probably longer. When the first German
Reich was foundering, in the fourteenth century, Schlitzerland became
the family's state, and the Schlitz counts ruled it pretty much as they
pleased. They built their castles and stocked their forests and enjoyed
a castle park by the Schlitz River, and no one but counts and countesses
and their friends could use the park until 1945, when American soldiers
parked their tanks there and liberated Schlitz by letting the Schlitzers
in. This left the count of the moment—Schlitzers refer to him as "the
old count," so as not to confuse him with his son, "the young count,"
who is forty-four now—the choice of sharing his park with his subjects
or giving it to them. In 1954, Otto Hartmann Graf von Schlitz genannt
von Görtz turned over the castle park—an event the town seems to
consider as important to its history as the Congress of Vienna, which
ratified the turning over of Schlitzerland itself to the Grand Duchy of
Hessen. The Schlitzers worried that a count who had lost his authority
over them would lose his responsibility for them into the bargain. Some
three hundred people depended on the old count for a living. He was
a rich man, but a lot of his family's money had come from forests
—especially forests on the Eisenberg. A hundred years ago, Eisenberg
firewood sold all over Schlitzerland. The coal mines of the Ruhr cut
shafts and tunnel beams from Eisenberg beech. The new chemical
industries of Hamburg and Berlin carved barrel casks from Eisenberg
oak. By the time the old count came into his inheritance, though, forests
were not so profitable for a family that wanted to keep up with the
Hessen forestry laws and its own traditions. The Eisenberg was a
symbol of the count's domain and the count's power. He was supposed
to use it nobly—culling carefully and replanting in kind and quality
—and never strip it and leave it bare to shame the family. In fact, the
old count kept the customs of the mountain. There were eight days
every fall when Schlitzers could climb the Eisenberg and take the wood
they needed for the winter. Schoolboys could climb the Eisenberg and
camp. Bird-watchers could climb it. Mushroomers could climb it and
pick morels. Families could climb it on summer Sundays, spread their
picnics and take their naps and watch their children go off courting on
paths that were bosky with willows and alderwood. Brides and grooms
could climb the mountain on their wedding day and gather wood and

light the first fire of their married life—and then the town would follow
with a bucketful of water, to put the fire out.

In 1967, the old count decided to have a wedding of his own. His
countess had died. His children were grown and his only son was
married, and there was not much for him to do in Schlitz once the
hunting season was over, so he married again, and his new wife had
four daughters who were also married or would be getting married.
Some of those daughters liked the kind of life that Germans refer to
lately as *Schickeria*—meaning the kind of fast, high life which would
cost the count a lot of money to maintain. They lived in places like
Munich. Their husbands drove racing cars and made movies. One
daughter was the Princess Salm-Salm. Another daughter was now a
Hohenzollern.

The old count started selling. He sold his brewery to a baron from
Lauterbach. He sold some of his farmland to Catholic peasants who had
come over from Sudetenland and Thuringia after the war and made
money. He sold his still, a small mountain, the oldest and most deteri-
orated of his four castles, and half his forests to the state of Hessen, and
he would have sold more forests later except that a terrible scandal at
the Hessische Landesbank left the bank with no money to lend the
government. His stepdaughters flourished, but in Schlitz the carpenters
and the craftsmen and the mechanics and the castle maids who had been
born into the service of the count watched a breaking up of Schlitzerland that, to their minds, had begun the day the Americans parked their
tanks in the castle park and invited the children in for chocolate bars.
In 1971, the old count divided his property. He gave about a third to
his bride and another third to his son, Rüdiger. Rüdiger's share was
7,400 acres on and around the Eisenberg, a sawmill, a couple of houses,
and a castle called Vorderburg, which was not the family's favorite
castle. In 1974, three years before the old count died, Rüdiger turned
the Vorderburg into apartments and the carriage house and sheep
stables into a tourist hotel, and then he built himself a split-level on the
edge of town.

Rüdiger Graf von Schlitz genannt von Görtz does not really like
Schlitz. He likes the South of France, where he has a villa, and he likes
Munich, where he was living when the old count called him home to
take over his share of the family property. He is a tall, wheezy person
who wanders around the Vorderburg parking lot looking a bit distracted, as if his mind were back in Saint-Tropez and he were somehow
trying to find a way to join it. It is hard to imagine the young count

striding over the Eisenberg with a wurst and a loaf of pumpernickel in his knapsack. Schlitzers say that Rüdiger's inheritance was an old man's revenge on a son who preferred his life away from home, and Rüdiger agrees that it was not friendly of his father to make him king of a castle he could not rule.

Rüdiger Graf Görtz describes himself as a businessman. He says that when he came home in 1971 he discovered himself paterfamilias of fifty Schlitz families, all of them explicit about their claims to his protection. Some of them went to work in his new hotel. A few still worked at the sawmill. But there were no jobs for most of them without him, and Rüdiger—who by leasing hunting rights to the Eisenberg and cutting wood with the discretion appropriate to his title was earning about one percent of the market value of the mountain—says that he had trouble enough supporting himself, let alone fifty families and a sixteenth-century castle with heating problems. Rüdiger had his eye on tax shelters in West Berlin. He needed cash, and so he offered the Eisenberg to the state of Hessen, figuring that Hessen, having already relieved his family of one mountain, might be persuaded to take the Eisenberg off his hands. The state said no, but it took two years to decide, and by then the word was out that Schlitz's mountain was on the market. Early in 1976, an agent arrived from Bavaria representing a couple of clients who, he said, were in the business of buying forests. Rüdiger sold them about four thousand acres of the Eisenberg, at ninety pfennig a square meter for the oak forest at the foot of the mountain and for the beech forest that runs the length of the mountain and along its crest, and at seventy pfennig a square meter for the pine and fir. The mayor found out about the sale when somebody dropped off transfer papers at the *Rathaus*. He told Schlitzers that eleven million marks—which was worth four million dollars at the time and is roughly what the count got for the forests—was a bad price, way below the mountain's value. He might have told the count, too, but the count was already out of town.

The North Atlantic Treaty Organization is said to have more than six hundred thousand acres of West Germany. A 1954 Status of Forces agreement between West Germany and France, Britain, and the United States gives NATO the use of West German territory, and the Allies themselves still have the right to own territory if they decide they need it. Germany has peace, but one of the ironies of that peace is that West Germany is something of a provisional entity, keeping its claim to a united Germany open, and probably will be for as long as the de facto occupation of the country is a Cold War convenience or—according to your point of view—a protection. There are appeals before West Germany's Constitutional Court right now that challenge the constitutionality of missile deployment in what, for practical purposes, is still the American Sector, but the West German constitution is in a way provisional itself. American military operations in West Germany are sovereign operations, whatever the courts decide or the Bundestag resolves. This makes America—and, through it, NATO—a steady customer for West German real estate, and a fairly reliable one. A class of middlemen—dealers and speculators and promoters—has come of age in West Germany since the 1954 agreement set down the terms for the occupation. People with friends in NATO or in the German High Command attached to NATO or in West Germany's Defense Ministry get their tips about NATO's plans—about where the Americans are going to start putting 204 new missiles this month, say, or where twenty or thirty thousand American soldiers are going to be restationed—and they buy property to sell to the Allies at a healthy profit. In France, they would be the *promoteurs* who make their money selling cheap boutique space four or five stories underneath Les Halles. In Spain, they would be the *empresarios* who hustle Costa del Sol condominiums to Japanese businessmen. In West Germany, they are the camp followers of the military-industrial complex. In 1976, two of them bought Eisenberg land from Rüdiger Graf Görtz and offered it to the Defense Ministry in Bonn, which eventually passed their offer on to the Americans. Their names were Josef Hörhammer and Hans Zahn, and for a while that was all most Schlitzers knew about them, besides the fact that they were both Bavarians (Hörhammer, who bought sixteen hundred acres, comes from Deggendorf, and Zahn, who bought about twenty-five hundred acres, comes from Starnberg, near Munich), and men of obvious influence and wealth.

Josef Hörhammer rarely came back to Schlitz after he had bought his piece of the mountain. Hans Zahn, on the other hand, seemed to like Schlitz. He moved his wife and his two sons to the Eisenberg and waited there for the Americans to buy. Schlitzers got used to seeing him on the mountain—a large Bavarian in a loden coat and feathered cap crashing through brush on his bulldozer or dragging tree trunks on his skidder, enjoying the life of a lumberman. He was not welcoming. The mayor, who has dealt with him now for seven years, says that he is "furiously shy"—meaning that strangers make him mad and that strangers on his property make him madder. People in Schlitz tend to regard that shyness as something willful and high-handed, something predictably Bavarian. No one in town was surprised when Zahn built himself a big white house on the mountain without applying for a housing permit, and then claimed that it was not a house at all but a machine shop for his logging tools. No one was surprised when he stocked a deer park, or when he added a strip of fluorescent driveway to the Eisenberg so that his boys could race their motorcycles at night or take turns at the family Maserati. The town got to know Frau Zahn, who came down sometimes to do the marketing, and then it got to know Frau Zahn's mother and father, who arrived one day and moved into a little house in one of the Schlitzerland villages. Frau Zahn's father organized an oompah band and, in what Schlitzers considered a fairly ecumenical spirit for a Catholic, offered his services to Klaus Steckenreuter, the Lutheran minister, as conductor of the church orchestra. But Zahn himself seemed to hate to leave the mountain except when he was leaving Schlitzerland. Friends would come in the fall to hunt on the Eisenberg with him. The Vorderburg parking lot would fill with Mercedes 500 SEs with Bavarian plates, and Schlitzers stopping by the hotel for dinner or schnapps would prowl the lot trying to figure out whom the cars belonged to. Once, they say, Franz Josef Strauss, the head of the Christian Social Union, came from Bavaria to shoot wild sheep at the Zahns', and it was the rumor of Strauss's visit that seemed to connect the new owners of the mountain to the German right and to plans that were not necessarily to the town's advantage. Bürgermeister Klee says that all he knew for sure was that Zahn and Hörhammer were political friends of Franz Josef Strauss. They may have been involved in one of Strauss's campaigns, or in one of his occasional attempts to turn his Bavarian party into a national party, a voice of the "true" German right, and give it more power in its coalition with the Christian Democrats. These friends of the Christian Social Union were buying land, and with it influence, all over Germany—weighing in, as it were, with their money. Hans Zahn had bought or was buying land in the Moselle, land near Hamburg, land near Lake Constance, as well as land in Austria, near the Yugoslav border. The land he bought was almost always land where there was talk of new military installations.

Jörg Brehm, at Schlitz's limnological station, says he began to notice changes on the Eisenberg in 1977. That was the year Zahn and Hörhammer started stripping the mountain—first the oaks, then the beech—with no regard for what Brehm, who is a passionate ecologist, considers "a perfect little ecosystem," a landscape whose richness and variety would take most mountains a couple of hundred square miles to duplicate. It is seventeen years since Brehm saw the Eisenberg for the first time. He wanted to know what happened to amino acids in running water, and he particularly liked the water that ran from the Eisenberg through Schlitz and on past his office, near the castle park. The limnological station was his first job, and he kept it. He married a local girl whose parents were Sudeten refugees, and started raising a family. Now he calls the Eisenberg "part of my home." Schlitzers are used to seeing him on the mountain, dressed for a climb in his old Raichle boots and torn corduroy hiking pants and down vest, squinting into brooks and marshes with pale-blue North German eyes as if he were a Viking who had strayed inland and was trying to find the sea. In Oberhessen, people tend to be small and dark, and Jörg Brehm —with a red beard and a big Saxon barrel chest—is something exotic there. He probably knows the mountain better than anyone else, and he can talk for hours praising it—the way the beech rises on the south slope, the way the alder, thriving in the wet ground, traces the path of every rivulet, the way the woodpeckers poke nesting holes for stock doves and owls in the old trees, knocking leaves into the water for the flea crabs' food, the way the rotting wood smells thick and sweet, nourishing larvae from beetles that have not been seen in the rest of Germany for fifty years. The Eisenberg is as familiar, as satisfying to Brehm as a kitchen garden. He can sniff the air of one of its old fish ponds and tell you what odd microscopic life is generating underwater. He can turn some soil with the toe of his boot and release the rich smell of mushrooms whose roots glow yellow in the dark. He can look at a pile of rocks from fifty feet and head for the one where a salamander is hiding. He knows the way to big, hidden meadows where the first Schlitzerlanders had their villages, and he can tell by the tone and texture of the soil and the plants that grow there where those Schlitzer-landers chucked their garbage, and where they piled their dead when plague and the Thirty Years' War were driving them off the mountain to the safety of fortified valley towns. Jörg Brehm is the sort of person foreigners sometimes imagine when they talk about a German roman-tic. Nature gives him a relentless eloquence. He talks about *Naturver-jüngung*—nature regenerating and rejuvenating—and about primal na-ture and chthonic nature and nature as joy and nature as harmony. He does not approve of anyone who interferes with that harmony, the way the old count interfered when he stocked a deer park on the Eisenberg, or the way Josef Hörhammer interfered when he started chopping down leaf trees that by Brehm's reckoning had stood on the Eisenberg for more than 150 years. Brehm got angry "in my way"—which means he disappeared into the library at his office and put together a brief for the Eisenberg and sent it to the Minister of Forests in Hessen, asking him to declare some five hundred acres of virgin forest on the mountain a nature preserve.

Forests are precious in Germany. They belong to a wilderness that is disappearing to the roads and factories of the *Wirtschaftswunder* and to war games and to the acid rain that has already ravaged a third of the woods in the country, and they are symbols out of the mythology of a mighty fatherland filled with *Übermenschen*—symbols to manipulate. The art of the Third Reich was about mountains and woods. Leni Riefenstahl's pure German woman who tied her yellow braids around her head and climbed through forests to breathe the air of an equation of alp and Aryan made for powerful populist propaganda in the 1930s. Nature was free in Depression Germany, and food and coal and a winter coat were not. There has always been a nature mystique in Germany—a belief in life forces and remorseless processes that will triumph over society, with its weakness for intellectuals and ideologies and its decadent notions of justice and a common good. Nature in Germany is an enthusiasm that often has less to do with land than with German land. It did not take long for the Wandervogel that Walter Benjamin and his school friends joined so innocently in 1910 to turn into the Hitler Youth, and it still does not take very long for *Boden*—soil—to begin to sound like *Blut und Boden*.

Jörg Brehm is suspicious of groups that make a cult of German soil. He is an enthusiast, but a loner in his enthusiasm. He did not, for instance, join the Greens, although the Greens are certainly an ecological party, well organized in Hessen, with seven seats in the Hessen parliament, and they particularly wanted to keep the Army off the mountain Brehm loves. The Greens' appeal in West Germany is enormous—it is hard to resist a delegation that drives to the Bundestag in a Volkswagen bus with its dogs and its babies and keeps flowerpots on its desks and passes out dried apricots and pumpkin seeds and stores its dossiers in rucksacks—and they add a cheerful, pagan tone to the dour proceedings in Bonn. Their "rules" about popular democracy are the only rules they seem to acknowledge. Colleagues in the state parliament say that the Greens stayed up so late at night arguing among themselves about the fate of the Eisenberg that by morning they were always too tired to argue properly with anyone else. They seem to have decided early on that expertise is a kind of terrorism, encouraging the arrogance of leaders and the abuses of leadership. They do not say much about the terrorism of ignorance, or about the arrogance and abuses of the

masses, despite the evidence of their own German past. Practicing
party democracy, they helped put their best politician, Petra Kelly, into
a rest home and they insulted two of their most useful and distinguished
converts—Otto Schily, the civil-rights lawyer who planned the defense
of Ulrike Meinhof, and Gerd Bastian, the infantry general who became
a leader of the disarmament movement. They believe that popularity
and information give people like Kelly and Schily and Bastian an
authority that is against Green principles. People outside Germany,
taking long hair and high spirits for ideology, tend to think of the
Greens as a party of the left, but left and right are not really words that
apply to the Greens' peculiarly German sort of populism or to the
appeal that put them into the Bundestag and six of West Germany's
state parliaments. That appeal has to do with nationalism, with a way
finally to be "German" again, with Germanness that is defined by
boundaries of land and language and not necessarily of culture or
historical conscience, or even history. It has nothing to do with "politics" because it has nothing to do with history. It is a way of being free
of history—a German unification no one before the Greens had imagined. It is why they can be as much at home with the dairy farmers of
Schleswig-Holstein as they are with the squatters in Kreuzberg or the
Eisenberg ecologists or the Christians for a Nuclear Freeze. The fact
that the same Green who started a debate to save the Eisenberg in the
Hessen parliament led a friendship delegation to Colonel Qaddafi dis-
tresses liberals in the state, but a lot of liberals vote for the Greens now,
hoping they will shake up Germany where Germany needs shaking up
—it was pressure from the Greens that pushed the Social Democrats
into passing a resolution last month against the new missile deployment
—and then conveniently disappear. People say that the Greens are
mellowing, anyway. When a group of pedophiles claiming to be
Greens occupied Green Party headquarters in Bonn in the company
of several schoolchildren, the Greens broke what amounted to a cove-
nant against authority and called the police.

The Greens got interested in the Eisenberg a couple of years ago,
when a Schlitzer by the name of Hans Hibinger asked for help. Hibinger is the workers' council representative at a packaging plant in Lauterbach and the trade-union representative in Schlitz, and he hates the
capitalist rich with an intensity that seems to have taken over his life.
In 1971, Hibinger bought what he calls "my Eisenberg property"
—about two-thirds of an acre of meadowland with three little fish ponds
and a toolshed. It is one of five private plots on the south slope of the
mountain, where Hans Zahn has beech forests, and when Zahn silted

up an irrigation ditch that ran between their land Hibinger decided to
sue, and told the Greens about it. Hibinger is forty-one and what he
calls an "original Schlitzer." His mother worked for a Schlitz count,
and so did her mother and her mother's mother, and Hibinger himself
had his education, as he puts it, in the old count's brewery. Hibinger
was determined to make something of himself. He saved his money,
and eventually he used it to take over a family restaurant on the ground
floor of his father's fine old half-timbered house on the *Marktplatz*. The
restaurant lasted seven years, and folded. It left Hibinger furtive and
resentful—full of schemes to save his pride. He had got on well enough
with the old count, but when Zahn bought his twenty-five hundred
acres of the Eisenberg, Hibinger began to do some "research" on the
rich Bavarian who was now, in a manner of speaking, his neighbor.

There were a lot of military maneuvers on the Eisenberg by the
time Zahn and Hörhammer took over. The Americans were testing
tanks, and NATO supposedly wanted to know how long it would take
those tanks to cross the mountain if the Russians came over from
Thuringia, and what adjustments to make for the terrain, and how
many atomic howitzers to order at the arms commissary outside Munich. The tanks were digging up meadowland and swampland, so that
water that had been trapped in the wet soil spilled out and killed the
plants around it. They were making deep furrows on the mountain
paths, collapsing the banks of streams, flattening the young hazelnut
trees. The American Army always paid for its damages. American
engineers would come out and make the repairs they could, and then
German Defense Ministry accountants would arrive to calculate what
the rest would cost. In 1981, there were important maneuvers called
REFORGER '81, and Hibinger claims that after those maneuvers Zahn
sent the Defense Ministry a big bill—and was reimbursed—for damages
he had invented. Hibinger conferred with the Greens in Wiesbaden.
Then he and the Greens moved to have Zahn charged with fraud
against the state.

Zahn and Hörhammer were notably cavalier as foresters. They cut
down trees so fast that they were earning five or six marks a square
meter on land that had cost them less than one, and Hörhammer was
selling his oak for as much as fifteen thousand marks a trunk. The forest
was theirs, and as far as they were concerned they were under no
obligation to spare it *or* share it. They painted the boom gates on the
roads into their property blue and white—the royal colors of Bavaria
—and started to keep them closed. When Schlitzers wanted their wood
that fall, Bürgermeister Klee had to present Zahn with an official list

of the villagers—how much wood, say, a farmer in the valley figured he would need to keep his *Kachelofen* hot through a bad winter, how much wood a village mother would need to cook for her children —before Zahn gave in and supplied it. The mayor says that Zahn chose his poorest wood for the town, and that he dumped it on hills and cliffs so that old farmers who went to collect it couldn't reach it and had to go home empty-handed.

The state of Hessen has foresters on the Eisenberg. One forester was assigned to Zahn and one to Hörhammer, and these foresters were supposed to supervise whatever work went on, according to Hessen law and their own sense, the way a game warden is supposed to supervise hunting. Zahn's forester complained, and Zahn ignored him, and he complained again, and Zahn threw him off the mountain and replaced him with a private forester, who was more agreeable. Hörhammer's forester—he lives in Schlitz and plays soccer with Willi Schäfer at the Sports Club—also complained, but Josef Hörhammer was back in Bavaria by then and didn't seem to care. According to Bürgermeister Klee—who had been making official complaints about the plundering of the forest—the state didn't seem to care, either. It was Hörhammer's forester who first guessed that the Army's interest in the Eisenberg went beyond the occasional use of the mountain for maneuvers. American purchasing officers started looking over the Eisenberg in August of 1982, and the forester saw them. In December, at a forestry seminar in Schlitz, a man from the Forest Ministry asked Hörhammer's forester what was happening on the mountain. Word had it that troops, and maybe even missiles, were coming to the Eisenberg, and once the forester heard that, he went to the Social Democrats in Schlitz and told them what he himself had seen.

On December 9, Bürgermeister Klee wrote a letter to Alfred Dregger, a Christian Democrat who is deputy chairman of his party and majority leader, so to speak, of the Bundestag. Dregger comes from Fulda. He is the undisputed ruler of the Fulda Gap, and he runs his part of Germany as what his friends describe as a family and his enemies as a political protection racket. The town of Fulda is a conservative town. St. Boniface converted some of the Frankish tribes to Christianity near Fulda in 719, and it is fervently Catholic. (People call it the Vatican of Hessen.) The most important men in Fulda are the Catholic bishop and his friend Alfred Dregger. Dregger is closer in his political style to Catholic politicians from the south than he is to northern Catholics, like himself, who are Christian Democrats. He likes to have his picture taken with the tanks and the troops he says are going to save the Fulda

Gap from the Communists. He likes to stand at the Wall reading statements about the defense of German democracy. He was as likely as anyone in the country—anyone, that is, outside the military— to know what was planned for the Eisenberg, and, in fact, he wrote right back to Bürgermeister Klee and promised him that all the Americans' new missiles were going somewhere else. On the other hand, he said, the Americans were certainly looking at the mountain. Someone *had* offered the mountain to the Defense Ministry. The Ministry had passed the offer along. The Americans were interested.

On February 25, the chief of staff for the American commander in Heidelberg wrote a letter to Schlitz's dentist, Heiner Müller (Müller was spokesman for the Eisenberg Action Community), and confirmed that the Americans had been offered about twenty-two hundred acres of the Eisenberg and were "evaluating the property offer to determine whether there is a defense requirement for the land." His letter arrived the week of the meeting that brought six hundred Schlitzers together at the community center to talk about the mountain. Their agenda was "What does the restationing on the Eisenberg mean for Schlitz?" And the speakers they invited were Jörg Brehm, representing the Max Planck limnologists; Peter Krahulec, a teacher from the technical college in Fulda, representing the peace movement; and Klaus Steckenreuter, representing the Lutheran ministers in Schlitzerland. They had also invited someone from the Hessen Forest Ministry, but he backed out at the last minute, saying that the meeting was "too political" to attend. That night, Schlitz decided to save the Eisenberg from the Americans.

Henry Kissinger once said that the Europeans' secret dream is that the Third World War will be fought over their heads—meaning that all that Europe will see of the war will be intercontinental ballistic missiles whizzing through the sky on their way from the Soviet Union to the United States and from the United States to the Soviet Union. It may be that the secret dream of the Americans and the Russians is that the Third World War will be fought on a battlefield, like Europe, where the antagonists can match their strengths and test their missiles as the observers but not the victims of their own conflict. The facts of nuclear war—radiation, a nuclear winter, a dying species, a dead landscape—are beside the point of secret dreams and, it seems, of the policies that secret dreams inspire. Those policies—with their language of "first strike" and "launch on warning" and "megaton parity"— have a kind of pure logic, the logic of mad poems. The little nuclear wars that Ronald Reagan started hypothesizing in the fall of 1981 are one of those pure, mad poems. There are said to be 141 nuclear warheads at eighteen American bases and depots in the Fulda Gap already, so Schlitzers are not much interested in arguments about whether America is putting itself more at risk or less at risk by deploying 572 Pershing II and cruise missiles in Western Europe over the next few years. They find the arguments abstract. First, they read that America is going to recouple its risks with *their* risks and has therefore decided to send them bombs. They read that if the Russians fire, say, an SS-20 missile at Schlitz to clear the way for a tank invasion through the Fulda Gap, and the Americans fire a short-range missile at Schlitz to stop the Russians from coming, then the Russians will destroy the United States—and this is what "recoupling risks" means, because the Russians consider any missile sent by America a missile sent *from* America. Or they read that America is taking away its "umbrella" from Europe. They read that by sending theater-nuclear-war weapons ("theater nuclear war" is the current euphemism for the destruction of Europe) to West Germany America is endorsing a double standard of protection among allies—that in a war the rest of NATO will suffer and die for the United States. And in the end neither argument moves the Schlitzers, because they know that if a Pershing II missile takes six minutes from launch to target and an SS-20 not much longer and both sides are talking about launch on warning, then the only advantage to Schlitzers of their friends' striking first will be the grim satisfaction of dying second themselves.

Watching the missile deployment this month—wondering whether America is really risking three million lives in Chicago with every Pershing II it puts in Neu-Ulm—Germans have become obsessed with fears of war and fantasies of salvation. It may be that they know from experience how easy it is to start wars, or it may be, as Alain Clément, of *Le Monde*, once said, that they have no faith in the restraint of others, having had so little of their own. But the fact is that all Germans seem to have those fears and those fantasies. East Germans are terrified because the Russians are moving more and more of their tactical nuclear weapons—SS-21s and SS-22s and SS-23s—into East Germany and Czechoslovakia and Poland every day. The Russians started deploying SS-20s along their western border in 1977 and have not stopped, and their logic seems just as odd in Schlitz as America's logic, since the Russians could already incinerate Schlitzerland with any one of their SS-4 missiles, whether or not that SS-4 happened to provoke a colonel in Fulda, say, to use the American atomic artillery in the neighborhood. That artillery already has seven times the power of the bomb that wiped out Hiroshima. Schlitzers worry that someone will use it to start a chain of radiation and fire. They feel gratuitously exposed by America, because America admits that a lot of its tactical nuclear weapons are obsolete. And they wonder whether those weapons are, in fact, at the disposition of some colonel in Fulda. They wonder whether those weapons have anything at all to do with the "permissive action link" they always read about in the paper—the fail-safe link with the White House that is supposed to prevent a nuclear disaster. They are assured and reassured by "experts," but they do not really know what to make of American experts who talk about nuclear war in the Fulda Gap and play war games accordingly, and at the same time plan to restation as many as twenty or thirty thousand of their own troops in the Gap, in the line of fire, in case the war turns out to be a "normal" war and requires a lot of soldiers in place, ready to move. The truth is that there is no agreement anymore among American commanders as to what kind of war a war in Germany would be. The only thing those commanders do seem to agree on is that the deployment going on around them now has to do with politics, and not with any military sense or strategy or advantage. They know their arsenals, and they are frightened. But some of them predict a nuclear war, and so they aim their bombs and ask that American soldiers be dispersed. Some of them predict conventional war, and *they* ask that American soldiers be concentrated. Those commanders are usually talking about the same place.

A couple of years ago, CBS made a series of documentaries about the defense of the United States. One of the documentaries was called *The Nuclear Battlefield*, and it involved a war game in the course of which the village of Hattenbach, in the Fulda Gap, was hit by one of NATO's ten-kiloton nuclear warheads to stop an invasion by Soviet tanks heading across the Gap from Thuringia. Hattenbach was Ground Zero, the movie said. Hattenbach, eleven miles north of Schlitz, was the place where the Third World War was going to start. Everybody in Schlitz knew something about the movie. Some Schlitzers had seen it two years ago, when a Hattenbach schoolteacher named Brunhilde Miehe borrowed a cassette from a social worker in the peace movement and arranged a screening in the village tavern. One of the Schlitzers who saw the movie then was Klaus Steckenreuter, the Lutheran minister who made a speech—"God, Nature, and the Master Restationing Plan"—at the Schlitz community center on the night the town decided to save the Eisenberg. Pfarrer Steckenreuter comes from a village near Schlitz. His father was a schoolteacher and then a school principal, so people in Schlitzerland knew him as a boy. He is forty-six now, and like many German ministers of his generation he is something of a pacifist, close to the tradition of a *Bekennende Kirche*—a "confessing church" that will testify to injustice—and he thinks a lot about the *Bekennende* ministers who "confessed" their faith to the Nazis and were martyred for it. Pfarrer Steckenreuter knew the Hattenbach minister, Karl-Werner Brauer. Pfarrer Brauer is something of a pacifist, too, and Steckenreuter says he understood his friend's anguish about *The Nuclear Battlefield*—his commitment to show it and his desire not to show it, because the boys and girls in his confirmation class would see themselves in the movie, ten pretty children walking home from church on a snowy afternoon while a voice in the background said that they would all be burned alive at 7,000 degrees Fahrenheit when the bomb fell. Hattenbach is a symbol now for the German peace movement. Brunhilde Miehe guesses that she has shown the movie a hundred times. But Hattenbach itself turned against Pfarrer Brauer after the minister told villagers to see the movie and think about the movie and talk about the movie, even in church. They called him a Communist, an "agent of the East." Some of the church elders wanted to fire him for bringing politics into his sermons, for disturbing Hattenbach's children with his talk about bombs, for associating with people like the social worker from the peace movement who came from Berlin and had known "terrorists" like Rudi Dutschke and Daniel Cohn-Bendit.

Pfarrer Steckenreuter says that, thinking about Hattenbach and what happened in Hattenbach, he understood that silence about the past and silence about the future were the same silence. He wondered how much more silence to expect from villagers of forty or fifty who kept pictures of their fathers in S.S. uniforms on the living-room wall and referred to them as "fallen soldiers." Some villagers were S.S. officers themselves once; they have a reunion every year in Bad Hersfeld and talk about the good old days. Pfarrer Brauer got up in church this fall—it was the Sunday after their reunion—and said it was obscene for torturers and murderers to be celebrating at reunions. One elder of the church walked out, and another elder—a Hattenbach farmer's wife—called the pastor "intolerant of those old grandfathers who only want to get together in their uniforms and reminisce, and who do no harm to anyone."

Last winter, Pfarrer Steckenreuter phoned Pfarrer Brauer for advice about the Eisenberg. He wanted to talk to people like Brauer who knew the kinds of experiences he might have organizing his villages, and who could be honest with him about failure—people who under-

stood this tendency of German country men and women to push their
fears out of consciousness, to defend themselves against reality with
such aggressive complacency. He wanted to tell the people of Schlitz
that their silence would be a kind of guilt. He wanted them to connect
the Eisenberg with the war they accepted in silence forty years ago and
with the war he fears will come if people like them are silent now. He
got his parish youth group together. The boys and girls from Schlitz
talked over their problem with the boys and girls in Hattenbach, and
then they started meeting every week. They wrote letters. They wrote
about their "Christian feelings" for the Eisenberg and they sent their
letters to the families of Schlitzerland and knocked on doors and asked
those families to talk to them about the Eisenberg. Mainly, they worked
on strategies of persuasion. They discovered that no one listened if they
started out talking about free-world problems and arms-control problems and called them Schlitz's problems. Schlitzers thought that their
problem was the Eisenberg. They did not spend time worrying about
soldiers on other people's mountains. What they wanted from their
minister was a kind of theological sanction for sending the Americans
somewhere else. What Pfarrer Steckenreuter wanted from them was a
chance to begin—a chance to encourage them in their first step out of
an almost endemic resignation. The Schlitzers trust their minister.
There is something comfortable about him. He has nice brown eyes
and a toothy smile, and he is not gaunt or ascetic, like his friend Brauer,
who has a Mephisto beard and comes to meetings in corduroy jeans and
a white crew-neck sweater, without a shirt. Pfarrer Steckenreuter is a
little overweight, and he wears dark suits off the rack, and white shirts
that Frau Steckenreuter usually forgets to starch. He is trying to recon-
cile his pastoral patience with his pastoral conscience. He likes to quote
the Social Democrats who broke with Helmut Schmidt at the beginning of the debate about missiles saying, "We cannot govern without
the Sermon on the Mount." That, in a way, is what he was trying to
tell the Schlitzerland villages that are his community—that private
morality and public morality must be joined.

Pfarrer Steckenreuter knew the Zahns—because of Frau Zahn's
father and his oompah band and his church orchestra—and once Frau
Zahn tried to persuade him that her husband had never really offered
the mountain to the Americans, that he would never sell to the Americans unless, as Frau Zahn put it, "they took the mountain from him."
Pfarrer Steckenreuter says that he was not much interested in whether
Zahn tried to sell the mountain himself or hired an agent to sell it or
—which he doubts—whether the Americans tried to take it away. He

says that it will not do the people in Schlitz any good to know who made the first phone call or signed the first letter—that the issue is not Hans Zahn's evasions but bombs and wars and the fragile consciousness of German people. He does not think Germans "see themselves right," as he puts it. He says that Germany's curtains are not iron curtains but ghost curtains. First, there was the ghost of the Russian enemy. Russians were bad, and their weapons were bad, and this meant that Americans were good and American weapons were good. Now the ghost is American. Americans are bad, their weapons are bad, and so the Russians and their weapons are, if not precisely good, then unimportant to the argument. Pfarrer Steckenreuter agrees with the mayor about enemies. He says that the Germans are still victims of their savage history —that they are weak and dangerous at the same time. None of the Schlitzers went to Zahn or Hörhammer and talked to them about the Eisenberg. None of them urged the Zahns to come to their meeting last February, or to a meeting that Bürgermeister Klee called in March —it was the annual town meeting—to continue the discussion. Pfarrer Steckenreuter wonders why he himself didn't drive to the mountain and try to persuade the Zahns to come down to the community center. He says that with no one talking to Zahn, with no one explaining, or even arguing, Zahn was bound to react badly to the thought that six hundred people were sitting around insulting him and accusing him of treachery and greed. In any event, Zahn reacted by insulting them. He closed the forest. He locked his blue-and-white gates against the town.

Some Schlitzers think that it was up to the Americans to come to their meetings and explain why they wanted to put ten or twelve thousand soldiers or, as rumor had it by March, eight atomic tanks in a town that was just beginning to prosper as a tourist town, a town for families who liked to walk and fish and admire scenery—which meant, really, admire the Eisenberg. Heiner Müller says that he invited American officers from Heidelberg to every meeting of the Eisenberg Action Community but that not one officer ever came or even replied to his invitations. Müller knows that there are Americans who believe that Pershing II missiles are important or that restationing troops is important. He assumes that they are reasonable people who could have discussed the Eisenberg reasonably, and maybe have tempered some of the bitterness that Schlitzers felt when Peter Krahulec, from the Fulda peace movement, showed them an American game called The First Battle of the Next War, which was all about the Fulda Gap and about choosing sides and bombs and strategies and "losing" towns like Schlitz when your turn came. Schlitzers heard that night about a valley in

Nevada where soldiers played war games in papier-mâché villages built to look like Schlitz and Hattenbach and the other Oberhessen towns. They heard about generals in Heidelberg who referred to the Fulda Gap as "the killing ground." They began to ask their speakers why the Russians and the Americans were making "little nuclear things," as the mayor put it, and aiming them at towns like Schlitz instead of at each other.

When visitors arrive at Heiner Müller's house, Müller goes to the bookshelf in his living room and takes down a big blue loose-leaf notebook that holds the clippings and the correspondence of the Eisenberg Action Community. Everybody in Schlitz seems to have one of those loose-leaf notebooks—Willi Schäfer has one, Jörg Brehm and Klaus Steckenreuter have one, Siegfried Klee has two and is starting on a third, and Hans Hibinger has a notebook entirely devoted to his lawsuits against Hans Zahn. Schlitzers like to refer to their notebooks when they talk about the Eisenberg. They look at the pages of daily clippings from the *Schlitzer Bote* and at the posters and stickers that the mayor paid for out of the *Rathaus* budget, the manifestos that Hibinger copied at his packaging plant, the lists that Willi Schäfer compiled, calling ten thousand people on the *Rathaus* telephone—as if Schlitz's memory were as tentative as Schlitz's courage and could disappear without a pile of bulging notebooks to validate it and give it substance. Heiner Müller's notebook is the most personal of the notebooks. Schlitz's year as an "action community" has been a kind of *Bildungs-roman* for him—maybe because he is neither a pacifist nor a leftist nor a Green nor a mystic of the German soil. He is a member in good standing of West Germany's economic miracle, a conscientious consumer who still looks a little awkward sitting on his olive Habitat couch in his coordinated olive slacks and sweater—as if everything in his life matched except Heiner Müller himself. This awkwardness is his charm. The town likes him, even though by Schlitz standards he is a foreigner. He has a reputation for fair-mindedness and respectability, and it made him the obvious spokesman when the town organized. Müller says that at first he thought that Germans themselves were responsible for what seemed like an "official silence" about the Eisenberg. He says that Germans thrive on secrecy, that secrets are marks of status in the Federal Republic, whereas Americans are known in Germany as people who never keep secrets, as garrulous, democratic people with no instinct at all for silence—and that even Schlitzers who claim to hate Americans could not really understand why the officers in Heidelberg told Herr Müller to stop writing to them. It was this secrecy, Müller says, that got him thinking about Americans and then worrying about Americans, and convinced him that Ronald Reagan, with his talk about limited nuclear wars and evil Russians, was up to something too simpleminded to be reliable—something that threatened the forty years of "nearly peace" that people on both sides of the border between East and West Germany had managed to endure.

The questions that were raised in Schlitz this year were the questions Heiner Müller raised to himself—questions, as Pfarrer Steckenreuter likes to say, about enemies, questions about being German and about the other Germans across the Wall in Thuringia, questions about the *Volk*, about how to turn this longing for a German *Volk* into something honorable and progressive, about longing that is free from corruption. Müller says that this was the year he "learned." He learned that if one Schlitzer put a SAVE THE EISENBERG sticker on his car window, three more Schlitzers would put stickers on their car windows, but that it took a lot of talking to get that first sticker on the first car.

On March 27, the Sunday before Easter, five thousand people from all over the Fulda Gap marched to a meadow on the Eisenberg and planted a little oak with two branches, telling reporters who had come from Hessen television and the big Hessen newspapers that they were planting a "peace oak," for a peaceful mountain. They had wanted to demonstrate on one of Zahn's meadows, but Zahn was furious about the demonstration, and he put a notice in the *Schlitzer Bote*—by way of an official no—warning the demonstrators off his property. They used someone else's meadow instead. Their peace oak disappeared —Jörg Brehm says that the next time he was on the Eisenberg the tree was gone—but their fight to save the mountain had started. People from the peace movement in Fulda got busy organizing. They led an Easter march to Schlitz, and the mayor met them in the *Marktplatz*, at the old fountain with St. George in the middle—Schlitzers think of St. George as the saint of linen weavers—and made a speech telling the merchants at the *Marktplatz* that eight tanks crashing through the *Platz* would surely do more to ruin their trade than all the peace people in Oberhessen. Then they had a big meeting in Lauterbach, and fifteen hundred Schlitzers came dressed in sacks and smeared with ashes, because they had been advised to "do something spectacular," and rather than shave their heads (which was the suggestion) they compromised with sackcloth, like the people of Nineveh. Pfarrer Steckenreuter's youth group cut the sacks. Willi Schäfer got a cowboy hat and put a little

Eisenberg sticker on the brim and wore it. Heiner Müller's committee was meeting every week, Pfarrer Steckenreuter was anxiously entertaining *Stern* in his front parlor, and the town council called a special session and took over the great hall at the Vorderburg, where twenty-one councilmen who had been notably quiet on the subject of the Eisenberg before the Schlitz elections—they were just over—started fighting about which councilman was doing most to save the mountain. They were country politicians, but their instincts were shrewd: suddenly the Eisenberg was the most famous mountain in Germany. Müller thinks it was the sackcloth and ashes that started the attention. Schlitzers in sacks were in the paper every day. People picking up the *Frankfurter Rundschau* saw them. People reading *Der Spiegel* and *Stern* saw them. People watching the nightly news in Hamburg and Düsseldorf and Berlin saw them. On Hessen Day, which is a state holiday, the Eisenberg Action Community put out a petition to save the Eisenberg, and nearly ten thousand people signed. A crew from West German Television came down from Cologne that Hessen Day. They spent two weeks filming, and they followed Pfarrer Steckenreuter on his pastoral rounds and on his peace rounds. They filmed the mysterious manhole covers near the Fulda Bridge, they filmed nuclear depots at the border, they filmed a wedding at Pfarrer Steckenreuter's church, and they would have gone on filming, except that their producer, in Cologne, called to say that the footage they were sending home would never make it past the network officials and onto the air. He turned out to be right.

May Day was Union Day in Schlitz. The trade unions took over the community center and ran *The Nuclear Battlefield* non-stop for seven hours. June 8 was the first day of the Kirchentag—the biennial convocation of the Lutheran Church in Germany. Pfarrer Steckenreuter drove to Hannover, where 250,000 West German Lutherans were meeting, and he took over Stand 511 at the Kirchentag Fairgrounds, and passed out flyers, and collected more signatures. July 9 was the Schlitz Folk Festival Day. Twenty thousand people came to that and saw the Schlitzers dance in their sackcloth. Then, in August, Jörg Brehm and his hiking club—which is the only organization Brehm belongs to —made a kind of Calvary to the mountain, carrying a long wooden rocket along the highroad out from Schlitz and setting it in the ground near the foot of the mountain. They scattered stones—"stones of sorrow"—around the rocket. Every Schlitzer who took that road was supposed to add a stone to the pile, and thousands did, until vandals came one night with a power saw and cut the rocket in half.

No one in Schlitz knows exactly why or when the Americans decided not to buy their mountain. By September, people were in the streets all over Germany protesting the missile deployment that is just starting, and, given the energy of their protests, it may have been simple common sense for the Americans to try to deflect that energy and seize a chance to look generous and responsive. Four new supermarkets had moved to Schlitz in anticipation of a base on the Eisenberg, and Bürgermeister Klee took it as a sign that, around September, the manager of one of those supermarkets began to talk about moving on. By September, too, Josef Hörhammer had sold a parcel of his land—it was land on the east face of the mountain—to a friend from Deggendorf who started appearing at the Vorderburg, weekends, in a green Mercedes, with an architect's model for what looked like a big mountain house lying on the back seat. It was about that time that Zahn and Hörhammer wrote to the Minister of Forests and asked him to buy the rest of their Eisenberg land. They wanted six marks a square meter, the minister says, which was more than six times what they had paid. The minister said no. He had just put five hundred acres of the Eisenberg —the virgin forest that Jörg Brehm had petitioned for in 1977— under the protection of the state, and this meant that some of the mountain, at least, was now a nature preserve and could not be used.

There were elections in Hessen on September 25. People were voting for a new state parliament, and every big politician in Hessen wanted the credit for saving the Eisenberg. Holger Börner, the Minister-President of Hessen and an old Social Democrat, had been helping the Schlitzers. The Social Democrats had run Hessen since 1949, and now Alfred Dregger's Christian Democrats were looking for ways to take it over. Dregger decided to change his mind about the mountain. He put pressure on the Chancellor, Helmut Kohl, and Kohl put pressure on the Americans, who were counting on Kohl and his coalition to approve the new deployment and spare them the political embarrassment of having to "pull priority," as one of the Heidelberg commanders put it, on an unwilling country. The final missile debate was coming up in Bonn. Kohl needed favors, and the Americans owed him favors —especially in places like Hessen, where so many American soldiers are based. On September 2, Dregger heard from the Minister of Defense that the Eisenberg would not be bought for military use, and on September 6 he saw to it that the minister's statement was in the *Schlitzer Bote* and the other Oberhessen papers—by way of an election ad for the Christian Democrats.

The Social Democrats kept Hessen after all. The Christian Democrats voted to approve the missiles. And late last month in Bonn the Green deputies presented Helmut Kohl with an origami funeral wreath made by schoolchildren in Hiroshima. Schlitz itself, after an Eisenberg celebration, is back to normal. Hans Hibinger is suing Zahn again; this time, he wants five thousand marks for water damage to his meadow. Bürgermeister Klee wonders if Ronald Reagan knows how beautiful the Eisenberg's meadows are. He says that "the taste of America is bitter now in Schlitz." He is happy the Eisenberg was spared, but he still cannot cross the bridge to Fulda without thinking about three atomic demolition mines planted there, making his town a target. Pfarrer Steckenreuter is hard at work marrying people and burying people —there were a lot of funerals this fall—and writing Sunday sermons after a year in which he had seen his speeches printed in the *Frankfurter Rundschau,* and even heard one broadcast over Radio Free Europe. He says that many Schlitzers were relieved in September, and talked about a victory, but that he never felt a victory. He felt "the stone weighing in my heart change places," but the stone, he says, did not fall out. Changing places is like changing mountains, and Pfarrer Steckenreuter wonders if many Schlitzers will care when someone else's mountain gets a tank depot or a Pershing launcher. He wonders, now that the mountain is safe, how many Schlitzers will remember *The Nuclear Battlefield* or the Fulda Gap game or their own terror—and understand that the Eisenberg is "only a chip in a mosaic that is *their* earth."

Oberhessen was always the backward part of Hessen, the reactionary part, the part that sent an old S.S. captain to the Bundestag as a Free Democrat at the same time students in Frankfurt and the rest of south Hessen were stringing love beads and playing Bob Dylan and hanging prison photographs of Ulrike Meinhof on their walls. It is still a heavy, closed world, and a poor world. There is no real industry so close to the frontier, no real investment. The people with money to spend are the American soldiers and—because of the state's subsidies to towns like Schlitz—the German tourists, who come for the castles and for a countryside that still manages to look bucolic despite the coded signs at every crossing. There are ten little hotels and guesthouses in Schlitz now. The mayor figures that thousands of people passed through Schlitz last year, but this contact with the world is new. Old people in Oberhessen got to know strangers only when soldiers came through or when they were soldiers themselves, heading out.

"I remember my father coming back from France," Willi Schäfer said last month when he was talking about the problem of enemies.

"My father was pulled out of the castle in '39 to march against France, and years later, before he died, he said to me— It was like a secret. He said, 'You know? France? I never saw an enemy there.' People my father's age, people my age—we never travelled, so we had enemies. But kids today travel. They hitchhike and they take part in the world, and when they come home they are a peace movement. They think about other Germans, Germans in the East, but they don't think enemies. They think, They're only Germans who'll be dead just like us if this craziness goes on. People in Schlitz say they were 'politicized' by the Eisenberg, but I don't know. They're not a peace movement yet. They haven't engaged themselves. Hattenbach is twenty minutes away, but a lot of them saw the Hattenbach movie and started worrying about Hattenbach only because the Eisenberg was involved and they were worrying about bombs on *their* mountain—bombs or troops or tanks that would make Schlitz a target. The story goes on. So many weapons. So much pain. I walk on the Eisenberg and look around—and the truth is I see no enemies anywhere."

December 1983

THE PARIBAS AFFAIR

*La stupidité de l'homme d'argent, quoique devenue quasi proverbiale,
n'est cependant que relative.*—BALZAC.

It is part of the folklore here that land and Catholicism have left the
French unfit for capitalism. The merchant bankers who were France's
first capitalists were the Jews and the Protestants of the country, following in the footsteps of fathers and grandfathers and great-grandfathers
who had loaned money to Popes and Kings in the days when usury was
a sin and a crime for the Catholic faithful. (The first Catholic bankers
with business in France were not French at all but Lombard, and it took
a Medici Pope, with one foot, so to speak, in faith and one in money,
to arrange that.) Some historians think the French Revolution might
have been avoided if Louis XIV had thought sensibly before revoking
the Edict of Nantes and forcing the country's thrifty and industrious
Protestants—and their money—into exile. The Protestants came back
after the Revolution, of course, and prospered. When Napoleon looked
around for the best people to start a Bank of France, he came up with
four Protestant merchant bankers and one Sephardic Jew. By the late
nineteenth century, there were two kinds of banks in France. There
were the private banks, run by the Jews and Protestants who began
them and dedicated to the great capital ventures of their time—
the wars and the colonies and the railroads and the visionary engineering projects, like the Suez Canal—and there were the big new public
banks, run by Catholics and dominated by the state and its institutions.
It was taken for home truth that those Catholic bankers out of the

landed bourgeoisie and the *petite noblesse* were, by definition, more concerned with what you owned than with what you made, and would therefore consider lending money and investing money to be shady and indelicate practices, on the order of indiscreet adultery. (A young investment banker I know with a Protestant father and a Catholic mother says that his Protestant relatives always thought of banking as big business, but that his Catholic relatives went into banking as if they were going into the civil service.) When the richest public banks were nationalized after the war—they are Crédit Lyonnais, Société Générale, and what is now the Banque Nationale de Paris—not many Frenchmen seemed to care, because those banks had never really been independent of the state to begin with. People went on putting their gold under the mattress, and the biggest trader on the Paris stock exchange was the French government.

Gaullist France, with its breadbasket rhetoric and its enthusiasm for *la France profonde*, was not encouraging to the old merchant bankers. The Protestant banking families—the Schlumbergers and the Vernes and the Mirabauds and the Neuflizes—had been merging or selling out or moving since the war. As for the Jewish banks, history had taught the Jewish banking families that discretion was the better part of power, and they kept their local operations small—though not small enough for the Banque Rothschild to avoid being nationalized by President François Mitterrand. ("Jew under Pétain, pariah under Mitterrand—that's enough for me," Guy de Rothschild wrote in *Le Monde* when the bank was put on the nationalization list.) Mitterrand nationalized thirty-eight independent banks, all told, toward the end of his first year as France's first Socialist ruler since Léon Blum. Every bank with deposits of over a billion francs was on his list, and when the list was published it turned out that the biggest and certainly the most aggressive independent bank in the country was not a rich family bank like the Banque Rothschild but a publicly held merchant bank and holding company called the Compagnie Financière de Paris et des Pays-Bas, or Paribas. Its offices were on the rue d'Antin, near the Opéra, in the *hôtel particulier* where Napoleon married Josephine. It was probably the only bank in the world where clients talked to their bankers in private rooms off a perfectly acclimatized *orangerie*, with an equestrian statue of Louis XIV for decoration.

The man who ran Paribas at the time was a banker named Pierre Moussa. He was the son of a Catholic midwife from Lyons and an Egyptian and (at least by origin) Muslim father, but the fact of a

Catholic mother did not seem to have kept him from becoming a dazzling capitalist. He had no ties to the old banking bourgeoisie. Nor was he connected to any of the great banking dynasties, like the Rothschilds, or to what economists sometimes call the "smart-people, no-money" school of banking, like his friends at, say, Lazard Frères. He was, if anything, a banking intellectual. He went to the École Normale Supérieure, became an Inspecteur de Finance, and taught at Sciences-Pô and at the École Nationale d'Administration before he was a banker. He had little interest in becoming a servant of the French state—the usual way for an intellectual to translate business into a form of statecraft and ease his squeamishness. People liked to say that there was something exotic, something not quite French, about Moussa, but it was really that he was sallow and heavy-lidded from too much work and too much reading. Coming to Paribas, he was solitary and a little elusive, even a little furtive. But in twelve years at the bank—three and a half of them as president—he made his reputation as the most enterprising international banker in France. By 1981, Paribas money was invested in forty-one countries. More than half the bank's business was outside France. It had rich banking subsidiaries—the French call them *filiales*—in Switzerland and Belgium, and assets of 238 billion francs (at the time, about $42.5 billion), increasing at the rate of 23 percent a year. Mitterrand called the nationalization of Paribas *"la récupération du patrimoine"*—the recovery of the national patrimony—but Moussa and his partners in Brussels and Geneva did not seem to consider *their* investments France's to recover. Moussa tried his best to talk the government out of nationalizing the subsidiaries along with the parent bank. When he failed, he put an old contingency plan into operation. It was called Noah's Ark, and it was a plan to spin the subsidiaries off—which meant right off the President's list. It took two days in the fall of 1981 for Pierre Moussa to "liberate" Paribas-Suisse and Cobepa, the Belgian Paribas. He simply sold France's majority holding in the Swiss subsidiary to the Belgian subsidiary, and vice-versa. For practical purposes, this meant that the control of Paribas-Suisse went to a Swiss holding company called Pargesa—it is the company of a Belgian steel millionaire named Albert Frère—which was acquiring the rest of the stock and had guaranteed the takeover. The liberation of Paribas-Suisse and Cobepa was an astonishing sleight-of-hand, and it was the scandal of France's first Socialist year. The Socialists accused Moussa of everything from "cosmopolitan influence" to having an "émigré mentality" (like the rich Frenchmen who fled to Koblenz with their money after the Revolution) and masterminding dark, Freemasonic plots against the people of France, but Moussa's only crime was that he loved his banks more than he loved his government.

There was nothing illegal about Moussa's selling 20 percent of the shares in two Paribas subsidiaries for what in fact turned out to be about twice their market value. A bank president in France has enormous power. Moussa had the authority to sign those Paribas-Suisse and Cobepa stock transfers without the government's—or even the Paribas board's—approval, and he took it. A lot of bankers here agreed with what he did, and said that, whatever their feelings about nationalization, they did not see how Belgium's second-largest holding company and Switzerland's fastest-growing bank could legitimately be considered France's property. Moussa himself believed that selling Paribas-Suisse and Cobepa for such an important profit was not really so different from selling, say, Crédit du Nord or any of Paribas's domestic companies. He said that in business everything has a price, and that in 1981, with the price right, it was his duty as a businessman to sell. Paribas had owned 60 percent of its *filiales* before the sale. Moussa sold 20 percent—which was enough to free the banks from French control—and he told his board that he found it much more interesting for Paribas-France to own 40 percent of a couple of prosperous, independent companies than to own 60 percent of subsidiaries that were bound to lose a lot of power if the government took them over. The Paribas board—fifteen men who, among them, controlled 260 billion francs in assets and employed more than half a million people—did not find it more interesting. Mainly, the Paribas board found it shocking. Some of the men on the board were shocked not because of what Moussa had done but because he had done it without telling anybody—and they felt foolish. Some were shocked because they shared a particular French pride in what they called "serving the legitimacy," and Moussa, to their mind, had abandoned France by serving the bank instead. The fact is that in France business and the state are not adversaries. The impulse is to reflect, to identify. *Le patrimoine* is a real, if exaggerated, notion, and it meant that, in the end, most of the people on Paribas's board accepted Mitterrand's decision to nationalize. One of the most powerful of them—Jean Riboud, the head of Schlumberger—was particularly close to Mitterrand. Riboud's advantage lay in his being the senior capitalist, so to speak, in a Socialist President's entourage; it did not lie in his being the champion of Pierre Moussa. He wanted Moussa out of Paribas, and so did the honorary chairman of the board, Jacques de Fouchier, who had run Paribas before Moussa took it over. De Fouchier was a banker of the old school, but it was he, more than anyone, who had sponsored Moussa. He had wanted Moussa for a dauphin, and he had fought hard for his appointment—but he had also expected to preside at Paribas afterward as an *éminence grise*. He never forgave Moussa for actually moving into his office (and moving him out). He and Riboud, with the board's approval, forced Moussa out of Paribas.

On November 10, 1981, Pierre Moussa was indicted under the French Customs Code and charged with being "interested in the fraud" in a case involving four bankers from Paribas's *service gestion privée* (its money-management service) who had helped some 385 clients send a total of 180 million francs illegally out of France and into numbered accounts in Paribas-Suisse, in Geneva. The four bankers were indicted, too, along with fifty-five of the clients, some of whom referred to Paribas's special Swiss service as Les Must de Paribas (after Cartier's jewelry boutiques, Les Must de Cartier). One of the bankers, Léonce Boissonnat, killed himself that winter. His superior at the bank, Jean Richard, eventually fled the country. And his most notorious client, Pierre-Jean Latécoère—Paribas had smuggled thirty-five thousand pieces of gold across the border for Latécoère—settled down in Switzerland, after a nervous breakdown having less to do with the indictment than with the fact that someone at the bank had skimmed eight hundred rare Indian-head dollars from his cache and substituted ordinary gold coins. (*Libération* then sent three reporters as couriers to Geneva with two thousand chocolate napoleons in their suitcases, and in two days—crossing and recrossing the border by train, by boat, by car, and once on foot—they had managed to deposit their "gold" at the front door of Paribas Suisse, to be eaten by the bankers.) As for Pierre Moussa, he waited for his trial and changed offices. He rented a small suite on the Avenue Montaigne and went from being the most enterprising investment banker in France to being the most enterprising financial consultant—and eventually he put together an investment company of his own with a safe Luxembourg base and a hundred million dollars of foreign capital to spend. Paribas itself did well enough without Moussa, but it missed the convenience of a Geneva bank whose assets were fuelled by flights of capital, and whose investment arrangements were much more interesting than anything a bank in France, under French constraints and French disclosure laws, could offer.

Mitterrand's economic experiments—basically, they involved the same sort of heavy-handed state socialism that British Labour had tried, to its regret, in the 1960s—were by most accounts a disaster. Laurent

Fabius, the new Prime Minister, had encouraged those experiments back in 1981, when he was a thirty-four-year-old budget director in Mitterrand's cabinet and enjoying his first year of power. He had fought for the nationalizations, and he had fought for Pierre Moussa to be indicted. He was a talented, ambitious, and, to some people, disagreeable young man—one of the real Jacobins of the Socialists' government. He was not hard up for cash himself, being the son and heir of the most important antique dealer in Paris. He liked show-jumping, and he drove the most elegant Maserati in town, but he seemed to identify with people who wanted to see the rich punished. In 1983, he was promoted to Minister of Industry and Research, and it was then that he took a sobering look at the companies that the Socialists had nationalized and at the state banks that were obliged to underwrite them. Mitterrand clearly took a look, too. He stopped nationalizing and talking about nationalizing. He stopped underwriting redundant jobs in redundant industries. He started firing and letting private industry fire. (Three thousand auto workers at Talbot, which belongs to Peugeot and is a private company, were the first to go.) He called this the second stage of French socialism—"*la politique de rigueur*"—but nobody else did. Robert Lattès, the head of nationalized Paribas's foreign-investment department, went off to America and came back talking excitedly about venture capitalists and "*la leçon Américaine.*" Mitterrand himself began to behave like a capitalist. He had soothed his party by making good on a decade of campaign promises, but he had antagonized millions of people who had voted for him believing that the promises meant nothing. Now he needed to persuade those people to invest in France. He pumped the Paris stock market, pushing up prices by ordering a lot of what would have been called institutional investing, except that all the institutions involved—banks, pension funds, insurance companies—belonged to him as President of France. He exhorted people to invest—people who still tended to believe the folklore about the French making bad capitalists, people who preferred objects they could dust and polish and admire to stock certificates locked away in a bank vault or a desk drawer. He reduced the capital-gains tax to 15 percent—the lowest French capital-gains tax ever. Last year, there was more trading on the Bourse than at any other time in sixty years.

It was around this time—toward the end of 1983—that the Procureur Général informed Pierre Culié, the presiding judge of the Eleventh Correctional Court at the Palais de Justice, that Jean-Pierre Monestié, one of his public prosecutors, was ready to argue the government's case against Pierre Moussa and his old officers and clients. By then, most people had forgotten that there was a case, or wanted to have forgotten. Moussa may have been bitter, but for two years he had kept his bitterness to himself—and, furthermore, he had done better, financially speaking, than the government. By the time he came to trial, the same people who had talked about dark plots and émigré treachery had decided that the treachery was Mitterrand's. They knew that Moussa was not being punished for sending money to Switzerland—he was being punished for selling Paribas's foreign banks when the President wanted them. Mitterrand had intended the Paribas trial as an object lesson. He had wanted the French to know what happened to bankers and businessmen like Pierre Moussa who tried to resist the state —and, while he was at it, he wanted the French to know what happened to people who got caught with them. But the French were mainly ashamed at the spectacle. Some of the men and women who went on trial last winter were in their nineties. Their bank accounts were illegal, but the stories they told were more like soap opera than like testimony. Denise Adam, who was said to be ninety-two, had kept her money in Switzerland for an invalid sister. She told the judge a long, sad story, and then she died before the verdict. Fernand Louis de Robert de Lalagade, who was also ninety-two, had held the French monopoly on Iranian caviar since 1937. He had opened *his* Geneva account for the purpose of paying the Shah the 10 percent kickback the Shah demanded, and he was now liable for some twenty-four million francs. He began to cry in court. "In 1914, I spilled my blood three times for France," he told Judge Culié. "To have lived through that and to find myself before you now, like a bandit . . . This is terrible, terrible."

The truth was that none of the Paribas clients felt like bandits —not even the ones who were. Swiss bank accounts are an old and ingrained French habit. (When Mitterrand declared a currency amnesty in 1982—people who brought their money back to France during the first three months of the year could do it openly, paying a capital-gains tax of 25 percent—practically everyone ignored it.) Most French governments have looked on Swiss accounts as a natural function of being rich and French and, by definition, parsimonious, and until the Paribas indictments they were never considered a breach of citizenship. People who got caught taking money out of the country usually made their arrangement with French customs—the Douane—and, by common consent, those arrangements had never involved more punishment than a quiet, negotiated cash settlement. Paribas itself had negotiated with the Douane and settled out of court the day before the trial started, paying somewhere between 27 million and 130 million francs to be institutionally absolved, as it were, of its own "interest in the fraud." (Pierre Moussa's lawyer, Jean Loyrette, represented Paribas in the negotiations.) The clients themselves had been negotiating for a year when they were suddenly indicted. Pierre-Jean Latécoère, for one, was arranging to pay a thirty-six-million-franc fine on his smuggled gold, and Paribas was lending him most of the money. To the clients' minds, the Paribas trial was not *their* trial. It was the trial of Pierre Moussa by François Mitterrand.

The trial ended in February, and Judge Culié delivered his verdicts on April 24. Pierre Moussa was acquitted. No one except, perhaps, the prosecutor was really surprised, because the charge of being "interested in the fraud" had involved a loose and rather fuzzy concept to begin with, and by April of 1984 Moussa's particular "interest" was less a question of the law than of the situation in the courtroom. (The concept is peculiar to the Customs Code. It has nothing to do with responsibility or foreknowledge, or even complicity; it has to do with someone being in a position to benefit, directly or indirectly, from a crime, whether or not he is responsible for the crime or for the criminals.) Twelve Paribas clients were acquitted, too, for lack of solid evidence against them. Forty-one people were found guilty. Jean Richard, the missing bank officer, was sentenced to prison in absentia, along with Latécoère and two other clients who had fled the country in March of 1982. Everybody else got a fine and a suspended sentence—the sentences ranging from two to eighteen months. It seemed as if the only people left in France who were still angry at Pierre Moussa on April 24 were Paribas's clients.

People in different countries cheat in different ways. Americans do it at work, in ways—from stealing pencils to stealing payrolls— that would horrify the French, but it is not their habit to expect to negotiate their taxes, as the French do, or to stash their money in a Swiss bank, or to be outraged when the government asks them to declare it. Maybe the French identify so thoroughly with the state that authority becomes a kind of household familiar, something they are bound to work around, like a strict father or an irritable wife. For years, there was more gold in private hands in France than anywhere else in the world. (Latécoère kept *his* thirty-five thousand pieces under the floorboards of the family château.) It stays in private hands because of the determination of people here literally to possess wealth, rather than to invest wealth productively in France and watch it grow. The French are patriots, and often chauvinists, but they are rarely, to their own mind, foolish enough to want to squander their inheritance on governments and wars and politics. When a Frenchman puts his money in a Swiss bank and then uses it to buy a piece of Southern California, he believes that he is preserving the wealth of France from the whims and manipulations of France's rulers.

In the past, when it was mainly Jews and Protestants who practiced the arts of finance, French bankers were considered not to have the same conservative, concrete, innocent attachment to the idea of France as their Catholic countrymen. Today, there is still a kind of innocence in the way their countrymen define "France." Mitterrand talks about *le patrimoine* as if it were a household inventory. People "preserve" France in Swiss francs and California quarter-acres. One of the prosecutors involved in the Paribas case said that it was an easy case to argue but a hard one to judge, because people in France have felt economically betrayed by their history for at least two hundred years —and their feelings are accurate. He said that the druggist or the piano teacher heading for the border with the family gold in a little suitcase really did see Switzerland as a magic place—a place of peace and stability, where "France" would be safe until the French got smart. The French franc has been devalued so many times in the sixty-six years since the end of the First World War that by now it is virtually another currency. It is not hard to understand why, in the course of those years, a lot of Frenchmen decided that their best insurance against the future was to convert their French francs into Swiss francs, if not directly into gold—which went from two hundred francs a kilo to a hundred thousand francs a kilo while the franc was weakening. (*"L'or bien caché monte"* is how the French put it.) Anyone here over the age of seventy has lived through two long wars and an enemy occupation at home, not to mention a war in Indochina and another one in Algeria. People at the Paribas trial often talked about wars—about losing everything in one war and then losing it all over again in another. They talked about the First World War, when the government asked the French to turn in their gold in exchange for war bonds; people from all over the country carried their coins and their wedding rings and their cufflinks to the war office, but then the war was over and nobody who had bought one of those bonds was ever able to redeem its value. They talked about 1944, when Fascist *miliciens* and even hustlers posing as Maquisards were demanding gold for guns, gold for "war taxes," gold that the French never saw again, either. There were times during the trial when it seemed as if wars were fought and people died in them simply to rob the bourgeoisie of its money.

There have been controls on exporting capital since the Liberation. Charles de Gaulle relaxed those controls for twenty months in the 1960s, figuring that the franc was stable enough to stand the change, but money literally poured out of the country when he did, and the controls were never relaxed again. In 1983, Mitterrand imposed a two-thousand-franc limit on French tourists who wanted to leave the country—and he enforced it. The limit was only five thousand francs per trip before 1982, but people then paid very little attention to currency controls, because they were rarely stopped at the border and, more important, because they could charge anything they wanted on their credit cards. There were officers, too, in most French banks who would open illegal accounts in Switzerland for their clients. (Actually, the biggest numbered-account scandal before the Paribas affair involved a nationalized bank, the Crédit Lyonnais. Customs agents raided Crédit Lyonnais in 1976 and discovered that bankers there were managing Swiss accounts for their clients by telephone.) Keeping your money in Switzerland was an arrangement with certain risks and certain rules and very few surprises. People who did get caught, because of a bank raid or a spot check at the border or a tip from an informer, would call their lawyers, and their lawyers would sit down with the Douane's lawyers and negotiate a settlement that, by tradition, involved the actionable amount—capital leaving France for Switzerland, say, or interest from Switzerland coming illegally into France—along with a nice fine for the government, a commission for the Douane, and a 10 percent *prime d'aviseur* for the informer. Nobody worried much about the outcome. People paid their fines—two or three times the actionable amount of money was the rule of thumb—and told their friends, *"J'ai transigé,"* which means "I compromised," and their friends always knew what they were talking about. These currency crimes rarely made it to the courtroom. In the first place, it was not in the interest of the Douane to bring a currency case to trial, because no respectable judge was going to demand the sort of fines and commissions and informers' fees the Douane expects. Then, too, the court itself was never enthusiastic about currency crimes. Cases involving capital flight and numbered bank accounts were at best exercises. They focused on a few people out of thousands, and they made the thousands uncomfortable. One of the prosecutors put it this way: "Suppose it was a matter of car theft instead of bank accounts. Suppose your car was stolen and the thief said, 'It's all right to steal cars because everybody does it.' Well, in the case of those Swiss accounts . . . It's *not* right. *And* everybody does it."

The law in France is based on the notion of the *bon père de famille*. This is what every Frenchman is taught to aspire to, and the problem for the fifty-five people who got indicted with their bankers during the Paribas affair is that a good father in this relentlessly bourgeois country is, by definition, a father who protects and preserves the family capital in any way he can. One of the defendants liked to quote Napoleon III: "I'll make the politics here, you make the money." It was because of Napoleon III, the defendant said this spring while he was waiting for the verdict, that he did not consider keeping a Geneva bank account a crime. He considered it merely a *petit délit*—a little misdemeanor. No one else quoted Napoleon III, but the fact is that a lot of Frenchmen do take their *petits délits* as a patriotic duty. The Douane has ended up with twenty-two thousand agents, including a special branch of four or five hundred investigators with what amounts to police powers. People who join the Douane are not apt to be well disposed toward the sort of men and women who have bank accounts in Geneva and gold under the floorboards of the family château. Like every other institution in France, the Douane is political. Politicians from every party will try to use it if they have the power, but nearly three thousand of the *douaniers* belong to the Confédération Générale du Travail, the union close to the Communists, and another three thousand belong to the Confédération Française Démocratique du Travail, the Socialists' union, and their reputation among the bourgeoisie is sinister. They have time and license, and (when it is not to their advantage to be tolerant) they are brutally unscrupulous.

There is a customs official by the name of Michel Danet whose job it is to sit in an office on the rue de Rivoli, at the Louvre, and reflect upon the nature of the French and the regulations they are likely to break. M. Danet is the Douane's house philosopher, responsible, as he puts it, for *"la conception de la lutte"* in a country with 1,841 miles of frontier and another 1,934 miles of coastline and about 250 million people going in and out each year. Given the likelihood that every one of those people is carrying *something* illegal, it is up to M. Danet to decide what, precisely, the Douane wants to find, and where to find it, so that an agent at the Belgian border knows if he is looking for heroin or diamonds or guns or rolled-up Fragonards when he opens a suitcase. Last year, customs agents reported 210,000 violations. According to their figures, the problem for France right now is not just the traffic in francs; it is the traffic in drugs and in what is officially known as *le patrimoine artistique et culturel*—in other words, Louis XV snuff boxes and the family silver. Only fifty-one hundred of the violations last year had to do with flights of capital. And in 1980—the year that ten customs agents raided Paribas and discovered a list of code names, like Nero and Britannicus and Rhododendron, for the 385 clients with Swiss accounts —Paribas clients represented nearly half of all the currency violations reported. Of course, it is easier to spot the family silver at the border than a Swiss deposit slip. Whatever their politics, customs agents are going to feel a little awkward about asking a family of five on its way to a hike through the Bernese Oberland to turn its pockets out. Still, one of the most important border arrests the Douane has made in years involved a man who was stopped for a spot check and asked to open his briefcase. The briefcase was clean, but as the man was leaning over to close it his wallet fell out of his breast pocket and then a Swiss check fell out of the wallet—and the *douanier* discovered that he had caught a currency runner who had been carrying huge sums of money back and forth across the border for twenty years.

Mainly, the Douane makes its big discoveries in banks, not at borders. As many as 10 percent of the people who work in Basel and Geneva banks are French citizens either living in Switzerland or commuting across the border to their jobs. Some of them are, if not actually harassed, at least under a certain amount of pressure from the Douane to cooperate—which means passing along names and figures—and others are obviously paid informers. Swiss Socialists organized a referendum on banking secrecy this spring, and the canton of Geneva, like every other canton in the country, voted to maintain it. This was distressing to Mitterrand—who seems to have held the belief that with the right encouragement people in Switzerland would be more Socialist than Swiss—because most of the French money in Switzerland is probably in Geneva banks. The Douane has been raiding Paris banks with Geneva branches or correspondents for years. Paribas itself was raided ten times—the last time in 1978—before those ten customs agents stopped in, on a tip, on November 28, 1980, when all the bankers were out to lunch, and found the information they wanted. There are people who say that that was the day the liberation of Paribas-Suisse started.

Valéry Giscard d'Estaing was still the President of France in 1980, and so it is reasonable to assume that any "political instructions" (as one man from the Douane put it) about Paribas came from the right, not the left. Giscard had been Finance Minister for a while, under Georges Pompidou, and he had close connections at the Douane, which officially falls under the jurisdiction of the Ministry of Finance. He also had an election coming up, and in those days Pierre Moussa was quite respectably connected to the French left. Moussa had put in time as *directeur de cabinet* for a colonial minister in Pierre Mendès France's Fourth Republic government. He had invented the phrase *"les nations prolétaires,"* and he had even written books about those nations. It may be that Giscard thought the threat of a banking scandal—or, at least, of a lot of long negotiations and expensive settlements—would help keep Paribas's money out of François Mitterrand's campaign. (This is the common wisdom among bankers.) It may also be that Giscard wanted some leverage when he asked Moussa to put more money and more credit into places like Creusot-Loire, the heavy-engineering company, which was in danger of going under. At any rate, there were about four thousand private accounts at Paribas at the time—which meant that 10 percent of the bank's clients were taking advantage of its accommodating Swiss service. Jean-Pierre Monestié says that the most stupefying piece of evidence he had, as prosecutor, was the number of illegal accounts that Paribas was managing. One woman who went on trial last winter said that Paribas's Swiss service was "the little extra" with which the bank wooed customers. People took Paribas up on that service because the bank could make transfers that were mainly paper transfers and that did not have to involve sending big bundles of franc notes across the border. The bank was also known to cover financially for its clients the way an expensive American accountant might guarantee his time in the event that a client was audited by the Internal Revenue Service. Most Paribas clients who admitted to having Swiss accounts told Judge Culié that Paribas had promised to provide this sort of protection—protection from prosecution, protection from publicity, protection from fines and commissions and informers' fees. None of the clients had expected to go to court. Some were able to deny having their accounts at all, once it was clear that they could not be traced conclusively to their code names. (Even now, no one knows who Henry IV, Praline, Faust, and Mephisto were.) The ones who could be traced had already spent a year negotiating with the Douane when they were indicted. There was never talk of indictment during that year. Most of the clients expected that their *petits délits* would be settled discreetly, for a price, and that the bank would help them pay. (Some of them say they had already settled.) They continued to believe this through the elections and through the first months of Mitterrand's Presidency

—and so, apparently, did Pierre Moussa, who did not even bother to remove Jean Richard, the man running Paribas's Swiss service.

Léonce Boissonnat was the banker most of the defendants knew best at Paribas. He was not the most important banker in his department, not particularly high in the pecking order of Paribas officers. He managed 385 Swiss accounts because somebody higher up told him to. He was by all accounts a decent man and a very kind one. Judge Culié himself interrupted the testimony one day to say that Léonce Boissonnat was "an eminently respectable man" and that the court would not tolerate attacks on his character. Boissonnat's friends say that when Laurent Fabius—in his capacity as budget director at the Finance Ministry—instructed the Procureur Général to indict fifty-five of Boissonnat's clients, Boissonnat believed he had betrayed those clients by his own helplessness. He believed, too, that Paribas was betraying him. Pierre Moussa went into seclusion in his apartment on the Quai d'Orsay the day the indictments were handed down. Boissonnat stayed in Paris. On December 19, 1981, he sent his family away to the country and put a bullet through his heart.

It would have taken years to try 385 Paribas clients—a few were so senile they had forgotten all about their Geneva accounts—and the government was more interested in Pierre Moussa than in his clients, anyway. Fabius needed a way to eliminate most of them, and he settled on a formula by which clients with less than two million francs to account for could continue negotiating their settlements and clients with more than two million were indicted. The statute of limitations in cases of customs fraud is four years in France, and most Paribas clients had had their numbered accounts much longer. This meant that they were not necessarily responsible to France for their capital. They were responsible for, say, interest they had drawn on their capital or for additions they had made to it—for money that, from the point of view of the Douane, had crossed the border within the past four years. It also meant that anyone with two million francs to account for had a lot more francs behind him. The people who finally came to trial with Pierre Moussa were known in Paris as *les plus belles clientèles*. One of them had been president of Motobécane, the bicycle company. Another was president of Darty, the chain of appliance stores where most of France buys its refrigerators and its washing machines. Some of them were simply too old and too ill to come to court, and others refused to come, saying that the prosecutor must have confused them with other Paribas clients of the same name. The people who did come to the Eleventh Correctional Court to testify insisted that their Swiss accounts had been Paribas's idea. One immensely rich young man by the name of François Rochas said that he had discovered Paribas-Suisse when his mother sold the family business—it happened to be Parfums Marcel Rochas, one of the biggest perfume manufacturers in France. Paribas handled the sale, and afterward, apparently, Jean Richard approached Rochas, wanting to know what he was planning to do with all the money he received. Richard told him that it was certainly too much money to keep in France—that it should be somewhere safe from scrutiny and taxes. As Rochas tells the story now, he flew to Geneva, where Richard joined him for a nice lunch at Paribas-Suisse with two of the bank's directors, and he opened his account that afternoon. Rochas went back to France and bought a vineyard in Bordeaux, and after that, whenever he wanted to check on how his money in Geneva was doing, he would stop at Léonce Boissonnat's office on the rue d'Antin and Boissonnat would place a call and make some notes and go over the figures with him and then burn the notes with his cigarette lighter. Rochas says that he was never really worried about the money —that even after the raid four years ago he was sure the bank would take care of him. He was not much troubled by the propriety of his banking arrangements, either. He came to court looking (according to *Libération*) "bronzed" and "elegant," and when he talked about Paribas in court he sounded less distressed than petulant. He seemed to hold the charges against him—charges that had to do with currency controls and moving money around—not in contempt but in disregard. Or, rather, he did not seem to accept the fact that there *were* controls like that, controls that most intelligent people agreed were ridiculous but that could still make rich young men like himself inconvenienced or unhappy. He regards opening a secret Swiss bank account as a particularly farsighted and energetic gesture. Right now, in fact, he is trying to sue Paribas-Suisse for letting the French Paribas know anything about him. He says that his Swiss bankers have violated their own laws of banking secrecy. His argument goes that they had no business passing information to his Paris bankers, even though it was information he asked for.

People like François Rochas—people with time and money and little to lose—will appeal the sentences that Judge Culié handed down in April. An appeal takes about a year in Paris. A second appeal —one to the Cour de Cassation, which is the procedural court— takes another year. This means that at least a few Paribas clients will have two more years before they have to pay their fines, and in two

years the interest they have earned at the bank will probably be enough
to cover them. Covering their costs is what most of them want, in the
end. There are other Paribas clients—clients who are less sophisticated,
perhaps, and more caught up in their humiliation—who want something more than their costs back, something they will never get in an
appeal. They are clients like the old caviar importer, or like Gérard
Avalle, who was convicted this spring and given a six months' suspended sentence. Maître Avalle is a bailiff, and bailiffs in France are like
notaires—they are a kind of caste, a closed society. Nobody knows very
much about them but other bailiffs and their families, because their
number is fixed by a numerus clausus—120 bailiffs for the city of Paris;
1,800 for the whole country—and they often pass the profession down
from father to son, the son taking his place among the 1,800 bailiffs
when the father dies or retires. It is a Balzacian sort of profession,
having to do with being there when banks foreclose or summonses are
served or debtors are thrown out of their homes or buildings expro-
priated or adulteries committed or bankruptcies filed. Every time a
French bailiff signs his name to a piece of paper—an act or a court order
or an affidavit—he makes some money. According to Claude Roire at
the *Canard Enchaîné*, there are bailiffs who make twelve francs on every
150-franc parking ticket processed in the city of Paris.

Maître Avalle is head of a Paris bailiffs' association, and he likes to
talk about his three years at Sciences-Pô, where his class included
Jacques Chirac, the mayor of Paris, and Jean-Yves Haberer, the man
who took over Paribas when Pierre Moussa left. He is frenetically
conservative—it is a tradition among bailiffs to cultivate shiny suits,
shabby offices, miserly dispositions, and right-wing views—but very
much a man of the court (*un homme de robe*, the French say), and he
keeps two Daumier prints called *Men of Justice* on his office wall. To
his own mind, Maître Avalle is a diligent citizen and a French patriot.
Once, after the trial, he said that the charges against him were "unhealthy," that they had to do with "*la volupté de ceux qui s'abstiennent*"
—by which he meant a kind of prurient asceticism inherited by the left
from Robespierre. In his way, Gérard Avalle represents what people
mean by *la France profonde*—Catholic, conservative France, where
every father is a good father of the family. Avalle himself has five
children. He is a man who looks after the interests of his friends'
widows and who lectures the ten clerks in his office on the fact that no
one spending 800,000 francs a year on salaries, as he does, and another
420 on social security and insurance charges should have to listen to talk
about turning his office into a cooperative. He admires people like his

grandfather, who had a little factory and produced the first automobile batteries in the country. His grandfather put the money he made on batteries into property in Paris, and retired young, to live, like the nobility, on his income. Avalle is an almost classic bourgeois, like that grandfather. The closest he gets to the demimonde is when someone calls him there as a witness, the way he was called this spring to a Paris nightclub, the Élysée Matignon, which belonged to a couple who were getting divorced; he "witnessed" the fact that the wife had locked her husband out of the premises.

Avalle was nearly undone by his indictment—humiliated as a man of the court, fearful for the career he would lose if he was convicted, bewildered by the events that were stripping the euphemisms of his life of their respectability. He told a strange story. He talked about going to Paribas in 1973 and meeting a "man of family" who had been a hero in the war and had lost an arm saving a minister or a general and wore the Légion d'Honneur in his lapel; the man was Léonce Boissonnat. He said that he and Boissonnat had had a conversation about how France was being ruined by its governments. After that, he left 2,500,000 francs with Paribas. He could have made a fortune there. Once, he flew to America to buy some land on Jean Richard's advice. He travelled by Concorde, he says, and spent the night in a Holiday Inn outside Norfolk—with a reservation under the name of one of Paribas's American employees. Then he flew to Mississippi, drove south in a camper with Richard and his wife, spent *that* night in a Louis XVI canopy bed in a house in Natchez, and finally was met by a driver who took him to see the land he was supposed to be buying. The driver came from Paribas's Houston office, and Avalle says he was the first person ever to suggest to him that his money was not in France but in Switzerland. According to Avalle, Jean Richard had a scheme for financing land purchases in America. It involved borrowing dollars at, say, 10 percent interest and then lending them out in Europe at 15 percent, and skimming off the difference—and it also involved a big commission to Paribas for putting the deal together and laundering the money.

Maître Avalle wanted out, but he says that according to the people at Paribas the only way he could safely bring his money home to France was to invest it in raw materials—in oil, say, or forests—because the income from raw materials was "free" and could enter the country undeclared. By the time he went on trial, Avalle was the owner of five thousand acres of virgin forest in Quebec Province. He was also planning to sue Paribas, on the ground that the real fraud in the Paribas affair was the bank's. "The bank has saved its furniture," he told the court, "and forgotten its clients."

Le Nouvel Observateur says that there are five million numbered accounts in Switzerland. It is one figure nobody seems to dispute. Right now, there are safer ways than Paribas's for opening a secret Swiss account. Some people incorporate themselves. They register as a Luxembourg company, and their Luxembourg company, in turn, incorporates itself. It forms what is known in the trade as an "offshore" Panamanian company—that is, an address or a post-office box and no product—and then the Panamanian company opens the account in Switzerland. There are lawyers in Switzerland who have set up hundreds of these Panamanian companies for their clients. They charge about five hundred dollars for their time, along with the three hundred and fifty dollars it costs to incorporate in Panama, and for an extra two hundred or so people can choose a name they like for their company, the way Paribas clients used to choose code names like Leopard and Rhododendron and Socrates. Paribas was always known as an aggressive bank, and, like any aggressive bank, it made whatever deals it could through Switzerland. Under Moussa's predecessors, Paribas began to devote itself to pure capitalism—that is, to money and power. It was Moussa's genius to combine this devotion with the liberal politics of a French Fourth Republic intellectual.

Businessmen here were a little scared of Paribas. They liked to say that if you dealt with Paribas—if, say, you needed cash and Paribas gave it to you for 5 percent of your company—Paribas would own you within the next two years. The bank had a certain reputation for unscrupulousness. It was known as the kind of partner that would call in its loans on the twenty-ninth of the month unless it got a few more shares of your business, the kind of partner that would cancel your credit unless it got a bigger cut of your profits. One of the ironies of the Paribas affair is that Pierre Moussa had turned the bank into a great entrepreneurial force, with engineering projects that were his own equivalent of a Suez Canal and financing projects that were helping to underwrite development in the Third World. There is not much buccaneer spirit left at Paribas now that Moussa is gone. These days, Paribas likes to invest in the agents, not in the creation, of capital. Last year, the bank bought a controlling interest in a Wall Street investment bank and brokerage house by the name of A. G. Becker—becoming, in effect, a nationalized stockbroker—and a couple of months ago called in all the remaining stock, which had belonged to the Becker-Paribas employees. Moussa himself announced this spring that *his* new company was buying 50 percent of the London subsidiary of another Wall Street brokerage house, Dillon, Read & Co.

Moussa is now "recuperated," as François Mitterrand would say. And so, indeed, is some of the patrimony Mitterrand wanted. About two weeks after Moussa was acquitted, the holding company Pargesa sold its majority in Paribas-Suisse back to France and announced that the banks had resumed their proper partnership. Pargesa had run Paribas-Suisse for a little over two and a half years. Its profit on the sale was somewhere between 280 million and 500 million Swiss francs—between $124 million and $222 million.

In the end, even the bankers were surprised. People in the business knew that Paribas and Paribas-Suisse had been working on a deal for most of those two and a half years—but it was a deal they assumed would save face for France while keeping the control of Paribas-Suisse in Switzerland. They expected, say, that France would get back its 60 percent of the old subsidiary—it actually got 72 percent—and that some formula involving voting shares would be devised to leave the Swiss bank independent. In fact, the new Paribas-Suisse was transferred to a holding company in which half the voting shares belonged to France and the other half to Pargesa. The president of the holding company casts the deciding vote if there is any argument, and the president is Jean-Yves Haberer, from Paribas. François Mitterrand has finally —maybe permanently—nationalized Paribas-Suisse. It may be that Paribas-Suisse was what he demanded in exchange for Moussa's acquittal. Moussa cannot have been pleased to see the bank he liberated returned to the French state, but he seems to have taught Mitterrand something about business all the same: When the price is right, people sell. Moussa's friends sold.

July 1984

COAL AND THE BISHOPS

We are enormously tenderhearted, but we are not ideological. The terrifying intelligence in the eyes of a French plumber alarms us.
—THE REVEREND RICHARD CHARTRES,
Rector of St. Stephen's, Westminster

It used to be that the colliers of the county of Durham went to church once a year, in July, on Miners' Gala day. Each pit village in the county would send a band to Durham, and the bands—there were nearly two hundred—would parade through Durham town, banging drums and blowing trumpets, and the colliers would follow them to the race track for speeches and on to the cathedral for a sermon and prayers. The colliers of Durham were not notably churchgoing men, even in the days before television football—the days when there was nothing on Sundays to keep them home. Coal miners who went to church regularly were not apt to be Church of England anyway; they were Methodist or Irish Catholic, and they probably thought of the fine Anglican cathedral on top of the hill in Durham as a place where the sort of people who owned mines worshipped, a place that served established faith to the established classes. When they climbed that hill on Miners' Gala day, it was an exercise in sentiment. They were playing their parts in the old folk drama of British class, which holds that under the vicious divisions of wealth and privilege there is a heartfelt social contract —that Englishmen, in the end, are devoted to one another as Englishmen. They expected a sermon dedicated to them, and to England's coal, and so they came to town from the miserable little villages around the collieries where they had to live.

The diocese of Durham is what is known in England as a "prince bishopric." There is a ducal coronet on the bishop's arms, and this means that the diocese once "belonged" to the bishop, and its rents and a share of its crops went directly to his palace, at Bishop Auckland —the way that Yorkshire, just south of Durham, once belonged to the Duke of York and paid a share of its wealth to him. When coal was discovered in Durham, a lot of it was under Church of England wheat fields and Church of England pastures. The Church was still in the coal business, with a couple of collieries in its name, when Durham's pits were nationalized, after the Second World War—which may be why the bishops had a patronly as well as a priestly interest in Miners' Gala day. They would polish their pectoral crosses and put on their best chasubles and preach to the miners in their charge the way a business-man might dress up for a company Christmas party and share a bottle with the staff and maybe offer up a toast—in a shrewd gesture of community. The miners seem to have been truly fond of the Victorian bishop Joseph Lightfoot, and of his successor, Brooke Foss Westcott, who settled a bitter strike in Durham in 1892, helped the miners to start cooperatives in their villages, and, when he was ill and had to retire, chose their Gala for his farewell sermon. But in 1926, the year of the worst general strike in British history, the Bishop of Durham was Hensley Henson, and he used his Gala sermon to try to frighten the Durham miners back to work. The miners got mad and decided to throw the bishop in the river Wear. They were drunk by then, and got the wrong man and threw him in the river instead.

The Church of England, the saying goes, is the Tory Party at prayer. Even now, it evokes images of pleasant country Sundays —the honest squire in the front pew of a village church, the local doctor behind him, and the tradesmen and then the simple folk, the farmers and their bonneted wives and daughters and the colorful, pious bump-kins out of some Dorothy Sayers novel before the murder makes every-body seem a little queer. There was never room in that imaginary village church for the children of an industrial revolution so wrenching and disaffecting that it produced, along with its coal and its steel, the model for *Das Kapital*. The nineteenth-century miners who joined Methodist chapels (and the other "chapel" churches) were not involved in theological distinctions; they were a defeated working class looking for solace, and it did not occur to them to look for it in the church of people they considered their oppressors. The churches that Anglicans in the countryside still call "nonconformist" or "dissenting" grew with that working class, and served it in places where the Church of England was serving soup and sympathy but rarely fellowship. There were vicars then who wanted to reclaim the working class. Some of them wrote books and tracts (in what they took for common speech) about the temptations of Methodism, published them as the confessions of, say, a repentant collier, and passed them out in pubs and at chapel doors. And, like George Eliot's estimable Reverend Amos Barton, a few actually believed in the existence of that mythical workingman "who out of pure zeal for the welfare of his class took the trouble to warn them in this way against those hypocritical thieves, the Dissenting preachers"—but not many. A hundred years ago, Methodist preachers were organizing in coal mines and factories and steel mills by way of church recruitment, and standing up with those workers they got in trouble when the workers had to account for themselves to judges who were as likely as not Church of England clergymen. (At one point, over a third of the magistrates in England were Anglican priests.) When the miners began to hold meetings, the preachers opened their churches. Some of the first coal miners' union meetings were held in Methodist churches in Wales and Yorkshire, and the miners, for their part, got in the habit of calling their union branches "chapels." They used to hand over their dues to the preachers for safekeeping, the feeling being that only a Methodist preacher would be strict enough and sour enough to hold on to a union's money instead of drinking it. The miners were puritan. English socialism had its roots in their puritanism, in their Sunday-morning testimony about the wages of Saturday-night sin —which were really the wages of poverty. They are still puritan, if not Methodist. Wales is Methodist in its pit villages, but only about 6 percent of England is Methodist, and most of the miners in the northeast would probably describe themselves as Church of England if they had to describe themselves at all. In the county of Durham, four or five thousand coal miners belong to Anglican churches, but so many of their mines have closed that there were only eight or ten pit bands left to lead them to the cathedral in the last Gala parade they had, in July of 1983—or, for that matter, to lead them back to work when the coal miners' strike that began in March of 1984 ended this March, after fifty-one weeks.

Durham changed bishops during the miners' strike. The old bishop—his name is John Habgood, and he is the Archbishop of York now—spent ten years in Durham and watched while the coal-mining population of the northeast was dropping from 125,000 men to 25,000. The new bishop, David Jenkins, was appointed just as most of those 25,000 miners started striking. By Miners' Gala day last year, they were five months into the strike, with no strike pay to spend, nothing to do, and no one to negotiate for them, because Margaret Thatcher, the Prime Minister, was using the strike to try to break their union, and Arthur Scargill, the president of the National Union of Mineworkers, was using the strike to try to break the government. They cancelled the Gala, and held a demonstration instead. Dr. Jenkins had sympathy for the miners. Like Dr. Habgood before him, he made what Anglicans would call a liberal bishop, to distinguish him from the evangelicals in the Church, who are fundamentalists and often charismatics, and who think of themselves as England's Moral Majority (some priests think of them as "suburbanized Methodists"), and from the Anglo-Catholics, who are the aesthetes of the Church, and extremely formal in matters of dogma, faith, and practice. In the Church of England, a liberal means someone who is either theologically liberal or socially and politically liberal or both. Dr. Jenkins was thought to be both.

It has been the tradition in Durham to have dons as bishops. Bishops of Durham have come out of the Theology Department of one university or another since the nineteenth century, and—despite the evidence from the days when bishops railed at miners and miners tried to throw them in the river for it—to a lot of the Anglican faithful a Theology Department is a radical and seditious place, where people talk about doubt and argue about doctrine and do whatever else they can to undermine the bland tranquillity of the Christian lives around them. The new Bishop of Durham had been a don at the University of Leeds. He had degrees (seconds) in classics and literature along with his first in theology. Before he went to Leeds, in 1979, he was fifteen years at Oxford, five years at the World Council of Churches, in Geneva, and another five with the William Temple Foundation, in Manchester, raising social consciences. His job in Geneva was director of "humanism studies." He was there when priests and pastors began to elaborate something they called "liberation theology." He read the Peruvian Father Gustavo Gutiérrez, and liked him. He met the Jesuits and the Maryknoll priests and nuns from Nicaragua and Guatemala. He was a pink-cheeked, white-haired English cleric nearing sixty —charming, voluble, distracted, a little cluttered in his library and in his thoughts. He loved to talk. He entertained himself talking. He talked as if the world were a fascinating dictionary he was leafing through, and rarely finished a sentence on the subject he had started. It was a common-room style—thinking out loud, discovering and defining and revising opinion that way, making up one's mind in discourse. Style, not doctrine, was what really separated the Church's dons from its parish clergy.

There is an acknowledged difference in the Church of England between intellectual responsibility and pastoral responsibility. A theologian is supposed to probe and provoke when he talks. A priest is supposed to correct and comfort. The trouble with David Jenkins was that he moved from his rooms at Leeds to his palace at Bishop Auckland as if it were the same job but with a bigger audience. The Bishop of Durham (like the Bishops of London and Winchester) is a "senior bishop," second only to the Archbishops of Canterbury and York in the Church of England hierarchy. He has a kind of automatic theological celebrity; people are immensely interested in what he has to say. Jenkins had decided somewhere along the way to Bishop Auckland that the great miracles of Christianity were not a Virgin Birth and a Resurrection but apostolic faith in a Virgin Birth and a Resurrection, and he often said so. The evangelicals and the Anglo-Catholics in the Church disagreed with him, but Dr. Jenkins was untroubled, because he had also decided that theological rigidity was like any injustice or intolerance—a symptom of despotism in moral life. He was known to have (his words) "a conscious theory of my mission and a sharpened social concern," which was really an extension of his conscious theory of miracles. He believed that it was the duty of a Christian leader to confront what he considered bad or inhumane politics. He liked to say that "a lively belief in God revitalizes all political commitments"; in his case, those commitments included the people who were losing the only way of life they knew to Mrs. Thatcher's cold economies. Durham was full of them. It had got to be almost emblematic of England's problems. Its mines were obsolete, and so were its miners, who had nowhere to go and nothing to offer except a dwindling supply of coal that no one needed anymore. It was disturbing to intellectuals in the Church, because it posed the fundamental moral problem of societies like England that could shape a proletariat to the needs of an industrial age and not know what to do with that proletariat once the age was over. Mrs. Thatcher wanted to abandon the proletariat to the marketplace. Mr. Scargill seemed to want to abandon the economy.

England's miners are a lost tribe. It is hard to think of any other people in the West who are literally left over, in the way the miners of England are left over. The government calls them "redundant workers." Mrs. Thatcher likes to talk about redundant workers making new lives for themselves—like the steelworkers whose mill was closed, and who went to work in a factory making marshmallows—but none of her stories really apply to the coal miners, because England's coal miners refuse to move. The miners have never lived in big towns or cities, where in better times than these there might have been something besides mining for them to do, some other way of earning money. Their pit villages are just that—villages that were built by coal companies around coal pits. They were built to save coal companies the cost and the trouble of getting the miners to the mines in the morning and getting them home again at night. They were cheap, convenient, and even profitable, because the companies usually made money out of their company stores and company clubs and company houses. Most miners who lived in pit villages rarely got to see anybody but other miners and a few bosses. The assumption was that they were less likely to be restless or disgruntled and start complaining than miners who had friends and neighbors with better jobs. There are counties in Wales and northeast England dotted with pit villages the way the Kalahari Desert is dotted with acacias: the villages look close enough from an airplane, but from the ground they are patches in an empty landscape. They lose everything when a pit closes. They lose their schools and stores along with their collieries and union locals and workingmen's clubs and lodges. Eventually, they are ghost towns whose people have refused to die. In Durham, where the coal seams run close to the surface in mid-county and deepen toward the coast, you can follow a seam east to the North Sea and trace the whole, sad history of British mining in the pit villages along your way. The first pit villages were built on farmland. The miners were local men, and had connections to that land. For a hundred years, as mines were exhausted and replaced by deeper mines, nearer to the sea, the villages were also replaced, and each new village had fewer local men and more strangers. Scots came down to mine. Irish came. The Irish were dropped at ports along the coast and started walking and didn't stop until they found a colliery. If the colliery was big, there would soon be two more churches—a Presbyterian chapel for the Scots and a Catholic church for the Irish—and two more workingmen's clubs, to keep the Scots and the English and the Irish from fighting. The pit "community" that Scargill talked so much about saving was appealing mainly to writers like W. H. Auden and D. H. Lawrence, who didn't have to live in one. (Auden wrote madrigals about miners: "O lurcher-loving collier, black as night, Follow your love across the smokeless hill; Your lamp is out and all the cages still.") Certainly the miners never thought of their villages as tender or romantic places until they heard on television how tender and romantic those villages were. It was mainly the greed of the coal companies that fostered community among miners. They needed to survive that greed. They needed to survive in the mines, too. Men who worked together a mile underground—helpless, at risk, depending entirely on one another to stay alive in a cave-in or a fire—had no choice but to learn community. In the end, it was all they had.

Last month, I met the young vicar—call him Reverend Denby—in a pit village south of Durham that was built over seventy years ago and is still producing. The vicar told me that the village is so inbred by now that you can recognize the children by what he called "their slow, special, round-faced look." He said that villagers only marry other villagers. Even their adulteries, he said, are in the village. There is a kind of extended incest to village life—a vicious circle of village marriages and the dulled-out children of those marriages, children incapable of any other life, any other job, any other kind of marriage themselves. Mr. Denby's village is big as pit villages go. There are a few thousand houses, and every one of them except the vicar's, the Catholic priest's, the Methodist preacher's, and the two primary-school teachers' belongs to a miner or a retired miner or a miner who is out of work. About six hundred of the men still work at the colliery (along with a couple of hundred miners from villages whose collieries have closed). Another six hundred have been laid off or have grown up since the mine stopped hiring, and the rest either are too old to mine or are dying of black-lung disease or emphysema. I did not hear any of them talk about "preserving a way of life" for their children and grandchildren. In the village, they say that you can dig a mine and a town will grow around it, like a farm town, and people will work together, live together, drink in the same pubs, and even starve for a year on the same picket line, but none of this means that miners believe in a "right to be underground" or in some sacred quality to their lives that they want their children to inherit. Mr. Denby has been in the village for four years now, and he says the one conclusion he has drawn in those four years is that sending a human being into a coal mine is immoral.

Denby is what the English would call a red-brick cleric. He went to a small northern seminary, not far from another mining town, though he clearly would rather have gone to Oxford or Cambridge, where Anglican priests from good schools and good families get their theology degrees. He is chippy—touchy about class. He does not like miners the way that young Oxbridge priests, enjoying a few years of real life in a pit village before moving on in their careers, like miners. He has worked too hard getting away from real life to enjoy a ministry in a dying village or to regard the people around him as friends, but he is precisely the sort of young clergyman the Church assigns to the collieries. In a colliery village, there is no way for Denby to offend the faithful with his accent or pick up the wrong fork at a party or serve a duchess meat-and-potato pie on a plastic dinner tray. On the other hand, there is not much for him to do in a village like his besides, as people in the Church say, "hatching, matching, and dispatching." Only a hundred families belong to Denby's church, and only six or seven men come regularly to the church at all. During the strike, there was violence in the village. Four men crossed the picket line and were badly beaten for it, and ended up in the hospital. After that, they left for the pit while it was still dark, and took a different road every day (the other miners who broke the strike arrived in armored vans), and often came home at night to find their windows smashed and their doors smeared with paint and their children crying from fights at school and their wives crying from fights at the co-op. One miner asked Mr. Denby for advice during the fifty-one weeks of the strike; his wife was complaining because he was home all day, and underfoot, and she was used to having the house to herself. Denby told him to go fishing.

The Church of England is a state church. It has never been disestablished. Its synod is a legal parliament, a kind of theological branch of the House of Commons and the House of Lords, and its bishops and priests are servants of the state—spiritual servants. They consider all England, and not just Anglican England, their responsibility. (Richard Chartres, the rector of St. Stephen's, in London, refers to the Catholic cardinal Basil Hume, who lives in his neighborhood, as "my parishioner.") Vicars like Mr. Denby take it as a parish duty to visit the picket lines during a miners' strike, and to lend their church kitchens to miners' wives, who use them for hot lunches for unmarried picketers and for soup-kitchen dinners. When a pit village dies, the Anglican church is the last to close. Occasionally, it survives the village. A historian I know at the University of Durham bought a house in an old pit village whose mine had shut down in 1967, when two hundred coal-mining families were living there. There are a hundred families now, but most of them are people like my friend from the university, who moved in when the Coal Board started razing, and "gentrified" whatever houses they could save. Three miners are left. They travel to coal mines near the coast to work. Their school, their store, their union club and offices, and their Methodist chapel closed years ago, but the Anglican church stayed open—with no parishioners. Now the professors go.

The Bishop of Durham had Methodist preachers for grandfathers, and that may help to explain what his colleagues refer to as "David's enthusiasm." He made no secret of the fact that he found Mrs. Thatcher's strike policy inhuman and Mr. Scargill, whose vision of England resembled Eastern Europe with a few free labor unions, "not unredeemable." There are 239 Church of England parishes in the county of Durham, and 330 Anglican clergy, and a lot of them felt, like Mr. Denby, that if their bishop-designate had spent his time in a colliery village instead of a Theology Department he would have thought twice about redeeming Arthur Scargill—for God or for anything else. Dr. Jenkins was consecrated as Bishop of Durham on July 6, 1984, in York Minster. His archbishop and predecessor, John Habgood, officiated, and a friend from the University of Bristol by the name of Dennis Nineham gave the sermon, taking for his text this passage from Joshua: "Ye have not passed this way heretofore." Professor Nineham was more acute, perhaps, than he suspected. There were a lot of places the new bishop was passing for the first time—the collieries of northeast England, for one, and the BBC, for another, where he had answered questions about miracles by saying that there was more to the Resurrection than "a conjuring trick with bones." Professor Nineham said at the consecration that the trouble with most bishops is that they are, "generally speaking, generally speaking"—something that Bishop Jenkins likes to repeat, because he is one bishop with very specific things to say. Nineham spoke for the theologians, who were mainly pleased by the appointment. The evangelicals in the Church were not at all pleased. They did not care for Bishop Jenkins's inventive readings of *their* realities—believing, as they did, that the appropriate exercise of Christian imagination took place not on radio shows and television panels but in charismatic visits from the Holy Spirit. The Anglo-Catholics were more sophisticated but not much happier. Anglo-Catholics think of their Church as a repository of ritual and doctrine, a kind of British Museum of the faith, surviving, as one of their chaplains put it, "through confidence, continuity, and censers." They enjoy the mysteries and the miracles of Catholic Christianity. They think that liberal bishops like Dr. Jenkins dilute those mysteries or muddy them up with explanations and explications and disclaimers. They blame the liberals in the Church for defections to tantric orgy cults and Hindu gurus and, lately, the Russian Orthodox Church. (The Metropolitan of Britain is an émigré doctor called Anthony Bloom, who has been drawing crowds for years with his riveting Easter vigils.) Anglo-Catholics tend to prefer the Orthodox Church to their own in, say, its American Episcopal version. They do not like the idea of women priests or

Apache Masses. The fact that the Episcopal Cathedral of New York can put on a proper High Church Easter Eucharist and at the same time invite a feminist sculptor—her name was Edwina Sandys, and she happened to be Winston Churchill's granddaughter—to exhibit a crucifix with a female Christ in the ambulatory confuses them. Some of them think that David Jenkins belongs in a country like America, where nobody seems to mind if bishops undermine their own authority by talking all the time about politics and economics. They like to quote Stanley Baldwin, who was Prime Minister during the strikes in 1926: he asked a group of meddlesome churchmen how they would like it if he asked the Iron and Steel Federation to take over the revisions of the Athanasian Creed.

Dr. Jenkins's consecration service was on a Friday. There were summer storms that weekend, and a little after two on Monday morning lightning struck York Minster. By two-thirty, the roof of the south transept was on fire, its big rose window lit like an unearthly diadem; by dawn, when the first firemen could enter, its thirteenth-century beams and vaults were cinders on the stone floor. It was said by people who did not like David Jenkins that the fire was an act of God. The newspapers put it this way: If God set fire to the largest Gothic cathedral in England, did He do it because He disapproved of Bishop Jenkins or because He thought the World Council of Churches was getting too left-wing or because He wanted to put a stop to people naming rock groups after the Holy Family? The principal of Westcott House, which is an Anglican seminary at Cambridge, apparently believed that God struck York Minster. The evangelical vicar of Jesmond, which is a Newcastle parish, believed it. Letters about Dr. Jenkins and the fire started arriving at the archbishop's palace, in Bishop Thorpe, south of York, and kept on arriving until (according to the archbishop's secretary) they made a pile over a foot high. Most of the letters came from evangelicals in the Church. Dr. Habgood, who is a cool, charitable man, referred to them later as "a small number of intellectually self-confident fundamentalists at the edge of the Church." They talked about "scum" and "Judas"—which was not altogether in the spirit of a national church that had always made a proud point of eclecticism and tolerance. Once they had exhausted the archbishop's patience, they started on the newspapers. The vicar of Jesmond—his name is David Holloway—wrote to *The Times* of London so often that the paper seemed to be giving him a columnist's space and credits. Holloway liked to point out in his letters that even William Temple, who, after all, was a Christian socialist, had "publicly stated his belief in the Virgin Birth and the empty tomb." Temple, as it happened, had led the meddlesome bishops in their "clerical initiative" during the 1926 strikes. He was Bishop of Manchester then; by the time he moved to Lambeth Palace as the Archbishop of Canterbury, he had begun to wonder about his "tendency to try to make capital for the church" out of crises that might be better served with less publicity and more discreet, if not "entirely private," pressure. Archbishops of Canterbury are supposed to be discreet—though not necessarily as discreet as Temple's successor at Canterbury, a public-school headmaster named Geoffrey Fisher, who in the 1950s told the English to stop worrying so much about hydrogen bombs. "At its very worst," the archbishop said, "all a hydrogen bomb can do is to sweep a vast number of persons at one moment from this world into the other, and more vital, world—into which anyhow they must all pass at some time."

Robert Runcie is the Archbishop of Canterbury now. He used to be known as Killer Runcie, but that was during the war, when he was a tank commander in Normandy. Today, he is known as a cautious, conciliatory sort of man, who tries to keep his colleagues from rushing into things like the ordination of women or clerical divorces and upsetting the Catholics and the Orthodox primates, whom the Church is courting. Dr. Runcie has worked for years with commissions on Christian unity. Mostly, the commissions involve people from the Vatican —whenever they agree on something, they draft a report to say that Christian unity is at hand—but Dr. Runcie's particular project has been unity with the Orthodox Church, and he is sensitive about his bishops' making "untimely" pronouncements about female priests and female Christs and in-vitro babies when delegates from the Patriarch of Moscow are in town. (The Orthodox Church is not so accommodating. Orthodox holy places like the monasteries of Mount Athos do not let Anglicans in for services but make them sit outside on the porch.) The Orthodox have been Dr. Runcie's portfolio, so to speak, since he was the Bishop of St. Albans, in the 1970s. If Catholics interest him less, it may have something to do with the conviction of Englishmen like him that, having been Catholics themselves for a thousand years, theirs is the true Catholic Church, free from Rome. The latest round of meetings with the Vatican ended a couple of months ago, after ten years of discussion. A commission issued a report about Christian unity being "closer," and said that there was now "sufficient convergence on the nature of authority in the church" to make another round of meetings possible.

Authority, of course, is what divides Anglicans and Catholics. Anglicans accept administrative authority, and even some liturgical authority, but the moral and theological hierarchies of the Roman Catholic Church are anathema to them. (Clifford Longley, a Catholic who writes about religion for *The Times*, says that "deep in the soul of the modern secular Englishman lies an ardent Protestant and religious nationalist, for whom the national church is not so much a place to worship in as a buttress against something threatening and sinister, whose shadow is bedded in the subconscious and which used to be called Popery.") When David Jenkins talked too much for Dr. Runcie's comfort, Runcie would say something about rash bishops who in their zeal forget to ask themselves, "How will this conduct look to my colleagues, my flock, my parishioners, perhaps less instructed or sophisticated than I am and yet still, as St. Paul says, brothers and sisters for whom Christ died?" He would never have claimed any sort of doctrinal authority over Jenkins, the way John Paul II claimed *his* authority over the Franciscan friar Leonardo Boff, in Brazil, who wrote a book about liberation theology and the longings for "freedom of divergent thought within the Church." There is no Sacred Congregation for the Doctrine of the Faith in the Anglican Church to tell a dissenting priest— as the Congregation in Rome told Friar Boff—that criticisms of the hierarchy mean "destruction of the authentic sense of the sacraments and of the word of faith." A country where there are vicars who take polls about the Resurrection (and congregations that answer them) is not a Catholic country. David Jenkins's Anglo-Catholic colleagues were distressed less by his views, in the end, than by the fact that he was asking "simple people" to consider symbolic distinctions that were beyond them. They thought that simple people needed certainty. (At the General Synod last November, one Anglo-Catholic theologian told Michael Davie, from *The Observer*, that the Orthodox Church was appealing to disaffected Anglicans because it was "unchanged, exclusive, and above all *certain*," and added that he was sure that if Cardinal Newman were alive today he would be an Orthodox primate.)

In September, two months after the fire at York Minster, David Jenkins was enthroned, and spoke for the first time in Durham's cathedral. He said later that any bishop preaching at an enthronement last September had to say something about the coal miners—and that is what Dr. Jenkins did. He described himself as "an ambiguous, compromised, and questioning person entering upon an ambiguous office in an uncertain church in the midst of a threatened and threatening world." He said that dogmatism of any kind was "outrageously self-righteous, deeply inhuman, and damnably dangerous," and that the present government was certainly dogmatic—dogmatic in its indifference to poverty, its indifference to the coal miners, its indifference to "community." Inasmuch as the strike was in its seventh month, he said, the "imported elderly American" by the name of Ian MacGregor who ran Mrs. Thatcher's Coal Board might think of stepping down in favor of a more conciliatory "local product." MacGregor was not noticeably moved by the bishop—who did not have anything good to say about Scargill, either—except to object to the word "elderly," and to remark that he was not actually born in America, although he had lived there for forty years before Mrs. Thatcher hired him. He was a Scot, and thrifty, and that is the reason the Prime Minister liked him. She paid him a splendid salary to "rationalize British industry" for her. MacGregor was head of British Steel until 1983, and shut down enough steel mills to put more than half the steelworkers in the country on the dole. Then he shut down twenty coal mines that were either unsafe or unproductive or were costing the Coal Board more than their yield to maintain. He had plans to shut down twenty more when the miners struck. There are 186,000 members of the National Union of Mineworkers (which is really a federation of local miners' unions). Scargill called them out without a vote. He wanted all the coal mines in Britain open, whatever the economic cost, and Mrs. Thatcher seemed to want all but the big, new, automated coal mines (like the mines at Selby and the Vale of Belvoir, in Yorkshire) closed, whatever the social cost, and the argument was really between the two of them. The miners themselves were almost incidental. So, for that matter, was MacGregor.

The Church of England officially entered the argument about the miners' strike after David Jenkins's enthronement. The Archbishop of Canterbury talked to *The Times* a few days before the Tory Party conference, on October 9, and in his interview he warned Mrs. Thatcher that the violence of the strike and the miners' despair and her own policies were changing British politics "from consensus to confrontation." He talked about the more than three million people who were unemployed and were waiting for the "jam" the Prime Minister had promised them with their breakfasts tomorrow. He talked about the awful rhetoric on both sides: "The cheap imputation of the worst possible motives; treating people as scum in speech; all this pumping vituperation into the atmosphere has a deep effect on the possibilities of physical violence." He said that if the human consequences of Mrs. Thatcher's economic objectives were poverty and despair, then those objectives had to be called into question. At times, he sounded like Dr. Jenkins talking. It was a matter of style for the Church of England, a Conservatives' argument. (Neil Kinnock, the Labour Party leader, didn't join a picket line until three months after Dr. Runcie gave his interview.) Mrs. Thatcher was not humane in the way that Tories were supposed to be humane. She was not, as they say in England, "wet." She had contempt for the miners because she had contempt for their argument, for their obstinate illogic. Being a grocer's daughter, she liked to say, she had never had the time or the money to cultivate the sort of sympathies that old Conservatives cultivate in the protection of their clubs and their public schools. She was like the "new Tories" who had voted for her. She was part of the self-made bourgeoisie that lived in southern suburbs and "carried no luggage" (as people here put it) from the past into their new ranch houses and their new offices, no sentiment, no paternalism—no hypocrisy, either. She had no use for the sort of discussion going on in the Anglican Church about whether Keynes or Milton Friedman was the better "Christian." She did not really understand that the old Conservative leaders would have given something—would have offered to keep a few more pits open, or invited the miners to Downing Street for beer and sandwiches and a chat about being British together.

In a way, Mrs. Thatcher was a proper match for Scargill, so full of class rhetoric and class bitterness himself. Scargill claimed to be a Marxist. He may not have read Marx, but he had gauged exactly how class-riven England was. He knew that beer and sandwiches at Downing Street were only Marx's old opiate of the people in some peculiarly British version, and he would have refused them. He is not a democrat. (That may be the real reason he called the coal miners' strike without a membership vote.) He organized his futile strike at the end of an uncommonly mild winter, when no one in England was worrying about heat and there were stockpiles of coal all over the country. The strikes that bring down governments are strikes like the ones seven years ago, when half the workers in the country were out, and there was no fuel of any kind, and hospitals closed and trains stopped and people died from cold and illness, and even hunger. No one joined the miners this time. Mrs. Thatcher must have talked to the Russians, because the Russians saw to it that Poland sold her whatever coal she did need and that East German ships delivered it. When the dockworkers in Hull refused to unload the ships or even let them into port, the ships (about 80 percent of them, the Archbishop of York says) were simply sent upriver to unload their coal at unregistered ports, where there was no dockers' union to stop them. What was clear, by March of 1984, was that Bevan's famous description of England as "an island of coal surrounded by fish" did not apply any longer. England was surrounded by oil, and its problem was not how to heat itself or generate electric power but how to compute its social costs—including in its computations the fact that doing so was against the philosophy of its government. There was a debate on Mrs. Thatcher's economic philosophy at the General Synod of the Church last November. The Tory Party chairman, John Gummer, is a lay member of the synod, but he was so furious that he refused to go to the debate, and went off to Cambridge instead and gave a sermon in Great St. Mary's Church, saying later that if the bishops could talk about politics in their synods politicians had every right to talk about God in pulpits. Gummer is a keen churchman of rigorously simple views, and he talks a lot about God and country anyway. Mrs. Thatcher likes him because he is not apt to get in trouble and disgrace her, like her last party chairman, Cecil Parkinson, who had to resign because his secretary was going to have his baby. Gummer is not noticeably passionate about secretaries. He is passionate about things like the Falklands war (he has never forgiven the Archbishop of Canterbury for saying a prayer for both the British and the Argentine dead at a thanksgiving service when the war was over), and his idea of moral uplift is Norman Tebbit, the Industries Secretary, telling the unemployed to get on their bikes, the way his father did in 1926, and look for jobs. One miner took Mr. Tebbit's advice. He bought bicycles for his family, and they all rode south to a village near Windsor and camped on the village green while the miner looked for work. They were still on the green at Christmas.

There are three "houses" in the synod of the Church of England —a House of Bishops, a House of Clergy, and a House of Laity —and Gummer is right when he complains that the bishops are much more radical as a group than either the synod priests or the parishioners. The bishops, in their way, are upsetting the traditional balance of church-state power—which is that the Crown appoints and the Church consecrates, and in its more recent version has been that the Prime Minister appoints and the appointed bishops bless the Prime Minister's politics. Without their blessing, the sacrifice of people to policy loses a kind of cover, and that is what is happening in England now. When the bishops here say that the Tory Party is involved in economic idolatry, they are also reminding the party that idolatry of any kind is a challenge to Christian doctrine. They are separating the Church from the resentments about class and privilege that can mark an ordinary churchman like Mr. Denby and his parishioners. The Church of England is really a pre–Mrs. Thatcher institution. The questions that it asks today were the accurate banalities of the days when conciliation and compromise were part of the rhetoric of every government, Labour *or* Tory. Today, neither the left nor the right talks about conciliation. Both of them have abandoned compromise. They may not care much when David Jenkins talks about bones, but when he talks about coal miners both sides think, Rid me of this turbulent priest, and people like Gummer apparently even say it. Homilies about class and compassion can sound like declarations of war when they are addressed to a strike leader who admires Lenin and solicits money from Qaddafi or to a Prime Minister who has reasons for assuming that England will never recover from the scams of socialism and the pieties of conservatism without a harsh adjustment to the marketplace and to its own capacities, whatever those capacities are. The Church is a service of the British welfare state; its authority as an institution comes from the state, and the state has a proprietary interest in it. The Church, of course, has a proprietary interest in itself. It is as rich as the Queen, with property all over the country and two billion dollars' worth of stocks and bonds and no taxes to pay on any of its income. It has a lot to lose.

Ever since Henry VIII got divorced, it has been the legal duty of the Crown to appoint the archbishops, the bishops, and 6 percent of the parish priests of the Church of England. George I, whose English was terrible and who needed help remembering what the Church of England was, let Robert Walpole pick his bishops for him, and after that it was really the Prime Minister who chose. (Gladstone and Disraeli took what the secretary-general of the Church, Derek Pattinson, calls a "particularly keen interest" in appointing bishops.) It was clear that a conservative Prime Minister would appoint conservative bishops and a liberal Prime Minister liberal bishops, and there was not much that even the Archbishop of Canterbury could do about it. The system changed finally in 1977. Donald Coggan was Archbishop of Canterbury then, and James Callaghan was Prime Minister, and the two of them arrived at a kind of unwritten concordat about Church appointments. Now a Church commission—the two archbishops, three clergymen from the House of Clergy, three laymen from the House of Laity, and four parishioners from the vacant diocese—picks two candidates for the job and presents them to the Prime Minister, and then the Prime Minister decides. Mrs. Thatcher herself has an "appointment secretary," a man named Robin Catford. Catford is supposed to advise her properly on prospective bishops, and it is a mark of Mrs. Thatcher's single-mindedness that she seems to have overlooked her own interests in the Church and appointed someone like David Jenkins to begin with. Her friends say now that if there is ever another list with a Dr. Jenkins on it they will see to it that Mrs. Thatcher sends it back. The fact is that bishops are news and synods are news, and reporters cover them and the BBC televises them as if they were one of Mrs. Thatcher's speeches.

There is a Board for Social Responsibility in the Anglican Church. It has been involved in politics since it opened its offices at Church House, in the Dean's Yard of Westminster Abbey, twenty-seven years ago. It has a social mandate—what Dr. Jenkins calls a Victorian mandate. Its job is to decide on the "goals for a proper society," to study those goals, and then to advise the synod what to do with them. There are biologists on the board, who think about Christian ethics and in-vitro babies and genetic engineering. There are professors of international relations and chaplains general to the armed forces, who think about the military and nuclear bombs. There are economists and bankers, who think about monetary policy and what the economic alternatives are in the parts of Britain where all the factories have closed over the past five years. They think about social desolation, about the millions of people with "strong arms and not much else," and about how to acknowledge the problem of "not much else" and maybe begin to solve it without falling into old class clichés. There are 150 industrial chaplains, who operate out of offices and mines and factories instead of parish churches and are the field workers, so to speak, of the Board for Social Responsibility. Universities in the northeast have courses in "industrial theology," which are supposed to give those chaplains what Geoffrey Sturman, at the Theology Department of the University of Hull, calls "theological understanding of industrial society." The chaplains' movement started in England with the Second World War; the Bishop of Sheffield sent a chaplain to an ordnance factory, and after the war the chaplain stayed in Sheffield, in a steel mill, and other chaplains joined him. In the 1960s, it was fashionable for young priests to be industrial chaplains; it went with social protest and anti-war protest and protest in the universities. Being a chaplain in a factory is not so fashionable now. In the sixties, the old parochial base of the Church was changing, too. People moved with their jobs, and a factory or a colliery was sometimes as much of a community to them as the strange new town where they had settled down. Today, a lot of working people in the Church say that they would rather have vaulted ceilings and stained glass and Sunday services than a chaplain negotiating overtime for them in a colliery yard. There was not much that the industrial chaplains could do for the miners when they struck, anyway. It made no difference to the miners that the Coal Board's offers of relocation and resettlement were fairly reasonable offers. Whatever the chaplains advised them, the miners' terror of leaving home was precisely what set them apart from other British workers and made their strike hopeless.

In February, the Church of England had its first General Synod of the year. There was a lot for the synod to talk over. The Church is losing priests. Seminaries have half the students they did ten years ago. There are still eleven thousand Anglican priests, but even so there has been no real recruitment into the ministry from the working class —except, not surprisingly, in Durham, where the university holds weekend ordination courses. The Church is losing members, too —some of them to the "house churches" that opened in the early seventies for evangelicals of all denominations and have managed to recruit 180,000 members to what is called the British Renewal. ("They like 'intimacy' and 'confession,'" an Anglo-Catholic from Lambeth Palace said, "which means, of course, that we have failed to civilize them on their way up in the world.") There were questions of faith and science to discuss, because theologians in the Church are arguing a lot about quarks and black holes, and about whether the spiral of quantum mechanics leads to God, and whether the thousand unfertilized eggs that hatched over the past twelve years at the agricultural school at Pennsylvania State University were just another case of barnyard parthenogenesis or had something to do with the mystery of the Virgin Birth. But there was also the Bishop of Durham, and he turned out to be the real subject of the synod.

There was a debate about the Bishop on February 13, the second day. The debate was not referred to that way; nor was Dr. Jenkins on some sort of ecclesiastical trial. The debate was called "The Nature of Christian Belief," but as the Bishop of Winchester, the chairman of the Doctrine Commission of the synod, put it, "The occasion . . . is, of course, the controversy and anxiety that were exacerbated during the summer and autumn of last year by a fortuitous succession of personal interviews, panel discussions and prepared programmes on this general theme presented or reported through the media." The Doctrine Commission submitted a lot of documents to the five hundred or so Anglicans who met in Church House that day—among them a lawyer's report on canonical interpretations of doctrine and clerical adherence to doctrine; and the texts of a gravamen and reformandum circulated by forty-five fundamentalist priests from the Vicar of Jesmond's "evangelical fellowship," who wanted all bishops to declare "I believe in the fact of the Virgin Birth of Jesus Christ and his Resurrection on the third day from the tomb as is clearly taught in the Holy Scriptures" before administering sacraments or confirming children. The fundamentalists also wanted the House of Bishops to "take all such further action as shall seem to them . . . pastorally requisite and remedial to the restoration of confidence, the renewal of strength and the setting forth and maintenance of 'quietness, love and peace' throughout the Church of England." In other words, they wanted David Jenkins to say that Mary was a virgin and that Christ had risen bodily from His tomb three days after the Crucifixion, or lose his job. The debate lasted all morning, and could have lasted all week, because, whatever the fundamentalists had to say about truth, there are four Gospels, and it is hard to maintain that any one of them is "more biblical" than another. John and Mark (as a young Cambridge theologian named Peter Eaton pointed out when the debate was over) never used the word "virgin" to describe Mary, and none of the disciples actually described the Resurrection. Arguments about biblical truth (the Bishop of Durham says there has been a "faith row" in the Anglican Church every twenty years since 1860) are mainly reminders that the fundamental beliefs of the Church of England —that "the Word became Flesh" and that "Jesus rose again on the third day"—are also the fundamental mysteries.

There was a lot of collegial sympathy for Dr. Jenkins. The Archbishop of York got up and made a speech saying that the Virgin Birth was only one weak part of the "empirical anchorage" of the Church, and that the empty tomb was probably "lower down in the hierarchy of the Resurrection" than Christ's appearances to his disciples. Jenkins's archdeacon in Durham, Michael Perry, said that *his* Church was "an ark full of sometimes very peculiar birds and beasts," an ark with plenty of elbowroom inside—and that, in any event, Christianity did not depend on gynecological details. Then Canon Leslie Houlden, from the University of London, said that *he* was worried about bishops' having to pander to "people's fearful wish that everyone should respond to God in the same way as themselves." He talked about belief as "a matter of engagement with truth, which is never fully apprehended," and about "the interaction of our personal story with the Christian story," and about the tradition of Anglicans like Frederick Denison Maurice and William Temple and Arthur Michael Ramsey and Roman Catholics like Karl Rahner and Edward Schillebeeckx

—not men whom the fundamentalists in the group were apt to have spent much time reading. The Bishop of Winchester wanted a calm day —"I hope that what will emerge quite clearly from this debate is that . . . we have kept that excellent middle way, which is the special heritage of the Church of England," he said at one point—and the Archbishop of Canterbury talked about bishops being the trustees of tradition and having "a certain conservative responsibility," but the debate was often ugly. The Vicar of St. Albans accused Dr. Jenkins of saying the Creed with his fingers crossed behind his back, and the Vicar of Jesmond, who had started it all, compared Jenkins to a cancer in the Church that had to be dealt with now, before it grew and killed everything. When the evangelicals talked about tradition, it was usually the tradition of Billy Graham and the Renewal. They had a list of what "God is doing worldwide," and circulated it. According to the list, Africa was up from 5 percent Christian to 30 percent in the first three-quarters of the century; Korea was up from 11 percent Christian to 22 percent in only fifteen years; more people went to the evangelical church in Seoul on Sunday mornings than to the Wembley Cup final. The evangelicals said that the "U.K. was certainly missing out" on what God was doing worldwide, and that they were ready to leave the Church and get busy for God in the United Kingdom if it came to that. They had plans to open "worship centers" in places like Durham all over northeast England, where "historic Christian principles have not penetrated." They wanted to talk about evil in northeast England, but they did not want to talk about the miners who were still striking in that unregenerate part of the country. They did not want another debate on economics or on the responsibility of the Church of England in times when the social contract was cancelled. If, as some of their colleagues suspected, they were not really Anglicans at all but suburbanized Methodists, using the respectable Church of England to show the world they had made it into the middle class (though not into that excellent, Anglican middle way), then somewhere on their travels to respectability they seemed to have forgotten the English poor who used to be their special charge and their honest passion. The Church, with its own snobberies, had neglected to educate them so that they could carry that passion into the suburbs with them, changed into something agreeable like social responsibility or social commitment, or even simple compassion. Talking about Christ's bones, they sounded a little like Mrs. Thatcher talking about the pound as if the pound were, *prima facie*, the meaning of British life and had nothing to do with the quality of that life, nothing to do with coal miners out of work—nothing to do with belief or identity.

In the end, the matter of Christian belief and Dr. Jenkins was referred to the House of Bishops for reflection, and the bishops promised to spend the spring reflecting. As for Dr. Jenkins, he turned to the matter of Durham. He went on London Weekend Television to say that unless the government kept faith (by way of benefits) with all the people in northern England who were unemployed, it would divide the country into the "we who bear the costs" and the "we who inflict the costs," and that the risk was violence. Once, when Dr. Jenkins himself was reflecting on Christian faith, he said that people who believed in God had to understand something about symbols, because God was so much more than His descriptions and could never be "pinned down" to the literal. He might have said that people who believed in England had to understand something about symbols, too. Money is a symbol. So is a strike that lasts a year.

April 1985

ELECTION
IN CASTELLINA

There were elections in Italy last month, and a lot of Italians working abroad went home to vote. The two plumbers on my street in Paris took the train to their village in Puglia. The tiny *dottore* who gives Italian lessons in the neighborhood went home to Chieti. Gae Aulenti, the architect who is turning the Gare d'Orsay, with its crystal-palace light, into a national museum of nineteenth-century art, went to Milan with her crew of draftsmen and designers, and so did the waiters from the Italian restaurant around the corner. Not voting is illegal in Italy. No one really knows what happens to people who forget to vote or refuse to vote or cannot get off from work to make a long trip home; the suspicion is that their absence at the polls is noted somewhere in their town records, like a bad mark in citizenship. There are more than two million Italians working in Europe outside of Italy and millions of others who commute from villages in the Mezzogiorno to work in northern factories, and all of them have to go home if they want to vote. Occasionally, someone gets up in the parliament in Montecitorio and says that absentee ballots might be a good thing for Italy, but that is as far as it ever goes. Most Italians are surprised to discover that people from other countries vote by mail when they have to. Italians prefer to *go* home. To accommodate them, the government prints some money and uses it to pay the fare (or part of it) of anyone who wants to personally drop his ballot into a wooden ballot box in the classroom where in all likelihood he learned to read and write.

I watched the elections in a little Tuscan town called Castellina-in-Chianti. There is not much unemployment in Tuscany. Not many Castellinans had to come home from factories in, say, Södertälje or

Hamburg, but, even so, the biggest posters in town were not the campaign posters or the party lists—they were the government's travel-reimbursement charts. Voting in Italy begins on Sunday and runs through Monday morning, so that people at home can take a half day off from work and feel that they have got the better of the government, whoever wins. And the government will pay for a round-trip second-class train ticket or boat ticket for anybody working abroad (or for 63 percent of a ticket for anybody working in Italy but away from home), provided that the trip begins before Monday and ends after Sunday —provided, in other words, that whoever makes the trip is actually around for the elections, and does not simply take his ticket and cash it in or use it for a summer vacation or a February ski holiday. Fifteen Castellinans were expected home from abroad to vote, and only one of them came, but there was still a lot of traffic through the town. The stationmaster reported that all the Neapolitans who worked at Big Blu, the local swimming-pool-and-stadium company, had caught the Friday *rapido*, and one of the mayor's two sons—a young man named Marco, who runs a combination shoe-and-antique store outside Lugano —said that traffic was backed up all the way into Switzerland because of Italian *Gastarbeiter* heading south. There is always a discussion in Castellina on election days about why Italian workers will get in a car or a train and travel for days to vote for a new town or provincial council, but the one thing everybody agrees on is that politics has very little to do with it. The men say that elections are an excuse—an excuse to see your friends and show off your new clothes and your new car and maybe have a holiday. The women say the men come home for their mothers' spaghetti.

Castellina has had a Communist town council—and thus a Communist mayor—for forty years, and no one, including the Christian Democratic candidates, thought the Castellinans were about to change. Whatever interest there was in the voting this year had to do with the fact that Italy's ruling coalition of Socialists, Christian Democrats, Republicans, Liberals, and Social Democrats—its forty-fourth government since the war—had lasted nearly two years, and the stability, such as it was, was making people nervous. In Castellina, they talked earnestly about the *instability* of the arrangement. They said that having a government in power for twenty-two months with no terrible crises and no votes of confidence meant that Italy was behaving peculiarly, and that it was time for citizens to get involved.

Castellina is one of four communes in the Chianti Mountains. About seven hundred people live in the village itself, and eighteen hundred more live in the country and in *frazioni*—hamlets—around the village and hardly ever see one another except on voting days. The mayor, Marcello Cappelletti, who owns a shoe store in the village, says that there is not much of a collective spirit in Castellina. Communists there would never think of putting their land together or of pooling their produce and making cooperatives, the way they do in places like Emilia-Romagna, where the Party's big Po Valley farms are. There were five thousand people in Castellina before the war, and as soon as it ended half of them simply agreed that there was no future for them at home—and got on the train and went to work in mines in Switzerland or Belgium and were rarely heard from anymore. The peasants who stayed were *mezzadri*—sharecroppers for one of the Chianti vineyards or attached to a rich farmer who owned their houses and barns and paid for half their grain and livestock in return for half of whatever they produced. By the time sharecropping was abolished, in 1964, a lot of those peasants had left, too. They went to the town of Poggibonsi, close to home, where there were furniture factories, and waited for Italy's postwar economic miracle to start so that Italians could put their money into bedroom sets and veneer sideboards and dining-room tables.

In time, most of the Castellinans who were not in Poggibonsi making furniture were farming on their own, or were on salary at one of the twenty family vineyards that were still producing, or were working for the Niccolai brothers' fodder mills and granaries. The Niccolai brothers, Franco and Giovanni, were Castellina's own economic miracle. Their father was a carpenter who married a tailor's daughter, opened a store, and started selling bread and, in a few years, flour, and eventually decided to make his own flour. There are so many Niccolai silos in Castellina now that the last few have actually edged into the main street, and you have to circle round them to get to church or to the village square.

Castellina was a beautiful village before the brothers made it prosperous with their salmon-colored silos, thrown up like fortifications of the town wall. The wall itself was begun by Lombards more than a thousand years ago, and the town hall was originally a wall tower. When the Guelfs took Castellina for Florence, they turned the tower into a fortress and used it to fight the Sienese. Villagers with houses from Castellina's fortress days—houses built into the wall—can literally seal themselves off in wartime. In 1944, when the Germans were retreating through Tuscany and taking every Italian male they could find for labor camps in Germany, Castellinans hid in attics and in tunnels along the wall, and the Germans never found them. The man who was mayor of Castellina then hid some of them. His name is Giovanni Falassi, and he still lives in Castellina, in one of those ancient houses—an old don with a white mustache who seems to have a piece of every deal in town. He was not, the Castellinans say, "one of the big bad Fascists," like the Fascists nine miles away in Montemaggio, who rounded up nineteen local partisans toward the end of the war and killed them. Castellina was one of the first towns in Italy with a Fascist Party. The party arrived in 1921, when the town was run by Socialists, and over the years people must have got used to it, because in 1944, when the big bad Fascists in Tuscany were shot, the mayor simply walked out of his office and turned his attention to gas-station concessions and real estate and vineyards. His wife took over the church choir. The Falassis, in turn, have had to get used to the Communists, the way people in Bologna did. Communists do not distress them anymore. They are more distressed by having a Polish Pope in the Vatican. It does not matter to the old mayor that the Pope shares many of his own views. Signor Falassi complains about the Pope because, to his mind, the Pope considers Italy "just another country, and not Peter's seat," and consequently does not pay enough attention to it. He says that an Italian Pope would never have made the concordat that John Paul II made this year with Bettino Craxi, the Socialist Prime Minister. It was the first new treaty between Italy and the Holy See since Mussolini's concordat with Pope Pius XI in 1929, and it disestablished the Catholic Church in Italy by taking away state salaries from the clergy. (Signor Falassi prefers to say that it condemned the priests to "living on the charity of their congregations"—which is, of course, the way they live in other countries.) Catholics like the old mayor do not have much confidence in the piety of countrymen who in the course of a few years have voted to legalize abortion and divorce and, according to the new concordat, will now be able to keep their children out of the religion classes that used to be obligatory in the public schools. They say that Italy needs an Italian Pope to get its people back in line, but when Signor Falassi looked at the list of cardinals John Paul II had just appointed and saw that only five out of twenty-eight were Italian (and one of the five an old sociologist-priest with no vote in papal conclaves) he shook his head and made some calculations and figured that it would be two hundred years before there was another Italian in the Vatican.

Mauro Neri, who ran for mayor last month on the Christian Democratic list, has a dry-goods store on Castellina's main street, not far from Marcello Cappelletti's shoe store. It is piled with socks and slacks and underwear and with the kind of flowered housecoats that

Italian peasant women wear, and Signora Neri works above the shop, making shirts for important customers, like Falassi. Neri himself is an important man in the province. He is on the Christian Democrats' provincial council, and has favors, and even jobs, for friends at his disposal. Inasmuch as he can call the elections in Castellina and rarely be off by more than ten votes, it is clear to everyone that Signor Neri knows exactly who those friends are. There are four priests in the commune, and he thinks it would have been appropriate for at least one of them to use the last Sunday sermon before the elections to tell whoever was in church—not many Castellinans were—to vote Christian Democratic. The fact that the priests (as far as he knows) did not has confirmed his suspicion that priests these days are merely "the official performers of divine services," and not much use for politics. Neri himself came to politics from a group called Catholic Action. He is a fervent Catholic, but he says that if the Church wants support from Catholic politicians for *its* causes—the Christian Democratic Party campaigned obediently against abortion and divorce, and lost voters because of it—then the Church has to support those politicians from its pulpits and offer more than an occasional papal speech about governments of "Christian inspiration." The Christian Democratic Party always had its churches, the way the Communists had their cells, and he does not know what to make of a Pope who never consults the party bosses and treats Italian politics like a spaghetti Western instead of like the sophisticated protection racket it is.

Marcello Cappelletti, being a Communist, has much less trouble with the Church than the Catholics in Castellina do. The mayor likes to remind people that most Italian Communists go to church—or, at least, the wives and mothers of most Italian Communists go to church—and that even Enrico Berlinguer, who died last year after twelve years as Party Secretary, was a nobleman with a Catholic wife. He says that, anyway, it is always easier to get along with the Church if you are a Communist, because then the Church expects nothing from you. The mayor does not have much to do with the village priest, who, according to a lot of people in Castellina, performs his divine services as fast as possible and then hides out for fear that someone might see him and ask him to do something useful, but he is an old friend of the parish priest in one of the valley *frazioni*. He and Signora Cappelletti take two or three weeks every summer and join the priest—his name is Don Dino—on trips he organizes to exotic places like the Rhine valley and Barcelona.

The mayor was born in Castellina. He was sixteen when the Germans came through town on their retreat, and inasmuch as no one hid him he was captured and put on a truck for Germany, and he figures he would have died in Germany if he hadn't shut his eyes and jumped off at a bend in the road, somewhere near Bologna. He managed to get to Florence for the liberation. He joined the Communist Party when he got home. He is in his fifties now, a cheerful paterfamilias in a new white villa with a view out over the farms and vineyards of the valley, not far from the Niccolai house. It is a sunny place, full of country pottery and books and low, pale couches—not at all like the old, dark houses, with their massive furniture and velvet chairs, where the important Christian Democrats in Castellina live. The mayor built his villa a couple of years ago, and planted roses, and he spends his free time looking after them or playing with his granddaughter. It is hard to see him there, dressed in a pair of gray flannels and a V-necked pullover, and then to imagine him sitting at a cobbler's bench mending shoes, which is what he used to do. The Cappelletti shoemaker's shop has been a "shoe boutique" for twenty years now, but Marcello kept on fixing soles and carving heels for people in Castellina until 1981, when the town council elected him mayor for the first time. The shoes and belts and pocketbooks that his wife picks out and sells at Cappelletti's now are chic by village standards, and the old mayor likes to say that the Communists in Castellina must be a little uneasy with this new mayor of theirs, who can build himself a fine villa and a fine shop, and even set up a son in business near Lugano. In fact, it is only the old mayor who is uneasy. He prefers Communists who stay in character, like the *contadino* called Gino Tattini, who became the boss of Castellina after the war and was mayor for twenty-seven years and always prefaced the advice he gave in the town council by saying, "Excuse me, I'm only a dumb peasant, but . . ." This gave the local bourgeoisie a chance to answer, "Yes, but what a lot of common sense you have."

The fact is that there is no such thing as a typical Italian Communist. If Berlinguer was a nobleman and the mayor of Castellina is a cobbler, then it is fair to add that the first Communist mayor of Rome was an art historian and that Alessandro Natta, who took over the Party after Berlinguer died, is a butcher's son who worked hard and went to the Scuola Normale in Pisa, which is a kind of Italian version of the École Normale Supérieure in Paris. People say it was because of Natta's being "typical"—by which they mean boring—that the Communists lost ground in May. They lost Turin and Rome, and their margin in

a lot of the towns and provinces they do control is weaker now
—but not because of a record of bad government or corrupt government, or even ideological government. What bothers Italians about the
Party is simply the possibility of its running Italy. No one wants that.
Not even the Communists do. Communists in Italy these days think
more about their *scala mobile*—which is the cost-of-living adjustment
in their salaries—and their next cars and their houses on the Adriatic
than they do about Marx. They are a prosperous working class that just
a few years ago was a peasantry out of the *miseria* of Italian folklore.
The Party, for most of them, has been a sort of *gran padrone*, just as
the Church was once a *gran padrone* for the Christian Democrats. In
a way, they have struck a deal with the country: power in nearly half
of Italy's eight thousand communes in exchange for fairly good government. They offered a respite from corruption during the twenty or
thirty years when they were too new to power to be noticeably corrupt
themselves. If they lost some in the elections now, it was as much as
anything a case of Italy's assuring them (and itself) that they would not
have to ask for a crack at running the country and get everybody else in
the West upset about NATO and the Common Market. It was also a
way of sparing them the attentions of the Russians, not to mention of the
old ideologues in factory cells in Turin and Milan who still hang pictures
of Stalin in their locker rooms and go on charter flights to Moscow to
look at Lenin in his glass sarcophagus while Communist mayors like
Marcello Cappelletti are on vacation in Barcelona with the local priest.

In Castellina, the fact that the old mayor complains about his
maid's long vacations at the beach and the new mayor says that maids
have as much right to long vacations at the beach as everybody else does
not really make an argument. Vacations at the beach are precisely what
no one in Italy wants to sacrifice—neither old Fascists nor middle-aged
Communists nor the parish priests who organize them. Italy has got
used to a way of life it cannot afford: a month of paid vacation a year,
plus a slew of holidays; fourteen months of salary every year if you
work in agriculture, thirteen months if you work in a factory. And
nobody worries about it anymore except the economists, because the
Italians have heard so much about their national genius for making do
that they finally believe in it.

The way to tell the Christian Democrats from the Communists on
Election Sunday in Castellina was this: the Christian Democrats were
dressed up in blazers and ties and sunglasses. You could see them
standing in a group in front of the Circolo Italia, which is a bar the

Niccolai brothers built and is considered the "Catholic" café. The Circolo Italia is the best café in Castellina. There are young Communists who go to the Italia, because the ice cream is better there than at the Communist café, the Circolo Sangallo, and because the place is bigger—good for hanging out—and the soccer scores are always posted. Strangers tend to stop at the Italia. On Election Sunday, ten middle-aged men from a bicycle club in Zurich were at the bar, sweating in their bright-blue nylon bodysuits and drinking beer, and comparing the bikes on which they had spent the week racing up and down the Chianti Mountains. No one had told them that Italy was having elections. They thought that the whispered discussion among the men in blazers and sunglasses had something to do with Ronald Reagan's trip to Bitburg or with the Pope's new cardinals or with the condition of Tuscany's olive trees after the worst winter in anybody's memory. Sunday in Italy is still the day the men go out and the women stay home. Men are supposed to stand around or sit in a café, making desultory conversation and playing *briscola* and occasionally wondering out loud what dinner is going to be. Marcello Cappelletti stays home on Sundays, and is considered odd for it, like the husbands in American movies. He used to go out, but that was years ago, when he was first elected to the town council. There were no cheerful villas then for people like the Cappellettis. There were no television sets in Castellina, no movies—nothing for a lively young man to do but join the Communist Party, no place for him to get together with friends and have a good time but the Party café and the Party headquarters, no way to get ahead but politics. Marcello Cappelletti's great-grandfather was a woodcutter in the mountains. Marcello himself quit school at eleven and at thirteen went to work, and while he wanted to be mayor, and his friends wanted him to be mayor, and even the Christian Democrats didn't seem to mind, it was years before he could afford the time.

It is the custom in Castellina for people to live together in a family house, the way they did when nearly everyone was poor. The Niccolai brothers are in their sixties, and they still live together, with their wives and children and, lately, their children's families. In Castellina, that is the appropriate arrangement. The stationmaster, taking a walk on Election Sunday, looked down at the big white house in the valley where all the Niccolais live and put it this way: "If they didn't live together, people would think they didn't get along." He said that the brothers had been making money together for so many years that by now it was impossible for them to know exactly whose money it was—that they could never separate themselves or their fortunes, even if they wanted to. Provincial Italy does not change habits as easily as it changes politics. Italy's habits have to do with that national genius for making do; its politics do not, and Italians know it. The old mayor keeps a room ready for *his* son, Alessandro, who is a professor in Siena and writes books about folklore, and even spends part of every year teaching in Los Angeles, California. Whenever the Professore comes home (everybody calls him Professore), he moves right into his parents' house and takes up the filial courtesies of an Italian child. The new mayor also has a son at home. His name is Mario, and he has a technical-college degree in chemistry and works for Big Blu. A couple of years ago, Mario was in Florence and met a lawyer's daughter from Chicago, and as soon as they got married they moved into an apartment the mayor had built for them on the second floor. This year, they bought the ruin of an old barn on a hillside in Radda-in-Chianti and—"just like Americans," people in Castellina said—started to restore it. They talk about moving to the barn with their little girl, but Mario's wife, Claire, says that no one in the village believes they will. The villagers think of the ruin as Claire Cappelletti's country house, because it is, after all, twenty minutes' drive from Castellina. They assume that the younger Cappellettis will simply pack the car and use it on weekends. Having a beautiful American daughter-in-law has given the mayor a certain cachet in Castellina. He and his wife and eight other Cappellettis went to Chicago for the wedding, which was a big German-Irish wedding, and the mayor likes to talk about how the family nearly had to leave without him, because none of the Communists in town knew that a Communist mayor could have trouble getting a visa for America.

There is a bit of commedia dell'arte in elections in any small Italian town. All the stock characters come out of the folklore and take their places and look their parts—much more than they do when there is nothing special going on to inspire them. In Castellina last month, the Maresciallo dei Carabinieri sat behind his desk (and under a cross) at the garrison wearing his black dress uniform, with its red trim and silver braid and its stripes and medals, and dispatching the four young carabinieri in his charge on what he called "the sacrificial service of safeguarding the democratic process." He arrived at four on Saturday afternoon, when Castellina's ballot boxes were carried under guard to the two schoolhouses, and stayed with hardly a break till two on Tuesday afternoon, when the ballots were carried to Siena. There was a procession of sorts to the schoolhouses. Each of Castellina's four election "presidents" led a little march from the schoolhouse gate to the classroom where his hamlet would vote, followed by his "vice-president," his "secretary," one carabiniere, one policeman, and observers from the Communist Party and the Christian Democrats. It was a serious occasion, except that the key to one of the schoolhouse gates had disappeared and no one could find it, and the mayor, who was at home babysitting, had to send to the town hall for someone who could pick the lock. The Professore was president for one hamlet. He had 267 voters to attend to, and accordingly, he arrived on Saturday from Siena in a pin-striped suit and funeral shoes, and a dark tie that he never loosened as he counted ballots and recorded votes and distributed his six official indelible pencils and, in general, kept a proper tone, so that people did not start shouting in the voting booths or put their colored ballots in the wrong boxes. He said later that elections used to be livelier back in the fifties, when everyone voted in his own hamlet. People made a big day of elections then. The grade school in the Professore's hamlet was always full of people, and there was bread and wine and salami on the desks, and the people sat around eating and drinking and having a terrific time and—when they thought of it—voting. It was clear to the Professore even then that there was something irregular about a peasant wandering into a voting booth with his ballots in one hand, a bottle of Chianti in the other, and a salami sandwich under his arm. When the Professore took over the elections, he and the peasants arrived at a solution: the bread and wine and salami were put on the windowsill, and the window was opened, and people who had voted could go outside and take their food and not have to interrupt their conversations. Nobody eats or drinks at elections now that they are held in the village. The Professore's classroom this year was as solemn as his shoes. Mario Cappelletti, who was his secretary, checked off voters in a big ledger, and the Castellina bus driver who was his vice-president saw to the ballot boxes, and everybody else kept quiet. Villagers out on their Sunday-morning walk would stop sometimes at the schoolhouse gate, hoping to get a look at some Castellina celebrity —a Niccolai brother, perhaps, or Lapo Mazzei, the banker whose ancestor they all believe helped out Thomas Jefferson with the American Declaration of Independence, or the Principessa Eleonora Ruspoli-Berlingeri, who has a big vineyard in the valley and bottles Chianti Classico. In the old days, the Principessa would come to the polls in style. Her game warden would enter the schoolhouse in his uniform and announce her, and then she would sweep to the head of the line while the *contadini*— some of them hers and all of them good Communists—parted and bowed and murmured their respects. When the Professore took over the voting in the hamlet, he told the peasants that they were not behaving democratically—that in a democracy everybody took his turn. After that, the Principessa stood in line, and had a good time talking, but the *contadini* were embarrassed and confused, and told the Professore that it was just not right for Eleonora Ruspoli to be standing in line with peasants like themselves. Now the Principessa calls ahead, and comes to the school when there is no one around to embarrass.

There are 2,106 eligible voters in Castellina, and 1,986 of them voted. It was a fine turnout, people said, even if a quarter of the local ballots did have to be disqualified for one reason or another, and the peasants were so dazzled by the regional ballot, which had eleven party lists on it—including the Tuscany Greens and the Pensioners' Alliance —that some of them forgot to choose one. Once the votes were counted, Marcello Cappelletti went back to his shoe store and Mauro Neri went back to his dry-goods store and Alessandro Falassi, the Professore, changed into a pair of jeans and thought about driving to Pisa to meet a girlfriend who was flying in from Los Angeles. By Wednesday morning, Castellina had a bus driver again, and Big Blu had a chemist. The train that brought the Neapolitans back to Big Blu and Molini Niccolai was filled with men on their way back to their own jobs in factories in Germany and Switzerland and Sweden. The stationmaster could tell by the size and shape of a shirt collar or the cut of a pair of pants exactly where those factories were.

June 1985

THE GROUPE
MANOUCHIAN

A couple of weeks ago, the historian Alain Besançon wrote in *L'Express*
that the great problem for the democracies of the West, including
France's democracy, was that they could no longer expect their citizens
to die for *"le salut de la cité"*—that is, to die eagerly, as heroes or
sacrifices. It was after the long TWA hijacking, and Professor Besançon's point seemed to be that in better times than these an American
President could simply have told the hostages to say their prayers, and
made his plans. Professor Besançon talked about better times. He talked
about the *Iliad.* He talked about a medieval Spanish governor of Tarifa
whose son was kidnapped: the kidnapper threatened to slit the boy's
throat if the governor did not give up the city, and the governor, by
way of a reply, sent him a sword. It is unlikely that any of the thirty-
nine American hostages who had just come out of Beirut would have
agreed with the professor that *their* dying was an appropriate, let alone
heroic, solution to the problems of Western democracy under terrorist
siege. But in France lately people have been obsessed with questions of
heroism and of what it means to die for your country and, specifically,
of what it means to be "French" and to die for "France."

Historians here are arguing about the political and moral uses of
sacrifice, and their argument began long before the hijacking. In part,
it began this spring, when the Communist Party tried to keep a documentary having to do with the Communist Resistance off French television. The documentary was called *Des "Terroristes" à la Retraite,* and
the retired terrorists of the title were the elderly survivors of a group
of wartime Communist immigrants—Polish and Rumanian Jews,
Spanish republicans, Armenian exiles—who had joined the Resistance

and were sent into the streets of Paris as a kind of hit squad to kill German soldiers. Late in 1943, two hundred of these immigrants were betrayed by a comrade and arrested, and in February of 1944 twenty-three of them were killed publicly by a Nazi firing squad. (All of them were killed eventually.) During the last days of the Occupation, their pictures were all over Paris on a famous Nazi propaganda poster —Aragon wrote a poem about it after the war called *"L'Affiche Rouge"* —which was intended to persuade the French that France was well rid of this "army of crime," with its foreign names and foreign faces. The handful of immigrants who had managed to avoid being arrested settled down in Paris after the Liberation—mainly in old Jewish neighbor-hoods in the Eleventh Arrondissement—and went to work as tailors and cutters and furriers. They were neither distinguished nor success-ful nor "French" in any of the ways one usually associates with Resis-tance heroes. They had been wild and impressionable young men, grieving for families who had died in German camps, and they grew into cranky and sentimental old men and were forgotten. Parisians driving up the Boulevard Richard Lenoir toward the Place de la Répub-lique were likely to remark that this was the street where Inspector Maigret had lived with his thrifty, comfortable wife, but not many of them knew that Jewish tailors from the famous Paris Resistance unit, the Francs-Tireurs et Partisans de la Main d'Oeuvre Immigrée, had met in its courtyard ateliers and plotted bombings and assassinations. The young filmmaker who made *Des "Terroristes" à la Retraite*—he is a Jewish immigrant himself, from Bulgaria, and goes by his Bulgarian first name, Mosco—believes that a lot of people wanted them forgotten, most notably the French Communists who had recruited them. His movie sat on a shelf at Antenne 2 for two years. When it was finally scheduled and the Party started complaining, it was quickly cancelled on the advice of a *jury d'honneur* of old Resistance people who were distinguished, successful, and unquestionably French. By the time the movie did get on the air, it was clear to most of the people involved that the Communist underground could have saved its "terrorists" in 1943 and, for reasons no one can really swear to after forty years, had chosen not to.

The honor of the Resistance is one of the sacred truths of French history, like the honor of the Revolution or of Joan of Arc. History, in France, has a pedagogic function. It is only as "true" as its usefulness in maintaining proper attitudes toward being French—including the fierce and oblivious identification Frenchmen have with France and with everything they mean by France. Strangers tend to see that identification as nationalism or chauvinism, but it is much more primitive than that. A Frenchman identifies with France the same way he lifts his chin and sticks out his lower lip when he is puzzled—as a kind of reflex action. Skeletons in the closet of the state are family skeletons, and he does not easily admit that they are there. It took Marcel Ophuls ten years to get *his* movie about Occupied France, *The Sorrow and the Pity*, on French television, and that was a much more important piece of work than Mosco's. The feeling here about the Ophuls movie seemed to be that it would confuse the children—that it would undermine whatever cheerful patriotism they had, and make life difficult for the schoolteachers whose job was to teach them that no one except a few criminals and psychopaths collaborated with the Germans. The French want to forget the violence of the war, including their own.

Most people in the Resistance had to kill, or be ready to kill, in the course of helping to liberate France, and memories of violence are not something that real heroes tend to cherish. Reliving the past is of little interest to them now. Some of the old *résistants* who saw *Des "Terroristes" à la Retraite* said they were shocked by the enthusiasm with which Mosco's tailors told their stories of shooting German soldiers in the streets of Paris and bombing Paris houses. It was hard for them to understand that those moments with a pistol or a homemade bomb were the only moments of importance most of the tailors had ever had. Mosco himself was "out looking for heroes" when he made his movie. He likes to talk about his life, and he often tells people that he spent a good deal of it trying to invent a heroic father, "a father with a past," to take the place of his real father, who died in Israel when Mosco was a boy. He says it was easy to recapitulate his father, so to speak, as one of those old East European tailors who sat at sewing machines in the Eleventh and stitched up trousers and had amazing secrets. He met his first tailor in 1979, when he was making a short movie with the actor Gérard Desarthe and Desarthe told him about a man he knew who had been an assassin in the Francs-Tireurs et Partisans de la Main d'Oeuvre Immigrée and was still alive and cutting suits in an atelier on the Boulevard Beaumarchais. The man's name was Jacques Farber. The first time Mosco went to see him, he hid in a dark doorway in his courtyard with a couple of old comrades and asked a lot of edgy questions. In his mind, it was wartime Paris again, and he and his friends were at great risk as far as strangers were concerned. They scrutinized Mosco from the doorway, and conferred in whispers —as if Mosco were a policeman, or an informer like their old comrade Joseph Davidovitch, who had fingered the twenty-three "terrorists" of the Affiche Rouge (and was soon shot by the Resistance for it). It took a while before Jacques Farber let Mosco in.

The field commander of the Francs-Tireurs et Partisans de la Main d'Oeuvre Immigrée—the FTP-MOI—in Paris was a young Armenian militant by the name of Missak Manouchian. His group was known to the police as the Groupe Manouchian, and his picture was at the center of the Affiche Rouge, which credited him with 56 attacks and 150 deaths. It was Manouchian who linked the "terrorists" to the Party —who reported back to the Party after each attack, and who carried home the instructions. His comrade Davidovitch was the politician of the group—the "political commissar." Davidovitch was captured in October of 1943 by the Brigade Spéciale of the Paris police. He was either tortured until he talked or threatened with torture, because by the time the police were done with him they had the name and where-abouts of every FTP-MOI militant in Paris. Manouchian, who was warned by a friend at the prefecture, demanded that those militants be *mis au vert*—put to pasture—until the danger passed. He wanted the Party to get them out of Paris—to scatter and hide them, the way it always hid its people in emergencies. This time, the Party refused. The Groupe Manouchian was arrested in Paris in November, and the twenty-three "terrorists" of the Affiche Rouge were "tried" by a German military court and moved to Mont Valérien for execution. The day Manouchian died, he wrote to his wife forgiving everybody who had ever harmed him or wanted to harm him except *"celui qui nous a trahis pour racheter sa peau et ceux qui nous ont vendus"*—"the one who be-trayed us to save his skin and the ones who sold us." It was an eloquent letter—"I am a soldier in the Army of Liberation, and I am going to die with my fingers raised for Victory. *Bonheur!* to those who survive and taste the sweetness of liberty and peace tomorrow"—and after the war the Communists published it in a book called *Lettres de Fusillés,* but they were careful to cut the sentence about treachery and betrayal from the text.

Most of the survivors of Missak Manouchian's group are still in the Party, including three of the old tailors Mosco filmed for *Des "Ter-roristes" à la Retraite.* The tailors are loyal. They talk with tears in their eyes about Stalingrad. They argue about Poland. Every February 21, they meet in a cemetery on the outskirts of Paris to honor the men they still refer to as *les vingt-trois fusillés,* and in May they meet again, in a big gymnasium the Communists have built at Vitry, and have a five-course dinner called Le Repas de la Victoire. All of them know that they survived by accident. One of Mosco's tailors was in Lyons, recov-

ering from a shoot-out, when the rest of the group was arrested. Another one shot the policemen who came for him, and a third had been
deported to a concentration camp. They were not much use to the
Party after the war. The Party gave them their annual cemetery vigils
and their annual victory dinners and otherwise ignored them, but in the
end the Party was all they had. Mosco says that their loyalty moved
him. They reminded him of something the anthropologist Jean Malau-
rie had written in *Le Monde*—something about looking into the hum-
blest man and trying to find *"la part de destin et de tragique qui sommeille
en lui."* He was not interested in the famous *résistants*—the ones who
meant something important about being French and a patriot. He was
interested in the *résistants* who meant very little, even to themselves.
His tailors went into the streets with him and reinvented their war.
They got used to the guns he brought them—the kind of guns they
probably hadn't seen, except on television movies, for forty years.
Handling the guns excited them. They started to remember, and then
it was as if their memories were dybbuks that possessed them. They ran
around gesturing and shouting and pointing their guns. They would
turn at a sound, as if they were being followed. Or they would whisper,
or lapse into the *shtetl* Yiddish they had used as boys. They talked about
what it was like to be twenty-five and full of ideals and told, suddenly,
to shoot someone. Jacques Farber described his first mission as a *franc-
tireur.* He needed a gun and there were none to spare, and so his orders
were to get a hammer and use it to kill a German soldier and take the
soldier's gun. He couldn't do it. "I'm not an assassin, a murderer!" he
shouted at Mosco. But he never blamed the Party for asking him to be.
None of the tailors blamed the Party. They sat and sewed and talked
about their families dying in the camps, and then they cried and said
that maybe they hadn't killed enough Germans, that they would kill
again if they had to.

There are theories, of course, about who "sold" Missak Manouchian's partisans to the Germans, and what the reasons were. Manouchian's widow thinks it was an old comrade of theirs named Boris
Holban, though she is hard put to it to say exactly how or why he did
it, since Holban had been moved out of Paris by the time the Germans
knew for sure who anybody in the Groupe Manouchian was. Stéphane
Courtois, a young historian who helped Mosco with the movie, says no,
it was the men on the Central Committee. He says that by 1943 the Party
was negotiating with de Gaulle for a piece of the General's provisional
government, and consequently wanted to justify its claim to Paris with

a lot of spectacular attacks. His theory is that inasmuch as Manouchian's group was the only Resistance army active in Paris in 1943 a decision was made to keep it active, whatever the risks, until the Germans destroyed it. Philippe Ganier-Raymond, another historian who helped Mosco with the movie, has a third theory. He says it was the Comintern. *His* theory is that the Comintern told the Communists in France to sacrifice their immigrant units—that Stalin's plan was to make the Party in France sufficiently "French" so that after the war it would attract a working class that had never been fond of foreigners, especially Jewish foreigners, and was apt to be even less fond of them after four years of Nazi propaganda.

People have been arguing about how Communists go about betraying their friends since 1917, and one short television movie about Jewish tailors is unlikely to settle their arguments. The fact remains that French Communists fought courageously for France. They were crucial to the Resistance (which is why de Gaulle joined forces with the Communist underground in 1943), and the knowledge that some of them were working for Moscow at the same time they were fighting for France does not diminish their importance—it only complicates our understanding of it. Some of the *résistants* who wanted to keep *Des "Terroristes" à la Retraite* off television said that they had no appetite for passing judgment now, and all of them complained about the movie. They thought it was tricky and amateurish and sentimental—which in a way it was. The movie was commissioned by Antenne 2, but the channel covered only about a third of Mosco's costs, and Mosco had to work on it piecemeal while he raised the rest of the money from little groups like the Jewish Veterans. Antenne 2 is a public channel. The people who run it are approved by the President of the Republic, and by the time Mosco finished *Des "Terroristes"* the Giscardian who commissioned it had been replaced by the Mitterrandiste, who didn't like the movie at all. The new man, Pierre Desgraupes, put it away and avoided the telephone and hoped that Mosco would forget about it. But that year—it was 1983—the movie was shown at the film festival in Cannes, and then it won a prize at the film festival in Grenoble, and people began to praise it. Simone Signoret, who narrated *Des "Terroristes"* with Gérard Desarthe, sat down and wrote a novel about an immigrant in Paris during the Occupation, and told everyone that Mosco's movie had inspired her. Mme Signoret and her husband, Yves Montand, have recently (Signoret's words) "crossed the frontier into anti-Communism," and they have crossed it to the immense interest of the French public, which regards the couple's private and political lives as a kind of national sentimental journey. The Montands have what might be called moral allure. Being political and having political causes and caring passionately about those causes is part of their glamour, and the French like to watch them at it because, with their actors' gifts, their concern is so much more vivid and gratifying and expressive than anybody else's. People hear Simone Signoret talk, in her wonderful dusty voice, about discovering how treacherous Communists are —they hear the fatigue and sadness in that voice, and they blame the Communists for having made her suffer. Signoret's novel—she called it *Adieu Volodia*—was on the best-seller lists this spring. Desgraupes had left Antenne 2 by then, and it was his successor, Jean-Claude Héberlé, who finally scheduled Mosco's movie. By spring, everyone was curious.

The Communists began to attack *Des "Terroristes"* before they had even had a screening. The Party paper, *L'Humanité*, ran articles against the movie every day. The Party historian Albert Ouzoulias—he is a kind of official spokesman when Communist wartime honor is involved —threatened to sue Antenne 2 for defamation. And Héberlé got scared. French television is supposed to be "honest" and "pluralistic," and anti-Communism is frowned on in respectable television circles. After a few days, Héberlé had no idea whether *Des "Terroristes"* was honest or pluralistic, or even worth the trouble it was causing. Once *L'Humanité* attacked the movie, the rest of the papers started to attack *L'Humanité*, and it turned out that no one but Communists believed a word of Ouzoulias's story that the arrest and execution of the Groupe Manouchian was just an accident of war—that there would have been no underground left in Paris if the Party had "retired" every partisan who asked. According to Héberlé, there was no way for him to settle the argument. He turned over a print of the movie to the Haute Autorité de la Communication Audiovisuelle—the Haute Autorité is a kind of media-watchdog agency appointed by the government—and asked for its evaluation, and the Haute Autorité, in turn, called up five important *résistants* who were in Paris and asked for *their* evaluation.

Stéphane Hessel, a retired diplomat who was finishing up a term on the board of the Haute Autorité, was in charge of *l'affaire Manouchian* at the agency. He had been a Resistance hero himself—he was one of de Gaulle's couriers and had spent the war commuting between the General's London headquarters and the French underground—and the five *résistants* he called were people he had known for years. Four of them had met with Hessel before, to look at a movie about the death of Jean Moulin. (It was a nasty little "documentary," produced in part by Klaus Barbie's lawyer, Jacques Vergés, and meant to discredit the prosecution in the Barbie trial by proving that Jean Moulin was betrayed and killed by his own comrades—and, on the advice of Hessel's friends, the networks refused to touch it.) They said later that they had thought of themselves as an informal group, meeting to talk things out among themselves, and not at all as a *jury d'honneur* convened formally to make a recommendation. In any event, they disliked Des "Terroristes." They said that it fell into simplistic, even damaging, clichés about Jews, and, worse, implied that the Resistance *was* these funny-looking old men who waved their arms around and talked with accents and lived miserably, bent over their sewing machines or occasionally heating up leftovers on dilapidated stoves, as if the war they helped to win had in fact defeated them. They said this to Hessel, and Hessel repeated it to Héberlé, at Antenne 2, and Héberlé pulled Des "Terroristes" from the schedule. It was only after the television directors' union *and* the Minister of Communications complained about the propriety of this sort of censorship that a deal was struck with the Communists and the movie was shown.

One of the things the Communists wanted was a television debate about the movie. In fact, they wanted a debate *before* the movie, but inasmuch as no one else saw any point in talking about a movie before either the Communists or the audience had seen it they had to settle for making their denunciations first and then waiting until the movie was over to discuss them. The discussion took place on July 2, after a week of fanfare that included the serialization of the script of Des "Terroristes" in *Le Matin* and interviews with dozens of MOI "survivors," among them the mysterious Boris Holban, who turned out to have spent the past forty years in Bucharest, and who had just come back to Paris to retire. Charles Lederman, an old Communist senator —and a Jew—whose own resistance had involved acting as a liaison between Soviet intelligence and the Party underground, delivered the denunciations and afterward joined a panel of nine experts who had been invited to debate. No one had thought to invite Mosco to the debate or, for that matter, anybody from the Haute Autorité or the *jury d'honneur*. No one seemed interested anymore in why a group of people who in the minds of the French stood for Freedom had got themselves involved in what amounted to an act of censorship. The people who debated that night forgot the present. Like Mosco's tailors, they relived their war. Jacques Chaban-Delmas was there for the Gaullist Resistance, and Colonel Henri Rol-Tanguy was there for the Communist Resistance, and, regardless of the interrupting and the shouting

that went on, it was clear that to them, at least, it was the honor of the
Resistance that mattered most. Chaban-Delmas, who in his time has
been a Fourth Republic minister and a Fifth Republic Prime Minister,
took over the debate like a smooth practitioner of reconciliation. He
said that they had *all* been brave young patriots and that—whatever the
arguments had been between the Gaullists, who wanted a disciplined
and purposeful Resistance, and the Communists, who wanted to disori-
ent the enemy with random violence—they were united in being brave
young patriots. As for the death of Missak Manouchian and his friends
—*"C'est ça la guerre, c'est ça la crauté de la guerre, c'est ça qu'il faut
comprendre."* The important thing, Chaban-Delmas said, was for the
children watching television that night to know that the Resistance was
"an explosion of youth," that they lived in France, in liberty, today
because of those other children forty years ago. He said that the smile
of defiance on the face of one young *camarade fusillé* was as beautiful
to him as the smile on the face of the angel of Reims Cathedral. He said
that it was never a question of Communists or Gaullists, Frenchmen
or foreigners. There was only the Resistance, and the young men were
lucky enough to be part of it. He talked about hope. Charles Lederman
mopped his forehead with relief and cried, *"Ah, l'espoir!"* The French
have always sent foreigners to fight for France. The Foreign Legion
began as a "company of foreigners," with orders that were probably
best stated in an inscription on the wall of Fort Saint-Jean, in Marseilles:
"You are soldiers to die, and I am sending you there—where death is."
The difference between dying and dying for France is what makes
French history.

July 1985

THE MAYOR OF DREUX

Françoise Gaspard, who used to be the mayor here, says she expected trouble from the right when vacuum-cleaner salesmen started to show up in the town housing projects, where everyone is poor. That was late in 1982, and not many of the old Dreux families, with their own houses in the *centre ville*, near the Église Saint-Pierre and the famous High Gothic bell tower, knew much then about the visits or about the projects, which are a mile southeast of what they consider Dreux—up on the long, bare ridge, on the outskirts of town, that everybody here calls the Plateaux. There are more than eight and a half thousand immigrants in Dreux—factory workers and the wives and children of factory workers—and in 1982 the old Drouais believed that the projects were really a giant dormitory for those immigrants. They had heard the stories about life on the Plateaux—about the racket at night during Ramadan, about the sheep slaughtered in the halls for the Feast of Abraham and the blood pouring down the stairwells, about the veiled Turkish women who cooked on braziers on the floor while their husbands fought outside in parking lots, about the Muslim preachers sent by Qaddafi to turn the little Moroccan and Algerian boys of Dreux into maniacs. Anyone driving out of town to the Route Nationale 12, the road to Paris, fifty miles away, had to pass the projects. People would look up at the gray cinder-block buildings, which seemed to darken and deteriorate with every trip they made, and Mme Gaspard says that as often as not they would turn away; perhaps it was because the buildings looked so much like a dance of death across that curious, barren ridge that separated Dreux and the rolling countryside of the Beauce from the rich, flat farmland of the Île-de-France. If the people were public-spirited and humane—the kind of people who belonged to civic clubs like the Cercle Laïque or the Patronage Saint-Jean, and believed in good works for the city—they would shake their heads and talk about how difficult life must be for the immigrants, cut off by poverty and by their own recalcitrance from the good influence of real Drouais like themselves.

Until the vacuum-cleaner salesmen arrived, it had never occurred to most of the old Drouais that more than half the flats on the Plateaux had French families in them, that Dreux's Third World was also its Fourth World—its world of native poverty, of peasants who had happened to pass through Dreux on their way from Brittany or Normandy to Paris and had simply stayed on, hoping for jobs, and of beggars and street thieves who had come out from Paris because they were *interdits de séjour*, banished from the capital and forbidden to settle anyplace closer to the Paris gates. But the fact is that Dreux was always on a *route de passage* that poor people followed toward the Loire and their dreams of an easy and bountiful landscape. Long before the signs went up in Saharan villages and Portuguese churches and customs sheds along the Marseilles docks—signs advertising work in Dreux for foreigners—those Frenchmen were camped on the Plateaux. There were vagabonds and squatters. Even a colony of gangsters came to Dreux, between the wars, when the government was trying to clean up Paris and was using the old banishment laws to send pimps and runners and drug dealers out of the protected circle of the Paris Milieu, which is what the French call their Mafia. Neither the Brittany peasants nor the Paris crooks ever made it down from the Plateaux and into the life of the city. But they and, in time, their sons gave Dreux a terrible reputation—which everybody but the old Drouais acknowledged. People in Châteaudun, and even in Chartres, twenty miles away, knew about the gangs from Dreux. They were notorious. They would prowl the Île-de-France on Saturday nights—ten or twelve of Dreux's worst children speeding down the Route Nationale on battered motorbikes, looking for an open café or a farmers' dance to terrorize—and whenever they stopped, the children of Chartres or Châteaudun would scatter, crying *"Les bandes de Dreux arrivent!"* The old Drouais did not really believe in these *bandes de Dreux*—that is, not until the immigrants arrived. After that, they simply accepted that the gangs were full of small, dark boys named Muhammad or Mustafa. In fact, when Françoise Gaspard took over the Mairie—it was in 1977—the undisputed leader of the Dreux gangs was a French punk, who specialized in knives, and who commuted, so to speak, between town and prison until he found an honest wife and Mme Gaspard put him to work gardening for the city.

There were never many jobs in Dreux for people like that, and when the price of oil went up in the seventies, and the price of the franc went down in the eighties, most of the ones who did have jobs lost them. The Turks and the Arabs here were losing their jobs, too, but no one seemed to care about that very much once the vacuum-cleaner salesmen got busy. The salesmen would cover the housing projects —the French call their public housing HLM, for Habitation à Loyer Modéré—block by block, floor by floor, knocking at every door with a French name on it and producing catalogues of the most beguiling vacuum cleaners anyone living on the Plateaux was likely ever to have seen. It didn't matter that by then most of the housing blocks were slums, or that the decorations ran more to graffiti and garbage heaps than to carpets. The housewives of the Plateaux wanted vacuum cleaners. A housewife would tell the salesman at the door her problems: how there was no work for her husband, no money coming in except a government check that barely paid the grocer, no way to buy *anything*, let alone the beautiful vacuum cleaner that would change her life, the vacuum cleaner that would transform her into a languid *femme d'intérieur*, like the women she saw in the catalogues—slim, beautiful women gliding across pale carpeted spaces with vacuum cleaners that matched their gowns. And the vacuum-cleaner salesman would look at the housewife, astonished. He would look at her and say, "What, no work? No money? That's funny, because, you know, the Arab family below you? *They* just bought a vacuum cleaner from me. They had plenty of money." And then the woman would call her husband to the door, and the salesman would repeat his story, and the husband would begin to bluster and swear and shout, and in no time at all the word around the projects was that foreigners were buying vacuum cleaners while honest Frenchmen, real Frenchmen, starved. Foreigners had the jobs that by rights belonged to Frenchmen. Foreigners were to blame if Frenchmen got fired, because there was plenty of work in France, and plenty of money, if only the foreigners went home. It was then that Françoise Gaspard decided that the Front National, the party on the far right of France's far right, must be "looking into" Dreux again. She had been the mayor for nearly six years, but there were new elections in March of 1983, only a few months off, and she says it was clear to anyone who thought about it that the leader of the Front National —a Breton named Jean-Marie Le Pen, who talked about *"France aux Français"* and *"les Français d'abord"* and called himself a nationalist and took you to court if you called him anything else—had looked at Dreux, with its woman mayor and its Socialist council and its eight and a half thousand immigrants and its punishing unemployment, and concluded that with the right timing and the right tactics he could get his own mayor—or one who owed the job to him—into the town hall.

It is a fine thing to be a mayor in France. Being a mayor means respectability. It connects you to the provinces and to decent and abiding provincial values and to the reassuring authority of provincial office. Politicians who get to be mayor of a town or village—preferably their own—will try to stay mayor, and inasmuch as until this year there were no limits on the number of jobs a French politician could have at once (now he can only have two), most of the important deputies and ministers in Paris, and even the Prime Minister, have regularly gone "home" to some small town for the pleasure and publicity of presiding over a town council that met across the street from the war memorial and the statue of Clemenceau holding his copy of the Treaty of Versailles. Georges Pompidou was a mayor, Valéry Giscard d'Estaing was a mayor, and François Mitterrand was a mayor while they were leading parties and sitting in the National Assembly, and even running for President of the Republic. Mitterrand's first Prime Minister, Pierre Mauroy, was the mayor of Lille, and his Prime Minister now, Laurent Fabius, who is thirty-nine, and young still, is the deputy mayor of a town in Normandy called Grand-Quevilly. If you are a mayor —even if it is a question of a village of fifty farmers, two days' drive from Paris—you refer to yourself first as Monsieur le Maire, and only then as Senator or Deputy or a man to be reckoned with in the Council of Europe or the European Parliament. It adds something to your reputation. It means that you are serious, and think about serious French things and, whatever the opposition says, do not spend all your time running around Paris talking too much and spending too much and eating lunch in restaurants with beautiful women who have worldly views. It means you are accountable to your neighbors, and not merely to the left or the right or whatever ideology is fashionable that moment at the Café Flore.

Dreux calls itself a city, because officially every town in France with more than thirty thousand people is a city, but for practical purposes Dreux is exactly what the French mean when they say "the provinces." No one in England or Italy talks about the provinces the way the French do. Englishmen talk about provincial English life, and Italians talk about provincial Italian life, but usually they mean nothing more complicated than a life that is a little leafier, a little less sophisticated, than life in London or Milan. When the French talk about the provinces, they are talking about everything in France that weights and balances and restrains the impulses of the capital. They are making the kind of distinction they are fond of, and describing the poles of "being French." They are saying that the provinces are the roots of the civilization, and Paris the flowering, and that France itself is really the tension between Paris (open, worldly, free, experimental, aesthetic, foreign) and what they call *la France profonde* (moral, constant, slow, native, and sustaining). The "Frenchness" of provincial France may be a myth, since a third of the country's population has at least one foreign grandparent, but it is a myth the French live by. The people who believe in it—Charles de Gaulle, who never got to be a mayor, was one of them—tend also to believe that the relation between Paris and the provinces is fixed and fragile, and that it is absolutely essential to the well-being of the country. They believe that a town like Dreux cannot survive Parisian arrangements any more than Paris could survive under provincial scrutiny.

The most famous mayor Dreux ever had was an old republican named Maurice Violette, who died in 1960, at ninety, after fifty-two years in the big brick Mairie, on the rue de Châteaudun. Violette had his own party—a "radical" party, in the civilizing tradition of the provincial left of the *entre-deux-guerres*—and he was much esteemed in Paris. Léon Blum, the country's first Socialist Prime Minister, liked him enough to make him a Minister of State in the Popular Front government that Blum ran for two years in the 1930s. They shared an interest in the people who would eventually become "the immigrant problem" here. Violette had been governor-general of Algeria from 1925 to 1929, and it was his idea that "Muslim students, while remaining Muslim, should become so French in their education that no Frenchman, however deeply racist and religiously prejudiced he might be . . . will any longer dare to deny them French fraternity." When he joined the Popular Front, he and Blum wrote a naturalization bill together. It was called the Plan Violette-Blum, and in those last years before Vichy—those last few years of vision and tolerance—Violette did his best to persuade the French to offer citizenship to twenty-five thousand young Algerians, who would become a kind of leadership cadre at home, friendly to France and, more important, confident in the connection. After the war, when the revolution started in Algeria, he talked about welcoming Harkis—Algerians who were fighting for France and would have nowhere else to go when the revolution was over. The fact that a thousand Harkis arrived in Dreux in 1962 was, in a way, his legacy.

Françoise Gaspard, who was fifteen when Maurice Violette died, likes to think of herself as his disciple. The first time she ran for mayor, she talked a great deal about her connection with Violette—about how she had gone to Violette rallies on her father's shoulders at the age of eleven, about how she had got involved in politics listening to his speeches, about how Violette had made her an apprentice and then a kind of political trustee. She studied his papers, and took on the job of putting them in order for the Dreux archives and for a biography she had promised to write, and a "collected Violette" that she is still editing. She keeps a poster of the old mayor on the wall of her office here —for inspiration and association. It was blown up from a snapshot taken in the 1940s, but there is something ageless about it, because the face is one of those emblematically French faces, like Jean Gabin's. It is a big, heavy-lidded, *pastis*-in-the-morning kind of face, with a skeptical look, and even a cigarette dangling. Françoise Gaspard does not have that kind of face at all. She has a small, intense, rabbity face. Her hair is bobbed. It is parted and cut with bangs like a boy's, and she herself is slender like a boy, and she has the anxious darting eyes of an *écolier* under the scrutiny of a decorous teacher. She was never really comfortable in Dreux, although her family was one of the old Dreux families. The Gaspards were artisans. They had been in Dreux since the fifteenth century, and by Françoise's time they were prosperous —some of them from making cheese and the rest from making tomb-stones. The Gaspard men were Freemasons, republicans, and, during the war, partisans. Jean Gaspard, Françoise's father, was a Socialist, and Clovis Gaspard, her uncle, was a Communist, but when Françoise was growing up there was no such thing in Dreux as a Socialist girl or a Communist girl. Girls in Dreux—even girls from the left—got married and had babies and stayed at home. Françoise says she decided that being a girl in Dreux was not very interesting. She started following her father to his meetings, because going to meetings was something girls were not supposed to do. She went to college because going to college was something girls were not supposed to do, either. She fin-ished Sciences-Pô—the Institute d'Études Politiques de Paris. Later, she finished l'ÉNA—the École Nationale d'Administration. It took her seven years to work up the courage to apply to l'ÉNA, because l'ÉNA is the graduate school that trains people to run the country, and being an Énarque was something that most girls did not even consider.

Françoise Gaspard was already a politician then. She had "made her 1968," as the French say. She had a card from the Parti Socialiste Unifié and went to meetings and listened to icy young Marxists from CERES (the Centre d'Étude de Recherche et d'Éducation Socialiste) talk about administering the future as if the future were a dose of castor oil. The Socialists kept a list of prospective candidates all over France —it was something the party leaders and their factions negotiated and revised at every party congress—and in 1971, when Françoise Gaspard was twenty-four, they put her name on that list. Three years later, they tried her out in a cantonal election. (A French canton is a little like a county.) She lost, and says she hated losing so much that it gave her a kind of mission as far as Dreux was concerned. When she ran for mayor, she had her degree from l'ÉNA for credentials and could wage what she calls "an American campaign"—by which she means that she knew the uses of publicity, and in the end looked indispensable. It was not really very hard for a smart young Socialist to look indispensable in 1977. The French had been talking for so long about saving France with a government of the left that by 1977 they were almost honor bound to vote for one. The fashionable issues then—though not for long—were Françoise Gaspard's issues. She talked about women's rights and abortion and a "new socialism." But she also talked about the fact that thousands of foreigners were living in squalor up on the Plateaux. She said there would be terrible trouble in Dreux unless people at least admitted that the foreigners were there, and that the town didn't like their being there. She said that Dreux had a "race problem" it had not begun to solve. Fifty-five percent of Dreux voted for her. She was the youngest woman mayor of a French city. Two years later, she was also a deputy in the European Parliament. In another two years, she had a seat in the National Assembly.

There are people who think that Françoise Gaspard never did get comfortable in Dreux. She had what the French call a *style technocrate* —efficient and distant and uncompromising and a little superior. She was shy, and it made her proud, and sometimes people took her pride for scorn. She was interested in Dreux but not so much in the Drouais. Jean Cauchon, who was the mayor for twelve years before her, says that the women of Dreux would see Mme Gaspard at the big Monday market, walking fast with her head down, because she wanted to get her shopping done and not waste time talking, and then complain to him that she had hurt their feelings. Cauchon had a keen interest in the smart young Énarque who had run against him—and beaten him —after all those contented years in the Mairie. It was a paternal interest, he says. He went to Mme Gaspard and said to her, "Listen, Françoise, don't look down on these people. You have to *love* them. You have to *love* Dreux."

It is obvious that Jean Cauchon loves Dreux. He never leaves unless he has to. Even now, when the senate is in session and Cauchon, who is a senator for the Eure-et-Loir, is due in Paris at the Palais du Luxembourg at nine-thirty in the morning, he gets up early and takes the train rather than spend the night away from home. He is seventy-two years old, and still commuting. He lives in the house where he was raised and where he and Mme Cauchon raised seven children (five of them settled down in Dreux), and he likes to receive people in the big law office on the Place Anatole France where his fourth son, Yves, practices. On Sundays, he walks through Dreux the way he walks through the senate's gilt and mirrored halls—a rosy and benign old gentleman beaming at everyone, shaking hands, asking after ailing parents and precocious babies, listening to problems, offering advice. He is the kind of paterfamilias the Drouais liked in their Mairie. He was soothing. He was never sectarian. He would go to meetings of the Cercle Laïque, where Socialists and Freemasons and freethinkers argued loudly about things like state education and independence for New Caledonia, as enthusiastically as he went to the Patronage Saint-Jean, across town, where Catholics like himself raised money for church schools and African missions. When a Portuguese couple from the Radiotéchnique factory got married, he would talk as proudly about "another Dreux wedding" as he did when one of the Orléans pretenders came to Dreux to get married in the Orléans family chapel, the Chapelle Royale. He liked to say that all of Dreux were his children —which may be why he left a lot of the dull daily business of running Dreux to his deputy mayors and saved the family pleasures for himself. Some people think that he left too much business to his deputies —that if he had been paying attention to what was happening here in those twelve years from 1965 to 1977 he might have tried to stop the developers and the recruiters from moving in, he might have tried to control the immigration that was choking Dreux. As it was, loving Dreux, he listened to the town councillors and the deputy mayors who told him Dreux was booming. He believed that he had simply got himself a bigger, more exotic family. He calmed a lot of the tensions just by refusing to believe that any tensions were there.

Françoise Gaspard says that she won in 1977 because of "the problem of race"—that people in Dreux do not admit it but that by 1977 everybody blamed the immigrants on Jean Cauchon. Cauchon says no, that she won because "the left was like a strong wind in France, blowing everything old away." The truth is probably that Dreux did not expect the left when it first voted for Françoise Gaspard. The town expected a kind of female Maurice Violette, someone in the tradition of the old provincial *radicaux*, who were not radicals at all in any Parisian sense but were, rather, republicans—anticlerical and progressive. Certainly it did not expect a Paris intellectual who thought about ideology and class and the redistribution of resources more than she thought about her neighbors. Provincial radicals were people who believed in progress, not in the proletariat. They were a French version of the great Victorians who read Darwin and the Huxleys and believed in eugenics and the Social Good and the Betterment of the Working Class, and preached that misery was ignorance—that happiness would cover England like a soft blanket as soon as an enlightened and righteous bourgeoisie applied itself to the problem. The French idea of progress was drawn not from dramas of class but from the dramas of the Revolution. For old radicals like Violette, 1789 was the moment when history began and French identity was established. This is what separated them from Catholics like Jean Cauchon, who would have said that history began with the birth of Christ. In Dreux, those radicals —real or sentimental—voted for Françoise Gaspard. They voted for her because they considered her one of them. They expected "progress." She had the proper credentials for enlightenment, and so they expected her to make Dreux happy, too. Like most people who voted for the left then, they did not really expect Socialism—and Mme Gaspard was a passionate Socialist. She thought that Jean Cauchon, with his cheerful benevolence, had let Dreux go. He had done nothing about the immigration into Dreux, nothing to temper the shock to Dreux of that immigration, or the shock of Dreux to the immigrants—nothing to prepare for the trouble that was bound to come.

People who watched Françoise Gaspard running Dreux for the next six years say that there was a scrupulous purity to her attentions. She was a Jacobin. She did not court anyone. She may not have smiled and chatted her way through the Monday market, but she kept her office hours every week, and anybody with a complaint or a proposition to make or a problem to solve could come to her and know he would be heard. She was never indulgent, like Jean Cauchon—either with the immigrants or with the French. She was fair by instinct and education and because she believed that not being fair was inefficient, irrational, and unworthy. She was never willing to *s'arranger*—to make her arrangements. The old Drouais, including the Socialists among them, found her fairness severe, but the immigrants admired her for it. Even the North Africans and the Turks, who were not well disposed toward women to begin with, and certainly not toward women with power, got used to having Françoise Gaspard in the Mairie, and there were forty-five hundred North Africans in Dreux then, and more than a thousand Turks. There were so many Muslims up on the Plateaux, in fact, that old Dreux had taken to calling the projects Mecca. The graffiti there were in Arabic. The hallways smelled of sweat and the defective dyes in the flowered acetate dresses the Turkish women wore. At the project called Les Chamards, on the southernmost plateau, someone had built a mosque and a hammam and painted them blue and white, like the mosques and baths of a Tunisian town.

Françoise Gaspard approved of color. She was determined to make the projects a little brighter, a little more cheerful, and so she built a grammar school and painted it crayon colors and invited Dreux's astonished Arabs to the dedication of the École Jacques Prévert. She built another school, painted *it* pink and purple, and called it the Maternelle Louise Michel. She painted the apartment blocks at the project called Lièvre d'Or. She added big windows at Le Faucher, to break the sad gray cinder-block façades and let the light in, and some of the sun's heat. Until the money ran out, she was an enthusiast of what was called "the new Socialist experiment." It was as if she believed that a coat of paint and a cultural center and a couple of earnest young *animateurs* organizing volleyball games and readings from Boris Vian could turn a housing project on Dreux's Plateaux into a neighborhood.

The year Françoise Gaspard was elected, a young Algerian I will call Hamid Benamid, who worked in one of the factories here and lived in a workers' barracks with a few hundred other immigrants, decided to bring his wife, Aicha, from Algeria. He found a flat for them in an HLM on the Plateaux, and looked in on the Dreux chess club and on the local theater club—Théâtre en Dreux. He wanted to introduce his wife to Dreux society, he says—to the class of ladies she would meet at home in Tebessa, where her father was an important man in the bazaar and had a big house in the center of town—and so he read the bulletin boards at all the community centers and tried to decide if Aicha would be better served by the ceramics workshop or the women's choir or the Wednesday-afternoon macramé group. There was a lot to consider, from night classes in French to ski weekends in the Jura—though Benamid was hard put to it to think of any Algerians of his acquaintance who went on ski weekends, or, for that matter, let their wives go on ski weekends. Benamid thought for a long time and came to the conclusion that Aicha would meet a better class of ladies if she stayed home in their apartment and he did the socializing. He started night classes himself, and even thought about auditioning for a part in one of the Théâtre en Dreux productions. He introduced himself to Carlos Guerreiro, who came from Portugal and was the elected head of an association of all the foreigners in Dreux, and then to Jean-Pierre Dubreuil, who taught English at the *lycée* and was president of the Cercle Laïque and vice-president of Théâtre en Dreux and, Benamid had heard, a man of influence in half the clubs and circles and associations a provincial city like Dreux produces. He was especially proud to have met the professor, who could walk across the Place du Marché and greet as many people as old Senator Cauchon—even though it was known that the professor allowed his daughter to go to the movies with a boy from Africa. Benamid did not approve of Muslim boys and Christian girls going to the movies together. He did not approve of boys and girls going to the movies together at all. When Aicha had twin daughters, and then another girl, Benamid took out a loan from a Tebessa bank at 4 percent and started to build a house there, next to his father-in-law's house. He told Aicha that when the girls were older they would all be going back to Algeria, where women stayed at home and were properly guarded from European thoughts and European longings and European scandal.

Tebessa is a desert town, about a hundred miles into the Sahara from the Algerian coast, and not many Europeans stopped there once Algeria was independent. But on a March day nineteen years ago (for reasons nobody in Tebessa ever discovered) a Frenchman showed up in town and told the sheep herders and the phosphate miners and the merchants at the souk that he was "chief of personnel" for a lot of big new factories in a city called Dreux, near Paris, and that anyone who could sign his name in French was welcome to take a test and come to Dreux and have a fine career. By the time Benamid took the test and got his trial contract, nearly half the factory workers in Dreux were foreign, and many of them were still living without their families in the sort of barracks where Benamid had found a bed. Radiotéchnique, a Philips subsidiary with two plants here for assembling television screens, eventually owned five of these barracks; that is, the company owned the walls and leased the maintenance contracts and the canteen contracts to local entrepreneurs, whose only real problem was how to provide the least service for the biggest rent and get away with it. Most workers tried to leave the barracks as soon as their trial year at a factory was over and they had a proper residence card and permission to bring their families, but when Benamid arrived, early in 1971, there were still more immigrants in Dreux than there was housing for them. Dreux was advertised in the North African papers as a *ville ouverte*—a town that by policy welcomed foreigners. People getting off the boats from Algiers and Casablanca saw signs that either Radiotéchnique or Renault or Actim, Dreux's new turbine company, was hiring. They heard that in Dreux you could bring your prayer rug to the assembly line. They heard that during Ramadan you had twenty extra minutes of free time every day for resting, or, if you were working late, twenty extra minutes at night to break your fast. They heard that trucks arrived in Dreux on Sundays filled with Arab food, that on Sundays the Place du Marché in Dreux was getting to look like the Tebessa souk.

What Benamid liked about Dreux was the immigrants' Sunday market and the muezzin's calls to prayer on the factory loudspeaker and anything else that reminded him of home. He liked having Algerian neighbors and he liked the fact that there was an old patriarch like Jean Cauchon in the Mairie—someone on the order of a local sheik. He was horrified when Françoise Gaspard took over. He was not used to having a woman tell him what to do, but, then, he was not used to being an "immigrant problem," either. When Benamid talks about the immigrant problem, he puts it this way: "One day, there was work in Dreux. Everybody loved the foreigners, because it was dirty work, work that Frenchmen considered beneath them, work for foreigners to do. The next day, there was an oil crisis. The factories started letting workers go, and then everybody hated the foreigners. They talked about sending the foreigners home. They told me how lucky I was and what a fine job I had. They said that any Frenchman would be proud to have a job like mine."

Hamid Benamid is not a man with a long view. He has a blunt, literal sort of understanding and does not know what to do when life contradicts itself. His father worked in the Tebessa phosphate mines. He died when Benamid was still a schoolboy trying to memorize the Koran, and Benamid would have had to go into the mines, too, to support his mother, if a butcher in the neighborhood hadn't offered to take him on, providing his meals in return for a day's work that began at five in the morning. Being a butcher gave Benamid prospects. He wanted to distinguish himself. He wanted a specialty to offer—something to take the place of the sheep and fields and jewelry he didn't have —when he went looking for a wife among the Tebessa bourgeoisie. He was a good-looking boy, slim and very tall, with shiny hair and the beginnings of a mustache, which he rubbed with oil and tried to coax into a fine, curved line, like a line of script or an arabesque. He reminded his mother of the handsome young men in the movies that one of the colonial administrators in Tebessa used to show at the high school every month—first for the women, then for the men, and finally for the French, who came together. Once, when Benamid was ten, the administrator decided that Tebessa ought to have a theater—a classical French theater, a little Comédie Française at the edge of the desert, with a repertoire of Racine and Molière and Feydeau. Benamid's mother sent him to join the group, and he could still recite from *Phèdre* and *Le Misanthrope* when he went to the medina ten years later to present himself to Aicha's father.

At first, Benamid did not know what to do with a delicate medina wife—a soft, plump, perfumy girl who spoke a chirping French and moved about the house in little high-heeled steps instead of speaking Arabic and walking barefoot, like the women in his own family. He worried that she was laughing at him with her friends, that she took him lightly, that she would forget her respect for him and her duty to him, and even the obedience the Koran demanded. His father-in-law had set him up in his own butcher shop. It was when the shop failed that he left for France. He was determined to stay in France until he was somebody. He tried a course for French butchers. Then he enrolled in a weekend course for mechanics. The course met at an "institute" near Chartres, and there were thirty other immigrants in Benamid's class. After they had paid for their weekends in advance, the teacher disappeared, and all that was left of the institute was a *bail à céder* notice on the door and a landlord screaming for his rent. Benamid wanted to impress Aicha, but it was clear that she was not impressed by two dark rooms in a housing project—even a French housing project. Aicha looked around the flat and out across the empty concrete "park" that separated their building from five identical buildings, and remarked that now that she was finally free, like a Frenchwoman, there was nowhere to go. She was isolated in Dreux. The Portuguese women across the hall did not return her visits, and she herself would never have visited the Turkish women in the flat next door. She avoided the Turks. She thought that the Turks were ignorant and coarse and noisy, and from the point of view of a well-bred Tebessa lady she was right. She had wanted to live in France, but the France of her imagination was really a French Tebessa—a place where ladies like herself drank sweet mint tea and had amusing conversations with other ladies from good families, and where there were no "immigrants" to annoy them.

The fact that she shared a cinder-block HLM with workers from fifteen or twenty countries was not as moving or exotic to Aicha as it was to the politicians who came through Dreux and talked about "the immigrant experience" and the French melting pot. Diversity did not impress Aicha. The most diversity she could tolerate was the Fête de l'Amitié, when all the foreigners in Dreux got dressed up in their native clothes and sang and danced to their native music and being an immigrant became a kind of folklore, worn for the day, like those clothes, and put away in a suitcase under the bed for the rest of the year.

Françoise Gaspard probably did not enjoy the Fête de l'Amitié much more than Aicha Benamid enjoyed it. It is hard to imagine Mme Gaspard spending a long day with the immigrants, talking sign language with Turkish housewives who hadn't been out-of-doors since the fête the year before, or making conversation with the parish priests, or giving little toasts with supermarket port to Franco-Portuguese friendship. But she saw to it that the town council voted a proper sum of money for the festival, the way she saw to it that people who needed a hall for a play or a meeting had their hall—and Socialist Dreux would pay the rent and the electric bill, and even post the announcements at the Mairie. She did not pretend that Dreux was a big, various, happy family—a UNICEF poster of a town. She accepted the fact that there were things bothering immigrants about other immigrants—things like race and class and culture. She accepted that immigrants were just as prejudiced against each other as the French were prejudiced against them. It was simply a problem for French Socialism to solve. Jean Cauchon had liked the immigrants well enough, but he had *loved* them indiscriminately—and when the immigrants thought about this they were insulted. They came to prefer a mayor like Françoise Gaspard, who could tell them apart. Mme Gaspard talked about Socialism and equality, but she was cool and a little snobbish herself, and she seemed to understand that a lady from Tebessa like Aicha Benamid could not really be expected to embrace the life on the Plateaux. Aicha wanted to move to a respectable flat, with respectable neighbors. She wrote an application to the Mairie, and a year later someone called to say there was a place for the Benamids at an HLM down where there were not so many Turks and not so many Africans and not so many of those noisy Brittany clans—quarrelsome all day, drunk all night—to frighten her.

Dreux is a sleepy town. The Drouais complain about its always being described in the papers as a "sleepy Beauceron town," but in fact it is sleepy. Everything in Dreux except a couple of restaurants closes up by eight, and the lights in most of the houses are out by ten. It may be, as Carlos Guerreiro once said, that the city slept through its immigration, and then woke up one day to discover that it had forty public-housing projects, eight and a half thousand extra people, and a new Sunday market, where the prices were bargained down in twenty or thirty different languages. Certainly the immigrants knew they were a problem long before the French did. The immigrants had been waiting for something like the Front National to come to Dreux, because they had contact with other immigrants, in the South of France, where there had always been foreigners, and tension about foreigners, and so they knew that trouble was inevitable. In places like Marseilles and Nice and Toulon, people had been hating each other and sometimes murdering each other with every wave of immigration. The "latest" trouble in the South of France had been going on since 1962, when the last of the *pieds noirs*—which is what everyone called the French settlers in Algeria —came home to find that more than half a million of the Algerians they had just spent eight years fighting were already there, working and earning money and getting as much of a welcome in de Gaulle's Fifth Republic as the *pieds noirs* themselves. The fact that people in the Midi who put Le Pen's *"France aux Français"* bumper stickers on their cars are often, from the point of view of purity, more Spanish or Italian than French does not in the least affect their fervent xenophobia or the prejudice at the heart of their political attitudes.

Mediterranean France is polyglot. Marseilles (where more than a quarter of the people voted Front National in the last cantonal elections) has been a port of migration and immigration for thousands of years, and there is virtually no one around but some Provençal peasants who was not at one time or another a foreigner. For a Marseillais, the vocabulary of racism is a way of marking territory in the ethnic bazaar, a way of being "French" by saying that someone else is not—a kind of legitimacy by proclamation. Racism in the north is rarely so overt, and never so noisy. The north does not indulge in the sort of three-way Saturday-night fights among French, Harki, and Arab-immigrant kids which are so habitual in southern towns that the other kids turn up to watch them instead of going to the movies or a discothèque. In the north, people fight alone in alleys. There is less bravado. The racism has to do with more furtive sorts of protectionism: with newsdealers who put the papers that support Le Pen on display and hide *Le Monde* behind the counter to see who asks for it; with doctors who leave foreigners in the waiting room until all the French patients have been seen, and then close early. It has to do with more obsessive notions of purity, with a France so narrowly defined that it rarely extends to the next commune. Jean-Marie Le Pen is a northerner. He comes from a village called La Trinité-sur-Mer, on the Brittany coast, and when he is out campaigning he likes to recite these lines: "I love my daughters more than my nieces, my nieces more than my cousins, my cousins more than my neighbors, my village more than your village, my province more than your province—I love France above all."

The people in Dreux love France. They never thought of themselves as the sort of people who sent vacuum-cleaner salesmen into housing projects or paraded with shaved heads and paramilitary clothes or brought German shepherds to socialist rallies or published tracts against immigrants and Jews and all the terrible foreign influences and foreign elements and foreign practices that were contaminating the country. People in Dreux remember Vichy, which was an informer's France—a France of local grievances and petty envies. It was a France where bitterness fed on inadequacy and neighbors watched each other from behind their curtains and plotted their small revenge on fortune and dealt in intimidation and accusation—like the people the French call *corbeaux*, or crows, who paste together newsprint letters and make anonymous phone calls—and were never very far in their hearts from the collaborators who sent their letters signed in return for privileges and a measure of safety for themselves. People like that had not had any power since the 1950s, when there were wars in Indochina and Algeria and a lot of violence and exalted xenophobia at home.

In 1956, a shopkeeper from Saint-Céré by the name of Pierre Marie Poujade founded a party that was not so different in appeal from the Front National, and managed to get fifty-two deputies into Guy Mollet's Fourth Republic parliament. They lasted two years there, and then, gradually, Poujade's party disappeared. It was a party of shopkeepers and small farmers who hated taxes at least as much as they hated foreigners, and when their taxes were cut a lot of them lost interest in politics. The constituency of the Front National is a different constituency—a much more various constituency—although Le Pen himself was one of those Poujade deputies. Le Pen left Poujade to volunteer to fight for France in Algeria. He made a reputation in Algeria interrogating revolutionaries, and used a network of informers who were mainly trying to avoid being interrogated themselves.

Twenty years ago, Dreux was a town with twenty-four thousand people, and when those people talked about who was "different" they usually meant that the dairymen who came down from Normandy for the big Monday market were different from the farmers who brought their wheat in from the Île-de-France, because the dairymen were slow-moving and liked their cider raw and strong and never said much once they started drinking, whereas the wheat farmers were lively and progressive and liked to sit in the cafés on the Place du Marché and talk about politics. There was an orderly look to Dreux twenty years ago. Most of the houses were the Thymerais houses of the northwest —squat gray limestone houses with the doors and the windows and the corners etched in dark-red brick and, sometimes, a turret or a dormer sticking out like an afterthought. Industry in those days was mainly mill-town industry. Little factories followed the Blaise River as it flowed through town, breaking into channels toward the *centre ville* and coming together again near the stadium. There were factories for making sheets and pillowcases and factories for dyeing them, and there were woollen mills for the Beauceron fleece and wheat mills for the grain from the Île-de-France.

Whatever jobs there were for the drifters camped on the Plateaux were in those little mills and factories, because Dreux took on changes slowly—which is the proper provincial way. About three hundred Spaniards came here after the civil war. (They came a few families at a time. It took them thirty years to arrive, and by then no one found it strange that a colony of Spanish Republicans had settled down in a city best known for a chapel where the princes of Orléans are buried.) The Moroccans came next, looking for the jobs that had disappeared with their French *patrons* on Moroccan Independence Day. Then the Harkis came, and the Portuguese, and then the Algerians who had fought for Algeria, and then the Tunisians and Malians and Senegalese and Turks. But by then big new factories were opening up in Dreux, and the factories took the immigrants on—and no one seemed to notice they were there until the winter of 1973–74, when the bankruptcies, and the firings, started.

By 1974, about a thousand workers, half of them foreign, were making color television screens at Radiotéchnique. Fifteen hundred workers were making automobile wiring at the Renault factory and precision tools at a new branch plant of Perfect Circle called Floquet Monopole. Refugees and immigrants from sixty-three countries had settled on or around the Plateaux or were living in barracks in Dreux, or in the town of Vernouillet, next door, waiting to settle in. Everyone wanted housing, and there was obviously money to be made supplying it for seven or eight thousand foreigners who were not likely to complain if the materials were bad or the work was shoddy. Developers

—the French call them *promoteurs*—arrived in Dreux and opened offices and looked for local businessmen who were not too scrupulous about progress and could get them contracts with the government. Every available acre of land on the Plateaux and then in Vernouillet was cleared for projects. There was so much housing in Dreux in a few years that the developers began to advertise the town as a bedroom community for Paris—a good working-class address in the suburbs.

Dreux by then had a queer, lopsided look. The old town—with its little rivers and grassy squares and its houses edged in red, like the houses in a child's drawing—no longer faded into fields of cows. Dreux spread like a mini-megalopolis. Every HLM gave onto another HLM that was distinguishable mainly by the number of cracks in the concrete and the state of decrepitude and the lyrical name—La Croix Tiénac, Lièvre d'Or—that some *promoteur* had invented for it in a Paris office. The projects loomed over Dreux—although Dreux, by some quirk of geography, dipped in on itself like a shallow bowl and actually blocked its own view of the projects that dwarfed it. It was a symbol of the distance between the two Dreux that people up on the Plateaux could not see down into the old town, either. When *they* talked about old Dreux, as often as not they meant the old parts of the Plateaux —the long row of little villas, out on the edge of the ridge, where the Harkis could afford to live, because the Harkis had got the first, and best, jobs in the branch factories that opened here in the sixties, when the state was offering money to companies that "decentralized" by putting some of their operations in the provinces. The Harkis never got along with the other Algerians on the Plateaux. They were enemies in Algeria, and they were still enemies in Dreux, but by the time those other Algerians arrived there was no space left in Dreux for the Harkis to be alone. Dreux was a crowded town, and then a much too crowded town. The people who had bragged in 1973 that with a few more factories and a few thousand more immigrants Dreux would come into its own as a city, the equal of Chartres or Tours, had stopped bragging ten years later, by the time the vacuum-cleaner salesmen came.

By 1983, all the foreigners in Dreux were sensitive about status. Some of them—the majority—were officially immigrants, residents of France but citizens of Morocco, say, or Portugal, with none of the political rights of Frenchmen. Some of them were "French"—Harkis who had taken French nationality after the Algerian war, or immigrants who had applied for citizenship and got it, or immigrants' children who were born in France and were therefore French if they chose. Some were here illegally. Some had six-month visas. Some had residence visas that were good for years. The decisions that could send them home had been as arbitrary as the decisions that had let them into France in the first place. Immigrants lived, as Mitterrand's Minister for Social Affairs, Georgina Dufoix, put it, "with a suitcase in the head." They were not much soothed by the statistics about staying: officially, immigration had stopped with the oil crisis; officially, only political refugees and people like Aicha, with husbands or children in France, got in at all; officially, therefore, 80 percent of the immigrants had been in France for at least ten years and were unlikely ever to have to go. In 1973, 6.5 percent of the country's population was foreign. Ten years later, it was still only about 6.75—not really any change. Every year, about thirty thousand foreigners requested, and received, French citizenship. And, every year, about thirty or forty thousand foreigners requested, and were refused, permission to come, and about twelve thousand illegal or out-of-work immigrants were expelled. The fact that the legal status of immigrants was being "regularized" (the government's word) as a matter of Socialist Party policy did not mean that the psychology of immigrants was being regularized, or their privileges. There was still nothing to stop a worker from a Common Market country like Italy or Greece from coming to Dreux if he wanted to —except, of course, the fact that there were no jobs for him anymore. There were still special arrangements for workers from Francophone countries—in other words, old colonies—and even those arrangements varied from country to country, and sometimes from government to government. The immigrants felt vulnerable, and the old Drouais felt invaded. They felt particularly invaded by Arabs, like the Benamids, who accounted for more than half the immigrants in Dreux and as much "foreignness" as Dreux could tolerate.

Early in 1983, a group of conservative local politicians—perfectly ordinary politicians everyone in Dreux had known for years—formed a coalition with strangers from the Front National to take over the Mairie. Later that year, the town voted for the coalition. Françoise Gaspard was reelected to the town council, but the new mayor was one of those local conservatives who had come to terms with the Front National, and three of his eleven deputy mayors had run as Front National candidates. All told, there were now nine people from the Front National, either Party members or independents who had signed on for the elections, among Dreux's thirty-nine councillors—and only eight people from Mme Gaspard's old socialist government. Dreux was the only town in France to have given the Front National any official political power, and a lot of people explained it by saying that Dreux had collapsed under pressures that more properly belonged to Paris. By Paris, they meant housing projects and overpopulation and factories opening in good times and closing in bad times—times that had nothing to do with good or bad times as a Dreux merchant understood the words. By Paris, mainly, they meant foreigners.

Jean-Marie Le Pen's father was a fisherman. In 1942, a few years into the war, his boat was torpedoed a hundred miles from home (*"Mort pour la France,"* the Front National handouts say), and Le Pen was thus, at fourteen, a *"pupille de la Nation"*—a kind of honorary orphan, with France for his guardian. Le Pen himself was so enthusiastic about serving France that as soon as he finished school (he was in Paris at law school) he volunteered as an Army paratrooper in Indochina. A few years later, he was in Algeria. In July of 1984, *Le Canard Enchaîné* printed stories to the effect that Le Pen had tortured his prisoners in Algeria, and early in 1985 *Libération* reporters in Algiers found witnesses to back the stories up. Le Pen sued the two newspapers for defamation. He was so moved by memories of Algeria that at one hearing he told the judge, "I never had the authority to conduct interrogations. . . . If I had, I would certainly have conducted them." He lost the first round of the lawsuits: the judges said that inasmuch as he had often, and publicly, condoned the use of torture in the Algerian war, he could not reasonably claim to be dishonored by accusations that *he* had tortured. But then the Cour d'Appel judges disagreed. They said, in effect, that Le Pen had been dishonored—whether or not he approved of torture, and whether or not he himself had tortured anyone. They ordered the newspapers (along with a talk-show moderator who had repeated the torture stories and a journalist who had written about them in a book of "open letters" to France's presidential candidates) to pay damages and, in the case of the papers, to print the verdicts against them. Now the papers have filed their own appeal with the Cour de Cassation, which judges not the facts of a case but the use of the law —whether the law was properly interpreted and applied—and is as high in the French judicial system as they can go.

Le Pen likes to sue the people who criticize him. The Seventeenth Correctional Court at the Palais de Justice in Paris has had a full docket of Le Pen's lawsuits for so long now that reporters call it *la chambre Le Pen*. The judges complain to reporters about abuse if not of the law then of their own patience, but it does no good. Over the past few years, they have had to hear cases against smutty songs about Le Pen and talking Le Pen dolls with German accents (the dolls were called

Cocorico Boy) along with the cases against newspapers that suggest Le Pen start answering some of the accusations against him. When reporters visit Le Pen, he likes to remind them of all the libel cases he has won. Then he begins to talk. (At one interview, Le Pen kept a big children's globe beside him in his living room. The globe was sliced through the middle like a grapefruit, and from time to time he fiddled with it, as if he were turning on a tape recorder somewhere inside.) None of this has made for much carefree discussion of Le Pen in the French press. His own newspaper, a weekly called *National Hebdo*, deals almost entirely with his virtues. It covers his travels, for one thing, and in a memorable issue not long ago it took a couple of words between Le Pen and Pope John Paul II during one of the Pope's Wednesday-morning public audiences and turned them into a solemn meeting, referred to as *la rencontre*, at which the Pope entrusted Jean-Marie Le Pen with the future of Europe. (Le Pen and his group had stopped the Pope to say that they were fighting hard for Christianity in Europe, and the Pope said, in effect, that that was nice, that Jean-Marie Le Pen should keep on fighting.) Some of the more sensational papers that support him—the weekly *Minute* and a right-wing Catholic daily called *Présent* —deal almost entirely in accusations against his enemies. *Minute* is known for its cartoons of thick-lipped Africans and drooling Turks and Arabs with stubbly beards and enormous noses, which strongly resemble the caricatures of Jews that were a daily feature of the French Fascist press when Jean-Marie Le Pen became an honorary orphan. *Présent* is known for monitoring Justice Ministry lists of people who change their names (Mohammed to Moland, Ben Ahmed to Reinhardt, Boulalouad to de Coninck, Mahbouli to Michel), and for its chronicles of the lives of contemporary Jewish politicians—men and women like Simone Veil, who used to be president of the European Parliament, and Robert Badinter, who is the Justice Minister. "The only morality that traditionally has *droit de cité* in French politics is that Christian morality to which you, Madame, are so perfectly a stranger" is what *Présent* had to say about Mme Veil, who lost her mother at Auschwitz and nearly died there herself. As for M. Badinter, a well-known law professor and civil-rights lawyer who has just finished revising the French criminal code, "he is the very symbol of a France open to foreigners. His father was a furrier." Most of the Jews who are attacked like this are reluctant to give the publicity of a reply, let alone a day in the courtroom, to the people who attack them. Most of the immigrants have no way to reply, no knowledge of the defamation laws, and no money for lawyers with that knowledge. Some of them are simply frightened. Le Pen's friends do not take opposition lightly. Le Pen himself broke with every one of the groups he joined before he founded the Front National, in 1972. His wife, Pierrette, who left him in the spring and divorced him in the fall, uses the word "violent" when she describes him to reporters. Pierrette is a good-looking platinum blonde, who likes to be photographed in tight white jeans and high white spike-heeled boots, and she seems pretty tough herself. In an interview with *L'Événement du Jeudi*, she said that by the time she left Le Pen he was getting soft—not much different, to her mind, from Jacques Chirac or Raymond Barre or Valéry Giscard d'Estaing.

Le Pen's appeal may have to do with intimations of violence. It is not the cool, heel-clicking style of the commandant but something cruder, something at the edge of control—"a shrewd, smiling fury," one woman who heard him speak in Paris called it. Le Pen makes a great deal of what he calls his peasant pedigree. In fact, he looks like a peasant—a *gros paysan*. He is big, and he is overweight, with a baby face and pale-blue eyes and pale-blond hair that is turning white. He flaunts his weight like a weapon. His shirts pop open. His holiday snapshots have him windsurfing in a tight black rubber suit. Serge July, the editor of *Libération*, calls him a French Rambo. He wrote that Le Pen fascinates the French because, unlike the dry, aseptic politicans they are used to, "Le Pen smells of life—which is to say he smells of death, shit, and deals."

According to Alain Rollat, a reporter at *Le Monde* who has written two books about Le Pen and his politics, there are police reports from Le Pen's student days that have him brawling and drinking and resisting arrest—he was arrested twice—and in general making a nuisance of himself in the name of France. Le Pen's followers dismiss this. They blame Communists and foreigners for provoking him, and say that he was never as bad as any of the people he was taking on. They say that a little violence was normal in a young man—a *pupille de la Nation* —of Le Pen's ardent and injured patriotism. And, inasmuch as they consider *themselves* the ardent, injured majority in a false France, they enjoy the trouble he made, and continues to make, and the real fear he inspires. Le Pen is France without its civilizing hypocrisies, without the famous *pudeur* that usually mediates between the things Frenchmen feel like doing and the things they do. Le Pen is shameless. He is successful because he is shameless. He knows that millions of Frenchmen are frustrated, and that their frustration has something to do with a conviction that history has betrayed them—and he exploits that conviction. Twenty years ago, they believed they were losing their colonies not because the time of colonialism was over but because history was betraying them. Now they believe they have an immigrant problem not because they invited four million immigrants to France but because of history again. They believe that "history" is aggressive and foreign, just as they believe that "civilization" is French, and the reason they vote for Jean-Marie Le Pen is that Le Pen has told them that the defense of civilization against history is a holy war that Joan of Arc began—and that he will win. In fact, Le Pen has taken Joan of Arc out of the hagiography and made her his political property. Every May, on the anniversary of her burning, he leads a parade through Paris to her statue on the Place des Pyramides, and the fact that he makes an odd acolyte to the young saint who was filled with God and so fiercely delicate is evidently not important, because very few people have questioned his authority. Le Défilé Jeanne d'Arc is now announced all over Paris with posters to the effect that Jean-Marie Le Pen is fighting in the saint's name to keep France Catholic and pure and free of foreigners. As the lawyer Jean-Denis Bredin wrote in *Le Monde*—Bredin has published a book on the Dreyfus case, and he was talking about elections a hundred years ago and about a right wing that wanted to expel Jews—the French have always suspected that if it weren't for foreigners they would be *"au travail et en famille, prospères, tranquilles, heureux dans leur vieux jardin."*

Le Pen is rich. For years, he earned his living from a record company (producing what could be called music for the far right— Nazi songs, German marches—with a partner who used to be an officer in the Waffen-S.S.), but he got rich in 1976, when a cement millionaire named Hubert Lambert died of complications from cirrhosis and left Le Pen his fortune. Lambert was forty-two, and besides being an alcoholic and a pill addict and a patron of right-wing politicians he suffered from what was called delirium back in the days when lunatics from good families were (depending on their sex) either delirious or hysterical but never lunatic, and were kept at home in dark, hot bedrooms, looked after by their mothers, and calmed by doctors with odd degrees. In Hubert Lambert's case, it was not his mother but his friend Le Pen —who knew him from an old right-wing party called Le Front National pour l'Algérie Française—who took over his convalescence. What happened then depends on who tells the story (and many people have told it), but in the end Le Pen got four million dollars and Lambert's mansion in Saint-Cloud, which turned out to be called Montretout, or Show All. Montretout sits in a private park, guarded by Dobermans, and it is filled with large, gaudy objects with odd shapes and uncertain purposes, including a collection of iridescent rocks that climb the front staircase and seem to be sprinkled with golden makeup dust. It looks like the sort of place that people from the Front National describe when they talk about the houses rich Arabs like to own.

. Le Pen lives and works in Montretout now, with a couple of secretaries and servants and, occasionally, one of three blond daughters for company. (One of the Le Pen girls ran for the town council in Neuilly last year, but she lost. She had trouble remembering the name of Neuilly's main street, which is Avenue Charles de Gaulle, and when a reporter from *L'Événement du Jeudi* asked about her platform she said that she would have to look it up.) Le Pen parted with some of Lambert's money when a cousin who considered himself the rightful heir sued and Le Pen settled out of court. But he still has what amounts to two million dollars of the Lambert fortune, and the house is his, and the palms in the park and the sparkly rocks and the gilded objects that are really lamps and the children's globe. Lately, it seems, he may have come into another fortune—five hundred thousand dollars from an old Rumanian diplomat by the name of Gustave Pordea who defected a few years after the war and took out French citizenship in 1983, and, in 1984, wanted a place in Le Pen's delegation to the European Parliament. According to Jon Swain, who followed the story for *The Sunday Times,* the money came promptly, and in cash—Mme Le Pen says that she picked it up—and Gustave Pordea just as promptly turned up as the fourth name on the Front National's parliamentary list and got himself elected. *The Sunday Times* says that Pordea is really a Rumanian "secret agent," in place in France for forty years.

Montretout today is a hilltop bunker where the world is barred and megalomania can flourish. Pierrette Le Pen says that her husband promised her the Élysée as "a Paris pied-à-terre," and in all likelihood he did. There is nothing around Le Pen for contradiction or contrast. He has thrived on what the French call a *culte du personnage,* and now he depends on it. A lot of his old friends left the Front National last year, saying there was no "democracy" in the party. They wanted to be consulted about the party's election lists in their own departments, and when Le Pen wouldn't consult them they quit to join new parties —some joined a party that Le Pen's (and Lambert's) old doctor has put together for the National Assembly elections next month. In any case, there was no way for them to stay in the Front National once they had complained. Whenever anyone in the Front National complains, Le Pen prefers not having him around.

One of the reasons the Front National chose Dreux in 1983 was the Party Secretary. His name is Jean-Pierre Stirbois, and he was looking for a respectable home base, a base in the provinces, and had a vague connection with Dreux because his wife's parents owned a house in the country a few miles from town. Stirbois himself lived in Paris. His wife was in Paris, and his children were at school in Paris, and his printing business was in Paris, but he was nearly forty and wanted to get elected to something important—the National Assembly or, at least, the European Parliament—and, inasmuch as every time he ran he lost, it was decided that Stirbois needed that reassuring association with *la France profonde* which goes along with a desk in some provincial town hall. There was clearly something about Stirbois that did not appeal to Dreux. Only about thirteen hundred people had voted for him when he ran here—first in 1978, and again three years later—for the National Assembly. He did a lot better when he ran from Dreux in cantonal elections, in 1979 and 1981. But having lost four elections in as many years, he nearly gave up on Dreux. He went looking for his *France profonde* in Normandy, and settled on the town of Mantes-la-Jolie, thirty-seven miles out of Paris on the road to Rouen. Mantes rejected him so quickly that he came back to Dreux to try again.

By the end of 1982, Stirbois was a candidate for mayor of Dreux. The reporters arrived then, and the television crews, because people were curious about the town the Secretary of the Front National had adopted as his *France profonde,* and their curiosity gave Françoise Gaspard a chance to talk about a race problem and Stirbois a chance to exploit it. The politicians from Paris came, too, because the situation called for comment, and comment meant publicity. And the gangs came, though they were definitely not the famous *bandes de Dreux* —French or Arab. Actually, the one thing everybody in Dreux seems to agree on is that the strange young men who started to appear that winter were volunteers from the Front National. Mme Gaspard says they were paid volunteers, and even the old Drouais made jokes about the *interdits de séjour* finally having something to do. Stirbois set up an office, where he heard complaints from people who claimed to have been abused or attacked or insulted or robbed by immigrants. Housewives reenacted the crimes against them. Harkis came down from the Plateaux to talk about "the Algerian problem" as if all the revolutionaries of the FLN were now in Dreux, working at Radiotéchnique. The streets were patrolled at night by strangers "keeping the peace" that nobody until then had thought was gone.

The Front National had candidates in hundreds of municipal elections that year, but Dreux was different. It was different because Stirbois was running here. It was different because so many people were paying attention. Mainly, it was different because Stirbois and those respectable conservative Dreux politicians had put together a common list of candidates. The politicians came from a local branch of the Rassemblement pour la République, which is the big neo-Gaullist party and the political property, so to speak, of the mayor of Paris, Jacques Chirac. They were used to sharing their candidates' lists with other Dreux conservatives, like Jean Cauchon, but this time, when Cauchon told them that they would have to choose between his Christian Democratic Party—the Centre des Démocrates Sociaux—and the Front National, they chose the Front National. The senator never really recovered from the shock. "The shame of it, the shame!" he still says whenever he talks about it. "Thirty-six thousand cities in France, and we are the only one that made an alliance with the Front National!" Cauchon never expected the alliance to last. He assumed that Dreux's conservative list would end up looking pretty much the way it always had—except that he thought it was time for his son Yves, who was getting into politics, to take over his place on the town council. Cauchon had been talking about Yves with one of his old deputy mayors, Jean Hieaux, who usually ran for the council as an independent on the RPR ticket, and who wanted to be mayor himself. But while the two of them were negotiating their list Stirbois was negotiating his own list with another, younger RPR politician, René-Jean Fontanille, and in the end Fontanille persuaded the party that Stirbois was the profitable partner. Cauchon protested by telling Dreux exactly what he thought of Jean-Marie Le Pen and Jean-Pierre Stirbois and the Front National. Eventually, the government sent two riot policemen from the Compagnies Républicaines de Sécurité to guard the senator's house.

The right in Dreux split over the question of the Front National. It split gradually, because local elections in France always involve two rounds of voting. People run from their own party or in little coalitions of parties in the first round—and there is rarely a majority. Then, after all the favors have been traded and the arrangements made, they either drop out or attach themselves to one of the parties or coalitions that came in first or second—and there is a new round of voting, which amounts to a kind of playoff, with the winning party taking over the town council and its leader taking over the Mairie. What happened in Dreux was that by March 6, 1983, the day of the first round of voting, there were two conservative lists—one with Fontanille and Stirbois at the head of it, and the other with Yves Cauchon and a Giscardian from

the Union de la Démocratie Française—and by March 13, the second
round of voting, it was Fontanille and Stirbois against the Socialists.
The Socialists won that day by eight votes, but the opposition asked
for a recount, and in June the courts decided that, because of counting
errors, nobody had won in Dreux—and scheduled new elections for
September.

By then, there was so much tension in Dreux that Françoise Gaspard had given up and quit her job. She said she was quitting "to cool
the climate of racist hate" that the Front National had managed to
produce in Dreux with just a few months of threats and provocation
and propaganda. Later, she wrote that she had been threatened herself.
There were three-in-the-morning phone calls to her parents telling
them to buy a coffin. There were days when her tires were slashed,
nights, she said, when gunshots woke her. The night after the second
round of March voting, she spotted two thugs waiting in front of her
apartment. She turned her car around and fled to Paris, and that night
she decided she could not go on. She said that if she ran again the left
would lose in Dreux. She said she would be blamed, and maybe should
be blamed, because by then even her friends—not the old Drouais who
complained that in another ten years their mayor would be called
Hassan or Muhammad but people she knew and liked—were sick of
foreigners and of Françoise Gaspard talking about foreigners, and
wished that she would disappear. The rumors about Françoise Gaspard
were punishing. It was said that she had let a Moroccan murderer out
of prison; that she had given birth to a "dark" child and was keeping
it hidden somewhere in the country; that eight hundred Turkish fanatics were coming to live in Dreux at her invitation; that she was paving
Dreux's new pedestrian mall with human skin. It had got so bad, she
says, that she began to hate Dreux. She took to spending whatever time
she had at the house of her friend Mme Claude Servan-Schreiber, in a
village near Dreux, just to get away. Mme Servan-Schreiber is a journalist and a feminist—privileged in her life and unconventional in her
views. She founded the first important French feminist magazine, *F*,
and she adopted a Tahitian boy once her own children were grown.
She and Mme Gaspard decided that women and immigrants had a lot
in common. They began to write a book together about immigrants.

The Socialist who ran for mayor in Mme Gaspard's place that
September was a proper *petit bourgeois* with a little shoe factory, a
family life, a repertoire of platitudes, and nothing odd or intellectual
about him. He was easy to beat, and, to make sure that he was beaten,
the local Giscardians forgot their scruples about Stirbois and Le Pen

and added their candidates to the list with the Front National. They were not the only people to forget their scruples. That summer, Jean Cauchon's old friend Jean Hieaux negotiated his own peace with Stirbois. He replaced Fontanille at the head of what was now a decidedly right-wing list—which meant that Hieaux would be mayor of Dreux if the right won.

On September 11, after another two rounds of voting, the Socialists here were out of power; 6,404 Drouais—a little more than 55 percent of the voters—had voted against them. When the results were read, Françoise Gaspard said she was disgusted that in democratic France it took so little for racism to become legitimate. Jean Cauchon said that in his opinion the problem was not a Le Pen or a Stirbois but the responsible politicians, like Chirac and Giscard and the young conservative deputy François Léotard, who had convinced themselves that "Dreux is not France" and let Dreux happen. Stirbois himself said, "We are going to reduce and then eliminate, case by case, welfare for the immigrants here." And Jean Hieaux, who was the mayor of Dreux now, said, "C'est dingue! All this fuss over a little election." When he moved into the Mairie, he says, the concierge spat at him.

Jean Hieaux is a banker. His family opened a bank in Dreux in 1906, and now it is one of the important Dreux families—Catholic, conservative, stylish in the pleasant and predictable way of the provincial rich. The Hieaux are bankers to all the other old families here, just as Yves Cauchon is the lawyer. In 1934, Hieaux's father was at the center of an argument among those families which was not so different from the argument among them now; he had founded a regional chapter of the Croix de Feu—a new nationalist movement that included, along with patriotic Catholics like himself, militant reactionaries who talked about purifying France, and sometimes even about the purity of Joan of Arc, burning for the country. Hieaux himself is a Gaullist. He is quite precise, and likes to say that he has been a Gaullist since November 8, 1942, when he was eighteen and the Allies landed in North Africa and not one ship in the Vichy fleet moved out from Toulon to join them. Five years later, he ran for the Dreux town council. He was one of the youngest councillors in France, and he is right, in a way, when he says he grew up in the Dreux Mairie. He has been there, off and on, as a councillor or a deputy mayor, and now as mayor, for nearly forty years. He says that there were never "politics" at the Mairie until Françoise Gaspard and the Socialists got there. Getting rid of politics in the Dreux Mairie is his favorite excuse for having taken up with the Front National. It may be, as Jean Cauchon likes to say, that Hieaux is an honorable man but that he wanted to be mayor so badly and for so long that "getting rid of politics" finally came to mean ignoring the politics of anybody who could help him win. In the end, he seemed to forget that the Mairie was any different from the family bank. He talked as if he had no more reason to ask his running mates about their politics than he did to ask his clients; he talked as if looking into a politician's politics were indiscreet. To a successful banker in a small town, the important thing is solvency and discretion, and Hieaux—slim and silver-haired and beautifully dressed in suits that look as if an English tailor made them for him—ran his campaign like a banker, letting the Front National spread the rumors and collect the volunteers and do the dirty work.

"Politics are always a choice," Hieaux said long after the election. "The Socialists were a disaster here. We had a conservative list that had to be voted in, and we knew it, and if we could govern—we on the right, that is—only with the Front National, well, we were going to do it. Choices are not always ideal. The people who criticize—the people like Simone Veil and Lionel Jospin, who come to Dreux from Paris and listen to the immigrants—well, those people live like me. Even Françoise Gaspard lives like me. They see immigrants for the space of a debate, and then they go home and wash and say, 'We have been to Dreux and there is no problem.' I say let them spend three weeks in an HLM and try to sleep at night. Let them live with the piss in the elevators, with the noise, the smells, and then ask themselves, 'Is there a problem?' I look in the mirror and ask *myself*. Am I a racist? If saying that I don't like piss in the elevators makes me a racist, then, yes, I am a racist. Remember, the Front National had a list, and on the first round 16.5 percent of the people here voted for that list. If you don't accept the fact that those people have a legitimate right to be represented, then you don't accept democracy. I accept democracy. If Charles Fiterman were still the Minister of Transportation and made an official visit to Dreux, I would greet him. I would say, 'He is a Communist, and not my type of man, but he is a legitimate minister of the President of the Republic and I accept him.' Well, I have two legitimate deputy mayors from the Front National, and if you accept democracy you have to accept them, too."

Stirbois, of course, is one of those deputy mayors. He is in charge of "civil protection," which means that the forty-five Dreux firemen report to him, and that one afternoon a month anybody with a "security problem" or a "civil-defense problem" can see him at the Mairie, if the person calls ahead for an appointment and if Stirbois keeps the appointment. Unless there are elections going on, Stirbois is not around very much now that he belongs to Dreux and has the roots in the provinces he tried so hard to plant. His real office is in Paris, in a dingy building on the rue de Courcelles, and his real work is keeping the Party in line and the country convinced that immigrants are contaminating France. There is no Front National sign on the door. There is a company name on the mailbox, but nothing, really, to announce to strangers who is in that office. It may be that Stirbois is afraid of terrorists, because left-wing terrorists from Action Directe have made the Front National a target. (Last fall, Action Directe bombed three of Paris's radio and television buildings to keep Le Pen from appearing on a television talk show called *L'Heure de Vérité* and a radio program called *Face au Public.*) Or it may be that because Stirbois himself is furtive he enjoys this odd approximation of clandestinity—that he likes to think of the Front National as the guerrilla army of Le Pen's holy war, or of himself as a kind of plainclothes general, directing the liberation of France from foreigners from a couple of rooms in the middle of the Seventeenth Arrondissement. Not very much is known about Stirbois, beyond the fact that his father was a tinsmith and his mother was a goldsmith. He has a degree in marketing from the École des Cadres et du Commerce, and today he is the expert who thinks up ways to market the party. He seems to have distinguished himself as a student mainly by joining groups with names like Mouvement Solidariste Français at a time when most of the students in Paris were deciding between Mao and Trotsky. Otherwise, he is unnervingly colorless—a perfect foil for Le Pen's violent exhibitionism. Stirbois is small and dark and sort of shadowy. He insinuates where Le Pen threatens, and smirks where Le Pen shouts. He is indirect.

Jean-Pierre Dubreuil, who teaches English at the Lycée Rotrou, came to Dreux from Paris twenty years ago. He had finished the Sorbonne and married the maid in the *chambre de bonne* next to his own room on the rue François Premier—"We were a sixth-floor romance," as he explains it—and when the time came for a posting the Minister of Education told him to go to Dreux. Dubreuil is forty-eight now. He has three children and a house in a pretty little development in Vernouillet, and a garden where his wife plants pansies and tulips and petunias in neat circles around a red maple and some birches. For years, the house in Vernouillet was always open. Then it was robbed, and the neighbors shook their heads and said to the professor, "What did you expect, Dubreuil? With the kind of people you invite, you should be standing at the front door with a rifle." Most of Dubreuil's neighbors are French. By "the kind of people you invite" they meant foreigners and hippies and intellectuals who come from Paris to plan Nagasaki memorials and poetry readings and raise money for the Kanaks in New Caledonia. Actually, the neighbors are proud of their professor. He is the sort of teacher all Frenchmen know from the books they read as children and the movies they saw—the teacher who arrives one day in a small provincial town like Dreux, a nice young man with a new *licence* and a buoyant and infectious faith in education, and who stays to make that town his life and his passion. In twenty years, Jean-Pierre Dubreuil has made Dreux *his* life and *his* passion, and the brightest children here —the ones who stay on at the *lycée* for an extra year and prepare for university—have been his particular charge. It was his conviction that "*on se rencontre profondément*" in public school, that the *lycée*, like the Army, is one of the great democratic experiences in a Frenchman's life —a kind of liminal space in the patriotic geography, where divisions of class and wealth disappear and the children of the country get to know each other and themselves and share a clean, competitive identity that will send them out into the world on equal and companionable terms. It was a conviction he held as easily and cheerfully and unquestioningly as he helped with the gardening or drank his beer at the Tourniquet Café with the other teachers after school. It came from a republican vision. It was Dubreuil's legacy from 1789, and it had survived the Terror and the Empire and the Restoration and the wars France fought and the villains France produced. Dubreuil fully expected it to survive Le Pen and the Front National. It was not a question of ideology. It had to do with a pride and an optimism about what being French meant, or should or could mean. Dubreuil believed that the civilization of France was civilizing, and that the civilization of the French Repub- lic was particularly civilizing—a trust held by its teachers and belong- ing, by rights, to everybody here.

Dubreuil is a Dreux *personnage*, like Jean Cauchon or Françoise Gaspard. He is short and solid, with a trim gray beard and steel-rimmed glasses, and during the school year you can usually find him at noon at the Tourniquet, dressed in corduroy jeans, a down vest, and, if the weather is terrible outside, a navy knitted cap. Dubreuil is at ease in Dreux the way Françoise Gaspard never was at ease—despite the fact that she is the old Drouais and he is technically the stranger. His table at the Tourniquet is like the back porch of his house. People stop with their beer and sandwiches and coffee to talk to him and to each other. Something about his being there is reassuring.

The Tourniquet is a student hangout. It is an old café on a small
street in the middle of Dreux, with sawdust on tile floors, and cracked
marble tables, and a *patron* named Jacques Duval, who is known to be
"correct"—meaning that he does not discriminate between "French"
and "foreign" when kids get rough and he has to throw them out.
Duval is a Socialist. He sat for six years on Françoise Gaspard's town
council, and, in fact, was deputy mayor for civil protection—the job
that Stirbois has now. He has made his bar a lively, tolerant place, a
normal place for any other city, and it was probably inevitable that after
1983 the grownups here would start to use it more, as a kind of refuge
from the tension outside. Simone Liard, the town librarian, eats lunch
at the Tourniquet, and provides a commentary on life at the library
now that Dreux's deputy mayor for culture is a woman from the Front
National who keeps cancelling the town's subscriptions—*Le Canard
Enchaîné*, *Différences*, and *Sans Frontières* were the first to go—and is
talking about censoring the children's books. René Maltête eats at the
Tourniquet. Maltête is a photographer, and he is Dreux's bohemian and
its most original dissenter. Last winter, when the Mairie took back the
key to a city building where his club, Art en Dreux, had always had
its exhibitions, Maltête put on a pair of bathing trunks and waded
around in the Blaise until he found an empty house on the riverbank,
and then he squatted. A young Portuguese I'll call Marcio, who volunteers at one of the community centers, eats lunch at the Tourniquet,
and so does a Moroccan boy I'll call Driss, who works at another center
in town. Marcio and Driss have been friends since school. They go to
the movies together, and once they rode their motorbikes to Paris in
a "ride against racism." (French motorbikes run on a mixture of gas and
oil called gasoil, and the slogan for the ride was *"La France est comme
les mobilettes; il faut du mélange."*) But Marcio has the confidence that
comes from being Portuguese—not so "foreign"—and he complains
that the Moroccan boys he knows are "scared of politics." Driss says
that they are scared with reason. They are scared because a Moroccan
boy from La Croix Tiénac was badly beaten at a rally last year by
vigilantes who came at him with dogs and rubber clubs. They are
scared because the police in Morocco keep track of Moroccans who get
in trouble here, or get involved in politics, and have started seizing
passports when those Moroccans come home on vacation. They are
scared because there are Muslim fundamentalists—people the French
usually call *frères Musulmans*, whether or not they are formally connected to the fundamentalists of the Muslim Brotherhood—in Dreux
now, who feed on the fear and hatred on the Plateaux, and have "indoc-

trinations" for the men, the disappointed men like Benamid, and Koranic schools for the little boys, and lectures to tell the women to put their veils back on and, with them, the proper subservience. Driss says that by now a Muslim boy from a poor project like La Croix Tiénac or Les Chamards who heads for the Tourniquet after school with his French friends, or his Spanish or Portuguese friends, can count on trouble when he gets home. The *frères Musulmans* will come to his house and harangue him, and sometimes even threaten him. They have their holy war, just as Le Pen has his holy war, and suddenly, quickly, they have made it just as legitimate.

The principal at the Collège Pierre et Marie Curie, which is a middle school for about eight hundred children from the Plateaux, says that by now there are undoubtedly many of these little Koranic schools in the projects. Muslim boys are expected to show up for nine or ten hours of religious instruction every week. If they stay home, or their parents keep them home, the *frères Musulmans* come for them. If they still refuse to go, the *frères* beat them—and the authority of these fundamentalists is such that not many parents try to stop them. The children come to the Collège Pierre et Marie Curie exhausted, or they do not come at all. Immigrant children account for half the students at the school, and by now most of them—especially the Turkish boys and girls, whose circumstances are primitive—are at least a year behind for their ages, and the dropout rate is so high that fewer than half of them finish out their four years, and only a handful of those who do go down to Dreux and the Lycée Rotrou and Jean-Pierre Dubreuil's humane and civilizing lessons. The principal of the *collège*—his name is Jean-Paul Béguin—is exhausted himself. He came to Dreux from a cheerful school in Champagne where nearly everyone was French, never dreaming what the assignment would be. The tragedy, the teachers here told him, is that these children are becoming the foreigners of Le Pen's propaganda. They live in poverty. Often, their mothers are afraid to ask the Mairie for money for medicine or food—either because they are forbidden to go to town or because they believe that immigrants who complain will be turned out of their flats, or even sent home to Morocco or Algeria or Turkey, which are the countries most of the Muslim immigrants in Dreux come from—and so the children take drugs. The drugs of the poor in France, Béguin says, are glue and the ink in felt-tip pens. By the time the children get to school (if they get to school), they are sick and hungry and tired from their late nights *and* drugged. They begin to hang around in gangs—little *bandes de Dreux*. They steal, and they break things (the lights and switches and circuit breakers in the school are often broken), and when they fail a test, or get a detention for not doing homework, they take it as an attack on immigrants —as discrimination, which is what the *frères Musulmans* tell them it is. Then they are violent. The teachers despise them for it. And as for the Collège Pierre et Marie Curie, French schools are supposed to be serious places, and tend to look a little like penitentiaries in the best of circumstances. The Collège Pierre et Marie Curie is grim.

There used to be a lot of resistance among immigrants to the fundamentalists. Now they are part of the life of the housing projects. And, as Françoise Gaspard said about the Front National, all it took was a few months of provocation and propaganda. They soothe the humiliation of the immigrants with a kind of fanatical obliviousness. They have the energy of their cause, and they are filled with hatred. There are graffiti in Dreux—graffiti about Jews and about Mitterrand stealing from Arabs to give to Jews—as vile as anything Le Pen's people come up with about Arabs. Dubreuil once said that the Arabs always carried their politics to Dreux with them—like prayer rugs or teapots. The problem now is that their politics are so alarming. Bright young men like Driss, who hang out at the Tourniquet and try to avoid the madness on the Plateaux, would normally be in universities studying, but the nearest university—the one you can get to cheaply and quickly on a train—is the University of Paris, and the University of Paris is not "available" to Dreux as far as the government is concerned. Dreux is at the northern limit of an education district that includes the universities of Orléans and Tours, and there is no train from Dreux to either place. The young immigrants stay home until they earn enough to move to Paris on their own, or to commute with their own money —without the allowance they would automatically get if they went to Tours, say, 108 miles away. Driss wants very much to go to a university. He is twenty years old, and full of curiosity, but for now he is an *animateur*— a kind of social and sports director at the community center—and in all likelihood he will be an *animateur* in another five years. He does not spend much time anymore in the project where his parents live and everybody knows him. He tries to organize the Moroccans there whenever there is a march or a demonstration involving immigrants, but there is no community center for him in the project —nothing, really, to occupy him. With a community center, he says, he could do something useful. He could offer the kids in the project an alternative to the fundamentalists and their "voluntary" schools. The kids run wild there. When someone calls a meeting—the way a friend of Driss's did when he wanted to get a group of young Moroccans together for an "association against racism and for legal rights"—the police are there to break the meeting up and to take the name of whoever organized it. A few days later, he will have to answer for himself, like Driss's friend, at the commissariat.

The deputy mayor for culture, Mireille Brion, worked for a lawyer in Neuilly when Stirbois put her on his list for Dreux. She still lives in Neuilly, but she has an office at the Dreux Mairie, and after taking care of the library (she subscribed to *Le Figaro*'s weekend magazine with the money she saved by cancelling *Le Canard Enchaîné*) she decided to devote herself to the theater. She opened what could be called Dreux's theater season with a production of Henri de Montherlant's *Fils de Personne*, and sent out invitations from the Mairie on Front National stationery. One of the Tourniquet regulars who works at the Mairie discovered the stationery in Mme Brion's office and told the people at the café, and created such a scandal that even *Le Monde* sent a reporter to the opening. After that, the only plays Mme Brion put on were comedies. Then, last spring, she announced that she was bringing an important dramatization of Victor Hugo's *Le Dernier Jour d'un Condamné* to Dreux, and people at the Tourniquet were bewildered, because *Le Dernier Jour d'un Condammné* is France's most eloquent argument against capital punishment, and Mme Brion, like everybody else in the Front National, was campaigning to bring capital punishment back. Mme Brion, it turned out, had heard about the play, but mainly what she had heard was that it was a monologue—with only one actor to pay and not much in the way of a set and no orchestra —and would therefore fit right in with her policy of keeping the culture budget to a minimum. No one knows if she ever did read it, but, then, no one knows if she read Montherlant, who is a hero to the French right, either. Still, word went around Dreux—and especially around the local theater club—that anything Mme Brion produced should be boycotted. On the night of the performance, most of the seats at the theater were empty.

There is a club for everything in Dreux. Jacques Duval, from the Tourniquet, is president of something called Limonadiers à Dreux (Dreux Soda Jerks). René Maltête is the head of Art en Dreux. Dubreuil is president of the Cercle Laïque and was vice-president of the theater club, and he belongs to the art club, the documentary-film club, the chess club, the clubs that run Dreux's Fête de l'Amitié and its Fête sans Frontières, and a couple he can never remember (there are something like two hundred clubs to keep the Drouais busy) until he gets the bills for his yearly dues. These clubs are important in Dreux, if only because they provide people with a room where there are lights and conversation and a kind of gentleman's agreement against hatred. Hamid Benamid never goes to places like the Tourniquet—places where there are hot dogs and alcohol, and girls and boys who kiss across the marble tables and leave Benamid filled with shame—but he was still thinking about joining the theater club a year ago, which is when the *frères Musulmans* found him.

Early last year, a stranger—I will call him Sidi Omar—appeared at the gates of Benamid's factory at the end of the afternoon shift and sought him out, saying that he had been sent to Benamid with the word of God. Sidi Omar had just arrived in Dreux. He stalked the projects, bearded and glowering under a filthy white turban, on the lookout for little boys playing soccer during Koran reciting time or women in miniskirts or men with wine bottles in their coat pockets. He did not approve of plays unless they were the old ritual reenactments of the lives of Muslim saints, and he certainly did not approve of the sort of plays Professor Dubreuil put on when he was helping to run Théâtre en Dreux. Sidi Omar told Benamid that the arrival of the Front National in Dreux was a sign that the Europeans were coming out from under the cover of their treacherous "tolerance"—the tolerance with which they had weakened the faithful, using friendship and conversation and all the other soft European weapons—and were preparing to finish the faithful off. He said that this would happen unless Muslim men armed themselves with the hard weapon of rejection. He took Benamid's disappointments and froze them into a kind of furious calm.

Sidi Omar invited Benamid to talk about the Koran, and introduced him into a class for men that met on the nights Benamid would normally have been at home or playing chess with his friends. Benamid stopped playing chess, even on his lunch break. Instead, he tried to organize the men from his project to demand a special room for answering the muezzin's five daily calls to prayer. Last spring, there was a lot of discussion in Dreux about New Caledonia. The best baker in town invented a tasty cake and called it a Caldoche, after the pro-French party there. Housewives on the right bought the cake, and housewives on the left refused to buy it, and this meant that everyone in Dreux with a sweet tooth became an expert on an argument about independence in a French colony halfway around the world. People were so excited about New Caledonia that Dubreuil organized a discussion on the future of the islands at the Cercle Laïque. He invited a sociologist from Paris, a Kanak from New Caledonia, and a student from Dreux to debate before the discussion, and then he posted notices. There were notices around the Place du Marché and in front of the Cercle Laïque, on the rue du Commandant Beaurepaire, and one at the post office, which Benamid saw. A year earlier, he might have gone to the debate, because he was interested in the world, and because the Cercle Laïque was a place that genuinely welcomed immigrants, and gave people like Benamid a chance to get involved with the intellectual life of the town and to make French friends. But on the day of the debate Benamid's twins came home from school with two slices of Caldoche, and were spanked and sent to their rooms and told not to involve themselves in France's arguments. That night, while Dreux debated, Benamid went to Sidi Omar's rooms and read the Koran and listened to Sidi Omar's lesson, which had to do with the ignorance of Europeans who accused the faithful of being primitive or brutal whenever they cut off a robber's hand, because cutting off hands was a complicated—even a scholarly —application of Koranic law, and there were many criteria to apply, many formulas to follow. Cutting off hands was a question of crimes that only a holy man could interpret.

These days, Benamid spends his time with Sidi Omar or at home, supervising his wife and daughters in their radical new Islam, and serving tea and sweet Algerian cakes to his visitors. Sometimes, when he talks, there is some of the old ease and curiosity in his voice, and some of the actor's charm, but then he shifts, suddenly, into a mono-logue of opinions and explanations and exhortations which is really a kind of talking to himself—and it is the voice of a fanatic. It is the voice you hear on hijacking tapes and on "Christian" radio stations in Ne-braska and at Le Pen rallies where people stand and recite the litany about loving their daughters more than their nieces and their nieces more than their cousins and their cousins more than their neighbors —and France above all.

Carlos Guerreiro is a French citizen. He became a citizen in 1980, saying that he had spent the first twenty-three years of his life in Fascist Portugal and whatever debts he had to Portugal were paid. The loath-ing he has for Fascism is as strong today as it was on the day he fled Lisbon, after eight days of interrogation in a soundproofed room at secret-police headquarters, on the rua Maria Cardoza. His crime was collecting food money for the families of political prisoners who had been arrested at Beja, in 1962, trying to start the revolution that took another twelve years to accomplish. Guerreiro was a special immigrant. He was not one of the million peasants who found their way to France

from the Alentejo or the Trás-os-Montes looking for work—any sort
of work that would keep their families alive at home—but a young
Lisbon clerk who had finished the *liceu,* served in Angola, and was
making good money with an American engineering company. He led,
he says, *la vie nocturne* of a Lisbon bachelor. It never occurred to
Guerreiro, in those days before the police took him in, that he would
ever work with his hands in a factory in a French provincial town. His
own plans were to emigrate to Canada and work for an engineering
firm in Alberta. He had letters from his American company, and he was
confident of a good job and a good life in Canada, but leaving Portugal
the way he did—north and across the border into Spain and France,
without his letters—meant ending up as a refugee in Paris, waiting for
the papers that would let him continue. He found a room in Paris, and
a job unloading trucks at the markets in Les Halles, and eventually he
met a Portuguese student who sent him off to a café on the Avenue de
Wagram where there was a mason with a list of *patrons* who paid in
cash and were not fussy about work permits or residence cards so long
as the worker was cheap and cost them nothing in social security and
insurance and taxes. The first thing the mason said to Guerreiro was
"Show me your hands." Guerreiro had pale, smooth, office hands, and
seeing them, the mason shrugged and told him he was useless. But *he*
sent Guerreiro to Saint-François-Xavier, a church in a workers' quarter
near the Boulevard Bonnes Nouvelles which had Portuguese parishioners and a Portuguese Mass on Sundays and a Portuguese curé who was
a kind of employment agent for the neighborhood. The priest got
Guerreiro a job in Dreux.

By the time Guerreiro had all the papers he would need for a
Canadian visa, he was a janitor at Radiotéchnique, cleaning sewers, and
lived in a factory barracks with a lot of other Portuguese immigrants.
They were mainly Braga and Bragança peasants, and none of them
could really read or write, but they were kind to Guerreiro. They took
him to restaurants to eat, they took him to the movies, and whenever
he had nothing left they chipped in and gave him thirty francs for a
hot meal. The experience, he says, changed his life. "I was doing the
lowest work, the filthiest work. I didn't have much French, but I could
speak English and I could read and write and so I had a certain prestige,
you might say, among the Portuguese immigrants. Those immigrants,
those illiterate immigrants I looked down on—they saw that I had
never worked with my hands, that I didn't have the strength for it, and
so they did my work for me. What I really learned those first few years,
when I was learning to work with my hands, is that no matter what

a man *is* or *does* he has something to teach you, something true. I
learned that the peasant cleaning sewers can be just as good as the
professor. All my life, I had had this very Portuguese illusion about
class. I was a good bourgeois. A monsieur. I felt superior. But in France
I discovered that I was not a monsieur to the French, I was a *petit
bonhomme* cleaning sewers in a factory—and, I tell you, there are centuries of difference between the man I was then and the man I am now.
I began to believe in *liberté, égalité, fraternité.* I married a Frenchwoman. I made my home here. I decided to stay. I thought that if I
stayed perhaps I could do something to help the Portuguese here to live
better, the way they helped me."

Carlos Guerreiro has a better job now. He works for a charter-bus
company, and does its marketing and accounting, and sometimes translates for it, too. He has his own desk and his own phone—in fact, he
has his own office. Three thousand Portuguese in the Eure-et-Loir
think of him as their spokesman, and so do a lot of the other immigrants,
because he has put *their* clubs together with his own Portuguese Club
under an umbrella club called the Association des Associations Étrangères de Dreux—of which he is the president. He wants to see the kind
of solidarity among older immigrants that he sees among the young
immigrants who belong to the group called SOS-Racisme. Kids in
SOS-Racisme cover for one another in the courts and in the streets and
in their own high-school corridors and wear bright plastic badges
—an open hand with TOUCHE PAS À MON POTE (Don't touch my buddy)
written on it—and talk about France as a "Melting Pote." *Their* president is the son of a Frenchwoman from Alsace and a schoolteacher
from Martinique, which is a French Overseas Department. He is
French, of course, although the Front National would say "second-
generation immigrant." (Arab kids, if they were talking about themselves, would say *beur,* which is their argot for the same thing.) His
name is Harlem Désir, and he studied philosophy at the Sorbonne and
history at Paris XII. The reason he got involved in race politics had less
to do at first with his own dark skin than with something that happened
to a Senegalese friend of his called Diego. Diego was coming home
from school on the Métro one day when a Frenchwoman in the car
opened her pocketbook and decided that her wallet was gone. When
she cried out, everybody in the car turned and looked at Diego. They
looked at him as if it were perfectly reasonable to assume that, of all the
people in a subway car at rush hour, the only black man there was the
culprit—and they kept looking at him, even after the woman dug
around in her pocketbook and found the wallet under a handkerchief

and a compact. That night, about fifteen of Diego's friends were talking at a café in the Latin Quarter. As Harlem Désir tells the story, they listened to Diego and decided it was time to do something. Now, less than two years later, they have offices in Paris and Marseilles, three hundred chapters, seventeen lawyers, and two roving investigators, who travel around France looking into racism cases. When they need publicity, they have a rock concert. There were three hundred thousand boys and girls at the first big concert they put on—it was on the Place de la Concorde—and now they have Melting Pote concerts all the time. Their badges are so chic among the liberal bourgeoisie that the manager of a boutique in the Sixteenth called Désir's office and asked if they came in pink, because she thought it would be nice to have a basket of badges for customers to take home, and pink was her "color scheme."

There are obviously French students who agree with the American girl from Brown who went to the Concorde concert on a date and said afterward, "It was terrific, except for the Moroccans." There are problems about foreigners in SOS-Racisme itself—the Arabs argue with the Jews and the Marxists argue with the liberals over real and imagined politics in the organization. But it is still easier for students in Paris or Marseilles to find some common ground than it is for workers in Dreux, where there is inflation to worry about and unemployment to worry about, and even age to worry about, because age usually means that the prejudices and politics of your old country pull you. Children born in France usually end up thinking of themselves as French—which is why racism bewilders them. They think that way until they are rejected or abused into making a kind of psychological retreat or replying to hatred with hatred or, like Benamid's girls, getting indoctrinated with crazy simplicities. Guerreiro is sorry when Muslims like Benamid stop coming to meetings of the Association des Associations Étrangères, but there is nothing he can do about it. The message of the Front National is race. It is about the contamination of Europe by Arabs and Turks and Africans, and so the Portuguese, being European and Catholic, are really peripheral to the argument.

"I am frightened," Guerreiro says. "I am frightened that I will discover in France exactly what I left in Portugal twenty-two years ago. It is not so bad for the *real* immigrants—the ones who come for ten or fifteen years to earn some money and go home. The indifference of the French is not at the center of their lives. It is not so important. But the children—the children who are born in France and are going to stay here . . . How does a boy growing up in France feel when someone says to him 'Go home, Arab!' or 'Go home, dirty Porto!' and he knows that *this* is home, that France is where he lives?" Guerreiro has two children. They are still in school, and Guerreiro has bought a house for the family which is not much smaller than the Dubreuils' house; in fact, it sits about midway between the Dubreuils' and the Benamids' —literally between two worlds. The house is filled with carved-oak furniture and velvet armchairs, with heavy, reassuring things that cannot easily be moved away. From time to time, Guerreiro goes to the oak sideboard—a small, dark, gentle man with graying hair and a fondness for checked wool shirts that look like the shirts in an American country catalogue—and pours a glass of his best port and drinks a toast to Otelo Saraiva de Carvalho or one of the other heroes of the Portuguese revolution, but his heart and his politics are in unhappy Dreux. He thinks a lot about Françoise Gaspard lately, and sometimes has a glass for her. He is, he says, "a bad, macho Portuguese who had to learn that this *petite bonne femme* was better than any man I knew."

Carlos Guerreiro thinks the Socialists would be in the Mairie now if Françoise Gaspard had not collapsed from the attacks on her and the strain, and had run for mayor again when it was only a question of eight contested votes. He thinks that her popularity would have carried her, though other people here doubt it. In the Socialist Party, they say that Mme Gaspard inherited too many of Robespierre's uneasy principles and not enough of Danton's easy charm. She herself says she is a "Mauroy Socialist"—meaning Pierre Mauroy, who is a bluff and homely character, a leftist fantasy of *la France profonde*. Paris bewildered Mauroy when he was Prime Minister. He was always getting into trouble, always saying what he thought (or not knowing what he thought), always covering for the President and getting the blame when things went wrong but never getting the credit when things went better. Mme Gaspard seems much closer in character to her friends from CERES—like Jean-Pierre Chevènement, the Minister of Education—who know what is good for "the people," and rarely get confused listening for what the people want. She is still incongruous in Dreux, the way the flat she keeps in the middle of town is incongruous, with its white walls and leather couches and shiny steel and glass and plastic surfaces. The old Drouais with leftist sentiments usually live in a more confident kind of eccentricity, with shabby couches, and animals all over the house, and ancient water closets that are sometimes across a courtyard from the kitchen. They are people like Odette Husson—pleasantly distracted and the wife of the biggest insurance agent in town—who believe in the Third World and solicit "sister cities" for exchanges and are always rushing around with delegations from Todi and cooking lunch for tours from Koudougou. Or they are anxious provincial intellectuals, like Gilbert Stenfort, who teaches at the Collège Pierre et Marie Curie and talks about noble Scots ancestors who came to France during the Revolution and ended up as *libres-penseurs*, involved with ornithology and Montessori schools and sculpture, but always had pious Catholic wives to choose the silver and raise the children. They are not really very different from the old Drouais with Christian sentiments, like Jean Cauchon, whose own wife goes off to Senegal on occasion to commune with the natives, and whose youngest daughter is a reporter in Cayenne.

The fact that Françoise Gaspard *is* different is the excuse the politicians used when they let Dreux down. It took two years and, in the course of those years, a round of cantonal and European Parliament elections for them to begin to understand that when Jean Cauchon said, "Dreux is broken, and I don't know how we can put it together again," he could have been talking about France, too. Now, of course, everybody in France is talking about France, and Dreux is less a scandal from 1983 than an object lesson for 1986. Since Dreux, ten people from the Front National, including Le Pen and Stirbois, have been elected to the European Parliament. (They are part of a sixteen-member bloc that includes the Italian Social Movement and the Greek National Front, and calls itself the Group of the European Right.) In all likelihood, some of them will be sitting in the French National Assembly before this spring is over. If they are, it will be because a significant number of men and women now believe that immigrants are at the heart of France's problems. Mitterrand, talking about Dreux, remarked that there were only 150 more immigrants in town when Françoise Gaspard quit than there were in 1981, when the Socialists took over the Assembly. He said that immigration was not something the Socialists invented, and that anyway, with all the talk about French identity and about what being French meant, it would be well to remember that in France "if I go to your house, if anybody goes to your house and you let him in, especially if it is someone you invited, usually you say to him, 'Dear Friend, dear Monsieur, or dear Madame, you are here at my house—my house is yours.' This is *French* politesse. This has been the *French* way to behave for a very long time."

The French are paying less attention to politesse lately. The fact that Dreux is calm—whether from fear or resignation, or even contentment—means mainly that racism is a little more respectable in Dreux than it was three years ago. This winter, Jean Hieaux invited some Paris journalists to Dreux for a kind of progress report on life with the Front National, and the journalists reported that Dreux was boring. They said that nothing was happening. The point, of course, is that nothing *is* happening in Dreux. Whatever spirit the town once had is dying. Its arguments about race are old news. *Le Figaro*'s magazine published an issue on race this winter with a veiled, Arab Marianne on the cover and a lot of fancy graphs and statistics about immigrants, and predictions —they were made by a "humanity expert" named Jean Raspail and confirmed by the head of something called the Institute for Political Demography—to the effect that in thirty years about 17 percent of France, or ten and a half million people, will be "non-European foreigners," and that most of those foreigners will be Arabs and Turks, producing dark little French citizens at the rate of more than 275,000 babies a year. The magazine is run by a onetime necromancer named Louis Pauwels, but *Le Figaro* itself is probably the most powerful French paper after *Le Monde*. Thousands of people who read *Le Figaro* before it changed hands, in 1975—who read it when it was a perfectly respectable conservative paper, with Raymond Aron for a columnist —still read it, as much from habit as from politics. They are much less wary of its graphs and figures than they would be if they came upon a "demographic study" in one of the more notorious right-wing papers like *Présent*. They read the statistics about immigrants draining France of its social-security reserves, and those statistics are so persuasive that the official ones—immigrants contribute about 7 percent of the welfare budget in France and take back about 6 percent in benefits—go ignored or unknown or discounted. They absorb the fear about immigrants. And, quietly, racism stops being a question of a few murders in the south or of the southern cafés that have put up signs saying NORTH AFRICANS NOT SERVED. It is a question now of mild and thoughtful people, like the professor from Nanterre who was mugged on the subway platform at Châtelet by two young blacks in Rastafarian getups and now "assists," as he puts it, "at incidents of retaliation."

The fact is that today much of the crime in France does involve immigrants. There are places like the Plateaux in nearly every city, and children in them drop out of school and hang around waiting for something to happen, and when nothing happens they go downtown and get stoned and end up in the Métro harassing university professors who go home saying that maybe Jean-Marie Le Pen is not so bad after all—that he is *brute* and exaggerates but maybe there is some truth in his misguided patriotism. Not long ago in France, race was the obsession of a few certifiable reactionaries, like the writer André Figueras, who went to a rally one day and announced that France was "under the eye of the barbarians," and that immigrants were "reproducing like rabbits" and would continue reproducing like rabbits until there was a Muslim President of the French Republic. Today, it is everybody's obsession. Politicians like Alain Peyrefitte, who was Giscard's Minister of Justice, argue publicly against the immigrants (Peyrefitte was debating with Harlem Désir), and say that every time an immigrant gets a job a Frenchman is deprived of his livelihood. No one listening is surprised.

There is a lot of talk right now about "the Dreux model." People are wondering whether the big conservative parties will do what they did in Dreux and include the Front National in a coalition of the right if that is the only way they can take over the National Assembly next month and force Mitterrand to resign—or, at least, as the French now put it, to "cohabit." Mitterrand changed the Assembly election laws last year—it was the tenth time someone had changed them since the French started voting for a National Assembly, in 1791. He had talked for years about doing it, because officially the Socialist Party never accepted de Gaulle's Fifth Republic formula for French national elections—which was really a version of the old municipal system, and had two rounds of voting, with the majority candidate in each election district taking the Assembly seat. But the truth is that many Socialists preferred de Gaulle's formula to any of the old ones, which involved various complicated attempts at proportional representation and were associated with most of the chaos and collapses during the Third and Fourth Republics. Some Socialists even believed that the system was a stroke of genius. They said that it was typical of the General, who understood the French so well and suspected that if he gave them a chance to vote noisily from their ideologies the first time around they would vote quietly, and thoughtfully, from their common sense, when it was important—that is, when it was a question of supporting *him*. Mitterrand himself was happy enough with the old formula while he was certain of his majority. He had the same imperial ideas about the Presidency that de Gaulle had (around the Élysée, people call Mitterrand "the Emperor"), and he was in no hurry to make the kinds of changes that would leave him with a divided and disputatious legislature and a dozen parties arranging and rearranging their relations at his expense. He changed the voting laws because the country began to change and the polls he ordered told him that, while he was likely to lose the Assembly anyway, he would lose "less" under a proportional system of voting. He knew that a divided and disputatious Assembly would have to cohabit in a government of *his* choosing, whereas an Assembly clearly controlled by the two big parties of the right could reasonably expect to cohabit in a government *they* chose—that is, if they agreed to live with Mitterrand at all. There is no one in the Assembly now from the Front National. The old system pretty much precluded it, and then, too, the last national elections were in 1981, and no one on the right in 1981 would have dared to present a list with Front National candidates. But the European Parliament has always been a proportionally elected parliament, and the fact that there are ten Front National deputies in Strasbourg now (out of a total French delegation of eighty-one) means that more than two million Frenchmen, or 11 percent of the country's voters, voted for Le Pen and his party less than two years ago. If 11 percent of the voters in France vote for the Front National next month, Le Pen could have as many as forty seats in the National Assembly.

A lot of people hold François Mitterrand responsible for this. Michel Rocard, who was his Agriculture Minister, quit the government last year, saying that Mitterrand's new election laws were cynical and irresponsible, and meant, sadly, that for the sake of a few more Socialist seats a Socialist President of France was willing to give Jean-Marie Le Pen and his friends the sort of political power they had not been permitted to have for thirty years. Then Chirac and Giscard hurried to assure the country that *they* would never make a deal with the Front National—even if not making a deal cost them the government. They did what they had neglected to do in Dreux three years ago: they forbade their local party leaders to deal directly with the Front National, either. The commotion that followed gave Jean Hieaux his moment. He was shocked at Mitterrand, he said. He was scandalized by the compromise of France that Mitterrand had made. "Blame Mitterrand," he said whenever you asked about Dreux, or about the problems in Dreux. "Mitterrand looked around and said, '*Voilà!* I have to have this proportional vote to divide the right, because otherwise the right will win the elections.' Mitterrand tells everyone, 'Look at Dreux, look at what Jean Hieaux has done to Dreux.' But I say, 'Look at France, look at what François Mitterrand has done to France.' There will be Front National deputies in the National Assembly, and it will be Mitterrand who has put them there—Mitterrand, who talks about Dreux and blames me."

Hieaux is much more confident these days. He is unctuous and debonair, and he has found a theme for himself, which is that in life most people are simply not very understanding. ("Instead of dreaming, isn't it better to admit that man is not naturally tolerant, that he doesn't like things that annoy him?" the mayor of Dreux wrote to the Catholic newspaper *La Croix*. "Noise, old people, people with long hair, people with short hair, children.") He talks about Françoise Gaspard now as "a little woman who wanted to climb too fast too far," and who took up immigrants because she needed what he refers to, smiling, as "political virginity." He talks about Stirbois as if Stirbois were somebody he never saw, not even at the monthly meetings of the town council —which have actually got so heated that three hundred people come for the spectacle and talk about how the Mairie is "the only theater in town." Stirbois has even taken Hieaux to task for something having to do with budget appropriations for immigrants; it gave Hieaux a new cachet and put him back in the good company of people like Jean Cauchon, whom Stirbois sued after the old senator went on Radio Luxembourg and called him a racist. When *Le Monde* put out a supplement on immigration—the headline was DREUX SYMBOLE, DREUX CALMÉE, DREUX MÉFIANTE—Hieaux was asked to make a statement. He said, "Peace has arrived."

There are polls saying that 600 of the 1,750 people who voted Front National in the first round of Dreux's elections in September of 1983 were people who had voted Socialist before, and this may explain something of how Dreux managed to survive three years with Stirbois as a deputy mayor and eight of his friends as town councillors. The town seems to have accepted its arrangement with the Front National. Stirbois is not running from the department in the Assembly elections next month (he is running from the Hauts-de-Seine, next door), but his wife, Marie-France, is running here, and the Giscardians and Chiraciens have put together a department list headed by an old Paris councillor named Michel Junot, who is best known as Caroline of Monaco's ex-father-in-law, and who belongs to a little party much closer to the Front National than to either of theirs. Françoise Gaspard is running for the Socialists, but she is second on the Socialist list for the Eure-et-Loir—after the mayor of Chartres—and this means that she will get to keep her seat in the Assembly only if the party wins at least two of the department's four seats. A lot of the old Drouais have either forgotten what happened to Mme Gaspard in 1983 or got used to it, or decided that it was not so terrible after all. Now that the elections are coming and the politicians are back in Dreux, there is some of the tension of 1983, but people talk about tension now as if it were a fact of life, and life goes on here. It is usually only strangers who remark on how odd it is—even for the provinces—to be in a city that shuts its doors so resolutely. Every now and then, Jean-Pierre Dubreuil tells his students to write their weekly essay on the subject of immigrants. One of them began this way: *"L'inconnu fait peur."*

February 1986

KURT WALDHEIM

Austria's affair with Kurt Waldheim is a little like the affair between the French diplomat and the Chinese tenor who have just been sent to prison in Paris for spying. The tenor, Shi Peipu, was a secret agent who liked to dress up in his courtesan's robes from the Peking Opera. He put them on one day for a party at the French Embassy, seduced the diplomat, whose name was Bernard Boursicot, and began a romance that went on for twenty years—providing China with a lot of interesting information from the Embassy's diplomatic pouch. The odd thing about Shi Peipu is not that he spied but that for twenty years he kept his lover convinced he was a woman (only "very modest"), and that M. Boursicot went to prison refusing, really, to change his mind. The odd thing about Kurt Waldheim is not his war file or the Nazi clubs he joined as a student but the fact that for forty years he dressed up in patriot's clothes, invented a past for decoration, and seduced Austria, and now Austria would rather defend those inventions than discuss its own interest in maintaining them.

A diplomat in Vienna with a clearer head than M. Boursicot's said the other day that postwar Austria is like an opera sung by the understudies, and there is some truth to the observation. There have not been many people of stature in Austria since the war. There have been people like Kurt Waldheim, pretending to stature, and there has been a public anxious to believe in them. Vienna is probably the only European capital where it is considered normal, among the intelligentsia, to be a monarchist. It is not that the Viennese miss the Hapsburgs—though there are certainly people who do miss the Hapsburgs. The Viennese miss the city they had when the Hapsburgs were around.

They miss what they call the thickness of culture. They may not know it, but they miss the Czechs and the Hungarians and the Jews who lived in Vienna with them. They miss the "joyous apocalypse" of art and design and thought which produced the work that is making the museum rounds—the Wien Künstlerhaus, the Centre Pompidou, the Museum of Modern Art—in various versions of the *fin de siècle* Vienna show at the last Venice Biennale. Vienna itself has been returned to the natives, and it is a provincial place, a kind of imperial ghost town. It is beautiful and full of charm, but the nostalgia is so desperate, and so deep, that it seems to have exhausted the Viennese. They long for prominence. Kurt Waldheim lied about a past that included three years of devoted service to a Nazi general who was hanged for war crimes when the war was over, but the Austrians elected him President this month, and the reason they did may have less to do with Nazi stirrings or anti-Semitism, or even stubbornness, than with the indisputable fact that Waldheim is prominent—by which they mean that people who are not Austrians recognize his name. Waldheim was Secretary-General of the United Nations from 1972 until 1982, and Austrians—nearly 54 percent of them, anyway—do not much care that he was a terrible Secretary-General for every one of those years, that he was greedy and cowardly and vain and laughably ambitious, or that he wanted to stay and was defeated, or that he tried to leave New York with the residence furniture and did, in fact, manage to leave with the silver. At home, he has let it be known that he ran the world from his United Nations suite, and by and large the people at home believe him. How he ran the world is not important. What is important is that the world was run by an Austrian.

The irony, of course, is that the rhetoric has been so xenophobic. Waldheim's posters said things like "We Austrians Will Vote for Whom We Want!" (Originally, the posters said *"Jetzt Erst Recht!"* and had a yellow stripe, but they were taken down when somebody pointed out that Hitler had used the same stripe and the same slogan on *his* posters.) Waldheim's managers talked about a conspiracy of Americans and Israelis and the World Jewish Congress, despite the fact that research into Waldheim's past had already been going on for months in Austria, and by Austrians, by the time the World Jewish Congress got involved. Voting for Waldheim, people said, was "voting for Austria." All the same, the poster everybody liked, the poster Waldheim always signed for the children, was not the one with the Alps in the background or the one with Frau Waldheim in a dirndl—it was the poster of Kurt Waldheim and the Manhattan skyline, the one signifying his celebrity. Austrians feel about Kurt Waldheim the way they feel about Gerhard Berger, who races in the Grand Prix in Monaco and talks to Princess Caroline and Princess Stephanie. He is an Austrian who made good away from home.

This much is known about Kurt Waldheim's career. He was always adaptable in his own interests. It was said to be a family virtue (the family name, Watzlawik, became a properly German "Waldheim" when German names got to be more desirable than Slavic ones), although Waldheim's father, Walter, was notably unadaptable. He was an admirer of Engelbert Dollfuss, the Catholic Fascist who ran the country for two years in the 1930s, abolished Austrian democracy, and was assassinated by Nazis. When the Nazis took over, Walter Waldheim lost his job. There is a report on young Kurt Waldheim from the Nazi leader in his home town, Tulln, about fifteen miles from Vienna, which says that before the Anschluss Waldheim was a diligent Catholic who opposed National Socialism in a "disgusting" way—he had stood on street corners handing out leaflets that said "Vote Austria, Not Nazi"—but that after the Anschluss he was a diligent soldier of the Reich and "served us well." In fact, two weeks after the Anschluss Waldheim joined the Nazi Student Union. One week after Kristallnacht, he joined a cavalry unit of the Storm Troopers—in German, the Sturmabteilung, or S.A. The Storm Troopers had made a name for themselves in Vienna on Kristallnacht, burning synagogues, but Waldheim seems to have joined because their riding club was a place where a young Austrian starting out on a law career would make the best contacts. He lived his whole life in the same spirit. When it was time to marry, he chose a girl, Elisabeth Ritschel, who held the right new National Socialist views, and had joined the Nazi Party as soon as she was eighteen. When it was time to write his law-school thesis, he chose for a subject a German nationalist named Konstantin Frantz, whose concept of the Reich, Waldheim said, had finally been realized in the "current great conflict . . . with the non-European world." Two years into the war, he got himself attached to the staff of the German High Command for the Balkans, under General Alexander Löhr, and that was a job with so many contacts that Waldheim ended up with a King Zvonimir medal from the Croatian puppet state. He also ended up as Case No. R/N/684 in the United Nations War Crimes Commission file, charged with "murder" and with "putting hostages to death." Officially, he was a translator, an interpreter, and a "special missions staff officer." His job involved verifying and transmitting special orders, and, eventually, recommending on those orders and making suggestions of his own. He was in Greece for the High Command when forty-eight thousand Jews from Salonika and Corfu were rounded up and sent to Auschwitz and Bergen-Belsen. He was there, after the Italian surrender, when a hundred thousand Italian soldiers who were left in the country were seized and deported to German camps. He was in Yugoslavia for the High Command when massacres of thousands of partisans and their families took place. As far as the record goes, Waldheim never murdered anyone himself or personally "put to death" any hostage. "I only did my duty," he says now. He initialled the orders that crossed his desk and the reports that those orders had been carried out, and sometimes he wrote the reports himself and kept the staff logbook. When the war was over, he walked into the Foreign Office in occupied Vienna and asked for a job. He carried three letters in his pocket—one from Tulln's leading Socialist, one from Tulln's leading Catholic, and one from the mayor. All the letters said what a good patriot Kurt Waldheim was.

No one knows when Waldheim actually began to reinvent his war —when he started saying that he was medically discharged from the Wehrmacht in December of 1941, after a grenade splintered in his ankle (the wound is real) on the Russian front, and spent the rest of the war with his law books in Vienna. Every Austrian with a connection to the Nazi Party had to fill out a "de-Nazification" questionnaire by the end of January 1946. Waldheim, answering his, listed his membership in a National Socialist "riding club" (but not the S.A. Reiterei) and not much else. He was never formally "de-Nazified." His file went to the Justice Ministry and then the Foreign Ministry, and in the confusion it was never closed.

There were half a million Austrian Nazis—more Nazis, proportionally, than in Germany—and a million Austrians in the German Army, and many of them had records worse than Kurt Waldheim's. What makes Kurt Waldheim exceptional is not his record but the trouble he took to erase it. There was no shame in Austria in having been a soldier. In 1943, in Moscow, the Allies had signed a declaration to the effect that Austria was not a Nazi state but Nazism's first victim, and after the war this was how Austria chose to see itself. So many Austrians had joined the Nazi Party for cover or protection that it was easy for people who had joined in weakness or terror, or even out of enthusiasm or ideology, to begin to believe the same of themselves. Of course, the real victims of Nazism were not around to contradict them. A hundred and ten thousand Austrians (sixty thousand of them Jews)

died in the course of the war in concentration camps. As for the Jews
—there were 189,000 Jews in Vienna in 1938; when the war ended, there
were 600.

The first accusations of any importance against Kurt Waldheim
were made in 1947, in Yugoslavia, by a Wehrmacht captain named
Karl-Heinz Egberts-Hilker, who was on trial for his life and was later
hanged as a war criminal. Egberts-Hilker tried to implicate Waldheim
as the responsible officer in a series of reprisal murders in Macedonia
in October of 1944 (three villages were burned, 114 villagers were
killed), and those murders were the basis of the dossier the Yugoslavs
passed on to the United Nations War Crimes Commission that year,
with testimony from a German Army clerk and a recommendation that
Waldheim be placed on an international "search list," arrested, and
extradited to Yugoslavia for trial. The recommendation was disre-
garded—either intentionally or for lack of evidence or because there
were more than thirty-six thousand war-crimes dossiers on file at the
United Nations then, and no way they could all be processed. When
the commission disbanded, in 1948, every member state got an index of
those thirty-six thousand dossiers, but Austria was not a member in
1948. Austria joined the United Nations in 1955, after the occupation
ended, and by then Kurt Waldheim was well along in his career in the
Foreign Service. He served under four Foreign Ministers before he got
the job himself, in 1968. The first was Karl Gruber, who had led the
Austrian resistance. Gruber had brought his friends from the resistance
into the Ministry with him, and one of them, his secretary, was a young
man named Fritz Molden, who had been the liaison between the Austrian underground and the Allies—and who spoke in Waldheim's defense during the campaign this spring. Molden still remembers the day
in November of 1945 that Waldheim walked into his office in the
Foreign Ministry, looking, Waldheim said, for personnel. The two
men started talking, and Molden says that it seemed to him that Waldheim, with his law degree and his "clean" war, would make a good
diplomat. That day, he recommended the young lawyer with the bad
ankle to Karl Gruber. Gruber hired him—conditionally. There were
rumors about Waldheim in Vienna, and Gruber had Molden check
those rumors with the political police and then with the Interior Minister, an old Socialist named Oskar Helmer, and finally with the Allied
Counter Intelligence Corps and the Office of Strategic Services. In ten
days, he had clearance from them all.

Waldheim was twenty-seven and useful, and, whatever the rumors were, most people figured that he was at worst an accomplice, the way so many Austrians had been accomplices. "He was no hero," Molden says now. It is easy to understand why Austria did not pursue him. The politicians of the Great Coalition, as the postwar government was called, were Socialists, Communists, and Catholics from the Volkspartei—the People's Party—and they had either been in the Resistance together or in Dachau together. But the people who did the voting were mostly former Wehrmacht soldiers and their families, and by the end of 1949 five hundred thousand ex-Nazis (nearly a tenth of Austria) were eligible to vote, too. The official story was that every old Nazi was a potential democrat, the way every soldier of the Third Reich was an Austrian patriot liberated by Hitler's defeat. Just about every young man in Austria who was not demonstrably a war hero or a war criminal had doctored his record in some way and arranged his protection, or was arranging it. Some people think that Waldheim may have arranged *his* by informing. He was, by all accounts, as pliant at the Foreign Ministry as he was at the United Nations—doing favors, currying favor, careful never to take a moral stand or, indeed, any stand that could isolate him or make him unpopular. Certainly the Yugoslavs never pursued their charges against him. None of the Allies seem to have looked him up officially until he was elected Secretary-General, in 1971, and then they either ignored the reports they got or used them for the Secretary-General's friendship. There are stories that he was an agent of influence, early on, for Yugoslavia. There are also stories that he was an agent for Russia and its allies, because the Russians backed him at the United Nations right off, vetoing the Finnish delegate Max Jakobson and campaigning against other candidates who were more impressive than Waldheim. He was the Austrian Foreign Minister when Russia invaded Czechoslovakia in August of 1968, and it obviously suited the Russians that he ordered the Embassy in Prague closed to everyone except Austrian citizens. (Waldheim's ambassador in Prague happens to have been Rudolf Kirchschläger, the President he is succeeding now. Kirchschläger ignored him and kept the Embassy open anyway.) But if Waldheim was an agent of influence for the Yugoslavs and the Russians, the chances are that he was also an agent for the Americans and the British and the French and just about everybody else with access to his file, including, in time, the Austrians. The curriculum vitae he gave to Fritz Molden late in 1945 lists his military service in the Balkans. Supposedly, no one outside the Foreign Ministry ever saw it until it turned up a couple of months ago—to great fanfare at Waldheim headquarters—as proof that he had always been an honest (if not an honorable) man. The fact remains that people in the Ministry saw it, or could have seen it, and not only did they give him a job—they never corrected his public story. There is no mention of the war at all in the vita that Austria sent to the United Nations in 1971 to support his candidacy.

It seems now that Tito may have known about Waldheim, and chose to use him. (Tito's old Vice-President, Mitja Ribicic, thinks so.) The dossier that left Belgrade for the United Nations War Crimes Commission in February of 1947 said that Waldheim was a fugitive, but not that he was a fugitive in Vienna, or that he was working, as he was by then, as a special assistant to the Austrian Foreign Minister— although the Yugoslavs knew exactly where he was and what he was doing. They told their ambassador in London in a cover letter that left Belgrade at the same time. The point is that since the war there have been people in high places who knew or could have known that Kurt Waldheim was an intelligence officer for a war criminal, charged with transmitting requests and permissions involving reprisals and deportations and civilian murders, and that every one of them ignored or suppressed the information he had, figuring either that it was harmless or hurtful or useful or even profitable to himself. Waldheim was obviously not a spy, a Shi Peipu in a three-piece suit, any more than he was, technically speaking, a murderer. It was simply that his secret made him obliging. Israel Singer, the secretary-general of the World Jewish Congress, says that Kurt Waldheim is like the girl who takes a quarter here, a quarter there, and builds a clientele that way—with two-bit favors that add up to a lot of time in bed.

All of Austria knows there is a World Jewish Congress. Ever since February, when the Congress hired a historian from the University of South Carolina named Robert Herzstein to trace Kurt Waldheim's war by going to the National Archives and looking for every piece of paper that Waldheim signed or initialled as a "special missions staff officer" for General Löhr, the World Jewish Congress has had the peculiar status of a great enemy power. Quite a few other people have been tracing Waldheim's war—most notably a young reporter named Hubertus Czernin, who works for the Vienna newsweekly *Profil* and who started to investigate Waldheim, and the charges against him, late last winter. But the Congress is, so to speak, the enemy of choice. It is not that Austrians have any idea of what the World Jewish Congress is or whom it represents or who supports it. (It is a kind of umbrella organization, with headquarters in New York, which looks after the interests of Jewish communities in seventy countries. A lot of its support came from the Zionist Nahum Goldmann, who helped to found it in 1936, and, recently, from Edgar Bronfman, the Seagram's heir.) The problem, as one Vienna psychoanalyst put it, is that World Jewish Congress "sounds Jewish."

Waldheim himself is not known as an anti-Semite. He seems to have initialled away the lives of Serbian partisans as easily as he initialled the transit orders for Greek Jews on their way to Auschwitz. The only prejudice that might have seriously interfered with his career was a dislike of short people: *Wiener* magazine says that when he was Foreign Minister he tried to introduce a height requirement for the Foreign Service, so that only tall people could join the diplomat corps. But Austria has what could be called an anti-Semitic "vocabulary of explanation," and Waldheim—apart from one speech about Jewish suffering, very late in his campaign—did nothing really to discourage that vocabulary. Occasionally, he used it himself. He let it be known that the World Jewish Congress controlled the foreign press. He lingered over Jewish names. He stood by, smiling benignly, at provincial rallies while the local *Bürgermeister* went on and on about the foreign conspiracy against Austria's most famous citizen. He stood by, here in Vienna, while "patriots" in *Trachten* beat up people demonstrating against him and the police looked on. Waldheim is not a clever man. He is single-minded and implacably insensitive, and nothing—certainly not the prejudices of his admirers—seems to embarrass him. He was not embarrassed to have been caught lying about where he was and what he was doing from 1942 to 1945 any more than he was embarrassed to have been caught using the United Nations diplomatic pouch to send soft American toilet paper to his family in Austria. He learned one gesture for his campaign: whenever he was at a loss for something to say or something to do, he would open his arms in a kind of big, empty welcome. The gesture was automatic, like the movement of a windup toy. He learned his lines the same way—automatically. (He always did. Once, when he was on a United Nations famine-inspection tour in Africa, he greeted a mother with a dying baby in her arms by telling her what a lovely child she had.) It was clear, once the rumors about him started, that a man with a murky past could easily become President of Austria if he was a victim of Jewish conspiracies, just as a country with a murky past could easily become a democratic republic if it was a victim of Nazism. It was clear to the people in the Volkspartei, who had already put him up for President in 1971 and lost, and it was clear to the people at Young and Rubicam who were planning his campaign this time around, and who took a leave of absence to continue with Waldheim after the scandal broke and the agency cancelled its contract. "We were looking for impact—you know, a strong color and a strong slogan," one of the advertising men said when he was asked about the poster borrowed from the National Socialists. "We'll ask a client if the product is in line with the strategy, but it's not our business to ask if the product is really washing whiter."

There are only about seven thousand Jews in Austria, so any anti-Semitism here is anti-Semitism in its purest form—anti-Semitism without Jews. Harald Leupold-Löwenthal, the head of the Vienna Freud Society, calls it the Austrian disease—the negation of reality in fantasy. His friend Peter Michael Lingens, the editor of *Profil,* says that once you are guilty of killing millions of Jews you don't really need more Jews around to know you hate them. Every couple of years, somebody here takes a poll about anti-Semitism and the results never vary—70 percent of the Austrian people dislike Jews, and about a third of those people strongly dislike Jews, and a third of *them* consider Jews "foul" and are physically revolted in a Jew's presence. Bruno Kreisky, who was Chancellor for thirteen years and is a Jew himself, says the polls are nonsense—first, because Austrians elected him, and, second, because you can't base anti-Semitism, as some polls evidently do, on whether people enjoy telling Jewish jokes. Hitler, of course, was Austrian, and claimed to have learned his anti-Semitism in Vienna. He said that his ideal leader was someone who could combine the radical racial doctrine of George von Schönerer, whom he heard about in Vienna as a young man, with the scapegoat politics of Karl Lueger, who got to be mayor, in 1897, by convincing Vienna's workers that there would be plenty of money for everyone if only the Jews were gone. Lueger held torchlight rallies and burned the Rothschilds in effigy while Schönerer and his friends carved Jewish heads on their canes and talked in parliament about Jewish devils, and between them they managed to create a theater of race and a myth of race which had their paradigmatic moment on Kristallnacht, when forty-two of Vienna's forty-three synagogues were destroyed.

Most Austrians alive today have never known a Jew or had a Jewish neighbor, though Kurt Waldheim certainly had Jewish neighbors when he moved to New York and took up residence in the Secretary-General's mansion, on Sutton Place. New York was obviously not the place for Waldheim to announce that he had spent the better part of the Second World War working for a war criminal. His biography "washed whiter" in New York. The story in New York (it was in a book of his called *The Challenge of Peace*) went: "The knowledge that I was serving in the German army was hard to bear. Deliverance from my bitter situation finally came when our unit moved into active combat on the Eastern front in 1941. I was wounded in the leg and medically discharged."

In 1980, when Waldheim was thinking about a third term as Secretary-General, the United Nations War Crimes Commission files were mysteriously closed. No one, as it happens, was looking for Waldheim's dossier at the United Nations. The French had already looked him up in the Allied War Archives in Berlin, and so had the West Germans and presumably the East Germans, and they all, for reasons of their own, said nothing. But by 1980 the Americans had an Office of Special Investigations to look for war criminals, and had asked for access to the commission files. The American Attorney General, Benjamin Civiletti, wrote to the Secretary-General, thanking him in advance for his cooperation—and it was after that that all access to the files was cancelled. When the New York Congressman Stephen Solarz wrote to Waldheim a few months later—Solarz had been reading a little about Waldheim's past in *The New Republic*—Waldheim was so offended that he replied, "I have not hitherto considered it necessary to react to slanders such as the one you quote."

It was Bruno Kreisky who suggested Waldheim to the United Nations in 1971. Waldheim was looking for something distinguished to do. He had already been an ambassador and a Foreign Minister, and once he lost the presidential election that year there was not much point for him in staying home. It was never a question of making Waldheim Chancellor. The Chancellor runs Austria (though not the world), whereas the President has very little to do besides, as Waldheim put it this time around, "moral renewal." Austrians were aware that Waldheim was cut out for something much more ceremonial than life at the chancellery, something on the order of Embassy receptions and official visitors. For Chancellor, they preferred Kreisky—a brilliant and irascible Socialist who was so assimilated that he could call Menachem Begin a terrorist and Muammar Qaddafi a patriot and never admit to the contradiction. Being "assimilated" has a special meaning in Austria. Once, it was a legal status. Assimilated Jews—under the Hapsburgs, the official word was *tolerierte*, or "tolerated"—had rights and privileges that other Jews did not. They were what Hannah Arendt called a "state-people." The Austrians called them "court Jews," and this was often what they called themselves. Becoming assimilated was like

changing nationalities, and there were not many assimilated Jews in
Vienna before the war who identified with the *shtetl* Jews who had
made their way here from Poland and Russia. They were very Austrian
in *their* negation of reality in fantasy. It was not that anti-Semitism
surprised them—anti-Semitism has always been part of Austrian life
and politics. It was being identified with other Jews that they found
difficult to accept. They agreed with Gustav Mahler, who wrote in his
journal that Jews were smelly people with black robes and long hair.
When someone referred to Mahler (who was by then Catholic) as "the
Jew Mahler," he replied, "I do not belong to the same people." Kreisky
might easily say that *he* does not belong to the same people as the Polish
Jews who came to Vienna from the camps in 1945 and opened cobbler
shops and tailor shops in the Ring, or the old Hungarian Jews who
arrived in 1956, or the Soviet Jews who live near Mexikoplatz, across
the Danube Canal, and run a rough black market with contraband from
the East European river freighters that make the Danube route. On the
other hand, it was partly due to Kreisky's diplomacy that 260,000 Soviet
Jews got exit visas during the thirteen years that he was Chancellor, and
entirely due to his authority that Austria opened its borders to every
one of them as a place to live while they were deciding where to go.
Most of the Jews here now are Eastern Jews. There are only a few
thousand Austrian Jews—Jews who came home after the war or the
children of those Jews. Kreisky himself spent the war in exile in Sweden and has a Swedish wife, and sometimes he calls himself a Jew and
sometimes he says that to call Bruno Kreisky a Jew you would have to
use the same crazy racial categories that the Nazis invented at Nuremberg. He dislikes Zionists and Zionism. This has made him something
of a pariah to Jews abroad, but in his day it made him the one European
leader who could negotiate for the West in the Arab world.

The intellectuals here like Kreisky. They say that he is authoritarian and proud and that he nearly ruined his party, but they consider
him one of them, because he reads what they write and shows up at
their Graz conferences and always drops them a note when they publish something good, saying, "Loved the book, Yours, Kreisky." Even
his enemies admit that he is the most interesting Austrian politician in
forty years. It may be that in his own way Kreisky is assimilated to
anti-Semitism. Erika Weinzierl, a historian at the University of Vienna,
says that whenever Kreisky attacks the Israelis or the "Jewish lobby"
(meaning American Jews who do not agree with either his Middle
Eastern policies or his Socialist politics) there are Austrians who think,
If the Jew Kreisky can talk like this, then we can, too. She says that

Kreisky has not done very much more than Waldheim to correct that vocabulary of explanation which has to do with Jews and Jewish conspiracies and Jewish power.

When Kreisky was elected for the first time, he brought a lot of old Nazis into Austrian politics. This is no secret. Kreisky says that in 1970 there were still more than a quarter of a million Austrians alive who had belonged to the Nazi Party, and that there was no way he could have run a government with those Austrians disqualified from political life. He says he took the old official story about turning Nazis into democrats and made it his working hypothesis. The truth is he would never have won in Austria in 1970 without making that hypothesis. He recruited politicians with as much to account for as Waldheim, and whenever anyone brought up *their* records the Chancellor would say, "I back them, so this has to be the end of the discussion." A lot of people who voted for Waldheim this month were really voting against Kreisky and the Socialists. They said it was unfair to talk so piously about Waldheim now, when there had been four ex-Nazis and one S.S. officer in Kreisky's first government. It was particularly unfair, they said, when only three years ago Kreisky backed a notorious old S.S. Sturmführer named Friedrich Peter as a president of the Austrian parliament. Peter had a small party of his own, called the Freedom Party, which was supposed to protect the "Germanness" of Austrian life from decadent Slavic influences, and which was clearly appealing to old Nazis like him. The Freedom Party is in a coalition with the Socialists now, but Kreisky had talked about a coalition as early as 1975, when a round of parliamentary elections was coming up and the Socialists were worried about their majority. Simon Wiesenthal—the man who tracked down Adolf Eichmann from a documentation center in Vienna—started investigating Peter then. He discovered that Peter had spent two years on "extermination duty," in the Soviet Union, with an S.S. unit that murdered at least ten thousand people—eight thousand of them Jews. Wiesenthal had already kept one S.S. officer out of a Kreisky government. He never forgave Kreisky for making peace with Nazis, and Kreisky never forgave him. This time, Kreisky accused Wiesenthal of slandering him, of slandering socialism, of slandering Austria abroad. He threatened to take Wiesenthal to court. He called him a mafioso, and then he said that Wiesenthal must have had an "understanding" with the Nazis to have survived the war at all and especially to have lived through some of it "openly" and "unpersecuted." Wiesenthal, who spent the war in concentration camps, thereupon filed suit against Kreisky, claiming that Kreisky, in effect, was calling him a Gestapo agent, and Kreisky replied by naming a parliamentary commission to investigate Wiesenthal's center. They were "the only famous Jews left in Austria," as one reporter put it, and before they backed off from their various suits and investigations they nearly destroyed each other.

Wiesenthal is a conservative man. He is close to the People's Party, and has been for years. No one here was surprised that he refused to challenge Waldheim this spring—he said that Waldheim was an opportunist but that nobody yet had proved he was a war criminal— or that he attacked the World Jewish Congress, instead, for interfering in Austrian politics and "undoing the work of years of reconciliation." Wiesenthal is old, and maybe he is getting sentimental about Austria, or maybe age has made him susceptible to what Dr. Leupold-Löwenthal calls "the other Austrian disease"—"the situation is hopeless but not serious" disease. As it is, a lot of younger Austrians agree with Wiesenthal. They know the Socialists are just as compromised as the People's Party in their arrangements. Fred Sinowatz, the Socialist Chancellor, quit after the elections this month. He was maladroit and not too bright, and the coalition he made with Friedrich Peter's party was a disaster. Three of Peter's friends joined Sinowatz's government, including a Defense Minister who went to the Graz airport one day last year to greet an S.S. major named Walter Reder, who had just been sent home by the Italians after forty years in a Gaeta prison.

Last year, the Socialists talked about approaching Kurt Waldheim and asking him to run as *their* candidate. When the People's Party got to him first, the Socialists attacked him. When he came within sixteen thousand votes of the Presidency in the first round of the election, they stopped attacking him. They decided that every attack on Waldheim had meant a vote for Waldheim—and announced that in the interests of Austrian unity and an honorable campaign they would not mention the Second World War or Waldheim's part in it until the voting was over. Peter Michael Lingens, whose magazine exposed Waldheim, likes to tell a story about his mother and the election this year. Frau Lingens was in the Resistance. Her husband enrolled her in the National Socialist Working Women for protection, but she was caught and arrested anyway, in 1942, and sent to Auschwitz, and since the war—at least, until now—she has been a devoted Socialist. She voted for Waldheim, she told her son, because of the hypocrisy of the whole campaign.

Some Austrians want to see the Socialists out of power so badly that they do not much care that they had to start by making Kurt Waldheim President. A President here may have very little to do, but he does choose the Chancellor, and there are parliamentary elections in another year and no clear indication of what the majority will be, or even if there is going to be a majority. The Socialists have already run Austria for sixteen years, and there have been so many scams and scandals over those years that until the Viennese began to amuse themselves by betting on the countries that would still let Waldheim in if he was President (Bulgaria led the list, followed by Czechoslovakia, Libya, and Syria) the favorite parlor game in Vienna was betting on how much money had disappeared that week from the federal treasury. The economy in Austria is a state economy. A lot of the industry belongs to the government, and there are planned deficits to keep that industry going, so that Austria can, say, sell a telephone system to the city of Cairo and then loan the Egyptians the money to buy it. There is room in the system for what Germans and Austrians call *Filz*. (*Filz* means "felt," and people use it when a deal is so matted with favors and bribes and padded costs and hidden charges that you can't separate the threads.) There are bureaucrats from the Vienna Rathaus in jail now because of a hospital-construction scandal that has lasted five years and put more than a hundred million schillings—seven million dollars —into their various pockets. The officers from a trading company of the country's biggest steel conglomerate have been fired for "borrowing" a quarter of a billion schillings to invest in oil futures—and losing them. It is not that the Socialists have a monopoly on graft. (The most interesting scandal this year involved an insurance company that the People's Party controls through one of its trade *Bunde*: everyone supposedly took home millions of schillings, including a Cistercian abbot from Syria who was interested in living better.) It is simply that state ownership and state partnerships and state banking and state financing and all the formulas of a state economy have created habits of mind and opportunity that are now "institutionally irresistible," as one banker put it. They are not so different from the corporatist formulas the Fascists invented in the 1920s and 1930s (which is really how Austria got them), but by now they are almost entirely associated with Socialism and with sixteen years of Socialist government. Kurt Steyrer, the Socialist who ran against Waldheim, is a doctor, and a decent man but not a strong one. In 1983, when he was Minister of Health and the Environment, the Socialists wanted to build a power station at Hainburg, east of Vienna, that would have flooded thousands of acres of rare wetland forest. Ecologists and students stopped the project by demonstrating, but Dr. Steyrer never said a word against it. His reputation suffered so much that even the Austrian ecologists came out for Waldheim after the first round of voting this spring. Waldheim himself began to talk solemnly in what is known as his headwaiter's voice about clean air and clean water for Austria's grandchildren. Kreisky pointed out that there is not much Austria can do about its grandchildren so long as the countries around Austria have thirty-two nuclear reactors of their own and thousands of nuclear warheads aimed across it. But the truth, as one young Austrian said, is that "none of these old guys helped us much —not Waldheim, not Kreisky, not Steyrer." It is not lost on young Austrians that Kreisky himself built a nuclear reactor (there was a referendum against it, and it was never used), or that Waldheim never said a word about nuclear risk until Chernobyl exploded, and the ecologists got 5.5 percent of the vote in the first round of an election Waldheim was supposed to win easily.

The fact is that no one really knows why Austria voted the way it did this month. No one knows whether Austria voted for Waldheim or against foreigners and Jews or for the People's Party or against Socialists. No one even knows whether the politicians in the People's Party like Waldheim. Waldheim was their Trojan horse, and he carried them a little closer to power, and it was a free ride. None of them had to climb down and say what they were going to do once they got there. All they had to say was "We Austrians Will Vote for Whom We Want!"

The first most Austrians heard about a problem involving Kurt Waldheim was last September. People came home from vacation, and by the end of the month anyone with a friend in the Socialist Party knew that something was up—something terrible about the war that was going to come out and finish Waldheim in a couple of days. It is curious now how many people did think that the news about Waldheim—not his past so much as his having lied so calculatingly about that past—would finish him. The Socialists figured it was a matter of time before he dropped out of the election. The World Jewish Congress gave him three or four days. The reporters at *Profil* concluded that the Socialists were in business for another sixteen years. The Socialists claim that they did not get interested in Waldheim until January, when the Minister of Defense—the same minister who had welcomed the S.S. major home—allowed some Air Force officers to hang a plaque in honor of Alexander Löhr on the wall of the National Defense Academy, in Vienna, and in the discussion that followed someone mentioned that Kurt Waldheim had been Löhr's adjutant. The truth is that the Socialists were interested in Waldheim for as long as they knew that he was running against them. A local historian by the name of Georg Tidl had been working on Waldheim's file for a year before anyone at *Profil* heard about Waldheim's being a lieutenant in Löhr's Balkan command—the Heeresgruppe E, it was called. Nobody knows whom Tidl was working on Waldheim for—he is supposedly a little odd, and sometimes he says *The New York Times* and sometimes the South Africans and sometimes the "cossacks"—but the Socialists must have known about his work, because even the People's Party knew about it. Hubertus Czernin, at *Profil*, says that Tidl went to the Secretary of the People's Party in April of 1985 and told him that Waldheim had some sort of Nazi past, and that the Secretary refused to listen. After that, the information was more or less available. Some people think that the Socialists bought it, and eventually leaked it to the World Jewish Congress. Other people say no, that it was not Tidl but a man named Leon Zelman—he runs the Jewish Welcome Service here—who got the information and told the Socialists *and* the Congress what was going on. Zelman is a Socialist and a Jew, a *shtetl* Jew from Galicia. He spent three and a half years in concentration camps—Auschwitz, Mauthausen, and finally a camp called Ebensee, near Mauthausen —and then he settled in Vienna, and the little Jewish community here has been his life and his passion. Early last year, Zelman arranged an invitation for the World Jewish Congress to hold its annual meeting in Vienna. It was the first time the Congress had met in Vienna since before the war. And it happened to be the moment the Italians chose to let Walter Reder out of jail. The government that welcomed the World Jewish Congress one day welcomed the S.S. major the next, and then, to everyone's distress, Chancellor Sinowatz appeared at the Congress to make amends and gave a speech about how much the Sinowatzes had suffered the day the Jewish family next door was taken away by the Gestapo. All the Sinowatz children cried and cried, the Chancellor said, and had to have a lot of candy to get over the experience.

Many of the Jews here are conservative, like Wiesenthal. They look after themselves, and they do not want any more trouble in their lives. They were embarrassed when people from the World Jewish Congress started to talk about leaving Vienna because of Walter Reder. They did not think it was sensible for foreign Jews to talk publicly about whether to stay in a country that sends its Defense Minister to welcome war criminals home. They did not want the attention. Like other Austrians, they did not want to confront the anti-Semitism here. They preferred to put anti-Semitism in a drawer and close the drawer and hope it would disappear, like an old letter that has been around too long to answer. They liked the euphemistic surfaces of Austrian life. They liked reality that curved like a baroque bow into something pleasing. What they did not like was Israel Singer—who is an abrasive character—coming to Vienna and making judgments in their name. Many of them thought it would be nice if Kurt Waldheim was President. They approved of Waldheim for the reason other Austrians approved of him—because he was prominent. Zelman's friends say that when Zelman saw this his heart was broken. Now he tells people that the city he loved so much, the city that gave him peace and let him live in safety, was an illusion. "I was selling an illusion," he said, two days before Waldheim won.

Waldheim made a trip to Jerusalem when he was at the United Nations, and Zelman sometimes talks about that trip, because Waldheim referred to Jerusalem as the Israeli capital, and then, when his aides told him that as far as the United Nations was concerned Tel Aviv was the capital, he refused to wear a yarmulke at the Yad Vashem Memorial. Zelman says that one of these days Waldheim will show up at the synagogue in Vienna to make his peace, but that this time "I am sure that he will put a yarmulke on, and I am not so sure that the congregation will refuse to let him in."

Hubertus Czernin started investigating Waldheim after the Defense Minister and the Minister of Buildings had an argument about whether to take down General Löhr's plaque from the Defense Academy wall. Czernin called the German military archives, in Freiburg, and the Germans referred him to a veterans' club in Linz, where an amateur historian was doing research on Waldheim's Army unit in Russia. The historian, in turn, sent Czernin to George Tidl and to the State Archives, here in Vienna, behind the Ballhausplatz. Czernin had nothing against Waldheim then. In January, when the argument about the plaque started, someone from the Socialist Party had called him and asked if he had heard the rumors about Waldheim. He said he didn't take them seriously at all. He made a crack about Waldheim's having been Löhr's right-hand man, and mentioned it to a reporter at *Profil* who was writing an article on the plaque. The reporter did take the rumors seriously, and said so, and the investigation began.

Czernin wanted to be fair to Waldheim. Actually, he was so fair that he called on Waldheim and asked whether Waldheim objected to his looking through some of the files at the State Archives; he thought that maybe he could help clear up the rumors that were going around. Waldheim, he says, was gracious, or maybe just oblivious. He sent his

secretary with Czernin. The secretary was a young diplomat by the
name of Ferdinand Trauttmansdorff, who had come home from the
Embassy in Bucharest for what he probably thought was going to be
a predictable and pleasant campaign that would put him in touch with
a lot of important people and look terrific on his résumé.

Czernin is Austrian by birth, Czech by origin. He is thirty years
old—a friendly young man with black hair falling in his eyes and a pair
of round wire-rimmed glasses on his nose—and he wears polo shirts
and bluejeans to the office and carts around two plastic shopping bags
full of books about Nazis and Nazism, which he has been accumulating
since the Waldheim story broke. To many people in Vienna, Czernin
represents what has always been best about Austria—the ethnicity, the
civility, the intelligence, the very "Austrian" understanding of how
complicated reality is. He is a fine reporter in a city where most of the
press is terrible. The fact that it is terrible gives people something to
complain about and another wistful comparison to make with the
golden days when the press was good. The papers and magazines in
Austria belong to businessmen or to banks or chambers of commerce
with official links to the various parties, and they are expected to serve
their owners' interests. It may be true—the Viennese say it is—
that the country is so corrupt that you have to queue up at the newspapers with your scandal, but it is also true that most newspapers will turn
you away. The papers identify with power. They are respectful and
obliging, and nearly all of them chose to protect Kurt Waldheim. A
piece of information to the effect that, say, Kurt Waldheim once approved orders for a "cleansing operation" that led to the deportation
of sixty thousand Yugoslavs to concentration camps would appear in
the papers here as JEWS ACCUSE WALDHEIM OF WAR CRIMES. The biggest
daily, a tabloid called *Kronen Zeitung*, with a circulation of a million,
belongs to a neighbor of Waldheim's on the Attersee. *Die Presse*, which
used to be the great Vienna paper in the days when it was the *Neue Freie
Presse* and had people like Theodor Herzl contributing, belongs to the
Chamber of Commerce and reads like a People's Party public-relations
bulletin on newsprint. *Profil* itself belongs to a daily paper called
Kurier, which, in turn, belongs to a syndicate of businessmen and an
agricultural bank that are People's Party fiefdoms. Lingens and his
partner sold the magazine to *Kurier* in 1975, when it was four years old
and they were having a hard time keeping it going, but they demanded
an independent charter, and guarantees, and to their surprise got them.
They tried to model *Profil* after a good German weekly. They made
it look like *Der Spiegel*, but they say they wanted it to sound like *Die*

Zeit. It had been so long since Austrians had read any news about Austria besides good news that they did not know what to make of a magazine that talked about "investigative reporting" and had people running around the country asking questions and printing the answers. They are used to it now, but the fact is that any Austrians who did not read *Profil* over the past six months could easily believe that Kurt Waldheim spent the war with his law books, because that is what the papers they did read told them.

Most young Austrians learn very little at home about the Second World War. In school, if they get to the war at all, they usually learn that the Second World War was the time that foreigners came here and stole the Austrian farmers' chickens. Hubertus Czernin says that his *Gymnasium* class never even heard that there was a war. The class went right from the Treaty of Versailles to the State Treaty of 1955, which established the Austrian Republic. Czernin was one of the lucky ones, he says, because he had parents who talked about the war. Czernin's father knew a general in the plot against Hitler and was sent to prison in Vienna, and his maternal grandfather was half Jewish and in politics, and he spent the war in the concentration camp at Mauthausen. Czernin and Lingens have the Resistance in common—which means they have the war in common—and it may be because of this that the magazine took it as a duty to establish a record of Kurt Waldheim's career. Not many Austrians are willing to make a distinction between the men who fought for Hitler and the men who refused. In 1947, the priest of a parish church near Linz asked his bishop for permission to print a story in the church newsletter about a devout Catholic farmer named Franz Jägersteter, who had refused to swear an oath to the Third Reich when he was drafted, and was executed. The bishop said no. He said so many other Austrians had lost their lives fighting that it would not be right to take one farmer who had lost his life for *not* fighting and call him a hero.

At first, a lot of the people at *Profil* and on Waldheim's staff believed that Waldheim represented those "other Austrians." When he talked about the war at all, he talked about the hundreds of thousands of Austrians who were in the Wehrmacht. He never missed a chance to mention that the only serious attempt at a coup against Hitler was the Wehrmacht coup in July of 1944, but he never addressed the war itself, or his lying about the war, or the cost to himself or to any Austrian soldier of having fought for Hitler. The problem—at least for the staff that planned his strategy and wrote his speeches—was that he could never really bring himself to identify with those hundreds of thousands of Austrians who were not heroes, who were drafted and given a uniform with a swastika and sent away to fight. Some of his staff wanted him to talk about the difficulty of heroism, to take the part of ordinary Austrians who had lacked the will or the courage or the understanding to resist, and to say something about a life spent working for a world in which decent, ordinary people like that would never have to confront such a terrible choice again—and fail themselves. It was, to say the least, a moment for statesmanship, but Waldheim, despite his years as an ambassador and a Foreign Minister and even a Secretary-General, had never learned statesmanship. He was too vain to understand the uses of humility and regret and failure and a properly stated *mea culpa.* The best his people got was the speech he made about anti-Semitism, late in May, at the Schwarzenberg Palace. (The irony of the *mise en scène* may have been lost on Waldheim; the Schwarzenbergs were an Austro-Czech family who had challenged Hitler by registering as members of the Czech minority instead of citizens of the German Reich.)

It may be that Waldheim was so used to the ceremonial euphemisms of United Nations high life that he had come to believe that life was protocol and truth was the last word spoken by the highest-ranking person. When Czernin called on him a second time, Waldheim denied everything his file from the archives said. Czernin says that Waldheim would look at the photocopy of his *Wehrstammbuch,* his Army record, with his signature on membership cards from the S.A. riding club and the National Socialist Student Union, and even at his own photograph, and say, "No, not me, not true," as if there were nothing there —no papers, no picture, no embarrassed reporter, no young diplomats with their mouths open. It was a photograph from the archives that interested Czernin most. It was a head shot, the kind of picture that goes on passports and identity cards, but it reminded Czernin of something, and then he realized he had seen a face like that in a picture somebody had sent to *Profil* that fall—a picture of a group of young Austrians waiting on the Heldenplatz on May 1, 1938, to welcome Hitler to Vienna. Czernin was so bewildered by then—bewildered by the two pictures and by the *Wehrstammbuch* he had seen and by Waldheim's always saying, "No, not me," and smiling so politely—that he went straight from the meeting to a café in the Hotel Erzherzog Rainer and sat up until one in the morning drinking and talking with Peter Marboe, who was Waldheim's chief of staff, and Gerold Christian, Waldheim's press secretary, trying to make some sense of the conversation he and Waldheim had had. "I told them, 'Wow! Waldheim must

have had terrific contacts to be able to stay in Vienna and study law
for two whole years in the middle of a world war,' and they went back
to Waldheim, and then Waldheim said, 'Well, maybe I was only sick
for two months, and maybe then I went to the Balkans.' But the thing
is, he would never tell the whole story and this was very annoying,
because it turned out that he was one of the best-informed officers in
the Balkans. He knew everything." In the end, *Profil* and one Salzburg
paper, *Salzburger Nachrichten,* asked that Waldheim withdraw from the
campaign. An "alternative" paper called *Falter* gave all the reasons why
he *should* withdraw from it. The rest of the press preferred to write
about how the World Jewish Congress was paying Greek partisans
—$150,000 is the latest figure—to say that Kurt Waldheim had beat
them up.

Eli Rosenbaum, the general counsel for the World Jewish Congress, flew to Vienna on February 4—two weeks before Czernin visited
the State Archives and met with Waldheim. Rosenbaum says that the
Congress had only just heard about Löhr and Waldheim—that one of
his researchers had read the article on Löhr in *Profil,* and showed it to
Israel Singer, who took it to Edgar Bronfman, who said, "Go ahead."
Not many people believe that, but it is the Congress's story, the way
the Socialists' story is that one of *their* staff happened to read about
Waldheim and Löhr in *Profil,* and showed the article around, and that
after that the Socialists got busy. The World Jewish Congress blames
the Socialists for their "deafening silence" after the first round of voting. Singer claims, with justice, that the Socialists were immensely
cynical in their campaign—which went from attacks on Waldheim to
silence about Waldheim to elder-statesman rectitude from Kreisky to
the resignation of Chancellor Sinowatz once Waldheim was elected
and the Socialists had nothing to lose, and a lot to gain, by showing
some appropriate indignation. On the other hand, the Socialists blame
the World Jewish Congress for a certain potshot style that does not do
well here. Some Socialists agree with Wiesenthal that the World Jewish
Congress is raising the level of anti-Semitism in Austria. But the argument between Wiesenthal and the World Jewish Congress has as much
to do with Jewish politics, which are at least as involuted as Austrian
politics, as it has to do with Kurt Waldheim. Simon Wiesenthal does
not really like the Congress's moving, as it were, into his territory (even
the Wiesenthal Center in Los Angeles has been at odds with him over
his reluctance to condemn Waldheim), and the World Jewish Congress
does not really like the attention Wiesenthal gets as a famous Nazi

hunter. Israel Singer says that Jews do not cause anti-Semitism—anti-Semites do. He is right, of course. When Michael Graff, the General Secretary of the People's Party, actually accused the World Jewish Congress of provoking "feelings that we all don't want to have," a Viennese journalist named Barbara Coudenhove-Kalergi replied that it was not a matter of whether you *wanted* to have those feelings—it was having them that counted. She said that the most painful thing in Austria right now is watching anti-Semites warn other anti-Semites against anti-Semitism.

Monsignor Leopold Ungar, who runs the Catholic Charities in Vienna, thinks that the Allies made a terrible miscalculation after the Second World War. They believed that the Austrians were going to recover, morally and historically, and that it was the Germans who were going to have to start all over again—the hunters and gatherers, so to speak, of modern Europe. In fact, it is the Austrians who are without a history. People who have seen the new Vienna shows (the Künstlerhaus version was called *Traum und Wirklichkeit*, which means "Dream and Reality") often remark on the passion with which the artists and intellectuals of prewar Vienna abandoned history. Harold Bloom, the Yale critic, could have been talking about Vienna instead of Wordsworth when he described what an "anxiety of influence" was. That kind of anxiety hangs over Vienna even now. If there is no real Austrian literature of the war—no *Tin Drum* of the Anschluss—it may be because the important Austrian writers of the past forty years, writers like Thomas Bernhard and Peter Handke, went right back past the war to the questions about art and language which the early modernists posed and never resolved. Austria's evasions are the same evasions that Karl Kraus wrote about in every issue of *Die Fackel*—they have a special language, whether it is the language of anti-Semitism or the language of the victim, and the writers believe that any true recovery for their country has to start again with language, as Austrians use it. They are more interested in Wittgenstein than in their military historians. Still, when Waldheim began to talk about doing his duty as a soldier, Peter Handke offered his services to Steyrer, twelve hundred intellectuals published a letter of protest, and another group of writers and artists took ads in the daily papers to say that, while they didn't really like the Socialists, Kurt Steyrer would do less damage than Kurt Waldheim as an Austrian President. The only "artist for Waldheim" seems to have been a Hungarian sculptor who spends his summer vacations in Gablitz, in the Vienna woods, and thinks that Waldheim is the "greatest living European." Last month, the sculptor sent a huge bronze bust of Waldheim to a People's Party rally in the Gablitz *Festhalle*. It was a striking likeness of the new President, and it could be the first gift in a long career of getting gifts that Waldheim will want to donate to a worthy cause instead of taking home and keeping for himself.

June 1986

MEMORY

MEMORY

Pierre Mendès France died in Paris on October 18, at the age of seventy-five. It was nearly thirty years ago that he ran Fourth Republic France —and then only for seven and a half months—and yet in many ways his death is a more significant loss for the left in Europe than, say, the loss of political power in West Germany now or of public civility between West Germany's warring Socialists Helmut Schmidt and Willy Brandt. Mendès France was a socialist and a Jew and a Frenchman—which in his case meant the most scrupulous sort of patriot. He had a strong belief in the French nation, and an even stronger belief in restraint in the exercise of nationality. Mendès France ended his country's war in Indochina. He drank milk, as every Frenchman knows. He sent his sons to Camp Wigwam, in Harrison, Maine, as a few old Wigwam boys know. And he fought bitterly with Charles de Gaulle, who wanted to shape a Fifth Republic to decorate his own authority. Mendès France believed in the lessons of the Second World War in Europe. He believed that any country given over to symbols of power could become monstrous. He was a passionate democrat. He preferred the chaos of his old parliamentary state to the chilly clarity of a new, presidential France, even when that chaos meant his own defeat. He took a long view. His family had fled the inquisitors in Portugal—settling in Bordeaux in the seventeenth century, changing its name from Mendès de Franca to Mendès France—and there are many French Jews today who see an object lesson in that family saga which ended with a Jew ruling France and being humiliated in power and then revered in powerlessness. Mendès France was indeed revered here, even if the homage came so often from a sense of shame.

The eulogies of the past few weeks were mainly about his moral authority, his moral rigor. Over the years of his forced retirement from socialist politics, he had become the conscience of socialist politics. His scrutiny was humane, and even humorous, but its effect was rabbinical. People who acted meanly or cynically or dishonorably in political life found that they could not look Mendès France in the eye any longer. They did not know what to do with this civilized man who talked about a socialism built on sympathies of heart and mind and who accepted failure but not dishonesty about failure and who was so different from the Jacobins of the left, whose own moral authority was really only ideology and intolerance. François Mitterrand inherited a Gaullist Presidency last year, but the father he wanted to acknowledge, embracing Mendès France on the day of his inauguration, was that frail old Jewish democrat in the receiving line at the Élysée. The papers like to recall that moment, that image, because the French are moved by images that are grand and sad and have to do with patrimony. Let me add another image—one that Mendès France recalled himself, talking to Marcel Ophuls in *The Sorrow and the Pity,* Ophuls's remarkable film about France during the Occupation, about French traitors and French heroes. Mendès France became a Vichy prisoner in Clermont-Ferrand after the country fell. He was in obvious danger, and elaborate plans were made for his escape. Finally, one night, disguised with glasses and a new mustache, he made his way to the top of the prison wall: "I should admit that I am not very much of an athlete, but I had prepared myself for this ordeal by doing a lot of exercise in the months before it. So there I was, on top of the wall. I had to jump. It was quite high, but I had to risk it, because once down I would be free—with all that that entailed. I was just about to jump—there were trees all along the road—when I heard an unexpected sound. Voices. I tried to see into the darkness. There was a couple under one of the trees. You can imagine what was on their mind. He had some very definite ideas. She couldn't decide. It took a long, long time, it seemed to me. She did say yes finally, but, really, it seemed as if she put up a very long fight. And then—well, then they left. And then I jumped. And I promise you that at that moment I was even happier than he was. I would really like to meet those two one day. It would give me great pleasure to tell them how I lived through that night with them, and how untimely her shyness had seemed to me then. Well, in the end love, luck, and flight triumphed."

Nathalie Sarraute has just written an autobiography, *Enfance,* that stops at the age of fourteen. Mme Sarraute will be eighty-three in July. It is hard to imagine that what we call the *nouveau roman* was an experiment that she began in the early 1930s, writing a book of prose images, *Tropismes.* She is still experimenting. *Tropismes*—she calls them "certain interior actions, certain indefinable movements, which slide very rapidly to the limits of consciousness"—remain her form, her obsession, the reason she was drawn to the nebulous memories of her childhood rather than to the records and recollections of respectable old age. Mme Sarraute sold *Tropismes* to the publisher Robert Denoël in 1937— the same year she and her husband, Raymond, moved to their apartment on the Avenue Pierre Ier-de-Serbie. It is one of those rambling establishments built for a nineteenth-century Paris bourgeoisie that expected to collect and accumulate its objects like memories, and Mme Sarraute has filled it accordingly. There is something severely feminine about her. She is a householder, and it seems to me that she has written her memoirs the way she keeps her house, rubbing memory into images as if she were raising the patina on a walnut table or a hardwood floor. She says that she does not disrupt her work with too much "experience." She travels a lot, but that, she says, is for herself. This year, she has already been lecturing in Wales and swimming in Cyprus. Occasionally, she teaches. Every year or so, she tries to get to America. According to her, there is only one truly disconcerting place in America, and that is the University of California at Santa Cruz, where a few years ago she came upon students eating copies of their professor's book —the professor was Norman O. Brown—in order to "absorb the text." Mme Sarraute does not read Norman O. Brown. She reads Rabelais and Shakespeare. She writes, mornings, at a neighborhood café. Afternoons, lately, she reads *The Tempest.* Or she receives her friends, sitting on her library couch and offering whiskey from a little tray with a doily on it, as if she were serving tea and biscuits. She knows, or has known, practically everyone in Paris over the last fifty or sixty years, but she never thought of her friends as figures in an autobiography, any more than she thought of herself past fourteen, or of her life as a writer. Once, she tried to describe those "movements of the mind" which were, in a sense, her characters: "They develop and fade with great speed, without our perceiving clearly what they are, producing in us brief but

often very intense sensations, and it is only possible to convey them in
images that produce in the reader analogous sensations. One must break
these movements down—unwind them in the reader's mind like a film
in slow motion."

Enfance is a dialogue with memory, a merciless coaxing of memory
into images and then into refractions of images, until memory is
stripped of sentiment and becomes something close to sensation itself.
Mme Sarraute says that she began to write the book because of one
suddenly remembered sentence: *Nein, das tust du nicht.* ("No, you
don't do that.") The words became an image, the image of a German
nurse she had at the age of five or six, on a summer holiday in Switzerland, and then of the scissors in the nurse's sewing basket. The image
became a longing, a longing to be naughty, to cut a big hole in the blue
silk couch in the hotel drawing room where Nathalie and the nurse
were sitting. The nurse said, *"Nein, das tust du nicht."* A classic Sarraute
tropisme. The book is rich in them. The facts are scattered, like asides:
she was born in Russia; her parents were Jewish; their milieu was
literary, political, worldly; they divorced when she was two. Her
mother brought her to Paris, fretted for a few years, took her to St.
Petersburg. She was a woman who found motherhood a touching but
troublesome experience. When Nathalie's father remarried and moved
to Paris himself, Nathalie's mother packed her off for a summer's visit
to him and never managed to collect her. Nathalie grew up on the Left
Bank, in Alésia. Her stepmother, Véra, was angry and resentful. Her
stepsister, Lili, took her Teddy bear and was never punished. Once,
Nathalie asked Véra, "Do you hate me?" Véra said, "How can you hate
a child?"

There are old photographs of Nathalie Sarraute—"Tachok," at
two, in a white pinafore; "Natasha," at eight, in the braided travelling
cloak she wore to Paris—in which one sees instantly the woman of
eighty-two, in her navy slacks and cardigan and her scarf. There is the
same grave face, the same bright brown eyes, and curve to the mouth,
and short straight hair. Old age seems to have distilled her, leaving only
the radiant, essential qualities that small children and great beauties
have. When she was six or so, she started to collect perfume bottles. She
would wash them and dry them and rub the labels off, feeling the last
thin, gluey layers of paper roll into little balls beneath her finger. She
loved to hold her bottles to a lamp, or take them into the garden and
watch the sun make them sparkle. Those secret sensuous moments
became the moments that disciplined her art. Jean-Paul Sartre, who was
her collaborator on the review *Les Temps Modernes,* came to dislike her

tropismes. He said that Mme Sarraute was not "engaged," that it was better to write novels about injustice than novels about moments spent with, for instance, empty perfume bottles. Mme Sarraute said that, as far as she could tell, all that Sartre's "aesthetics of engagement" did for him was to make him give up writing novels of any sort. Back in 1960, she signed a famous manifesto against the Algerian war, but she still argued with friends like Sartre about her responsibilities as a writer, saying that the fact of a cruel war in Algeria did not preclude her right to what she calls a *"littérature d'ailleurs."* "The question," she says, "of whether a worker can appreciate Swann's love for Odette is not a question that concerns me."

June 1983

A few days ago, the anthropologist Claude Lévi-Strauss gave a talk called "Histoire et Ethnologie" to more than a thousand people. Lévi-Strauss is seventy-four, and he has just resigned his chair at the Collège de France. There will be no more of the famous Lévi-Strauss seminars at the Collège, and consequently this month's talk—it was the annual Marc Bloch lecture, named for the historian and sponsored by the École des Hautes Études en Sciences Sociales—was by way of a farewell from France's most important scholar. Lévi-Strauss spoke in the Grand Amphithéâtre of the Sorbonne, a wonderful Third Republic auditorium, lit from cupolas and draped with flags; above the rostrum is Puvis de Chavannes's 1889 mural of a sacred wood where the Spirit of the Sorbonne reigns, and the Arts and the Sciences frolic, and Eloquence celebrates the conquests of the mind of man. The amphitheater is usually saved for great occasions—the announcement of the first modern Olympic Games, the Pasteur centennial, the fiftieth anniversary of the Third Republic. An anthropologist of about forty, sitting next to me at the talk, said that the last time he had seen the amphitheater was in May of 1968, when students occupied the Sorbonne, and Daniel Cohn-Bendit was the lecturer.

Lévi-Strauss is very much a *maître*—in the sense that the French use *maître* to honor the scholars and teachers who are the living culture of the country. He is an almost Cartesian presence for his colleagues and his students—an intelligence so confident, so precise, so forceful that it translates into a kind of physical correctness. It is not hard to imagine him as a young man in Brazil with the Nambikwara and the Bororo Indians, doing the field work out of which he produced *Tristes Tropiques,* and which was the inspiration for the four landmark texts in structural anthropology that make up "Mythologiques." Tribal cultures like the Nambikwara and the Bororo are also correct. Lévi-Strauss would say that in their correctness they are beyond history, beyond the authority of events and personalities and time in which historians believe. Historians, on the whole, have not been very receptive to structuralists like Lévi-Strauss, who insist that they look beneath the chimera of change to the timeless structures of human social life.

Lately, Lévi-Strauss and his students have been writing "structuralist" French history—applying the kinship models of their research to France's noble families and marriages and alliances. They have taken those models, which were derived from tribal incest taboos, and, with Saint-Simon for a text (rather than, say, Bororo myths), used them to describe the France of the Condés and Bourbons and Dampierres. This is the work that Lévi-Strauss discussed in his lecture, taking the discipline that he himself did so much to define and setting it down, so to speak, on its proper course—on what he called its "legitimate direction." Thirty-five years ago, Lévi-Strauss described the elaborate structures of kinship and taboo, the rules of marriage and exchange with which tribal peoples organized their world. Now, standing under Puvis de Chavannes's sacred grove, he told the thousand Paris intellectuals who had come to hear him, and, perhaps, to say goodbye to the *maître* as a public man, that those same structures were the origin of the civilization they venerate. The audience was solemn, but it seemed to me that sometimes, listening to himself, Lévi-Strauss was amused by his discoveries, and maybe even by his own conclusions.

June 1983

There is a watercolor I like by the Italian painter Valerio Adami, who lives in Paris and is getting ready for a retrospective at Beaubourg. It is a study for a painting called *Incantesimo del Lago—The Spell of the Lake*—but it is not the final study. Adami says that it is awkward, that it misses somehow, that a line or a shape went wrong and he did not know really how to fix it. The watercolor moves me, perhaps because of its awkwardness. Adami is a narrative, and in some ways an autobiographical, painter. His work is about the history of artists. His paintings have names like *Archeology* and *Metamorphosis* and *The Return of the Prodigal Son,* and the black outlines he always puts around his cast of characters are really the boldface print of an ongoing life in which old winking gods conspire with temple goats and Wagner visits Marat in his bathtub and Sigmund Freud casts trout flies into pools of consciousness. In an Adami, massive bodies out of a Raphael or a Michelangelo flatten themselves into the curves and planes of a bright acrylic surface. Landscapes flatten, and with them time seems to flatten, and one is left, suddenly, with a collapsed iconography of the civilization.

Adami, at forty-nine, is one of a generation of European painters with what could be called an unrequited sense of history. There is an intensity of nostalgia in Adami's work, masked by the intensities of color that have become his trademark. It is a nostalgia that has to do with the war, with growing up to a shattered past from which there was only "history" to recover, and I think that one reason I like the watercolor study of a woman in a rowboat which Adami calls *The Spell of the Lake* is that it fails to resolve its nostalgia into elegant pop surfaces, it fails at the stylistic devices that are really Europe's devices. It is a little like the pencil drawings that Adami keeps for himself in a drawer in his studio. They are full of false starts and rubbings out and smudges, and they are not very pretty, but they are also full of the gestures and the concentration of translating ideas into lines on a piece of heavy, three-hundred-gram paper. Adami is known mainly for his paintings. But he himself is uncomfortable with painting, as if his paintings begged the questions they raise, by their crafty beauty and satisfying surfaces. He prefers drawing. He says that he thinks by drawing, and that his drawings are as close as he can get to thought and longing. It is this longing—the awkward longing of a woman in a rowboat who turns her back and strains into a brown Italian landscape—that separates so many European artists of Adami's age from their confident, painterly predecessors, and even from their followers, and gives them as much of an affinity for the intellectuals they know, the writers and philosophers, as for their own colleagues. The great old painters of the Paris scene are nearly gone. (Jean Dubuffet is about the last of them; I see him sometimes walking around my neighborhood, small and solid, and with the same sort of bald bullet head Picasso had.) Most of them were gone by the time Adami came here, from Italy, in the early seventies—one of those young European painters who were looking for a capital and who were to discover in Paris that the capital was New York, that there was no way for Europeans of their age and their bewildering experience to make the same sort of buoyant strides that painters were making in America. There was, to those European painters, an intimidating innocence to American art—even the F-111 bombers and the supermarket cans of the 1960s had that innocence. Europeans who stayed at home in Europe worried about this. They talked about "the terrorism of American painting" (and stopped only a couple of years ago, when Americans started raiding Europe again for paintings). Or they talked about *"l'espace américain,"* meaning a kind of free Wild West of the imagination. Memory is heavy in Europe even now, and Adami says that it amounts to a baggage that people like himself carry. He says that a childhood spent with a Caravaggio hanging in his local church and a Jewish lieder singer hiding in his basement, waiting out the war and occasionally giving family concerts, was bound to produce in him a very particular sense of memory, a fascination with memory, a bond. He and the other young painters he knew from Italy tried hard to work out concepts of modernity that would involve the rearticulation of memory more than they involved newness. Newness was an American problem. The problem in Europe had to do with making honorable connections with tradition—and with being written off in New York as either too "intellectual" or shallow. Adami is a painter of references, of indirection. The painters who have taken on the mythologies of the century more brutally are (almost by definition) younger, and they are mainly German, like Anselm Kiefer, who is an artist of extraordinary passion. They are more of an event, in their way, than an exquisitely civilized Italian like Valerio Adami, out looking for history, but they are not more important. Adami remembers standing in front of one of the cool Canova nudes at the Brera after classes and wondering who in fact were the proper predecessors of a seventeen-year-old art student in Milan seven years after the Second World War—the Canovas of eighteenth-century Rome or the Futurists of his own century, who easily lent their images to Fascism, or the Expressionists in Germany with their prophetic nightmares. It is not surprising that he and so many of his contemporaries—people like Ronald Kitaj, who lives in London and is fifty-one years old—became painters of allusion trying to translate the questions and propositions of the mind into corroborating images, obsessed with the sly combat between civilization and mortality.

May 1984

Christo has wrapped up the Pont Neuf in polyamide. His wife, Jeanne-Claude, who orchestrates his projects, is French and a general's daughter, and the general—*his* name was Jacques de Guillebon, and he was Maréchal Leclerc's *chef d'état-major* during the Liberation of Paris—tried to use his influence to see that Le Pont (as it was called by the climbers and divers and carpenters and bargemen who did the wrapping) went off smoothly and discreetly, without too much trouble from the politicians. Even so, wrapping the bridge took Christo ten years. He needed permission from Jacques Chirac, the mayor of Paris, and Chirac could not make up his mind, because he was worried about what two weeks of a wrapped Pont Neuf would do to his reputation as a presidential candidate. It was never a question of the people in Paris. It was the people in the provinces who worried Chirac. Their values did not involve wrapping the cultural patrimony in polyamide, and then, too, what they knew about Christo was mainly that he was a troublemaker who had once barricaded the rue Visconti with rusty oil barrels—the barrels were up for six hours before the police removed them—and therefore must have had something to do with 1968 and their rebellious children, with riots in the streets and poems to Che Guevara and Mao Zedong and all the other terrible, anarchic things that broke Charles de Gaulle's heart and sent him away to Ireland to grieve among strangers. By the time Chirac agreed to Christo's project, it was 1983, and Chirac was running for mayor again, and this time his friends said that he would probably lose votes in Paris, too, if the Front National found out and started identifying him with something as *louche* and "foreign" as a bridge wrapped by a Bulgarian artist from New York. Christo got his permission from the Mairie only after Chirac was safely installed there for another term, and then he had to start all over again, with the Socialists, because the Pont Neuf belongs to the city *and* the state as far as permissions are concerned, and the city and the state are usually more interested in sabotaging each other's projects than in sharing them. François Mitterrand's Préfet de Police de Paris, for one, thought that Christo was a public nuisance. It took an order from the President to start the project, and two hundred people working from barges and hanging from ropes and negotiating the bottom of the Seine in frogman suits to finish it—and when the hundred tons of ballast and chain and the three miles of steel cable and the nearly half-million square feet of polyamide were all in place and the bridge wrapped up and tied, Paris accommodated it like any other piece of the city, the way Paris accommodated in their time the Eiffel Tower and the colored pipes of Beaubourg and the arches and obelisks and Orientalist fantasies that Parisians have been putting up since the Gauls pitched skin shelters in the woods that are still under the Pont Neuf on the Île de la Cité.

The interesting thing about the wrapped Pont Neuf was that in a few hours it looked as if it had always been around. It looked comfortable. It was not witty, like Christo's pink-petaled islands off Miami, which were a corsage for the city, gaudy and exuberant and touching. It had none of the breathtaking beauty of his Running Fence of white nylon that had dipped and curved across a couple of California counties until it dropped, suddenly, into the Pacific and disappeared. The Running Fence had involved a whole community of ranchers in an almost Keatsian apprehension of time and loss, and the best part of it may have been the moment that Albert and David Maysles caught in a wonderful movie they made about the fence—the moment some of those old Sonoma Valley ranchers came out to see it for the first time. The best part of the wrapped Pont Neuf was the moment when Parisians began to ignore it. The polyamide on the bridge, which was dyed the pale-gold color of old Paris stone, got dirty the way Paris's buildings and monuments get dirty, and after about a week it faded into the city and people began to joke about getting it sandblasted, like Notre Dame or the Assemblée Nationale. In fact, in certain light, if you were coming from the east, it looked like the ramparts of some ancient Île de la Cité fortress—of a piece, really, with the Conciergerie, around the corner on the Quai de l'Horloge. About two hundred thousand people came to see the Pont Neuf every day and walked it and touched it, and it gave the Paris intellectuals something to talk about. They observed that the wrapping, with its long, deep folds, was "remarkably French in its commentary." They compared Christo wrapping the bridge to a great couturier dressing a woman: they discussed the "firm softness" of the pleats and talked about the "lovely revealed curves" of the arches. Afternoons, on the bridge, you could hear the students and professors from the neighborhood discoursing on the meaning of the pleat, on the "evident outside and mysterious inside," on the "vaginal folds" in Mallarmé's poetry and the "grimacing folds" of the mourning coats that Baudelaire's women wore. Sometimes they talked about Jacques Derrida's deconstruction of le pli, and sometimes about the "wrapped space of the bourgeois interior," with its art collections and its private household objects, which Maeterlinck wrote about and Walter Benjamin described, and a young professor from my building whom I ran into on the bridge decided that Christo had made a kind of ultimate statement about bourgeois capitalism—he had "collected" the Pont Neuf for himself by wrapping it up. When the professor and his friends got bored with the Pont Neuf, they said that perhaps it was Roland Barthes who had had the really interesting idea about surfaces. They quoted from Barthes's famous essay on the Citroën DS19, with its smooth and molded surfaces signifying perfection, "like the tunic of Christ," and the professor went off to write an article to the effect that the fundamental opposition in Western culture was the opposition between draped and flat things, with Christo for the moment on the draped side of the argument. Thus, the wrapped Pont Neuf entered what Parisians like to call *le discours.* Then it was time to take it down.

October 1985

EIGHT REFLECTIONS

THE WEST OF THE EAST

Lech Walesa came to Paris this fall and was photographed backstage at the Olympia, where Yves Montand is singing in a one-man show. In the photograph, Walesa and Montand are laughing; Walesa is nearly doubled over laughing, and Montand is holding out an arm to support him. They are sharing a story or a joke, sharing a moment—the hero of Poland's social revolution and the performer best known for playing heroes like him in movies like *La Guerre Est Finie* and *Z*. Walesa's face is still a new face to the people who buy French picture magazines. It is, anyway, Montand's familiar, funny, practiced face—melted a little by experience, touched by world-weariness and amusement—that holds you. Alongside Montand, Walesa seems ordinary and diminished. This is the response the eye has to the photograph—the first, sentimental reaction—and it is not so odd, really, because such images are often more seductive and satisfying than the reality on which they draw. There is a kind of aesthetic of politics in Paris. People are "attending" Poland now as if it were a theater. They are dropping in on the Polish revolution the way Europe's aristocrats drove their best carriages to Waterloo in 1815 to watch the Duke of Wellington take on Napoleon. Everybody goes—students, reporters, tourists, timid scholars hoping to attach themselves and their careers to something important. And occasionally the Polish revolution comes here, with its fine ironies (Walesa wanting to meet not François Mitterrand but Brigitte Bardot) and its confusions of identity (Simone Signoret in the background of the Olympia photograph, ample and radiant and modest, like a Polish wife).

The young man next to me on the plane from Milan to Budapest looked at the picture in the magazine and decided that Yves Montand must be the Polish revolutionary and Lech Walesa the performer. He had never heard of Yves Montand before—though this had less to do with his being Hungarian than with his being twenty-three and never having seen *Z* or *La Guerre Est Finie* or, for that matter, any of Montand's movies. He had heard of Walesa, of course, but he had never seen his picture in a Hungarian magazine or paper. When I told him who was who at the Olympia, he said that maybe the tall French singer in the terry-cloth robe *should* be leading the Polish revolution—that maybe Poland would be in less of a mess with Yves Montand running Solidarity. It was his idea of a Polish joke, and he liked it so much he repeated it, unbuckling his seat belt and leaning out into the aisle to pass the magazine to some friends in the row behind him. *En bloc,* he and his friends were the Szombathely soccer team. Milan had beaten them, 2–0, in a match that day, and now they were flying back to Hungary; they said that Szombathely was just a small city, off near the Austrian border, and they had never expected to beat a big city like Milan anyway. They were open and agreeable, a little shy, and obviously proud of their new team travelling clothes: every one of them had on a gray pinstriped suit and vest, a bright-blue drip-dry shirt, a navy tie, and "Western" boots from Italy—the pointed, orange kind that stop short just above the ankle. They may have missed *Z,* but they *had* seen *Kramer vs. Kramer* in Szombathely, and they could describe in detail the various adventures of Charlie's Angels, Kojak, and Columbo.

The Hungarians and the Poles were friends, the young man said, handing back the magazine. He did not like the Czechs. He certainly did not like the Rumanians. He liked the Poles best of anybody else in Eastern Europe, but his life in Hungary—to judge from the pinstriped suit and the shiny boots and the new family house he described and the money he made moonlighting as a mechanic and his trips abroad with the soccer team—was a good life, and he thought that the Poles were risking *his* good fortune with their wildcat strikes and their romantic revolutionary posturing. The man across the aisle thought so, too, and *he* was Italian—a Genoese in the container-shipping business, who passed out cards to the astonished soccer team and was rather downcast that none of the Hungarians on Malév Airlines Flight No. 411 (three times a week out of Milan) had heard of Brooks Brothers, where he had bought his tie. He liked the Poles as much as anyone did, he said. Poles and Italians were friends. They were so much alike, really—warm, impulsive, Catholic, *Latin.* But no smart businessman would invest in

Poland. Hungary was the place to make a deal. Hungary had got so rich since 1956 that the country was exporting grain surpluses. Hungary was joining the International Monetary Fund and the World Bank. The Hungarian forint was about to become a convertible hard currency, like the lira or the dollar (though only for foreigners making deals, and not for ordinary Hungarians). The Genoese was a rich man, obviously a *nouveau riche* man, one of a generation of European entrepreneurs whose network of trade and profit had nothing to do with East-West politics or border tensions or détente. He was a good twenty years older than the soccer player across the aisle, but there they both were, sharing a chilled Hungarian Tokay with their airline sandwiches and talking a rudimentary English—which the soccer player was studying nights, because the Russian he had studied for four mandatory years in school was useless when the team travelled. Each of them was a materialist in his own way, and neither was much interested in any new liberties in Eastern Europe that might disrupt an equilibrium they had come to count on.

The soccer player (I'll call him Otto) was born after Hungary's two-week revolution. He had read a paragraph or two about the revolution—it was called a Fascist uprising—in a school history book when he was twelve, but no one in Szombathely had ever really talked to him about it. Once, on a trip with the team to Budapest, he took a bus up the Buda hills to the Hapsburg royal palace, which is now the National Museum, and visited the big permanent exhibit on the history of the city—but the exhibit stopped with 1949 and the triumph of Socialism. He knew that the palace, along with most of Buda, had been rebuilt with Russian money over the years since the Second World War, but he had no idea that it was Russian tanks that had destroyed so much of Buda in 1956, or that the Russians' restoration was political— a way of erasing two weeks of Hungarian history, like expurgating a textbook. Early last month, Otto was practicing for the match in Milan and was too busy to read the paper when his government commemorated the anniversary of the Hungarian revolution for the first time—that is, when the Central Committee of the Hungarian Communist Party, anxious about the bad influence of Poland, decided that it would speak out about the counter-revolution that had threatened Hungary in 1956, and about the Communists who were martyred, and about how János Kádár, the Party Secretary, had saved the nation on November 4 with his new "Revolutionary Worker-Peasant Government." (Most Hungarians thought it was tasteless of the government to remind them.) Otto was coming home on the twenty-fifth anniversary of the day the uprising ended—the day the Russians completed their occupation of the country. And when we landed, Budapest was getting ready for its celebration of another revolution: the Russian Revolution of 1917. All the public buildings in the city and a lot of shops and restaurants, and even houses, were hung with the red-white-and-green flag of the Magyar Republic and with the red flag of that revolution, and it was instructive to note that while no one neglected to hang a red flag next to his country's flag, only a few people had thought or cared to add a hammer and sickle to the upper left corner.

There is something dashing about a city hung with red flags. Budapest, at any rate, enjoyed its flags. People talked about how festive the city looked that weekend, and they even seemed a little sorry when the flags came down, like children after the Christmas ornaments are put away. It may be that Hungarians have lived by their wits for so long —through centuries of occupation by Turks and Austrians and finally Germans—that by now they are able to persuade themselves that they are one up, as it were, on their own repression. They seem to believe that their tolerance of the Russians since 1956 has been a kind of ruse —a smoke screen thrown over what in Hungary is usually referred to as "the political arrangement." A lot of Hungarians are frankly relieved that nothing is demanded of them anymore in the way of heroics. It is as if they thought of liberty (when they thought of it at all) as a long-lost Hungarian cause, and of their two weeks of resistance in 1956 as an aberrant moment in Hungarian history. There are eleven million people in Hungary. Two hundred thousand left in 1956, and, according to the economist Péter Kende, who left with them and lives in Paris now, a few thousand more have been emigrating every year since then. The émigrés of 1956 were an odd lot of Communist idealists and bourgeois liberals and Catholic conservatives. (Cardinal Mindszenty, who took refuge in the American Embassy and stayed for fifteen years, and was consequently taken up by Americans as a kind of official spokesman of the uprising, was an outright reactionary and, by some accounts, a Fascist.) The émigrés of 1968—the "Prague Spring émigrés," people call them, because their disenchantment had to do with Russian (and consequently Hungarian) intransigence about Czechoslovakia —were mainly dissident Marxists. Some of them were old students of the philosopher György Lukács, and some of them settled as far away as Australia, trying to avoid the lecture-circuit notoriety of political exiles, and especially of Russian exiles, for whom dissidence becomes a kind of career in itself. Hungarians have a keen sense of the ridiculous. They do not have much appetite for spending their working lives as

gloomy, wandering prophets of some Communist apocalypse. A lot of
them leave Hungary—and then come home. Mihály Vajda, the political
philosopher, left for the University of Bremen in the late seventies, and
after two years was back in Budapest. György Konrád, the novelist,
went to Berlin and then to Paris and New York, and came back, too.
He says that it is simply not very interesting to be an exile—that
intellectuals who stay in Hungary (and the sort of people who think
about staying or leaving are almost by definition intellectuals) may be
isolated, but they are not alone. They have an adversary role to play.
Konrád himself was detained for a week in 1974 for writing a book
called *The Intellectuals on the Road to Class Power* with his friend Ivan
Szelényi, the sociologist. He was offered emigration then, and refused
it. His novels are banned in Hungary now, and it seems to be forbidden
to mention any of them in the newspapers. But he keeps on writing,
and his books are published abroad and find their way back to Hungary,
and that, he says, is mainly what he wants as a dissident and a writer
and a Hungarian—to live and work in his own language and be understood.

Everybody in Hungary had the day off in honor of the Russian
Revolution. The important Communists went to their summer houses
on the Danube. A lot of less important people stayed in Budapest,
walking through Buda, window-shopping in Pest, sitting down to
coffee and pastry at the Vörösmarty confiserie, and wondering what
was happening that day in Poland. Hungarians talk about Poland with
all the mixed emotions of people who have tried the same thing and
failed. They talk with bitterness and arrogance and shame, and with a
fear that is the real legacy of 1956. They genuinely do not know why
Russian tanks entered Hungary two weeks after *their* uprising, while
Poland has gone free for seventeen months. "We are the Sancho Panzas
of Europe, and for two weeks we were the Don Quixotes—it nearly
finished us," a woman I met for coffee at the Vörösmarty told me. It
was another way of saying that Hungarians have traded regret for an
image of themselves as cautious, practical, shrewd people—as people
who have "survived" Russia. They like to compare their history and
Poland's. A hundred years ago, they say, Hungary had to contend with
the Hapsburgs and Poland had to contend with the Romanovs, but
then it was the Poles who adapted, while the Magyars dreamed on
about a great and independent Hungary. Now it is the Poles who are
dreaming and the Hungarians who accommodate, talking about things
like the commodities market and the balance of trade, biding their time,

making money, making contacts, telling jokes about their own corruption.

People in Hungary love telling jokes. It is a kind of pseudo politics in a world where real politics are forbidden—a way of talking about that world. Two old Budapest Jews called Kohn and Grün have always been the stock commentators on socialism in Eastern Europe, and so I was struck by the fact that in Hungary last month Kohn and Grün were gone from the stories. The jokes had lost their edge of self-irony and self-knowledge. They mocked the Poles and their poverty. There were jokes about cats with mouse rations, jokes about meat—or, rather, about no meat. (Why is there not enough meat in Poland? The American says, "What is 'not enough'?" The Russian says, "What is 'why'?" The Pole says, "What is 'meat'?") I spent an evening with some middle-aged establishment literati—an editor from the state publishing house, a one-novel novelist with a job reading manuscripts for the editor, and a poet they publish who has made a name for himself representing Hungarian literature at international conferences, and was, in fact, just back from a P.E.N. seminar abroad. The evening began with Polish jokes, and with everyone agreeing that "the trouble with Poland is the Poles," and ended with everyone agreeing that Hungary was winning the fight for freedom slowly, with vegetables, not strikes—sounding just like the propaganda they claimed to despise. The litany, public and private, goes like this: The Poles are lazy. The Polish worker will not work, and, furthermore, expects the hardworking Hungarian worker to feed him with meat and grain that Hungary could be selling to the West for hard currency. (A Pole is carried off, chained to two policemen. A friend, seeing him in the street, asks what happened. "I killed my wife," the Pole says. "Ah, good," says the friend. "I thought they were taking you to work.") The Poles are striking and carrying on now, the litany continues, but it is the Hungarians who will have to send their sons to fight and die for that extravagance when Russia invokes the Warsaw Pact and calls the troops out. In the end, there will be a terrible backlash, and it is the Hungarians who will lose the liberties they have won with their vegetable revolution. "Now, for the first time, we are beginning to crawl out of the mess of our history," the poet said. "For the first time, we have a sense of the future, a more or less decent way to handle our problems, a new possibility to be clean—and the West says no, stop, dissent. The West wants to know our terrible secret compromise. The West says that we must be morally crippled if we admit that it is not so bad here after all." On another evening, in another apartment, an economist whose theory about "shortage" in traditional socialist societies has got him guest professorships at Princeton and Stanford says that maybe Hungarians like him have made compromises, that maybe the compromises don't look very attractive to a Westerner, but that revolution, close up, does not look very attractive, either. He does not have a very high opinion of the masses, he says. Millions of people will sacrifice themselves for a while—he calls it the adrenaline of revolution—but in the long run if it is a question of liberty or meat the masses will choose meat. Then, there is the historian who takes me to lunch at the cafeteria of his institute and makes a list of the bad things in Hungary and the good things in Hungary. He is very courteous and shy. One of the good things, he says finally, is his salary and his wife's salary. Together, he and his wife make the equivalent of about twelve hundred dollars a month, and this means that now, twenty-five years after the Russians came, he can relax and travel, and even send his children to the West, to America, to study.

The West is the real privilege in Hungary. Kádár's genius was to introduce a generation of Hungarians to the West—to have made the West the particular reward of being a compliant citizen of his Communist state. The compliant citizen obeys a few easy rules: Do not complain about the Communist Party or ridicule the Party or challenge its authority; do not criticize the Warsaw Pact or Hungary's part in the Pact or Soviet expansion backed by the Pact; do not condone neutralism, pacifism, or revisionism; hang out a red flag on Russian holidays. Then the citizen can put away his red passport—which is a special passport for visiting other socialist countries—and get his blue passport stamped for Western travel. He does not have to vacation in Bulgaria anymore, or spend his free semester in Moscow. He can go—as the poet and his two friends had gone—to the University of Iowa's Writers' Workshop. He can teach for a year at a time in America, like the shortage economist.

Hungarians like to call their country "the West of the East." Kádár had nationalized the farms by 1962, but he left the peasants their garden plots, and eventually even the state started buying produce from those plots. By now, the 15 percent of the land that is farmed privately accounts for over 40 percent of the agricultural output. A peasant family these days can mean a father working in a factory, a mother working on a farm cooperative, the children studying in school, or even college, and all of them getting together nights and weekends to tend the garden and feed the pigs and chickens they will eventually sell for whatever the market brings. Everybody works in Hungary—or, rather, everybody saves his best effort for the work he does for himself, by himself. Some 80 percent of the population makes money in what is always delicately referred to as "the second economy." It is pretty much acknowledged that whatever energy the Hungarian economy has depends on people working on their own or in cooperatives they control. The adrenaline, clearly, is not in revolution but in enterprise. Kádár began loosening up the state system in 1968—persuading Moscow that this was the best way to avoid another Czechoslovakia. He introduced profit sharing and left most factories free to indulge in a certain amount of market economics. Now Budapest women, who like to dress well, remember 1968 not as the year the Czechs begged for freedom but as the year the shoes in the stores began to resemble the shoes they actually wanted, which were French shoes, rather than the shoes they had been getting, which were designed by five-year planners and produced in lots of no fewer than a hundred thousand. Now there is so much private business going on in Hungary that the government has divided it into official categories—making it legal, first of all, so as to claim some of the enormous profits in income tax. There are already private restaurants, private shops, private services like plumbing and garages. In January, there will be "private collectives," too, which means, in effect, that people will be able to "associate" and start businesses and hire other people to work for them. Hungarians working in a state industry—a munitions factory, say—can get together now and manufacture bicycle parts in that factory, or hair restorer, or anything the market will bear and the Party will tolerate. Family businesses can take on apprentices. A group of editors at the state publishing company are even planning a private press within the company, and no one is at all worried about their publishing dissident books, because their one object seems to be to turn out bad novels for a mass market and make a lot of money. And in a few weeks' time Hungarians will be allowed to invest as stockholders in private collectives like that new press and count on realizing their investment in two or three years.

It is hard to be a dissident in Hungary today precisely *because* there is so little overt injustice, or evidence of injustice. Where other Eastern European regimes throw their dissidents in jail or lock them up in mental hospitals, Hungary punishes dissidents by firing them from their jobs. András Hegedüs, who was Prime Minister during the fall of 1956 (and, some people say, the man who called in the Russians), is a dissident now. He has lost his job at the Sociology Institute, and rides to Pest on the public bus to lecture old students from the institute at a kind of floating Monday-night free university. His oldest son has just quit *his* job to open the first Chinese restaurant in Hungary—a private Chinese restaurant. All this makes it difficult to say what kind of country Hungary is anymore—beyond being a police state that runs less on brutality than on the memory of brutality and the tension of capricious reprisal. Hegedüs had been a protégé of Mátyás Rákosi, and it was Rákosi who had János Kádár imprisoned and tortured in 1951, when Rákosi was running the Party and Kádár was considered a revisionist. Kádár himself is a mystery. He dropped out of sight during the Hungarian revolution, and everyone assumed that the Russians had shot him, until he reappeared in Szolnok a few days later in a Russian armored car to take over the country. Since then, he has survived all sorts of palace plots, quietly compromising his enemies until they retire, in disgrace, from Party politics. There are pictures of Lenin in every ministry—the favorite seems to be an inlaid-wood mosaic, with the famous bald head in sandalwood—but never of Kádár. He is not so much modest as mindful of the risks of exposure. He would never tolerate what is now referred to in East Europe as "a Poland"— where important apparatchiks skim money from Party dues for lavish villas and private planes and trips to Paris for their wives' haircuts. Occasionally, he will purge the Party of some extravagance; a few years ago, he called in the fifteen hundred Mercedes-Benzes the Party owned, auctioned them off, and instructed his people to make do with Russian Ladas, which are a kind of Communist-bloc Deux Chevaux. At the same time, he has cynically bought off social discontent in Hungary with department stores full of clothes and gadgets, and has encouraged such a consumer lust in workers that Hungarians have started calling the 1980s their "Eisenhower years."

Ulrike Meinhof, in prison in West Germany as a terrorist, talked about *Konsumterror*—the terrorism of things and of the society that valued the objects it sold more than the clean conscience it could not sell. There is a kind of *Konsumterror* in Hungary. People have chosen things. They say that the sacrifices they must make for those things are rhetorical—a vote with Russia in the United Nations, an invasion condoned—and don't matter very much anyway. They say that they have got the best of the bargain—that the regime in Budapest is at least benign, and has long since stopped dragging dissidents out of bed at night or executing unruly politicians the way that Rákosi executed his Foreign Minister, László Rajk, in 1949, or that Kádár, for that matter, saw to the execution of Imre Nagy after the 1956 revolution. Today, László Rajk's son has organized a *samizdat*, a do-it-yourself dissident press, and supervises a clandestine weekly distribution of its publications. There is, in short, a psychology of compliance and a psychology of dissidence, and the chasm between them is so profound that no one in Hungary talks anymore about levels or degrees of protest. Dissidents say, simply, that it is humiliating for a man or a woman to be grateful or obligated to the state for whatever liberty the state allows. They are what they call "outside." They do not accept the humiliation. Other people do accept it. They exercise a kind of self-censorship that is effective in that nobody really knows what the limits of expression are; they do not risk their jobs by saying the wrong thing, writing the wrong book, meeting with the wrong people.

The Hungarian who does not actively, formally dissent is apt to overlook little incidents of repression and go shopping when he feels bad, or take a walk across the beautiful Chain Bridge to Buda. He can choose his information. He "knows," for example, that the head of Hungary's official labor union wrote a long answer to Lech Walesa's appeal to Eastern European workers, but he does not know what the answer really was, because only the tough parts were published in the paper or read on television. He knows that the government is nervous about Poland, but unless he makes it his business to find out he has no way of knowing that fifty young Hungarians had their red passports taken back for trying to leave the country for Poland; he knows, instead, how many Poles are coming to Hungary and buying Hungarian medicine and food. Most of all, he knows that he has no choice except to work for the state. There is usually no other way for him to do the job the state has taught him.

Hungarians are always taking polls. There are thousands of sociologists in the country, and most of them spend their time doing surveys for the government. They believe that the right sociologists asking the right questions of the right sampling of Hungarians every couple of months will give them the key to their society—the answer to what makes Hungarians happy and what keeps Hungary compliant. The government believes it, too. The government believes so much in the power of the information it receives this way that it keeps the polls secret and the conclusions secret—though inevitably word gets out and people talk about them. Early this year, there was a poll to determine what Hungarians considered the most important thing happening in the world. The reply was supposed to be the Soviet Party Congress then in session, but to the government's distress, two thousand typical Hungarians said that it was either Ronald Reagan's election or the

Russians' war in Afghanistan or Solidarity in Poland. Now the government has asked a much more convoluted question, and discovered that 80 percent of the people in Hungary think of themselves as being more favorably disposed toward the revolution in Poland than their neighbors are. This is considered a very Hungarian answer.

December 1981

GROUND ZERO

The war panic in Germany is real. A lot of Germans are convinced, or are trying to convince themselves, that there will be a war soon and in Germany, and that they will all die in minutes in what the military discreetly calls a "theater nuclear exchange" between American Pershing II missiles and Soviet SS–20s. Young Germans carry around the Stockholm International Peace Research Institute yearbook on nuclear weapons. They march for disarmament—300,000 Germans marched peacefully through Bonn this winter protesting NATO's plan to deploy 204 new American missiles in West Germany in the next two years—and their demonstrations have the quiet fervor of the Ban the Bomb marches of the 1950s. They are obsessed with the idea of war. They seem to have no faith in the restraint of others—perhaps because Germany has had so little of its own. Germans, of course, are not the only Europeans worrying about the practicality, and even the sanity, of adding more nuclear artillery to their small, dense, fitfully civilized continent. But Germans think of themselves as ground zero—as somehow singled out by geography to be sacrifices to other people's politics. (The irony escapes them, though rarely any of their neighbors.)

The French are skeptical about German pacifism. I was in Hamburg a few weeks ago, and ran into a French television crew from Antenne 2 which was travelling around Germany documenting what the producer called "the daily life" of people involved in the peace movement—tracking them, so to speak, to their native habitats, for the observation and edification of his home audience. The producer thought these people were crazy. He had just finished interviewing

Freimut Duve, a forty-five-year-old Social Democratic deputy to the Bundestag and the editor of a distinguished collection published by Rowohlt which includes some fourteen or fifteen books about nuclear weaponry, the Peace Institute yearbook among them. Tomorrow, he said, he was going to film Duve at home with his wife and his daughters. He said that it was important to see exactly how someone who claimed to fear neutron bombs as much as he feared Russians spent the day.

Certainly there is not much of a pacifist tradition in France. Pacifism, the French believe, is precisely a weakness of Protestants in places like Germany (or England, for that matter, or Sweden or almost anywhere else in Northern Europe). The French believe in what they call "dissuasion." They believe that de Gaulle left NATO because defending NATO did not come down to the same thing as defending France. They believe that being able to defend France themselves and at their own discretion is their only security. Back in the sixties, François Mitterrand voted in the National Assembly against the *force de frappe* —France's nuclear-strike force—but now he argues for extending it. He worries that any "Europeanization of defense" will leave France at the mercy of those neutralists and pacificists who have not learned what he now sees so clearly as the lesson of the Second World War: France fell because it had no real way to dissuade the Germans, no bombs in silos on the Plateau d'Albion that might have spared it the pain of occupation and defeat. He worries now that the defense of Europe will end up meaning no defense for France. He does not worry about blowing up the world, and says so.

Actually, no one in Catholic Europe—call it Southern Europe or Mediterranean Europe—seems particularly worried about blowing up the world, about nuclear weaponry or nuclear war. This is a fact of Mediterranean life, and it seems to have nothing to do with whether people practice their Catholicism or whether Socialists or Conservatives are in power. People who try to explain it come up with the same applicable clichés about the ancient, accommodating, surviving, cynical, fatalistic South. They talk about a God that Southerners can possess in baroque sunbursts and gaudy cathedrals and all the sumptuous trappings of a worldly church, about Southerners' being drawn to pleasure and hence to sin and the confession of sin and arriving at the peculiar innocence of the absolved. Or they speculate that Catholic countries with strong Communist parties are "immune" to the kinds of arguments one hears in the North about shaming the Russians into disarming by disarming first—because history has taught those countries to have confidence in neither shame nor Communists. All this is really a way of saying that, for reasons no one understands, Southern Europeans are not at all guilty about having nuclear bombs. They are not guilty about daily, or even millennial, injustices. They do not really understand the spiritual scrupulousness that began in Northern Europe when Ulrich Zwingli melted down the Catholic crowns and scepters of Zurich's churches, turned them into Protestant gold bricks, and then used those bare churches to admonish the burghers and bankers who got the bricks about cupidity.

About ten years ago, the French historian Philippe Ariès ended a series of lectures on Western attitudes toward death by asking, "Must we take it for granted that it is impossible for our technological cultures ever to regain the naïve confidence in Destiny which had for so long been shown by simple men when dying?" Certainly the Germans have lost that confidence. The French, on the other hand, seem to have come full circle—to a naïve confidence that it is their own destiny to *survive*. They get excited and complain, but they do not have gloomy fantasies. Babar is their fantasy. The France they long for is a peaceable kingdom ruled by a benevolent bourgeois elephant—a family politic where little old ladies converse with monkeys in tennis shoes and learned professors take baby elephants on picnics. (Laurent de Brunhoff, who has written and drawn Babar for thirty-five years, says that his French readers will not tolerate discord in Celesteville; a few years ago, he wrote a book about an angry pig, *The One Pig with Horns,* and had to send it straight to America, because his French publisher was too horrified to print it.) They fall asleep at night to the television sight of Folon's little animated-cartoon gentlemen, in their long black overcoats and homburgs, flapping their arms and flying to twinkling stars, to sweet bedtime music. They listen earnestly to politicians who tell them that people who eat a lot of potatoes, like the Germans and the Irish, are prone to violence, whereas people like the French, who eat a lot of bread, are by nutrition agreeable—and can safely have all the bombs they want. In France, *"Non à la bombe à neutrons!"* is a hostile, Communist slogan. It was broadcast, full blast, over the fairgrounds at La Courneuve when the Communists had their annual Fête de l'Humanité. It was printed on Party posters. And by now to everybody in France but the Communists it has begun to sound subversive. The result of this, of course, is that the proper anti-Communist in France supports the *force de frappe* and a new French neutron bomb and the country's extraordinary fleet of missile-bearing submarines. His arsenal is a correlative of his identity. In a way, his bombs end the humiliation he suffered in the war.

Pierre Bourdieu, the sociologist, says that one reason the French have been so fervent about Poland is that the Polish military crackdown on December 13 provided them with a real *événement*—a piece of history to witness and corroborate, an act of oppression they could measure and interpret. They are relieved to be cured, if only temporarily, of their habitual weakness for abstraction, and so they are bound to be wary of Germans asking questions about nuclear morality. The French do not want to be left contemplating the end of Europe if the end of Europe turns out to be another embarrassing abstraction, like structuralism or Mao Zedong. And so they call the Germans, with their desperate pacifism, hysterical, and the Germans call them vain and foolish. For young Germans, and for some Germans who were young during the war, the idea that their country has a mission in a damned world is a kind of redemption. They have had no history to attach to with any pride, and it is intoxicating for them now to think of themselves as victims of a madness other than their own. This is why there is an almost expiatory fervor to so much of the new pacifist politics. Duve himself worries about what he calls a "traumatic idealism" in the German character. He compares it with the idealism of the French, which since the war in Algeria has tended to play itself out in rhetoric and rarely interferes with the real business at hand; German idealism, he says, consumes the idealist and with him whatever chance for a healing, ordinary life the world around him offers.

Some of the pacifists in Germany now say that the problem is not just weapon systems and weapon economies but energy systems in countries like their own and France and Switzerland, which try to export their breeder-reactor technology—and thus, inevitably if not intentionally, potential bombs—to the Third World. They say that whatever trading is done at the Geneva arms-control talks this year —the United States, say, agreeing to cut back production of its new cruise missiles, and the Russians agreeing to pull some of their SS-20s out of Eastern Europe—will not solve that problem. The current pacifist cliché that being a little nuclear is like being a little pregnant is, of course, accurate. NATO can argue about putting new mobile ground missiles—Pershing IIs—in West Germany, but there are already something like six thousand nuclear weapons in a country roughly the size of Oregon, and there are perhaps three thousand nuclear weapons in East Germany, which is a lot smaller—about the size of Virginia. They are medium- or short-range missiles for "flexible response"—not for blowing up the planet but for providing a kind of nuclear sampler. They are functions of an absurdist belief in deterrence—of a not very comforting logic which holds that he who fires first dies second. It is possible that this absurdity is what has kept the peace in Europe for more than thirty years. Helmut Schmidt thinks so. Most Germans, in fact, think so. But people in the peace movement say that there is more to "peace" than a thirty-year ceasefire between armed camps. Some of them are pacifists, and they dream of complete disarmament. The majority would never describe themselves as pacifists. They simply do not want to be defended (if the word applies) by neutron bombs or by chemical warheads or by any of the weapons being considered by both sides now. They are nervous when the American President who can push the button to release those weapons starts talking about a limited nuclear war in Western Europe, as Ronald Reagan did last fall. They say that when Americans start planning "theater nuclear war" it means that Americans have sanctioned a difference in the quality of security at home and the quality of security in Western Europe. America is the citadel, they say, and Europe the glacis. Günter Gaus, who opened the first West German mission to East Germany and is now one of the Social Democrats lobbying to keep out the new Pershings, argues this way: Europe since the war has been a not very commendable but very secure island of peace. The principle of divided influence is respected in Europe, and therefore Europe is the one place on earth where war is not necessarily the result of failed East-West politics. Europe cannot afford to take risks for Latin America or Africa or the Middle East. Europe's proper concern right now is Europe; whatever happens in the rest of the world, the equilibrium of a divided Europe must be kept. This was NATO's charter, and America, by insisting on nuclear rearmament in Europe and confusing its role as a superpower with its role as a NATO partner, has ignored that charter and left Europe vulnerable.

Wolf Graf Baudissin, who runs the University of Hamburg's Institute for Peace Research and Defense Policy, was the general who helped develop NATO's "flexible response" strategy, and *he* says that it is meaningless to talk about security gaps between America and its allies, since if America decides to drop a bomb on Soviet tanks invading West Germany, the Russians are more likely to shoot one back to America, where the order originated, than to the countries where America's bombs happen to be stored. He says that definitions of nuclear self-interest depend entirely on who is doing the defining. There are the missile-counters, with their theories of nuclear parity. There are men who, like Baudissin himself, do not think that a hundred new Pershing missiles will make a critical difference, one way or the other, to the defense of Europe but want to see them deployed now that NATO has agreed to it; they say that NATO should honor its decisions if for no other reason than that at the Geneva arms-control talks America needs arms to talk about controlling. There are politicians on the left, like Erhard Eppler, who want Germany to reject any new missiles proposed by the United States. But the fact is that most of them agree (at least in private) that strategic stability does not depend entirely on numbers—that there are important psychological factors to what we call the nuclear balance. They know that for twenty years the Russians had seven hundred medium-range missiles aimed at Western Europe and nobody in Western Europe seemed to care.

The real accomplishment of the peace movement may be in convincing people that there is no such thing as a nuclear-war "expert" —that the generals sitting over drinks, betting our cruise missiles against the Russians' SS-20s, are only a fraction better informed about the perimeters of destruction than the eighteen-year-olds sitting in their student bars in Hamburg and talking about *Heimat* and a new German consciousness. In a way, it was youngsters demonstrating near Hamburg against nuclear power plants who forced their parents to start thinking about nuclear bombs. Hans Ulrich Klose, who was mayor of Hamburg for seven years and finally quit in disgust last spring when his own cabinet voted to support what will be the city's fourth nuclear power plant, in Brokdorf, says that for him, as for a lot of people in the city, arguments about nuclear safety turned from ecological into political, even ideological, arguments. People in Hamburg began to ask whether nuclear policy could—or should—be left to businessmen or politicians or generals. They raised questions of accountability. They got frightened. Two hundred and fifty thousand German Lutherans were in Hamburg last June for a national assembly, and though the official text of the assembly was "Be Not Afraid" ("*Fürchte Dich Nicht*"), young pacifist ministers and their parishioners changed it to "Be Afraid" ("*Fürchte Dich*").

The decision to deploy 108 new American Pershing II missiles and 464 new American cruise missiles in Western Europe was made in Brussels on December 12, 1979. It was made ruefully, but it was made by all fourteen participating treaty countries, insofar as the generals who work in Brussels can be said to represent those countries. Later, the Europeans complained that it was the bad end of a deal they had had to make with the Americans. They wanted the United States back in Geneva for new arms-control talks, and Jimmy Carter wanted mobile tactical missiles in Western Europe. It was his idea of parity, and no one in Washington then expected so many Germans to oppose it, inasmuch as it was Helmut Schmidt who had first brought up the question of nuclear parity in Europe, in a speech at the International Institute for Strategic Studies, in London, two years earlier. Schmidt has always considered himself a nuclear expert. (He enjoys arguing missiles with pacifists like Eppler, who is fairly fanatical and can get carried away and ruin his own argument.) Schmidt *believes* in missile parity. He thinks that the new Pershings are important to West German security. He has been nervous about that security ever since the Russians started deploying SS-20s in the late seventies. His friends say he is convinced that there would be no peace movement of any consequence in West Germany today if Ronald Reagan and the "nuclear cowboys" (as they like to call them) in the White House had not started talking so casually about little nuclear wars in Europe. There is obviously more to the movement than Ronald Reagan's lack of tact. Freimut Duve talks about young Germans' loss of trust in the ability of any elected parliament or congress to control military fantasies. They inherited a Weimar complex, and now, Duve says, they have a Hiroshima complex, too. They are convinced that Hiroshima could well have been Dresden, say, and that their protests against Schmidt's nuclear policy and—by extension—Reagan's are a kind of last democratic option. Duve thinks that peace-movement people tend to focus their panic on America because America is, after all, an ally and a democracy, and they can hope to affect American policy, whereas they have no illusions at all about affecting Russian policy. Some of them say they worry about what they call a peace double standard. But the fact is that a lot of people in the peace movement seem to trust Russia much more than the United States when it comes to the question of nuclear war in Western Europe. They say that Russia and Germany shared one binding experience in the Second World War—they were both battlefields for civilians. And they conclude that for a Russian war in Europe means war at home—it means twenty million dead Russians—and that this, if anything, protects them. They make Americans furious. The French look at them and say that there has clearly been something dangerously romantic, dangerously German, in their education.

March 1982

DANTON AND ROBESPIERRE

There is an argument going on in Paris about a movie called *Danton*. The argument does not have much to do with whether *Danton* is a good movie or a bad movie, although it probably should, because by any reasonable standard *Danton* is terrible. The argument is about whether the Polish director Andrzej Wajda, who made *Danton*, has a correct appreciation of the French Revolution—a correct appreciation from the point of view of the French government being that "the people," in their passion for liberty, were the true heroes of the Revolution and that a strong man of the Grande Terreur like Maximilien de Robespierre was merely a servant of that passion, carried away by a conviction that "the Terror is nothing more than prompt, severe, and inflexible justice" in the people's name. The government here gave Wajda about half a million of the four million dollars that *Danton* cost to produce, but more important, it gave him the blessing of a Socialist Élysée and a year of fussy service from the Ministry of Culture. The government in Poland, where Wajda still lives and works and has a theater company, gave him another four hundred thousand. He raised the rest of the money privately. Most of it came from Gaumont, the French production-and-distribution company, which figured that a movie about revolution and oppression made in France by a famous Polish director during the year that Solidarity was crushed (and opening in forty-five Gaumont theaters) was not a very risky proposition.

No one really knows why the Poles invest in Wajda. *Man of Iron*, his movie about Solidarity, was not much better than *Danton*, and its sentimental images of Church and family were about as popular with the Party in Poland as Marc Riboud's photograph of little Magdalena

Walesa in her christening robe. Still, Poland has been backing Wajda's movies for thirty years. Dissident or not, he belongs to one of the country's few profitable export industries. His movies bring in hard currency. To worldlier apparatchiks, confronted now with sullen neighbors and angry children, Wajda seems to fill what Nadezhda Mandelstam once called that margin of bourgeois hypocrisy where illiberal people flatter themselves with the kinds of liberal attitudes and gestures that in no way threaten their power and their privilege. It is obvious that General Jaruzelski would rather give Andrzej Wajda money to make a movie about a dead Frenchman—a movie he can easily suppress at home—than let jailed intellectuals like Jan-Jozef Lipski and Jacek Kuron out of prison or invite the young leaders of the Solidarity underground up from clandestinity.

Danton's Death, of course, is the great work about Robespierre and the comrade who turned against him to plead the cause of his own weaknesses—and for a moment of respite and tolerance for France. Georg Büchner wrote it in 1835. He was twenty-two and a revolutionary himself—on the lam from the German police, passionate about the revolution of 1830 in France, composing tracts about the overthrow of the princes at home. Wajda's *Danton* comes from a Polish play of the 1920s. The play was called *The Danton Affair*, and it was written by an ardent young Communist named Stanislawa Przybyszewska, who despised Danton as a kind of proto-revisionist. Her play covered the last eight days of Danton's life—his trial for corruption and his execution —but her hero was Robespierre, who sent Danton to the guillotine. Przybyszewska's Robespierre was the first Communist. He was the vanguard through which the will of a people expressed and realized itself. She gave him a mandate that made conventional notions of political liberty obsolete and discussion irrelevant, and turned dissent into betrayal. A Polish historian in Paris tells me that her play is a kind of *Our Town* of the East Bloc, a set piece in the provincial repertories of Poland and the German Democratic Republic. He says that Przybyszewska's Robespierre and Danton are such broad caricatures that all it took was a few words here, a few gestures there for Wajda and his screenwriter, Jean-Claude Carrière, to stand the play on its head and make heroic Robespierre bad and bad Danton heroic.

Wajda has made some good movies in his time. *Ashes and Diamonds* —he shot it in 1958—is one of them. But the French did not give Wajda money because of movies like *Ashes and Diamonds*, which is complicated and personal in its judgments. They gave him money because they wanted to encourage a French *Man of Iron* or *Man of Marble*—

a movie in which "the people" of the late eighteenth century, like workers in Gdansk's shipyards, would shine with force and solidarity. They wanted to start celebrating their Bicentennial of 1989 now. The government in France kept a paternal eye on the social revolution in Poland. During the sixteen months of Solidarity, there was constant contact between the French and groups of dissidents in Poland. A fair number of Poles were visiting in France when the military took over their country on December 13, 1981, and suspended their workers' movement. Many of them stayed. The Centre National de la Recherche Scientifique and the universities gave jobs to about twenty Polish scholars in 1982. The Maison des Sciences d'Homme was suddenly full of Polish historians and Polish economists. They were welcomed by Hungarians of 1956 and Czechs of 1968, who referred to the place as *"notre coin de dissidence."* France adopted Solidarity because the French tend to see reflections of their own Revolution in other people's struggles and easily mistake those people's various ideas of freedom for their own ideology. The Socialists, who brought Wajda here (and campaigned for *Danton* to win a critics' prize called the Prix Louis-Delluc), were confused when Wajda presented them with a movie in which *le peuple* and their Revolution counted for very little. The French people were at the heart of Büchner's play. Wajda's people rarely do anything but wait in bread lines and watch the executions. His movie is an argument between Robespierre and Danton, with Saint-Just and Camille Desmoulins as seconds in a kind of social philosophers' duel. Robespierre (Wojciech Pszoniak, a Polish actor who used to play the part in *The Danton Affair*) is a sociopath who soaks his bed with sweat and cringes if a woman touches him. Danton (Gérard Depardieu, who roams around the movie like a big bear caged in a cliché, too cheerful and too generous to be bored) is a slob and a libertine and a lush who drinks his wine in gulps, like Polish vodka, but in the end would rather be executed than executioner, and defies the Terror he helped to theorize.

It is hard to imagine why anyone here expected a fifty-six-year-old Catholic from Communist Poland to like a French revolutionary who hypothesized a dictatorship of the people (not to mention permanent revolution and government by central committee) some seventy-five years before Marx wrote *Das Kapital*. The right thinks that *Danton* is a terrific movie. Michel Poniatowski, who was Giscard d'Estaing's Minister of the Interior for three years (and had such enthusiasm for state security that he himself was sometimes referred to around the office as Robespierre), wrote Wajda a thank-you note in *Les Nouvelles Littéraires*, as if the movie were a small gift to the right from an admirer.

The left took *Danton* personally, too. François Mitterrand went to a screening at the Palais de Chaillot and endured the experience with what was described as "glacial courtesy." Michel Vovelle, the historian who is next in line for the chair of French Revolutionary studies at the Sorbonne, refuted Wajda's "revolution" in the Communist Party paper *L'Humanité.* Then the Socialists took Wajda on. *Le Monde* devoted a page to the argument. Louis Mermaz, who is president of the National Assembly, complained that *Danton* was a confrontation out of context —which in a way was true—but what bothered him most was how the French themselves had been neglecting Robespierre. He was distressed, he said, that there was no rue Robespierre anywhere in Paris. (Actually, there is a rue Robespierre, with its own Robespierre Métro station, in Montreuil, in the *banlieue rouge* around Paris, but Danton has a street and a four-hall movie theater right in the middle of the Latin Quarter.)

Robespierre was a prig. It was to Danton's credit to have loved him once, and to Saint-Just's credit to have kept on pretending to love him until they went to the guillotine themselves, four months after Danton died. Wajda's Danton tries to woo Robespierre with a feast in the Palais-Royal, and the sight of the rich food revolts him —which in France is a sure sign of repression. Büchner's Danton was more to the point with Robespierre: "You and your 'virtue,' Robespierre! You've never taken money, you've never been in debt, you've never slept with a woman, you've always worn a decent coat, and you've never got drunk. Robespierre, you are appallingly upright. I'd be ashamed to walk around between heaven and earth for thirty years with that righteous face just for the miserable pleasure of finding others worse than I."

Mme Roland described Danton in her memoirs as a man whose great gift was his ability to charm people less cruel than he into murdering for him. "*Voilà* Danton," she said. "I defy the artist who wants to paint a two-faced man to find a better model." Mme Roland went to the guillotine on November 8, 1793. Five months later—it was April 5, 1794—Danton and his friends followed. In Büchner's play, his last words are to the executioner: "Do you want to be more cruel than death? Can you prevent our heads from kissing at the bottom of the basket?"

An actor in Wajda's *Danton* told me that to his mind Americans project their own secularism onto European life. He said they tend to forget that in Catholic Europe (and in a lot of Protestant Europe, too) renouncing the Church usually amounts to an act of faith in something else, and that this is what gives the European left its baffling fervor. The first guillotine lists went "Aristocrats, libertines, and fanatics." "Fanat-ics" meant Catholics. Catholics were dangerous not just as reactionaries or monarchists or mystics, or whatever else the Revolution called them; they were dangerous because they competed with the Revolution for an idea of history, because *their* history, their moment—the moment from which their time and meaning and explanation derived—had nothing to do with the moment of July 14, 1789, when the Bastille fell, or the moment of November 10, 1793, when Liberty danced on the altar of Notre Dame and the Cult of Reason was declared. François Furet, the historian, says that when Frenchmen today talk about the Revolu-tion they are really talking about two revolutions—the Revolution of 1789, which was about freedom, and the Revolution of 1793, which was about the suppression of freedom in the interests of "the people," most of whom were too hungry by then to care about revolution anyway. Furet says that the French try to absolve themselves of the Terror in their enthusiasm for Bastille Day, which is a moment that everyone in France but the most ardent monarchists can claim. They make their Revolution a kind of sister to the American Revolution, which was liberal and pluralistic and not, strictly speaking, a revolution at all. If they are on the left, they make it father to the Revolution of 1917 in Russia and grandfather to all the independence wars in Africa and the civil wars in Latin America. 1789 is the reason the French could fight for years to keep their colonies in Indochina, and then, losing the war, turn ideological confessor to those colonies. It is why the French could claim common cause with the Algerians after eight years of war and torture. It is why Mitterrand today can go to Mexico and, in all sincer-ity, adopt the Third World as France's special spiritual province. It gives a kind of moral logic to a foreign policy that otherwise seems whimsical and exasperating. And it explains, at least in part, why so few Frenchmen seemed to expect a Polish dissident to take on Robespierre just because of his own experience with a failed people's republic at home.

Despite the evidence of Solidarity, the French left does not actu-ally believe in the reality of Catholic revolution. Socialists here think of the phrase "Catholic revolution" as a contradiction in terms. They regard the Church in Poland as a family—conservative and reassuring, a refuge from the reality of Communism, but not a part of any reason-able person's strategy for change. They do not really understand the lush Vatican Catholicism with which the Poles defend and sometimes delude themselves. They prefer to think of Polish revolutionaries as acolytes of 1789.

There has been a chair in French Revolutionary history at the Sorbonne since 1886. It goes, by tradition, to historians of the left —Georges Lefèbvre, Albert Mathiez, Albert Soboul, and now, in all likelihood, Vovelle. They are party to a sort of scholars' *compromesso storico*, which divides French history so that conservatives control the monarchy, Marxists the revolutions, and liberals the two world wars. Of course, some of the best writing about the Revolution was done by men who were not, properly speaking, historians at all: Chateaubriand and his *Mémoires d'Outre-Tombe;* Alexis de Tocqueville and his *L'Ancien Régime et la Révolution.* Chateaubriand and Tocqueville are for the grownups. Children in France learn their history the way American children learn their times tables. They memorize the canons of citizenship. Their teachers are apostles of a rigorous and quarrelsome national identity. Their education has to do with forming a proper attachment to the state—Freud would have called it transference. It has to do with the conviction that truth for its own sake has no particular pedagogic value. No one, for instance, expects the press to be objective, or even fair. English and American papers seem strange to the French, because they serve no persuasive purpose as the French understand it. A Frenchman reads the paper to corroborate his prejudices, or he reads many papers and makes a sort of collection of prejudices. He is not much interested in information without a strong attitude attached to it.

A schoolteacher down the street from me who teaches history and geography at the local *lycée* uses one textbook that describes bananas as yellow fruits grown by peasants in poor, hot countries for 11.5 percent of their market value and exported and sold by foreign intermediaries who pocket the other 88.5 percent. Last week, the teacher had a visit about bananas from an angry mother. The mother wanted the teacher to tell her twelve-year-old son that while bananas were indeed yellow fruits grown in poor, hot countries and sold for a lot of money by wicked foreign intermediaries, the exploitation of banana farmers was not really part of the essence of "banana." She had tried to tell him this herself, she said, but he did not believe her. He believed his textbook, which had a page about bananas in a chapter entitled "The World Today." Another page in "The World Today" was about happiness in China. Another was about the wealth and health and culture of France's old African colonies. Another was about wanton power in North America, and another was about misery in South America. (It was called "315 Million Men Under the Shadow of the United States.") There was no page about the Soviet Union or Eastern Europe—

in fact, nothing to suggest that there was a Soviet Union or an Eastern Europe besides the initials "U.S.S.R." on a chart about oil producers and oil consumers. The schoolteacher, who happens to be a Socialist, agreed with the mother about bananas and said he certainly found it odd that the Soviet Union had disappeared from the modern world. On the other hand, he saw nothing odd in the fact that Francophone Africa resembled a set of Chamber of Commerce postcards, whereas New York City looked as if it had been photographed by a police photographer on a slum homicide case.

Not so long ago, every French schoolchild learned his history from little catechism textbooks known as Malet-Isaac. Albert Malet was a history teacher at the Lycée Louis-le-Grand, in Paris. He wrote the first of these textbooks alone, around 1900, but eventually he took on Jules Isaac, who was a teacher at another Paris *lycée*, as a partner, and when Malet died, in 1915, Isaac kept writing. Albert Malet liked Danton. Back in 1908, children all over France read in their Malet that Danton was one of the country's great statesmen—"incapable of hatred, or even rancor, an ardent patriot, the best of the men of his time"—whereas Robespierre was a hateful, jealous man, a puritan dandy who devoted his mornings to clothes and to a wigged and powdered "sober elegance," and his afternoons to guillotining his friends. Isaac, on the other hand, preferred Robespierre. After he started to work with Malet, another generation of children read that while Robespierre may have been given to a few "odious excesses" Danton was brutal, cynical, and venal—a statesman, yes, but certainly not a great one. The children of the next generation got Isaac alone and then Isaac with some new colleagues, and they had it on authority that Robespierre was the preeminent democrat of the Revolution, champion of universal suffrage, more than worthy of his nickname, which was "the Incorruptible." As for Danton, he was not only brutal, cynical, and venal but also ugly and —the ultimate disgrace—"a revolutionary opportunist."

This was the Danton that Wajda's critics—they are in their forties and fifties now—inherited, and, in a way, the Revolution they inherited. They are not much interested in revisions of that Revolution —especially foreign revisions. Probably, they never were. Büchner is loved in France, but it took fifty-four years for anyone here to publish *Danton's Death*. Charles Dickens is loved in France, too, and yet *A Tale of Two Cities* was out of print until the 1960s. The Petit Robert, which is the standard French desk encyclopedia, does not include *A Tale of Two Cities* in its list of Dickens's novels; it commends his other books for their insight into "British hypocrisy" and "American rapaciousness." The first Dickens scholar in France dismissed *A Tale of Two Cities* as "a novel with neither humor nor originality." The most recent Dickens scholar—his name is Sylvère Monod, and he likes Dickens well enough to have been the first Frenchman elected president of the Dickens Fellowship—says he does not care for the novel, either. French children weep for Oliver Twist in the workhouse and for lonely David Copperfield, but they do not weep for Sydney Carton on his way to the guillotine. To the French, *A Tale of Two Cities* is Dickens under the influence of Thomas Carlyle, and Carlyle, with his peculiar ideas about geniuses being more important than *le peuple* when it comes to cataclysmic social changes, is not a favorite here. The kindest thing I ever read about Carlyle in French was that his history of the Revolution was not history but a kind of epic poem, "sublime and uneven."

February 1983

THE VATICAN

Not many of the Romans waiting in St. Peter's Square on the evening of October 16, 1978, recognized the name Karol Wojtyla. Reporters who were there claimed that a rumor went round the square that the new Pope was an African, because "Wojtyla" sounded so exotic—coming, as it did, in the middle of Pericle Cardinal Felici's Latin invocation. People said there must have been a Third World takeover of the College of Cardinals—making Wojtyla's nomination to the Papacy something on the order of a resolution about Zionism in the United Nations General Assembly. Later, when they realized the Pope was Polish, they changed their minds, and said that Stefan Cardinal Wyszyński had taken advantage of an Italian stalemate—about a quarter of the College of Cardinals is Italian—to put one of his own countrymen into the job. Everybody knew that the Italian cardinals had lost a lot of their old authority when they settled on the first John Paul, a friendly cardinal who wrote poetry to Pinocchio and was expected to be accommodating but who had some fairly progressive ideas about overpopulation in a hungry world. When John Paul I died suddenly, thirty-three days after his election, his friends announced that the Papacy had killed him —that the thought of his own terrifying new significance had literally stopped his heart. A few skeptics said that he was murdered. They wrote about sinister Curia conspiracies, about poisonings and blue fingernails and Mafiosi in the Papal Palace. But none of them, to my knowledge, mentioned Bulgarians.

Italians know from trials going on in the country now that Bulgarian spies and Bulgarian businessmen and common Bulgarian criminals are busy in Italy. They know that Bulgarians have been involved in selling drugs and trading arms and recruiting workers to report on Solidarity activists in Poland, but, unlike almost everybody else in Europe, they are not much interested in Bulgarians. Italians tend to take a short view. The Sicilian novelist Leonardo Sciascia calls this their protection against too much history. Right now, that short view holds that Bulgarians are the least of Italy's problems. The plot to kill John Paul II, insofar as it involves Turks or Bulgarians, or even Russians, is less important to them than, say, the plot to kill Aldo Moro when Moro was the head of the Christian Democratic Party and was evidently on his way to a *compromesso storico* with the Italian Communists.

Moro died after fifty-five days in the hands of the Red Brigades, and his ordeal obviously gave Italy an occasion for a *mea culpa*. But Moro's murder also raised questions that were quintessentially Italian. Five years dead, Moro still raises those questions—questions about the ethics of negotiating or not negotiating with terrorists, about the failures of police and government, about the corruption of the secret service, about political blackmail, and, finally, about the abject fear in the letters that Moro sent to anyone he thought might save him. It was a fear that moved and shamed the Italians, and with which, in spite of themselves, they identified. Sciascia, for one, was moved to the point that he left the village in Sicily where he lived a life of legendary shyness and ran for parliament in order to sit on a commission investigating the government's conduct of the Moro case. He says that he wanted to test a hypothesis about Moro—that the government could and should have saved Moro during the two months of his imprisonment. He is convinced now that his hypothesis is right. He has no hypothesis about the Pope. Aldo Moro, in his way, was a Sciascia novel —a genre crime, intensely local. John Paul II, Sciascia says, is more a novel by John le Carré.

Italians maintain that the only "Italian" thing about the attempt on the Pope's life on May 13, 1981, was the fact that Mehmet Ali Agca fired from that piece of the Vatican between Bernini's glorious colonnade and the doors of St. Peter's which, while not actually in Italy, falls under the protective jurisdiction of the Italian police. They are surprised that friends from abroad expect them to be up-to-date on whether a Russian told a Bulgarian to tell a Turk to shoot a Polish Pope. They have little to add to the argument about whether or not John Paul II wrote to Leonid Brezhnev threatening to march into Poland if the Russians invaded. They saw more of their own confused reality in Aldo Moro's ordeal, and now they see it in the trial of Toni Negri, a philosophy professor from the University of Padua who led a gang called Workers Autonomy (which had no workers but a lot of the professor's friends and students) and was considered a theoretician of Italian terrorism.

The Italians have a saying that goes *"Morto un Papa, se ne fa un altro"*—meaning that if one Pope dies you can always make another. It is a saying they are fond of. They practice a hard-won anticlericalism. Even their priests sometimes practice it. The fact that they are so pointedly uninterested in the shooting of the Pope is a way of letting the world know that Italy cannot afford to be seduced into the kind of papal aesthetics the French took up when they exhausted an enthusiasm for Marx and Lévi-Strauss and Freud and became, in a sense, enthusiasts of the Vatican—"choosing Rome," as the writer Philippe Sollers put it. Catholic attitudes may hold in France (and pilgrims pray on the rue du Bac), but no one here really questions the fact that, two hundred years after the Revolution, church and state are vigilantly separate. Italians have to renegotiate their secular rights at every election. The Christian Democrats in Italy count on some twenty-seven thousand parishes to deliver Catholics on Election Day, the way the Communists count on the Confederazione Generale Italiana del Lavoro to deliver workers—and, in return, the Christian Democrats have given those parishes enormous authority over schools and family life. The lay parties in Italy (except, notably, the Italian Communist Party, which resembles the Church enough to get along with it) mainly try to ignore the Papal State sitting in the middle of the capital and the Polish Pope who flies all over the world proselytizing and brings back problems more ecumenical—if the word applies—than anybody bargained for.

John Paul II is not popular among the Roman bourgeoisie. Romans, as the Poles suspect, would prefer an Italian Pope, but not so much for his nationality as for his inconspicuousness. They are used to thinking of their Pope as a local politico with connections—a sort of *porte-parole* to God from the government. Six Popes (four of them tenth-century Popes) have died violently in the 1,950 years of the Papacy, and with one exception they died in Italy at the hands of Italians because of Italian politics. Right now, only the Socialists in Italy have a real political interest in the attack on John Paul II. The Socialists are a small, slick party, prone to scandals, and they have nothing in common with the other European Socialist Parties, or even with their own Italian predecessors. They are trying to revive their respectability by way of a fairly gratuitous anti-Communism, and they get a lot of publicity out of the Bulgarian connection, talking about coverups and making speeches in parliament about mysterious radio

signals from the East, which filled the air of Rome just before Mehmet
Ali Agca fired his automatic and which, presumably, were ignored.
The other parties, seeing no particular political advantage in exposing
Bulgarians, keep quiet in public and, in private, long for the days when
Paul VI was in the Vatican. Pope Paul VI was timid and retiring. His
idea of a fight was a disagreement over Latin grammar with his friends
the Jesuits, across the street on the Borgo Santo Spirito, and the kind
of trip he preferred was a walk up the aisle of the General Assembly
with a white lily in his hands. The Christian Democrats liked him,
because he left them alone in the Vatican. During the fifteen years of
his pontificate, the Christian Democrats went about their business un-
disturbed, and the Italians in the Curia looked after the interests of the
Church in Rome, arranging appropriate favors for their political friends
through the Vatican's bank—the Institute for Religious Works—
or through "Catholic" banks, like the Banco Ambrosiano, which was
founded by a priest late in the nineteenth century and in which the
Institute had a share. Now a lot of those Christian Democrats are
complaining that Pope John Paul II has shut them out of the Vatican.
They say he uses the Vatican for his own politics, and those politics
have to do with Poland—Yalta politics, they call them—and not with
the hegemony of the Christian Democratic Party in Rome. John Paul's
politics carry no votes, no favors, no guarantees. He has no interest in
the domestic courtesies of the Holy See. He does not consult his bishops much, or his administrators in the Curia, unless they happen to be
Poles. He is a shameless populist. He says he wants to speak directly
to the Catholic poor, and if the things he tells them are often at the level
of a parish sermon his effect on them is charismatic. He seems ravenous
for the corroboration of crowds. His huge weekly audiences and his
restless travelling are the way he stirs his faith: through contact. His
critics say that he has made the Church a festive Church but a Church
without substance. The Christian Democrats say no, that there is too
much substance in the Church right now—meaning that the issues
Catholic politicians hope to avoid, issues like divorce and birth control
and abortion, and even Catholic education, are precisely the issues the
Pope keeps bringing up. They say that John Paul II reminds Italians
that the Christian Democrats are bound by those issues, and so Italians,
being sensible, vote against them. (A few days after the Pope was shot,
Italy had a referendum on abortion. People were expected to vote
against a liberal abortion law, out of respect for the Pontiff. They voted
to retain one.)

I was in Rome this month and took a walk with a parish priest I know, and the priest said, "If you want to talk about how much the Pope loves Poland, it will take all day." I asked a writer I know about the Pope, and the writer said, "Where do you want to begin? Polish issues? Polish priests? Polish lunches?" I stopped in at the Jesuits, on the Borgo Santo Spirito, and the Jesuits said that clever Popes were like garlic ("in everything") but that this Pope was like a kielbasa and took up the whole stew and considered everyone around him small potatoes and sauerkraut. In October of 1981, John Paul II suspended the Jesuits' constitution. Their Superior General, Father Pedro Arrupe, had had a stroke and was in the infirmary, and the Pope sent him a message with the news that he was replacing Arrupe's Vicar with a Jesuit of his own choosing. The Pope did not really approve of the Jesuits to begin with, and he certainly did not approve of the Jesuits' Vicar, Father Vincent O'Keefe, a priest from Jersey City (and an old president of Fordham University), who, according to their constitution, should have run the order until a General Congregation was called and a new Superior General elected. Jesuits ask embarrassing questions about the proper Christian response to situations like this one: It is Sunday in Paraguay. Hundreds of peasants have walked to town to confess and receive Communion, but there is no priest in town, and there is not likely to be one for the next month. A couple of nuns run the parish. They care for the peasants every day—when the peasants are sick, or hungry, or in trouble. Today, what should these nuns do? The Pope does not think that this sort of situation raises any questions. He is against this sort of situation. He says that the answer to an absent priest is for parishes to share their priests, but Jesuits in Latin America say that there are often no priests to share, whereas, given papal exhortations to multiply, there are getting to be more and more Catholics. Of course, Jesuits rarely get along with the Vatican. They are a worldly order, and they have a reputation for independence which no other order has. They are subject only to "extraordinary interventions"—interventions by the Pope— and while there have been a lot of these interventions in the 443 years since Ignatius Loyola and his followers took vows, the Jesuits still consider themselves a kind of fourth estate of the clergy. They are planning to meet in September and restore their constitution by electing a Superior General—and they say they are praying that the Holy Father has no cause to intervene again. At their last General Congregation, in 1975, they redefined the Jesuit vocation as "service of faith and promotion of justice," and the result was that Jesuit missionaries felt free to enter governments like the Sandinista government, in Nicaragua, or formulate a "People's Church," or simply take up the cause of poor people who are oppressed and terrorized by their regimes. The Pope, for his part, ordered the Jesuits out of Central American politics. The Jesuits replied that it was difficult to avoid politics, let alone to promote justice, when terrorists under the protection of right-wing governments kept trying to kill them. Thirty nuns and priests have been murdered in Central America over the past four years, and the Jesuits conclude that this makes any nun or priest a charter member of a People's Church, since in Central America "the people" are always dying.

The Polish Church is also a People's Church. Poles are close to their Church, and their Church sustains them. It is also one of the most conservative churches in Europe, and insofar as John Paul II is a product of that Church and the society it reflects he is bound to be at odds with Jesuit intellectuals who say that, being Polish, he is more concerned with liberty than with democracy. A lot of people at the Vatican say that, too. The Vatican has never been known for democracy, but Curia people seem to regard their elaborate intrigues and manipulations as a kind of democracy—only more artful than what the rest of us are used to. (Actually, the process is pure social Darwinism.) Curia people say that John Paul II decided to open the Vatican doors for a Holy Year this year without letting them know anything about it. They say that he chose eighteen new cardinals and that no one in the Curia but his Polish friends knew who the candidates were, or even when the consistory would be. There were a lot of late changes in the new canon law. For one thing, abortion was put on the list of seven excommunicable offenses, whereas in early drafts abortion was forbidden but was not on the list itself. For another, a clause was added permitting the establishment of "personal prelatures" for lay orders —prelatures that would place those orders outside the jurisdiction and scrutiny of local dioceses and, for that matter, archdioceses, making them responsible only to the Pope and giving them something of the status of religious orders like the Dominicans or the Benedictines.

Within a few days of the publication of the new canon law, the Pope appointed a "personal prelate" for the lay order called Opus Dei. The Opus Dei is a shadowy organization of about seventy thousand Catholic laymen and women, with a thousand priests for counsellors, and it is a kind of private army of the faithful, pledged to enrich the Church, to obey the Church, and to uphold what appears to other Catholics to be the values of the Inquisition. (One of its Vatican patrons is Silvio Cardinal Oddi, a papal nuncio who was retired from Church politics—"released for prayer"—by Paul VI but was taken up by John

Paul II and, at the age of sixty-eight, given the powerful job of Prefect of the Congregation of the Clergy.) Not many people outside the Opus Dei or the Vatican know very much about the group. Its priests recruit in universities like Oxford where the Catholic elite is apt to send its children. Young Catholics who join the Opus Dei often take vows of chastity and secrecy, and even mortification, and then go out into the world to recruit their friends. (Right now, some of the Opus Dei people in Paris are said to be working against an American bishops' "draft pastoral" on nuclear war—Joseph Bernadin, the new cardinal from Chicago, presented it at the Vatican in January—which described non-violence as a "legitimate mode of Christian witness" and called the idea of a just nuclear war a contradiction in terms.) For a time, the Opus Dei was like a good club for the offspring of the Spanish and Por-tuguese oligarchies. The new prelate, Alvaro del Portillo, is Spanish, and a few Spanish bankers say that as many as fifteen out of every twenty private trusts in Spain involve money in trust for the Opus Dei. Some Jesuits say that the Pope, finding Jesuit education too disputa-tious for his taste, wants to replace the youngsters they train with a generation of boys and girls who are rich, respectful, and practically guaranteed to stay in line.

Mme de Sévigné once wrote to her daughter about Pope Innocent XI, who was having a fight with Louis XIV about appointing bishops: "What a strange Pope! He talks like a sovereign! You would think he was every Christian's father. He doesn't tremble, he doesn't flatter, he threatens . . . This is such a new style for us that we in France tend to think he's talking to some other people." Mme de Sévigné might have been a Roman writing about John Paul II. Some Romans regard him as a pilgrim from the Moral Majority who has strayed, by chance, into the Dolce Vita and decided to blast it with righteousness. He talks to the Eternal City about Christian memory and Christian destiny, not really understanding that the Eternal City has too much memory and is waiting, in its way, to be released from destiny. Rome is not so much cynical as weary. It is a subtle, existential town, and all its ardor is for the here and now. It does not know what to make of a moralizer like John Paul II, who seems so fanatic and foreign in his passion for a better, purer world. It is said in Rome that the Pope has a mystical, almost an ecstatic, sense of mission. He expects his clergy to have it, too. Paul VI released some thirty thousand priests from their vows during his pontificate, but John Paul II put off considering the petitions of priests who have asked since then to renounce their vows, and, perhaps, marry. He has told his friends that a Polish bishop at the

Vatican named André-Marie Deskur prayed for his election, offering his own life in the bargain: he considers this a sign. In the same way, he considers the attempt on his life a sign—a kind of personal Golgotha. Sometimes he seems to be saying that he has taken on our sins with Agca's bullets and we had all better measure up. He is still suffering from those bullets. He tires suddenly. He seems to be fighting weakness, and this may account for some of the urgency of his trips —eight countries in a week this month.

Vatican scholars have noted that in the new canon law Freemasons, like Communists, have been taken off the Unbelievers List. Enrico Berlinguer, the Communist Party Secretary, can now accompany his wife to church in good conscience, and the few thousand Italian Catholics who belong to a secret organization called Propaganda 2 may go to jail for their sins but not necessarily to hell. Propaganda 2 is a Masonic lodge. It has rituals of initiation and instruction, and its members ascribe to fancy Freemasonic touches (compasses, squares, white hats and pinafores), but its last Venerable Grand Master was an old Fascist and a blackmailer, and those fancy touches mainly cover a lot of plain criminal activity. Two years ago, the police raided the Venerable Grand Master's office in Arezzo and seized a list that included about half the Propaganda 2 membership. They discovered several of their own superiors on that list along with businessmen and bankers, not to mention a fair selection of cabinet ministers, Army generals, past and present heads of the country's secret service, and one ambassador from the Knights of Malta. Some of the people on the list are already in prison for banking fraud and business scams, some for plotting a right-wing military coup in Rome. Some, like the publisher Angelo Rizzoli, who owns the paper *Corriere della Sera,* are being arrested now. And at least one—Roberto Calvi, who was chairman of the Banco Ambrosiano—has died under extremely peculiar circumstances. Roberto Calvi was a charter member of Propaganda 2 and a diligent schemer. In 1971, when he was general manager at the Ambrosiano, he sold the Vatican a small interest in the bank. By 1975, it amounted to 1.6 percent, and 1.6 percent was evidently enough to allow him, over the next five years, to make the Vatican the major investor in— and hence the titular owner of—ten or twelve dummy holding companies with their mailing address in Panama. Late last spring, Calvi was found hanging under Blackfriars Bridge, in London, washed by the tides of the Thames and carrying five pieces of brick in his pocket. He was under indictment at the time for illegally exporting currency, and he was talking to magistrates, and people in Italy assume that he was murdered because Freemasons who inform against other Freemasons are supposed to be murdered and their bodies washed twice a day with running water and weighted with masonry. His creditors—among them ninety-two foreign banks, which in 1980 and 1981 loaned Calvi $788 million that went directly through Ambrosiano subsidiaries in Luxembourg, Peru, Nicaragua, and Nassau to his dummy companies —say that the Vatican, as paper owner of those companies, is ultimately responsible for a debt that by now amounts to $1,278 million.

In 1968, Italian tax law changed, and the Vatican suddenly became liable for taxes on income from its Italian stocks and business and property. Pope Paul sold what he could and looked for a financial adviser—and he chose a banker named Michele Sindona, who was the chairman of the Banco Privata Italiana and the Franklin National Bank, in the United States. Paul gave the Vatican's cash to Sindona with orders to diversify—which in Italy means to invest it somewhere besides Italy. By 1974, Sindona had cost the Vatican anywhere from twenty million to a billion dollars (depending on who is counting). This was hard on the Vatican, and it was especially hard on the man who ran the Vatican's bank, the Institute for Religious Works— a Damon Runyon bishop from Cicero, Illinois, by the name of Paul Marcinkus. Marcinkus was under enormous pressure at the Vatican. When he took over the Institute, in 1969, it was already short. The Vatican "treasure" he had expected to find was really treasure— art and objects that could visit museums as much as he wanted them to, but were in trust for God, so to speak, and could not be sold. Vatican II had cost the Church a great deal of money. Then Sindona came along and cost it money, and so, in his way, did Pope Paul VI, who did not draw crowds and the contributions of crowds—their St. Peter's pence. John Paul II, who drew crowds, looked promising, but he began to cost nearly as much as he brought in, because of all his messianic travelling. It was up to Marcinkus to keep the Vatican liquid. He could not afford to lose anything, and once Sindona dropped out, in 1979, by arranging to have himself kidnapped, Roberto Calvi had the Church to himself, and he had Marcinkus cornered. When Calvi started looting the Ambrosiano—hustling the loans for his dummy companies and using them, in fact, to buy a controlling interest in the Ambrosiano itself—Marcinkus, wittingly or unwittingly, provided a sort of fiduciary cover. As head of the Institute for Religious Works, Marcinkus sat on the board of Ambrosiano's Nassau subsidiary, the Cisalpine Overseas Bank of Nassau, presumably looking after the Vatican's 1.6 percent. The problem was that the Vatican's interest in all of Calvi's dummy companies had pushed its paper investment in the Banco Ambrosiano up to more than 15 percent, and this meant that when some of the foreign creditors—in particular, the ninety-two foreign banks— got nervous and started calling in their loans, Calvi knew that he could go to Marcinkus for "comfort letters," vouching for his reliability, and that Marcinkus would probably decide to write them. Comfort letters are not letters of credit. They are not binding, and, legally speaking, they are not worth much, but the ninety-two banks that lost their money say that a comfort letter from the Holy See is something on the order of a letter from God. They say that it carries the moral authority of the Church. In court, they would probably say that the Institute for Religious Works used that authority to misrepresent Roberto Calvi with its endorsements. The Church, however, is not being sued. People are asking the Bank of Italy for the money, and the Bank of Italy, in turn, is trying to negotiate with Marcinkus, who still runs the Institute for Religious Works. It has offered to help Marcinkus borrow a billion dollars, but Marcinkus says that the Vatican cannot afford the interest on a billion dollars—which would amount to a hundred million a year.

Marcinkus rarely leaves the Vatican. As a citizen of the Holy See, he cannot be extradited across the street to Italy, where he is under investigation as a possible accomplice in Calvi's schemes. Marcinkus is a golfer. He does not enjoy being shut away in Vatican City, where there is not even a putting green, and where, he says, the definition of a workout is taking a walk in the garden between prayers. Marcinkus and Roberto Calvi did not have much in common. Calvi did not play golf, and by all reports he was a cold, colorless soul who wanted mainly to own a big bank like the Ambrosiano and make himself powerful. In fact, he courted the Opus Dei more than he did Paul Marcinkus. His wife claims that at one point the Opus Dei offered to take over his debts and the Vatican's liability in those debts—in other words, take over the Institute for Religious Works and the Vatican's money—on the condition that it get to determine Church strategy toward Communist countries and the Third World. Calvi himself claimed that what he and Marcinkus did share was an interest in Poland. In September of 1981, when Calvi was first indicted, he told his lawyer that he had "recycled" some forty or fifty million dollars to Solidarity for the Pope. What is unknown to everybody but the lawyer is whether Calvi meant hot Ambrosiano money recycled through the Institute for Religious Works or Institute money recycled through the Ambrosiano.

It is hard for one Bulgarian airline clerk to get much attention in a country where the competition includes the Red Brigades, a Masonic lodge plotting military coups, a Church in debt for over a billion dollars, and a bishop who has to worry about the police every time he leaves the Vatican. Italy has had its share of Bulgarians anyway. Bulgarians were involved in every one of Luigi Scricciolo's adventures—Scricciolo is an all-purpose secret agent who worked as a trade unionist in Milan while spying and smuggling and putting together dossiers on Solidarity activists, and even, apparently, plotting to murder Lech Walesa and helping to kidnap General James Dozier—and Sergei Antonov, the Balkan Bulgarian Airlines office manager who is in jail in Rome as Mehmet Ali Agca's accomplice, may have been among them. Whatever his connection was (or was not) with a plot to kill the Pope, it is likely that Antonov was involved in some spying and smuggling in Italy, because spying and smuggling are what Eastern European bureaucrats in Western capitals are expected to do. Antonov's Italian lawyer, Giuseppe Consolo, says that Antonov is fairly simple, not really up to masterminding anything. Antonov's wife, Rossitza, works at the university in Sofia and is not simple, and some people suspect that she is the family mastermind, the real secret policeman, with an airline-office manager for a cover. Rossitza Antonov left Rome in September of 1981. Two diplomats at the Bulgarian Embassy who were indicted along with Sergei Antonov left in November of 1982, just before the indictments went out and Antonov himself was seized. The diplomats say that the fact of their having stayed at all once the Pope was shot and Agca was in jail and, presumably, talking makes them innocent.

Over the years since the war, Italy has turned into a crossroads for spies and terrorists. Bulgarian spies are considered fairly obvious among them. Turks are considered the way Turks are usually considered in Italian folklore—ugly and treacherous. People in Rome who have seen Agca describe him as they would an animal—smart, sly, liable to turn. Not many people see him now, though. He is a witness in the case against Sergei Antonov, and that case will be sub judice for as long as it takes the examining magistrate to decide whether there is evidence to bring Antonov to trial and, if so, what the charges against him will be. Agca's prison guards see him. Ilario Martella, the magistrate, sees him. And now another magistrate, Ferdinando Imposimato, who is investigating the case against Scricciolo and has indicted Agca and Antonov for conspiracy to kill Walesa, sees him, too. Agca has a television set in his cell; it is doubtful whether he knows much Italian, but he does know how much publicity he gets each time he elaborates his story and somebody else is charged. Martella himself is remarkably discreet. Romans talk about this with astonishment. A judge who is honest and earnest, owes no favors, and is not on the take from any party is a rarity in Rome, and so they wonder if maybe Martella is a little naïve, too, a little unworldly—if Agca enchants him with all the plots and conspiracies he elaborates, the characters he introduces. They like to compare Agca to Scheherazade in *The Thousand and One Nights*, determined to prolong his time and his comfort by keeping Ilario Martella curious. One theory has it that Agca waited, quiet, for a year to be sprung by the Turkish religious fanatics—the Gray Wolves —he first described as his accomplices or by the Bulgarian spies he describes as his accomplices now or by whatever other contacts he had in terrorist circles, where right and left are indistinguishable. The theory goes that when no one saved him he began to complicate his story, tying his attack on the Pope to the drugs-for-arms trade that seems to be a Turkish-Bulgarian specialty. He was almost certainly in the pay of Bekir Celenk, a Turkish smuggler who worked out of Sofia and is either in police custody or under police protection in Sofia now, and he could have been in the pay of some Bulgarian smugglers, too. Agca arrived in Bulgaria on the lam three years ago and left with money to lead the life of a rich punk on his way to Rome. The Pope was his obsession, whoever was paying him. He was talking about killing John Paul II when he broke out of a Turkish prison in November of 1979. Bulgarians may have paid Agca to kill the Pope. Or Bulgarians may have simply covered for him in Rome, because of all the other dealings they had had with him. They may have been frightened themselves, knowing Agca. They may have set him up to die—with a Polish Pope in the bargain. They may have weighed the odds against a papal assassin's leaving St. Peter's Square alive, and figured that the Swiss Guards would shoot him, or the Italian police, or that the crowd of pilgrims in the Square would finish him off. They may have planned to kill him themselves in the confusion. They may have hired him or simply agreed to help him—and either way decided to sacrifice him in the Square for their own protection. As it was, a nun caught him by the sleeve, and pilgrims held him until the police came.

This week, *The New York Times* ran a story about a Bulgarian named Iordan Mantarov who defected in Paris in April of 1981, and who supposedly has told the internal intelligence agency there—the Direction de la Surveillance du Territoire—that the KGB ordered John

Paul II killed. A few Paris papers picked up the story and reported it like any other (*Le Monde* on page 4, *Libération* on page 16), and there was not much of a reaction from anyone except an anonymous agent at the DST, who told *Le Monde* that Mantarov had never said that at all. People in Paris seem to take it for granted that Yuri Andropov knew about the plot against the Pope and, whether or not he ordered it himself, did nothing to stop it. They say that to Andropov the fact of a Polish Pope, alive and speaking out for Solidarity, was tantamount to a call for revolution in Poland. They point out that once the Pope was hurt—warned off, presumably—General Wojciech Jaruzelski was able to take over, and the Pope began to make a measure of peace with the Communists for the sake of saving his country. The Pope's choice then, they say, was between a Vatican Ostpolitik and a civil war, and the Pope made it realistically, remembering his experience in St. Peter's Square. Parisians tend to believe that one day soon we will know everything there is to know about May 13, 1981. Romans tend to believe that we will never know. Romans say that there is no trump card called Andropov in America's hand waiting to be played, because, wherever the proof of conspiracy ends—in Ali Agca's cell or in the Balkan Bulgarian Airlines office in Rome or in the secret police station in Sofia, or even in KGB headquarters in the Lubyanka—Yuri Andropov will disavow it as the handiwork of mad employees, something on the order of a Spanish priest with a bayonet.

March 1983

MITTERRAND'S
MONARCHY

A couple of months ago, a West German photographer named Konrad Müller, with a "specialty" in heads of state, produced a coffee-table book of pictures of François Mitterrand. The book was announced in *Le Monde* by way of a full-page sample in which the President of France sat under a tree in his country clothes (Cifonelli tweeds, cashmere pullover, casual hat with the brim down), airbrushed by Herr Müller so that the lines of presidential stress softened into crinkles signifying wisdom and amusement and the cheeks shone with an inner glow. Then the book was spread over the display tables at La Hune, reminding the intelligentsia that the iconography of Fifth Republic France was indeed intact—that their President made his lonely decisions at a Boulle desk, took his inspiration from rare tapestries, and knew the kind of solitude that forests and clouds over cornfields confer.

Maybe it takes a shrewd German romantic with a book contract to catch a French President at the moment when self-regard slips innocently into self-parody. It is hard to imagine an art book about Helmut Kohl or, for that matter, Margaret Thatcher or Felipe González, although Müller has evidently done a job on Bruno Kreisky and Anwar Sadat. The French like their Presidents looking historically important. Charles de Gaulle had *his* official picture taken in the manner of an imperial portrait, hand resting on his new French constitution, and, according to the novelist Michel Tournier, who wrote a foreword to the Mitterrand book, it did so well that the General's photographer got calls from every Prime Minister and President-for-life in Francophone Africa requesting "Charles de Gaulle portraits" of themselves. Tournier himself keeps a skeptical distance from the iconography and its august symbols of citizenship. He is probably France's best-known writer, but he lives quietly in a converted presbytery in a Chevreuse village, attended by the son of a local peasant, and works there on his brilliant and perverse novels, and comes to Paris not for the scene but to read out loud to schoolchildren. He thinks of a French President the way he thinks of God, as a promoter. Talking about God, he says: "Having created man and woman in His image, in His likeness, He said to them: 'Be fruitful and multiply and replenish the earth.' Thus, having produced His self-portrait, He saw to His self-promotion. Ever since the Second Commandment was handed down, there has been a divine monopoly on images: 'Thou shalt not make unto thee any graven image.' We have had to wait a few thousand years for the politician—God's monkey—to discover His triple formula: picture, distribution, monopoly."

François Mitterrand is nearly three years into his seven-year term. In his lugubrious and rather moving self-esteem, he has been one of Tournier's true *singes de Dieu*, working out a monopoly on history. The instinct to pose at dusk in silhouette in the woods, contemplating a sapling, or to offer his wrinkles to the sort of filtered mercies usually reserved for movie stars is the same instinct that makes him keep 3,000 French combat soldiers in the deserts of Chad or 1,250 French soldiers in downtown Beirut when everybody else's troops have moved back to their warships. He seems to identify utterly with France—with its beauty, its poetry, its power—the way de Gaulle did, or, for that matter, Napoleon. It gives him great clarity of purpose abroad, and confusion of purpose at home. Mitterrand has money problems at home. His indifference to people scrambling for themselves and their own advantage instead of for the good of France is one of the reasons six thousand truck drivers stopped their trucks in the middle of the country's highways and left them there during the week this winter when most of France was on the road looking for a place to ski; it is one of the reasons twenty thousand Paris schoolteachers and government clerks and utility workers went on strike last week and shut down all the public services in town. His indifference to people who are not convinced that their money is part of the national patrimony has put a ninety-one-year-old businessman on trial for the crime of keeping a bank account in Switzerland. The intellectuals he invites to lunch at the Élysée come hoping to hear him out on, say, the prospects for French socialism or the European currency basket, and discover that he would rather talk about Civilization. In a way, Mitterrand is much like France right now

—masterly at self-delusion, self-serving in its choices, and self-righteous in explaining those choices to itself.

If Mitterrand makes people here uncomfortable, it may be because they see in his crafty vanity an acknowledgment of their own. Confusions of power and presence, of reality and what the French call *pur apparence,* are confusions that they are trained for. Their confidence —which is their great natural resource—depends on how well they learn. They have spent two years arguing about Mitterrand's nationalizations, but the fact is that most of the companies Mitterrand took over —it was during the winter of 1982—were already mortgaged to the state, and by taking them over he relieved a lot of nervous French industrialists of enormous debts and reimbursed them in the process. He substituted for an unwieldy state capitalism an equally unwieldy state socialism, and called it change. He nationalized banks that were already dominated by the state and its regulations, and called that change, too. He put a stop to people's exporting money, but people with money had already done their exporting, under Valéry Giscard d'Estaing. France's old money did not like Giscard any more than it likes Mitterrand. People said that Giscard was sabotaging the country with sleazy schemes, and then, by putting their own money in California, they sabotaged it more. They explained that the kind of business the French admire is the business of the state or the business of the corner grocer, not the business of the President. They thought of Giscard as an arriviste, with his doctored pedigree and his wife out of the aristocracy and her Bokassa diamonds.

It is not that the French despise the wheeling and dealing— the business of introductions and commissions and arrangements —that Giscard d'Estaing got involved in during his seven years at the Élysée, or that they are incapable of it themselves. It is, rather, that the French—whatever their private financial vices—prefer a rhetoric of "France" when the state does business for them. De Gaulle understood this. De Gaulle considered the fortunes that had been made in guns in the course of his career as a soldier, and proceeded to turn France into the third-biggest arms exporter in the world, but the image of France he always used was "the breadbasket of Europe." Giscard seemed to think that his family château made a better image than a breadbasket or a rifle. He underestimated the legacy of land and country that had been the real legacy of a Catholic *ancien régime* to a secular republic. When the oil ministers came calling, some of the women in his family started Arabic lessons. When the Oklahoma oil bankers came calling, the family ordered Popsicles and threw barbecues. Giscard himself got mixed up in a scheme involving a Belgian con man with a plane that "sniffed" offshore oil from the air; he took a billion francs from the state oil company, Elf-Aquitaine, and gave it to the Belgian and, "in the interests of national defense," neglected to mention the fact to anyone in the government except his Prime Minister, Raymond Barre. He was a snob, but he was a snob about class, not a snob about France, and the French would not forgive him for it. That, as much as anything, is why they voted against Giscard and for Mitterrand, who was always campaigning in front of churches and in wheat fields and forests, talking about roots and tradition and the richness of France and its great civilizing mission in the world.

Mitterrand invented a kind of Gaullist socialism. Like de Gaulle, he suspected that the Americans and the Russians had divided the world without considering France at all. He is often less concerned with arguments between the free world and the other side than he is with arguments between the French world and the other side. He spent a lot of time in December of 1981 grieving for Poland. His Socialists met day and night, making plans, talking strategy. They gave long and emotional speeches in the National Assembly. They issued warnings from the Élysée. They marched to the Russian Embassy, on the Boulevard Lannes, and carried candles during nighttime vigils outside the Polish Embassy, on the rue Talleyrand. But when somebody asked Pierre Mauroy, the Prime Minister, if France was going to cancel its natural-gas deal with the Russians because of the crackdown in Poland, Mauroy consulted the President and replied, in effect, "Surely we don't want to add to the tragedy of the Polish people the tragedy of the French people without heat."

Mitterrand had produced his first surprise at his inauguration. He had given the French a spectacle that even de Gaulle would have been hard put to it to improve on. It was called La Cérémonie à la Mémoire. Walking solemnly, with one perfect, long-stemmed red rose in his hand —a red rose is the French Socialist Party symbol—Mitterrand left the Right Bank (bourgeois, conservative, elitist, aging, *ancien-régime*) and crossed the Île de la Cité and then the Pont Saint-Michel onto the Left Bank (*populaire*, democratic, intellectual, young, free). He walked up the rue Soufflot with his rose, followed by a cordon of Socialists —arms linked, and every one of them a *personnage*—who were in turn followed by a cheering crowd representing, naturally, the people. He climbed the steps of the Panthéon, where Rousseau and Voltaire, and many of the heroes of republican France, are buried, and where the words on the lintel read *Aux grands hommes, la Patrie reconnaissante.* He waited while Daniel Barenboim, stationed across the Place du Panthéon on the law-school steps with the entire Orchestre de Paris and a chorus of 150 voices, raised his baton. And then the new President of the Republic, alone with his thoughts (and with the television crew that was broadcasting his pilgrimage live to fifty-four million Frenchmen), entered the Panthéon crypt, with his footsteps echoing on the marble floor and Beethoven's Ninth Symphony echoing behind him. He laid one rose on the tomb of Jean Moulin. He laid a second rose on the tomb of Victor Schoelcher—it was Schoelcher who, in 1848, wrote the act abolishing slavery in the French colonies. Finally, he laid a third rose on the tomb of Jean Jaurès, who could be considered the founding father of modern French socialism. Mitterrand left the crypt in time for Schiller's "Ode to Joy." Placido Domingo sang the *"Marseillaise."* The crowd kept cheering. And there was dancing in the streets, and the dancing went on all night, despite the fact that it was pouring. After La Cérémonie, no French Socialists believed—as many had earlier —that Mitterrand was going to relinquish, if not abolish, the fairly royal attributes of a Fifth Republic President. *Le Monde,* in a particularly rapturous "review" of Mitterrand, spoke of "his face . . . full of majesty, a Roman emperor's head." Then Jean Baudrillard, the sociologist, wrote an article in *Libération* called *"L'Extase du Socialisme,"* and in it suggested that socialism in France today was a kind of "gigantic special effect," that it had more to do with the mournful ecstasy on that face in the Panthéon crypt—with the aesthetic and moral imagination of the French people—than with any concrete ideology or concrete consequences, and that a true left, in fact, no longer existed in France, and hadn't for a long time.

Christian Bourgois, the publisher, says that to understand Mitterrand you have to imagine a Third Republic President in Fifth Republic France, meaning that Mitterrand is right in the tradition of Jaurès and the other seminal nineteenth- and early-twentieth-century French socialists—a tradition that is at once republican, secular, populist, nationalist, and, above all, *French.* People today tend to forget just how French that socialist tradition was, because two world wars and the Depression obscured it for more than fifty years. They tend to associate that sort of patriotic populism with de Gaulle, who was obviously no socialist (though an ardent believer in the rights of the state over the rights of the marketplace). De Gaulle, of course, was committed to a Catholic France. He read in Catholicism France's special destiny, and he had an obsession with "legitimacy," which evidently began to haunt him as a military man, the way it had haunted Franco, whom he despised; people say that once, in his old age, de Gaulle seriously considered naming the Bourbon pretender, the Comte de Paris, as his successor. The man he did choose, Georges Pompidou, was genial and shrewd —less than rigorous in his Catholicism, and more agreeable to the idea that the state and the market shared an interest in making money. Pompidou's Paris was the Paris of the *promoteurs;* they arrived en masse at the state banks, and Pompidou indulged them with easy credit and with a law to "liberate" the height of Paris buildings, so they could speculate on gigantesque projects like La Défense and Le Front de Seine and La Tour Maine-Montparnasse. They said they were "promoting" France with these projects, and Giscard, coming after them, looked at first like a relief from that brazen Gaullist chauvinism —an international man. In the end, he was not so much international as multinational. He was at heart an *homme d'affaires.* Mitterrand came close to beating him in 1974. The difference in 1981 was that a lot of people who may have had much more in common politically with Giscard voted Socialist *faute de mieux,* to spare themselves seven more years of his unsettling petulance. They were not expecting much of a leader in Mitterrand. They underestimated his lugubrious enthusiasm for the Presidency, and talked instead about his staying power, about his tenacity, about the skill—some said the sinister skill—with which he had survived in politics for forty years. They expected Mitterrand to patch together a government the way he had patched together the Socialist Party in the 1960s, taking a fractious collection of syndicalists and armchair Marxists and Social Democrats and sitting out their quarrels. They expected him to be crafty—but not so crafty. He put their old quarrels to his own court uses. He took the most *gemütlich* Socialist in France out of the Lille *mairie* and installed him in the Matignon as Prime Minister. He left his only serious rival in the party, Michel Rocard, anxious and vulnerable in the cabinet. By putting four Communists in the cabinet, too—it was the one place where they could not abuse him—he left their Party Secretary, Georges Marchais, with almost no influence in the government, and with not much more among his own comrades. He comforted Ronald Reagan by being anti-Soviet. He went to Yorktown to celebrate the last battle of the American Revolution. Nothing embarrassed him. He was measured, rational, severe.

Mitterrand's foreign policy is mainly about presence. It has to do with French influence and French prestige in a world where French power is really at the discretion of bigger, richer countries. The same instinct that made de Gaulle dress down the Russian ambassador —"*Alors, monsieur l'ambassadeur, nous allons mourir ensemble*"— when the wall went up around West Berlin and that made him cable encouragement to John Kennedy during the Cuban missile crisis operates at the Élysée today. Mitterrand has discovered that talk is cheap and talk is powerful. With France out of the North Atlantic Treaty Organization, Mitterrand can be fierce about wanting the security of NATO troops and NATO missiles in West Germany. For the French, being fierce is a way of being there. They remember the fractious parliamentary years of the Fourth Republic as years of war in Indochina and Algeria. They have made a hero of Pierre Mendès France, who ran France during one of those years, but they did it only after Mendès France was out of office and could not disturb them anymore with his passionate democracy. Now that he is dead, they cherish him. They like to talk about his dream that could not work in France. It confirms the fact that they are cynical, tough, realistic people—that they are not *moralisateurs*, like Mendès France, who was a Jew, or like their Protestant neighbors. They smoke. They do not understand the fuss about Watergate. They do not understand the fuss about missile deployment. They say that people with nuclear bombs do not have war and that therefore there is a kind of Cartesian logic to Mitterrand's argument for "nuclear dissuasion" ("dissuasion" is the President's word for deterrence).

The remarkable thing about French colonialism was that it created an identification with France, a desire for "Frenchness," in the same people who were fighting to compel the French to go. When de Gaulle signed his peace treaty with Algeria, after eight years of war, he left behind the seductive power of France, and that power had colonial uses that sometimes make real colonial power sound like a nuisance by comparison. The conversion of Francophone Africa into Francophile Africa meant more than preferential trade contracts and mining concessions in the Sahara. It meant that the power of shadow ministries and *lycée* teachers out of the École Normale Supérieure and manufacturers of "Frenchness" in places like Lille and Clermont-Ferrand was fixed in independent Africa. This is the sort of power that Mitterrand, with his nuclear technology for sale and his factories and his *force de frappe* for inspiration, is trying to "reclaim" in the Middle East. He has an insistent—almost an obsessive—idea, a history-book idea, of a Middle East with France as the source and center of its identity. He calls this idea "*tiers-mondiste*," because it has to do with the Third World, and "socialist," because it has to do with helping people in the Third World arrive at their particular kinds of freedom, and so he has few qualms about selling the guns and the grenades and the mines and the airplanes that the Third World uses to go to war with itself. Three hundred thousand Frenchmen earn their living in the arms business, and now that the government is taking it over, most of them can say they work for France. France has sold steel sheets for tanks to the Soviet Army and guns to Ethiopia. There are not many orders it refuses. It does not sell guns to South Africa—not directly, at least—and, according to people in the Foreign Ministry, on the Quai d'Orsay, it sells "practically none" to Chile, but it has sold guns to Libya. The argument for Libya seems to be that France did not sell the Libyans the particular guns that the Libyans are using against the French in Chad.

France has no economic stake in Chad. No one has thought of what an economic stake in Chad would be. The country is enormous, but it is one of those Third World countries which people have started referring to as the Fourth World—meaning that there are no resources, no export agriculture, no industrial capacity, no way to survive alone and no reason to have to beyond the political reason of being independent states at a time when independence is considered a proper conclusion to colonialism. France ruled the desert that is now called Chad until 1960, and then came back twenty years later because the heads of six or seven African states that had also been ruled by France at one time or another did not want Libya moving south of the Sahara, and they reminded France of some of the obligations of "presence." During his first year at the Élysée, Mitterrand thought about having a presence in Latin America, too. He went to Mexico and promised everybody freedom. He said that France thought all the time about freedom in Latin America, that tyranny in Latin America was unacceptable to France, that Latin civilization, after all, had France as its center and Paris as its capital. But then he went home and, in effect, dropped out of the hemisphere, and the Sandinistas in Nicaragua and the freedom fighters in Guatemala and El Salvador are still waiting for their francs. Partly, this was Mitterrand's way of calming an American administration that, to begin with, was not temperamentally well-disposed to a French President with four Communists in his cabinet—and that also seemed to believe that there were more human-rights problems in the neighborhoods of Sandinist Nicaragua than in the torture chambers of Guatemala and Chile. Partly, it was Mitterrand's gentleman's agreement about spheres of influence.

France cannot really afford Latin America. Its experience, its history, is in Indochina, Africa, and in the Middle East, and—inasmuch as Indochina doesn't want the French around anymore—Africa and the Middle East are where Mitterrand has to settle its influence. At one time or another, France was the mandatory power in half the Arab world and Africa. Generations of diplomats at the Quai, of ministry *fonction-naires,* of teachers and technicians and doctors and farmers and mission-aries have put in time in France's old colonies. Their connections are deep, their sense of place is proprietary. They were the field hands of a colonial empire. Now they are professional empathizers. The diplo-mats among them are attached to Arab causes and African causes. Some of them are genuine in their attachments. Some are paternalistic —practicing the kind of colonial affection that is still a badge of sophisti-cation in France.

Traditionally, there is an argument between the Quai d'Orsay and the Élysée about policy in the Middle East—an argument between the professionals and the politicians. The professionals, who like to con-sider themselves men of insight, tend to favor Arabs; the politicians, who like to consider themselves men of heart, favor Israelis. (It is a French version of the argument that has been going on for years between Whitehall and Downing Street, and between the Middle East desk at Foggy Bottom and the White House.) The argument stopped for a while under Giscard, because Giscard was such a fanatic about oil. He wanted to be an oil power, and the problem was that France has no oil. One of the few things that the Gaullists and the Socialists agree about is that Valéry Giscard d'Estaing would have sold his country's soul for a couple of cut-rate oil deals in the Middle East. The country has always been less enthusiastic than its field hands about Arab causes, and Giscard was committing it to policies that ignored this. Stability in the Middle East was not his real concern. He did not worry about whether his manipulations were acceptable to Israel, or even politically tolerable. A 1980 European Council declaration that was supposed to be Europe's response to the Camp David agreements was really Gis-card's declaration, and it was a fairly magical piece of work, offering up at once self-determination to the Palestinians, security to the Israelis, and a future where everyone would live happily ever after within borders that had not existed since the 1967 war. As a "solution," it needed a deus ex machina to make it work. A lot of people at the Quai liked it, although any diplomat with experience should have known that solutions in the Middle East are not made overnight with a hand-shake and a signature but are a matter of slogging along collecting obligations and sensitivities about obligations, of bargaining and drink-

ing tea and saving face and drinking more tea—that they follow a
rhythm and an etiquette that have nothing to do with Paris.

Giscard, by then, was in Iraq. He and Jacques Chirac—Chirac was
Giscard's Prime Minister for a while, and then they fought and Chirac
got to be mayor of Paris and started his own campaign for the Presidency—were courting the Gulf sheiks and the Saudis and, in general,
looking for business in the Gulf. They wanted a steady source of oil
and a market for their arms, and at the time Iraq seemed like both. In
1975, billions of francs in aid and investments started going to Iraq. In
1979, the French government broke ground for a nuclear reactor near
Baghdad. In 1981, when the Israelis bombed the reactor, the government
started building another. By the time Mitterrand took over, France was
committed to Iraq the way banks are committed to clients who have
already borrowed too much money to be allowed to default. Mitterrand
inherited Iraq from Giscard, but not all his biases. Mitterrand likes
Israel. People who consider Mitterrand to be the most treacherous
politician in France since Robespierre admit that the President has two
quite genuine public passions—his contempt for the Soviets and his
admiration for the Israelis. His ties to Israel go back over years of
meetings of the Socialist International. (Shimon Peres, the Labour
Party Secretary in Israel, was a special guest at his inauguration.) Mitterrand once spent time on a kibbutz, and years later he sent his son
to work on the same kibbutz. He sees in Israel a way to prove France's
constancy as a friend and a patron. Israel and Iraq and Lebanon are trial
runs, so to speak, for that constancy. But if French interest in Iraq has
to do with money and in Israel with old friendships, then Lebanon, as
the President likes to say, is "about history." Jacques Huntzinger, who
helps run the French Socialist Party for Mitterrand, was asked by a
reporter last month why France stayed in Lebanon, and he answered,
"Le Liban, c'est la France qui l'a un peu créé."

When Mitterrand talks about history, he invokes a French adventure in the East that began with Napoleon's Egyptian campaign. He
invokes 180 years of wild and exotic places to settle and explore
—the wars and voyages, the grand tours of Nerval and Flaubert and
Delacroix, the heady Orientalism of Paris itself. The war in Algeria
burned up a lot of that adventure. After Algeria, there were years when
the French avoided any kind of Arab policy, for fear of doing something disastrous—which may be why Mitterrand talks so much now
about France's "reclaiming" its historic role. He makes a heavy point
of involvement. He flew to Beirut last fall after terrorists blew up a
French Army base and killed fifty-eight French soldiers, and his trip

was all the more effective in that Ronald Reagan, who had lost 241 Americans that same day, didn't bother to go. Mitterrand obviously wants his soldiers out of Beirut now. He tried to persuade the United Nations to send a force to replace them, but the Russians vetoed his resolution in the Security Council late last month, and now those soldiers will have to go anyway, with only the grim satisfaction of being the last "peacekeepers" to leave the war.

The Foreign Ministry is a curious place. The driveways and the iron gates and the doors that run along the Seine are barred and locked, and to get into the Quai d'Orsay you have to turn a corner and find a little door on the rue Robert Esnault Pelterie that leads to a kind of reception barracks, where a couple of elderly North African porters sit behind a counter leafing through out-of-date directories and dialling numbers that are almost always busy. Their simplicity is a tactic. It enforces the pace at the Quai. It announces imperturbable rhythms of diplomacy, even of clandestinity. The Quai does not pretend to the sparkling competence of the Élysée, where brisk young men in gloves and morning coats skip up and down an *escalier d'honneur* dispensing presidential hospitality. There is, rather, a kind of siege mentality at the Quai. Some of it comes naturally to an office of career diplomats out of a tradition that does not credit the "outside" with having much information, or even much intelligence. People at the Quai like to complain about *"la déprofessionnalisation"* of diplomacy. They say that Mitterrand is turning his embassies over to party cronies instead of proper professionals—meaning, in numbers, that there are now eleven instead of four "amateurs" among 150 French ambassadors. (One of these amateurs is Bernard Vernier-Palliez, the Ambassador to the United States; he used to run Renault.) The Foreign Minister himself —his name is Claude Cheysson—was one of France's commissioners at the Common Market for eight years and, before that, the director of a big multinational chemical company. Mitterrand chose him for sophistication. He was supposed to represent an opening out of French policy —toward Europe, toward the *sottogoverno* of international banking and multinational business. In reality, Claude Cheysson is a romantic. He likes freedom fighters and resistance movements. He can look at, say, Yasir Arafat and think of the heroes of 1789. Mitterrand's Francophile Middle East and his Francophile Africa are, for Cheysson, facts of nature, appropriate brotherhoods. He was not prepared for the discretions of diplomacy, or the hypocrisies. He suffers injustice loudly, with what the French call a *maladresse*—by which they mean that he blurts out whatever is on his mind. Most people at the Quai like him anyway, because he is full of energy, he is loyal, and he tends to share their views. They like the cachet of having a real Catholic radical in the Foreign Minister's office, even though that Catholic radical has no more power than any other minister in Mitterrand's government.

Over the twenty-five years of the Fifth Republic, there has been a real movement of status away from the ministries and into the Élysée. The French have got themselves what the historian Stanley Hoffmann calls a republican monarchy. They have a King they can overthrow every seven years, and the King has a Prime Minister (actually, a cityful of ministers) he can blame for all his problems and fire by way of solving those problems. The government here is entirely at his disposi- tion—it is a little like a collective vice-president—and depends on him for whatever authority it has. De Gaulle, for example, gave people at the Quai a measure of power. He had great esteem for the Quai. He trusted his diplomats—because a number of them had been with him in the Free French in London and Algeria during the Second World War, and because his own lieutenant from the Free French, Maurice Couve de Murville, was Foreign Minister and looking after them. Georges Pompidou, on the other hand, put a man he didn't like much into the Quai and then ignored him and often insulted him, and re- ferred to the diplomats he sent abroad as *les tasses de thé et les petits fours*. Giscard, for his part, got to the Élysée and took over the foreign-policy establishment completely, so that even the French have trouble remem- bering his Foreign Minister's name.

As for Mitterrand, his cynical, sentimental policies are too personal to share (if the word applies) with strangers. He sits at de Gaulle's Boulle desk and consults himself, and when there are important jobs to be done abroad he sends people like Roland Dumas, an old party friend and lawyer from Limoges, who is by now adept at paying secret calls on Qaddafi and Assad and taking night flights incognito to Gabon. (Officially, Dumas is Mitterrand's special Minister for European Af- fairs.) Mitterrand is comfortable with his old political friends. He is a little like Lyndon Johnson in his loyalties, and, like Johnson, he has a memory for betrayals. The younger men who are his Élysée counsel- lors—Jacques Attali, his economic adviser, is one of them—lend a kind of bubbly, busy style to the place, but they are house intellectuals, fancy pets who are important mainly because Mitterrand would rather talk to someone like Attali, who owes his career to the President, than to the stony, critical types on the Quai d'Orsay. Mitterrand remembers the years he had to travel around as France's opposition leader, and the condescension of diplomats at the Embassy in Washington or London when he wanted an Embassy dinner party or an introduction to the people who counted. A lot of those diplomats are back in Paris now, and they remember the dinner parties, too. They say that Mitterrand could sit down with a group of the most conservative American businessmen and start talking solemnly about his roots in the provinces, his Catholic values, his deep family feeling—and the businessmen would go home thinking that they had eaten dinner with a French Barry Goldwater, and that the young diplomats who had called him a radical and otherwise insulted him were idiots.

Mitterrand is hard for the French to love, with his chilly pride and his wealth tax and his 65 percent income tax and his Socialist managers trying to run complicated banks and businesses and doing it badly. But most people here agree with him about the world outside France. They agree with what he says about the Middle East and about the Soviet Union and about the French hydrogen bomb. Mitterrand surprised people who thought that a Socialist President would be "socialist" abroad and perfectly innocuous at home, where it counted. They did not expect the old politician who had held together that shaky coalition called the French Socialist Party (and in ten years' time brought it from 4 percent of the vote to the Élysée) to turn into the impresario who staged an emperor's inauguration for himself in the crypts of the Panthéon and started talking like Napoleon. They did not expect surprises. They did not expect anything original. They did not expect statesmanship. And they certainly did not expect François Mitterrand to rule France instead of govern it.

March 1984

BEING GERMAN

Every Sunday night this fall, fifteen million Germans—East and West —watched a television serial called *Heimat*. *Heimat* was Germany's version of a Masterpiece Theatre production. It covered a century in the life of three families from a Hunsrück mountain village, and it was about what people on my street in Paris would probably call *Allemagne profonde*— deep Germany. The Germans thought of calling it *Made in Germany* until someone at West German Television decided that *Heimat* was the best title. *Heimat* means home, but in the way your family or your country or your great-grandfather's farm means home. It is one of those maddening words, like *Innerlichkeit* or *Weltschmerz*, with which Germans suggest that their experience is too complicated for anybody else to understand. When a German talks about *Heimat*, he is collapsing home and homeland into one invigorating sentiment. The word was useful for the Third Reich, and it was not much heard in civilized company once the Reich fell.

A couple of years ago, home and homeland were taken out of the closet of suspect German enthusiasms and dusted off like a thirties boa or a feathered hunting hat. People talked about "being German again," about a special quality of Germanness that was defined by boundaries of land and language—but not necessarily by culture or conscience or even history. They talked about a new kind of *Ostpolitik*, about a longing for "Germany" and a reaching out to Germans across the wall to share that Germany. The country they meant was the Germany they reinvented on Sunday-night television. It was a little Hunsrück village where honest farmers spoke their honest dialects and kept their old, honest German ways, and where children inevitably returned, suffering from worldliness, to be welcomed and forgiven. It was the Germany of the Romantics, of Hölderlin's poetry and Eichendorff's stories, and because it seemed to exist beyond time and politics and accountability it was a much more comfortable place to live than that other Romantic Germany which radicals like Ulrike Meinhof were talking about ten or fifteen years ago—a Germany obliged to light a cleansing moral fire and burn for its crimes, and restore itself by repudiation and penitence. In a way, it was an escape from that exhausting, impossible enterprise called the German past—not so much an evasion as a surrender, a collapse into simplicities that are not very different from the simplicities of the right in America now. V. S. Naipaul, writing about the Republicans' convention this year, described a political fundamentalism that "rolled together many different kinds of anxieties" and "offered the simplest, the vaguest solution: Americanism, the assertion of the American self." Substitute "Germanness" for "Americanism," and "assertion of the German soul" for "assertion of the American self," and you have a pretty good description of *Heimat* at the service of German politics. *Heimat* today is a code for German fundamentalism; it takes the landscape for its text, a catalogue of simple, selfish, "rural" values for its theme, and "being German again" for its intention.

The Greens, with their pastoral politics, are fundamentalists. The Bavarians, with their raucous rightist patriotism, are also fundamentalists (although the Greens and the Bavarians' Christian Social Union are obviously worlds apart on every subject except "home"). So are a lot of ordinary West Germans, liberal Germans in big cities like Frankfurt and Hamburg; they are also talking about "home" and about "being German again." Some of them say that prosperity has seduced them out of "being German." They say that they are just beginning to understand that the terrible division of Germany was not the political division but the sentimental one—that the Cold War followed so quickly on the war Germany fought and lost that within a year of the surrender it was more profitable for them to hate Communists than to join with other Germans in hating Nazis. They often blame America, because it was Americans who encouraged them to put their past aside, so to speak, and concentrate on the Russians. The fact that the exorcism of Nazism in East Germany was a cynical ritual, performed for politics, does not console them in the matter of what they call their American seduction. In a way, they envy the East Germans. To them, the harsh world that the East Germans inhabit may be the appropriate one. East

Germany is the Germany that has confessed its crimes and—at least in this—recovered.

Five or ten years ago, the division of Germany into a German Democratic Republic, in the East, and a Federal Republic, in the West, was not that much of an issue. One of the clichés of a divided Germany was that there had been no "Germany" anyway until Napoleon forced the three hundred little kingdoms and duchies and principalities and city-states he overran on his way to Russia to consolidate into about thirty-five slightly bigger kingdoms and duchies and principalities and city-states, and Bismarck, in turn, forced those "Germanys" into one Germany that was really Prussia and its unwilling satellites. (Goethe once wrote about waking up in Weimar, when he was Prime Minister of the duchy and its five thousand citizens, to the sound of his state shepherds herding his state sheep to pasture.) But the rhetoric of one Germany was always an issue. German unity was what Augustine would have called the civil theology. After the war, it became more of a millennial than a practical theology— "Not in our time" was the disclaimer whenever politicians talked about uniting Germany—and it was a theme that Adenauer used to great advantage. I have a friend in Hamburg who remembers the day (he was eleven, and it was the summer of 1953) that Konrad Adenauer came to the barracks outside town where he and his mother were living with thousands of other refugees from the Eastern Sector. Adenauer promised that they would all be home within the year, and he got six thousand votes with that one sentence. It was not that any of the refugees believed they were going home; they believed in the theology, and Adenauer, with his purity and his prestige, had made it respectable again.

The idea of a German *Volksseele*, or "folk soul," is much older than the idea of a German state. The philosopher Johann Gottfried von Herder (who was Kant's student and Goethe's tutor) believed that the soul of a people lived in its ancestral language, its ancestral poetry, and that belief led straight to Hegel's theory of history and Hölderlin's poetry of "home." Herder invented the *Volk*, who became the German *Volk*, and he described the *Volksseele*, which, with the rise of the nation-state and its ideology, was identified as the soul of Germany. His eighteenth-century speculations about the folk soul degenerating whenever its language was "invaded" by other languages became the truths of nineteenth-century German nationalism. By that time, the Germans were masters at taking history from its context and passing it through filters of language—Romantic language—until they had distilled it into mythology.

This fall, Erich Honecker, the East German Party Secretary, cancelled a visit he was going to make to Helmut Kohl, the West German Chancellor. Helmut Schmidt had issued the invitation to Honecker back in 1981, and Kohl had reminded Honecker of the invitation when they met in Moscow at Andropov's funeral. Honecker's visit would have been the first official visit to West Germany of an East German leader, and if not many West Germans got very excited about it at first, it may have been because they assumed he had made a visit before. When Honecker cancelled his visit—it was three weeks before he was due in the Federal Republic—the Italian Foreign Minister, Giulio Andreotti, started saying how dangerous it would have been to let two German leaders get together unsupervised, anyway. Then the West Germans got excited. Andreotti made one speech about Germany at a rally in Rome in September, and nobody knows why he did unless he wanted to say something alarming to entertain his audience, and hit on Germany for a subject. He made another speech at a press conference in the middle of a state visit to Saudi Arabia. He said that while everybody wants to see Germans getting along together, no one wants to see "pan-Germanism" encouraged or the status of either Germany challenged. It was a reasonable enough statement, inasmuch as no one in Europe *is* really comfortable with German enthusiasm for "Germany." People in the West tend to overlook the family reunions and emigration visas and trade and marketing arrangements that are the real achievements of West Germany's *Ostpolitik*. They think that any East German influence in West Germany is, at best, "neutralist"—meaning that it makes West Germans worry about having missiles around or about West Germany's turning into the battlefield for a Third World War—and, at worst, Communist. If they are liberals, they think either that Willy Brandt's *Ostpolitik* has been distorted, or that Kohl has improvised an *Ostpolitik* of his own—one that does not really comprehend the facts of defeat that, as Helmut Schmidt once put it, "are the roof under which Germany will exist." They are alarmed but not surprised when Kohl's Minister of the Interior, Friedrich Zimmermann, starts talking about the "real" Germany of the 1937 borders.

The subject of Germany comes up at every meeting of the Council of Europe—and, in all likelihood, at every Warsaw Pact meeting, too. Günter Gaus, who opened the first West German mission in East Berlin, in 1974, likes to say, "We share this with East Germany: neither of us is free to decide our important questions, our life-and-death questions, for ourselves." The Russians have taken to calling *Ostpolitik* "revanchism." They consider every friendly gesture of Kohl's to Honecker an infiltration, and they were mainly responsible for keeping Honecker out of West Germany this year. The Americans tend to consider every friendly gesture of Honecker's to Kohl a sign of Honecker's longing for democracy—a cheering thought, but not one that is likely to help their own relations with the Russians. Europe may be the only place in the world where the battle lines are clearly drawn and the alliances (relatively) respected. The fact is that neither side is much willing to risk a change. Solidarity was blessed publicly in the West, but privately every NATO government considered Lech Walesa and his workers' revolution a nuisance—a cry for help they could neither afford to answer nor explain not answering. In the same way, West Europeans who are not actually alarmed at the prospect of a revived and independent German nation are alarmed instead at the prospect of an unstable and insecure continent. The West does not intend to unite Germany any more than the Russians do. Everyone knows this, but the working arrangement is that no one admits it. Andreotti, talking the way he did about pan-Germanism, broke what one irritated Paris diplomat called the "gentleman's agreement."

West Germany is not exactly a country. The arrangement is a formality, but the fact remains that West Germany's constitution is still a provisional constitution, the capital at Bonn is a provisional capital, and the supreme court at Karlsruhe is a provisional court. Legally, West Germans are waiting to become "Germany," with Berlin for their capital. The Allies have nothing to do with the way West Germany leads its domestic or its diplomatic life, but as signatories of the Status of Forces agreement of 1954 they have powers they would never have in another NATO country—powers involving the use of German land and the deployment of troops and weapons—and they want to keep those powers for as long as the Russians are in Eastern Europe. They want to stay in West Germany whether the Germans like them there or not, and they want to keep the question of Berlin open.

All this really means is that the subject of "Germany" is complicated. It means that German reunification is not just the civil theology in West Germany but the argument on which all of West Germany's political institutions are based and the military intrusions of 350,000 foreign troops and their bombs and missiles are justified. One reason Honecker had trouble—trouble at home as much as in the Soviet Union —explaining his plan to visit Kohl was that Kohl had refused to receive him at the Federal Chancellery in Bonn, and had insisted on meeting him in a hotel outside town, in Bad Kreuznach. What he meant was that *he* did not want to be obligated to meet Honecker in Honecker's residence, in East Berlin, when he returned the visit. As long as West German leaders stay out of East German leaders' houses, they avoid having to admit that East Germany exists and that, at least for now, East Berlin is someone else's capital.

René Wellek, the critic, had three criteria for a Romantic culture: belief in myth, belief in the power of poetic language to deepen reality, and belief in the oneness of nature. By those criteria, one can assume that Germany has never really recovered from Romanticism. The myth of "Germany" and the language of home and landscape mean some-thing to every German, regardless of what he thinks about chancelleries or where the capital belongs. In a way, Giulio Andreotti shamed the Germans by admitting so bluntly that the real interest of the West was in maintaining the Yalta borders—that the rhetoric of "one Germany" was a strategic convenience and had nothing at all to do with uniting the country one day. Andreotti is a politician who usually gets his name in the German papers when someone at home is accusing him of having friends in the Mafia or of suspicious dealings with Michele Sindona —but after his speech in Rome he found himself at the center of an argument about Germany that still goes on. Horst Ehmke, who is a Social Democratic minority leader in the Bundestag, tried to end the argument by saying that inasmuch as there *were* two Germanys, and everybody knew it, Andreotti's thoughts on the subject were hardly surprising. But the Christian Democrats resented the fact that an Italian —and a fellow Christian Democrat at that—was talking as if Italy had been with the Allies at Yalta, parcelling out Central Europe. They were furious about the word "pan-Germanism," which by now is a dressed-up way of saying Nazism, and about the implication that their feelings about being German were suspect. Kohl himself asked for an apology. His Foreign Minister, Hans-Dietrich Genscher, summoned the Italian ambassador—and then changed "apology" to "explanation." The am-bassador called his Prime Minister, Bettino Craxi, and Craxi wrote what he called a letter of clarification to Kohl, but the "German question" was still no clearer than it had been for forty years.

Rudolf Augstein, who publishes the newsweekly *Der Spiegel,* says that people abroad often have a bad conscience about the conundrum they call the "German question," but that to his mind having a bad conscience about something that *is* and cannot be changed is like having a bad conscience about the weather. The politics of the two Germanys have such a mad, topsy-turvy quality that it is often easier to imagine Helmut Kohl and Erich Honecker bumping into each other in *Through the Looking Glass* than in East Berlin or in Bonn. Russia talks about two Germanys and probably wants them both. America talks about one Germany and is much happier with two. What Ronald Reagan means by "normal relations" between the two Germanys does not really include the discussion about "Germany" which normal relations would involve. Freimut Duve, a Social Democratic deputy from Hamburg who is important in the German peace movement, says that the country is in a classic double bind: as the law stands now, Honecker himself could walk into any West German police station during office hours and demand a West German passport and get one. Duve likes to imagine Honecker at the police station. Sometimes, he says, he also likes to imagine three million Communist bureaucrats crossing over from East Germany and claiming their right to keep working for the "German" government. The trouble in Germany is that being abnormal is normal. It would be normal for the two German leaders to visit, but in Germany the fact that Honecker doesn't visit Kohl and Kohl doesn't visit Honecker is more "normal"—more appropriate, somehow —than the visit that Honecker cancelled.

When Willy Brandt started to negotiate his *Ostpolitik,* in 1969, people in Germany talked about doing "history's business"—which was the business of bringing the people of two German states back into contact. The East Germans (and the Russians) maintained that there were now two irreconcilable German peoples—capitalist and decadent in the West, Communist and worthy at home—who, presumably, could meet safely, but Brandt's was a subtler politics, having to do with the culture that Germans shared. The fact that East Germany did so much to undermine his *Ostpolitik*—from keeping attack dogs along the wall to harassing travellers at the checkpoints—obscured the progress that was made under Brandt and, later, under Schmidt. Families that had been separated for twenty or thirty years started visiting. Trade began—to the extent that East Germany is now among West Germany's most important European markets. Businessmen in the Federal Republic took advantage of cheap East German labor and started exporting things from the G.D.R. to Common Market countries as protected "German" products—making East Germany a kind of junior partner in the European Community. Diplomats started negotiating the repatriation of millions of Germans who were scattered across Eastern Europe. It cost West Germany a lot of money (by now the price is about twenty thousand dollars for one refugee), but the result was that six hundred thousand Germans from Poland, Rumania, Czechoslovakia, and Russia became West German citizens.

People suspicious of Brandt and his German policy (Helmut Kohl was among them) saw in his *Ostpolitik* a chance for the Soviets to exploit a certain enthusiasm for neutrality which was beginning to surface in West Germany during Brandt's time and has got stronger over the years, as the left turned against NATO and Brandt himself talked more and more about a neutral Northern Europe. But détente was also established during those years, and inasmuch as East and West German relations then were really a reflection of the state of East-West relations in general, *Ostpolitik* was as logical as it was humane. The mood in West Germany began to change in the late seventies— just as it was changing in America. When Jimmy Carter started building new missiles—more than two hundred of them intended for the Federal Republic—and "theater nuclear war" became the euphemism for nuclear war in Germany, the German left started having arguments about deployment and neutrality, and the German right discovered a passion for "Germany" which in educated conservative circles passed as a kind of German Gaullism but in the *Bierstuben* of Baden-Württemberg and Bavaria sounded like old-fashioned nationalism. It is reasonable for a country that supplies half the soldiers in NATO's land armies to want some say about NATO's plans, but NATO is mainly an issue here for the Greens and the left wing of the Social Democrats. The constituency tapped by right-wing politicians is united by its deep, almost narcotic anti-modernism, by its longing for *Heimat*, more than by any policy. Its vision is only "Germany." The rural values it cherishes are really rural simplicities. They are the values that young German idealists talked about early in the century when they were skipping through German forests and bounding up German mountains, worshipping nature and calling themselves the *Wandervogel*. "Germany" turned them into the *Hitlerjugend*. Some people think the Greens are a little like the *Wandervogel*. The Greens have twenty-seven seats in the Bundestag, but they still come to work with their babies on their backs and oatmeal cookies in their pockets. They have a bludgeoning kind of sanity and they are often intolerant. They can put their friends—not to mention the rest of parliament—to sleep with their lectures about the good countryside against the bad city, about nature against civilization and cows against power plants. Most of them have more "truth" in their heads than experience, but they work hard and they know Germany down to its smallest village, and, for now, they seem to be the conscience of the country, not its problem.

Helmut Kohl was elected early in 1983, a few months after Brezhnev died and Andropov took over in Moscow. There was not much left of détente by 1983. The Russians had already invaded Afghanistan and were busy making SS-22 missiles for East Germany. America was busy making cruise missiles and Pershing 2s. Reagan was two years into his first term, and seemed to consider détente a treacherous preoccupation —something that liberals spent their time on. Kohl was at a loss when Reagan started saying that détente was a pact with the devil but implied that Kohl could exploit his part of it under another name—like a spy on a mission. Kohl himself is a simple character. He sometimes sounds like the Good Soldier Schweik with a government—always trying to do the agreeable, patriotic thing and doing it wrong. A documentary called *War and Peace* that was made in West Germany a couple of years ago shows Kohl in a tank during Army maneuvers. The Chancellor was in *Bundeswehr* fatigues, and a reporter asked if this was the first time he had worn a uniform. Kohl cheerfully replied, "Oh, no, once I was a *Flakhelfer*"—an anti-aircraft spotter—"and I wore a uniform, a real uniform!" (The London *Times* called Kohl "the first German postwar leader not to have fought against the French," and one wonders what Willy Brandt, who spent the war in exile in Scandinavia, had to say about that.) People who like Kohl describe him as sincere, and say that his being a little plodding, a little maladroit, only adds to his "German" charm and confirms that sincerity. People who do not like him say that his rusticity is a ruse. They say that big business in Germany depends on Kohl to look after its interests. They consider the fact that Kohl took over the Christian Democratic Union in 1973 from a man who, for practical purposes, was paid off to the amount of $700,000 by Friedrich Karl Flick's holding company to step down in Kohl's favor to be proof that his friends find him either efficient or useful. Kohl himself testified at the Bundestag last week about some Flick money that *he* received. He admitted getting about $55,000 in thousand-mark bills stuffed in plain envelopes. It turns out that, over the years, Flick has handed out nearly $2.8 million in contributions to the Christian Democrats, $2 million to the Free Democrats, and $1.5 million to the Social Democrats. The company wanted tax writeoffs and friends in every party, in or out of government. There are no disclosure laws in West Germany, but there will undoubtedly be some soon.

Kohl did not really understand that détente was over. He was an amateur when it came to the rest of the world. What Reagan meant when he talked to Kohl about his "moral concept" of foreign policy was that East and West Germany should be enemies for as long as Russia and America were not getting along. Kohl, to his credit, did seem to understand that it was important for the two Germanys to be, if not closer, at least easier in their relations. He liked the idea of *Ostpolitik* now that he had inherited it. It was an imprecise affection; *Ostpolitik* seems to have reminded him of the 1950s, when the Christian Democrats were so popular and politicians could talk to people about "going home" and be cheered for it. Since then, one and a quarter million refugees from Eastern Europe have started voting in West Germany. They were the margin that put the Christian Democrats in power in 1983, and they are blunt in their prejudices: they hate Communists. Kohl, being agreeable, hates Communists, too. He does not talk about uniting Germany, but he does seem to believe in *recovering* Germany. The war ended when he was fifteen, and this may be why he has so much trouble with the "roof" of history that Helmut Schmidt described. Brandt's *Ostpolitik*—and, later, Schmidt's—involved very specific agreements about trade and West Berlin and family contacts, and those agreements were ratified in treaties with Moscow, Warsaw, and East Berlin. After the Helsinki Accord, in 1975, they were extended to include human rights—in particular, the rights of families who had been separated by the wall between the two Germanys to be together. Kohl's *Ostpolitik* was different. The most surprising thing about it was that it went along so smoothly for so long—more than a year and a half —because there was no real policy behind it, no particular intention. Kohl likes to read his treaties with the East Germans, but, as one man in his cabinet said, he does not read between their lines.

Erich Honecker confuses a lot of Christian Democrats. The fact that he can be a German and a nationalist and, at the same time, an ardent Communist confuses them, and the fact that he is willing to accept Russian policy, and even stand behind it, confuses them, and so, inevitably, does the fact that he gets angry when something like a visit to Bonn is publicized in the West as "Erich Honecker's turning toward democracy." Günter Gaus, who knows Honecker well and admires him, says that to understand Erich Honecker you have to think of those nineteenth-century German Catholics who gave Bismarck so much trouble when he had put Germany together and was trying to persuade them of their patriotic duty to obey their Chancellor first and their Pope second, if at all. The Catholics considered themselves as German as

Bismarck, but they still listened to the Pope when it came to who would choose their bishops and who would educate their children. They were called ultramontanes, because Bismarck complained that they were always looking across the Alps to the Vatican, and Gaus says that in his way Honecker is an ultramontane, because on questions of faith *he* looks across to the Kremlin. Gaus also says that "looking across the mountains" to Moscow is not at all the same as phoning Moscow every morning for permission to shave or to eat a soft-boiled egg for breakfast —which is what a lot of West Germans imagine Honecker doing when they are not imagining him renouncing Moscow by visiting their country. Last year, Honecker admitted Martin Luther into the official East German hagiography with a five-hundredth-birthday party that went on for months. He put Frederick the Great and his horse back on their marble pedestal on Unter den Linden, in East Berlin. He is concerned about East Germans' enjoying some identity of their own, but he also knows that they would rather travel than look at an equestrian statue or have a birthday party for Luther; they would rather be a little more prosperous, and their children would rather dance in American jeans to Japanese Walkmans than devote themselves to puppet-theater productions of the Diet of Worms.

Ostpolitik is important to Honecker. East Germany is one of the twelve industrial powers in the world, and this gives it a measure of economic freedom and a leverage with Moscow that Poland, say, or Czechoslovakia does not have. Honecker can make the same sort of argument for *Ostpolitik* that the West Germans make. He can say that East Germany bears the burden of defense for Eastern Europe and the burden of risk in its battle plans, and must get something special in return. There are as many as three thousand nuclear weapons in East Germany; there are 400,000 Soviet soldiers. A lot of East Germans think that they are being sacrificed to Russia and the Warsaw Pact, just as a lot of West Germans think that *they* are being sacrificed to the United States and NATO. They all know what "theater nuclear war" means, whether it is a Russian or an American talking. They also know that right now Germany is the key to political stability in Europe. A French diplomat I know who works on what could be called the Cold War desk at the Quai d'Orsay says that, like the Hungarians in 1956 and the Czechs in 1968, the East Germans have had to make a trade with Moscow—their political liberty in exchange for any economic, or even personal, contact with the West—and that they are in a position now to see that trade honored. Their price is high, because the Communists are as unpopular in East Germany as the Greeks are in Turkey (West

Germans figure that if there were free elections in East Germany the Communist Party would be lucky to get 10 percent of the vote), and because the Russians are, if anything, more terrified of a real understanding among Germans than the Americans are. The Russians want Germany to suffer all the traumas of the Cold War. They want to avoid a little German oasis in the middle of Europe where nationality could overrun ideology, the way it did for a while in Poland. Honecker can say to the Russians, "Pay up," because he knows that they would rather pay than find themselves with a German Walesa on their hands.

When Honecker cancelled his visit—the official word is "postponed," since he is apparently going to try again, in 1985—everyone in West Germany told a different story. Some people said that he cancelled because Alfred Dregger, the Christian Democratic majority leader, had insulted him. (Dregger, who is a reactionary, and a bitter one, had told *Die Welt* that "our future does not depend upon whether Herr Honecker pays us the honor of a visit.") Other people blamed Kohl's adviser for East Germany, Philipp Jenninger, because of some of the things *he* had said—among them that the terrifying new nuclear weapons deployed this year in East and West Germany were really going to bring the two Germanys closer. Then, there were the arguments about where to meet (heads of state do not usually receive other heads of state in suburban hotels), and the embarrassment about papers like *Die Welt*, which were printing headlines on the order of HOW FREE IS HONECKER? There was also Kohl's reluctance to talk about the things that Honecker, free or not, had to talk about to please the Russians —things like whether West Germany was ever going to recognize East Germany and stop tempting East Germans with "German" citizenship. There was the question of having embassies instead of missions, of exchanging ambassadors instead of envoys. There was the question of "security"—meaning missiles. Honecker wanted to talk about security. He is not at all free to disarm East Germany (he is free only to demand that Kohl disarm West Germany), but disarmament was first on his agenda, because East Germans talk about it a lot, because it embarrasses America, and because it makes terrific propaganda. It was not on Kohl's agenda. Kohl would not agree to a joint statement about the two Germanys' working together toward disarmament—a statement that Honecker wanted to carry home. The only subjects that Kohl would take up with Honecker were the environment and human rights.

People here say that Moscow stopped the visit, but Honecker could just as well have stopped it himself, before Moscow had a chance.

Honecker is practiced in the kinds of self-censorship that keep Eastern European leaders in power, and the arguments in the Soviet bloc about his visit were much more violent than he might have predicted when he agreed to come. In July, *Pravda* was already printing cartoons of goose-stepping West German soldiers in Nazi uniforms (actually, it is the East German Army, not the West German Army, that goose-steps), and *Red Star* was reporting that the Bundeswehr was training "along Hitlerian lines . . . for an attack on the Soviet Union and its socialist allies." Honecker held out as long as he could. He saw to it that the *Neues Deutschland*, in East Berlin, printed every side of the argument, from the editorials in *Pravda* to the rebuttals to *Pravda*—which came, surprisingly, from Hungary. After he cancelled, Todor Zhivkov, the Bulgarian Party Secretary, cancelled *his* visit to the Federal Republic. The only Eastern European to visit Helmut Kohl this fall was Nicolae Ceauşescu, the Rumanian President, who seems to have invited himself.

A Swiss playwright I know who spends a lot of time in West Germany says that for reasons he cannot explain he has been asking every German he meets this question: How do you define progress? The East Germans have removed the shrapnel guns from their emplacements along the wall and replaced them with guns they say are "better." Is that progress? They have turned over the railway that runs through West Berlin to the West Berliners. For a time, they even lifted some bans on emigration—which they never did while Germans from the rest of Central Europe were leaving for the Federal Republic. In February this year, twenty-six hundred East Germans crossed over into West Germany; by May, twenty-five thousand East Germans had arrived. Emigration was stopped then, because "being German" began to mean being West German to too many of Honecker's subjects. There are now anywhere between 200,000 and 500,000 East Germans waiting for their exit visas—including the 180 East Germans who started camping this fall in the West German embassies in Prague, Budapest, Bucharest, and Warsaw. Is that progress? East Germany was in trouble when Honecker started talking about letting people go. The country needed hard currency—fresh money, the bankers say these days—the way Italy had needed fresh money in 1976 and Turkey had needed fresh money two years later. In a way, East Germany sold twenty-five thousand East Germans to the West for West German Deutsche marks. When the emigration began, West German banks had already lent East Germany a billion marks—"You see, we are not cold warriors," said Franz Josef Strauss, the Prime Minister of Bavaria.

When the emigration stopped, those banks decided they had better send a billion more.

It was Strauss who arranged the first loan—not Kohl, or Jenninger, or Hans Otto Bräutigam, Kohl's envoy to East Berlin. Strauss runs the Christian Social Union, and for years he has harassed his Christian Democratic partners just by being around. They used to call him a Fascist. Now that he has taken up East Germany, they say that he is "too Catholic" for Fascism—that he is more of a crusty old nationalist, a sentimental lover of "Germany." It is true that, given the mood here, Strauss does not seem nearly as dreadful as he did five years ago. Strauss hates Communists, but he loves "Germany" more— and this has always made his politics eccentric. He wanted to be Chancellor, but he and his party were an embarrassment to the silky capitalists behind every conservative German government. He was Defense Minister in 1956, and Finance Minister for three years in the 1960s, but those were the only times he was invited to Bonn. He is almost seventy. Stories still go around about wild parties at his hunting lodge, and every once in a while someone publishes a snapshot of the beefy Herr Strauss with a young blonde on his lap, but now that he is determined to leave his mark on German politics (he says he wants to show the Christian Democrats how to do it) he has started sending himself on "diplomatic" missions, in the manner of, say, Jesse Jackson. He sent himself to China and Albania and Hungary, and then he sent himself to East Germany. In East Germany, he did not talk about state visits or treaties or protocol. He talked about simple German folk sharing their money with their neighbors, and about other simple German folk packing up their belongings and heading west, like cowboys. It was a down-home *Ostpolitik* that Strauss concocted: with it, he made the rounds of West Germany's banks and negotiated one of the most spectacular—and complicated—loans in the country's history. The difference between him and all the other politicians who wanted to "save" East Germany was that Strauss had never doubted his freedom to make a deal anywhere. All of a sudden, he looked original—avant-garde, people said. Even some Greens decided he was (in the words of one) "a nice old guy," and went to visit him in Munich. "Is that progress?" my friend from Switzerland would ask. Is it progress when Strauss is applauded for calling Andreotti "scandalous and treacherous," and when Horst Ehmke is pointedly not applauded for saying that, whatever one thinks of the Italian Foreign Minister, Germany is two states now and it is stupid to deny it?

François Mauriac once said he loved Germany so much that he

was grateful there were two of them. According to Strauss, if Mauriac could see Germany now he would find another way of expressing his affection. When Franz Josef Strauss talks about François Mauriac (he did it in a special "Germany" issue of *L'Express*, which followed *Der Spiegel*'s *Heimat* issue and had the words *"Une nation dans ses états"* on the cover), it means that something curious is happening in Germany, something that shows up in the art young Germans are producing —even when they are working far from home. Wim Wenders won the prize at the Cannes Film Festival this year with a movie, *Paris, Texas*, about a little boy who lives quite happily in Los Angeles with his aunt and uncle until his real father—a lost American soul who used to tie cowbells to his wife, and then tie his wife to the stove, so she wouldn't stray—rescues the boy from that happy life and "reunites" him with his real mother, a pure girl in a Texas brothel. When mother and child meet, they seem to fuse, to melt together in front of Wenders's camera. They are one flesh, one blood. The movie, I am told, is a statement about America. It may be just as much a statement about what is addling Germany.

A couple of years ago, Walter Abish wrote a novel called *How German Is It*. People I know in France who read the book called it a *policier*, but it is a *policier* in the way that, say, *The Golden Bowl* is a love story. It is about Ulrich Hargenau, a young man from a family of famous Germans. Being a writer, Ulrich himself is occasionally famous. His father is more than famous; he is a hero in the "new" Germany, because forty years ago he led an officers' plot against Hitler and got shot for it. Ulrich has dropped the "von" from the family name, and has done the ungentlemanly thing of testifying about some friends of his wife's who used to hang out at their apartment eating everything in the icebox, and who turned out to be terrorists from a gang called the Einzieh Group. Ulrich loves his wife—his ex-wife now—and is trying not so much to find her as to discover how "German" she is. He is an embarrassment to his wife, to the terrorists he used to feed, and, especially, to the third famous Hargenau, his brother Helmuth, an architect who designs police stations and wants to keep his commissions coming. One reason Ulrich is so embarrassing to have around is that someone in a yellow Porsche is trying to kill him. Someone is always either sending him warnings in coloring books or blowing up his brother's police stations or producing lovers for Ulrich who betray him not with other men but with other identities. He does not know what to make of this "Germany" where people are so murderous and congenial (and only his mother's old servant, another kind of architect, with a matchstick concentration camp in the basement, is considered crazy), and where the important observations have to do with your tennis serve and the important accusation is "You don't love me anymore."

Abish was born in Vienna, which he left in 1938, at the age of seven, and eventually he made his way to New York, married there, and settled down. He had never been in Germany when he wrote *How German Is It*, but his novel is the most remarkable description of postwar Germany I have read. When people ask Abish about the book, he says that "Germany" has always been an imaginary place, an idea of Germany. He says that anyone who knows anything about the country —about its language or its history or its philosophers or its cruelties —will invent a Germany of his own, and there is no reason that Walter Abish's Germany should be less "German" than, say, Kohl's or Honecker's or Strauss's. When Abish did finally go to Germany, in 1982, he was a little bewildered. He liked Germany. It was a beautiful country. He started wondering whether the Americans and the Englishmen who flew over Germany in 1943 and 1944 had looked down when they dropped their bombs and thought that they were bombing something beautiful. When he came home and talked to some of them, he discovered, of course, that they had not thought about beauty at all. Abish is a Jew and an intellectual, and questions about Germany are often on his mind. He says that the Germans he met were agreeable. They would drive him around, trying to find his Germany, but it was always they who asked "How German is it?" when they saw or heard something disturbing. He still gets letters about the places that he made up —the police stations that are bombed; the bland new suburbs built on the sites of mass graves and concentration camps; the Frisian islands where pretty terrorists retire and "good Germans" and "bad Germans" walk the beaches together, drinks in hand, in cool complicity. The Germans who write to him have discovered those places at home, just as he described them. Germany may be the only country in the world where people check up on reality with such persistence, anxiety, and desire.

November 1984

GREENPEACE

The Greenpeace affair is not really about the ecology of the South
Pacific or secret agents blowing up the protest boat called *Rainbow
Warrior* or France's right to test its bombs at a safe distance of halfway
around the world because it happens to own some suitable atolls there.
Everyone I know in Paris seems to have a good idea of what it is not
about, but nobody can say for sure why, exactly, it is so absorbing. A
conseiller d'état who lives around the corner from me and is following
the affair from what could be called a constitutional point of view tells
me it has a lot to do with the country's obsession with "honor." He says
to think of honor as a kind of wrapping for authority that is taken out
and dusted off and aggressively adjusted whenever the country is feeling defeated or weak or humiliated—as a way of rearranging history
and of announcing what the authority of the future will be. Honor, he
says, has nothing to do with morality or integrity—it has to do with
the appearance of integrity. He says he cannot name one Frenchman
who questions the morality of blowing up a boat because it was heading
for French territorial waters to protest French nuclear testing or the
morality of the government's having lied about Greenpeace for at least
two months, or of the Army's having lied. Lying in politics is not the
sin in France that it is in what my friend the *conseiller* calls "the
touching Protestant countries." Incompetence *is* a sin, and incompe-
tent deception is unpardonable. One of the first things French children
learn in school is that Fifth Republic France is as smooth and seamless
as one of Roland Barthes's Citroëns, with none of its insides showing,
none of the adjustments and interventions and compromises that it
takes to keep it running—a triumph, so to speak, of political technol-

ogy, and not at all like the jumble of institutions in other countries, disputatious and exposed. The French were ashamed not because they were blowing up Greenpeace boats but because they were caught blowing up Greenpeace boats and became disputatious and exposed themselves. "Criminal and stupid," Mitterrand said, when he finally had to say something.

France and the Greenpeace flotilla—seven sailboats and tugs and trawlers that travel to nuclear-waste and nuclear-test sites carrying protesters—are old antagonists. In 1972, a French minesweeper rammed a Greenpeace boat off Mururoa, a Polynesian atoll where the French do a lot of their underground testing. In 1973, French marines boarded the same boat and beat up David McTaggart, the Canadian ecologist who founded Greenpeace, and his crew, and after that there were run-ins every few years. The commander of France's test-site forces has come to expect trouble of some sort from ecologists whenever the country schedules a round of testing, and last spring, when tests on Mururoa were announced, the commander—at the time it was an admiral by the name of Henri Fagès—wrote to Paris requesting permission to "anticipate" a Greenpeace protest. Sometime in March or April, French secret agents—at least two women and somewhere between five and ten men—started moving in on Greenpeace groups in the South Pacific. The men who have been identified or accounted for belonged to an Army underwater commando unit based in Aspretto, Corsica, and attached to something called Action Service, which is itself a kind of elite hit and sabotage squad of the Direction Générale de la Sécurité Extérieure, the French Secret Service. The women were officers directly assigned to Action Service by the DGSE. Three of these agents went to New Caledonia and signed on as crew for a doctor from Dieppe, who supposedly wanted to have a South Seas sailing holiday. Two more agents—a man and one of the women—arrived in New Zealand for a "honeymoon" and set off in a hired camper to be alone. Eventually, other agents appeared in Auckland. Working with the honeymooners (who carried Swiss passports and called themselves M. and Mme Turenge) and with the doctor's crew, two of the frogmen managed to attach two bombs to the hull of the *Rainbow Warrior*, which exploded on July 10 in Auckland harbor. Everybody fled the boat when the first bomb went off except a young Portuguese photographer, who ran belowdecks to save his camera equipment. The second bomb killed him.

There were not many people in New Zealand to arrest. The frogmen disappeared. The doctor's crew managed to get away after a couple of policemen found them on Norfolk Island and started asking questions. The doctor himself came back to Paris, claiming that all the talk about frogmen and secret agents on his boat had ruined his holiday. But the honeymooners were picked up by the Auckland police when they returned their camper to a rent-a-car garage, and they immediately used the police station's telephone to call a secret emergency number at DGSE headquarters in Paris and report that they had been arrested— thus letting anyone who happened to be listening in know precisely who they were. Eventually, the people who knew included (along with the Auckland police and the DGSE switchboard operators) the British Secret Service, Interpol, and the French Interior Ministry, which has its own secret police, the Direction de la Surveillance du Territoire, and spies regularly on the DGSE in the manner of an FBI spying on a CIA. But that was July, and no one in France seemed very interested in Greenpeace in July, least of all the President, who knew that *les faux Turenges* (as everybody calls them now) were agents because his Interior Minister, Pierre Joxe, drove right to the Élysée and told him. It was not until August, when a reporter from a weekly tabloid called *VSD* (for Vendredi, Samedi, and Dimanche) recognized a Secret Service contact in a picture of the crew on the doctor's sailboat and started to track the story down, that people in Paris realized what a summer scandal they had. The Élysée replied to the news with an official disclaimer in the form of a report, dutifully, if cynically, compiled by an old Gaullist named Bernard Tricot, who had been called in to make an "impartial investigation" for the President.

Last month, *Le Monde* took up the Greenpeace affair, and then Mitterrand had to say something—if only that "we are learning from the newspapers what we cannot get from our own intelligence." In fact, most people said that the paper was getting its information from Mitterrand's Interior Ministry, and presumably with the blessing of the minister, who, for reasons having to do with party problems and election politics and his own ambitions and simple common sense, wanted the government to come clean and save whatever face it could before the public prosecutor in Auckland brought *les faux Turenges* to trial on murder charges. *Le Monde* had been waiting for something like Greenpeace. The paper had been having problems for almost as long as France had been having problems with Greenpeace boats—money problems and the problems of boring too many of its readers with meditations called "Whither the Left?" and anxious headlines about the rising dollar followed by anxious headlines about the falling dollar, not to mention its own weakness for the honor of the state and its reluctance to subject a Socialist President to what is known in France as "Anglo-Saxon journalism." The paper had got a new director not long before the Action Service commandos started for the South Pacific, and the director—his name is André Fontaine, and he has been at *Le Monde* for nearly forty years—was determined to make *Le Monde* snappier. It was his good fortune to have a "deep throat" (a *gorge profonde*, the paper put it) as reliable as the Interior Ministry, and the paper's reputation as the country's journal of record to back him up. There is not much of a muckraking tradition in France. It has been considered disrespectful for any paper but *Le Canard Enchaîné* (which is there to be disrespectful) to discuss the country as if it were an ordinary place, like England or America, and this is probably why *Le Monde* has often been so brilliant in its foreign reporting and so tedious in its reporting from home. It was something of a revolution when *Le Monde* took on the Greenpeace affair. The paper's Paris circulation went up twelve thousand copies in a single day. Parisians were elated and talked about the brave young reporters who must have spent their summer holidays keeping dangerous rendezvous in bad neighborhoods to get their story. (The paper itself ran articles modestly comparing them to Robert Woodward and Carl Bernstein.) Actually, the most dangerous rendezvous any reporter in Paris seems to have had was at a pleasant café across the street from DGSE headquarters. *Le Monde* reporters supposedly got their "leaks" hand-delivered to their offices on the rue des Italiens.

What *Le Monde* confirmed was that the government had been covering for a bungled act of sabotage that was probably (as Mitterrand said) stupid to have undertaken in the first place and certainly stupid to have bungled. The bombs on the *Rainbow Warrior* were never intended to kill anyone. They were set to go off in Auckland harbor rather than at sea, where the boat would certainly have sunk, and they were timed so that the crew would flee after the first explosion, leaving the boat empty for the second, stronger blast. It was, as Joseph Fouché, the man who created France's Secret Service, put it when Napoleon ordered the execution of the Duc d'Enghien, "worse than a crime—it was a blunder." People in the government began to take it for granted that Mitterrand had lied in saying he knew nothing about Greenpeace until he read about it in the paper, although by then Mitterrand's office was orchestrating its own leaks to the press, which had to do with the President jumping up at cabinet meetings and crying, "I want to know! I want to know!" They took it for granted that Laurent Fabius, the Prime Minister, must have had to lie, too. They started accusing each other of lying, and by the time they stopped, nine people had been implicated in either the decision to bomb the *Rainbow Warrior* or the decision to cover up the bombing, including Mitterrand's (at the time) military adviser, Fabius's military adviser, the admiral in charge of the French Secret Service, the Minister of Defense, and the *chefs de cabinet* from Matignon and the Élysée. The Minister of Defense resigned then—or, rather, the Prime Minister announced his resignation. His name is Charles Hernu, and he was one of Mitterrand's oldest and closest friends in the government—loyal during the twenty years that Mitterrand fought for the Presidency and, it turned out, immensely useful once Mitterrand had it. He was a gendarme's son who had grown up loving soldiers and soldiering and had never lost that fascination. The generals trusted him, and it was his job to persuade them to trust Mitterrand, too. Not many of them were notably well disposed to their Socialist President, but Hernu won them over and became a kind of lobby for the Army at the Élysée. In the end, it was a question of whether Hernu controlled the Army or the Army Hernu. He would not blame his generals for Greenpeace. He would not "sacrifice" his army, he said, to save face for his government, or even for his friend François Mitterrand, and so, reluctantly, he sacrificed himself—and refused to answer the people who wanted to know if Charles Hernu had been the man to say about the *Rainbow Warrior,* "Who will free me from this turbulent priest?" In a way, the admiral who ran the Secret Service sacrificed himself, too. His name is Pierre Lacoste, and by all reports he was the most prudent of conspirators—the one who had held back, insisting that bombing the *Rainbow Warrior* would accomplish nothing that could not be accomplished simply by turning it back or putting it out of commission (the way protest boats were often said to be put out of commission when they got near French waters, with a little damage to the engine, or a little something in the pot-au-feu to give the crew indigestion). But he refused to account for Greenpeace when the Élysée demanded an accounting. He said he had a "professional duty" to protect his men, and by saying that, he challenged Mitterrand's right, as President of France, to any information he sought. Lacoste was fired, and five DGSE agents were arrested on charges of leaking secret information to the press. One of them, it turned out, had been stationed for a while at the underwater commando base in Corsica. He was evidently troubled in Corsica—troubled not only by the fact that the agents there were fanatically anti-Socialist but that *le discours,* as *Le Monde* put it, was subversive. He had written to Hernu, and even to Mitterrand, to complain.

The Secret Service used to be an independent service, responsible to the Prime Minister. It was turned over to the Minister of Defense in 1965, after the Moroccan dissident Mehdi Ben Barka was kidnapped in Paris, outside the Brasserie Lipp, and killed by French policemen and agents presumably in the pay of the Moroccan Interior Minister, General Muhammad Oufkir. Its name was changed and, more to the point, it was directly connected to the military. There are twenty-five hundred agents in the DGSE, and some fifteen hundred of them are Army or Navy officers on loan to the agency—which is why the honor of the military came into the Greenpeace affair, and not just the competence of the Secret Service. The officers in the DGSE are clearly happier with an admiral like Pierre Lacoste in charge than with the civilian chiefs they sometimes have. Mitterrand's first director of the DGSE was a civilian. His name was Pierre Marion, and he started out at the office by firing agents he considered reactionary. Some of those agents broke into his flat one night and carried him off, and the next morning he woke up adrift in a dinghy in the Mediterranean. When he was fired, Admiral Lacoste took over. And when Lacoste was fired Mitterrand replaced him with another military man, a general named René Imbot. Imbot is tough, in a steely, Foreign Legion sort of way—which seems to be what Mitterrand wanted. A week after he took over, he put on his uniform and the medals and ribbons and sashes from a dozen North African and Indochinese campaigns and went on television to glare at the country and talk about how he had uncovered a dark plot at the heart of the DGSE, whose intention was nothing less than the destabilization of the French Secret Service and thus of "one of the five great nuclear powers in the world." Without saying any more, he announced that the matter was in good hands—his hands—and, as far as the rest of France was concerned, closed. By then, it seemed as if a lot of people wanted it closed. *Le Monde* had already renounced some of the pleasures of its "underwatergate" to say that the honor of France and of the men who ran France was never in question, nor was the "deep unity" of the French people and their Army or the "fundamental consensus" on which the nuclear authority of France rests. And after that, as is the custom here in a crisis, everybody with a name and an opinion on the crisis contributed that opinion to the *Débats* page of the paper. The director Patrice Chéreau wrote in to say that the obsession with Greenpeace was distressing him personally. He said there was a lot of false naïveté in expecting a Secret Service to function perfectly—which means in perfect secrecy—and at the same time to be perfectly "transparent" about its orders and directives. Certainly it would have been naïve to expect Pierre Lacoste to check with the Élysée every time one of his twenty-five hundred agents went off spying or sabotaging or "neutralizing," or whatever else secret agents do, and it is unlikely that he could have checked if he had wanted to—the real secrecy in agencies like the DGSE is secrecy in the field. And certainly it would have been naïve to expect important people to sit around at the Élysée all day examining DGSE dossiers as if they were *baccalauréat* scores. But the problem with Greenpeace seems to be that a lot of important people *did* sit around discussing what to do with the *Rainbow Warrior,* and for the French this raises the question of why those people decided to bomb the trawler when the correct—if that is the word—procedure with protest boats is to track them until they reach your territorial waters and then either turn them back or seize them. It raises the diplomatic question of France's "right" to plant bombs on boats in a friendly country's harbor. It raises the tactical question of what good blowing up a Greenpeace boat would do besides providing the ecologists with a lot of free publicity—which is what their missions are for. It raises the question of security which was so darkly suggested by General Imbot and then much taken up by the papers—the question of whether there was in fact a sabotage plot within a sabotage plot. (The plot-within-a-plot theory is that the Greenpeace operation was planned to fail, and people who hold this theory say that the evidence is on their side: the *Rainbow Warrior* was bombed right in Auckland harbor; agents seem to have left a trail for the British Secret Service, along with providing the New Zealand police with such clear clues as a traceable rented camper; spies and saboteurs who by all accounts could not speak English were sent to an English-speaking country; *les faux Turenges* called home from a foreign police station on open lines.) On the other hand, it just as easily raises the question of military competence, because the operation was so misguided it might just as well have been sabotaged from the inside.

The important question, of course, has to do with the quality and calm of the leadership here, and this is probably why the French got interested, and then obsessed, with Greenpeace. It has to do with why some of the most powerful people in France were so upset by the idea of an unarmed protest boat that they decided to destroy it. It is not usually France's policy to treat its passive resisters and dissidents and protesters like terrorists. The disturbing thing about Greenpeace is the sense one has of discipline out of control.

There has always been something puzzling to foreigners about the way the military is courted in France. The assumption that a strong army will defer to civilian authority is supposedly at the heart of the social contract in a democratic state—and not quite at the heart of the social contract in France. Mitterrand permitted the arrests of the five talkative secret agents to calm his generals down. Hernu resigned talking about the honor of the Army. Lacoste himself warned Mitterrand that his responsibility in the affair was a military one. It may be that Joxe and, later, Fabius were asking Mitterrand to choose between the Army and the government when they delivered their own ultimatums about Greenpeace; Mitterrand did choose, in a way, by letting Hernu and Lacoste go, and by putting Fabius on television to blame them, but he was as nervous as the president of a shaky banana republic until he had restored its "honor" to the armed forces. It was General Imbot who appeared in his ribbons and medals to "close" the Greenpeace affair, and not the President himself (or his new Defense Minister). People were surprised at first that Mitterrand had asked Imbot, and then they were surprised because asking him meant that Mitterrand believed—or had been persuaded—that what the country needed was military rather than political assurance. The Army today is not the old French Army, with its officers tied by privilege and family to the other ruling classes of the country and an authority that had to do with the conquest and maintenance of an empire, and with the wars France fought. Today's Army is really Charles de Gaulle's. He patched it together in 1944 and 1945 of Resistance fighters, Free French officers, Communist *maquisards*, agents from the prewar secret services, old Pétainists, and just about anybody else who came along. It was mainly their humiliation in Indochina that united them. "A bitter *rassemblement*," Jean Planchais, who used to be military correspondent at *Le Monde*, says, and not much sweetened by the war in Algeria that followed, or by the orders to withdraw that put France close to civil war. The classic way to console an army without wars to win or colonies to pacify is to give it weapons, and this, of course, is what de Gaulle did with his *force de frappe*. He assigned the prestige of what the French call *le nucléaire* to the Air Force, which supported him—and withheld it from the Army, which was giving him trouble. He conferred that prestige like medals, and so have his successors. It is not so hard to understand why France's officers despise the Greenpeace boats that sail, so to speak, right into the waters of their prestige and mock it by refusing to go away.

John Ralston Saul, a Canadian writer who lives in Paris and is best known for a novel about the assassination of the Gaullist general Charles Ailleret, said last week that the most important moment in the Greenpeace affair was not René Imbot's speech but a radio speech by another general warning that if French military men were used as scapegoats "there would be a *malaise* in the army"—meaning a withdrawal of support from the government which, according to Saul, would amount to a highly sophisticated coup d'état. French politics have been punctuated by this sort of military withdrawal since the Revolution. De Gaulle came to power not in an election but because the military had had enough of the Fourth Republic and of the wars no one was allowed to win, and so it withdrew, as it were, from France until the President—René Coty at the time—had no choice but to ask de Gaulle to form a government. De Gaulle began to lose that power when the military left him with 1968 on his hands. It may be true that *le nucléaire* is what keeps the military from "withdrawing" now. It is certainly true that *le nucléaire* is what links French men and women, whatever their politics, to the Army. The French like being the great nuclear power that General Imbot invoked. They have no argument with the Army about nuclear weapons or about the policy that is always referred to in France as "nuclear dissuasion." (*"Ma bombe est indiscutable,"* Mitterrand said to Mikhail Gorbachev when Gorbachev was in Paris this month and asked for negotiations on the *force de frappe.*) They have no argument about nuclear power of any sort. Brice Lalonde's Écologistes are rarely heard from anymore, except when something like Greenpeace happens and Lalonde is called on to give "the ecologists' view." When the *Rainbow Warrior* tried to block Cherbourg harbor a couple of years ago to stop delivery of twenty-four tons of atomic waste to the city, people talked about Communists and hippies interfering the way they talked about Communists and hippies this year when someone reported that Greenpeace was going to "invade" Mururoa atoll with a fleet of rubber kayaks armed with flowers. People in France do believe that their authority and independence and influence rest on an arsenal of bombs and a capacity for "dissuasion"—and they believe it all the more because authority and independence and influence are precisely what they lost with the Occupation and the wars in Indochina and Algeria and the dismantling of France's considerable empire. They believe the reason that any of the South Pacific is still French has to do with France's nuclear presence in the world. Not even the Frenchmen who live in territories like Tahiti or New Caledonia are moved by arguments about the risks of underground tests so close to home—the risks of radioactive leaks through the porous coral of a test atoll or any of a hundred accidents. When photographers from Gamma-Télévision, a French company that started filming aboard the Greenpeace flagship this week, needed a boat for their equipment, they had trouble finding anyone in Papeete who was willing to rent them one. The *force de frappe* may be a symbol, insofar as no French leader could really consider using it on his own—but it is a powerful symbol. It represents what the French think of as their strength and their sanity in the middle of a morally weakening Europe. People in France look at pacifists in places like West Germany and assume that they have been either maddened by romanticism or indoctrinated by Communists or simply drugged. They look at politicians in the South Pacific—politicians like David Lange, the Prime Minister of New Zealand, and Bob Hawke, the Australian Prime Minister—who talk about a "nuclear-free ocean" and assume either that *they* are staking claims to other people's (including France's) territory or that they are simply as ignorant as Europeans have always suspected they were.

October 1985

KLAUS BARBIE

I was in the Swiss village of Sils-Maria the week the Bolivians arrested Klaus Barbie and sent him back to France. The village was getting ready for the annual spring cross-country ski marathon over the Engadine lakes. Serious *Langläufer* in narrow blue jumpsuits and blue stocking caps were out on the frozen Silser See at dawn, going so fast that from any distance at all they made a smooth, dark ribbon on the lakes, hung in motion like thoroughbreds on a track. Families on holiday explored the mountain paths and glacier trails. Or they skied into the Val Fex, awkward on their long, skinny skis, falling sometimes but always caught by the lovely white rise of the valley toward the Maloja-pass and Italy. Down in the village, the five councilmen of Sils-Maria (three of them innkeepers) met to discuss a German speculator who had ended up controlling some valuable village property, and whom the councilmen were courteously, conscientiously discouraging with lists of building codes and regulations and restrictions. Lights went on in the little Sils house where Friedrich Nietzsche spent his summers —which meant that the teacher from Poitiers who presides over a philosophers' fan club called the Nietzsche House Foundation had arrived, with his family, to ski and to count the linens and check the bedsprings for the Nietzsche scholars who come in summertime and pay the foundation to sleep on Nietzsche family beds and sit on the rock where Nietzsche invented Zarathustra and cook in the kitchen where Nietzsche ate his suppers after the Hotel Edelweiss, next door, barred him from the dining room because of bad table manners.

There is an old dairy farmer on the path to the sister village of Sils-Baselgia who says that his father used to deliver milk and butter to the cranky Herr Professor Doktor Nietzsche, but not many villagers know the name of any of the cranky professor's books, or that it was in Sils-Maria that he settled his conscience and broke with a composer called Richard Wagner because of what he said was the composer's wild and dangerous Aryan theology. Sils-Maria is a protected place, impossible to reach except by alpine passes like the Maloja. It is hard to imagine Parsifal stalking one of its snowy pastures (in another month, those pastures will be covered with *Alpenrosen* and violets) in search of purity or Rhine Maidens bathing in the Silser See. People in Sils-Maria talk about the Second World War as the time the village inns went into receivership. When a German who was staying down the hall at my *pension* came back from a night out in St. Moritz bringing the week's magazines, and then left one of them on a hall table for the other guests to see, it was pointedly ignored until the maid discovered it and took it away. The magazine was something of an anniversary issue—memorabilia of Hitler's appointment as Reichskanzler, fifty years ago—with a spread of "September Morn" watercolors of Eva Braun, signed, supposedly, by the Führer. The anniversary was not noted at the *pension*. Nor was the news that the man who in all likelihood had tortured to death the French Resistance leader Jean Moulin, in 1943, was in a French prison waiting to be tried for crimes against humanity. The guests of the *pension* were a friendly group—mainly French and German—and back home in Stuttgart or Bordeaux they would probably have been talking about Klaus Barbie. In Sils-Maria, they were party to a shrewd discretion that is remarkable even in a country as discreet as Switzerland. That discretion is a legacy from the days when any stranger who made his way over the mountains to the village was on a quest for some sort of forgetfulness, and the villagers offered as their "neutrality" the eloquent sanctuary of hidden lakes and meadows—and silences.

Klaus Barbie was the S.S. commander of Lyons from November of 1942 to November of 1944, and in the course of those two years he murdered, or ordered the murder of, 4,342 Maquisards and deported 7,591 French Jews—men, women, and children—to concentration camps in the Reich. He was known as the Butcher of Lyons, though he was only twenty-nine when he killed Jean Moulin. Lucie Aubrac, who helped found the Resistance group Libération-Sud, and who is a grandmother now and lives in Paris with her husband, says that Barbie's youth was somehow the most shocking thing about him.

Mme Aubrac was thirty-one in 1943, and she was pregnant. Her husband, Raymond Aubrac—he was a young engineer then, and in charge of the Army of the Resistance for Southern France—was in prison with Moulin, and Mme Aubrac encountered Barbie a couple of times in the course of trying to rescue him. She is a remarkable woman. Someone once called her "the woman who domesticated fortune," and, like most real heroes, she does not so much wear her past as reflect it in the elegance of her character. She taught history to a generation of Paris *lycéens*. Then, in Morocco, she took up archaeology. She would rather talk about the ruins at Volubilis and Mogador, where she used to dig, than about Lyons. But the story of her confrontation with Barbie is in virtually every high-school history book in France, and now that Barbie has been arrested and is in Lyons people ask her about him all the time, and she keeps telling them to remember that monstrous agents of the Third Reich were just as young and ordinary as the people who risked their lives to fight them.

By all accounts, Klaus Barbie had neither the intelligence nor the talent—if "talent" is a word that applies to torturers—for interrogation. He could kill people, but he was not good at getting information from them before they died. The few people in Lyons who survived his interrogations say that he always worked with a bullwhip or a black-jack, and that his rage betrayed his incompetence; once he started beating, he usually could not stop himself until his prisoner was either dead or dying. Capturing Jean Moulin was Barbie's great good luck, because Moulin had united the right and left wings of the Resistance behind the Free French of Charles de Gaulle, and he was the one man in the country with information on every aspect of the underground and of Free French strategy involving the underground. And yet Barbie seems to have beat Jean Moulin to death with what amounted to uncontrolled dispatch. His real passion was destruction. Moulin himself was only forty-four when he died. He is often called "the father of the Resistance," but then, as Lucie Aubrac says, the men and women who fought with him were usually so much younger. Mme Aubrac wants youngsters today to know that it was simple people their age who behaved like heroes during the Occupation and simple people their age who behaved like bastards. She is seventy-one now, and she belongs to a generation that knows how it behaved then and can say, with some authority, how it would behave again. Not many people who are younger can.

There has been a lot of talk in France lately about the "wisdom" of extraditing Klaus Barbie. Raymond Barre, who was Valéry Giscard d'Estaing's Prime Minister, says that he is uneasy about "abandoning a fundamental rule of law which holds that after thirty years it is up to God to judge the criminal." Simone Veil, the president of the Judicial Commission of the European Parliament, who was denounced as a Jew in the South of France in 1944 and sent to Auschwitz, says that the trial could tear the country apart, and at the very least distract it from its proper business—which, according to Mme Veil, is the business of getting on with the future. Many people believe it would be better for Barbie to get sick and die, or be killed in jail, or manage to kill himself, than to survive until a trial and turn the people of Lyons against their neighbors.

Robert Badinter, the Minister of Justice, is one of the people who wanted Barbie back. He worked for months to persuade the Bolivians to send him, and once they did he put Barbie right into the prison in Lyons—Montluc Prison—where Barbie held Jean Moulin and Raymond Aubrac and so many of their friends from the Resistance forty years ago. Badinter wanted to give the occasion of Barbie's capture a kind of symbolic weight, like a homecoming, because the trial itself is supposed to be another sort of occasion, a scrupulous exercise in French restraint and due process. There are thirty million Frenchmen who were not even alive during the Occupation, and a few months ago most of them had no interest in the fact that Klaus Barbie had been living comfortably in La Paz, under the protection of a succession of junta generals, for the past thirty-one years. The trial of Klaus Barbie will be the first French trial of a Nazi war criminal since Karl Oberg, the S.S. commander for Occupied France, and his adjutant, Helmut Knochen, were tried in Paris in 1954 for sending eighty thousand people to die. It was only nine years after the armistice, but even in 1954 there was not much interest in the trial. People wanted to be proud of themselves and their country. They wanted to believe that France had had no part in the atrocities of its occupation. They were distressed when professors arrived from England and America and started looking at the Vichy files, and made such a great deal of the fact that there were probably no more than 2,200 Gestapo policemen in Occupied France, whereas there were at least twice as many French policemen in the Gestapo's local auxiliary and up to thirty thousand *miliciens,* which is what the Vichy security police were called. Pascal Ory, a young "historian of collaboration" who teaches in Paris at Sciences-Pô, says that when all the counting was done there turned out to have been about the same number of card-carrying Combattants Volontaires de la Résistance as there were official collaborators—collaborators indicted by the special courts of the postwar *épuration,* or purge. His figures are 160,000 resistants to 170,000 collaborators.

Some people think that Barbie belongs in Germany (which had also asked the Bolivians to extradite him), because there are no real arguments about accountability in Germany, as there are in France. Germany has to acknowledge its accountability for Nazi crimes, because those crimes were part of the official ideology of the state —natural extensions of the doctrine of racial superiority and necessary genocide. The problem for Germans right now is not so much a desire to preserve memories of Nazism as a desire to integrate those memories into the German past—to settle the Third Reich into "history" instead of maintaining it as a central trauma, a defining moment. Young Germans still cannot be sure whether that desire is understandable, or even appropriate, or whether, as Ulrike Meinhof once said, "history" is another word for their own evasions—a way of avoiding the pain of what being German means. A lot goes on in Germany today in the name of history. Eva Braun becomes a nude centerfold. Hitler's "secret diaries" are peddled to the highest bidder—a scoop on the order of Prince Andrew's Caribbean frolics with Koo Stark.

A couple of weeks ago, the *Frankfurter Allgemeine* said that the great myth in Germany about the war was that the Occupation of France was a gentlemanly affair, a "beautiful victory," with courtesies on both sides, a kind of real-life remake of *La Grande Illusion,* having nothing to do with men like Barbie or like Paul Touvier, the notorious commander of the Lyons *miliciens,* who apparently lives in a convent in Italy now and is still wanted by the French police for his own crimes against humanity. The "gentlemanly Occupation" was a soothing Wehrmacht fiction, and it appealed to the sort of respectable Germans who voted for Konrad Adenauer—Germans who wanted to be reassured that too many gestures of expiation would be undermining and indulgent. In France, the fiction has sometimes been that every Frenchman was a hero and sometimes that every Frenchman was a collaborator, but that either way guilt and expiation were sophisticated exercises, suitable only for a few Left Bank grownups. The French identify with their state. They think it is healthy for their children to identify with the state. The children of radicals have family feelings about the kings of the *ancien régime.* The children of monarchists have been known to weep for Marat in his bathtub. Real dissent, when it occurs—as it did with the student protests of May 1968—amounts to an almost Freudian drama, a breakdown in the nation's psyche. Children here are educated to argue well but not to doubt who they are or what France is. This is why people like Raymond Barre prefer to leave Barbie to "God's justice," and people like Simone Veil say that any trial that exposes a wartime France of bastards and cowards cannot be very good for the country. They are really saying that history is too dangerous to be left to its own surprises and its own truths.

Charles de Gaulle landed in Bayeux on June 14, 1944, and congratulated the city for "beautiful collective resistance." His wholly heroic wartime France was a myth that began that day, in Bayeux, and it lasted for as long as de Gaulle was paterfamilias to the country —for as long as official history gave Frenchmen one splendid collective memory to replace their difficult memories of the Occupation and its ambiguities and compromises. A lot of the people who went to bed Pétainists and woke up Gaullists were not so much repudiating the past as acting with fairly consistent chauvinism. Unregenerate Fascists went on trial during the *épuration*, and then to prison. By the end of 1948, about 70 percent of them were home, and in another two years the special courts of the *épuration* were dissolved. By August of 1953, when the National Assembly passed a general-amnesty law, there were practically no collaborators left in prison or in detention to free. The old Maquisards involved in the *épuration* say that it was fast and fairly harsh but that most of the magistrates who did the investigating for them and handed down the indictments had been Pétainists themselves. After a couple of years of peace, a lot of people simply decided that the way to get on with reconstruction was to say that, after a fashion, everyone had collaborated, or that, after a fashion, everyone had resisted, and let it go at that. In fact, most of the *gens de doctrine*, as some of the French called their Fascists, started referring to themselves again as "conservatives" or "traditionalists," or even "Catholics." As a respectable right revived, old Pétainists stood out and were considered spooky. (Last month, a group of them showed up at a Paris church called Saint-Louis d'Antin for an anniversary Mass for Colonel François de la Rocque and heard the priest compare them to "followers of the reviled Christ.") The solidarity of postwar France was impressive. No one talked about collaborators, even at trials like the Karl Oberg trial. The reporter who covered that trial for *Le Monde* wrote that it was a trial "without passion" and that the French were "preoccupied with more timely problems." It had seemed to him, he said, a kind of indispensable formality—*"la liquidation d'un mal déjà oublié."*

May of 1968 made for a kind of spontaneous revisionism. Students decided that the authority of the generation they thought they were

taking on at the barricades had a lot to do with the images that generation claimed—images of great patriotism and valor. And so they challenged those images along with the authority. France began a negative
investigation of itself. Intellectuals announced that Nazism was pornography, and spent a lot of time writing about movies like Luchino
Visconti's *The Damned*, with its feverish equations of sex and evil, and
Liliana Cavani's *The Night Porter*, which *was* pornography (people
called it "erotic projection"). The historian Michel Foucault, talking to
a reporter from *Cahiers du Cinéma* in 1974, said that he was baffled by
the connection: "Here is a problem for history. How is it that Nazism,
which had to do with pitiful, pathetic, puritanical boys and with nasty
Victorian spinsters, could have become, in France, in Germany, in the
United States—in the pornography of the whole world—the ultimate
referent of eroticism?" Louis Malle made *Lacombe, Lucien*, about a
young peasant who torments chickens and is not very smart, and for
whom collaboration becomes a sort of voluptuous awakening. Patrick
Modiano wrote stories about shadowy and ambiguous Vichy characters. There was an almost cult interest in a Jewish writer named Maurice Sachs, who had joined the Gestapo. Politicians tried to catch the
mood and use it, and inevitably failed. Giscard went so far as to cancel
the national Armistice Day holiday on May 8—the implication being
that it was unkind to keep celebrating Germany's defeat now that West
Germany and France were friends. (François Mitterrand put Armistice
Day back on the calendar as soon as he took over.)

Lately, it has been fashionable to treat Vichy France as a kind of
secret Germany—a country of Fascists and anti-Semites happy to col-
laborate. There was always anti-Semitism in France. The history teachers of 1944 who warned their pupils about "the ancient Jewish practice"
of stealing French girl babies and selling them into white slavery were
not really much worse than, say, the Chalon housewives of 1974 who
accused the Jewish merchants in the town of chloroforming women in
dressing rooms and shipping them off to oil sheiks and African chiefs
and South American dictators with slave harems. "Dreyfus" is still a
loaded word here. Vichy, of course, produced the only official collaboration in anti-Semitism in occupied Western Europe. It played on the
notion of what the French call *l'état protecteur*—the guardian state
—to give French Fascism under Marshal Pétain a pretty, sentimental
explanation of itself. After the war, Pétainist historians, among them
Alfred Fabre-Luce, claimed that France had been protecting the majority of its own Jews by collaborating. Actually, the Pétainists were
enthusiastic collaborators, occasionally offering more Jews to the Ger-

mans than even the Germans asked for. Maurice Papon—Secretary-
General of the Prefecture of the Gironde under Pétain, Prefect of
Police in Paris under de Gaulle, Minister of the Budget under Giscard
—is under indictment now on charges of deporting Jewish children to
Auschwitz. The fact that he was a Pétainist and then a Gaullist is
something that surprises only foreigners. A lot of the country was
Pétainist and then Gaullist. It may be that not many people but the
militants on either side saw any real contradiction between Pétain's
legality and de Gaulle's legitimacy. Papon was converted, so to speak,
toward the end of the war, but his conversion was not considered
dramatic in the sense that a Nazi's conversion would have been dramatic in Germany. Most of what we call "collaboration" now was
acquiescence—the small daily betrayals of small people looking out for
themselves and their privilege. Vichy did not produce many real mon-
sters of ideology; evil was not the official strategy. The seduction of
Vichy was that Pétain and his friends did not preach doctrines of hatred
and extermination. They simply saw to it that Maquisards were shot
and that neighbors informed on one another and that Jews registered
with the police and carried the proper *carte d'identité*, so that the
Germans would not be inconvenienced when the time came to kill
them. Mme Aubrac says that in July of 1942, when the French police
were ordered to round up Jews for deportation, some eight thousand
Jews went quietly to the Paris Vélodrome d'Hiver in buses the police
had commandeered. It never occurred to most of those Jews that
French policemen in French buses would be delivering them to the
Germans. They went because they needed to believe that French fraternity, and even a measure of French justice, still existed in Vichy France
in 1942. Mme Aubrac says that if Germans had come for them that day
in the Marais and Belleville, the way Germans came for the Jews in
Warsaw, the Jews of Paris would have known that they were going to
die, and then, like the Warsaw Jews, they might have fought, to die
nobly. As it was, she says, only one Paris policeman refused to participate in the *rafle des Juifs*. He quit his job.

It is obvious that Klaus Barbie will try to inflict a last cruelty on
the French—that he will try to name names to the point of making an
accomplice of everyone in Lyons who was not his victim. He claims
that he has "forgotten" everything about his two years in France except
who his helpers were. He likes to tell people that the denunciations of
Jews and Maquisards "rained" while he was in Lyons. In his interviews,
he has half the city lined up at his office in 1943 turning in friends. He

is arrogantly unrepentant, and his one pleasure in prison seems to be anticipating a showdown that will turn children against their parents and old neighbors against one another. No one doubts that, whatever he says, Barbie will be lying, but the Lyonnaise are curious and frightened. Last month, the Archbishop of Lyons said that Barbie's presence had created an atmosphere that he believed was dangerous and unhealthy—though he had trouble understanding just why he believed that. He knew only that passions that had finally cooled after forty years were being stirred by the fact of Klaus Barbie in Lyons. Some thirty-five thousand Jews live in Lyons today. Nearly every one of them is related to somebody or knew somebody who was tortured and killed by Barbie or deported to be tortured and killed because of Barbie. They fear that the Second World War is passing out of memory. The anguish of memory is that it dies with the people who remember.

May 1983

The *rentrée* is always an instructive season. Through September, Parisians coming home from five weeks of obligatory leisure turn the city into a kind of street theater, parading their Corsican tans and their sun-streaked hair and the gauzy pink and white and yellow clothes they bought for the Île de Ré or Saint-Tropez. There is something touching about Parisians on display. They try so hard, they trust so much in appearances, that their gaiety carries a sense of loss to enhance it, like a Christo fence, or a butterfly. This is what makes the *rentrée* instructive. It is a small, yearly exercise in the conviction Frenchmen share that with the proper earnestness and attention they can arrive at a perfectly illuminating moment, an exemplary image of themselves. The Barbie trial was meant to be one of those illuminating moments. After four years and twenty-three thousand pages of testimony and instruction, S.S. Hauptsturmführer Klaus Barbie, the butcher of Lyons, has been convicted of crimes against humanity committed during the German occupation of that city, forty-three years ago. But, as one of my neighbors put it, "nobody understands more."

I was in Burgundy after the trial, and, in a small village near Meursault, I visited an old *vigneron* whose family library had been put together during the Enlightenment and, by the looks of it, never expanded by a single volume. I had come for the wine, but I stayed for

the *Encyclopédie*. It was, astonishingly, the third set off the press, and
it was printed to last forever—printed with such confidence in the truth
of its definitions and distinctions that two hundred years later the
vellum was white and supple and I could browse through the twenty-
eight volumes with less worry about wear and tear than I would have
felt approaching a shelf of airport paperbacks. My friend's *arrière-
grands-pères* believed in the *Encyclopédie*, and in the massive textbooks
they used to buy to cover every human "science," from Philosophy to
Trigonometry to Justice. Understanding was their creature comfort.
Their ideology of the rational man and the perfected mind was an act
of faith as much as the miracle-counting Catholicism of the peasants
who worked their vineyards, and it occurred to me, sitting in their fine
library, that something of that same faith—that stubborn, fragile Enlightenment faith in the ability of a well-intentioned man to understand
his way to truth, to *maîtriser* his history—had affected every day of the
Barbie trial and was still affecting the people who thought about the
trial and were not "understanding more." The French expected Justice
in Lyons. They got justice instead.

When Barbie was arrested in Bolivia, in 1983, and turned over to
the French police for extradition, he had already been tried twice in
Lyons, in absentia, and sentenced to death twice, for war crimes. Since
those trials, capital punishment had been abolished in France—it was
abolished by Robert Badinter, a Jew whose father was deported to
Auschwitz by Klaus Barbie in 1943, and died there—and the statute of
limitations on carrying out those sentences had expired. It was hoped
—by Beate and Serge Klarsfeld, the people who had tracked down
Barbie and compiled the new evidence against him, and by Mitterrand
and Badinter, who had bargained for his extradition—that this time
Barbie would stand, in France, as what they called a "symbol of Nazism," that in the person of that one murderous S.S. Hauptsturmführer
all of German National Socialism, state and system, would be tried and
judged and condemned, and "history" would be served. On the other
side, Barbie's lawyer, Jacques Vergès—whose own father was a French
colonial diplomat forced out of the Foreign Service for marrying a
Vietnamese—seemed to expect, or pretended to seem to expect, that in
Klaus Barbie's trial other crimes against humanity would be exposed.
He meant, very specifically, the crimes of the French Army in Algeria
and what he called "Zionist crimes," as well as the "crimes" of treachery and betrayal within the French Resistance. Barbie in fact stood trial
on five charges involving 341 separate counts of crimes against humanity—accounting for the torture or deportation to death camps, or both,

of 737 Jews and resistants, including forty-four small Jewish children from a shelter in the village of Izieu—and in the end he was found guilty of those charges by a jury of nine Lyons men and women and sentenced to life imprisonment by a tribunal of three judges of the Lyons Cour d'Assises, which, like any criminal court under a democratic rule of law, is in business to try criminals, and not systems or symbols or honor or memory or history.

There has been a peculiar vogue for "history" lately. The journalist Mary Blume, who lives in Paris, thinks it is part of a turn-of-the-century mood, not so different from the mood in France at the turn of the last century—only starting earlier, as befits a speedy age full of speedy people not eager to be scooped by reality. Some of this has to do with the French preparing for the bicentennial of their Revolution, which, given the national passion for talk, will probably be less a matter of mock battles and costume villages and *son et lumière* at the Place de la Bastille (though there will certainly be some of those) than of solemn colloquiums about what the Revolution really meant and who the real heroes were and why Danton has more movie theaters and big streets named after him than Robespierre. But mainly, I think, this vogue (it is more of an obsession, actually) has to do with settling the history of France's most humiliating, if not inglorious, century—the four years of German Occupation, and then the lost colonial wars in Indochina and Algeria. The statisticians of the Occupation say that 98 percent of the people who stayed in France during the Second World War were neither active collaborators nor active resistants, and one of the footnotes to the Barbie trial—*en marge des débats,* the French say—was about them. They are a subject Frenchmen usually avoid, but once the trial started and the survivors told their stories of other Lyonnais watching, fearful and silent, while they were herded into concentration-camp convoys, it seemed an important thing that these ordinary, uncourageous people should be restored to "history"—dusted off and polished and presented to their children and grandchildren if not as heroes then at least as patriots and, in their hearts, resistants.

The Resistance has been the healing symbol of a country that chooses to believe that it did not capitulate, that it was never in spirit occupied or broken, and the French are not prepared to give up that symbol now. They prefer a past that corroborates and confirms an idea of France, a kind of collective national identity. They prefer a history that binds them. History is their patrimony, and lately they have made a cult of it. They have meetings called "La Mémoire" and "L'Oubli," at which important scholars sit around talking about what remembering means and what forgetting means, and the most ambitious piece of scholarship all year was four long books of essays called *Les Lieux de Mémoire*—after a seminar at the École des Hautes Études on what the historian Pierre Nora, who taught the course and edited the collection, describes as "the rapid disappearance of our national memory." *Les Lieux de Mémoire* is a kind of catalogue—an explication of the symbols that constitute the collective memory of Frenchness. It covers an enormous field—Verdun, the Panthéon, Reims, Versailles, Paris statues, lineage, landscape, the Code Napoléon, the patrimony, the republican calendar, "*La Marseillaise,*" the *mairie,* the Fourteenth of July, Voltaire versus Rousseau, Victor Hugo's funeral, the Colonial Exposition of 1931, and fifty other *lieux de mémoire*—and a range of "histories" from art history to literary history to ethnographic history to the history of the Revolution. I doubt if anyone took *Les Lieux de Mémoire* to the beach this summer, but it is sure to be taken out and displayed, like a *rentrée* tan, now that people are home.

The book that people took to the beach—the season's philosophy —was something called *La Défaite de la Pensée,* and it was appropriate to the summer of the Barbie trial, because it is really a book about France and Germany. It is about the battle between the Enlightenment (France) and Romanticism (Germany), and about how France lost its "reason" and its moral clarity, not to mention its intellectual authority, and Germany took over, with that dangerous and seductive cult of innerness which passes for thought across the Rhine. It was written by a reporter turned media *philosophe* named Alain Finkielkraut, who is usually referred to by his critics as Alain Finkielfrance. Finkielkraut is one of those enemies of relativism who have got so fashionable lately, like the Chicago professor Allan Bloom, by fixing on relativism as the cause and symptom of a collapse of values—they mean their values —and talking a great deal about "the fight for Western civilization." Finkielkraut confuses relativism with romanticism, while the conservative Bishop of London calls it "subjectivism" (and blames Rousseau), but mainly these new pundits have borrowed "relativism" from a discourse that actually could be said to have begun in France, with Montesquieu and the Enlightenment, and reached Germany only to produce Hegel and the idea of history they are so fond of. Relativism, of course, has very little to do with romanticism, which is about the absolute authority of the self. Nor does the argument here really involve romanticism. It is a reaction to the sort of historical revisionism that was also very much *en marge des débats* at the Barbie trial—

and troubled a lot of Europeans, French and German, besides Finkielk-raut. It had to do with a group of anti-Semitic historians and publishers busy "revising" the Holocaust into a piece of Zionist propaganda, or, at most, a "relative" unpleasantness in an unpleasant world.

As it happens, the original revisionists were Dreyfusards. The word was used for people like Émile Zola, who wanted to "revise" the judgment on Alfred Dreyfus after Captain Dreyfus was framed as a German spy and convicted of treason in a trial that itself is one of the most complicated and revealing *lieux de mémoire* in France's history. There is an obvious and not very comforting irony in the fact that "revisionism" has been appropriated by French neo-Nazis who main-tain that the Holocaust never happened, that there were no camps or crematoriums, that six million dead Jews were a Jewish invention intended to weaken Europe with guilt and doubt—to perform what one revisionist has referred to as "the circumcision of Aryan man." There is nothing new about the lunatic fringe of the French right. Whatever people called it, its propaganda and its publications have been around for years. But by the time Klaus Barbie was arrested a historian named Robert Faurisson had submitted a doctoral thesis to the Univer-sity of Lyons in which he claimed to prove that gassing six million Jews was technologically impossible in Germany in the 1940s, and the thesis had been accepted, and his colleagues had complained—and then, for reasons it is hard to credit or explain, Faurisson was taken up by a group of fairly prominent academics on the left, among them the Swedish anthropologist Jan Myrdal (whose prominence came mainly from peo-ple confusing him with his famous father, Gunnar Myrdal) and the American linguist Noam Chomsky, a Jew, who contributed the preface to one of Faurisson's books, defending his academic freedom. Faurisson has said that his thesis is "simply a scientific denial of the existence of the gas chambers"—that he bears the Jews no ill-will or disrespect, and doesn't even particularly approve of Nazism. He is a seeker after "his-torical truth," and in the interests of truth he is now devoting himself to a magazine called *Annales d'Histoire Revisionniste,* which went on sale all over France the day before the Barbie trial began (and was seized and banned by the government). The second issue of *Annales d'Histoire Revisionniste* appeared this fall. It is distributed through a right-wing Paris bookstore that turns out to have been financed by the chief politi-cal officer at the Iranian Embassy.

Revisionism was news during the Barbie trial. Revisionists gave press conferences and started writing to newspapers, and their letters were so offensive that one *Libération* editor lost his job for publishing a selection that included someone's calculations of how many man-hours and how much oven space an extermination of any "importance" would have taken at Auschwitz. The French revisionists were so obviously crazy that in one way they were less troubling than the revisionists writing and teaching in Germany now—the "respectable revisionists," who contest not the facts of Nazism but the common understanding of Nazism as something morally and historically unique, something that sets Germany apart and gives it special burdens of responsibility. The new German revisionists are well-known scholars, and most of them have reputations abroad, where they are acknowledged for the sincerity of their work, if not for the credibility of their conclusions. They do not have very much in common: the philosopher Ernst Nolte, for example, has a theory that Hitler killed Jews because he was frightened of Russia and Bolshevism and the Gulag, whereas the historian Michael Stürmer thinks that Germany has to "demythologize" the Holocaust, to put the war and the Holocaust into some kind of historical perspective that will provide the country with "directions to identity." But all of them have been taken up by a new German right, which makes a great deal of Goethe and Beethoven being just as German as Hitler (Hitler, of course, was Austrian), and talks about restoring the "real" fatherland to young Germans, as if Hitler could be slipped into the cracks of history, somewhere between Hölderlin and Günter Grass—a bad man, a terrible, shameful time, but not impossible to understand in light of the mess at home in 1932 and Stalin in the Kremlin. People like Jürgen Habermas have spent the past year answering these revisionists—one side in what quickly became a kind of national debate-by-newspaper. Habermas thinks that the revisionists are romantic and irresponsible and, in the end, extremely dangerous for Germany. He says that the only possible point of departure for a German identity is the moment postwar Germany was born and a constitution signed and a democracy established.

Jacques Vergès, who is neither a modest nor a noticeably sensitive man, says that there were only three people who "counted" in the Barbie trial: André Cerdini, the presiding judge of the Cour d'Assises; Pierre Truche, the public prosecutor; and Vergès himself. He does not include the witnesses, with their harrowing stories, and he does not include his client. Barbie was not in court after the third day. He refused to appear, on the ground that he was "not in France," having been "illegally" extradited, and after that Judge Cerdini ordered him back to court only three more times—twice for witnesses to identify, and at the end for the summation and sentencing. Absent, he seemed almost beside the point—except, of course, to those witnesses, who had come to the court in anguish to confront him, to try to describe what sort of man Klaus Barbie was, and who were mocked by his absence. Some of the reporters in Lyons literally walked out with Barbie. Eight hundred reporters were accredited to the trial, and there were nearly four hundred press seats in the courtroom, but the reporters seem mainly to have come for courtroom theater, and once Barbie began his boycott they began drifting in and out of Lyons. There were days —when the thirty-nine lawyers representing the various *parties civiles,* the Jewish groups and the Resistance groups and the families of survivors who had joined the trial as morally interested parties and were suing for a symbolic franc, made their depositions—that only thirty or forty reporters were in court.

In a way, the trial took place somewhere else—which was pretty much as everyone but Barbie's victims had intended. Jacques Chirac told teachers to devote a history class to the Holocaust. They were provided with books and instructions for the occasion, and the result was that in May this year millions of French *lycéens* talked about Jews and concentration camps (and apparently some classroom revisionists argued that the extermination of Europe's Jews was a "relative" unpleasantness in a world where cowboys had exterminated Indians). Mitterrand, for his part, sent his wife, Danielle, to Lyons, and saw to it that Claude Lanzmann's movie about the camps, *Shoah,* was shown on state television. Lyons financed a production of *The Investigation,* Peter Weiss's play about a Frankfurt trial of twenty Auschwitz camp guards. There was an official pilgrimage to Izieu; and a Holocaust exhibit, *Mémorial de la Déportation,* went up on the Place des Terreaux, in Lyons, just across from the *mairie* and down the street from the Palais de Justice. Two hundred thousand people saw the exhibit —many more than saw the trial or, apparently, wanted to.

Some of the people who did both said the exhibit was "more real" than the trial, with its thirty-nine squabbling lawyers and its defense counsel talking about Zionist crimes instead of Nazi crimes, and its absent S.S. Hauptsturmführer. Often, they said they wanted to forget the trial—that it was a show trial, a media spectacle for reporters who filed stories about restaurants when the spectacle bored them, and who were much more interested in the posturing of Maître Vergès than in the heartbreaking testimony of the survivors of Barbie's interrogation rooms at Fort Montluc. Suffering like theirs is not an easy story. It is not news, like revisionism, once it is repeated. It is impossible to match the horror of those repetitions in a column of newsprint, and this may be why a lot of the reporters who were there (I was not) said they felt like voyeurs in the Lyons courtroom, listening in on grief that was so deep and ultimately so private. They had expected a release, a kind of collective exorcism, from the Barbie trial, but Barbie himself had neither conscience nor remorse, nor even any particular attachment to the crimes he had committed. What they got instead was the obliviousness of an elderly psychopath. Criminals rarely achieve the dimensions of their crimes, and Barbie was no exception. The fact that he was literally beneath contempt put him, in a sense, beyond retribution. It made the trial a gruesome entertainment, appropriate to the couple who said they had come downtown for a movie, discovered it was sold out, and wandered over to the Tribunal "so as not to waste the afternoon."

Jacques Vergès was one of a group of young French lawyers who got together in the fifties and volunteered to represent Algerian revolutionaries on trial in French civilian and military courts. He made his reputation in that lawyers' cooperative. He had a strategy he called *"défense de rupture."* He did not plead innocence for his clients. He did not bargain with the prosecution. He did not claim extenuating circumstances or poverty or insanity or desperation or influence, or even coercion. He acknowledged whatever crimes his clients had committed. He said that his clients were proud of those crimes, because they were not crimes at all but acts of revolution by freedom fighters struggling to liberate their country. And for a time, to the extent that he was accurate—there was a war for independence in Algeria, and young Algerians working and studying here had brought that war to the Métropole and were joined by young French men and women who supported them—Jacques Vergès became a kind of minor hero. He was a hero to the French left, and to many ordinary people, of no particular politics (and even, occasionally, fairly conservative politics), who simply wanted to end their country's colonial adventure with a measure of dignity and responsibility and peace. They did not know very much about him, but they admired him as a man who stood up in French courts, ten years after Nuremberg, and accused the French of terrible war crimes in Algeria—accused them of the same sort of crimes that many of them had suffered under Germans.

Vergès was a child of colonialism and, psychologically, a creature of the colonial predicament. His Vietnamese mother died young and far from home, on a French island in the middle of the Indian Ocean. His French father stayed on, on the island—it was the Île de la Réunion

—making what Vergès calls an "adventurous" exile, practicing medicine, organizing for the Communist Party, working on a novel about colonialism that people say was one of Ho Chi Minh's favorite books. Vergès himself left for London when he was seventeen. He fought the Germans with the Free French Forces, and ended up in Paris, studying law. He was right when he talked about how much he "counted" at the Barbie trial—though not, perhaps, for the reasons he imagined or the courtroom reporters claimed. Vergès counted because he was a "yellow" (his word) whose family had been shattered by racism, whose career had begun in racist military courts—and now he was representing Klaus Barbie. He counted because somehow, in the sordid story of why Jacques Vergès had come to defend Klaus Barbie, the "other" costs—the moral costs—of colonialism were grotesquely clarified.

Vergès never got what he wanted from France. He was successful, but never in the French way. He was never a *conseiller*. He was never called to the Élysée for a conversation. He was not quite accepted, not quite respectable—not quite French enough. He was, instead, a Frenchman who lived to expose the French, to humiliate them, to turn them against each other. Once, briefly, he was a Muslim. He married a revolutionary he had defended—an extraordinary Algerian named Djamila Bouhired, who had been tortured by French soldiers and was said to have laughed in court when she heard her sentence—and converted and took an Arab name. But he never handed in his French passport. He was always a provocateur. His ambition was to drive the state crazy. (He would say to "destabilize" it.) The genius of colonial France was to create in its subjects a great longing for the French, an identification that survived rejection and racism, and even revolution. Vergès has lived in Czechoslovakia as a Communist and in Algeria as a nationalist. He has spent a honeymoon in China, paying his respects to Mao Zedong. He has disappeared—or seemed to disappear, for nearly eight years, in the 1970s—and the rumor then was that he had moved to Cambodia to advise his old Paris school friend Pol Pot and the Khmer Rouge on foreign policy. But he has always come home to Paris. He lives in a *hôtel particulier* on a pretty street between the rue Blanche and the Square Berlioz, with a Louis XV desk in his office and a fine old Aubusson on the wall behind it. He receives visitors with immaculate French manners, and defends terrorists—they are by now his enthusiasm and his specialty—with what seems like contempt for life and law. He is a man of good Paris friends and notorious connections, the most obviously notorious right now being a Swiss arms dealer and "political financier" named François Genoud, who considers himself a Nazi, and who in fact made his first fortune as literary executor for Hitler, Bormann, and Goebbels. Genoud has helped finance a magazine for Vergès—a glossy magazine that was called *Révolution Africaine* and then *Révolution*— and he has paid the legal fees and costs for several of Vergès's clients, among them two terrorists from the gang that people call "friends of Carlos" and now, supposedly, Klaus Barbie.

Vergès is usually described in the papers as a shadowy figure —"the mysterious Maître Vergès," an article will say—but there is nothing mysterious about him except, perhaps, his reputation. Georges Kiejman, who argued against him in the trial of the Lebanese terrorist George Ibrahim Abdallah, says that there is not much courtroom evidence to justify that reputation. Vergès's famous strategy of a *défense de rupture* is not meant for judges and juries; it is propaganda, addressed to people outside the court who will be moved and perhaps converted. It is based on the understanding (at least, on Vergès's understanding) that the client is going to be convicted anyway, and can thus be sacrificed to his particular cause. Vergès's own cause is always France. He wants, he says, to expose the hypocrisy here, to shatter the social and political equilibrium. When he took Barbie for a client (replacing an old Lyons lawyer who for all practical purposes had appointed himself), he called a press conference and announced, smiling, that he was going to tear France apart with "revelations" about collaborators in the Lyons Resistance. His strategy then, it seems, was less a *défense de rupture* than what Pierre Truche, the prosecutor, called a *défense de dérivation*— an argument that "in this world everyone is rotten." Vergès had already said that he had no particular interest in Klaus Barbie. (He calls the appeals he has filed on Barbie's behalf a *service après vente.*) He took the case, he claimed, to publicize French crimes against humanity during the Algerian War.

French law has a reputation for being cold, narrow, and oppressively literal, but that is in the writing down. French justice can be a free-for-all. (American lawyers following the Lyons trial often remarked on how little of the testimony would have been admissible in a court at home.) The bench here has tremendous discretionary powers. It can admit, and even solicit, the testimony of people known as "historical witnesses" or "moral witnesses"—the Catholic writer André Frossard came to Lyons and told the story of a Jew before a firing squad who had to repeat the words "A Jew is a parasite who lives on the skin of Aryans, and must be exterminated," and Elie Wiesel said, "The man I am, the Jew I am, must speak out, in the name of memory, until the day the dead speak, and on that day the earth will tremble"—and it can admit defense lawyers who plead not for their client but for, say, Algeria or Palestine or Africa. Vergès took on two "colleagues" in the Barbie defense, and no one who knew his tactics was at all surprised that one colleague was Algerian and the other came from Congo-Brazzaville. The Algerian, Nabil Bouaïta, spoke once. He was there, he said, to accuse Israel of crimes against humanity, and to talk about the massacres at the Palestinian refugee camps at Sabra and Shatila, in Lebanon, which he compared to the German massacre of French villagers in Oradour-sur-Glane in 1944. He did not mention that it was Lebanese Christian Phalangists who carried out the massacres at Sabra and Shatila, although he talked at length about "slavery and the Enlightenment." Vergès's other colleague did better. His name was Jean-Martin M'Bemba, and *he* talked about why crimes of colonialism were also crimes against humanity. He told a story about the black workers who had built the French a railroad from the Congo to the sea. They were forced labor, and they were sent to die in the jungle, he said, as surely as if they had been put on one of Barbie's concentration-camp convoys. The lawyers on the other side saluted him.

There is, of course, no acceptable answer to the question of what constitutes a crime against humanity. There are only legal distinctions. France was the first—and is still the only—country in Europe to take the concept "crime against humanity," as it was written into the Nuremberg statutes, and give it a binding legal definition within its own penal code. This happened, in part, because the French wanted to settle on a formula to keep the dossiers on Nazis like Klaus Barbie open. In 1964, the Cour de Cassation—the court that defines and interprets law here—determined that inasmuch as "humanity is an ongoing concept," extending beyond particular people victimized at particular times in particular places, there were no limitations on the prosecution of crimes against humanity. Legally speaking, a crime against humanity was committed everywhere and forever. French justice could claim Klaus Barbie in Bolivia because French justice did not recognize a distinction between Bolivia and France where Barbie's crimes were concerned. And it could claim him in 1983—or in 1993, for that matter—because humanity did not die with Barbie's victims. Legally speaking, humanity was always there to represent them. This is why, when Barbie was in fact extradited, hundreds of people filed claims against him with the *juge d'instruction* in Lyons. Jewish groups filed. Human-rights groups filed. Resistance groups filed, because from their point of view Barbie's crimes against the Lyons Resistance, including his torturing to death of the Resistance leader Jean Moulin, could also be counted as crimes against humanity, and not proscribed by any statute of limitations. Lawyers—not only Vergès but liberal jurists and legal philosophers—began to argue about "colonial" crimes in their journals, because to their minds the question of crimes committed by the French Army in Algeria was morally, if not legally, unresolved. That question had been complicated for them by an amnesty after the Algerian War, which made it libellous to talk about those crimes, and even to print the testimony of victims.

The Cour de Cassation had to sit three more times before Barbie could be brought to trial. The last time—in December of 1986— it resolved that crimes against humanity were "inhuman acts and . . . persecutions which, in the name of a state practicing a politics of ideological hegemony, have been committed systematically not only against people as members of a racial or religious group but also as opponents of that politics, whatever the form of their opposition." In other words, persecution institutionalized by official ideology. This meant that Klaus Barbie could be charged with crimes against resistants as well as crimes against Jews—something the French had not anticipated when they arrested Barbie, and Vergès threatened to "put the Resistance on trial." The prosecution added two cases involving resistants to its dossier; they were fairly simple cases and not likely to involve the Resistance in any scandals, and, in fact, Vergès could not come up with even one. (The *juge d'instruction* is considering a new trial, based on the testimony of two survivors of the famous meeting in Caluire at which Jean Moulin was betrayed to the Gestapo, and Vergès claims to be waiting for *that* trial.) On the other hand, the Cour de Cassation avoided the question of colonial crimes—or, indeed, of any crimes against humanity that France had committed, or might have committed, or might commit sometime in the future—because "a state practicing a politics of ideological hegemony" is another way of saying a totalitarian state, and this means that a democracy like France is by definition excluded.

After the trial was over, Pierre Truche said that there was no jurisprudence in the world adequate to the questions raised in Lyons. How could there be? Convicting Klaus Barbie does not settle the matter of six million Jewish deaths; it does not even stop old officers of the S.S. from holding their yearly reunions. There is no way to say that Stalin's terrible purges were not crimes against humanity, or that Pol Pot's massacre of two million Cambodians was not genocide simply because the Khmer Rouge happened to be Cambodian, too. The raid on Shatila was no less inhuman because, legally speaking, it was a war crime, or because the Phalangists who carried it out participate in free elections. The crimes of the French officers who were secret-army terrorists in Algeria—the OAS—are no less crimes for having been amnestied by a French President under threat of an Army coup d'état at home.

Mourad Oussedik, who founded the Algerian lawyers' cooperative, is an old man now, but he still practices law in Paris and is a kind of paterfamilias to the aging idealists of Algerian independence. Oussedik did not really approve of Vergès's performance in Lyons, though he is too discreet to say so publicly. He says, instead, that it was never up to the French to accuse themselves of crimes in Algeria—to put themselves on trial and condemn themselves and send themselves to jail. It was up to the Algerians to try colonial crimes in Algerian courts, the way the French had tried Klaus Barbie—in absentia. Oussedik says that until they do the French will still own Algeria. He says that the French do not need any soldiers to police a country that even now —twenty-five years after independence—considers it awkward or impractical or impolitic or unprofitable to risk offending them by condemning the crimes of the OAS with so much as a watch list on visitors. It was not Algeria or Brazzaville that sent Bouaïta and M'Bemba to Lyons to raise colonial ghosts. It was Jacques Vergès who hired them and a Swiss Nazi who paid.

In the end, there could be no satisfaction in Lyons. The Holocaust remains the Holocaust, and at the same time—and perhaps because of this—it is the emblem of a thousand other atrocities, committed in the name of a thousand other systems. Vengeance in the name of memory —even clean, clear, necessary judicial vengeance—diminishes memory as much as it restores or dignifies or enshrines it. There was never any question of Barbie's guilt, whatever the charges were against him this time. His guilt was determined years before he was extradited. He talked about his war all the time in Peru and Bolivia. He advised a succession of junta policemen on how to torture. It was probably impossible to give him what we would call a fair trial—only a correct one. In the end, it was appropriate that he was absent. It was a measure of his depravity that the trial was so unsatisfying. And maybe, too, it was a measure of how little is ever really learned from history. Before the trial was over, a teenage gang was spraying swastika graffiti on the shopwindows of a Jewish merchant on my Paris street. A month later, kids in Germany were laying roses on Rudolf Hess's grave. Jean-Marie Le Pen, who is running for President here on a platform of deporting foreigners, controls 15 percent of the French vote. His party, the Front National, is in city halls all over the country, in coalitions with the respectable conservative parties of Jacques Chirac and Valéry Giscard d'Estaing. While Barbie was on trial, Le Pen was busy campaigning on the beaches. He decided this summer that foreigners were responsible for AIDS—foreigners carried AIDS to France and then mosquitoes spread the disease to pure French men and women—and he said that when he was President of France he was going to put those foreigners into camps until they were deported or died. Le Pen was a paratrooper in Algeria during the revolution. He has sued—under the amnesty laws —every newspaper that printed evidence to the effect that he tortured prisoners there, although, like Barbie, he often brags about his war. Two months after Barbie was sentenced, Le Pen went on the radio and said that Hitler's gas chambers were a "minor detail" in the history of the Second World War. He wanted to know why people kept harassing him about gas chambers when historians, right now, were debating the existence of gas chambers. He did not think gas chambers were "a revealed truth that everybody has to believe in."

October 1987

Index

FOR THE BEST IN PAPERBACKS, LOOK FOR THE

In every corner of the world, on every subject under the sun, Penguin represents quality and variety—the very best in publishing today.

For complete information about books available from Penguin—including Pelicans, Puffins, Peregrines, and Penguin Classics—and how to order them, write to us at the appropriate address below. Please note that for copyright reasons the selection of books varies from country to country.

In the United Kingdom: For a complete list of books available from Penguin in the U.K., please write to *Dept E.P., Penguin Books Ltd, Harmondsworth, Middlesex, UB7 0DA.*

In the United States: For a complete list of books available from Penguin in the U.S., please write to *Dept BA, Penguin, Box 120, Bergenfield, New Jersey 07621-0120.*

In Canada: For a complete list of books available from Penguin in Canada, please write to *Penguin Books Ltd, 2801 John Street, Markham, Ontario L3R 1B4.*

In Australia: For a complete list of books available from Penguin in Australia, please write to the *Marketing Department, Penguin Books Ltd, P.O. Box 257, Ringwood, Victoria 3134.*

In New Zealand: For a complete list of books available from Penguin in New Zealand, please write to the *Marketing Department, Penguin Books (NZ) Ltd, Private Bag, Takapuna, Auckland 9.*

In India: For a complete list of books available from Penguin, please write to *Penguin Overseas Ltd, 706 Eros Apartments, 56 Nehru Place, New Delhi, 110019.*

In Holland: For a complete list of books available from Penguin in Holland, please write to *Penguin Books Nederland B.V., Postbus 195, NL-1380AD Weesp, Netherlands.*

In Germany: For a complete list of books available from Penguin, please write to *Penguin Books Ltd, Friedrichstrasse 10-12, D-6000 Frankfurt Main I, Federal Republic of Germany.*

In Spain: For a complete list of books available from Penguin in Spain, please write to *Longman, Penguin España, Calle San Nicolas 15, E-28013 Madrid, Spain.*

In Japan: For a complete list of books available from Penguin in Japan, please write to *Longman Penguin Japan Co Ltd, Yamaguchi Building, 2-12-9 Kanda Jimbocho, Chiyoda-Ku, Tokyo 101, Japan.*

FOR THE BEST IN HISTORY, LOOK FOR THE

FOR THE BEST IN HISTORY, LOOK FOR THE

☐ **MOVE YOUR SHADOW**
South Africa, Black & White
Joseph Lelyveld

Drawing on his two tours as a correspondent for *The New York Times*, Lelyveld offers a vivid portrait of a troubled country and its people, illuminating the history, society, and feelings that created and maintain apartheid.

402 pages   *ISBN: 0-14-009326-5*   **$7.95**

☐ **THE PELICAN HISTORY OF THE WORLD**
Revised Edition
J. M. Roberts

This comprehensive and informative survey of the growth of the modern world analyzes the major forces of our history and emphasizes both their physical and psychological effects.

1056 pages   *ISBN: 0-14-022785-7*   **$11.95**